THE COLLECTED INTERVIEWS
VOLUME ONE

IAN GLASPER

Published by Earth Island Books
Pickforde Lodge
Pickforde Lane
Ticehurst
TN5 7BN

www.earthisland.co.uk
© Copyright Earth Island Publishing Ltd

First published by Earth Island Publishing 2022

First edition printed February 2022

The moral rights of the author have been asserted.

ISBN 9781838356781

Printed and bound by IngramSpark

Front cover photo - Earth Crisis - by Danielle Dombrowski
Back cover photos - AFI, by Danielle Dombrowski; Agnostic Front & Breakdown,
by Naki; The Damned, by Morat; Exodus, by Doralba Picerno; Extreme Noise
Terror, by Gutterpunk Photography
All used with permission & much gratitude
Cover design - Welly

Terrorized – The Collected Interviews

Introduction – Volume One

Prior to writing for Terrorizer, I had dabbled with doing my own fanzine, a scruffy xeroxed collection of scribblings called, aptly enough, Little Things Please Little Minds. Featuring interviews with some of my favourite bands, a few gig reviews and various naive ruminations, it ran to five issues, and whilst it will never be mentioned in the same breath as such legends of zinedom as Raising Hell, Ripping Thrash and Problem Child, it was my first foray into writing.

That would have been 1985 or 1986, and Terrorizer started in 1993. I started writing for them by happy accident really. I was already in touch with the first editor, Rob Clymo, as he ran a music distro, Round Diamond Records. I remember ordering 'Cowboys From Hell' by Pantera from him in the very early Nineties, back when the album was just trickling in on import, and I'd be ringing him up every week to see if it had come in yet or not. I became a regular customer, and from what I ordered off him, he could see I was into heavy music but especially punk, hardcore and thrash.

When he told me he was starting an extreme music magazine, I was excited to see it – I had always loved Metal Forces, and then Thrash 'N' Burn and the short-lived Xtreme Noize (which I believe Rob may have had some involvement in?)

So I ordered issue # 1 from our newsagents, the next road down, which was the very same newsagents where I did my first paper round that helped pay for my early record collection. This was back in the day when the newsagent ordered specialist magazines in for you (titter all you like...!) and put them under the counter with your name on them, and would even ring you up to let you know they had come in. Named after the grindcore band Terrorizer, of course, the inaugural issue didn't pull any punches with the bands it covered, and Rob was chuffed to bits when I told him how much I enjoyed it. Which was when he asked me if I would like to try my hand at writing a punk and hardcore column for # 3 (# 2 was already away to the printers by then). I wasn't too sure if I'd be able to pull it off – after all, this was a glossy 'High Street' magazine - but my girlfriend of the time, Donna, encouraged me to give it a go, so I agreed, and he told me he'd get me a parcel of stuff sent out to review. A few days later a big box of goodies arrived from Plastic Head Distribution (they pretty much distributed all the labels who worked with Terrorizer back then) – I was like a kid at fucking Xmas - and a few days after that I submitted my first Hardcore Holocaust column to the mag, which I handwrote and faxed over to Rob. He liked it and typed it up, complete with bonus typos, and I remember being absolutely thrilled when I saw it in print a few weeks later. It was well enough received for Rob to make it a regular feature, and by issue # 4, I was contributing features and reviews as well. I carried on buying the magazine from my local paper shop for several more months, despite writing for it, before Rob started sending me it out for free. And he eventually started sending me cheques for £25, and sometimes £50 depending upon how much I contributed, every few issues for my time and effort. This was great... not only was I being sent tons of free CDs, and even getting into some gigs for free, but I was now being paid, albeit a token amount, for the pleasure. It was never going to pay the rent, but that wasn't why I was doing it; I just loved getting the opportunity to talk to my favourite bands and hear lots of new music, and as Rob grew to trust my judgement, I could sneak some of my friends' bands in the mag as well.

Over the next twenty-five years I wrote at least something for every single issue; I outstayed every other writer, I saw many editors come and go (two of the most influential of which have kindly agreed to write forewords for these volumes) and I never missed a single deadline. I almost became editor myself at one point, but it wasn't the right thing for my circumstances at that particular moment in time, although I sometimes wonder what might have transpired if I had (to be fair, the mag would probably have turned into a more hardcore Punk Lives or something!)

Of course, the musical landscape ebbed and flowed, and there were several years when the type of bands I wrote about weren't as in vogue as others, but I hung in there even through the fallow patches, because I always thought that, as flawed as it was, it was the best magazine out there. So, it was quite a wrench in the summer of 2018 when it eventually folded, in a rather messy fashion it has to be said. However, I'm not here to dwell on its demise, I'm here to celebrate its legacy, and more specifically the bits I wrote, with these two volumes collecting every single interview (but not the hundreds of columns and thousands of reviews...) I had published in the magazine, and even a few that didn't make it to print.

I would never profess to be a good writer now, and I was even rougher around the edges back then, so reading some of the earlier interviews in particular has me occasionally wincing with embarrassment, but I've not revised any of this retrospectively, and what you get here is what I wrote then, for better or worse. Instead of just reproducing endless scans and PDFs from the original mags, I've salvaged the text files and then hunted down new photos (from the relevant period wherever possible) to accompany them.

I'll always have a soft spot for Terrorizer. It opened so many doors for me, paving the way for me to write for more mainstream magazines like Record Collector and Bass Guitar, and ultimately enabling me to fulfil a lifelong ambition to write books of my own. When I look back at all the bands I interviewed over those 280+ issues, it was quite a ride and one I hope you'll enjoy revisiting as much as I did.

Ian Glasper, October 2021

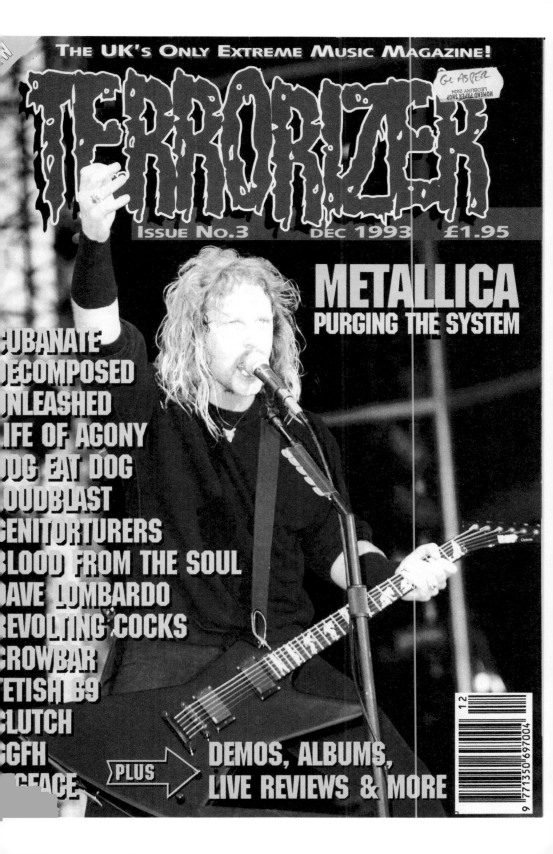

THE UK's ONLY EXTREME MUSIC MAGAZINE!

TERRORIZER

ISSUE No.3   DEC 1993   £1.95

GLASPER
HOMEND PAPER SHOP
LEDBURY 2804

METALLICA
PURGING THE SYSTEM

CUBANATE
DECOMPOSED
UNLEASHED
LIFE OF AGONY
DOG EAT DOG
LOUDBLAST
GENITORTURERS
BLOOD FROM THE SOUL
DAVE LOMBARDO
REVOLTING COCKS
CROWBAR
FETISH 69
CLUTCH
GGFH
GFACE

PLUS ➡ DEMOS, ALBUMS,
LIVE REVIEWS & MORE

12

9 771350 697004

HARDCORE HOLOCAUST

WANT TO KNOW WHAT'S HAPPENING IN THE WORLD OF HARDCORE? IAN GLASPER HAS ALL THE LATEST INFO...

Welcome to hopefully the first of many hardcore columns in Terrorizer, which will feature all the bands no one else has the balls to touch - for fear of getting their fingers bitten!! Well, I sat and racked my brains for hours to think up a flashy intro for this; I was considering trying to define H.C., and what it means to me, but why limit ourselves? H.C. isn't the sort of music that sits comfortably in a convenient pigeon hole...it's a middle-finger salute to establishment, a thorn in the side of complacency. It's an attitude, and it's not meant to be defined. Anyway, enough verbosity! Onwards!

ANAL CUNT have shortened their name to A.C., in what is probably a wise career move, but their music remains as extreme as ever...extremely crap. Their new LP on Earache 'Everyone Should Be Killed' (Mosh101) has some hilarious song titles (like 'Brutally Morbid Axe Of Satan'... Ahem) but the music is about as funny as a visit to the dentist. If you're into short pointless bursts of apocalyptic noise, it might turn you on, but otherwise avoid like 'Neighbours'.

An infinitely better bet for H.C. heads perusing Earache's catalogue would be LAWN-MOWER DETH's recent effort 'Billy' (Mosh098), which is, quite surprisingly, a very competent and powerful piece of poppy punk. Complete with a few cover versions, this is perhaps their best to date.

Ruptured Ambitions Records have just released a double LP full of cover versions of that seminal UK anarcho-punk outfit CRASS, entitled 'You've Heard It All Before'. It features some of the best English H.C. bands, such as OI POLLOI, FLUX, DECADENCE WITHIN, CITIZEN FISH, etc, and it's a benefit for Rape Crisis

Centres, so what're you waiting for? Get your hands in your pockets! Write for details to: Chris Willsher, Old Forge Cottage, Rushford, Lamerton, Tavistock, Devon, PL19 8RY, England. By the way, Chris drums for those maniacs C.D.S., who are also on the LP.

ANTI-CIMEX, from Sweden, have slowed down considerably for their latest, 'Scandinavian Jawbreaker', on Vinyl Japan, but haven't compromised any of their customary ferocity. It's a potent mix of DISCHARGE-style H.C.

and primo-metal riffing, and well worthy of your pennies. Their extremely raw live album 'Made In Sweden' is still available - ANTI-CIMEX captured at their abrasive best! Equally as intense, and also from Sweden, DISFEAR's newie 'Brutal Sight Of War' (Lost & Found), certainly delivers the goods. It could rip your face off at 30 paces! Both are available via Plastic Head distribution.

They also stock Epitaph releases, the label established by Brett from BAD RELIGEON - which is a big clue as to what their bands sound like. In some parts of their latest opus, 'The Unknown Road', PENNYWISE sound uncannily like B.R. (that's BAD RELIGEON, not British Rail, dummy!), which showcases their melodic rockin' Hardcore, brimming with more hooks than a 'Hellraiser' movie.

Epitaph also offer up the self-titled debut from California's RANCID, who play their own brand of groovin' catchy punk rock, and

the long awaited newie from the near-legendary SNFU, strangely entitled 'Something Green And Leafy This Way Comes'...NUCLEAR ASSAULT eat your hearts out!! It's no let down either. Packed with their trade-mark off-the-wall energy. Copacetic, indeed.

Those mourning the demise of POISON IDEA could do worse than check out the APARTMENT 3-G 'Punk Machine' LP (on Germany's Bitzcore Records). APARTMENT 3-G play a similar blastin' H.C. to P.I. (maybe not quite so powerful as the overweight ones), which isn't surpris-

ing really seeing as they come from Portland, and feature 2 ex-members of P.I. Until earlier this year, APARTMENT 3-G were known as MULE, and under this equine monicker they released four very limited 7"s.

And if you're missing AGNOSTIC FRONT, you ought to try to catch up with MADBALL, from New York, the band put together by various members of A.F. back in the late 80's and fronted by Roger Miret's young brother, Freddie. He was only 12 when they released their 'Ball Of Destruction' EP on Wreckage Records. It's slower and heavier than the first 7", but still real angry. It's been out a while, but what

the hell? It kicks ass.

Also, keep your eyes peeled for CONCRETE SOX's recent 'No World Order' (Lost & found LF048), which was probably their best work to date, slower and heavier than their previous output, and choc-a-bloc with some chunky rifferama spiced up with a few amusing samples. It's worth buying to see the lads in their suits on the cover!!

HERBGARDEN, from Bristol, are another UK act going from strength to strength. They are an eclectic bunch, letting their musical muse carry them wherever it fancies, as proven on their recent LP, 'HMS Disaster' (WOW LP30), and their 3-song EP '?' on 42

Records. Unusual, and manic, and worth checking out.

Well, time to wind down for this month, which is always difficult to do. I could talk a glass eye to sleep, me!

FOREWORD - BY MIKE SCORE (ALL OUT WAR)

I remember when I first came into contact with Ian Glasper. I knew of his band, Stampin' Ground, from the European metallic hardcore scene and knew of his contributions to the almighty Terrorizer magazine, but I don't believe we had ever spoken prior to 1997. That all changed when I received a message from Mario Weltmann from Fire Engine, who was doing PR for Gain Ground Records. All Out War was about to release 'Truth in the Age of Lies' on the label, and Mario dropped me a line expressing Ian's interest in the band. Mario had stated that Ian became aware of the band through various compilations and was really excited about the release of the album. Ian requested a copy of 'Truth in the Age of Lies' and said that if it was as good as they anticipated, Nick Terry (his editor) had given him the green light to run a feature on All Out War in the magazine. The possibility of being in Terrorizer was a huge step forward for the band and we were very humbled to hear about their excitement about our upcoming first full-length release. At the time there were very few major magazines delving into the underground metallic hardcore scene as it was mostly relegated to fanzines and very 'beneath the surface' publications. Terrorizer was one of the few exceptions. They covered it all - metal, hardcore, industrial, black metal, death metal/grindcore, doom/stoner metal, punk, noise, ambient/experimental gothic – you name it. Terrorizer didn't just pay attention to the metal genre's heavy hitters; they gave the underground bands a chance to gain some notoriety, which was a rarity in those days. All Out War very much appreciated the opportunity to gain some exposure on a larger scale than what we had previously been accustomed to.

Even before being contacted about the potential feature, I was already a regular consumer of the magazine. I picked up every issue from the local Barnes and Noble. At that time in my life Terrorizer, along with a few others, was essential reading. I looked forward to thumbing through it to keep up with new releases, reading the reviews, and in order to follow some of my favourite bands. I really enjoyed the live reviews as it gave me the opportunity to vicariously attend these shows through the eyes of the reviewer. As a huge fan of all things heavy, Terrorizer was everything I was looking for in a magazine. It was glossy and slick, but covered all things ugly and dark. The magazine addressed the obvious bands of the time, but also took a much deeper dive into the obscure. Terrorizer was not afraid to give exposure to things that were happening underneath the surface; Ian, and the magazine as a whole, gave a platform to underground scenes that were being ignored by the more mainstream publications. They offered an in-depth look at multiple scenes of all things falling under the metal umbrella, which was extremely thorough and seemingly all encompassing. Most heavy and/or dark bands from the 1990s were being featured and reviewed in Terrorizer.

Looking back now I realize the impact the vast diversity in the coverage had on opening metal fans' eyes to more eclectic styles within the genre. Not everyone was going to fall in love with every band out there, but at least each genre was getting a fair shake at catching on. Terrorizer gave upcoming underground acts the chance to appear in the same pages as the already established powerhouses. At the time, I don't know if people consciously realized the type of impact this was having on heavy music, but in hindsight, this type of coverage was catching on and opening doors. All anyone needs to do is revisit those old issues from the '90s and they will see such a variety of bands appearing alongside one another. Bands who normally would not have been mentioned in the same breath were colliding and appearing side by side. This approach managed to keep things fresh and interesting. All Out War is very honoured to have appeared among the pages of Terrorizer. Thank you, Ian Glasper, for the opportunity and thank you for your friendship.

Mike Score
Vocalist of All Out War, New Paltz, NY
November 2021

Foreword – by Nick Terry

(Terrorizer editor, 1996 – 2000)

February 1996: I've just taken over as editor of Terrorizer magazine, working out of a tiny attic office above Smithfield Market in London. The internet is still a year away from installation, mobile phones are down to roughly half-brick size and are still too expensive for anybody but yuppies, and the phones have actual cords plugged into sockets. I have inherited a minuscule writing staff, and they are scattered across the country. So it was on the phone that I first got to know the author of these two volumes, before email and emojis changed how we converse.

And, as you'll see in these two volumes, it was on the phone that we did much of our business at Terrorizer, arranging interviews with bands across Britain, Europe, the United States and elsewhere in the world. Call #1: please, please, please let me do an interview with Anthrax? Yeah, that's a great idea. Call #2: hey, record company, can we interview Anthrax? Sure! Call #3: it's all set for this time. Call #4: I'm on the phone with Anthrax! Call #5: the feature is in the post. Because yes, honestly, we were posting floppy disks back and forth to each other, things were that backwards in the mid-Nineties.

Ian Glasper probably doesn't need much of an introduction to many fans of extreme music, after writing five definitive histories of British hardcore, punk, anarcho punk and thrash metal in fifteen years. Back in 1996, however, I certainly needed an introduction to him – Ian was our hardcore and punk expert, the curator of the magazine's 'Hardcore Holocaust' review column, and my knowledge started getting hazy much past metalcore. Ian gave me a crash course in the full range of hardcore and punk styles and scenes that were exploding at the time in the US and across Europe, and I think we made the right choices about who to feature from those scenes over the next four years.

Our common ground, however, was metal, especially thrash, doom and metalcore. Reading back through these interviews spanning 25 years of Terrorizer, it's clear just how much metal we editors got Mr Hardcore to cover – Ian would alternately beg and be begged to write about everyone from Annihilator to Xentrix (and that's just the bands on Roadrunner in 1990), from Candlemass to Witchery. You'll also find Ian documenting the rise of metalcore through the Nineties into the new millennium, while steadfastly chronicling the comebacks and breakthroughs of crossover, NYHC, Cali-punk, as well as Swedish and Belgian hardcore.

Re-reading these interviews in some cases 25 years later, I can't help but be amazed at how fresh they feel today. Ian wasn't just the longest-lasting contributor at Terrorizer, writing for almost a quarter of a century for the magazine; he was always the most reliable writer we had. Every feature wasn't just turned in on time, it was written with palpable enthusiasm, encyclopaedic knowledge and sound judgement. You'll find yourself not only reminded of some classic albums, but also introduced to some records that you might well have dismissed out of hand Back In The Day, whether that was 1997 or 2007. With luck, the Gods of YouTube will provide; if not, there are gems to be hunted down in the second-hand and used markets for the true collectors out there.

I left Terrorizer in October 2000 to become a historian of the Holocaust, so it's ironic and apt that I can now look back on the writings of the 'Hardcore Holocaust' columnist who has himself become a noted historian of punk rock and extreme music; my university even has Ian's book 'Burning Britain: The History of UK Punk, 1980-1984' in our library! Time will tell how we look back on the extreme music scenes of 1993 to 2018 in the future, and whether Ian will write more of his histories of these decades for different scenes and genres; for now, these two volumes chronicle and recall a remarkable time in hardcore, punk, metalcore and metal that should be long remembered.

Dr Nick Terry
Department of History, University of Exeter
September 2021

CONTENTS

CHAPTER B

CHAPTER C

CHAPTER D

CHAPTER E

CHAPTER F

CHAPTER I-J

CHAPTER A:
No Gods No Masters...

100 Demons - issue 83 (October 2000)

100 Demons. Now, there is a name to conjure with – and what horrors could be summoned forth, I'm sure! Far from being a bullet-belt-toting black metal band, da Demons are a metalcore band out of Connecticut featuring ex-members of Yuppicide, Pushbutton Warfare, Higher Force and Bloodbath, whose 'In The Eyes of The Lord' debut for Good Life is a furious diatribe of hatred in the fine style of Merauder meets Hatebreed. And don't be deceived by that album title into thinking that these boys are god-fearing do-gooders... oh no.

"Yeah, I do have some animosity towards religious zealots, both in and out of the scene," reckons vocalist Bruce. "Most of it comes from my Catholic upbringing, and the struggle I've had in my life accepting the concept of blind faith. I also never understood how they can claim victory for god's glory whenever something good happens, but wash their hands of everything really bad. I guess the bottom line is that I have more than enough hate for everybody...!"

As you might have guessed by now, and as you'll know if you've already heard the awesome smack-down that is their debut album, and experienced first-hand the utter nihilism of songs like 'Wake Up And Hate', 100 Demons take as much inspiration from the negative as the positive.

"Positive hardcore is an oxymoron," spits bassist Steve, "Like political integrity or military intelligence. Bruce calls things as he sees them; it's reality, not wishing for a touchy-feely world of rainbows and fucking unicorns. Our music and lyrics aren't positive OR negative; they're just telling you how we see the world around us.

"For me, 100 Demons is very cathartic; I get a lot of my *100 Demons, by Stage* frustrations and aggression out on stage – it gets your blood *Hog Photography* running and your sweat flowing. You feel alive. And besides, there is some positivity in our music: in Bruce's resolve and determination not to quit or be counted out. For me that counts for more than a bunch of crud about holding hands or a better world full of flowers and bunnies! This is reality, and it isn't always pretty, but 100 Demons are not going to flinch or tone down the crunch. If you can't handle 100 Demons, you might wanna try INXS; they might be more your speed..."

25 TA LIFE – ISSUE 49 (DECEMBER 1997)

New York's 25 Ta Life must rank among the hottest prospects in the hardcore underground right now. And with good reason, says Ian Glasper, who talked to singer Rick Healey about the Big Applecore band's long-awaited MCD, 'Strength Through Unity'.

Among the hardcore underground, I think it's safe to say that the new 25 Ta Life MCD, 'Strength Through Unity – The Spirit Remains' has been as hotly anticipated as the Second Coming by Christians. 1994's EP on Striving For Togetherness Records sure seems like a long time ago now, and the 'Keepin' It Real' MCD on We Bite in '95 only served to heighten our appetite.

So, with only six songs, clocking in at just over twelve minutes, has it been worth the wait? Well, yeah – from the Slayer-esque 'Loose Wit Da Truth' to the propulsive 'Loyal To The Grave', which guests on vocals none other than Madball's Freddy Cricien and Ezec from Crown Of Thorns, it's every bit as brutal as we dared hope for. But why the delay?

"Well, we've toured a lot," explains vocalist Rick Healey, "All across America, Puerto Rico, Japan, Europe, and we've had problems with labels and contracts and band members. We've had a lot of delays, y'know, but I'm very involved with da scene, and I have another band, Comin' Correct, so I was still out there, one way or another. It's not like we've been inactive."

You mentioned problems with labels. I think most labels that put out hardcore music

25 Ta Life, CBGB's, 1997, pic by Carl Gunhouse

25 Ta Life, Coney Island High NYC, 1995, pic by Carl Gunhouse

25 Ta Life, The Wetlands (NYC), 1995, pic by Carl Gunhouse

have been mentioned on the grapevine as in the picture to release this MCD at one time or other, but now it's finally emerged Stateside through Triple Crown, a New York label, and through the rapidly rising Good Life in Europe.

"We have a problem with labels who have nothing to do with hardcore, and who just want to make money off it. We know the guys from Triple Crown really well from when they did Another Planet, so we know we can trust them. And Edward [Good Life - IG] is a friend of ours, and he does a lot for the scene. We know that any money made will go back into releasing more hardcore music."

You'll hear Rick talk about the 'scene' an awful lot, just as you will hear him mention 'unity' in every other breath. Metallers may scoff at this, but understand that it's these things that are the glue that binds hardcore together, and to some of us they aren't just empty concepts to be bandied about in interviews.

"A lot of people laugh at it," agrees Rick, "But without unity, without the kids sticking together, hardcore would be very weak. Without kids promoting their own shows, without the underground distros helping new bands out, it would all be meaningless. The scene is built on a foundation of helping one another out.

"Every band has its own crew, you know, but there's still unity between us, especially in NYC," he responds, when I ask him how he reconciles the two seemingly opposing concepts of unity and individual crews. "It's what helps the scene grow, but yeah, there are crews that will start fights, and 25 Ta Life try to put that down. We want to bring people together and violence only divides us. You have to speak out; if there's a fight, you can't just let it go on. And in this band, we've taken a stand against all that. At our shows, we try to encourage singalongs and pile-ons, where everybody can have a good time, no matter how big or tough they are. We want to see kids go home having had a positive experience so they will bring their friends to the next show, not with black eyes so their parents moan at them and stop them coming. We want to see the scene get bigger, not smaller."

Rick's commitment to the scene is well documented. Not only does he front 25, he also sings for Comin' Correct, a slightly punkier hardcore band and does his own label (see the sidebar for more details), his own distro and zine, and finds time to book shows and tours for other bands. He even makes Pierre from Knuckledust look like a lazy bastard! "Everyday I wake up and I'm working for hardcore," he affirms, "Whether it's mail, the bands, or just booking a show, the best thing in life is to be able to do what you love and be able to get by. I'm not looking to make a lot of money, just enough to live and help my friends' bands out, and let people know what's going on. I do make time to chill with my girl, go to the movies or something, and hang with the guys. But almost all my other time is dedicated to hardcore. If it wasn't for this music, I don't know where I'd be - when I was younger, I was into drugs and drink, all that stuff, but hardcore changed my direction for the better. And that's why I put so much into it - I want to give something positive back."

When a band are this focused on the underground, it always sits uncomfortably if/when

5

they start to break big. This is already happening to 25 Ta Life, having just toured the States with Biohazard. How can Rick reconcile his DIY ethics with the higher door prices and the tough security they virtually advocate by taking such a gig?

"We definitely had to compromise a bit, but we're playing in front of more people, which is always a cool thing. A lot of them don't know what shows are about; they've seen a video and they come into the pit as tough guys, and it's good to let those people know what it's really about."

Seeing as he mentioned 'tough guys' – just like All Out War featured elsewhere in this issue, his own band too have actually been dubbed as such themselves. Having discussed this with the softly spoken Healey, it's obviously an opinion held by those armchair critics that the scene is so rife with, but having written songs like 'Short Fuse' doesn't actually help...

"I think a tough guy is an ignorant person who can't think things through, so they have to rely on their fists," claims Rick indignantly. "And that's not true with this band, everyone knows what we are about; we're a band who really cares about da music and da kids – just read the lyrics. But if you're going to disrespect me, or my friends, or hardcore, I'm going to stand up for myself. I won't start some senseless violence over nothing, but I won't let people walk over me either. At the end of the day, people can think what they want about us. It doesn't make any difference to me, 'cos I know how many benefits shows we've played, how many small hardcore shows we've done. We'll always be a hardcore band, it's in our blood, it's our lives."

Sidebar: Back To Basics Records

You now know that Rick does his own label, so why the hell didn't he release the new 25 MCD himself?

"Basically, I didn't have the money for the recording, or to take out the ads for a 25 Ta Life record. I've got my hands full as it is, and I just couldn't handle a new 25 release. We've been around for five years now anyway, and a lot of people know about the band – Back To Basics is more geared towards new bands who are just coming out, who need a push."

What about the past?

"So far I've put out 24 releases. I started in '95 as a DIY label going through small distributors, just kids in the scene. Not that bigger labels don't want to carry my stuff, but I'd rather they didn't, 'cos I want any money made to go directly back into the scene."

Favourite releases?

"Everything I've put out has been special to me. Whether it's sold thousands or I ended up giving them all away, 'cos I did each one for the music and the lyrics, 'cos I liked it or was friends with the band. A lot of work went into every release."

Will he ever graduate from the DIY sleeves?

"I could release stuff in glossy sleeves," he says, dismissively, "But I'm putting out the message; the cover doesn't matter to me. I put a lot of my own time into making those covers 'cos I don't want to waste money. That way I can release even more stuff!"

And the future?

"Oh, there's a new Comin' Correct split with Stormcore from France, a new split between Strength from Japan and No Compromise outta PA. I also have releases coming from Overthrow, No Submission, Backlash and Billy Club Sandwich. There's tons of new stuff coming out all the time..."

25 TA LIFE – ISSUE 70 (SEPTEMBER 1999)

Ian Glasper has been keepin' it real ever since we took the guy on all those years ago to pen the Hardcore Holocaust column, so who better qualified to get da lowdown on the new 25 Ta Life record, 'Friendship, Loyalty, Commitment', than him? Right – nobody.

Over the years, 25 Ta Life have built themselves a huge reputation within the worldwide hardcore underground, one more befitting a band that has released two or three albums at the very least, but these guys created the buzz about their band through just a few MCDs and, of course, some concerted touring. So, the arrival of their debut full length, 'Friendship, Loyalty, Commitment', for Triple Crown, has been greeted with great interest and anticipation, and not without reason. From the incendiary opener, 'Let The Past Be The Past', which is somewhat akin to having your teeth kicked in by a particularly bad-tempered Sumo wrestler, to the unrestrained brutality of closer, 'Smackin' You Up', it's blatantly obvious that 25 have not compromised their savage take on metalcore one fucking iota. It is gloriously violent and rawer than a fresh tattoo – just what the hardcore doctor ordered.

"Yeah, it takes this band a while to write new songs," sighs vocalist Rick Healey, calling me from his label's New York office, "And we play out a lot. We didn't wanna rush our first album; we wanted to do it right, on our own terms. A lot of bands don't really deserve to put out albums, and when they put out a CD no one knows them, so no one buys it, but we've played and played and played..."

And that's still an understatement! These guys tour like maniacs, so it's no wonder they've taken so long to unleash their debut album – but even after this big wait, there's still only ten brand new songs, boosted with a Warzone cover (of 'As One'), and re-recordings of four hoary old 25 classics. So, were you unhappy with the original recordings, or what?

"Oh no, we were happy with them first time round," explains Rick, "But all those recordings - the We Bite and SFT [Striving For Togetherness Records, the band's first label – IG] CDs - are now out of print. Those four songs are the ones we still play live, and everybody knows the 'Strength Thru Unity' stuff, but the newer kids have never heard some of that early material, y'know?"

One very cool thing about 25 Ta Life is that as soon as you hear them, you know who it is! You have a very distinct style, partly due to the septic guitar riffs. but mainly 'cos of your unmistakable vocal snarl. I guess that you and Fred [Mesk, guitar] have been playing together so long now, you've got a damn fine chemistry happening?

"Yeah, it's been seven years now," replies the talkative frontman, "And we've been working hard at this. I mean, the band's fun, and we do it 'cos we love hanging out with all our friends, but it is stressful when you come to record. Too many bands churn out bad songs, and we really wanted to release the best album that we could. We've developed our own sound, and people expect more from us than, say, Comin' Correct [Rick's other, more old school, band - IG]. That's more of a fun thing; it's not thrown together or anything, but it's much simpler; it's an older style of hardcore. It's definitely easier to do; 25 is much more in-depth."

I notice that you've had another line-up change since the last disc... dare we ask what happened to the last members? Or was it the inevitable pressure of all that touring?

"Well, me and Fred are very happy with how the band is going - we've been doing this for a long time, and we know exactly how we want to do things - but there was just a difference of opinion as to where the band should go. Our old guitarist, for example, is now with Madball, and they're a band who are definitely on the next level, and that was more what he wanted."

Surely you're 'big enough' now in your own right, to call the shots in most aspects of the band's business dealings, anyway?

"We're having a blast touring and stuff, but we are still doing it on our own terms," states Rick. "We're working with Triple Crown and Good Life, and we have a say in everything that gets done - if I'm not a big part of all that, if I'm not in control of what my own band's doing, then it wouldn't be the same."

Unfortunately, this hardcore scene that I love so much, like all things in life, is both good and bad, and one of the worst aspects of it is how fickle it can be. One minute a band can be flavour of the month, the next they can be sell-out motherfuckers... 'cos they bought some fries at McDonalds. I've heard 25 copping some flak recently, for daring to earn a living off the music they spend so much time perfecting. How dare you, Rick Healey!

"Half these kids," sighs Rick resignedly, "A year from now, they won't even be into hardcore. A lot of them are already set for life, and mummy and daddy will pay for their college, and they won't have to worry about paying bills or anything. That is what they do, and this is what we do. And we can't pull into a gas station and say, 'Yo, we're 25 Ta Life, fill her up - for free', y'know? Unfortunately, money makes the world go round, but it's what you do with your money that really counts.

"And a lot of people have no idea how expensive it is to keep a band going! I don't care what people say, or what other people do. Some kids are too judgmental when they don't even know us, who we are, or what we do. They think hardcore is all about them and their five friends... and it's actually about opening up your mind. I don't care if a band's doing good and they've signed to a bigger label - I'll love you or hate you for what you do, not what label you're on. Whatever happened to tolerance, and supporting each other?"

Truer words you won't find anywhere else in this issue, and that sincerity shines through every pounding beat of 'Friendship, Loyalty, Commitment'. It manages to be both a rousing hardcore record, and a scathingly hard metalcore one, too. Songs like 'Positive Hardcore, Go' add a very definite death metal vibe to the usual 25 Ta Life beatdown - all searing guitar torture - and the result is pleasingly Belgian, but still undeniably 25.

"We've always been metallic, mixing bands like Slayer with the Cro-Mags and Agnostic Front [couldn't have put it better myself - IG], whatever. We've always been a heavy band, even tho' my heart is more with the old school stuff, like 'Hardcore Rules', Fred is really into a lotta metal, so we try and mix it up, and this record is definitely the closest we've come to the perfect combination.

"Too many people are too quick to say, 'Oh, that's not hardcore', but who's to say? HC is an attitude; it's what is in your heart. Everyone should be able to do their own thing. And we get a lot of different kids at our shows, from punkers to metallers to vegan sXe kids... whether they all get it? Who cares?

HC will get stronger with more diverse people involved, 'cos that's how I got into it; when bands like the Crumbsuckers and Leeway and C.O.C. started crossing over..."

Sometimes it seems that all you guys are worried about is scene unity, and a lot of people would argue that there are more important things to fight for.

"We're an open-minded band," reasons Rick, "We're not a political band; we'll play to anyone and everyone. People say that unity can never happen, but I would rather strive for that, even if it is impossible, than just be content with ignorance. The world is a fucked-up place right now, and unity may never happen, but we are a positive band, and we are trying to make a difference... even if it is just to one kid on a purely personal level.

"There's more to life than money; take control. If you're not happy with your job, get another; if you're not happy at school, do something else. I want to be able to look back at my life and say that I had some fun. I lived how I wanted and I was basically happy. Life's too short to do otherwise."

3 INCHES OF BLOOD - ISSUE 126 (DECEMBER 2004)

Inventive thrash/power metal fusionists or post-modern piss-takers, taking liberties with orcs, axes and boiling seas of blood? Canada's 3 Inches Of Blood have been dividing listeners since their 2002 debut, and now they've been signed up to Roadrunner for their troubles. Ian Glasper heard their latest, 'Advance And Vanquish', and joined in on the battle cry.

"We've had our fair share of criticism, and still to this day get people who think we're making fun of metal. Just our age, you know? We don't look like a metal band; we're not dudes in our 40s, so they think we can't appreciate it or take it seriously. There's too many people wrapped up in the image side of things, and we just don't look enough like a heavy metal band! But when they see us live, they usually change their minds. We've had a lot of people say that they couldn't take us seriously until they saw us play."

Unbelievably the above statement is from Cam Pipes, one half of the deadly vocal duo that fronts Vancouver-based 3 Inches Of Blood, the latest heavy fuckin' metaaal sensation about to take the scene by storm. 'Unbelievably' because one listen to their 'Advance And Vanquish' album will leave you in no doubt as to the utter seriousness with which these metal warriors approach their art, said art being the dramatic fusion of traditional power and thrash metal into a molten mass of galloping rhythms and virtuoso riffing. Think 'Painkiller', only a lot faster. Or how about King Diamond covering 'Master Of Puppets'? Excited? You damn well should be; this is one of the best metal albums of the year – and to think that their debut nearly slipped by unnoticed.

"When we did our first record [2002's 'Battle Cry Under A Winter Sun'], we had a friend who put it out for us, and just sold it from his record store. When he sold out of the first press of that pretty quickly, we decided that we could probably do something with it ourselves, we repressed it on our own label. Then we got picked up by Death 'O' Clock in the UK, but unfortunately it never got a release in the US. Maybe it will one day in the future."

How does he regard it with the benefit of hindsight?

"Well, it did really well for us, it definitely helped get the word out; we toured on the back of that record quite a bit. And obviously Roadrunner liked it when they heard it!"

Ah yes, a coveted deal with Roadrunner. But not only have they signed to one of the biggest labels in the genre, they also secured the services of the very best producers it has to offer, Neil Kernon and Colin Richardson.

"Oh man, Neil brought the best out of all of us," gushes Cam proudly. "We were kinda nervous before the recording, because we had never really worked with a proper producer. Certainly not one with Neil's background. All the legendary bands he's worked with, all the recordings he's worked on that we think are absolutely stellar. But as soon as we met him, all the tensions were instantly gone; we warmed to each other really quickly and had a great rapport. It was really easy to work with him. He's not a ball-buster, but he knew how to push us and get the best out of us.

"Then to get Colin Richardson to mix it was the icing on the cake. The fact that those two guys were so enthusiastic about doing it is still kinda unbelievable. We haven't actually met Colin yet, because he did all the mixing on your side of the pond, but he would send us mixes every now and again, and we had no complaints."

No surprise there though, 'cos spinning 'Advance...' at volume is akin to a rollercoaster ride round the hallowed halls of Valhalla, the band hardly pausing for breath as they immerse you in wave after wave of soaring melodic thrash. The crystal-clear sound allows every note to embed itself beneath your skin with a surgical precision, whilst every falsetto shriek rips urgently at the ear. And all without even a hint of irony in song titles such as 'Axes Of Evil' or 'Destroy The Orcs'.

The striking Ed Repka artwork merely adds to the overall effect of OTT sensory overload, enhancing the certainty that your hands are feverishly clutching a modern classic in the making.

"We were trying to decide what to do for the cover, and we had a few artists in mind, but had no idea how we were going to approach it. Then the label suggested we try to get Ed Repka, and we thought that would be amazing, and sure enough, he did an incredible job. His work is so recognisable, and to have someone like him do artwork for us – this little band from Canada – is kinda overwhelming. I'm sure we all own at least two or three albums with his art on the front, which just added to the air of amazement to work with him."

They may not have realised it yet, but these unassuming youngsters have picked up a torch – now let's see how far they can run with it.

59 Times The Pain – issue 22 (August 1995)

59 Times The Pain, 1997, courtesy of Eelco Klein Overmeen (EpitaphEurope)

Swedish hardcore is right up there with the best of 'em, so reckons Ian Glasper, who meets up with guitarist/vocalist Magnus Larnhed of newest Scandinavian sensations 59 Times The Pain.

Sweden has been taking the hardcore world by storm recently with a constant and consistent output of quality bands. One such band is the oddly-named 59 Times The Pain, who have their first full-length, 'More Out Of Today', out on upcoming Swedish label Burning Heart.

On the back of their 'Blind Anger And Hate' MCD, the band billed themselves as 'hard-hitting, honest, straight on hardcore', a cap they seem happy to wear and one which fits them admirably. Let's just say that if you like Agnostic Front, you'll love these guys...

I caught up with guitarist/vocalist Magnus Larnhed recently, and talk began, where else, but with the new album...

"We recorded it in less than ten days, really quick; we wanted to capture the energy of our live performance. It's got sixteen songs on it, a lot like the last record I guess, but still a little bit different..."

I think it sounds groovier than 'Blind Anger And Hate'....

"We tried to get a bit more variation, even the vocals have some melody 'n' stuff. I'm really pleased with it."

As always, I was keen to hear about some of the lyrics. What's 'We're In, Now What?' all about?

"Sweden's just joined the European Community," explains Magnus in his careful, but fluent, English, "And that song title is a question of mine. The lyrics go, 'Too many questions, and not one of them answered...' I don't think Europe should just be one big map."

What about 'Two Minutes Remaining In The Third'?

"That's a hockey song," he laughs. Considering that two of the band aren't just hockey fans but players, and that Magnus was actually ringing me from a mobile phone whilst sat in a hockey arena, his answer isn't too much of a surprise. "But it's not just a hockey song, it has a meaning behind it. It's about never giving up; in a hockey game, when there's two minutes left, that's when you've got to give it all you've got, your best shot. And it's the same thing with life."

A lot of your lyrics seem about inner strength - is this something you think a lot of people are lacking?

"Definitely," agrees Magnus. "You've got to be able to believe in yourself, and a lot of people lack this ability. They also prefer to blame others for stuff that they could put right themselves. The title track of the new record, 'More Out Of Today', is actually about me because I was unemployed, feeling really down and depressed, but you've just got to pick yourself up. You can blame the politicians if you like, but in the end, it's up to you, I think."

Is it really that bad living in Sweden?

"Well, I'm from a small town, and the main problem here is you can't get a job. So everyone's very bored; the people just drink at the weekends and don't do anything else. And you start to wonder what life is all about. Like in all countries, I guess, the climate's getting rougher on the streets."

Is the band formed as a direct result of that boredom?

"Actually," he confides, "We formed the band after I saw Youth of Today in '89, and Biohazard in '90. When I saw those bands and that aggression on the stage... and their whole attitude. They were so friendly; they talked to us like normal people. I was like,

'Yeah, I wanna do this.'"

What other bands have influenced 59 Times The Pain?

"All the New York bands like Gorilla Biscuits, Judge, Burn... also, bands like the Beastie Boys. Even some metal bands - I think Entombed are really good. Also stuff like the Mighty Mighty Bosstones and Rancid."

Ever think you'll incorporate some of those styles into 59 Times The Pain? A bit of ska perhaps?

"Never!" comes the emphatic reply. "Actually, we think there's too many bands out there who change too much from one album to the next. I like it when you know what a band's new album is going to be like. They should change - change is always good - but they should also stay true to their roots and develop within that framework."

I know that you play guitar as well as sing when you play live. Don't you find this a bit limiting?

"When we do our live set, I play guitar at the beginning, then I put away the guitar. I only want to sing but the other guys want me to play guitar as well, so I'll play guitar for like twelve songs, then I take it off and there's something new in the show. When the energy level is slacking, at that point, I take the guitar off and it's, wow – boom!"

So what touring plans do you have for the new album?

"Peter from Burning Heart is talking about us doing some shows in Germany, then we might go over to the USA in September. But I haven't heard anything about England yet. Hopefully we'll get there, 'cos that's what we want to do: just get out and play, 'cos that's what we do best."

59 TIMES THE PAIN - ISSUE 38 (JANUARY 1997)

59 Times The Pain may be Swedish, and they may have worked with underground wunderkind Dan Swano on their new album, but they're as hardcore as they come. And what more, says Ian Glasper, could anybody want?

"It's a good record, there's something for everyone, I think." Oh, come on, Magnus, blow your own trumpet fercrissakes, it's a great record. "Well, there's more variation in the songs, I like it a whole lot more than our previous records", he eventually concedes. "We've improved in every aspect of song-writing, but it's still got that 59 vibe. We've never had a plan when we write songs, and this time was no different - this is how they came out."

For those who've just joined us, Magnus Larnhed is the guitarist/vocalist of Swedish hardcore combo 59 Times The Pain, and I just can't seem to get him as excited about their new record, 'Twenty Percent Of My Hand', as I am. I guess I'll just have to do all the drooling for him. Personally, I can't see how any hardcore fan can fail to get off on this vibrant disc in an instant. Opening salvo of 'With Instead of Against' and 'Can't Change Me' immediately demonstrate that here's a band who can combine the old

59 Times The Pain 1998, courtesy of Eelco Klein Overmeen (EpitaphEurope)

school and the new, the fast and furious with the groovy and sassy, maybe even the underground with the overground...

Its only shortcoming, for some folk, at least, 'cos I know I couldn't give a fuck, is that it is so flagrantly hardcore. "We all listen to different kindsa music, even bands like Civ, Rancid, and Pennywise", reckons Magnus. "One day I'll be listening to Uniform Choice, the next it could be Sepultura, or rap, whatever. But when we get together, we're 59 Times The Pain, and we're a hardcore band."

So, there, in a nutshell, is the crux of the matter. If you want your hardcore with some metal, or some industrial, or some death influences thrown in for good measure, walk on by. Stay out of this kitchen, 'cos the heat of this band's unashamed focus will singe your eyebrows off.

Anyways, 59 hail out of Sweden, where it's possible for a band to stay hardcore and become huge, as has been amply demonstrated by the likes of Millencolin and No Fun At All, who may not be big names here, but back home their record sales make impressive reading.

"Oh yeah, it's still really good for hardcore here", claims the reticent frontman. "The bands you mentioned regularly make the national charts, but we're a little too hard for the radio – hopefully! We still play with those bands, we'll play with anyone, anywhere, that's our thing. There's a really young audience here, which is great, 'cos they will end up growing with the band. We know that the older people go out and buy the CDs, but they don't go to the shows quite so much. I guess it's the snowboarding here that helps attract the younger crowd, and they really put out a lot of energy when they go see a band, too."

Mmm, I think the UK scene could maybe use an injection of that youthful energy 'n' all, to counteract the inbred cynicism we've inherited as a nation, which even extends into our alternative music scenes. That's why I hate to hear the snobbery of older fans, who seem to begrudge new kids getting into 'their' music. Listen up, those kids are the future of the music; otherwise we'll end up playing to halls full of faded tattoos and Zimmer frames, and shows won't be so much fun then, will they?

Anyway, back to the plot, what little there is, and 59's ripping new disc, which is even better when you consider the band hate recording full-stop. "No, we really don't enjoy studio work too much", Magnus sighs. "It's great to get the finished CD and, of course, you need to release records to be able to go out on tour, but we'll never be a studio band. This sort of music wasn't made to be perfectly recorded, analysed in minute detail, or for it to take two weeks to record the drum tracks. It was made for the stage, and that's where we feel comfortable."

Maybe you should have done a live record then. "We did record a lot of first takes, to try and capture the live energy. We were only in the studio so long because we had some problems with our guitars, none of them wanted to work! Dan [Swano] was really cool about it though. He's really nice to work with, and that's really important, to get on well with your producer. We couldn't think of anyone we'd rather record with after he did the last one ['More Out of Today', also on Burning Hearts – IG], and we're very pleased with what he's done for us. It sounds real big."

As for that enigmatic title, Magnus refuses to enlighten me as to its meaning. I hazard a guess that seeing as twenty percent of a hand is one finger, it refers to the traditional

- no matter where you're from - middle finger salute. Are they 'flipping the bird' to someone with that title, or what?

"Hey, man, I told you I'm not saying", he laughs. "It's a secret; we want to leave it to the imagination, and that's all I'm going to say right now. You can all think on that one yourselves."

For a band so blatantly hardcore, it's good to see they don't over-romanticise our proud subculture, as I discover when I probe him about the song 'Neither Question Nor Disagree'. "That's about how people live their lives, and I'm talking all people now. Some people in hardcore are in as much of a rut as normal people. Listening to hardcore music doesn't make you special, or exempt from problems. Some people are just content to live out the same life as their parents, and their parents before them, without stopping to wonder 'Why?' Life's too short to not enjoy it now."

A PERFECT MURDER – ISSUE 136

(OCTOBER 2005)

"Of course, we have a Pantera influence in our sound!" declares Carl Bouchard, guitarist with brutal Canadian metallers A Perfect Murder, unapologetically, on the subject of our Leander's review of their recent 'Strength Through Vengeance' album (Victory Records), that basically wrote them off as Pantera clones. "Everybody that plays heavy music today surely has a Pantera influence, in the same way that they will all have been influenced by Metallica and Black Sabbath, you know?"

"But, lyrically, all of the songs are drawn from my personal experiences and observations," interjects new vocalist Kevin Randel (formerly of Tennessee's Skard). "There is nothing fake or contrived about the lyrics on this album; they are about as real as you can get when it comes to dealing with life and all its struggles. Personally, I'm influenced by everyone from Elvis to Slayer, and everything in between. Southern rock, old outlaw country... I was raised on that shit, man. It's what helps me write honest and meaningful lyrics... something that metal these days so often lacks."

Yes, Leander was right, the shadow of Anselmo and co. looms long and large over 'Strength Through Vengeance', but that doesn't change the one indisputable fact about the new album – it rocks. Really damn hard. Guitar riffs cut like surgical steel, huge strident drum patterns nail everything through the floor, and Randel's bitter bark is a litany of dark, violent rage. Best of all, its earthy, organic tones are a refreshing change from the cold, ultra-processed productions so favoured of late.

"Getting a raw, natural drum sound was probably the main goal for this album," reveals Carl. "We ended up putting twenty-five mikes on just the drums! It was pretty insane, but we really wanted to capture that natural sound, y'know? Everybody uses triggers these days, and I'm not saying they're shit or anything, but we're just tired of them and wanted to do things a little differently."

"I decided to use a hand-held microphone as opposed to a condenser mike," adds Kevin. "We all approached this record with the same goal, to capture the band at its most raw and powerful. No bullshit, no tricks, just pure aggression; we went for a live vibe and that's what we got.

"And it is a release for me, for sure," he adds, when considering the hateful nature of many of his lyrics. "A form of therapy if you will... I'm actually a very physical person; I work out and train in various combat sports to keep myself occupied when I'm at home between tours. As far as getting in the right frame of mind goes, that all depends on how creative I'm feeling. I may write 100 songs in two months and then not write again for a year. Fortunately, right before I joined A Perfect Murder, I had just gone through one of my most productive periods ever, where I wrote upwards of 150 songs!"

A18 – issue 123 (September 2004)

A18, pic by Dale Rio

"We're very hit and miss; we seem to always get that love/hate response," laughs Mike Hartsfield, guitarist with straightedge Californian hardcore band, A18. "Some people are blown away and others can't stand the sight of us. But I guess it's up to everyone to choose for themselves; not everyone's a fan of heavy hardcore. Some people don't want to get showered with broken guitar parts, and some don't want me bleeding all over the stage. Really we just wanted to give the SoCal scene a kick in the pants because we felt it needed one about now."

Never mind the SoCal scene, sometimes it seems that hardcore worldwide needs a wake-up call, and 'Dear Furious', A18's second album for Victory, is as rude an awakening as you could hope for. A lumbering brute of a record, bringing to mind the visceral forcefulness of classic era Integrity, it's also imbued with an intelligence that belies its gruff exterior, and it's all delivered with the assured confidence that only comes with first-hand experience.

"Yeah, Isaac [Golub, vocals] was in A Chorus of Disapproval," explains Mike of their to-die-for pedigree. "Steve Larson [a founder member who left the band in 2002] was in Carry Nation and Insted, and I was in Outspoken, Strife and The Suppression Swing. But A18 is a far deeper band than anything we've done previously. The lyrics are much more interesting and take a bit more thought; you find that some topics in hardcore are just too spelled out and obvious. And musically it's much heavier, of course, because our writing abilities are fifteen years more refined!"

'Stab You Through The Everything' sounds as pissed off as it's possible to get without actually beating someone to a pulp, but has that ultra-violent vibe got you tagged as 'hatecore'?

"I've seen a few reviews for the new record where the 'hatecore' label has come up, but anyone who really listens to the record will obviously see that we're no such thing. We don't talk tough and don't reference the streets all the time; it's just not our thing. Although I agree that the band is very much a release for our more extreme emotions.

"Our name itself comes from the 18th Amendment in the US constitution," says Mike, closing on a positive note. "It made drinking and the possession of alcohol against the law. Personally, I've been straightedge for almost twenty years and, honestly, it's been a lifesaver. I don't waste my time and effort, getting distracted from doing what I believe I need to do in my life; I am always focused, every day, and how many people that drink can honestly say the same?"

Abhinanda – issue 37 (December 1996)

"We took it from the first Shelter album", explains Jose Saxlund, vocalist with Swedish hardcore hopefuls, Abhinanda, laughing as I relate our editor Old Nick's problems getting his head round the band's mouthful-of-a-moniker.

"It means 'never-ending well of bliss', and we just thought it was a cool name. It's not your typical hardcore name at all."

Now, assumption is the mother of all fuck-ups, and a lot of people assume that Abhinanda are a Krishna band 'cos of that name. Sorry to piss on your fireworks, everyone, but...

"No, we're not a Krishna band", he replies with admirable patience for someone who's no doubt answered this question a million times. "It's 'cos of the name, and also the long tour we did with 108. People are quick to jump to the wrong conclusion. I don't personally relate to Krishna consciousness, but I have absolutely nothing against

18

Abhinanda by Naki

anyone who does. Like everything in life, there's some people into it who are very cool, and there's some people who aren't. I don't want to waste my time complaining about them. Religion is a personal issue, and there are more important things to sing about."
Such a statement against the negativity so often prevalent in hardcore music seems to have been perfectly articulated in 'Illumination', the opening track of Abhinanda's new, self-titled, album on Desperate Fight.

"People should confront each other, and learn from each other," elaborates Jose, "But don't let's waste each other's time fighting each other for no real reason. There's too much energy wasted arguing over petty differences, don't you think?"

I sure do, and it's great to hear a killer new record with the potential to blow away some of the barriers that create such trivial rivalries. Abhinanda's newie takes that prime hardcore fury and batters it through a rock, as in Rock, filter, resulting in something uniquely exciting, yet utterly listenable. It's no surprise then that the band have achieved considerable success in their home country, where hardcore is big news, and bands like No Fun At All even make the Top Ten!

"Sweden is such a small country, but HC is really big here, so bands like us, or Refused, can get into all the big papers. We're 'bigger' here than, say, in Germany, but we sell more records there. ln Germany, which is a much bigger country, you can sell a lot more records, and still stay really underground. "

And underground is where l think this particular band would rather stay. Their music is just a little too hard, and their lyrics too real, for pop kids.

"l don't think it's too hard", reasons Jose, destroying my romantic notions with old-fashioned logic. "Look at how big bands like Pantera and Rage Against The Machine are, and they're very hard, with very real lyrics... l just think our music isn't so mainstream. And basically, we don't have the kinda money needed to push a band like us into the big time. Besides, even if we had, we wouldn't want to, y'know? We've reached a level that is cool for us. We can record albums whenever we want, and do a couple of really good tours each year, but we have other interests, too. We don't want to do this full-time; we have social lives outside the band. Refused tour all the time, and we've learnt by watching them. Whenever they're home, they're just too exhausted to do anything!"

Jose is in the happy position of being able to decide just when his band records and tours, because he runs the label they are signed to, Desperate Fight, who are now enjoying being licensed in the States by the mighty Victory. The label has been responsible for unleashing not only Abhinanda, Refused and the Doughnuts, but also rising stars, Separation, Purusam ("They have a new singer, and are even heavier than before..."), and Said I Was.

"ln the beginning, when I signed bands", he recalls fondly, "It was 'cos all my friends liked them. Now, we're under a little more pressure to sell records 'n' stuff, so we have to put some of that pressure on the bands, to make the best records they can. It's good that the bands and the label have had to grow together. We hang out with all the bands every day, so it's a great working relationship. At the end of the day, we're all friends first and foremost."

Above All, at the Esplanade, Southend, by Phil Howes

Brutal, heavy, grinding, hard as nails... just some of the words we like to use when we're talking about Above All here at Terrorizer. The Southend-based metalcore band have excited more than a few of us here with their debut album, 'Domain', not least our man Ian Glasper, who buttonholed vocalist Tony and guitarist Ben to find out more about Above All's bid for domination....

You can count the number of bands to burst out of the English underground hardcore scene and move onto bigger things without losing their integrity on the fingers of one hand. In fact, so judgmental and unforgiving is that scene, you could probably say the thumbs of one hand! Southend's Above All are no doubt hoping to fly in the face of such

Above All, at Saks, Southend, by Phil Howes

adversity with the imminent release of their debut album 'Domain' for Roadrunner Records. l caught up with the guys at a bit of a loose end, really, having turned up at the Century Media Crossover 2000 show in London, where they were meant to be halfway up the bill, only to find that, due to several unfortunate misunderstandings, they weren't playing at all. I managed to calm down their vocalist Tony enough to tell me more about the forthcoming album, which is definitely a bit, well, metal, compared to his previous band Stand Off.

"It's very metal," he confirms unashamedly, "But that's something we always wanted to do from the beginning anyway. Ben [guitars] and Hallam [bass] both come from a metal background, Mark [drums] kind of, and before I got into hardcore, I was into the metal thing. We've just progressed, and this is the sound that came naturally... and we're really happy with it!"

So, Roadrunner exerted no pressure on you whatsoever to pursue that direction?

"No, not at all. We can do what we want. Actually, they were kinda shocked when they heard it, 'cos it was so much more metallic than what we'd previously done. I mean, we'd only done two demos anyway, and the last one was headed in this direction, but this album has fulfilled what we wanted to do. The new stuff is in a similar vein, too, but a bit more... well, metal!"

Are you worried about losing some of your original fanbase? "Yeah, but most of 'em are into the metally side of hardcore anyway," Tony ponders. 'We've only ever really appealed to the metal-hardcore kids - the 'emo' kids aren't really into us, 'cos we're a completely different thing. I'm sure we will lose a few fans, but I hope we'll gain more, and people will realise that we haven't changed our sound to suit anyone. There's no preconceptions about what we do... we've always been metally, y'know?"

"At the end of the day," adds Ben, "We're doing what we want to do."

One obvious advantage Above All now have over their peers since inking a deal with such a prestigious label is a bigger recording budget. Alex 'Fudge Tunnel' Newport was flown in to produce 'Domain', and, axe-specialist that he is, he's brought out the venomous crunch of the guitars, even if the drums could have sounded a little punchier. I wondered how much of a hand Mr. Newport had in the arrangements of the material? "He came down to Southend three days before the recording," Tony recalls, "To watch us rehearse, and we played him the songs. It was kinda rushed; we didn't have too long but we played them to him, and there were a few bits where he gave us his opinion, said maybe this could be extended, this could be shortened, try something like that, y'know?"

Did AIex's input have anything to do with Tony mellowing his vocal style? "A lot of that was to do with production, anyway. Before, when we've done demos, the music would get done, and then it'd be like, 'Tony, do your vocals!' And I'd get two takes, in there for twenty minutes, screaming my throat raw. I know what you're saying, though, it's not as raw. We were trying to appeal to a wider cross section of people, but there's still a lot of urgency there. I didn't want to limit us, so l tried to incorporate something a bit different."

"We tried to make the lyrics work with the guitars, not like some musicians who write music with guitars and then just put words over the top," Ben interjects. "That just doesn't sound right, y'know?"

Ah yes, the lyrics, so often as - if not more - important as the music in hardcore, and that title 'Domain' has a distinctly 'concept' ring to it! "A lot of the songs are about life, survival, destruction, that kinda thing," Tony explains. "General existence, and how we're destroying things. They're not preaching or anything, they're just a point of view from a third person, if you will. There is a link between them. We're not trying to thrust things down people's throats, because they just reject them then, straight away. l don't pretend that I know everything, and I try not to see through this blinkered vision. The lyrics are based around what I believe in, but there's four individuals in this band."

Above All got signed remarkably early on in their careers, mainly on the strength of Miles Leonard, then the A&R man at Roadrunner, liking Tony and Hallam's previous band Stand Off so much. One disadvantage of a band getting signed so early is that they do all their growing in front of the public...

"At the time, we didn't think of it like that. It was more like, 'We're in a band, let's go and play some shows, let's just get out and do it...', but looking back, I wonder why we did this or that! But we learnt a lot, we had to deal with a lot of pressures, and we got the nerves out of our system. We just go and do our thing now."

How are they finding it playing in front of metal audiences? "We're going down great, and they're not as reserved as hardcore audiences. Don't get me wrong," Tony reassures me, "We don't want to cut ourselves off from that scene. We just want to expose our music to a totally wide cross-section of music fans, hardcore kids, metal kids - even a lot of hip-hop kids listen to heavy stuff..."

The band have a 7" just out on Bradford-based Sure Hand Records, which, while a formidable slab of metalcore, isn't a patch sound-wise on the impending album, and seemed a little badly timed?

"We recorded it a year and a half ago," Tony explains, "Way before we signed with Roadrunner. It'll mainly be sold to the kids who were there for us in the beginning, rather than the general public. It's an underground hardcore record, recorded on a very small budget, and people will have to accept it for what it is, y'know? It's not like our album by a long shot, but it's good in a way, because we came from that scene and this is something that represents us from that time. But I'll stress again, it was done a year and a half ago, off a demo we financed ourselves."

And finally, what would he say to the critics in Terrorizer who claim that hardcore has no place in the magazine?

"If the black metal kids think their form of music is the only extreme form of music, then they're very mistaken. If it's not their cup of tea, then fair enough, but any heavy hardcore band is definitely extreme! Too many people associate hardcore with just melodic or punk stuff. They'll moan about something, but when they hear it, it'll be like, 'Oh, right, cool!' I'm sure there'll be a lot of death metal kids who'll like us, 'cos we're not Green Day and we're not Offspring!"

THE ACCUSED - ISSUE 136 (OCTOBER 2005)

Accused, circa 2005, by Tasha Sawabini

24

Accused, circa 2005, by Tasha Sawabini

'Oh Martha!' heralds the long-overdue return of Seattle's most rabid metal act, The Accused. Ian Glasper entered the dark world of raped nuns and buxom serial killers inhabited by vocalist Blaine Cook to find out more.

"Oh Martha...!" cackles The Accused vocalist, Blaine Cook, gleefully, when asked to reveal the origins of his band's sinister mascot, Martha Splatterhead. "The name 'Splatterhead' was actually taken from a series of BB-gun wars that me and some buddies used to have back in, like, '83. We'd put on heavy clothing, homemade helmets and stuff, and chase each other around the woods, taking careful aim and unloading with the BB. One of the guys was called Splatterhead; he was the singer for an old Seattle punk band, Solger. If I didn't know any better, I'd even say that King Diamond got the idea for 'Nuns Have No Fun' from the Solger song, 'Raping Dead Nuns'...

"Anyway, one day I'm riding the bus home from work and I'm writing this lyric about some mad psycho killer who just happens to be a buxom female who's prowling the streets in a zombie-like state. I figured that if we had a female killer we wouldn't be poo-poo'd by the more politically-correct hardcore scene of the time, haha! And we've continued to use her as a visual for the band and a source of lyrical inspiration ever since. The one drawback though was that the only songs that anybody ever talked about were the horror-themed ones, and anything we did that had any other message was overlooked. But Martha keeps growing... or rotting. Her teeth are getting longer and sharper, and her tits... well, for a rotting old corpse, she's got some pretty firm ones!"

And thus we set the scene for the new Accused album, 'Oh Martha!', on their own Condar label, the first studio full-length they've unleashed since 1992's 'Splatter Rock', and a more raging slice of frenzied hardcore thrash you're not likely to hear any time soon. These guys wrote the book on intense crossover, and the passing of the years has done little to dim their enthusiasm for good-natured carnage.

"We just started playing together about two years ago," explains Blaine, on how the band coalesced again after such an extended hiatus, and what they've all been doing in the meantime. "When we got it going again, we had no idea which direction we'd head, but after playing a bunch of shows it

Accused, circa 2005, by Tasha Sawabini

just seemed natural to at least attempt some new songs. As for the past ten years...? Well, I had a kid, and that's pretty great; we both get the summer off to screw around! "But we've all been doing different stuff. I had a band called The Black Nasty going on for a few years; we released one lowly little old DIY CD. Then, back in '99, Alternative Tentacles contacted me about re-releasing all the old Fartz stuff [The Fartz were Blaine's first band, responsible for the oft-overlooked classic EP, 'Because This Fuckin' World Stinks', way back in 1981 – IG]. So, of course, we had to play some shows, and one thing leads to another. Paul Solger, the Fartz guitarist, couldn't pull his weight so we replaced him with the Accused bass player... the one and only Alex 'Maggot Brain'. Alex had been playing guitar in his latest outfit, the Hot Rod Lunatics, whilst [Accused guitarist] Tom [Niemeyer] had been doing some stuff with Gruntruck. I think his last deal was called Soul Killer, and he was also playing second guitar for River Red."

So, your reformation didn't have anything to do with that 'Mechanized Death: A Tribute To The Accused' album on Transparent?

"No, but that was really fucking cool, all sorts of different bands on that thing. We're like the bastard step-children locked in the closet, y'know? Lotsa bands got some stiff shots of inspiration from The Accused!"

'Oh Martha!' will give any fan of extreme deranged thrash a stiff something, that's for sure, it being an awesome OTT collection of Jack Endino-produced, tear-ass metal (the band even tackle a Tank cover, 'Filth Hounds Of Hades'!), bound in a gloriously tasteless full-colour booklet, every song a bizarrely realised reflection of the depravity Mankind is capable of.

"Yeah, there's a couple of songs on the new disc where the lyric is taken right out of the newspaper headlines so to speak. 'The Body', for example, is about a small, fanatical religious cult - with some very disturbing child-rearing practices! Whilst 'Fast Zombies Rule' was the first new song we wrote... the line 'fast zombies rule' was actually etched into the matrix of one of our old LPs. Remember how some bands would have a cryptic message scratched on the vinyl? Well, fast zombies are just that much more sinister, aren't they? No matter how crafty you are, those flesh-chompers are going to run you down!"

Much like The Accused then; believe me, there's nowhere left to hide this time.

AFI - ISSUE 89 (MAY 2001)

AFI, Nov '99, by Danielle Dombrowski

Across the course of five albums and two EPs, Californian punkers AFI have metamorphosed from an above-average melodicore band into something that can only be described as... well... AFI! A potent combo of hardcore, punk, and gothic metal, the band really came into their own with their recent 'The Art of Drowning' album for Nitro. Ian Glasper got the lowdown on the eve of their first headlining UK tour.

27

AFI, 1999 by Danielle Dombrowski

You may or may not have noticed, but San Francisco punkers AFI have featured highly in the writers' poll in this here magazine for the last two years running, which might have raised a few eyebrows out there in readership land. What the hell was a 'pop punk' band doing featuring in the playlist of an extreme metal mag? Well, AFI are no ordinary 'pop punk' band; sure, they may be melodic, and they may be on Nitro Records, but there is a dark heart beating at the core of their being, pumping blood as black as pitch through their veins! If you scratch the surface, you will see that they have more in common with the usual 'Terrorizer band' (if such a creature exists?) than you might suspect, as the opening comments of vocalist Davey Havok confirm, when I call him up in readiness for their imminent UK headlining tour.

"Oh yeah, I do really like black metal, and to cross over to those fans would be cool. We all have the same dark qualities in our sound, and similar themes behind our music..." But whereas black metal is dark like a winter blizzard, AFI proffers a rich gothic tapestry of vibrant decadence that positively throbs with a passion for life. Until recently, the band were punk rock's best kept secret, but you can't help have noticed them these last few months, especially since they opened up for the Offspring in Wembley fucking Arena.

So, Davey, how was it opening up for a band as huge as the Offspring all across Europe? "It was really different every night. Some nights it was wonderful," he recalls fondly, before adding with a sigh, "Other nights it could be horrible. In the UK it was amazing for us; we were, like, 'Oh my god, we're playing Wembley Arena [laughs]', and it was really good for us, a dream come true. We're very pleased with the response we've gotten from England, especially seeing as we've done so few shows there. But in Europe, it was harder... especially Germany. We'd have, like, one really great show, then one really bad show. In Italy, we had an amazing gig in Bologna, then we had stuff thrown at us the next night in Rome [laughs]!

"They had no real idea where we were coming from, some of the kids didn't understand it at all. Bands on that level are always going to be hard to tour with, 'cos their fans are so fanatical, and have very little time for any support bands."

Of course, you're on Nitro [Dexter from the Offspring's own label – IG], which seems to me like the perfect label for you guys. It's big enough to have clout, but small enough for you to really matter, and what a roster they're slowly amassing! They've just signed the Damned, right?

"Yeah, that's right, I met Dave Vanian [The Damned's vocalist – IG] at that Wembley show, and he said he liked our show. I was, like, 'Fuuuck!', cos they are one of my favourite bands ever. They were one of the first bands doing that dark punk thing that I really got into...

"And being on Nitro is wonderful. They've got great distribution and are great business-wise, but more importantly, we get very personal treatment; they truly care about this band and our music. Most labels are about numbers, and if you don't do the right numbers, you're not on the label anymore! But we know everyone at Nitro on a personal level, and we're all from similar musical backgrounds."

AFI, Nov 1999, by Danielle Dombrowski

As the years have passed, AFI have become darker and darker with each release. Was this a natural progression, or was it an intentional decision to take the band in this direction?

"Actually, it was really natural. I think that the influences you hear on our later albums were always there, but we just had to learn to play and grow as a band."

So, it was just a case of unlocking your own potential?

"Yeah, I guess so," agrees Davey. "We became more cohesive with each line-up change. It was really when Jade [Puget, their guitarist since the awesome 'Black Sails...' album – IG] joined that we made that big turn and became the band we are now. He was a friend of mine, and someone I respected very much as a musician and had always wanted to work with, and we really started to solidify as a band very quickly after that. "We like to push ourselves, and we wanna keep changing. I'm sure that the next album – whenever that will be, and it won't be anytime soon – will be quite different to this last one. We're never content to stand still; we always want to challenge ourselves.

"We're very lucky," he reflects, "It can go either way for a band like us. If you're a band who doesn't fit in anywhere easily, sometimes no one ends up liking you [laughs]!"

That said, the last album itself [2000's 'The Art of Drowning' – IG] was as subtly eclectic as any other melodic hardcore record I've heard in recent years, and it was met with nothing but unanimous praise. One listen to, say, the opening track 'Initiation' should be enough to convince even the most sceptical of our readers that you guys have nothing to do with the carefree pop punk so beloved of the mainstream media right now. The band really seems to be at a peak of eloquence.

"Thank you! We do try to combine beauty with aggression, sombre music with high energy stuff... anger with..."

Tender Fury?

"Ah yes, good ol' Jack Grisham," laughs the likable vocalist. "That whole era of LA music was so great, wasn't it? I love TSOL, DI, the Adolescents, Christian Death... I grew up with that West Coast punk rock thing, but also listened to some of the DC and east coast stuff too... and a lot of English bands too, of course! Like the Damned, the Bauhaus, the Sisters of Mercy, Siouxsie and the Banshees – you English did it first, and the best!"

My turn to say thank you then! What about your own Bay Area scene?

"Oh yeah, that whole Gilman Street [famous alternative venue in San Francisco – IG] scene was very, very influential... Operation Ivy, Samiam, Jawbreaker, and Rancid, of course. They've been great friends of ours for many years. Our influences are all across the board, to be honest. Adam loves The Clash, I like Metallica and Slayer too... it varies hugely. But if we all had to agree on just one album, to listen to on the bus, I guess it would have to be 'Appetite For Destruction'... we'd all be happy with that one!"

Lastly, your lyrics are wonderfully provocative, full of dramatic metaphor, and hinting at intense profundity. They beg further explanation, yet you remain steadfastly tight-lipped about explaining them too much.

"They're intentionally ambiguous," he admits. "For two reasons really; they're very introspective and personal, and I like a little buffer between me and the world, a shield of sorts, I don't wanna lay myself too bare. And also, I'd prefer people be able to take what they want from the lyrics, rather than me spell it all out for them word for word; I think music means more that way... if you have to discover some of it yourself."

Suggested side-bar: SON OF SAM

You just know that any band named after an infamous serial killer is gonna be darker than the shithouse in the London Dungeon, and Son of Sam – Davey's one-off side project - don't deliver any surprises as such, just ten tracks of amazing gothic punk rock in the vein of early Misfits and Samhain. Not surprising really when you consider that the band comprises guitarist Todd Youth (moonlighting from Danzig), drummer London May (Samhain) and bassist Steve Zing (also Samhain). Add to this already-impressive line-up guest appearances from Glenn Danzig and his current drummer Joey C. and bassist Howie Pyro, and you have the recipe for a truly heady witch's brew. If you have even the remotest taste for any of the above-mentioned bands, you have to hear their 'Songs From The Earth' (Nitro) album right now.

"In a way it is a homage," agrees Davey when I suggest that Son of Sam sounds like a blast from all the members' glorious pasts. "It was London and Steve and Todd's project long before I became a part of it. They called me up, and asked if I wanted to sing, and of course I jumped at the chance.

"They intended it to be in the vein of their own classic material, and it turned out exactly like it was meant to. I mean, when they sent me the tapes of the music, so I could start to put the vocals over it, I couldn't help but come up with stuff that sounded like Samhain [laughs]. It was totally derivative, and they were cool with that, because they wanted to capture that original spirit again.

"Samhain were the first band to ever sound like that, and no one's ever touched them since either, so those guys are the only ones really qualified to do an album like this and make it work."

So how was it working in the studio with Mr. Danzig?

"Oh, I didn't meet him; he came in the studio after me to do his parts. To be honest, I was kinda glad that he wasn't there the same time as me; it would have made me very nervous if he'd been watching me doing my tracks!"

And will we ever get to see the band live?

"There are no plans for that right now. We're all in other full-time bands, and we all have very busy schedules. If we were all in the same place at the same time, maybe a show might happen... but it's not likely, haha!"

AGNOSTIC FRONT – ISSUE 42 (MAY 1997)

Agnostic Front, by Naki

At one point, Agnostic Front weren't just part of the legendary Eighties New York hardcore scene, they were the NYHC scene. Now, with their influence and importance at an all-time high, the original four-piece line-up have reformed five years after the last AF line-up split, with live gigs and a new studio album due very soon. Ian Glasper gets the skinny from guitarist Vinnie Stigma and bassist Rob Kabula.

The whole idea behind hardcore, especially the punk strand of it, was/is that the audience are on par with the bands. Anyone can have a go, it's music for everyone, and, as such, hero worship of any band seems a bit at odds with the original concept of the genre. And for a band to take on 'legendary' status should be taboo, but hey, even a republic has its elected representatives, and long ago, Agnostic Front were unanimously deified. This band defined the old school sound back when 'old school' was still new school, established New York as a Mecca for the hardcore underground, and courted just enough controversy so as not to become too good to be true. Their ex-members can be found in almost every NYHC band of note, and their songs have been covered by bands across the fucking globe, keeping their legacy alive.

When they split in 1992, the news was met with disbelief by the faithful, and resignation by the rest of us. The signs had been there for a while – less than convincing material on their latter albums (that's not to say they were shit, hell no! AF at their worse were better than most bands at their best...), and two live albums in as many years. Vinnie, Matt and Will concentrated on Madball, and vocalist Roger went off to be a Harley mechanic, and managed to break his back stage-diving to his kid-brother's band.

1996 was a good year for comebacks. The Misfits, another lot of legends in their own lifetimes, returned to the fray, and towards the end of the year, whispers began of Exodus's rebirth, and mebbe even the reinvention of Suicidal Tendencies. Those whisperers told of Agnostic Front reforming too, and not just some cheap cash-in either. This was going to be the real thing – the original first album line-up that so many people wanted so desperately to see for so many years, but never did. I greeted the rumours with scepticism until Ray outta Warzone assured me it was all true, and he should know, having been their first drummer for the 'United Blood' EP.

Actually, scepticism is how most people view reformations, but founding member and living personification of the NYHC scene Vinnie Stigma is keen to reassure me that this was not a planned occurrence.

"It was a fuckin' accident", he exclaims on the phone from his band's management's offices in the Big Apple. "We all happened to be at a Madball show, 'cos we're all down with those guys, y'know, and they got me up on stage, and they got Roger up to sing. The next thing, Hoya, the bass player handed his guitar over to Rob, and we were nearly all there. It just happened, and it felt good. We'd talked about it often enough, so we just decided to do it. We thought, why not?"

When you were in Madball, and playing AF covers in the set, did it inspire you to get the band back together, seeing how many people still loved those songs with such passion?

"The kids never forgot us", he replies humbly, before adding in a more Vinnie Stigma style, i.e. his voice rising to a yell with enthusiastic excitement, "At all the shows there'd always be kids in AF shirts... there's always one Agnostic Front guy at every hardcore show!"

Agnostic Front, Birmingham 1991, by Andrew Giles

I'd wager more than one actually, but anyways... it seems slightly weird that Vinnie left Madball because he was starting a family, and now he's back in a band already – surely he's not sick of changing nappies already?

"Yeah, I know," he laughs, "But that's just the way it happened. Before my boy was born, I was really building up and anticipating it, and when it happened, it became so natural. I could handle it, and I knew that I could do this as well as that."

Roger Miret was quoted in a New York zine as saying that 'Vinnie's a kid in an adult body...'

"Well, that's true, too", he concedes, "I just can't stay off stage."

Now, it's well documented what Roger and Vinnie have been doing, but what of the other members from that original line-up now thrust once more into the limelight? Rob Kabula was until recently in Against The Grain, a NYHC band, not dissimilar to AF in their 'Cause For Alarm' phase. You know, high-speed metallic hardcore with big mosh sections. ATG were - or should I say 'are' - much better than most of the wannabe pack, too, resulting in them being the object of attention of several labels, including, if my sources are correct, Victory.

"Well, I got so busy with AF that I had to leave them", reckons Rob, taking over from Vinnie for a moment. "Against The Grain have two guitarists, and one of 'em switched over to bass to take my spot."

Would you agree with the Agnostic Front comparisons Against The Grain garnered?

"Maybe. I wrote a lot of the songs, y'know? They're young kids, and I went in, and I was like the coach, and got their shit together, and we started playing out and things were moving... but then I jumped up onstage with Roger and Vinnie, and things have got real busy since, and I didn't want to stop them. I said, 'You guys go on without me,' but I still get up for them once in a while. Things are still cool between us."

Is this a permanent comeback, 'cos I read that it might only be for a 7" to start with?

"No, this is a real comeback," Vinnie's back on the line, and still bubbling. "We've got fifteen brand new songs, and we should have a new album out by September. I mean, we don't even have a record deal yet, but we have some good offers."

No doubt some interest from some majors, too? I'm sure they can't resist something as potentially lucrative as an AF reformation. With the Misfits on Geffen, and hardcore punk seemingly booming, the sky's the limit.

"Yeah, they're sniffing around, of course. We've got offers on the table, but we're shopping around, to see who'll do the right thing by us, who's not gonna bury us, who's right for a hardcore band like ourselves."

In actual fact, by the time you read this, there will be new AF material committed to tape, and we're all wondering what direction the band will be pursuing. Judging from other interviews I've seen with Roger stating that on this reformation tour they'd only be playing stuff off their first EP and LP, I guess we can anticipate a return to their roots.

"It's hardcore!" yells Vinnie. "We're going back to the traditional hardcore style."

But are you disowning your later material? "Uh, we'll do a few songs off the later albums, too. It'll be all the old classics, and lots of new material, and a bit in between. We've got a lot of songs to draw on, we'll be doin' a 55-minute set, which is plenty of time for a hardcore show, y'know? The kids are killin' themselves out there."

So, spill the beans on the new record. It's certainly gonna be the hottest hardcore album of the autumn for most of us, but what can we expect?

"It's all-new Agnostic Front hardcore! And we ain't fronting on hardcore, either. It ain't got no metal tint, or no hip hop feel, it's just straight-up hardcore."

Well, that's probably turned Old Nick off straightaways. The concept of old school is becoming a little abhorrent to Da Ed lately, despite the Path of Resistance record, but mebbe hearing it done by the masters will change his mind? [Mebbe - Ed] After all, these guys pioneered those big singalong breakdowns that send us hardcore afficionados into frenzied pile-ups down the front of those macho pits that everyone pours scorn on. Yes, it's probably got something to do with male bonding. Yes, it's chest-beatingly primitive, but every time I hear 'United Blood', the hairs start prickling on the back of my neck, and I want to flip off a stage. It works on you at a very base level: you either instinctively love it, or find it awfully boring and regressive.

Do you sit down and write that shit intentionally, or does it just flow out of you naturally?

"Oh, naturally, very, very naturally", boasts Vinnie, good-naturedly. "It's all coming out of me so smooth, it's scary. I'm still the best hardcore guy out there! I've already got another album in my head; I can't stop it."

"It's probably gonna be called 'Do or Die'," adds Rob, the voice of reason. "We have song titles like 'Gotta Go', 'Rage', 'Bloodsucker'... it's been a total band collaboration, musically and lyrically. They're

hardcore lyrics, about being angry, about authority putting you down, about the hardcore kids of the world uniting together. We're going back to the old school way of hardcore thinking."

Of course, those doubters will still have their doubts about the sincerity of Agnostic Front's timely reformation, what with everyone from Slayer to Obituary citing them as a major influence. With a major deal highly likely and big money changing hands every time they play out, there's plenty of ammunition there for the people who'd like to cry 'Sell out!'

Vinnie is, of course outraged. "No way, no one better say that, 'cos it ain't that way, and never has been, never will be."

And so is Rob! "At our Wetlands shows [where they played two sold-out reformation shows last December – IG], we just took a percentage of the door, depending on how many people came in."

But not as much as Vinnie! "When they've done as many fuckin' benefit shows as Vinnie Stigma then they can fuckin' talk! I've probably done more benefit shows than they've been to fuckin' hardcore shows..."

"And they can talk when they've been around as long as we have", adds Rob. "A lot of people drop out after a year or two, but we've always been around the scene. We've been around forever, we're fuckin' lifers."

Strangely enough, Agnostic Front were one of the bands who turned me onto metal,

Agnostic Front, by Danielle Dombrowski

actually! I started off listening exclusively to punk, UK punk, in fact, but then got into the USHC thing, and eventually the crossover style, and from there, it was only a short step to 'Hell Awaits' and 'Ride The Lightning'. When I think crossover, I always think of three albums immediately - DRl's 'Crossover', of course, COC's 'Animosity' (still their finest moment, if you ask me, which you didn't, but hey, that's the advantage of being a writer, so go hang), and AF's 'Cause For Alarm'. You can't beat the adrenalin rush when the tight-ass riff and pummelling double bass kick in out of the tremolo dive intro to 'Eliminator'. Thankfully, this is one of the songs not off the first LP that they'll be keeping in their set. After all, it's still their biggest-selling album to date, a fact which probably speaks volumes if you care to analyse it.

And their opinions on influencing a death metal band like Obituary, who last issue said they'd like nothing more than to tour with AF? To your humble scribe, it seems like the Agnostic Front sound reached far beyond the confines of the HC scene, whether they like it or not.

"Oh, we've played a few shows with them", recalls Vinnie, of his Madball days. "They're good guys, and we're friends with 'em. Madball were on the same label as them, of course, and we did tours with 'em, so we were all down with each other, y'know? It's cool to cross over here and there, to break down barriers. We never wanted to segregate ourselves or anything, y'know?"

And now a question that I posed the Misfits, Obituary, and Warzone when they each returned to the action after long hiatuses. Things change, especially musical tastes, and kids can be fickle sometimes, and unforgiving, so how does it feel to be back on the scene, with all the new faces and their higher expectations?

Agnostic Front, by Sam Lennox, Lecky from Voorhees on the mic

"Hardcore's changed since we've been away", replies Vinnie, beating the other guys to the phone yet again. "It's a whole different ball game now. We used to play to all punks, we used to mainly play squats... and now, well, hardcore has a different face. The kids dress differently, think differently... I dunno," he laughs. "It's all a lot different! It's matured basically, but there's still room for Agnostic Front.

"I go to all the little hardcore shows", he adds, on the subject of the upcoming new wave of NYHC, "Like Breakdown, Rejuvenate, or Down Low. They don't pull big crowds, but I go and support. I love goin' to HC shows, I love fuckin' hardcore!

"You know I have a British Bulldog?" he asks, changing tack with gleeful disrespect for my line of questioning. "Yeeaah, I took him to a show here last week, and he bit somebody. He was goin' after everyone! His name's Paulie, I flew him in from England. I'm flyin' the flag for your fuckin' country out here!"

Vinnie wanted Paulie on the front cover of the mag, but we figured it wouldn't sell too many copies, despite him being a better vocalist than most black metal frontmen, so the least I can do is give him the final word. Woof.

With another of their notorious Unity tours underway, and a blinding new album, 'Dead Yuppies' on Hellcat/Epitaph, nestling in the racks, it seemed high time to catch up with New York yobbos Agnostic Front once again. Ian Glasper went a few rounds with outspoken vocalist Roger Miret.

Agnostic Front's Roger Miret, by Naki

"Someone better give me an Oscar or something," guffaws amicable Agnostic Front vocalist, Roger Miret, when I congratulate him on the fact that 'Dead Yuppies' is in fact the band's tenth album. "I honestly never thought we'd get this far; in fact, if you'd told me how far we would come back in '81 or '82, I would've laughed in your face. Who would've thought that New York hardcore would have had such an impact around the world?

"But I never went to high school, y'know? This is what I do best. I don't have diplomas on my wall – I have ten albums up there instead. Over the years I've got a lot of music out there, and I've been thinking about framing all those discs, just to show that I did something with my life."

Of course, as well as singing with the mighty AF, Roger plays bass with Lady Luck, a much mellower proposition musically, and one where he even gets to play alongside his wife, but now you can soon add into his burgeoning discography a 'solo' album, although he doesn't want it to be perceived that way at all.

"Yeah, in February Hellcat will be releasing an album by Roger Miret And The Disasters!

It's much more Oi! or punk in style, but with a definite New York flavour to it. There's no hardcore in it as such, and no pop punk, altho' the lyrics are similar to what I write in Agnostic Front. I guess if you like 'Crucify' or 'Gotta Go', you'll like this too."

Back to the matter at hand, and the new AF album, is possibly one of their best ever – despite losing Rob Kabula, their original bassist, to the pressures of relentless touring. "Oh, Rob just wanted to spend some proper time with his family," explains Roger. "Now we've got Mike G. from On The Rise, a NYHC band kinda like Killing Time. I just produced their new demo actually, and I'm seeing if I can help sort them out a little deal.

"But yeah, I'm very pleased with the new album too. It reminds me of a cross between 'Victim In Pain' [their seminal debut – IG] and the last two releases, but with some of 'Cause For Alarm' in there too – Vinnie put his crazy leads all over this; we just let him do whatever he wanted [laughs]!"

It's also good to hear a little bit of that mid-period AF creeping in on occasion, albeit subtly. There was a time when the band seemed to disown that material, only playing either songs off the first or last albums.

"Well, we play certain songs better live than we do others, and a lot of those mid-period albums were recorded with a totally different line-up. But I still think they're great records. 'Cause For Alarm' was a minor classic, a real ground-breaker. We always move with the scenes and go with the flow, and we helped set a few trends along the way too. 'One Voice' really paved the way for that whole new school thing. If you took my vocals off it, and dropped in Freddy's, that could actually be a Madball record!

"But we've come full circle again, and we're happy doing what we're doing right now. We just play to our strengths, y'know?"

So it isn't a case of you guys mellowing with age?

"Oh, not at all; I'm even more pissed off now – at being old," he laughs. "I've got a fourteen-year-old daughter, too, so I have a lot to be pissed off about! But you do get mellower in some respects. I used to act before thinking. Back in 1980, I once threw a garbage can through a McDonalds' window. Actually, I wrote song about it on the Disasters album; it's a story about me and Harley Flanagan [bassist with the one and only Cro-Mags – IG]. Of course, I wouldn't do anything like that now, even though I'd like to! In my heart I still wanna do those crazy things, but I can't afford to get into trouble with the cops again, so I go to my anger management course, Agnostic Front, where I sing about doing them instead!"

So, here we have a happier, more relaxed band than ever before, but 'Dead Yuppies' is still a tense piece of agitated punk rock, with Vinnie wringing classic hardcore riff after classic hardcore riff from his guitar, and Roger spitting his vocals over the top like a dentist's drill bit burrowing into a nerve. And of course, with the September 11th tragedy still fresh in everyone's minds, the title of the album has taken on a hideous new double meaning.

"We actually had the title long before all that happened," explains Roger. "It's a true story from Hoboken, New Jersey. A lot of New York is being overrun by yuppies, but we'd never wish death upon anybody, not even our worse enemies. What happened was horrible, but it has brought everyone together, through a whole lot of unity and patriotism – and I don't mean patriotism in any sort of negative, nationalist way, but in a positive way; between people, between races. There's a lot of anger too, of course. But now none of our ads are coming out, none of our posters are going up, and our record's hardly going to get promoted; it even has to go in the shops with a big sticker on the front of it, explaining all about the cover and title. Your average person in the street just wouldn't understand where we're coming from and would take it all the wrong way. It's a real pain, but all part of the black cloud that follows this band around..."

'Dead Yuppies' is also the end of the Epitaph deal for AF, and the end of a very fruitful period for both band and label, but do you have any idea where you're going to go next? "To be honest, we don't even know if there will be another album," he says, pausing for thought. "Yes, the Epitaph deal was a very positive time for us, but we have no real idea whether we'll get another deal. And if there is a label out there that wants to work with us, would we even wanna work with them? The main thing we want is good worldwide distribution, so our records are available everywhere – and at a reasonable rate, not as expensive imports. But we take everything on a day-to-day basis. First, we'll tour on the back of this one, and then we'll see what happens next."

There is a weary resignation and a cautious optimism about Roger Miret nowadays, as though the only thing he can count upon is his own music, his own band. There are no extravagant claims to be the best in his field, no naïve aspirations at world domination. When we discuss bands that preach, he dryly informs me that he puts himself "on a very low pedestal", so he "doesn't have so far to fall", and when we discuss nu-metal and the influence of rap upon hardcore and metal, that's when he really starts spitting bullets.

"I guess, the focal point of a song like 'Club Girl' is that I don't like rap or hip hop. I'm talking specifically about the gangsta movement, and the negative connotations it had for the hardcore scene, especially the new school thing. Now everyone's a tuff guy, and everyone's in a crew. I especially don't like the way they treat their women, calling them 'bitches' and 'hoes' all the time; I don't understand that whole way of thinking, and I really don't want to – and they probably feel the same way about Agnostic Front's music too, so that makes us about even, huh?

"And that whole Adidas rock thing?" I can almost hear him shaking his head in disbelief down the phone-line. "I don't like it at all! They all sound the same, they all look the same, they all got the dreads happening, every song is the same fucking song! And it's all over the skate and surf videos now, too, where once upon a time you'd get all the hardcore and punk!"

Thing is, I know a lot of nu-metal kids say that it's actually punk rock that all sounds the same; in fact, some of them go so far as to say that nu-metal is the new punk rock! "No fucking way! How can they say that? How can they say that Discharge sounds like The Exploited? At least all those bands had their own identity, rather than some corporate approved image. Hey, when you put the phone down, you go listen to some

punk rock – some real punk rock – and then listen to some nu-metal. Nu-metal is not the new punk rock, no matter what anyone says..."
You know what? He's dead right.

Agnostic Front – issue 126 (December 2004)

Agnostic Front's Vinnie Stigma, by Danielle Dombrowski

New York hardcore veterans Agnostic Front have returned with a new studio album 'Another Voice', produced by Hatebreed frontman Jamey Jasta, and it's being hotly tipped as the unofficial follow-up to their 1992 classic, 'One Voice'. Ian Glasper discovered just why they chose now to turn back the clocks from vocalist Roger Miret.

In 1998, old school hardcore fans rejoiced when Agnostic Front, widely regarded as the godfathers of NYHC, returned to their street punk roots with the spirited comeback album for Epitaph, 'Something's Gotta Give'. And now new school kids have something to crow about as well, 'cos the band – never ones to plough the same furrow for too long – have rediscovered their more metallic direction of the late '80s/early '90s. Whereas 'Something's Gotta Give' harkened back to AF's classic early albums, 'Another Voice' leans heavily towards the riff-heavy grooves of their just-as-seminal crossover period. Which may seem weird to many as the band have steadfastly not played any songs from those albums for over five years. "Let me tell you the story, and I'll try to keep it as brief as I can!" chuckles Roger in explanation. "I stopped playing with AF for a while in '93, 'cos I wanted to focus on my family, spend some time with my daughter, and that was right after all the touring we did for 'One Voice'. I still went to shows, I still loved the music, and I even played bass in Madball with Vinnie [Stigma, AF guitarist] for a while until Hoya joined.

"Then when the AF thing came up again, I went to a rehearsal with Vinnie, Rob [Kabula, bass] and Jimmy [Colletti, drums]; I walked into that room and it was like walking into a time warp. All those guys were around back when we did 'United Blood' [1983], and when we played all those really old school songs again, they just felt so good we went out there and did what we did best.

"We did attempt a couple of 'One Voice' songs when Mike [Gallo] joined on bass, but they only really sounded right when Steve [Gallo, Mike's brother] eventually joined on drums. I'm not dissing Jimmy or anything, but some drummers are good at playing one style and others are good at another. And Steve just made those 'One Voice' songs sound fresh all over again. Plus, we were on tour with Hatebreed, and Jamey's a huge 'One Voice' fan. One drunken night when we were hanging out, he just started on about doing 'Another Voice' – and before we knew it, he'd already named the record and promised to produce it! So, in many ways, he started it all rolling for this album and I have to give him his due; he's been like a sixth member of the band. A true producer, he's been a co-pilot every step of the way, and he's been so enthusiastic because all along he's been helping make the AF record he's wanted to hear since 1992!"

Not only was it intended as a musical return, 'Another Voice' was originally imagined as an exact continuation of 'One Voice' – even as far as band personnel.

"Yeah, although Lenny DiSclafani is our guitarist now - he's been with us about a year - he didn't play on the record. Matt Henderson played lead on the new album. For nostalgia's sake, I did originally want to put the exact 'One Voice' lineup back together in its entirety. Matt was totally up for it, but Craig [Setari] is too busy now with Sick Of It All, and Will [Shepler] has just had a baby, so he couldn't commit either. So I figured why not do it with Mike and Steve anyway, they were both itching to play all those songs again.

"And it's really refreshing to be playing like this once more," continues Roger, obviously enthused with his latest work. "As soon as I sang the first line in the studio, we were all amazed at how awesome it sounded; it all came flooding back, the vibe of 'One Voice' all over again. But we're leaders, not followers, we've always moved with the times and reinvented ourselves, and helped refresh our scene with each new record. We helped pave the way for old school hardcore, new school hardcore – even crossover. And always by just doing what felt right at the time, by being honest to ourselves, and that's all we're doing again now. This is as honest, real and true as anything else we've ever done."

Roger's claim that AF have never sounded better is no idle boast. From the furiously intense opener 'Still Here' (that features guest vocals from Karl Buechner, late of Earth Crisis) to the vicious title track that closes out the album (and sees Scott Vogel from

Terror lending his formidable tonsils to proceedings), 'Another Voice' is an incredibly tight, focused assault that doesn't relax its grip on the listener for an instant. Packed with exactly the sort of huge, crunching singalongs and driving metallic riffage that ignite moshpits into maelstroms of blood and sweat, it sees Agnostic Front joyously rediscovering a facet of their musical arsenal that many had resigned themselves to never hearing again. And nowhere do the band lock together more convincingly than on the fluidly menacing 'Peace', the first video from the record, and a song that reveals Roger's disbelief at the state of the world today.

"Exactly; it's an open statement about the troubled times we live in. Ironically enough, the line, 'One man's freedom fighter is another's terrorist' came from when I was in Ireland, something I saw written on a wall that really made me stop and think. It truly is all about perspective; one man's good is another man's bad. I'm not taking sides, but it's sad that the world has come to this. Do we even have the right to choose between war or peace anymore? Does it really make any difference what we want?"

On a more jubilant note, 'Take Me Back' is a celebration of an important moment in hardcore history.

"Yeah, that's going back to when NYHC was just starting, when the scene was still in its infancy. All the bands I mention in that song were very important in my life. I know I left Madball out, but the period I'm talking about was even before those guys got started, and I use the phrase 'Demonstrating my style' to acknowledge the part they played. AF are NYHC and proud, and I'm not going to let that be forgotten.

"You see, hardcore is not just music to me, it never was, it's a movement. That's why we called our band Agnostic Front, in the first place; it's a way of life, you've gotta feel it. When I first got into punk rock, it really was a place to go if you were a misfit, an outcast. And hardcore is the same, it's about belonging somewhere. CBGBs was always like my second home, and those other bands I hung out with were like family. That's why it's so real to me, and the kids that love this band can feel that commitment. We've seen 'em come and we've seen 'em go, but we're still here. People say, 'Oh, you'll grow out of it...' but I'm representing New York City with my music and I don't ever wanna 'grow out of it'!"

And no Agnostic Front interview would be complete without mention of the one and only Vinnie Stigma, livewire rhythm guitarist and Roger's long-term sparring partner since the very inception of the band.

"We have a true friendship, it's genuine brotherhood," he says sincerely, in closing. "We love each other basically, we really do, straight up – and we're like the parents, haha! We stay together for the kids! We have a very deep understanding; we each know how the other does things. He was one of the four people who always came and stood at the front when my old band before Agnostic Front, The Psychos, used to play. And I really do mean four people! It was a small, tightly-knit scene back then, and we might get 25 people at a show, if we were lucky, but Vinnie was always there. He's the Joe Pesci of hardcore, a real character. They broke the mould after they made Vinnie Stigma... and thank God! I don't think the world is ready for two of him!"

Alehammer, by Meg Manley

If such a thing as a 'DIY crust punk super-group' is actually possible, Alehammer are probably more entitled to the accolade than anyone. Featuring guitarist Scoot from UK heavyweights Extinction Of Mankind, bassist Shrub and drummer Shrew from grind legends Prophecy Of Doom, and vocalist Karl Patton from cult Chicago crossover act Impulse Manslaughter, their sound is every bit as gnarly as their pedigree suggests.

"Being spread around the world, we don't exactly rehearse very much, which keeps it totally fresh for us," reckons Shrew. "But we had a right fuckin' laugh last July, playing the 'Death Pints Across Europe' tour, and in September we're going to chug the U.S.A. to a screaming pulp!"

Next up though is a split 12" with Sweden's Tyrant for Italian label Agipunk, hilariously entitled 'At War With Straightedge' and slated for release February 2009.

"That's all the details we have right now," laughs Shrub, "And believe me, details are few and far between in Alehammer!"

ALL OUT WAR – ISSUE 49 (DECEMBER 1997)

Pacifists we may be here at Terrorizer, but that doesn't stop us loving the name of NYC's All Out War. Oh, and the Slayercore on their 'Truth In The Age Of Lies' debut album utterly kills too. Ian Glasper announces hostilities along with vocalist Mike Score.

How the hell could I not love a band called All Out War? Especially when the name is so

All Out War, New Jersey 1995, by Carl Gunhouse

gloriously apt? Especially as their music reflects perfectly the imminent Armageddon evoked so effectively in their lyrics? And before you start thinking, 'Oh no, Glasper's off on another trip again...', go and have your ears singed by their 'Truth In The Age Of Lies' CD on Gain Ground Records. Then tell me I'm getting excited about nothing. And it's not every day that Da Ed rings me up gleefully ranting about how much a hardcore band sounds so much like Slayer, Slayer and more Slayaaargh.

"Oh, really?" Vocalist Mike Score, crackling down a crappy phone Iine from New York, sounds surprised at the comparison. "I don't pay too much attention to labels, but I've heard Carcass mentioned a lot, and I don't really know why. I guess a lot of our reviews are in hardcore zines, and they don't know too much about metal, so it's inevitable that they'll mention Slayer and Carcass. If we do sound like Slayer, I'd like to think it was a cross between them and the Cro-Mags' 'Age of Quarrel' album."

Well, rest assured, the big T. isn't some hardcore zine that knows little about metal, and Da Ed still thinks you sound like Slayer, so there! It is pretty damn metallic, isn't it? How come you're in so many HC zines, and hardly any metal ones?

"WelI, we all grew up in the hardcore scene," reckons Mike. "We know lots of people from NYC, and it's easier to get shows in that scene. 25 Ta Life always look out for us, and get us shows, Inhuman, Blood For Blood, Confusion... the thing is, there's not so many small metal shows in the North East, just these huge shows that we could never get on, so we end up doing the hardcore gigs. We've played with Agnostic Front, and we've played with Deicide, and felt comfortable on both bills. We went down real good. I guess I prefer to play hardcore shows, though, 'cos there's more energy than at metal shows. Except the show we did with Napalm Death, where there were lots of hardcore kids anyway, all having fun together with the metal kids."

Are the walls coming down between the two genres as quickly there as they are in Europe?

"Sure, 'cos most hardcore bands are just playing metal nowadays, anyway. That's why I can't understand why some hardcore kids snub their noses at the metal scene."

People often say that hardcore is all about attitude, and that the tone of the guitars, the style of the music, is all secondary to being sincere, to being true to yourself and what you believe in. That's what it's always meant to me anyway, and that includes being tolerant towards others. Mike tells me how All Out War have seen their fair share of the closemindedness that ironically plagues our scene.

"I don't see why we still get tagged as this 'tough guy' band! Other bands play just as brutally, and put on an aggressive live show, but don't get called it. In the USA, there's a lot of very separate, cliquey scenes, and they're quick to dismiss you if you don't fit in with their little circle. We hardly get any violence at our shows anymore, and when we did, it used to be because of the kids that were there, not the band. They weren't into the music, they were into the image. They knew they could go to a hardcore show, beat someone down, and not get arrested. You can bet they didn't go home after the show and put on an All Out War CD! But all those idiots have gradually been weeded out.

"It's not meant to be a battleground, or a cage match," the singer emphasises. "You should be able to go off on the dancefloor, but it can be controlled. Hardcore is hard music, and a lot of us got into it because we were angry, but it isn't about violence. Violence nearly killed the NYC scene. None of the clubs wanted to book the shows – and who could blame them?"

After having spoken to Mike, I can vouch that he's far removed from the 'tough guy'

All Out War, at This Is Hardcore 2019, by Danielle Dombrowski

misnomer. In fact, despite the band logo, the sinister artwork, the tattoos and bare chests, there's a very definite spiritual awareness weaving its way through the detuned grooves of their debut full-length.

Something given away when Mike thanks God in his section of the thanks list.

"Yeah, I believe in God, I believe in a higher power, but not in organised religion, which seems to defeat the object, especially when you see the sheer number of wars fought in the name of God. I see the hypocrisy and greed of this modern material world, and how it's destroying the planet, and everyone seems blind to it. They all see technology as a good thing; they can't see the damage it's doing, they don't want to. Sometimes I wonder if there's a cure to all this! There's some good people out there, but the majority just take, and I lose all faith in humanity in general. On the whole, people don't care, as long as they're doing okay, and sometimes I think we deserve to be wiped out."

ALL OUT WAR - JULY 2015

All Out War, unknown photographer

New York hardcore doesn't get much harder than All Out War. Over the last 20 years, these guys have spat out five albums of truly vicious metalcore – imagine Cro-Mags, Merauder and Slayer in a particularly violent scrum and you're halfway to the intensity AOW can generate – and they show little sign of letting up, with new MCD, 'Dying Gods', still as virulent as anything on their classic (1997) debut, 'Truth In The Age Of Lies'.

"It's very easy with the current line-up," reckons vocalist Mike Score, when pondering how AOW maintain their inspirational energy after two decades. "These are all the guys from the 'For Those Who Were Crucified' (their 1998 breakthrough release on Victory) era line-up; although Andy wasn't on the album, he still played all the shows that supported it. We are all committed to the musical direction of the band and it just works. Everyone in the band is on the same page, which is a rarity. It has been a rebirth of sorts; everyone is totally into it and comes to crush, even at rehearsals."

Five albums and five EPs over twenty years isn't exactly prolific, but it's not exactly lazy either, and whenever All Out War do drop new music, you always know it's going to be sick, they never disappoint... which is more than can be said for many of their peers, who would kill for such consistency.

"Some would argue that we have been incredibly inconsistent due to our on again/off again status, but thanks for saying that," laughs Mike. "I think now, after all this time, we've finally reached a spot where we are really merging all our influences and are very comfortable when writing with each other. I'm very happy with the way 'Dying Gods' came out; it really is my favourite All Out War release. I know everyone says that about his or her latest effort, but I really mean it. And the intensity just comes from our love and confidence in what we've been doing.

"It all just clicks lately, and I'm grateful for that. It feels like it did when we started, mainly because there are no expectations at all. It's just been hanging out, writing music, and playing the occasional show. Everything is on our terms. We do what we do for us and don't let

All Out War, unknown photographer

outsiders influence us at all. It's been awesome. Not caring is liberation. There are too many bands that let outsiders influence them... but that's not us. We don't give a shit about naysayers or trouble-makers on social media. Those people are a dime a dozen. This is our thing."

So, does that mean we shouldn't expect too many shows in support of 'Dying Gods'?
"We've actually been playing a lot lately... well, a lot for us anyway. We just did two release shows in NYC and both were incredible experiences. So many old friends came out to support, which was great. Alan Blake [Sheer Terror and Darkside NYC] even made an appearance yesterday. Then we did This Is Hardcore in Philadelphia, where we got the pleasure and honour to play with The Exploited and Negative Approach just to name a few. Then we hit Europe for some festivals and club shows.

"We plan on playing as much as possible before we get down to recording our next full length, and we leave everything up on that stage every time we get up there. We know how special it is just to have some people come out and watch your band play, so we don't hold back at all. We really appreciate people coming out and we are not afraid to get involved with the crowd... as I'm doing this interview right now, I'm doing it with shattered front teeth from last night's gig!"

ALL SHALL PERISH ‒ ISSUE 148 (SEPTEMBER 2006)

Having toured with everyone from Agnostic Front to Hate Eternal, Oakland's All Shall Perish look set to finally take the extreme music scene by storm with their rather stunning sophomore album, 'The Price Of Existence', for Nuclear Blast. Ian Glasper buckled up in the face of much ferocious turbulence.

"Well, it's a complete record," offers drummer Matt Kuykendall proudly, when pushed to comment on the progression he feels the band have made since their 'Hate. Malice.

All Shall Perish, courtesy of Claire Harris, Nuclear Blast

Revenge' debut. "Eleven tracks, and all diverse; musically it's years beyond our last one... maybe because it's actually been years since our last one, haha! It definitely still has the brutality of that first record, but brings a lot more musical elements to the table, and we really get a chance to show what we are capable of and expand on our varied tastes in music..."

'The Price Of Existence' also introduces new vocalist, Hernan 'Eddie' Hermida, who has a fine set of face-flaying pipes on him, but the whole band actually excels in what is a shameless display of crushing modern metal. From the thudding Pantera-like beatdowns of 'Wage Slaves' to the melodic blasting of 'We Hold These Truths', the album is a vertigo-inducing ride that convincingly embraces most metallic sub-genres whilst snaring the listener with some truly exhilarating musicianship and too many dynamic guitar flourishes to mention.

"We just sit down with a bunch of riffs we think go together," explains Matt, of the All Shall Perish writing process, "And we just start piecing together sections until we have a structure, and then we refine that through each band member's opinions, until it sounds exciting to all of us, and we end up with a nice compacted ASP song that we then write lyrics to. We have some computer recording software we use to keep everything in front of us, and that helps a lot, I think, in getting an objective opinion on any brand-new shit you are putting together..."

The band's esteemed Bay Area heritage possibly shines through strongest on the beautiful acoustic piece, 'Interlude' (what it lacks in the imaginative title stakes, it more than compensates for with a subtle pathos that recalls Testament at their world-beating best), a legacy (excuse the pun) that Matt is justifiably proud of.

"Yeaaaah, we were definitely takin' a few cues from our roots when we wrote that; we always loved the super melodic stuff bands like Metallica did, and it serves as a cool contrast to the brutal-ass songs that surround it on the CD! And when you write eleven songs for a record, it's hard to just keep writing the same type of thing over and over... I don't know how some bands can do it.

"A lot of bands have an old school vibe to them right now," he adds cautiously, on the subject of the thrash resurgence we're enjoying at the moment, "And are trying to capture some of the remaining light from the glory days of Bay Area metal. I don't think we really fall into the category of those newer thrash bands, but we definitely incorporate a lot of that style into certain songs and love the hell out of all the old records; this is definitely a labour of love, in the sense that we hate the bullshit that comes with it, but couldn't live without the music. The future is most definitely about world domination and putting the Bay back on the map for innovative metal!"

With songs such as 'The True Beast' and 'There Is No Business To Be Done On A Dead World' (never mind that evocative album title and apocalyptic moniker), it's also very apparent that All Shall Perish are as heavily lyrically as they are musically.

"Our inspiration comes from all the many themes of life, and we tend to write about whatever is on our minds. 'The True Beast' is a weird one to define though... there's a lot going on in that song, and you kinda have to read the lyrics and make your own conclusions..... 'There Is No Business...' is a little more cut and dried, and is all about the institutions who rape our environment for profits, and the consequences we all face for their greed and our ignorant acceptance of it. It's written with a lot of first-person anger and frustration at the subject.

"As for the album title?" concludes Matt, on a suitably ominous note. "In the USA, the price of existence includes war, poverty, inequality, torture and slavery... the general raping and pillaging of our world and our minds by those who care not of the future!" In the face of which, all may well indeed perish. Happy holidays!

AMEBIX – ISSUE 162 (OCTOBER 2007)

'ARISE!' – classic album piece
ALTERNATIVE TENTACLES 1985

Tracks:

'The Moor', 'Axeman', 'Fear Of God', 'Largactyl', 'Drink And Be Merry', 'Spoils Of Victory', 'Arise!', 'Slave', 'The Darkest Hour'

Personnel:

Rob 'The Baron' Miller (bass and vocals)
Chris 'Stig' Miller (guitar)
Robert 'Spider' Richards (drums)
(with George 'The Dragon' Fletcher on keyboards)

Amebix, 2011, by Morat

Why is it a classic?

No one who has heard this album has remained unmoved by it, and if that's not the acid test for a true classic, then what is? Throbbing with a dark, visceral atmosphere that has never quite been replicated since, 'Arise!' was the first punk/metal album to truly capture the raw intensity of instinctive crossover, loaded with a timeless primeval power.

"I was only twenty years old, and didn't know shit from pudding, but even I realised we were doing something untoward," laughs Spider. "At the time, we were one of the first bands really crossing metal with punk... and we were getting all this shit off the punks and all this shit off the metal guys, and it was only years later, when we'd split up, that everyone realised it could be done..."

What were its inspirations?

"We were into a lot of stuff," explains Rob, trying to elaborate upon the dark melting pot that spawned such a magnificent folly. "Black Sabbath, Crass, Killing Joke, Discharge, Accept ('Restless And Wild!')... but there was also the constant influence of people like Joy Division providing the emotional intensity."

How was it received at the time?

Considering that Alternative Tentacles almost didn't put it out when they first heard it (having signed Amebix on the strength of their rather-quite-different 'No Sanctuary' 12"), it's safe to say that 'Arise!' ruffled feathers upon its release, but its true worth wasn't realised until several years later, as more and more people were exposed to the band's cataclysmic force-of-nature live experience.

"We were a bit surprised that it wasn't appreciated initially," sighs Rob, "But it clearly illustrated to me that the whole 'punk' scene was actually very conservative, and becoming more and more regimented; the punks didn't like it because it was heavy and the metal heads didn't like it because it wasn't full of guitar solos. It was completely ignored to begin with, like some strange curiosity..."

"Don't forget, it was recorded right in the middle of the Eighties," adds Spider. "Around the time of The Battle Of The Bean Field, when Stonehenge got all nasty and unpleasant, and we actually dedicated the album to the spirit of the travellers that used to go there... the record was immersed in the spirit of that whole period – it was called 'Arise' for a reason!"

How important was the artwork?

Rob's stirring front cover, silhouetted warriors rallying themselves for a final victory against the backdrop of a brooding sunrise, is as evocative today as ever, and married rudimentary anarcho punk aesthetics to some full-on heavy metal thunder! Hell yeah!

Amebix, mid-Eighties

"I do like to think that we developed a very original style of artwork," reckons Rob. "It was crucial to try and transmit our ideas in a very simple form - hence the silhouettes - in the same manner that we were transmitting a very simple musical style. Both were potent and ultimately symbolic... I suppose the artwork was like a sort of ink blot test, and people saw what they chose reflected in it..."

How influential did it prove to be?

Just ask Sepultura, who not only ripped off the title for one of their own albums in the early Nineties, but obviously took great inspiration from the band's heaving hell-for-leather punk/metal fission. And it's safe to say that Neurosis would never have developed into such an ominous collective if they hadn't locked themselves in a very dark room with 'Arise!' for several years. In fact, the whole international crust-punk trail leads right back to Bristol and the Amebix.

"A few years ago, I was in a band called Muckspreader," recalls Spider proudly, "And we were doing this tour of the West Coast of America. We were in this bar, and this guy came up to me, saying, 'Hey dude, were you in Amebix?' And he bought me a drink and said, 'I'm buying you this beer because you saved my fucking life!' He told me how he'd been on the verge of suicide until he got 'Arise!' and how it changed his life for the better, and I thought, 'Shit, we really were doing something important after all!'"

American Nightmare, by Albert Licano

American Nightmare are American hardcore's best-kept secret. Sad but true, 'cos their 'Background Music' debut full-lengther on Equal Vision is a truly potent blend of old school energy and new school dynamics. The band have recently assaulted these shores yet again, and are currently fighting desperately for the right to just use their name, so I caught up with guitarist Tim Cossar for the latest.

"Yeah, we're currently being sued by another band called American Nightmare," sighs Tim. "We can't even have our album re-pressed right now, because we were served with a 'cease and desist' notice by this other band, and it's really frustrating because they're just a rock band who play local bars maybe once a month!"

Anyway, onto happier topics, namely the music. Our American Nightmare bust out some truly scathing old school jams, tempering their ferocious intensity with some astoundingly poetic lyrics and a few clever arrangements. Hardly surprising when you consider that they include in their ranks some ex-members of old school heroes Ten Yard Fight, but this isn't an angle the band want to dwell on at all.

"That whole old school tag is a bit of a bummer really," admits the guitarist. "People can't see past the label, and a lot of people don't give us a chance to prove ourselves. Metalcore kids think we're way too fast, and the punk kids probably think we're too metal, or whatever.

"Our roots are obviously in that old school scene, but we're actually quite different, if

American Nightmare – by Albert Licano

you listen to our stuff properly. In fact, we've gone out of our way to avoid that whole Ten Yard Fight connection; it's even in our contract with Equal Vision that they can't market us that way. We really don't wanna be an 'ex-members of...' band; we have always wanted to stand on our own two feet."

Well, they've certainly managed to do that, choosing to build a solid fanbase the good ol' fashioned way. Their first two 7"'s appeared on the well-respected Bridge Nine label and garnered such great reviews the band soon found themselves touring from coast to coast, which led to the Equal Vision deal and the blistering 'Background Music'. Incidentally, those two EPs have just been compiled onto one CD, entitled 'Year One', recently released by Dutch label, Reflections (and be sure to check out the hidden Cro-Mags cover, if you pick it up!).

And talking of old school, the band will soon be appearing on a Black Flag tribute CD being compiled by Initial.

"Yeah, we're doing 'Depression'," Tim enthuses. "Black Flag were a big influence on us, as were most of those early hardcore punk bands like The Misfits, Youth Of Today and Bad Brains.

"You know, we meet a lot of kids whilst out on the road who have no idea about some of those amazing bands; instead, they grew up with Earth Crisis, and they have no idea of what real punk rock sounds like!"

Yet some of those kids would swear black was blue they're more punk than you!

"We were even asked, 'Would we be offended if we were ever called a punk band?' Hell no, we much prefer that punk ethic to the modern hardcore one. I mean, we still sell our own merch, drive our own van, load in our own gear... and I'm more broke than I've ever been! And then for some snobby hardcore kid to go and accuse us of selling out just 'cos we have a booking agent or whatever? Our booking agent is one of our best friends – virtually our sixth member – and if it wasn't for him, we could never stay out there on the road the way we do."

Such are the trials and tribulations of playing hardcore music for a living, folks, but as long as they can keep a-hold of their name, I'm sure you'll see American Nightmare rising above such trivial bullshit to raise hell in a club near you again soon. All thanks to the power of positive thinking.

"Well, it's hard sometimes, but we're just trying to put it all aside and concentrate on what matters – the music and our next record."

ANARCHO PUNK – ISSUE 96

(JANUARY/FEBRUARY 2002)

Winston Churchill's turf mohican planted in the aftermath of the May Day anti-capitalist riots symbolized a debate that been raging within punk ever since the late '70s. Was it a situationist joke, or a political message? Chaos or anarchy? And if punk was supposed to change the order of things, how far down into the roots of society were they willing to tackle? After 'Anarchy In The UK' inspired a generation, Ian Glasper talked to those who put their money where their mouth is.

"Punk belongs to the punks, not the business men. They need us, we don't need them; punk will never be dead... as long as some of us refuse to be lead."

What better way to start an article on anarcho punk than with a quote from those seminal anarchists Flux Of Pink Indians – taken from the song 'Take Heed', off their highly influential 'Strive To Survive Causing Least Suffering Possible' 12". Not the snappiest of titles, I grant you, but definitely one to live your life by. In fact, if ever there was an antidote to the myth that music can't change your life, that band would be it. It was their 'Neu Smell' 7" that actually prompted me to re-evaluate my attitude and diet and go vegetarian twenty years ago, and I've never regretted that choice since.

Originally punk rock was a bold statement against the deplorable staleness of music and fashion in the mid-'70s, but it soon became a parody of itself when it began to take on many of the characteristics of the scene it set out to depose. Enter stage left hardcore punk; faster, harder, nastier and heading back underground to nurse its wounds. And from there, but a small step to anarcho punk, defiantly DIY in approach, and railing against far greater wrongs than outdated dress codes. Here was a musical magnet for anyone who felt let down by our leaders, cheated by our 'superiors' and threatened by our peacekeepers.

"Those who are obsessed with categories and genres seem to think anarcho punk

Anarcho Punk - Britt of Assert, Birmingham 7-12-98,
by Andrew Giles

means looking like a crusty and singing 'Fuck the system' 30 times in every chorus," claims Britt, vocalist with political hardcore thrashers, Assert. "I think it was a reaction to major label punk rock and the acceptance of punk into the mainstream; a more hardcore reply was needed. I suppose a lot of people (some still do) did look like crusties, as an anti-fashion statement, which also tied in with the squat scene and the roots of DIY, with all the anti-corporate, anti-consumerist ideas that went with it.

"To me it meant a reclamation of the original ideas of punk; an intelligent, anti-corporate, counter-cultural, subversive, anti-authoritarian, agitational musical movement. The years between 1950 and 1980, or thereabouts, saw a major upturn in the world economy and capitalist representatives propagandised the triumphalism of their system, claiming we had reached the highest stage of societal development. Anarcho punk gave a reply and a reminder of the reality of the world..."

So, bands like Crass, who put all their emphasis on lyrical content rather than the listener's musical pleasure (that's not to say that they didn't write some bloody great songs, but some of it was a gratuitous racket too), set out to not only discredit the system, but also the punk bands who they felt had discredited the scene.

So, do anarcho-thinking punk bands actually view themselves as 'anarcho punk'? Or are they keen to distance themselves from any such rigid pigeonholing?

"That all depends on whether you're comfortable with being boxed or labelled, doesn't it?" says Stig, vocalist of the Icons Of Filth, anarcho stalwarts from the '80s, recently reformed and sounding better than ever. "Some of us are more comfortable than others with it. People will always find a box to drop you in. Some would question, why volunteer it yourself, when the new material we are doing is both analytical and varied. I suppose categories are inevitable, even if just quickly to describe something. Collectively, it's really not important to us. We're just a bunch of freethinkers really. Speaking for myself, I have no real problem with that description."

Obviously anarcho punk was achieving its aim of upsetting the status quo, because bands were making the front pages of the tabloids with some of their more controversial releases (Crass' 'Sheep Farming In The Falklands' springs to mind); the police were monitoring where and when these bands were playing and to who, with great interest; and there was even a backlash from the chaos punk faction. Special Duties released their 'Bullshit Crass' 7" (the title a 'clever' play on the 'Bullshit Detector' compilations put together by Crass to release unsigned demo bands), and The Exploited declared Crass 'a big bunch of wankers' on their 'Punk's Not Dead' album.

But the anarcho punk scene was exceptionally diverse, a whole host of great bands united by a common set of strong values. On the one hand, you had the apocalyptic grind of the Amebix; on the other, the mellow, haunting strains of The Mob. You could see the raging Anti-System opening up for the poppy, theatrical Chumbawumba (yes, they sold us down the river in the end, when they signed to the very label they had slagged so bitterly a few years earlier, but for a while there, they were truly inspirational). You had the politically vehement Conflict, probably the most militant and outspoken of all the anarcho bands, who unleashed a whole slew of awesome albums, and the Subhumans, who mixed clever music with even cleverer lyrics, provoking with thought rather than confronting with force. And let's not forget the morbid meandering of those eccentric death punks, Rudimentary Peni, whose first two EPs and visionary debut album still sound as disturbing as they did all those years ago. All were as vital to the overall vitality of the scene as the others, each complementing the whole with their own unique personality.

The burning question, as I mentioned earlier: was it all just so much hot air? Or could this music effect real change?

"Music can play a significant role in changing one's view of the world and what we may think is our historical mission in life," reckons Britt. "It will be nice to play Assuck when we take over the airwaves! Punk rock changed the musical landscape forever and will continue to inspire or frustrate our world and personal perspectives..."

And what of this whole concept of anarchy? Some bands interpreted it as 'anarchy and

Anarcho punk – Stig fronting the Icons of Filth in the early Eighties, by Mick Slaughter

peace', others as 'anarchy and chaos'... whilst many of us felt that anarchy was an unrealistic concept, as people can't be trusted enough to share with their fellow man unless they have to.

"Um, how much time have we got...?" laughs Stig. "I think the former suggests the abolition of government, replacing it with a social system based on voluntary cooperation, which would seem a very good idea. The latter suggests the widespread misconception of the coupling of the two words so that they become synonymous in people's minds with having the same meaning. This is represented throughout all forms of the media as it suits the beneficiaries of the status quo to perpetuate that myth. It's not just the principles of anarchism. Any alternative is readily dismissed as an unworkable pipe dream, so we end up believing it. Things aren't possible because we believe we're all rotten to the core, can't be trusted and are incapable of making rather basic decisions, and failing in the prospect of having even a modicum of readiness to accept responsibility for anything, even things that directly affect our own lives and interests. Things can change. People change. Therefore, people can change things. It's a realisation thing. War is over, if you want it. Thought patterns can be infectious!"

Stateside, bands such as MDC, Crucifix and Final Conflict (with their 'Millions Of Dead Cops', 'Dehumanisation' and 'Ashes to Ashes' albums respectively) were generally playing faster and crazier than their UK counterparts, but based their lyrics on the same high principles. Poster covers, with gruelling images of war and torture, were the norm; music ceased to be mere entertainment, now it was alternative propaganda.

Banned from most regular venues, these bands were forced to look elsewhere for outlets, and often ended up playing squatted buildings – the infamous 1 in 12 Club in Bradford springs to mind as a prime example. Not just a music venue, it is also a café and anarchist bookshop, and for a long time was the hub of the northern scene here in the UK. Similar collective endeavours sprang up all across Europe, enabling bands to tour the continent with no reliance upon the established music industry clique. Of course, there is a fine balancing act to be done if you don't want to be tainted by all that music biz bullshit...

"By not kissing arse," is how Assert stay true to their roots, reckons Britt. "By not changing to fit in with the latest trend; by not lying, stealing, cheating or ripping people off. We (mostly) book our own tours, take care of our own merchandise, sell records dirt cheap within the venues and don't ask for silly money to play. We lend other bands our equipment and always offer a helping hand; it's about give and take... if you take from the scene you should be prepared to put something back. I have also put out compilation CDs to help bands get more well-known and help them get gigs. I'm not saying we are perfect; we still get a lot of criticism and it's extremely difficult to reconcile DIY ideas at all times, but the bigger things get is not a pre-requisite for ethics to fly out of the window."

"You'll never do right for doing wrong," says Stig, in closing. "If it's not the record labels, it's the promoters, or the venue proprietors. If it's your own label, it's the people you have to deal with in order to get the distribution required. We live in a capitalistic state. We operate within that environment. It exists. It's everywhere you turn; every avenue has just about been cornered. You can't be Jesus Christ in an imperfect world. Just watch your backs, and share information with each other to reduce the effect they can have on us all.

"Almost everything seems to be, in some way, a subsidiary of something more corporate or multinational somewhere down the line. Everything seems to belong to the Hansom Trust or Unilever, or whatever. The umbrella is growing over an increasingly small world. One man will eventually purport to 'own' everything. Of course, alternatives do exist in many small ways, and should be utilised and encouraged, but there's virtually no such thing as 'clean'. If it gets too big for its boots, it's the subject of some financial offer because it's affecting the market controlled by the big boys; otherwise it gets the big squeeze put on it to nullify its effect, and ultimately is put out of action by their friends in the legal profession and other dubious circles. We have only ourselves and each other.

"It's corny, but united we stand, divided we fall. Better to fail than not having tried at all. There has to be hope, but there has to be effort also. Otherwise, we might as well all just give up, go home and sit in front of the TV, taking endless zaps of the 'truth' according to the Mind Police, dribbling out of the corner of our mouths and rubbing rice pudding in our heads!"

Anarcho Punk Art - Robert 'Mid' Middleton

ANARCHO PUNK ARTWORK - ISSUE 154

(FEBRUARY 2007)

The World In Black And White

Despite its rudimentary, mainly colour-free aesthetic, the artwork for anarcho punk bands such as Crass, Discharge, Conflict and Amebix has proved to be not only one of the definitive styles to have emerged from the extreme music scene, but also responsible for much of its most searing imagery. Ian Glasper looks into its history, in the company of its most noted artists.

Anarcho punk, peace punk, hippy punk, positive punk – call it what you like, but the well-meaning, political punk movement originally spearheaded by Crass at the arse end of the '70s spawned not only some incredible music but some incredible artwork as well. These were hard-hitting images that left the audience with nowhere to hide, no possible salve for their conscience and no other option but to confront the implications of the art and decide how best to deal with them. And punk rock as a genuine movement for social change – as opposed to mere radical fashion statement – lurched into reluctant life.

Gee Vaucher, the often over-looked visionary behind the unforgettably distinct Crass sleeves, nowadays only makes pictures for people that she likes, but the stark, unflinching works she produced for not only Crass themselves, but the bands they released on their eponymous label, suited the stripped down, abrasive music to a tee. Her terrifying collages of charred corpses and mutilated squaddies, usually realised in glorious fold-out poster form, remain some of the most shocking images of the whole punk era, and launched a thousand respectful imitations. No stone was left unturned in getting a point across. A scale model of a house was built from paper-maché (and burned) for the cover of Conflict's 'The House That Man Built' EP and a brave photographer sent into an actual abattoir for Flux Of Pink Indians' 'Neu Smell' booklet. As well as on numerous other memorable sleeves, more of Gee's work can be found in either of her books, 'Animal Rites' (Pomona) and 'Crass Art And Other Pre Post-Modernist Monsters' (AK Press).

Of course, punk rock is all about expression, and the most celebrated artists of the genre didn't just regurgitate the ideas of Crass, they absorbed their core concepts and then took them to fantastic new places. There was none more fantastic than Nick Blinko, vocalist and guitarist with the supremely secretive Rudimentary Peni. Heavily influenced by 'outsider art' – the deranged scribblings of those that mainstream society have deemed 'insane' – his incredibly detailed 'disasterpieces' take the viewer to nightmarish worlds inhabited by festering idols, flying coffins and bloated amputees. Every piece he's done is a total hoot, but the immense poster sleeve to 1983's 'Death Church' album takes some beating in the peculiarity stakes. Once seen, never forgotten. "The thing that Blinko generated was this marriage between music and artwork, which was quite unique for punk," reckons Mark Farrelly, guitarist with early '80s death rock band, Part 1, and himself an artist that shared Blinko's fascination with the unspeakably macabre. "You had that back in the prog rock days with Roger Dean; this, dare I say, conceptual thing going on, without anyone actually knowing what was happening. There was all this really lovely packaging that complemented the music. The thing is, me and Nick weren't really that interested in doing the music, we were more into our artwork and HP Lovecraft!"

"The artwork for those Peni EPs was a great inspiration to me as well," explains Squeal, the man who gave the mighty Icons Of Filth their strong visual edge, also providing stunningly dark visuals for Poison Idea, Septic Death, and Excrement Of War. "Correspondence with Nick ensued, letters more often than not accompanied by crazed drawings, which he actively encouraged. Similarly illustrated correspondence with [late vocalist] Stig from Icons Of Filth drew an invitation to provide some artwork for their 'Used, Abused, Unamused' EP, and the doom-laden drawings for this and subsequent IOF releases were largely based around the lyrical content of their songs. Most are self-explanatory, and beyond that I'd prefer to leave people to interpret the work for themselves as they see fit. Why so many skulls? I see dead people!"

Infinitely simpler than Blinko and Squeal's finely-lined exercises in excruciating detail, but no less atmospheric, was the cover art of Amebix, the Southwest's seminal grind band, whose crushing 'Arise!' album boasted a truly dramatic scene of desperate warriors surveying a war-torn battlefield, and was the next logical step for a band who were motivated by unfettered primal expression.

"Looking back, I think there were a few contributing factors in the way that the style developed," says bassist/vocalist Rob 'The Baron' Miller, from his blacksmith forge on the Isle of Skye. "One being that I was not a particularly talented artist in either colour or 3D, so these silhouette figures were an ideal way of expressing my ideas: dark and brooding images that lent themselves to individual interpretations. The modern-day Longinus with the crucified figure on a telegraph pole, the recurring motif of the bird breaking away from its chains, the struggling figure drawing power up through the earth itself – these were all very primitive expressions given very primitive life.

"The 'Arise!' cover itself was basically another silhouette," Rob continues, "A group of figures pointing to the horizon, their spears and axes intimating the idea of warriors on a cliff's edge looking over a landscape which we can't yet see. And remember this: when I drew these pieces, all that black ink and scratchy writing, it was not in some art studio propped up against a nice clean desk, more often than not it was in some seedy squat or other, the walls sprayed vertically with blood from syringes, a scrap sheet of paper and a single Rotring pen in hand, often by candlelight, with the sirens of the city night all around.

"When I look back from where I am now," he ponders, "I see a lot of weaponry, swords, axes, spears – a sort of subconscious prompt for the way that my art expresses itself now. The artwork of Amebix was very much in tandem with the principles and working practice of the band itself; we were not musicians, we struggled hard to find a way to draw every ounce of energy out of our musical illiteracy, and succeeded. Likewise, I was no artist, and in a similar way expressed myself through a very simple style. Again, power through simplicity."

Some other artistic highlights in the UK anarcho punk canon came courtesy of Antisect (their 'In Darkness There Is No Choice' album featured some exceptionally bold images), The Mob (whose 'Let The Tribe Increase' LP even eschewed the anarcho preoccupation with black and white) and the Subhumans, who found in Nick Lant a very capable, playful illustrator ("I swear his covers were half the reason the records sold so well," laughs vocalist Dick Lucas).

Not strictly 'anarcho' as such, but taking many of their creative prompts from the likes of Crass, Discharge offered up two of the most powerful anti-war covers of all time wrapped around their 'Why?' 12" and 'Never Again' 7", the former rubbing the horrors of collateral damage in our horrified faces, the latter a poignant portrayal of a dove impaled upon a bayonet.

Across the Atlantic, the tradition of art as a weapon of truth was embraced by the likes of Crucifix, MDC, Septic Death, and, most famously, the Dead Kennedys, who employed the devious montages of Winston Smith (a specialist in subverting the American Way through the clever displacement of innocent images) to great effect, especially with their 'In God We Trust' 12", which saw a bullion Christ crucified to the almighty dollar. Those interested in seeing more are advised to check out Winston's books, 1994's 'Act Like Nothing's Wrong' and 1998's 'Artcrime'.

Leeds-born John Yates, who now resides in California, also picked up work with Jello Biafra and the DKs before beginning his own Stealworks graphics company, who have since designed striking sleeves for the books of such radical luminaries as Noam Chomsky, Paul Avrich and Ward Churchill, not to mention CD covers for Against All Authority, Anti-Flag and Chumbawamba.

In more recent years, the ideals and aesthetics of anarchic art have been kept alive by the likes of Robert 'Mid' Middleton. Now guitarist with Bait but once the driving force behind crustcore legends Deviated Instinct and Spinewrench, he has been illustrating record sleeves since 1986, for the likes of Napalm Death, Gorefest, Extreme Noise Terror, Stampin' Ground, Hellchild, Disfear, Medulla Nocte and Underule amongst others. But even more impressive than his CV is his knack of unnerving the observer with his raw, twisted deities of skewed flesh and bone.

"My initial influences were all the killer black and white illustrators of the '80s like Pushead, Nick Blinko, Nick Lant and Squeal," he begins, rather unsurprisingly. "But a great deal of my influence just comes from the everyday world. I get more inspiration from what I see on a day-to-day basis than from looking at other artists, architectural forms, urban decay, organic matter – just running about with my camera. I see possibilities in everything, even the way a wall of cracked tiles looks on a rundown subway wall. I can just stop and stare at stuff like that for ages, recomposing it in my head.

"Most of the bands I work with are after something very dark or angry. On the rare occasion I've had to take on something with some sort of uplifting vibe I'm normally really struggling. Having said that though, I don't go out of my way to make simply depressive work. People often say, 'What on earth goes on inside your head?' and I've had my fair share of demons to conquer, but who hasn't? I'd like to think I'm generally a positive person, although I guess I just feel more aesthetic power in a negative worldview. I don't really want to make happy work, although I'd like to think that, however ugly the image, it's all beautiful in its own way."

ANDY SNEAP (PRODUCER/FOZZY/SABBAT) –

ON THRASH METAL – ISSUE 108 (APRIL 2003)

"I guess it was the energy that got me into thrash in the first place. And also the great playing of some of those bands. Metallica were actually great from the word go. I remember getting 'Kill 'Em All' and Anthrax's 'Fistful Of Metal' at a record fair - I actually part sold my Status Quo collection for them, one of my wiser moves I have to say. I was about 15 at the time and had been playing for a few years. I had just started playing in a band from Nottingham. We formed Sabbat in May '85.

"I can't remember for sure the first thrash record I bought, either 'Fistful Of Metal', or Exodus' 'Bonded By Blood', or maybe it was Slayer's 'Show No Mercy'? I can remember that it made me feel my down picking was somewhat inadequate anyway!

"As for the best thrash album I ever bought? There's a few: 'Fabulous Disaster' by

Andy Sneap, when in Sabbat, by Tony Mottram

Exodus - I still enjoy Mark Senasac's production work on that, and what great guitar playing too! I also really liked Forbidden's first album and Testament's 'The New Order', both for the riffs and solos.

"I think my first thrash show was probably Metallica and Anthrax on the 'Master Of Puppets' tour at Sheffield and Birmingham. The spitting during Anthrax's set was outrageous. I remember poor old Malice getting virtually spat off stage supporting Slayer on the 'Reign In Blood' tour... poor bastards!

"On that same tour, I saw Slayer at Nottingham Rock City, and that was probably the best thrash show I've ever attended. There was a great vibe. Also, Anthrax and Metal Church at Hammersmith would have to rank up there as one of the all-time classic shows - Metal Church were great that night.

"Anyway, I had a small recording studio set up at our rehearsal room, where I was demoing my own stuff, and I started getting more and more bands coming to me after they'd heard what I was doing. One thing led to another and I ended up doing a couple of projects with Colin Richardson, which saw me working in the US and it's just kept snowballing really.

"The essential ingredients of a great thrash production are basically good playing and a good drum sound. If the drums sound like shit, the album will really suffer. That's where all the clarity is. To be honest, I don't think the current metal scene stands up when compared to the thrash heyday in the '80s. Back then there were some ridiculously good guitar players. Kids these days just tune to A#, play no higher than the third fret, play on single strings, and try and touch their toes! Whatever happened to riffs and solos? Thank God for Sweden that's all I can say!"

Angel Crew, by Rudy De Doncker

The Eurocore old guard need to watch their backs, 'cos there are some new kids on the block. Angel Crew, who feature members of Backfire!, Deviate, Length Of Time and Arkangel, are about as close to a 'hardcore super group' as you're likely to find this side of the Atlantic, and their debut offering on Good Life, the scathing 'Another Day Living In Hatred', wastes no time whatsoever laying waste to the opposition.

"Uh, yes, we are really, as we don't see ourselves that way at all," laughs guitarist Danny, when I ask if that term 'super group' embarrasses them. "That seems to imply that we think that we are better than everyone else, but that's not the case at all. Angel Crew members have all been friends for a long time, and it just seemed the right time to finally get together and do this. It's something special that we all have in common, that we can look back on fondly in the future."

But being in all these other bands must surely make it a nightmare to schedule stuff to promote Angel Crew?

"We have problems every day," he sighs. "Obviously it's very difficult to make plans for the coming months when most of your musicians will probably be on tour already! But we manage as best we can, by talking to each other every day, to make sure we have at least some sort of agenda. It means we are all really busy all the time, but music is our life, and putting more and more pressure upon ourselves is something we all like to do!"

For those still unfamiliar with the band, Angel Crew specialise in ultra-hard riffing arc-welded onto devastating rhythms, for maximum damage on the dance floor. These guys sound like the missing link between Merauder and Fury Of Five, and that means total heaviness and full-on aggression.

Of course, you've already been misunderstood as some kind of tuff guy band, not least of all by Fracture magazine who ran a damning review of your lyrics...

"Hey, 'Another Day Living In Hatred' was never meant to please everyone," counters Danny. "Most of the messages are directed at/related to past experiences, with certain people, with the scene, explaining that times are changing and that we aren't prepared to take shit from them anymore. It is not a message directed at the world, and neither is it a tough guy affirmation; it's just how we feel and how we deal with people who try to pass judgment on our lives."

So, there you have it, an all-too-brief glimpse at Eurocore's next big thing. The band are currently on tour with Biohazard as you read this, and are planning to unleash their follow-up this coming summer, to be entitled 'Kings Of Dogs'. Until then, though, 'Another Day Living In Hatred' should be on the shopping list of all fans of brutal crossover.

ANGER MANAGEMENT – ISSUE 202 (OCTOBER 2010)

Anger Management

With ex-members of such bruising UK metal acts as Murder One, Underule and Next To Nothing in their ranks, it's no surprise that Evesham's Anger Management channel the psycho-grooves of prime-time Pantera via the intensity of hardcore and the aggression of death metal.

"The metal scene in Britain really sucks right now for a number of reasons," spits drummer Jamie 'Jammer' Airns. "The main one being that it seems the image or look surrounding metal appears to be more important than the music itself, which is ridiculous. Seen to be scene, you might say! We don't have any stupid gimmicks, and we're not just another beat-down band. We are who we are: straight-up, in-your-face, brutal metal... there's something for everyone in what we do - but we need to kill off those fringed hair cuts!"

RIP Jammer

Annihilation Time, pic by Nick Ulmer

"We didn't make it into your country, man, and we're kinda bummed about that!" Annihilation Time guitarist Graham Clise is speaking from Den Haag, when this interview for Terrorizer was actually scheduled to take place face-to-face in Newport. "The guy booking our shows was supposed to get us work permits, but he didn't... and we got stopped at the border and denied access! It sucks 'cos we were so looking forward to coming to the UK again; we always have a good time, and we've got a lot of buddies there too.

"Last time we had a full UK tour booked, I broke my hand really badly a month before we were coming over, so we had to cancel then as well... I don't know what's going on, but we're pissed about it! I hope people there don't think we're just flaking out on them or anything..."

The band are (meant to be) on the road to promote their ballsy new album for Tee Pee, 'Annihilation Time III: Tales Of The Ancient Age', a volatile cocktail of don't-give-a-flying-fuck rock 'n' roll unleashed with the furious energy of the gnarliest USHC acts. Just don't call them the missing link between Black Sabbath and Black Flag (even though they are)!

"That's all we ever hear, man," laughs Graham. "I dunno, it's cool in one way, 'cos I totally dig both bands, but we've got our own sound down a bit more now, and it's less obvious than any one particular influence...

"If anything, I like being called 'hardcore punk', 'cos that's what we do first; we play punk, but we all listen to a lot of rock music... and I mean a LOT of rock music. It's almost like we try to write a rock song, but then we can't help but skate it up, play it with more attitude... make it uglier, I guess... if that makes any sense? We're just really into a lot of different music, and it's not a deliberate attempt to 'cross over' or whatever, it just comes out this way...

Annihilation Time, by Chris Carey

"That's the funny thing," he adds in closing, explaining away that grandiose title that would be more at home on a Candlemass album. "We decided upon it because it sounds all epic, y'know? But actually, Ancient Age is a type of really cheap whiskey we have here in the States, and it's horrible stuff! But it always makes for a crazy night!"

ANNIHILATOR – ISSUE 68 (JULY 1999)

Annihilator, courtesy of Olly Hahn

Nine seems to be the number of the moment right now, doesn't it? You've got Mercyful Fate returning to awesome form with their ninth record, and lo and behold, here's Annihilator back with a vengeance as well, with their ninth record, and the year being 1999, 'n' all. Many feared these Canadians were doomed to be also-rans after a few mediocre records that didn't exactly Set The World On Fire (groan), but 'Criteria For A Black Widow' sees them over their Rocky patch (shit, sorry...) and thrashing with the best of 'em again. Here's Ian Glasper with the low-down.

After the anomaly (when placed alongside their other releases) that was 'Remains', you could've been forgiven for thinking that Canadian thrash pioneers, Annihilator, were all washed up. It was their eighth album, and apparently saw main-man, Jeff Waters, flailing about for inspiration, incorporating all sorts of unworthy influences (such as Ministry!) into the band's traditional speed/power metal sound. But thankfully, nothing could be further from the truth, 'cos now Jeff has reassembled the original line-up (well, okay, most of it) that was responsible for their ground-breaking 'Alice In Hell' debut, and the latest offering, 'Criteria For A Black Widow', which also sees them safely back on Roadrunner once more, is possibly their strongest to date.

"Back in January '97, my marriage got really messy," recalls Jeff, calling me from his home in Vancouver, of the unfortunate incidents that led to the below-par 'Remains', "And until the summer of '98, I was right out of music. I hardly picked up my guitar once! And when I recorded 'Remains', I wasn't too interested in my career at all, and I just put it out basically for contractual reasons. Yeah, I know it could've been better, but I can live with it, and looking back, there's a few good songs on there... and some of the playing is pretty good... but it's no comparison to this new one."

And that's an understatement right there, too. 'Criteria...' eats its predecessor for breakfast, combining all the best elements of previous Annihilator incarnations – technicality, melody, power, speed, craftsmanship... the whole nine yards – into one satisfying whole, sure to please even the most demanding metalhead. It's harder, faster, leaner and meaner than any of their records since

'Alice...' first smashed onto the scene back in '89, which obviously begs the question, how calculated a move was this 'reunion', given the current resurgence of thrash, and all those other, um, high profile metal acts getting it back together again after long layoffs?

"If you'd seen how fucked up I was back there, you'd know exactly why the songs on here sound so hard," laughs Jeff wryly. "l went through a year of custody and courts for my boys, which I eventually won, but it was a bad time for me, as you can imagine. Then one of my friends dragged me along to see a Slayer show here in Vancouver, and as soon as I saw such an aggressive metal concert again, it kinda breathed some life back into me. I had a lot of anger in me, and seeing that band again, who I had always loved, brought it all back, and I started writing again.

"It was only when I demoed it all on my little four track that I realised how heavy the material was. I had originally intended it to be just me playing all the instruments and singing – like on 'Remains' – but once I'd written the stuff, I knew it needed a real drummer for it, not a drum machine, so I got in touch with Ray Hartmann, who had played on my first two records. When he heard all the old Annihilator influences coming through in the songs, it was actually Ray who suggested I call Randy Rampage up, and within a week he was down here demoing the songs!"

So, with four-fifths of the 'Alice In Hell' touring line-up reunited once again, Jeff then proceeded to batter out his most potent Annihilator album in ten years. 'Criteria...' literally buzzes with the ripping riffs and rhythms that we all fondly remember from the very best thrash of the late '80s, but all delivered with the benefit of a '90s production job, and thicker than a stegosaurus' hind leg. Put it on and you'll be assaulted by all manner of influences from right across the spectrum of metaldom.

"I'm not offended when people say that my solos sound like this or that," reveals the amicable axeman. "If anything, I'm actually pleased... as long as they're not saying that I've just blatantly ripped people off! Even the best guitarists are totally influenced by their predecessors, no matter how much they deny it, and I'd rather acknowledge those influences than be ashamed of them, y'know?

"I mean, I can sit down with any one of our songs, and pick out the obvious influences, just like anyone else can. For example, on 'Bloodbath' [the kick-ass opener on the new record - IG], there's some Slayer, and even Destruction, in the verses, whilst the chorus is very early Metallica. The first solo is similar to that guy from the Scorpions, whilst the second one is quite, um, Kirk Hammett... but it all adds up to Annihilator when taken as a whole!

"I'm just winging it here, but that's how easy it is to extract influences from my writing. There's everything in the Annihilator sound, from Slayer to Rush... and that's not how record companies usually like a band to work. It's easier for them if we keep churning out carbon copies of our best-selling work, but really, because of all the different line-ups, none of my records have ever sounded the same... until now. 'Criteria...' is the first Annihilator album that has bore a strong resemblance to any of the others. Once upon a time, I would've said that I'd written it for the fans, and it wouldn't have been an intentional lie, but truth be known, I don't ever tailor songs for the fans... I write for myself, and just see what comes out."

And readers, trust me when I say that what came out this time ROCKS. Really. Nine albums down the line, but Jeff has proven once again that he is a guitarist and writer the equal of the very best out there – Dave Mustaine springs to mind (and Waters was one of the people that the Ginger 'Deth Man seriously considered for his own band before plumping for Marty Friedman to replace Jeff Young) – and the reunited band behind him aren't exactly slouches either.

"The whole thing this time round is very relaxed, and a lot more fun because of that fact," he reckons. "It's the first time we've been together for nearly ten years, and we're leaving rehearsals with big smiles on our faces, so we must be doing something right again.

"Those first records, I was very young and selfish, very focused and egotistical... it was my band, and having fun was not an option. I was always stressed – we had to be as tight and perfect as possible. I was too wrapped up in myself to realise what great musicians I had around me.

"On these warm-up shows we did recently, I was just loving it, and looking around at all the others, who were loving it too. We're just very lucky, and very glad to be doing it again. To be back with this line-up is so great for me, and the fans – we can finally do those old songs the way they were meant to be."

Ah yes, those old songs! Who could forget mosh pit anthems such as 'Welcome To Your

Death', 'Wicked Mystic' and 'Human Insecticide'? Classics one and all, that rightly went on to see that first album become Roadrunner's biggest-selling debut record.

"Nobody knew how successful it was going to be," recalls the laid-back guitarist. "I was just some kid from Canada playing thrash in his basement, and I was so excited at even selling, say, five or ten thousand albums... and then it went on to do a quarter million really quick! Of course, we were young, and it went to our heads - we thought we were going to be the next Metallica!

"Getting a deal with Roadrunner was probably one of the three greatest things to ever happen to me in my musical career. Another was doing an interview with Bernard Doe from Metal Forces – I bought that zine religiously when I was a teenager... it was my Rolling Stone, so I was freaking out big time. The other highlight was probably touring with Judas Priest. That band were like gods to me when I was a kid."

Do you think you're maybe just a bit of a control freak, seeing as you write, engineer, mix and produce your material?

"Uh, yeah, on those first two albums I definitely was," admits Jeff, "But on the third, I eased off a little bit. I got my own studio, and it became more of a fun hobby for me, where I could just vanish downstairs and record riffs whenever I had a new idea.

"I would like to produce other bands one day," he adds, on the prospect of the future, "Because I do know a lot about engineering, but being a single dad with two kids, and the band, is not easy. The anxiety and stress levels are brutal beyond belief!"

ANNIHILATOR – ISSUE 138 (DECEMBER 2005)

Fuckin' hell, what do you say about the kind of review Paul Stenning crucified Annihilator with last issue? 3/10? I mean, c'mon... their new album, 'Schizo Deluxe', is actually a mighty enjoyable slab of melodic metal. Sure, it falters in places, but it's heavy enough to appeal to fans of Megadeth and Pantera, and more than catchy enough to hook fans of mid-period Metallica and latter-day Judas Priest, and whilst current singer David Padden comes across as a bit of a chameleon vocally, he didn't deserve to be hung, drawn and quartered quite so vehemently by our Paul, turning in a spirited performance despite his tender years. 3/10 is a mark that should be poured with liberal scorn on releases enjoying no redeeming features, and let's be honest, 'Schizo Deluxe' is not a bad record, not by a long stretch of the imagination. In fact, this particular scribe has been having problems prising the track 'Warbird' from his car CD player, and I'm sure that most old school metal fans would find much to rejoice about here.

"The overall reaction has been incredible," enthuses garrulous main man and axe wielder extraordinaire, Jeff Waters. "It's been about ten years since I had this kind of press reaction to a record. Usually I just go into the interviews thinking, 'Okay, it's work, I've gotta talk about my record again...' And it's nice to talk to people from different countries and stuff, but you kinda do it, and sometimes you already know some of the press are going to be like, 'I don't like your new album because it's

Annihilator, and you've had too many changes, too many different styles, you never stick to the same vocalist...' Sometimes it's difficult to do interviews when you know they've got the negative side covered even before you pick up the phone to them! But this time it's been really exciting and energising for me because it's all good, and I'm like, 'Oh cool, I must have done something right this year!'

"Yeah, I know every artist out there always claims their latest LP is 'the best thing they've ever done'," he adds with a wry chuckle. "And I said it myself on the last CD I did, but the reasoning is simple... when you're a musician or an artist or whatever, and you create something, it doesn't really matter how good it is compared to anybody else or what you've done previously, you're usually proud of it, like 'Hey! Look what I did!' But over time – sometimes a month, sometimes six months or a year – you look back and see it totally differently, more realistically. I have songs I write, and as I write them, I'm all excited... 'Man, this is easily the best shit I've ever done!' Then six months later, I'm like, 'Jeez, there's only four or five really good songs on this record... it's actually quite mediocre!'"

One thing that can never be described as 'mediocre' though, not even on Annihilator's least memorable offerings – and there have been a few, oh yes – is Jeff's playing, and this time the guitars are nicely to the front of the mix, enjoying a wonderfully hard, sharp edge that allows every note picked to gleam with a surgical precision. All the better to enjoy the sort of dazzling display of fretboard gymnastics we've come to expect from Jeff Waters over the years.

"Yeah, physically I went right to the edge, because I'm not eighteen years old anymore," he admits affably. "I'm not fifty either... I'm thirty-nine... right in the middle there, right where you gotta get in a bit of shape and do some stretches before you try and become one of the fastest picking guys out there.

"The thing is, Sid, a friend of mine who lives pretty close and calls by my studio once or twice a week, always bugged me by saying, 'You're writing some okay songs... but I'm not looking forward to yet more typical 'Waters solos'...!' 'Cos a lot of guitar players, as they settle on their own style over the years, probably think that their 'typical solo' is a pretty fine thing. But he kept telling me that I needed to light a fire under my ass and push myself... not just cruise through this shit. I didn't realise exactly what he meant to begin with, but he was basically saying that I had an opportunity to push myself to the fucking limit with my playing... to go as hard, as fast, whatever... to the point where there can be only the one take, because you'll never get it that good again. And I had the attitude of, 'Right, I'm going to hurt my hand, hurt my wrist, hurt my neck... but I'm going to play this thing until it's something fucking special.'"

There's certainly some stupidly fast picking on the album... 'Drive' and 'Pride' both teetering on the brink of being flat-out speed metal.

"But you know what? I don't care how fast you can play, it's a load of bullshit... and I said in jest recently that, 'I was the fastest, tightest rhythm guitarist in metal'... and actually, if you take my words and analyse them, I might be pretty close. But I was joking! And a lot of people were up in arms about it, when deep down, I don't care if you only play three chords, if you're Malcolm Young from AC/DC, you're a god! Those players who can do the simple, powerful stuff are amazing... they write great songs, and Angus' blues solos are some of the best stuff out there. You don't have to play fast to be good, and I don't care about speed, but I sure stirred up some shit saying that – like, thirty thousand hits on our forum from one stupid comment.

"Remember, I'm Canadian, and I have a strange, immature, goofy side to me, that sometimes gets me into a lot of trouble. I've met a lot of people touring who not only don't get my sense of humour, but they don't get how I can be so unserious about life sometimes... I have to laugh when I see bands turn into these rock stars overnight, because I never had that goal of selling millions of records, seeing my face on the cover of all the magazines, having people telling me how great I am... that was never, ever my intention. My number one thing in life – beside family and friends and health and all that shit I'm supposed to care about – is heavy metal music, and I don't have to prove the validity of that claim, because I've been playing this stuff for eleven records, so you can figure that one out yourself. But number two is, I'm a guitar player... and number three, I'm in a band called Annihilator. I never wanted to be famous! I was a metal fan, then I was a guitar player, and then I found a vehicle that allowed me to do the stuff that I like – and I've been pumping albums out ever since. Some of them are better than others, some of them have classic songs on them, some of them have crappy songs on them... but an album like 'Schizo Deluxe' comes round once every ten years or whatever, and all the pieces of the puzzle fit together for once."

Those 'pieces' being Tony Chappelle on drums and Chris Coldrick producing (Jeff handling, as per most other Annihilator releases, all guitar, bass and engineering duties at his home studio in Ottawa, Canada), both of them going above and beyond the call of duty to help deliver a record the equal of anything the band has released since 1994's 'King Of The Kill'. So, does Jeff feel under pressure to recapture the commercial glories of his earlier years?

"The easy thing for me is that I don't have anything to live up to, because I change all the time. Some of my favourite bands – like AC/DC and Slayer – have perfected their own styles, and you know what every new album is going to sound like... you know the style of drumming you're going to get, you know the style of guitar, the types of riff, the kind of singing you'll get...

"I went down a totally more ridiculous route business-wise, haha! Instead of creating my own sound and sticking to it, I decided I wanted to do something different with every album I did, so I've ended up with different singers, different drummers, different song-writing styles, different productions... but I've stayed on the same path of playing metal... apart from maybe one album in '96 or '97, when I fell off the whole game plan of doing what I want and trying my best; it was when metal looked like it was totally over, totally beaten into the ground. When I was doing 'Remains', man, I was so depressed about the state of the metal scene... it sounds cheesy, but bear in mind that heavy metal has been – is – my life, and I'm sat in the studio thinking about writing a new album, and I'm looking down this long tunnel, and there's just no light at the end of it. What I was doing didn't seem to be important anymore for anybody, and that was a depressing time. However, I stuck with it, and in '99 I did a record that returned a bit to my thrash roots, and slowly but surely it's been building for me again since then. I ended up doing more tours, and here we are – just toured with Judas Priest last year, and back with my strongest record for years."

And, as with previous releases, there seems to be a certain sly sense of humour at work on 'Schizo Deluxe' (the album apparently named after the band's fans who have referred to themselves as 'Schizos' ever since the track 'Schizos Are Never Alone' that appeared on the triumphant 'Alice In Hell' debut), in both lyrics and music.

"Well, there's two kinds of heaviness for me," ponders Jeff. "The old style... you know, Judas Priest... that real simple, slow, grinding stuff... and then there was that fast evil stuff, like Slayer. And that aggression of early Metallica and Exodus was all lumped in there with the different styles of heaviness. I always wanted to come up with that, but I've never been as genuinely angry about life and stuff to come up with anything as brutally heavy as what those bands did. My life has had some ups and downs – I've been through divorce and alcoholism, and every good and bad thing that could happen – but I never had that fucking anger that those guys were able to produce... and believe me, I've tried! I've come close a couple of times too... but I look out my window here, look out over Ottawa, and it's beautiful! Life is good, my kids are fine; I'm living a good life! It's hard to pretend to be angry if you're not.

"I mean, I can channel stuff and find the aggression for my music, when I'm angry at people who fuck me around in this business, but there's always some humour that comes through. It might sometimes be cheesy, but a lot of it's on purpose, 'cos I'm a goofy kind of guy. If you cross the pure aggression of Metallica and Slayer with the fact that I'm a Canadian, you have a pretty original take on metal."

That's not to say that there aren't some songs that are deadly serious; tracks such as 'Like Father, Like Gun' and 'Plasma Zombies' have a pertinent socio-political opinion to impart, the latter inspired by an incident a little too close to Jeff's own heart for comfort.

"I basically had this problem with my son where I bought him an X-Box and almost let it be his babysitter every day. I'd turn the computer on for him, so I could get some of my own work done, and I had no clue what I was doing to him, and he was sitting there in a daze in front of that screen. And one day I woke up and realised, 'My god, our son doesn't go out to play anymore! He's going to school and thinking about video games all day!' I went 'Holy shit!' and cut him off straight away, and within a week his behaviour was just so much better. He was getting exercise, playing with his friends, drawing pictures, doing normal things for kids his age... and I put this poor kid through that for about six months, and now I'm aware of it, I notice that a lot of my friends and their kids are glued to their TV sets, obsessed with the Play Station... and when I went to his school, I realised that most of the kids there were the same. It's just an observation though; it's a very important subject, of course, but I'm not here to preach.

It's almost like alcohol to me... I quit drinking many years ago, and I was playing video games, and I was so amazed at the quality, at how fucking cool the games were... and I could see why some people find it so addictive, and I had to hide the X-Box away in my basement on the top shelf, so I wasn't always tempted to pull it out and waste my time. The thing is, some people can go out and smoke just one cigarette at the weekend, and they don't go and smoke another one for a couple of months, but if I smoke a cigarette, I'll be smoking a pack a day within a week; that's just the kinda guy I am, haha!"

FROM THE CUTTING ROOM FLOOR:

The intro to 'Maximum Satan' is pretty cheesy, now you come to mention it!

I just held a microphone up to the shitty little TV in my studio and flipped through the channels. The song is about how the mainstream media portrays the world as a generally nasty, evil place, and make out that the human race is dying out, it's all going to hell. But I see the reality as different, and in most places, the mortality rate is improving... there's so many good people out there, so many good things going on, if you wanna sit there and get depressed and blow your head off, just sit there and listen to the fucking news non-stop.

It's like a knowing nod to heavy metal tradition!

Yeah, you gotta remember, I know all about the words 'Hell' and 'kill' and 'Satan'! I grew up on 'Haunting The Chapel' by Slayer, grew up listening to Venom... I'm not sat here pretending that I'm writing poetry! I know it's not 100% original... it's meant to be entertaining. I just sit here and write whatever comes out of me, and sometimes you'll get some pretty serious subjects and sometimes you get a song like 'Braindead', off 'Set The World On Fire', which has gotta be one of the craziest, goofiest songs ever, haha! I put things on there for myself; there's jokes on there about my sister and my friends... I do silly things because sometimes that's what I want to do.

How much of the testing of the songs comes from actually playing them live?

Um, I think I've figured the way to road-test the songs without even leaving the house, haha! Without even getting a band together to tour... without even releasing the record! And that is, do it through the press this time... you go to the press 'cos you wanna get the message out, you wanna let people know you're there, and it's cool if people wanna talk to you 'cos they like what you're doing – but now I'm kinda gauging the strength of the album.
For example, the album I did last year was the first album with a new singer, Dave Padden... who's now our veteran singer! And the press reaction was 50/50... some people liked it, and some didn't. And back then, as now, I was saying, 'Oh man, this is

one of my best records!' And that was the feeling I had... and is the feeling I'm having now, but this time I'm keeping my mouth shut and listening to something happening that hasn't happened since my album called 'King Of The Kill'... they're all saying good things. 'Cos the minute I start yelling, 'I love my baby!' I'm setting myself up as a target for some people... I've learned that one quick.

There's a strong Halford influence on the song 'Too Far Gone'... in fact, each song sounds different, the album as a whole taking influence from all aspects of metal...

The thing that saved my ass on that front is that the actual record sounds consistent; the guitar, bass and drum sounds are the same all the way through, which gives you a little more room to experiment with the style and theme of the record, y'know? I only see it from my own perspective, usually as a burnt-out musician, having spent so many months on the record, I don't even know what I'm listening to, but I picked the strongest songs, that sounded like they all belonged on the same record, as the first seven tracks. Then the last three songs, that I thought were three totally different tunes, with the only thing they had in common being the sound... so I put them at the end, thinking that at least people would have six or seven songs of pure adrenaline, just pounding for most of the record, and then they can kick back at the end and listen to these weird and varied things. In a way, to start with, I thought that was almost like admitting I should have written three stronger songs, but after having done 150 interviews since starting press on the album, and there's songs that I think might be weaker ones that are the favourite songs of some journalists. And other people are saying, 'Obviously this song is the best one on the record...' and I'm just shaking my head. And that's a good thing, when there's not just two obvious 'hits' on a record; all these people having all these different opinions, it must mean something is going down well. And everybody has a different opinion on each album I've done too, which is fucking great, because it means if you don't like a record I put out, you might like the next one! And that's what's kept us going...

I kinda draw parallels between your career and Dave Mustaine's – the way he's steered the Megadeth ship through all the stormy waters, changing the band's style with each record...

One of the differences is, I didn't have the pressure he did. Dave and I are good friends, and we've talked a few times about this, and he had all the pressure. I came in as an unknown, and had a great first album that sold very, very well, but really Annihilator has been a solo project, with me hiring in a drummer for the studio, using all these different singers... I've always played guitar, played bass, engineered all the records, mixed all the records... I've never had to deal with that whole 'band thing', with band members being fired all the time, having to struggle to find replacements and stuff. Sure, it might have looked that way to the public, that I had a revolving door of musicians, but it's my own fault that I advertised this thing as a band called Annihilator, when really it was the Jeff Waters project!

And that's a double-edged sword; the big negative is that people see all those members coming and going and don't take it seriously at first glance, but at the same time, I can tell you now, that's why I'm still here, putting out my eleventh CD. To deliver something different every time is a lot better for me and my fans than just pumping out the same shit over and over again.

There are some similarities with Megadeth though... we both love metal, we're both reasonable guitar players...

You may be a little more modest than him as well, haha!

Well, I honestly respect guys like Malcolm Young... sometimes the simpler guys are the best players technically... it doesn't matter to me if you practise fourteen hours a day and play like Steve Vai, it doesn't appeal to me. I'd rather hear three great chords at a concert than some guy noodling fast... the thing is, I can noodle fast if I want, but it's not a priority for me. I'm not interested in running to the front of the stage and having a spotlight on me! There are so many better guitar players out there, to be honest. I'm not up there to be acknowledged as a great guitarist, I just wanna write some good music that people like to hear, and I try my best to be a good guitar player...

ANNIHILATOR – ISSUE 247 (APRIL 2014)

'Alice In Hell' – classic album piece

It's possibly hard to comprehend when you look back at such a classic album as Annihilator's 1989 'Alice In Hell' debut that the band were still finding their feet and battling all the hardships that come with the territory of being a new unknown act in an anti-social genre like thrash metal. With our rose-tinted specs on, we look upon it retrospectively as this perfectly formed defining moment in the evolution of melodic speed metal, but the truth is we're lucky it ever got recorded at all.

"For me, it's kinda weird looking back," muses Annihilator main man Jeff Waters, whose single-minded determination has kept the band rumbling ever since, "Because I originally started the band back in late '84 or early '85, with an old friend of mine called John Bates, who co-wrote a few songs that eventually appeared on 'Alice In Hell' and [1990 follow-up] 'Never, Neverland', but it was four years before I got to record them properly. I had to record two demos before I got a deal, and that took four years – which was a long time to get signed, especially at the height of the thrash scene. That album came out at the very tail-end of that killer wave of metal that ran from 1980 to 1990. I sometimes wonder what would have happened if it had come out in '86 or '87!

"Anyway, I did that last demo on my own, because there were no musicians in Ottawa,

79

and then I went to live in Vancouver, to try and get the band off the ground. I was in total poverty for two years; it was a really tough time, and I didn't have the heart to tell my family and friends back home that I didn't even have enough money to eat. People talk about 'starving musicians', but I literally was... I lost about 30 lbs. I really paid my dues! But it did keep me focused on making something good happen, writing the best music I could and finding the best musicians...

"It was the 'Phantasmagoria' demo I did in '86 that eventually got us the deal with Roadrunner. I kept sending it out there and eventually people started picking up on it, and it got bigger and bigger on the underground, and it took a long time but it paid off in the end, because when the album did come out, we actually had a fan-base waiting for it, and it went pretty big around the world straight away. So it was basically a really long, drawn-out overnight success story, haha!"

As well as ripping thrash metal anthems such as 'W.T.Y.D.', 'Wicked Mystic' and 'Human Insecticide', 'Alice In Hell' is probably best remembered for its virtuoso guitar work, and [DOA bassist] Randy Rampage's aggressive vocal turn. Mr. Rampage was unfortunately a short-lived member of the band, 'Alice In Hell' his only appearance with Annihilator.

"I think it was the opening two songs [classical piece 'Crystal Anne' running into the title track], that made an impact with metal heads around the world," reckons Jeff. "People just remember those songs, from the radio play and the videos. It seems to me that those two tracks really stood out, but it wasn't just about those songs; some of that stuff is really raging as well as catchy. Apparently, the Megadeth guys were singing those songs on the way to the studio each day to record 'Rust In Peace', which is crazy to consider.

"I wrote it all, played all the bass too, arranged the drums, wrote the lyrics, engineered and produced it... I'd found Ray [Hartmann], this great drummer, and we'd written this killer album, and we needed a singer. Randy Rampage was this really rough guy, who looked like he was on drugs and couldn't sing a note. But he didn't give a shit, and just wanted to be a rock star. He only had one voice, which was pretty good, to be honest, but he had this awesome punk/metal attitude, and I knew he'd be the perfect front-man.

"Anyway, we went on tour with Testament, who were touring 'Practise What You Preach', and 'Alice In Hell' had just hit and was blowing up, so the tour was amazing... then Randy quit! None of us could believe it – why would anyone leave when their band was just breaking big? He said it was his job back at home, but years later I realised he was a self-confessed drug addict and alcoholic, and he just went home to get a fix, because it was too difficult to get one on tour, crossing borders all the time. It put me in total shock, because it was all going so well, so we were stuck – with a very successful album, the world was ours for the taking, and we lost our singer. Thankfully we found a replacement [Omen's Coburn Pharr] really quickly and the next album was even bigger!"

Admittedly the production on 'Alice...' wasn't the best either, but it did the job, and certainly the album sounded good enough for the songs to shine through and Annihilator to be guaranteed a long illustrious career. Of course, Jeff has just re-

recorded some of those classic cuts on the bonus disc of latest album 'Feast', and against the odds they manage to trump the originals.

"'Alice In Hell' is not well recorded, but the songs and performances made up for it," he agrees. "I'm not usually into re-recordings – why would you even touch a classic recording again? You can never get back the feeling of the original. But Dave, our singer, suggested doing the bonus 'Re-Kill' CD, because no one has to pay for it, and we could have fun doing it. Just don't think of it as a 'best of'; it's more a collection of the songs we're going to play live. We have a lot of younger fans who are still discovering the old stuff like 'Alice In Hell', and that has to be a good thing.

"And I truly appreciate the fact I'm still able to do this. Every time I get on a plane out of Ottawa, I look out the window and think, 'You lucky son of a bitch!' I had all the ego and dreams squashed out of me years ago, but it's not about my bank account and it's not about ticket sales. I'm still making a living from this band after 25 years, I still have artistic control, and I'm still enjoying every single day."

ANOTHER VICTIM – ISSUE 59 (OCTOBER 1998)

Another Victim

No one had ever heard of Syracuse, New York, until Earth Crisis unleashed their 'Firestorm' EP, irrevocably changing the face of modern hardcore as we all knew it with their pyretic mixture of heavy music and revolutionary lyrics. From then on, the name of that town became synonymous with the vegan sXe wing of radical music - the straightedge capital of the US, if you will - and with EC all poised for mainstream

Another Victim

success, please welcome in Another Victim, who, with their new 'Apocalypse Now' MCD for Equal Vision, look all set to continue flying the flag for Syracuse as a birthing place for sonic savagery.

"The scene's still strong here," reckons their drummer, Tony Tornabene, "Although attendances at shows have dwindled off a bit in the last year. I guess a lot of people are getting older and moving on. But as far as the sXe capital of America goes...? I dunno!"

"There is always twice as many sXe kids when we play here compared to anywhere else," interjects Andy Bradshaw, who is responsible for the vociferous roar topping off the metallic mayhem to be found on 'Apocalypse Now'. "It probably is 'cos Earth Crisis originate from here; I would attribute a lot of it to them. They got so big, so fast, despite being so militant, and a lot of people really took to them. That said, it is a very open-minded scene; all kinds of bands do really well when they play Syracuse, the kids co-mingle just fine, y'know?"

How do you feel about the Salt Lake City 'hardline' straight-edgers, who have been doing drive-bys on McDonalds, etc.? It's this sort of fanaticism that turns so many people off what is otherwise a very positive healthy lifestyle (with a killer soundtrack, to boot!)

"I guess, um, in their hearts they mean well," begins Tony, carefully, "But they sometimes go too far. For me, the whole idea about sXe was never to force your ideas on others, but to try and see the overall picture, and how your actions affect others."

"None of us are hardline," adds Andy, "But it's like everything else - there are certain aspects of that philosophy that we totally support, such as the human and animal rights stuff, but there's others that we don't agree with at all."

As well as continuing the ideology so inherent in their home town, Another Victim pick up the baton cast aside by EC after their mighty 'Destroy The Machines' opus. There is a similar base brutality coursing through the six steel-plated slabs of undiluted aggression that comprise the new MCD, and all driven by the same kind of unrelenting rhythms that made the Hatebreed CD such a choice morsel for us metal fans.

"Once this record's out properly, we hope to crossover even more," claims Andy, when we discuss the inordinately high mineral content of their dense guitar tones. "We'd like to turn a whole lot more metal kids onto our record, and in turn, our lyrics. Reaching a bigger audience is not selling out, not if you have important things to say with your music. Stuff like animal rights needs to be taken into the mainstream, and some day, even tho' we are totally happy where we are right now with Equal Vision, we would like to take this to the next level. On the next record, with the new material we've already written, we've actually made a conscious effort to balance our songs between the hardcore and metal styles."

One thing that sets 'Apocalypse Now' apart from the faceless masses of riff-mongers out there on the East Coast are some interesting percussive flourishes that lurk deep in the mix, unobtrusively enhancing your listening experience. Unfortunately, it looks like these may be a thing of the past, as Tony explains.

"That was their old drummer, who had a rack of bongos and a timpani and stuff, which I don't use at all. But I try to do some of that stuff on the regular toms, which makes it all a lot heavier and punchier. Anyway, I try to compliment the guitars a lot more, rather than complicate things too much..."

And, with their debut full-length planned for 1999, fans of metallic hardcore can rest easy knowing they have plenty more AV earache to look forward to. Just don't expect the band to share any such optimism about the future, okay? With that ominous MCD title, and a record that is steeped in dark prophetic visions of a dog eat dog world, where the strong run rampant over the meek whilst the planet burns on its skewed axis, it's fair to say that Another Victim don't relish the imminent millennium with quite the same enthusiasm as, say, Carol Vorderman.

Another Victim

"We are kind of pessimistic about the future," admits Andy, "But who can blame us? Earth resources are dwindling, third world countries are virtually owned by big corporations, who are descending into chaos... we came up with the title, 'Apocalypse Now', with the outlook for the next century in mind. We won't say that it's the end of the world, but it sure could be soon. And people need to realise what's happening beyond their day-to-day lives. We all need to decide what kind of a future we want for our children."

Anthrax

Hailed as part of the Big Four in the Eighties, Anthrax are still going strong in the Nineties. This month sees the release of 'Volume 8 – The Threat Is Real'; yes, you guessed it, their eighth album, and first for their new label. Ian Glasper called up drummer Charlie Benante to find out why the New Yorkers nearly went missing in action after their last album, and to hear all about the new one.

"Oh wow, one of the high points would have to be the first time we did one of the big festivals, like the Monsters of Rock, at Donnington - that was a real big deal for us, a definite high point. We didn't know what to expect when we got there, but it was just crazy... people were so receptive to us, it was a great feeling. We made a lot of friends in England, a lot of people took a liking to us right away. It was the first place that we enjoyed any real success."

Okay, whaddya expect? I'm talking to Charlie Benante, drummer of the legendary Anthrax, a band with a brand-new record, 'Volume B - The Threat Is Real', still hot in the racks, a band I've been listening to for thirteen years, a band responsible for some of the best, and funniest, moments in thrash metal, and you think I ain't gonna chew the shit with him about their past? Get real! There's too many good memories there not to indulge in a bit of nostalgia.

The first time I saw Anthrax, they were opening up for Metallica, who were on the '...Puppets' tour, and it was at the Birmingham Odeon. It was £3 to get in, and Billy Milano introduced them as 'the heaviest fucking band in the world!' Needless to say, it was an awesome show, my memory of it only besmirched in hindsight by the knowledge of the tragedy that befell the headliners a few weeks later, when Cliff Burton sadly died in a bus accident.

Then, of course, I saw 'em on the 'Among The Living' tour, with a young, and very hungry, Testament snapping at their heels as support, but the Noo Yorkers held their own admirably. Charlie laughs at the memory of shows he hasn't thought about in a long while, and the enthusiasm with which I recall them. Unfortunately though, for the band, they don't have to dredge so far back in their career to summon to mind a low-point for me.

"Oh, the release of our last record, the 'Stomp 442' album," sighs the amicable drummer, still sounding non-plussed at their turn of fortunes. "No one even knew it was out. That took a lot out of us actually, we didn't really know what to do. This was at the height of alternative music, and there we were, trying to exist, trying to survive, in a world where 'metal' was a dirty word. We didn't know how to take it back then, but what we tried to do was just be ourselves, not go along with the trends and write some alternative album. We just decided that to give what we felt inside us was right, but that was a low point, believe me."

Being honest to themselves, and consequently their fans, has always seemed to serve Anthrax well, and has led them to where they are today, with another ground-breaking, especially for a one-time thrash metal band, new album under their belts, an album that pushes the envelope probably further than even they have dared, until now. Like its predecessor, the ill-fated 'Stomp 442', and also 'The Sound Of White Noise', the watershed album that introduced ex-Armored Saint John Bush to their mic spot, 'Volume 8 - The Threat Is Real' sees the band in a more sober frame of mind. It explores subtle moods in a way that, prior to '93's 'Sounds Of...', we would never have associated with Anthrax. After all, they were the most cartoonish of the Big Four of the late Eighties metal scene (rounded out by Metallica, Slayer, and Megadeth, of course), seemingly obsessed with Bermuda shorts, Stephen King and 2000AD.

"See, what happened, keeping it brief... for so long, after we did ' State of Euphoria', people just thought we were becoming a novelty act, and we thought, 'Fuck them, that's not what we're about, we gotta put a stop to this right away.' So, when we decided to part ways with Joey [Belladonna, their old vocalist - IG], we wanted to bring out the serious side to our music. We didn't wanna do any more 'I'm The Man' or 'Starting Up A Posse' stuff, so in a way, we put our sense of humour to one side for a bit, and we did two very serious records.

"And you know what? We started to miss that humour, so on this record, we bought it out again. We have a coupla songs like '604' and 'Cupajoe' [a 40 second blast of S.O.D.-like mayhem - IG], and they are serious songs, too, in a way, but we thought, 'Hey, let's have a bit of fun here', too."

Once upon a time, your name was synonymous with the term 'mosh'... but you don't mosh it up on the new record, anywhere! You didn't on 'Stomp', either. What gives?

"Oh, it's still there," Charlie claims, "But it just doesn't say it on the cover. It's still an ingredient, it just comes out in different ways. Whenever I hear the media talk about 'mosh pits', or whatever, I still cringe, even now. I half expect to walk into a Burger King and see a Moshburger, or a Moshwich. It's kinda stupid. We never took credit for that mosh thing - it was something already in the hardcore scene. I swear that it was Vinnie Stigma who came up with the term. We just used it, and people just really picked up on it; that's the way that whole thing went down."

Oh well, don't go expecting any monster crunch mid-sections a la 'Indians', and the album grows slowly but surely on you, rammed as it is with more hooks than a fisherman's tackle box. And it throbs with a dark undercurrent too, not unlike Alice In

Anthrax, Scott Ian ©Doralba Picerno

Chains in places, that adds a sombre feel to even its more uplifting White Zombie-like groove passages. I wonder how much of this newfound gravity can be attributed to some of the personal problems the band have had to deal with these last few years; Scott Ian in particular has seemed to teeter on the brink of more than one personal crisis recently.

"Well, it's kinda stupid that Scott's been pinpointed for this whole thing," he explains carefully, "Okay, he did something he maybe shouldn't have, but the rest of us had the same demons, but we kept them to ourselves. I'm way more private when it comes to those sort of things. A few years back we were protecting someone in the band, and that someone was Joey, our old singer, who was an alcoholic. We used to hide all the drink from him, 'cos he would get fucked up and ruin everything otherwise, so we were perceived as some sort of SXE band almost, and that wasn't the case at all, really. But when John joined, it all got blown up again, and when you go on tour with your friends, especially Pantera, shit's gonna happen. Scott was going through a tough period - he was separating from his wife, things weren't working out, and he got drunk, and he fucked up [he was arrested for breaking and entering the Yankees' spring training camp in Florida – IG]. It happens to everyone, y'know? We were all dealing with our own shit, but Scott's ended up getting well documented.

"Nothing brings people together like a common enemy," he adds, "And that enemy was our own record company. We just felt like we got fucked, and I kept that inside, and maybe that did motivate me to write some of the darker songs on this album."

What about the music you were inspired by during writing this time out?

"There was a couple of things that really clicked with me. I've always been from that Led Zeppelin school of thought, y'know? And Black Sabbath, the Sex Pistols... Husker Du, of course, and that whole Bob Mould thing."

They're all simple arrangements. Did that rub off on Anthrax? "Yeah, 'cos on some of older records, we had these ridiculous arrangements, and now we leave that to those other bands who are kinda, like, where we were at that point. When you're younger, you just wanna play as much as you can, it's hard to learn restraint. A lot of the time they could just condense everything and cut to the chorus."

Less really is more in a great song. "Yeah, exactly. Listen to a band like Husker Du, and they have everything, the best of everything. You've got this incredibly abrasive, loud guitar in your fucking head, it's total punk, but they put a great melody over it all. I hear so many bands who've ripped them off, it's crazy."

Probably what threw me with the new record was the more mellow stuff, the, dare I say it, country-inspired songs like 'Toast To The Extras', which seemed to sit uncomfortably with the other material at first, but now they seem to add a necessary depth to the record. 'Volume 8' is certainly the most diverse incarnation of Anthrax to date, but what will those die-hard fans make of it all?

"I had to fight to keep that song on there," Charlie reveals. "The rest of the guys were unsure of it, I think they were scared, but I was, like, 'No, this is an Anthrax song, we have to be brave enough to put it on here, and put it as the fifth, or sixth, song...' If we'd put it last, it would've seemed like a novelty song, and I was, like, 'Fuck that, we have to make a statement.'

"It's weird," Charlie concludes. "We're still a metal band, or a rock band with heavy guitars, or whatever, but we're gonna explore as much as we can, and I'm sure we can pull it off."

THE ARGENT DAWN – ISSUE 194 (MARCH 2010)

"Yeah, it just feels so good to be able to walk into an HMV or wherever and see our name on the shelves," beams an obviously chuffed Tom Scobie, guitarist with fast-rising Swindon death metallers, The Argent Dawn. "Ever since we started that's always been the goal and to finally have it happen feels incredible, even more so that we have done it without making any compromises when it comes to the music. We wanted to make our debut as heavy and relentless as possible!"

Said debut being 'A Blank Eternity' for Rising Records, and said statement being happily 100% accurate; this is a slobbering beast of an album with its phasers set defiantly to kill, its precision picking and relentless blast-beats snapping at the heels of Annotation Of An Autopsy [with whom the band undertook their first UK tour several years back] and [Rising label-mates] Trigger The Bloodshed.

"Without a doubt, we've produced some amazing young bands capable of holding their own over in Europe and even the States," reckons bassist Grant Anthony, on the rather healthy state of the UK death metal scene right about now. "It's great to see the likes of Trigger The Bloodshed, who we've known for years, touring and holding their own on huge bills. The major UK festivals like Download and Bloodstock are finally paying attention to the up-and-coming bands and giving them decent slots which means the chance to play to thousands of people who wouldn't normally be exposed to death metal..."

"As far as our influences go, we're definately European death metal boys!" adds Tom. "Bands such as Aborted, Kronos, Napalm Death and Opeth are what we're all about, but that's not to say the occasional American band doesn't exert themselves on our music. Skinless and The Black Dahlia Murder are both big influences."

So, what exactly takes a young death metal band out of the back room of Swindon pubs and onto the international stage in three short years? A combination of hard work, tireless touring and plain old luck, of course. You slackers at the back, pay attention to this bit... pay your fucking dues!

"Yeah, I guess like most bands these days, we started by recording some demos and putting them up on MySpace," offers Grant. "It just so happened that we were lucky and straight away had a lot of interest from promoters wanting to put us on all over the country. We just made as many friends as we could really, whether they be promoters, other bands, or the people at the shows, and I really do think this is what helped us get to the stage we are at today; if I had to give just one piece of advice to new bands starting out, it would be: speak to as many people as humanly possible!"

"From a technical point of view, it's helped us get much tighter, both individually and as a collective," continues Tom, on the subject of all that touring. "It's also given us the opportunity to play with some amazing bands. But really the main reason for us doing it over and over again is that it's just so much fun! I can't think of anything better than hanging out, travelling around the country with your mates playing metal, and meeting so many legends along the way. We have had so many good and bad times on tour, it's certainly shaped who we are as a band, and for the better at that... "We always put everything we've got into our performances, whether we're playing to fifteen people or 150, so expect headbanging and plenty of circle pits, with a side order of blast-beats and down-tuned guitars!"

ARKANGEL - ISSUE 74 (JANUARY 2000)

Arkangel, by Rudy De Doncker

Once upon a time, it seemed like every other issue Ian Glasper was singing the praises of some Belgian band or other, but now he tends to only get excited by the very sickest, nastiest shit (and we mean that in the nicest possible way, of course!) our continental neighbours have on offer. And Arkangel are very sick and nasty indeed...

Potent riffs lash and thrust like an irate venomous snake, whilst a blackened soul vents its considerable spleen in an outpouring of lacerated vocal chords. A cloud of malevolence settles slowly after the decimation has passed, and you're left wondering just what the hell hit you... welcome to 'Dead Man Walking', the debut Arkangel album, for Good Life (fast becoming Belgium's answer to Victory), which will steamroller you all the way to Judgement Day and back. If you thought their 'Prayers Upon Deaf Ears'

MCD for Released Power Productions was intense, wait until you sample the world of pain they have in store for you this time out!

"We signed to RPP because we knew Alain, and he was in the same city as us," recalls vocalist Baldur, explaining the reasons for the recent label change. "We thought he would do a good job, but his distribution wasn't so great, so when another label came along and offered us something better, we went with them; it wasn't like we were ever under contract to RPP or anything. He just didn't do enough for the band really."

So now you're ensconced on Good Life, surely the biggest underground hardcore label in Europe... but aren't you concerned you might be swallowed up in their deluge of releases?

"No, not really, 'cos our CD is strong enough to stand out from the rest of them," claims the frontman, "And like you say, Good Life is the only hardcore label over here that is well distributed all across Europe, and even the rest of the world now. But it's not just the distribution; everything is better - the promotion, the advertising, the merchandise... now when we go to shows, we always see Good Life - and Arkangel - stuff there. If people want to get our stuff, now they can."

And the new CD is certainly strong enough to stand up to mass scrutiny, and hopefully really cross over between genres, too. I honestly can't see how any true metalhead can fail to be moved by such an assault of skin-stripping guitar riffs, and add to that the raw Integrity-like vocals, and you have a release of the utmost extremity. If it's possible, what with the increased reliance on evil-sounding harmonics, you sound even more Slayerish than before!

"Well. we've always been compared to Slayer [hey, there's worse brushes to get tarred with! – IG]," says Baldur defensively, "But we have a lot of other influences apart from them, y'know? Our guitarist is a big Slayer fan - and he does write all the riffs admittedly - but the rest of us hardly listen to that band at all. Slayer's just an easy label to stick on us because of the style of guitar playing, I guess."

Of course, Arkangel aren't the first – nor the last, I'm sure! - overtly metallic hardcore band to crawl forth from the Benelux. For many years, scenes like the H8000 were held in worldwide regard for the sheer quality - and quantity - of their bands. Arkangel come from the slightly less known (but just as infamous for savage music) Brussels area, also the spawning ground for the mighty Length Of Time. So, how's the scene out there now? Just as healthy as ever, no doubt?

"Actually, no," he sighs. "It's getting a little bit like, uh, everybody's against everybody else - but it's like that all across Belgium in general. Everyone's trying to get ahead of everyone else if they can.

They're always saying this or that about a band's attitude, or lyrics, or spreading rumours about what someone said at this gig or that gig...

"The H8000 was always very competitive, but it was always very good for us over there, and we used to play a lot of shows, and would always get a great response. But now people say that we're too violent, and that there's too many fights at our shows... which of course isn't our fault really..."

But isn't it? Aren't bands accountable for the actions of their fans if they don't attempt to dissuade their followers from stupidity? And it's a thin line between a violent pit and a violent gig...

"We won't tell people what to do at our shows: when we play, they can do whatever they please. That doesn't mean that I agree with violent dancing, but I'm not here to tell people what is right and wrong. It's their choice - as long as they're a bit careful, and they don't go around hitting on people who aren't there to dance that way too...

"There was never a problem with violent dancing - everyone used to do it and enjoy it - until the fights started. And obviously that's a problem for us as a band, but we can't be held responsible for what happens when we play - and we certainly won't preach to people about how they can or can't dance."

Serious stuff indeed. And one look at the dark imagery that the band steep their lyrics and artwork in will convince you that Arkangel aren't happy bunnies... but in a world where it seems everyone is motivated by greed, at the exclusion of all consideration for others, are any of us? Really? No, and bands like Arkangel are just the very necessary mouthpieces for our anger and hatred at society's gross injustices.

"We started out just singing about veganism, and the awful things that man does to animals, but now we've branched out a bit, and we write about the things man does to himself, and others. We've given up trying to tell people what to do with their lives; we're not a political band, just a band with strong lyrics. We just try and share our opinions with the people who come to our shows... and the rest is up to them!"

ARMORED SAINT - ISSUE 76 (MARCH 2000)

Armored Saint

Yet another metal reunion - yawn! - hardly an excuse to hold the front page, is it? But this is Armored Saint we're talking about now, one of the original and the best. Never mind the fact that their vocalist John Bush has a day job fronting Anthrax, their new album for Metal Blade (who else?), 'Revelation', is yet another milestone in unchained power metal. Ian Glasper donned his armour and went forward into battle. . .

"We had always talked about it ever since the break up in '92, but obviously Bush was busy with Anthrax for several years. And all along the way, when he was going to places he'd never been before, he was meeting all these Armored Saint fans! Asking him what we were up to! And I had the same experience on tour with Fates Warning. It was amazing; I went to Italy, for example, twice with Fates Warning, and it blew me away how many Saint fans I met there. We had never been there, and yet we had somehow achieved a big underground cult mystique..."

"After 1995, the talk began to get a bit more serious, and from that point on, it was more just a case of timing, and when we could all fit it into our schedules. This has been on the cards for three or four years, but it was just a question of organising it all properly."

So says Joey Vera, bassist and one of the founding members of LA metal legends, Armored Saint, on the subject of their brand-new studio 'comeback' album, 'Revelation', for Metal Blade. And in keeping with other recent returns to the fray from such metal gods as Agent Steel and Artillery, it certainly won't disappoint any of the band's old fans - it might even win them a load more new ones in the process, with its melodic, yet fiery, take on power metal. Ultra-catchy riffs chug along on waves of rock-solid percussion and spiralling leads, with John's vocals soaring enthusiastically over it all. It seems like their last album, 'Symbol of Salvation', was recorded only yesterday - and not back in '92 - so effortlessly does this timeless music gobble up the years.

"Oh, we knew from the beginning that we had to make a classic old school Saint record, and that was always the intention from day one. Really, we wanted to avoid anything modern creeping into our sound, but I think that, although it's mainly classic metal, it does sound modern in some way..."

That's kinda strange - because you used a real old school producer, Bill Metoyer (readers long in the tooth will recall his name being all over those vintage 'Metal Massacre' compilations like a bad rash).

"We brought him in because we wanted to recapture that feeling that so many new bands have lost," reckons the bassist. "He was on our first recording we ever did, back in '83, so it was like a big metal family reunion! We figured, why the fuck not? We were going full circle anyway..."

Well, you're back on Metal Blade too — back where you started all those years ago, despite stints on several major labels. Some bands would have a hard time dealing with such a change in fortunes...

"It's been quite a long time since we were on a major," chuckles Joey wryly, "And I learnt a lot from John's experiences with Anthrax, and he will attest that being signed to a major label isn't all it's cracked up to be! The most important thing is having a good relationship with your label, and we do have a good history with Metal Blade. We know that we can work together; in a huge corporation, it's much more 'them and us'. And at least everyone at Metal Blade is genuinely into this music - you can go into their offices any day of the week, and everyone is listening to heavy metal. Somehow I doubt that happens at Chrysalis!"

After all the ups and downs of your musical career, how on earth do you manage to approach writing music without it sounding swamped in grim cynicism? Because 'Revelation' doesn't sound like a band that has taken the knocks you guys have - it's way too joyous a celebration of pure metaldom for that.

"Don't be fooled, I am most definitely a cynic when it comes to the music biz," he sighs wearily. "But that actually makes it easier for me in many ways. I've learnt to deal with false expectations; I have a much clearer grasp on reality, on what is and isn't possible. But I try to keep that totally separate from my state of mind for writing songs. I've gained a lot of knowledge and experience over the years, and it's helped me be smart when writing music; I don't mean breaking new ground theoretically or anything, but the overall delivery, the dynamics. I'm now a better writer, who is also able to deal with the uglier side of the business, too. Unfortunately, a part of you has to become ugly as well, just to survive - and I have no interest in being totally ugly! I know what the balance between the two needs to be now."

And I guess you all have other bands that are your 'bread and butter', so the pressure is off to an extent for Armored Saint. Does less pressure equate to more fun?

"Well, we spent ten long years trying to conquer the world," comes the philosophical reply, "And that battle very nearly fucking destroyed us. We never ever gained the success that everyone thought was due to us, either! But we don't have to do that anymore. We're just celebrating the fact that we can still do this music we love so much, and that there's still a small group of fans out there who actually give a shit about this band."

ARMY RISING - ISSUE 218 (DECEMBER 2011)

"In general, it's pretty poor," laughs Army Rising guitarist Noel O' Brien candidly, of the Tipperary metal scene that spawned them, but judging by the band's debut album for Rising Records, 'Impending Chaos', it hasn't stopped them developing their own brand of melodic Irish thrash.

"We gather a lot of influence from NWOBHM bands," he adds, "And we do draw motivation knowing that Ireland isn't exactly known for its metal heritage... we want to be the band that changes that! We have a big sound with brutal breakdowns and fast rhythms, so the crowd can fuck the place up and have a great night, and we just love what we're doing, so we always put in 110% for our fans and give people a relentless show they'll be talking about for ages."

ARTILLERY - ISSUE 73 (DECEMBER 1999)

Who would ever have thought that we would see Artillery back together again? Let alone returning to the fray with a record that is not only their best yet, but more than capable of taking on the might of Scandinavia's new battery of melodic metallers. In the current climate of a thrash resurgence, anything seems possible. Ian Glasper investigates.

Artillery

Any thrash fan worth his mettle - bad pun intended - will wax lyrical about 101 'second division' bands who in his/her esteemed opinion should have made it, but didn't, for one reason or another. In the case of all those bands like Atrophy and Acrophet, love them all as much as I did, it was usually down to the overtly generic nature of their material that they failed to lift themselves above the masses of flailing hair, black jeans and big trainers that was suffocating the scene back then. But there were actually one or two of those underrated outfits who really did deserve greater success. And when the serious minds gather and true thrash is discussed in hushed tones (usually in the queue for a show), there is one name that rears its head with undeniable regularity: Artillery.

These Danes first started honing their formidable skills back in 1982. Yes, we're talking pioneers here. And three years later, they released their 'Fear of Tomorrow' album, an impressive debut by anyone's estimation, which was followed two years later by 'Terror Squad', a record which set new standards for European thrash metal. By rights, the band should have taken the world by storm right there and then, but circumstances conspired against them. As I found out from guitarist Michael Stutzer, who called me to chat about the band's recent reformation, and the imminent studio album, 'BACK' for Diehard. Their story is a veritable catalogue of disasters.

"Neat Records, our label at the time had a lot of problems with budget," recalls the guitarist with a weary sigh. "It was mainly 'cos of Venom who they spent a lot of money on, and it resulted in 'Terror Squad' being delayed for over a year, which was obviously very frustrating for us all. And then it got all these great reviews, but nothing happened, and 'cos of all the delays there was no tour support, no adverts. We ended up touring with our own money, and consequently, we couldn't afford to do many shows."

Undeterred, the band went on to sign with genre giants, Roadrunner, and unleashed the amazing 'By Inheritance' album. But again, nothing went the way it was planned, and despite the band being the first extreme metal band to play Russia, they eventually split in 1991.

"I was just tired of the singer," explains Michael. "We weren't friends at the time and we were all tired of the whole music business. Thankfully, a lot of things are very different now. Some of us went into different bands; I ended up in Missing Link which was more melodic, thrash mixed with true metal. We ended up doing three albums, and we're actually still together today. Flemming Rasmussen produced our last LP which was called 'Lobotomized'."

And so one of Europe's most exciting metal hopes bit the dust. But enough of the history lesson, let's cut to the chase. Like I said, the band are back together, as the title of the new record might suggest to the more astute amongst you, and their comeback release is everything you could hope for from Artillery. Rip-roaring leads dart with savage grace all over a soundscape of cascading riffs and lightening, precise rhythms, and even those piercing 'acquired taste' vocals of Flemming Ronsdorf have been preserved in all their unique glory. We can even forgive them the blatant Hetfield-isms, i.e. the intro to 'Final Show' or 'WWW', seeing as they were plying their trade in thrashy riffs before Metallica had ever set foot outside the Bay Area.

"Metallica used to hang out in our rehearsal room when they came over to record the 'Ride...' and 'Master...' records. At the time we were sharing a rehearsal studio with Mercyful Fate; it was a very exciting period in music.

"This time we tried to mix 'Terror Squad' with 'By Inheritance' [and they succeeded – an excited IG]," reckons Michael. "We just did what we know; we can only write from the heart after all, and we didn't look to modern metal for influences. Although obviously we have heard and absorbed all those albums by bands like Machine Head – I couldn't really avoid that 'cos I work for a radio station. But when we came to write 'BACK', we just sat down and wrote an Artillery album. I really hope that people can hear this is a genuine album. It's true metal, and it's from the heart."

The master stroke, as far as I can see, was managing to mix the classic Artillery sound with a '90s feel, so it didn't just seem totally retro - despite the cover suggesting to the contrary... very Whiplash, lads!

"Well, we got Andy Sneap to produce it, which really added a modern edge to the sound. We'd heard his work on the new Testament album, and the production is totally good. We knew he could bring out the best in this band."

And he certainly has brought out the best in them, because 'BACK' throbs with an urgency that you wouldn't normally expect from such a bunch of wizened old-timers. For me, having been a fan of the band before, it's as great a return to form as I could have dared hope for. Songs like 'How Do You Feel?' rage with that intensely melodic edge that bands such as The Haunted seem to specialize in. But one has to wonder whether those aforementioned, eccentrically metal vocals might still throw younger music fans off the scent somewhat?

"A lot of people still say that Flemming's voice is weird, but if it's 'weird', it must also be different. People either love it or hate it, there is no middle ground. Which could also be a great thing for us, 'cos once you've heard them, you certainly never forget them. Besides, we wanted to stay true to our old style; we could never do an album just to please the modern market."

It all started - second time around, I mean - with the Mighty Music release, 'Deadly Relics', of those old Artillery demos, right?

"Yeah, 'cos we ended up doing a show in Copenhagen to help promote it, where we just got up and played four songs and Diehard were there and saw the show. It all felt so good and we got such a great reaction. We knew we couldn't leave it there. Anyway, a lot of people had been looking for those songs for a long time, so it was really a release that was for the fans who were still into the band after all these years."

Is this a permanent reunion or just a flash in the pan?

"We really don't know," admits Michael, "But if we get the opportunity to tour, we will. It really depends on the reaction to the record. Flemming also plays in another band who are professional, and that takes up a lot of his time. But we did have a lot of fun with this record, so I know we would like to take it a bit further. I have a lot of contacts through my radio show, and I've talked to a lot of good bands, so who knows?"

And finally, how does it feel to be 'BACK' from the dead, lucky enough to have another shot at the cherry after all these years?

"It feels great," chuckles the guitarist, enthusiastically. "I just hope the critics and the people out there like it as much as we do. We had a lot of fun making it, and it's a true Artillery album that we're all very proud of. And that's the most important thing of all – to be able to look back at this album and know that we stayed true to what this band has always been about."

ASSERT – ISSUE 48 (NOVEMBER 1997)

Assert, 1995

Some bands come from nowhere, and go nowhere. Some bands come from nowhere, and, if they're lucky, hang around for a while, before then going nowhere. And some bands, such as Medulla Nocte still do it the old-fashioned way - the right way, if you ask me - by working their way up through the ranks, garnering a following, slowly but surely, through persistent gigging.

Assert, Shropshire's only hardcore export at the time of writing, band-wise, are one of the latter, and like the Nocte lads, they are one of the bands on the metal crossover fringe of the UKHC scene who've always seemed a bit distant from the rest of the pack. Britt, their opinionated frontman, explains to me how it's not through any fault of his band. "Uh, I think that's changing all the time, and I'm not sure that 'distant' is the right word, either. We've got our own individuality - we're not trying to sound like Earth Crisis, we're not trying to sound like Agnostic Front, or Downset. We're not old school, we're not particularly new school, we're just the AssertCoreGrooveMachine, and it takes people a certain amount of time to get their heads around it, to suss out where we're coming from.

"Everyone wants you to come straight out with an amazing demo, but we started slowly, and have just honed our sound naturally. We've improved as a live band to where we're at now, where we blow people away at every show.

"Like Medulla, we had people saying we weren't enough of this, we weren't enough of that, but we stuck to what we wanted to do. And it's very difficult to stick the tail on the donkey as far as this band's concerned."

Well, the new 7", 'Four Fingers And A Thumb Fold Into A Fist' on Household Name, demonstrates that the band have a whole lot more to offer, and are developing at a frightening rate into a force to be reckoned with. That title's pretty aggressive, tho', isn't it, Britt? In fact, the band name itself is pretty confrontational full stop.

"It's not saying four fingers and a thumb fold into a fist to punch someone in the face with, y'know?', says Britt in his throaty growl. "It's actually saying that everyone has the ability to stand proud, to put their fist in the air for something they believe in. It's all about working class solidarity.

"And you've gotta remember that the word 'assert' isn't necessarily about aggression. It comes from the word 'assertion', which is an act that doesn't have to be achieved through aggression. We have to provoke a reaction, one way or another. It's a waste of time if you're not stimulating people, and making them think. Hardcore is meant to be a challenging genre."

ATAKKU - ISSUE 135 (SEPTEMBER 2005)

"We were actually going to call ourselves Otaku which means 'obsessive'!" reveals Matt Ryder, vocalist with promising UK metallers Atakku. "It's what they call people in Japan who are totally immersed in things like anime and clothing etc., but we found out that there was already a band called Otaku, and then we just thought Atakku... was that even a word though? We looked it up and sure enough it means 'attack' in Japanese, so we thought it was pretty fitting for our sound... no one ever spells it correctly though, haha!"

Atakku it is then, and, before you ask, no, Matt isn't pulling our collective pissers when he claims that it suits the band's style. Hailing from deepest Hertfordshire, Atakku have been honing their craft for but two short years, yet have wasted no time finding their stylistic feet because their 'Dark Acts Of Friendship' MCD for Misadventure is as stridently confident a debut as you're ever likely to hear. Ponderous rhythms, massive riffs, intense screamy vocals and great swathes of dynamic atmospherics have garnered the band considerable critical acclaim already, not to mention an endless stream of comparisons to Will Haven and Sikth.

"They're both really cool bands, but as for being able to hear them in our sound? I personally can't," reckons Matt. "We're more into bands like Mastodon, Pantera, The Red Chord, Meshuggah and Fugazi, so we draw our influences from all over the place really. And besides, we're not trying to sound like anyone else! We're going to record again in February, and then you'll see; hopefully it will be a full album, but obviously money dictates what we do. We recorded the EP over a year ago now, and it's cool for what it is, but our new stuff is so much better and we want to move onto the new rather than the old. The new stuff is 100% us; we know where we're at and where we're going."

Fighting talk indeed, and in keeping with such aggressive focus – in keeping with the metalcore scene in general, in fact - the bitter lyrics of 'Dark Acts...' lead the listener along a very bleak, lonely road indeed.

"We don't class ourselves as 'metalcore' in any way, shape or form actually. I think what we're doing is incredibly different to the usual bog-standard metal that's out there right now. And I wouldn't say that any of my lyrics are particularly bitter either; they're just honest. I can only write about things that are connected to me and I've had a lot of shit happen in my life that I feel very angry about. I don't think anger is a negative thing though; used in the right way it can be a very powerful tool."

Avail – issue 34 (September 1996)

Avail

Virginia's Avail must be the closest you can get to hardcore heaven reckons Ian Glasper. Musically diverse, politically active, phenomenal live, they're also resolutely underground enough to have turned down the chance to play with Slayer...

"It's impossible to describe. There's a lot of chaos, there's a lot of dancing, there's a lot of interaction between the band and the audience, but it's absolutely not violent or macho like it might be at a Biohazard show. There is a lot of stage-diving and slam-dancing, but it's not ever aggressive..."

The hardcore heaven you're seeing described above is an Avail show, ladies and gentlemen, rightfully one of the most happening bands on the US underground as we speak. Europe's catching on fast, too, but in true conservative fashion, England's lagging behind, yet to be won over by the charms of this exciting band. Still, they'll either win us over on their own terms, or not at all. This is one band who will not pander to the industry one jot. Rather, they've achieved their not inconsiderable success

Avail, 1993, by Vique Simba

through hard work, especially on the live front. These guys gig all the time, so it's amazing how small a percentage of their shows are ruined by violence.

"I just don't think our music has that violent feel to it at all," ponders Tim, their exceptionally nice vocalist, from an Ohio payphone. "I don't think there's anything wrong with that Biohazard or Madball sorta thing, but we just attract a different set of people to the show. We get all sorts, skinheads - obviously not fascist ones, punks, hardcore kids, straightedge kids, and at any other show that would cause an awful lot of tension. I can't really pinpoint why it is, but at one of our shows, everyone just comes together."

You get the definite feeling that Avail are one of those bands whose forte is their live show, and studio work is very much a secondary consideration. "We have come to the conclusion that we just use records as a way for people to get familiar with our music for the live show, so they know the lyrics, and can join in..."

But our readers shouldn't write off their third album, '4am Friday', on Lookout Records, as surplus to requirements. You may remember me raving incoherently about it in one of my 'Holocaust' columns not so long back. It's a great record, chocka with classic hardcore references, given that special Avail twist.

"We all live in Richmond, Virginia, now, which is two hours from DC, but we all grew up in the suburbs of Washington, but we've also all sorta got into the traditional music of the southeast, such as bluegrass music... which actually comes from Ireland," adds Tim, laughing, "But it has progressed in Virginia to what it is now. And shitty southern rock bands, like Lynyrd Skynyrd! Somehow all that combines in our music, just don't ask me how. A lot of people thought the little 'Swing Low' ditty we did on the new album was a joke, but it's absolutely not. We think hardcore people need to branch out a lot more and look beyond their realm of music."

The thoughtful approach to composition doesn't stop at just the music, either. The lyrics are a similar revelation, being neither obvious nor pretentious. A song like 'Nameless' operates on several levels; at first glance it's a damning condemnation of scene violence, but it can be read in a much wider context, too.
"You can attribute that song to almost anything in life, not just tension at punk shows," Tim confirms. "It can be about daily life, anywhere where people beat the shit out of each other. I just try to write about things that I see, or that affect me. If I write about general issues that don't touch me personally, it just feels fake. But whenever anything inspires me, I go write a song about it. We do social issues too, like the song 'Monroe Park', which is a park in our hometown where all the homeless live during the summer, but then get run out of in the fall, when the rich kids go back to their boarding schools, so their parents won't see the area as an eyesore."
In true anarcho-peace-punk fashion, Avail don't just talk about the problems they identify in their songs. Rather than just mouthing empty platitudes, they take direct action (another reason no doubt for them being championed by those in the know in hardcore circles), hence their involvement in an organisation such as Food Not Bombs.
"They're basically a group of people who take food that society wastes and gives it to people who are hungry, that's not homeless people in particular, just anyone in need," explains Tim, for the benefit of anyone who may be unaware of the organisation. "It's not a free hand-out, it's a true community effort... if it was a hand-out, it would make the poor feel patronised. It's more like a huge picnic. What Avail does is we donate about $1500 a year to them. When I get a chance, I cook for them, and other members go down and serve. We try to look beyond just the musical aspects of what we do as a band..."

When Tim talks about 'the poor', the empathy in his voice is genuine. He walks it like he talks it, eking out a living from what he loves best, but it seems the geographical location of the band is crucial to their solvency!
"Our town is an economic disaster," he says. "We all live in the same six-bedroom house, and our rent is only $500 a month, and I end up paying less than $100 rent each month. And Lookout Records send us a royalty cheque every three months, so we are able to scrape by. I left for this tour with $2 in my pocket, but then again, I haven't 'worked' for two years. We're not rich, but we get by."
And there's not a lot of hardcore bands who can do that. "Y'know, a lot of people say that, but the people who are surprised by it live in New York or Philly or Oakland or Berkeley. There's absolutely no way we could live off this band if we lived in any of those cities - the cost of living is just too high."
The fact that they rely on the band's income to live makes their utter commitment to the DIY ethic even more commendable. Just consider that every penny they save their

fans by remaining loyal to the underground could be another penny in their empty pockets if they did the easier, greedy thing and went through a big booking agent. All the more remarkable then, that they booked their current European tour (which hits England for a handful of shows this month) themselves, with each promoter individually, to ensure things like low door prices.

"Control is the key word," Tim admits. 'We're complete control freaks. We try to be as ethical as possible; we don't want to fuck people over to survive. We want to make our shows as accessible as possible to everyone, An example. where I am right now, in Cleveland. We had the option to play in a huge rock 'n' roll club that would have been $7 on the door and is run by a load of dupes. So, instead, we're doing two shows, in a much smaller punk pock venue, where it's $4 flat-rate, so everyone can afford to get in. We consciously try to do that everywhere we go.

"Sometimes we get kinda torn... like on this tour, we had a chance to play with Slayer, which was really tempting, but we had a show booked already, with three local bands, and the idea of saying, 'No, we're not playing, you don't have a show tonight 'cos we're playing with Slayer for $15...' seemed so lame, we turned it down and did the underground show for $5.

"As soon as you start going down that road," Tim concludes, "Who knows how far you'll go? It's basically a question of maintaining your integrity."

AXEGRINDER – JUNE 2018

Almost thirty years after their 'Rise Of The Serpent Men' debut was unleashed by Peaceville Records in 1989, and their subsequent premature disbanding soon after its release guaranteed them underground kvlt status, Axegrinder have returned with the glorious 'Satori' for Rise Above Records.

Of course, 'Rise...' was released at the height of the crust punk movement in the UK, and tapped into such formidable peers as Amebix and Antisect for influence, both of whom can still be heard in the DNA of 'Satori', but a lot has changed since the heady Eighties.

"I really liked the diversity of the scene, for want of a better word, back then," begins vocalist Trev. "It always struck me as odd that so many different sounding bands were categorised into one thing; bands like Ripcord sounded nothing like Deviated Instinct, and Electro Hippies sounded nothing like Axegrinder, but it made gigs very interesting.

"However, the scene became very restrictive, with its own set of codes and rules. I remember the band deliberating for days whether to book a photo shoot for PR and then spending just as long deciding whether a colour, posed photo would be seen as too 'rock star-ish'. Then there was all the 'crustier than thou' stuff... who had the dirtiest dreads, the most ripped combats etc. For me that was the call to go and get a haircut!"

"The best thing back then was the whole vibrancy of the scene at that time," adds guitarist Steve Alton. "If you wanted to play in a band, you formed your own; there was

Axegrinder, by Ester Segarra

the whole DIY aspect, with great bands all coming together from all parts of the country... people who I still know now. For me, it gave me a new-found energy for punk again.

"And it's funny how the brain after so many years edits out all the bad parts, but I remember being slagged off for having a guitar case... spat at for the colour photo on the album. I was called a fucking popstar, and had people scream 'I hate you!' in my face. Yet now I see guys doing crust with Marshalls and BC Rich guitars... jeez, I couldn't have got away with that back then – how times change!"

A pulsating knot of tightly wound metallic punk fury, imbued with a melancholy and majesty exceeding its meagre recording budget, 'Rise...' is rightly regarded as a crust punk classic, but its inception was anything but a smooth one, and much of the kudos it received was only bestowed upon it posthumously.

"The album was pretty much written at various squats throughout north London, where rehearsal spaces popped up all the time," recalls Trev. "It wasn't unusual to have dogs brushing past your legs as you were writing new songs. Rehearsals were fuelled by Thunderbird wine, but home brew, night clubs, lack of sleep and hot knifing breakfasts were the four major drivers behind the actual recording of the album. To be honest, we were going through a tough time; [drummer] Darryn had just been ordered home to Dover by a lenient judge over drug charges so we weren't such a coherent tight unit as when we were all living in London.

"Add to this our exuberance at being given the opportunity to record an album, a horrible studio [Lion in Leeds] and an understandably limited recording time and you get the picture as to why the album had many faults. Hammy [at Peaceville] was kind enough to give us another four chances at remixing though, so for that we are forever grateful..."

"I'm still proud of it to be honest," continues Steve of the album, "I made a choice in my life not to have children, so it's my legacy really. My stamp on the world, no matter how small. Stupid, I know, but yeah, I walked out on the final day of remixing thinking, 'No one will even remember this in twelve months' time...'

"I'm not sure how well it went down on release though; I think it did alright, but for a while we were stuck in limbo: too metal for punk and too punk for metal. The RAW magazine interview we did really helped us to pick up a more metal following, and Q magazine called us 'Motorhead in a bucket falling down a flight of stairs...' That certainly got us a few more sales!"

Fast forward three decades and against the odds Axegrinder have reformed, with expectation for their comeback album spiralling dangerously high, especially when they are not the type of band content to just repeat themselves by raking over past glories – despite what hardcore fans of 'Rise...' might demand from the band. Thankfully no one will be disappointed with the latest glorious noises they're making. But what prompted the reunion, and do they think they can avoid the sort of blinkered backlash Antisect received for their 'The Rising Of The Lights' comeback album (also on Rise Above)?

"Well, Trev and I have stayed in contact over the years," explains Steve. "I'd always had in the back of my mind about doing another album, but something just never felt right about doing it; it was never the right time. But then I sat down and wrote a couple of tracks, sent them to Trev and bang! It just clicked, and I then wrote the rest of the album. Trev went away and came back with a most amazing set of lyrics and ideas, so massive I was shocked. It blew me away when he got in the booth. And for a guy who's not done this for a while... stunned is not the word.

"How does it differ now to back then? Well, I can play better, I know what the hell I'm doing in a studio now, but apart from that I'm not sure really. It's not 'ROTSM 2', but is it Axegrinder? Yeah, it's Axegrinder - but a 21st century version!

"There were no issues; we agreed on everything from the start. It was an interesting process from my point of view. Engineering Trev's vocals was a brilliant journey for me... translating someone's ideas within minutes and them going 'Yes!' is quite satisfying. Have I achieved what I set out to achieve with the album? I think so. I've carried this second Axegrinder album around in my head for years, and I needed to get it out, haha! But spending time with Trev making music and chatting about the highs and lows from the old days ignited a spark in both of us. I certainly feel a different person after writing this album, so everything else is a bonus."

"I don't think we set out to achieve anything except to please ourselves and not get hung up on the mythical Axegrinder legacy," adds Trev candidly. "We often joke that if anyone has the right to fuck up the so-called legacy then it has to be me and Steve. I think we have made a great little album and I hope others will get what we're doing. We certainly haven't made 'Rise… II' though, as we aren't twenty-somethings anymore and I just wouldn't be interested if we didn't stay true to ourselves in the here and now. Yes, we are still angry about things - age certainly doesn't dissipate your feelings on certain subjects - but I think in youth you look at everything as either black or white, and age helps you to see different perspectives and explore new ideas.

"I also think with age you're less concerned about fitting in, or indeed what others think of you. Back in the day I was very driven, opinionated and very stubborn, and the band was a major thing in my life. Nowadays I am more laid back and my focus is on being a good dad to my kids, so Axegrinder isn't so precious to me. I had a blast with Steve in his studio experimenting with sounds etc. and it was good to spend some time with him again after all these years.

"And then I just started exchanging music with Lee [Dorrian, at Rise Above], almost like, 'I'll show you mine if you show me yours, haha!' We were obviously aware of the bands on his label but didn't think anything would come of it, so we were just stoked that Lee got to hear it and like it. He then kindly offered to put it out for us and right from the initial meeting we felt comfortable with him, and we have done ever since. Rise Above have done so much for us, leaving us to get on with what we want to do but also giving us a guiding hand when we need it. We had a set vision when we started this album, including the packaging; the whole aesthetic and feel was really important to us. We never set out to be contentious, only to challenge what is accepted as the norm in the crust genre. If you don't challenge yourself, why bother?"

RIP Darryn Garlinge

CHAPTER B:
AGAINST THE GRAIN...

BACKFIRE! – ISSUE 36 (NOVEMBER 1996)

Backfire – Richard Bruinen (RIP), pic by Dave Thomas

"Our band is a reaction, that's why we chose the name we did," explains Rich, drummer with rising Dutch coremongers, Backfire! "We're really in your face, with our music, our lyrics, our live show. We want to move the listener in some way."

Well, saying his band are in your face is no idle boast, as anyone whose heard Backfire! [yes, there is meant to be an exclamation mark after their name, it's not just me being sensational – it's like that fucking question mark in Therapy?] will vouch. Their 'Rebel 4 Life' CD on Lost And Found kicks off like some hardcore hybrid of Extreme Noise Terror, before settling down into a rabid old school maelstrom, the kinda raw-throated, high-speed frenzy whipped up by the Rykers. Seeing as we all seem to float out expressions like 'old school' far too often, mebbe we ought to start clarifying their meaning a bit... if we can.

"Um, it's just about musical style", reckons Rich. "The new school is bands like Snapcase or Earth Crisis, whilst the old school is represented by, you know, Agnostic Front, or Sick Of It All. I like a lot of both style bands, but I've been into hardcore for ten years, so I guess that makes me old school."

Shit, such a literal interpretation would make me Grandad School at the very least... better change the subject quick! Rich used to play drums in the late, great Right Direction, and like his old band, Backfire! seem to have copped some flak for their lyrics, songs like 'Hate' and 'The Stakes Are Too High' being especially open to misunderstanding...

"We write personal lyrics, about real experiences, about our immediate surroundings. Some people seem to think we're a macho band, but they can't see beyond my shaved head and tattoos. You can never do it just right for everybody; there's always someone who will complain about you, so we just let them get on with it. If they don't like our band then that's fine!"

For a scene that's meant to be open-minded, hardcore kids are so often quick to judge. "It's getting better now," reckons Rich. "It was really bad a few years back, but we're getting accepted by a lot more people now, including straightedge kids. Even those self-righteous edgers, who are sixteen years old and think they are going to change the world."

You'll get chance to catch Backfire! later this month, when they open for Warzone, but if you'd like to check out how their (barely) controlled mayhem comes across in the live environment, then you can pick up their new MCD, which contains some concert recordings, as well as their first 7", made available again.

"We're releasing the 7" on CD, 'cos although I still buy vinyl, a lot of the new kids don't so much, so we want it available for them, too. There's some bonus live songs on there, which have come out really well. It's a bit special; we recorded it in France, when we played with Madball, and we did a cover song with [Madball vocalist] Freddy [Cricien] singing. It sounds really cool. Besides, we're definitely a live band first, before being a studio band, so it seemed a logical step."

BACKFIRE! – ISSUE 48 (NOVEMBER 1997)

Though label problems have forced them to change their name to BF, none of that seems capable of stopping Maastricht's Backfire!, who've bounced back with a new album on Century Media, 'All Bets Are Off'. Ian Glasper hooked up with vocalist Patrick Toenen.

European hardcore has been on the up for so long now, it was only a matter of time

Backfire, courtesy of Laurens Kusters

before some bigger labels sat up and took notice. Of course, Rykers led the way by signing to Warners, or at least a sublabel thereof, and now Century Media seem keen to get a piece of the action, having set up their own nursery label, Kingfisher, for the blatantly hardcore bands under their wing. They can no longer ignore the talent on their own doorstep, especially as it's every bit as fierce and potent as anything pumped outta America.

Promising French metallers Kickback have found a home there, as have Holland's Backfire, who you might have seen last year, opening up for Warzone on their Euro trek. If you thought our Dutch friends were cool back then, wait 'til you hear their coming-of-age second album, 'All Bets Are Off'. But a lot of turbulent water has flowed under this particular bridge over the last year, so I hooked up with vocalist, Patrick Toenen, to hear all about it. First off, what the hell are you guys called now? I heard you were forced to change the band's name to just B.F.?

"Oh no, we're still called Backfire! There's still some bullshit going down, though, and I think the CD will have to go out with a sticker saying 'BF' over the name Backfire!"

If you're late joining us, the reason for this rumoured enforced name change was apparently due to some, er, unpleasantness between the band and their old label, Lost And Found.

"We don't really want to slag off Lost And Found," says Patrick, very reasonably. "We had a lot of problems with them, which started about the time of the Warzone tour, but that's all in the past now. We're not bitter, and a lot of our friends' bands are still on that label, so we don't want to say too much. There are a lot of rumours about those guys, but we can only speak for ourselves. For about six months, we were uncertain about how we ought to go forward, and it was a difficult time for us. We actually split up for two weeks, but we soon realised we're all into it too much to give it up. It wasn't worth losing it all."

Things certainly seem to be going right for the band now, a killer new album nestling in the racks. tours with Belgians Deviate and even Madball planned for the New Year, and they're sitting pretty on one of the most respected labels around.

"We'd wanted to be on Century Media for a long time," enthuses the frontman, "So it's almost like a dream come true that they were interested in us too. They'd already heard the first album ['Rebel 4 Life (L&F, 1996) – IG] and liked it, and Marc from MAD [the band's booking agent – IG] got them to check us out live. They came to see us at a couple of the big hardcore festivals, and it wasn't long before we'd sorted out a deal."

The label obviously knows a good hardcore band when they clap ears on one. 'All Bets Are Off' is fourteen short, sharp shocks, M-Town-style, pure Eurocore in that fast 'n' furious vein of the aforementioned Rykers, but also showing enough of a progression – with no cop-out, mind you – so you know they're not some flash-in-the-pan fly-by-nights.

"The Rykers comparison doesn't really bother me," claims Patrick. "They are good friends of ours, and I like their music, so why not? There's definitely worse bands to be likened to. We've matured quite a lot as musicians. Our musical tastes have changed quite a bit since the first record, there's so many good bands out there. We all love Crowbar, for example, and they've had quite an influence on us."

And that influence is noticeable, but don't go thinking that they've slowed it all down to a crawl. They might grind out a few passages here and there, but there's still plenty of that Maastricht speed which put bands like Right Direction [who Patrick tells me are back together again! – IG] on the attacking edge of new school hardcore.

"We have a great scene here, one of the best," he says proudly. "Everyone respects each other, there's no bullshit. All the bands have really come along, and they all help each other out, which is exactly how it should be."

Bad Religion – courtesy of Jeff Abarta @ Epitaph

Ian Glasper talks to Bad Religion vocalist Greg Graffin on the eve of the release of 'Stranger Than Fiction', the band's eighth studio album.

I recently caught up with Greg Graffin, vocalist with LA's Bad Religion, whilst he was over in London promoting his band's eighth album 'Stranger Than Fiction', their first for the Atlantic label, which is where we begin the following conversation...

Tell us about some of the guest appearances on the record. "There's a couple of rather interesting people on it," opens Greg. "Wayne Kramer who used to be the guitar player for MC5, plays a solo on 'Incomplete'. Then we have the singer from Rancid, who are an Epitaph Records band; he sings on a song called 'Television'. And some of the guys from Pennywise sing backing vocals on 'Marked'. It's always been fun to share musical insights with people from diverse musical backgrounds."

What are the lyrics about to 'Tiny Voices'? "That was a song originally inspired by the tragedy in Yugoslavia, and as I was writing it, I tried to make it more relevant to everyone. It's basically a song about dead people. The dead people in this respect are the people we hear in our conscience and the reason for their death is because of our ignorance."

What about 'Slumber' and 'Hooray For Me, And Fuck You'? "'Slumber' is about suicide and also a song about extinction. The setting is someone who feels his or her life is unimportant and meaningless. I guess I give a somewhat atypical way of thinking of your life as being equal to everyone else's; there is great equality in extinction and death. 'Hooray For Me...' is about individuality and rejoicing in the ability to think and act independently."

So they hold no truck with that LA gang mentality that some bands seemingly revel in? "We're not into that at all; we're the opposite, in fact. We're the antithesis of gang thinking and group mentality. We think it should be applauded whenever anyone steps outside a group. It has a utilitarian place in music because commercial reality and marketing success depends upon group thinking and thoughtless impulse, but I think music would be a much richer source of entertainment if people would step outside of that and think for themselves."

Weren't they happier being a big fish on Epitaph Records as opposed to a small fish on Atlantic? "We considered heavily before we made the switch. We were perfectly happy with Epitaph in most respects, except there's no chance of an independent label getting the same kind of distribution you'd have on a major deal. And as for being a small fish, we insisted in our deal that we would be given priorities that are not usually given to new bands or new signings. We got assurances by presidents of both companies, in America and in Europe, that we would be prioritized."

I know that you are an assistant teacher in biology at Cornell University when you're not off with the band. Do you ever get frustrated by the education system's shortcomings? "Oh totally, I'm very outspoken about it. I've written songs about it in the past, like 'The Answer' on the 'Generator' album; that song takes a cynical view of the notion that there is one correct answer for a given question. I think our education system is based around not praising people for looking for answers, but just getting the right answer. The point is, there is no one answer. One of the greatest things in life is to search for an answer, share information with others, then see how they come up with an answer."

The LA Times said, 'Bad Religion is the living incarnation of the theory that hardcore punk is in fact folk music'... do you feel a closer affinity to folk than, say, rock or metal? "Yeah, I personally do, because I grew up in my family singing that kind of music, and I'm not talking about the '60s folk revival; I'm talking about real traditional American folk music, and that's always shown up in my delivery right back to the earliest Bad Religion records. I think that folk music in its purest form is simply music stripped down to the bare basics. You have some kind of accompaniment, some kind of melody, and some kind of relevance to the lyrics. And those three elements are what you find in Bad Religion."

Do you still view yourselves as a punk rock band? "Yeah, I would say that the original concept of punk where we came from, Southern California in 1980, was individual thinking and independent motivation. And being free not to associate with any advocacy groups, having the self-dignity not to affiliate with tribes... social tribes, that is. In that respect, I think we're still a punk band because it's very hard to categorize us, both as individuals and as a band. The independent spirit is still very strong with Bad Religion."

Wise words that should hopefully reassure any of the band's fans doubting the wisdom of the label change. Regardless of the label putting it out, there's no doubt that 'Stranger Than Fiction' is their strongest yet, and well worth investigating. Greg told me the band should be hitting the UK in late October, hopefully to play three shows, probably London, Glasgow and Wolverhampton. See you there.

BAD RELIGION – ISSUE 29 (APRIL 1996)

Bad Religion, courtesy of Jeff Abart @ Epitaph

Cats have nine lives, and melodic hardcore veterans Bad Religion now have their ninth album, 'The Gray Race', out. Is there any connection between these two statements? Have Bad Religion run out of juice after all these years? Have they used up all their lives? Not according to our man in Hardcoreland. A relieved Ian Glasper snuck off to talk to guitarist Greg Hetson, and got the lowdown on one hardcore institution that isn't quite ready to be institutionalised...

Bad Religion have long been leaders in the melodic hardcore field, and they've just returned to the fray with album number nine, 'The Gray Race'. It's been a while since they spoke to Terrorizer, so I hooked up with the ever-so-slightly reticent guitarist Greg Hetson for an up-date. Before we talk about the new record, I bring up the subject of the interim 'All Ages' compilation, because they hardly seem like your typical 'Greatest Hits'-mentality band. I was wondering whether it was a contractual thing...?

"No, it wasn't a contractual motive behind it," Greg replies. "It was Brett [Gurewitz]'s idea, I think, being an ex-band member and Epitaph head honcho. I think 'Greatest Hits' albums are kinda lame, myself... but it was going to come out no matter what, so we figured we'd make it as, uh, less cheesy as we could. Some people liked the idea, some people didn't care, but I was real happy with how good it came out, with the cool packaging and everything."

You guys toured a lot on the back of 'Stranger Than Fiction', how has that shaped the band?

"l think it's had an accumulative effect," he reckons, "Seeing the world and questioning what you see at home. Being on the road exposes you to different cultures. We'd never been to Japan before and we hadn't been to Scandinavia either, and we did a bunch of dates there."

How do you stay sane out there on the road for those long stretches of time? "We get on pretty well, we joke around a lot. We try to do a bit of sporting stuff. In Germany, we staged a football match between Bad Religion fans and us. We tied 7-7 – we were lucky, those kids were good players!"

Any exceptional lows to report? "Not really, we're just happy to be out there doing it. Most bands don't last as long as we have, and have such consistent popularity, so I think we're lucky. We really can't complain, it's more than we ever expected."

Talk eventually turns to the new album, 'The Gray Race' – I knew there was some reason for this phone call! Being a (so-called) musician myself, and knowing full well the multitude of different ways to approach composition, I'm always curious to learn about a band's writing process. And Greg's more than happy to let slip some trade secrets...

"Greg Graffin [vocalist] writes the majority of the songs. Then we send demos to each other and add in our own ideas, and bring it into the studio to record it where everyone adds their touch to it, and it becomes a Bad Religion song!"

So, you mainly write by mail then? "Yes, we never rehearse unless we have to. For example, we just rehearsed four or five days last week and then did a show in LA, before flying out here to tour. We know the old songs really well, anyway; we just had to nail down the new stuff."

What prompted you to record the basic tracks live in the studio? "We thought a live feel would give it a little more energy, which might have been lacking on the last few records. We haven't recorded like that for a long while."

Were you aware of much pressure to follow up the success of 'Stranger...'?

"Not really," he reveals, "Although I think pressure came from Brett leaving the band, and that really challenged Greg to write a bunch of good songs. We just try to write the best album we can every year and expand as much as we can within this style of music, and the level of musicianship that we have. And it's kinda tough, but it's a challenge, trying not to sound the same but keeping the Bad Religion sound."

If you've not heard it yet, 'The Gray Race' is a strong, powerful album. Comfortably-paced, simplistic punk with folk undertones in the harmonies and arrangements, and Graffin's gently hypnotic vocals lead you into the dance. There's nothing to quite rival 'Inner Logic' or 'What It Is', but 'Streets Of America' comes close in the anthemic pop stakes, and the uneasy melody of 'Come Join Us', complete with Dickies-ish backing vocals is another highlight. They've obviously got this formula down pat, and they demonstrate a total command and understanding of this material. The biggest criticism you could level at it is that it's another Bad Religion album, and you know exactly what to expect and when to expect it.... this is, surely, an approach that will only maintain their fanbase without expanding it?

"Yeah, that's possible," Greg concedes. "It's just a balance you have to strike. We know what we like and we enjoy it, and we just try to put out new records that are always better than the last - and hope others enjoy them, too!"

Bad Religion's lyrical insight is almost as renowned as their musical consistency. I wonder if the concept behind 'The Gray Race' is that modern life is leeching us all of our vitality...?

"It's basically a metaphor for the human race. Human beings tend to see things in black and white, one way or another, and we all fall into this trap of giving in and not bothering to look at both sides of an issue, just giving in to the flow and not struggling to stay individuals."

And what about 'Ten In 2010'? "That's just a kind of warning. Greg read a prediction somewhere that there'd be ten billion people by the year 2010, which means the population will have doubled. Countries like the US are pretty much zero population growth, it's the Third World nations in Africa and Asia that are really going to get into trouble. All the natural resources will be drained. If it seems bad now, think what it'll be like then!"

Did the label exert or attempt to exert any influence on your writing? "No, there's really not much difference to when we were on Epitaph, except that instead of five guys in LA running the show, there's now people in every country in the world marketing and promoting our records."

On the touchy (within punk circles, at least) subject of major labels, Greg has the following words of wisdom: "It's really down to the band and the label and the relationship they have and the style of music they play. When we signed with Sony and Atlantic in the US and Columbia for the rest of the world, they knew this is what we do, and we have a certain way of doing things, and if they were going to infringe on it, not to bother talking to us. They said, 'You guys have been doing it a long enough time, we can maybe learn something from you'. So, we were lucky enough to dictate the terms from the start."

How can you talk to a band like Bad Religion, for so long lynchpins of the US hardcore-punk scene, and not discuss the changes they've seen over the years in that myriad-faceted genre?
"It goes through phases, y'know," Greg offers, after a thoughtful pause. "There was the initial late Seventies wave, then in the mid-Eighties it turned very speed metal, then it died out a bit, and now you're having your punk rebirth. The thing I see right now is that there's a lot of edge missing from the music that there used to be... it's gotten a little bit wimpy, a little watered down. There's not the anger or backbone to the lyrics, which is fine, but I personally would like to see more bands with a message in their songs!"
Here, here! If punk gets diluted as it grows in popularity, it just becomes pop music...
"Some of the bands, yes," comes the careful reply.
What's 'Punk Rock Song' on the new album about? "It's basically saying that there's so little we can do as a band except offer you our music. It's kinda pathetic, but is this the best we can do? We can't really change anything as a band, just being five guys on stage, all we offer is the songs."
Do you still listen to much hardcore? "The general influences of the band would be early punk rock... The Ramones, Buzzcocks, Sham 69, The Germs, Black Flag... mix in some new wave Devo and AC/DC, and you get Bad Religion!" (laughs)
But what do you slap on in the bus on tour when you're out there on the road surrounded by it?
"I can guarantee no one will put on a punk rock album in the bus after a punk rock show! It's anything from bluegrass to country to classical guitar..."
Any folk? BR are undeniably folky in their simplicity... "Greg's the one really into folk music, but I don't mind it, not too much. The appeal of a good song is you can sit around and just play it on an acoustic guitar and all sing it. Punk or folk, it's that simple, anyone can do it. That's what attracted me to punk rock in the beginning."
Truly music for the people! "Exactly! There's such a connection between the band and the audience."
Finally, and seeing as you brought it up earlier, Bad Religion have been together a long, long time. Are you wary of becoming an institution? "Mmm, that's a good question! I guess at some point we may become an institution... I dunno what kind... a mental institution, p'raps?" laughs Greg.
But when would you decide to knock it on the head? "I dunno! You have to step to one side and look to see if you're really still good, or just pitying yourself. If enough people ever came up to the band and said, 'You really should quit', if enough people said that, I guess we'd eventually say, 'You're probably right!'"

It's bounty time for fans of California legends Bad Religion. Not only have they released a new, highly topical album, 'The Empire Strikes First', they've also just put out a DVD document of their '89 European tour, and reissued their (almost) entire back catalogue, charting the rise of a band long considered the keepers of US punk's conscience. Ian Glasper got the long view from founder Brett Gurewitz, and even uncovered a period the band would rather forget...

OBEY YOUR REMASTER

"That's actually a reissue of a VHS tape that came out back in... uh... well, a long time ago!" laughs guitarist and founding member Brett Gurewitz, of Bad Religion's new 'Along The Way' DVD. "It's still of great interest to our fans, I think; it captures a moment that was very notable. There we were, this Californian punk band, who were doing okay in our own area but were still to blow up over here, yet we were huge in Germany! And it wasn't a result of marketing or anything either, just that for some reason the music alone captured the imaginations of all these kids in Europe."

So the band broke in Europe long before it did in the States?

"Oh yeah. We did real good around LA, but not really anywhere else. And if we hadn't taken off in Europe like that, I don't think we would have had the same impetus that we did. What's really interesting on the DVD though is that we were still playing in squats on that tour, still doing the underground shows, and those venues were quite small really, so not all the kids could fit inside, it was a very exciting time for us. We were still driving around in an old German bread van or something, haha! I think it's cool for the kids nowadays to see that side of punk rock, and we just wanted to preserve it for posterity."

And what about these CD reissues? Surely they were already 'preserved for posterity' anyway? Or did you feel they needed tidying up a bit after all these years?

"We just remastered them," explains Brett. "We didn't change anything else at all, and certainly didn't 'tidy them up', as you put it. A lot of kids don't understand the concept of remastering anyway, because they've only ever known the CD format. But all our records were recorded on analogue, which sounds better than digital anyway. They were originally intended for vinyl.

"Then when they came out on CD, they sounded pretty horrible. Sure, the discs were tougher and more convenient, and there was no hiss between songs, but on those early CDs the top end always sounded like someone frying an egg! Nowadays CDs sound a lot better, so we've just remastered those early albums to sound like the original tapes and vinyl. We wanted to restore that sound, plus we wanted to bring them up to an equivalent volume as the more modern CDs. 'Cos let's face it, everyone in a band – especially a punk rock band – wants their records to be loud!"

HOW TO LOSE FRIENDS AND ALIENATE PEOPLE

As raging as all those early albums still sound, not many people know that there was actually a Bad Religion record – their 'lost' (although 'abandoned' might be more accurate) second studio album – that was anything but punk rock. So, how come there's still no new version of 'Into The Unknown'?

"Hmm, I really don't know," ponders Brett. "I see it as the black sheep of the catalogue really, but maybe we'll do a limited reissue just for the fans one day."

Even though 'Into The Unknown' wasn't a proper Bad Religion LP in the traditional sense of the word, it nevertheless played its own important part in the band's evolution. "Sure, it was important in that 'Suffer' was a reaction to it; we realised what we were good at, what we wanted – and needed - to do, and we really applied ourselves. So, yes, it does have a place in our development, but it might confuse new fans of the band. We don't have the marketing power to release it and let everyone know the whole story behind it, so there'd be all these kids picking it up thinking it was the new Bad Religion album... and taking it back to the store because it sucks!

"It nearly destroyed us once already. We went from having all this critical acclaim, being local punk heroes, to being the biggest dicks ever, haha! But a lot of LA bands were getting experimental at that time – TSOL, and Christian Death, and we felt the need to experiment ourselves. And me and Greg [Graffin, the BR vocalist] had these common roots in progressive rock, stuff like King Crimson and Emerson Lake Palmer..."

The whole antithesis of punk rock then!

"Well, yeah, exactly. We were just trying to do something artistic, but some of that sound snuck in there somewhere. But at the end of the day, I hear a lot of serious prog elements creeping into the hardcore bands of today... it's all to do with luck. Luck and timing. After all, there's only twelve notes, but what you can do with them depends upon how fashionable you are at the time."

WHO'S THE BOSS?

"Well, I still own Epitaph... despite the rumours that we're owned by Sony or whatever!" explains Brett, as to just what his role is right now in the band. The astute reader will have seen his name on the new album, and wondered why he wasn't on stage helping to promote it. "The truth of the matter is, Epitaph is owned by me – I don't even have a partner or anything - and it's a job, a real job, with a lot of responsibility, which is why I don't tour. But the other guys understand; we're the oldest and best friends... we're like family, and we've all settled into our roles.

"But it's not like I don't do any work for Bad Religion... I've heard people say that I do all the fun stuff, and then the other guys go off and do all the hard graft! What those people don't know is, I'll spend months and months writing before we record an album, then we all go in and spend maybe three weeks recording it all, then those guys leave again, and I spend months doing overdubs and mixing... so we all play a part. And mine is during the recording - and the initial gigs here in LA, sometimes the odd special show. I'm flying out to Boston soon to play the tenth anniversary of the Warped Tour; it'll be a huge punk rock extravaganza, and I'd like to be there. But most of the time I have to take care of business here, 'cos it's not like we only have five bands anymore, as we did when I used to tour full-time.

"In actual fact, I'm just getting ready to write for another Bad Religion album for some time next year. And I love to write! I stopped for a while, and it was only when I started again that I realised how much I missed it. That this is what I do best."

SIDEBAR: 'SIX OF THE BEST...'
The new album and those reissues in detail, and why you need to own them... right now.

'HOW COULD HELL BE ANY WORSE?'
Epitaph [1982]
The one that put the band on the map, and certainly a record that is widely regarded to this day as an important chapter in the history of Californian punk rock. Opening with the powerful 'We're Only Gonna Die (From Our Own Arrogance)', that was covered to great effect by Biohazard on their breakthrough 'Urban Discipline' album, Bad Religion's debut full-length also featured several other songs that are still staples in their set even today, not least of all 'Fuck Armageddon... This Is Hell'. And the CD version includes the band's ultra-raw 1981 '1st EP' and the 'Back To The Known' EP from 1984. [7.5]

'SUFFER'
Epitaph [1988]
Now, pay attention: if you're only gonna own one Bad Religion LP, this is it. 'Suffer' saw Bad Religion finally arrive in style, and remains their defining moment, a gloriously driving, melodic slice of intelligent punk rock. Where 'Hell...' was the band's mission statement, 'Suffer' was their manifesto, and it still throbs with a genuine spontaneous energy. Also features the two best Bad Religion songs ever, 'You Are (The Government)' and 'Give You Nothing'. [9.5]

'NO CONTROL'
Epitaph [1989]
If you've stumbled upon the perfect formula, why change it? The albums came thick and fast after 'Suffer', the band apparently an overflowing well of inspirational lyrics and music. From the joyous title track to the measured introspection of 'Sanity', 'No Control' is hot on the heels of 'Suffer' as the most essential Bad Religion release. Immaculately produced, it oozes class and confidence. [8.5]

'AGAINST THE GRAIN'
Epitaph [1991]
With their fifth studio album, Bad Religion proved they were here to stay, and that there was no limit to the amount of pathos they could wring from a few power chords and some simplistic folky arrangements. Honourable mention should be made of both Greg Graffin's lyrics and voice, the profoundly honest passion at the heart of Bad Religion's richly layered sound. And let's not forget that this was the album where '21st Century

(Digital Boy)' first appeared – a song so good they had to record it twice (it later appeared on 'Stranger Than Fiction', their 1994 major label debut for Sony). [8]

'GENERATOR'
Epitaph [1992]
The title track challenged the listener's preconceptions about the band with its intricate discordant chorus, whilst elsewhere, 'Too Much To Ask' and the insistently lustrous 'Atomic Garden' for example, could be found some of the best Bad Religion compositions to date. And on songs like 'The Answer', Graffin's lyrics reached new heights of self-awareness; during 'No Direction', he even declared, 'I don't believe in self-important folks who preach, no Bad Religion song can make your life complete.' If only more bands were so knowingly humble. [7.5]

'THE EMPIRE STRIKES FIRST'
Epitaph [2004]
And just to prove that Bad Religion are as fiercely relevant today as they've ever been, once you've made your life complete with the above reissues, check out the brand new studio album for yet more vibrantly infectious, sublimely tuneful punk rock. Not to mention some scathing lyrics aimed at the current US administration and their evangelical warmongering. Intelligent and uplifting, 'Social Suicide', 'Let Them Eat War' and 'The Empire Strikes First', to pick but three choice cuts, all prove that Bad Religion can still hold their own against the likes of Pennywise, NOFX and any of the other Californian melodicore bands that sprang up in their own considerable wake. [8]

BAIT – ISSUE 126 (DECEMBER 2004)

Ever wonder what happened to Deviated Instinct, the crustiest of all the '80s UK crustcore bands? Their stinking corpse was still cooling when main-men Robert 'Mid' Middleton and Steve 'Snapa' Harvey formed Bait back in 1992, so why has it taken them this long to unleash their stunningly brutal debut album, 'Anatomy Of Disaster'?
"We were just experimenting with samples," reckons Mid, of Bait's earliest incarnation. "After DI, we wanted to do something even heavier, and it had this down-tuned, early Godflesh vibe."
It was only in 2001, with the addition of a real drummer, the ubiquitous Nick Barker, rather than a pesky drum machine, that Bait really started to come into their own.
"Even though we adapted some of the earlier stuff that we wrote as a two-piece, when Nick joined it was pretty much a totally different thing, apart from the name. Hopefully, we've thrown off any misconstrued industrial connotations now, as well. I think we've gone full circle back to what we're really all about – heavy-duty, twisted punk rock."
'Twisted' is certainly a word that springs to mind when one first confronts Bait: a molten mass of menacing metalcore that sounds like a psychotic fusion of early

Bait

Neurosis, Rudimentary Peni and 'Killing Technology'-era Voivod. If that strikes you as more than a little nasty, well, that's 'cos it is, with Mid's red-raw vocal outbursts like so much pus squirting from the centre of the gangrenous wound.

With Mid singing, playing guitar, writing the riffs and lyrics, and doing the artwork, isn't Bait something of a democracy being run by a dictator?

"Don't let the other two guys hear you say that, but, er, yeah, I'm a tyrannical control freak!" he admits. "I never actually wanted to do the vocals, but we found nobody else suitable. But we do operate as a total democracy; putting the songs together is a three-way argument and everyone brings something to the floor. As far as graphics go, here I will hold up my hand to some control freakiness. But seeing as I spend so much of my time doing art for other bands [from Napalm Death to Knuckledust], I'll be damned if I'm not gonna do it for my own band. Thankfully, the other guys trust me, but if they were to disagree, I might have to kill them. This is a band and we're all driving... although not necessarily in the same direction all the time!"

BARRABUS – OCTOBER 2016

After originally forming about ten years ago, as one of the many projects to spew forth from the demented musical vision of Medulla Nocte's Paul Catten, Barrabus are finally

Barrabus

about to issue their debut album, and it's as noisy and barbaric as you might imagine. "Yeah, we formed in 2005, or 2006, as a bit of a project, because Murder One were not sure whether they were going to carry on or not," confirms Paul. "It was me, and my usual partner in crime, Mark [Seddon], and [Matt] Keen and Dan Marshall, who were both in and out of Murder One at times. We just wanted to get a band together that was more eclectic than what we were doing, and just wanted to do some gigs, so we got together and went out and did stuff with SikTh and Skindred and My Ruin... just generally jumping on bills and having a good time, without having any business ties to it all."

But there were no official recordings, other than some home studio demos that made their way onto You Tube, and once Murder One split in 2007, and Paul and Mark began the Sontaran Experiment, Barrabus drifted apart.

"And then at the beginning of last year, or the end of 2014, Dan stumbled across this rehearsal recording of all these old tracks," continues Paul, "And next thing, I hear from Keen, saying, 'Fuckin' hell, we gotta record this stuff, it sounds great!' And I thought back to those songs, and thought, 'Yeah, there was some really good stuff there, I wish we had recorded those!'

"Anyway, before we knew it, Dan had recorded the drums, and some of the bass and guitars, and sent the files up here. Of course, I couldn't hear a thing, and couldn't make any sense of some of the lyrics from the old recordings... I could just about pick out key words – like 'Merrick' and 'Porn'! It was all quite dark... and the last song on there didn't even have any words, I don't think."

So that recently-discovered rehearsal tape – recorded back in 2006 - was like a time capsule, a snap shot that captured the material and spirit of the band at the time. Are you picking up exactly where you left off, or are you tempted to update everything with the benefit of hindsight?

"Mmm, yeah, the drums are pretty much the same... there's a few changes to the guitar parts, and the vocals are a bit different, but the songs are basically as intended, and they actually sound really fucking fresh... better than most stuff that's around at the minute. But no one really got it at the time! And when you listen to these tunes now, they're still pretty full on!"

Do you think people will get it now? Do you even care?

"No!" he laughs, "But I hope so. To me it sounds super fresh, it doesn't sound ten years old; it sounds like a new band, and we treated it like a new band, do you know what I mean? When we recorded it, the only people that saw each other were me and Mark. I still haven't seen Dan... because he left once he did his bits, so we've got another geezer called Adam [Evans] on drums. And I've only seen Keen a couple of times. So we recorded everything separately, and it worked – no arguments, no hassle...

"But Barrabus was a great band. The last gig we did was to a packed-out Islington Academy on the Sikth farewell tour. We had a country and western song in the set, just to annoy everyone... in fact, our aim was just to annoy everybody; it was great!"

People who can remember catching the band first time round will remember they used to wear suits onstage – are those coming out of retirement too?

"Absolutely, yeah, we're dusting them off, the moth balls are out!" enthuses Paul, before adding, "Although we might need to get some bigger sizes...

"I'm actually really excited about it all, really excited about this record – because it sounds great, but it still sounds punk rock. It's not super glossy in its production; the songs sound exactly how they should, and we're very proud of it. Mark and I did pretty much all the production here [in Paul's home studio]... which was great, very chilled, especially vocally, where we could do all the over-dubs we wanted. You know what it's like when you go in a studio, when someone else is paying for you to be in there, and you listen back to it and end up saying, 'I wish I'd had time to try that...!' I've got records that I fucking hate in my back catalogue, but I'm not making that mistake again..."

So, this is the first proper Barrabus record, and it's been worth the wait. It's an explosive mix of weird and wonderful influences, lurching and violent and explosive, with the deranged vibe of Mr. Bungle looming large over proceedings, and Paul seemingly taking great influence from Mike Patton with his vocal delivery.

"Yeah, to an extent, even though I don't give a fuck what he's up to now – but that was how the songs were written at the time. Certainly the vocal characters were written in that style. We were just trying to be as far away as possible from the other stuff we were doing then, both musically and lyrically. We wanted to get some quirky riffs in there,

121

and avoid normal, run-of-the-mill lyrics... we didn't want to sound like anyone else; it was definitely way more eclectic than our other stuff we were doing. I can hear some Melvins in there, and lots of punk rock... even some Dead Kennedys."

Apart from a set of Medulla Nocte songs at Damnation festival four years back ("It was horrible, there were no monitors!"), Paul's been away from the live circuit for quite a while. "I did a wedding gig actually!" he laughs, "Yeah, I did a Pearl Jam song at a wedding... that's what it's come to!"

And probably made more money off that one gig than everything else put together?

"No, I did it for fuck all, same as usual, haha! But I'm definitely ready to get back out there; life has just got in the way really. It was tough a good few years back, when we lost Morry [Murder One's vocalist John Morrow], you know? And then we lost Jammer [drummer Jamie Airns]... another partner in crime for many years. And when he went, I thought, 'You know what? This was never in the script...!'

"After his funeral – which was the last time Barrabus were in a room together actually – I just thought, 'Fuck this...' But I've been keeping busy. I did some stuff with Ginger Wildheart on his 'Mutation' albums. And I did a noise album last year... and then the recording and mixing of this album. So, I've been around - but I definitely lost the taste for it for a while.

"Plus, I did a bit of tour-managing, so I saw what a bunch of knob-heads musicians can be! And I thought, 'You know what? Fuck you guys!' I saw it from a different side, and it was horrible, absolutely the worse... you've driven for ten hours, and all the band vanish off to some strip bar, and you know you're going to be sat in the van waiting for them all until three in the morning... I got sick of it. So I took the easy option and got a job in a school, haha! But tour managing taught me a lot of patience, which I was able to bring across to my current role...

"Despite all that, I'm looking forward to getting back in the van, and getting around again. We're calling in a few old favours, so we'll do exactly what we did first time around, and just jump on whatever bills we can get on – but I couldn't give a shit whether it's a little DIY show somewhere, or something in a big club or whatever... we just want to go out and play.

"There probably won't be as much jumping around as last time, but it's still pretty full-on... probably more full-on now, with this new drummer, because he's a proper hardcore drummer, nice and fast and intense... prepare to be underwhelmed!"

How do you stay relevant with the scene constantly evolving?

"I don't give a fuck what else is going on. The majority of the bands I've done never fitted in, and that's fine. This will be interesting. We're not doing this for any other reason than we want to put these songs out, just for posterity. We were actually a pretty good band, and recording those songs, and just being in a room together, has made us think, 'Let's get out there and do this!'

"But going on tour for three or four weeks at a time isn't going to happen, because physically I couldn't fucking manage it, to be fair... but I'm looking forward to being a front man again, just getting the mic and smashing it."

Black Dahlia Murder, by David E. Jackson

If you're looking for sheer bloody-minded death metal wrapped up in the ambiguous trappings of hardcore thrash, you need look no further than true crimesters The Black Dahlia Murder. Ian Glasper grilled vocalist Trevor Strnad about his alibi.

"It's been great!" enthuses Trevor Strnad, vocalist with Missouri metallers, The Black Dahlia Murder, whose new album for Metal Blade, 'Miasma', has seen them scaring the bejeezus out of Ozzfest crowds across the US. "It's kind of a weird situation for us, being the only death metal band on the bill, but that's a good thing in many ways because at least we stand out, and it's certainly a perfect platform for a band like us to reach a lot of new kids. And the crowds have been cool... for a lot of them, it's the first time they've even heard us, and admittedly some of them are dumbfounded by it all, haha! But a lot of them are totally into it straight away, which is awesome...

"The thing is, heavy music is cool again right now; MTV's playing heavy stuff again, and it's really big with young kids, who are at high school and college age. I guess it's enjoying a resurgence, but I'm not so naïve to see that it'll be in a recession again soon, so we have to make the most of it while we can. And, to be honest, I'm also not so naïve that I can't see it was probably money that got us onto this tour, simple as that. I'd like to say that the industry is waking up to the potential of extreme music, but the truth of it is, Metal Blade bought us onto these Ozzfest dates because they know that we'll be playing to 8000 new people every day... and who can blame them? It's a great opportunity."

Things have certainly been afoot in the Black Dahlia camp since the release of 2003's

'Unhallowed', and not all of them conducive to inter-band harmony, but you seem to have turned it all around and made a superb record.

"This new album is a more developed record on every front; even the recording is a lot better, it's turned out really heavy. We just tried to take everything we've learned since 'Unhallowed' and bring it to bear on the new material. Being on the road so much has helped the band as well, and even [old drummer] Cory [Grady] being asked to leave last year, for personal and professional reasons, played a part. When Zach [Gibson] joined behind the kit it was like we were reborn, a whole new start for us; he's a very inspirational player, and that's helped push all of us to up our game.

"It's just a breath of fresh air for us to have a new record out and be playing these new songs live. There was so much turmoil between the two albums, and 'Miasma' really is a product of all that tension, so to have it turn out so well was very therapeutic in many ways."

Whatever lies behind it, there's no disputing that 'Miasma' is a ferociously unique take on death metal, its bludgeoning blast beats counterbalanced by frenetic fretwork and layer after layer of schizoid vocal savagery. And don't be fooled by their name into thinking that these guys are some sort of pretentious metalcore troupe suffering delusions of intellectual grandeur; the 'real' Black Dahlia murder is actually an unsolved homicide case from 1947 that saw a young Hollywood wanna-be, Elizabeth Short, cut in half (yes, cut in fuckin' half) under most suspicious circumstances.

"It's just something that I stumbled upon really," reveals Trevor, of their intriguing moniker. "I found that, as a metal fan that listens to all these bands like Cannibal Corpse and Carcass, I'm normally fairly jaded as regards shock value, but when I read about this murder, it really freaked me out for some reason. It was just so weird, so unbridled and macabre; I had to investigate it further, even though part of me really didn't want to. Like a car accident or something, where you don't want to look but you feel compelled to anyway, the whole case repulses me and fascinates me at the same time, especially with all the superstitions and fake confessions surrounding it. And people are still obsessed with it nearly sixty years later...

"We're not dwelling on it thematically though – it's not as if we're respecting Elizabeth Short with our band or anything like that – but we just wanted to tap into the whole creepy vibe that surrounds the case.

"We're frequently lumped in with this whole 'New Wave Of American Metal' thing, but we don't feel a part of it at all," he adds carefully, when pressed as to where his band fits into the current grand scheme of things. "A lot of metalcore is obviously Swedish-influenced, but it's so bastardised, so inbred, those bands don't even understand themselves where their roots lie. And a lot of today's heavy bands seem to just be products, nothing heart-felt at all; they're too safe to even be considered 'metal' in my opinion, too watered down. I mean, if you're going to rip off Swedish death metal, why not go straight to the source and be done with it? Metalcore won't last forever, perhaps another few years... it's another fad is all, it'll pass; MTV will lose interest and it'll all be over!"

Bleak Zero, by Ian Gotham

"Shit happens, and most things are beyond our control, but in general we are positive and at least try to theorise in an introspective and sometimes ambiguous way, to satisfy our own miserable existence," ponders Rob Hunt, guitarist with Stoke-on-Trent's nihilistic metallers, Bleak Zero.

Formed in July 2013, following the demise of doom band, Raven Of Odin, Bleak Zero are a thoroughly uncompromising and cathartic experience, remorselessly beating the listener over the head with their measured mix of hardcore, doom, sludge and black metal, yet still managing to surprise with thoughtful, intricate passages as well.

"We are hoping to rationalise all of our different influences into a unique sound, and move forward from the generic forms that are around at the moment without becoming contrived. The last thing we want to do is become a fusion band, but we try to incorporate what we appreciate as individuals."

BLO.TORCH - ISSUE 72 (NOVEMBER 1999)

"It's been a pretty hard, tumultuous time for metal over the last few years, especially here in Holland, where all the bands crossed over to other genres, and basically drifted away from the scene; they almost seemed ashamed to be playing extreme music! So, it's amazing that Earache are putting their agents back into the underground, and Wicked World is supporting all the upcoming metal bands. It's a really breath-taking

Blo.Torch

experience to be involved with the label that released so much of the stuff that influenced us over the years..."

So says Marvin Vriesde, guitarist with rising Dutch death metallers, Blo.Torch, and well might he sound so ecstatic, having just inked the deal of a lifetime with his favourite label - Earache's Wicked World off-shoot, for those just joining us - with the first fruits of this unholy union being a savagely melodic self-titled debut album of epic metal proportions. Veering smoothly from At The Gates to Candlemass, and back again, 'Blo.Torch' is a dark, twisted vision of searing speed and soaring (guitar) harmonies, and worthy of investigation by any discerning metalhead.

"We all played in other bands that were very technical," reveals Marvin, in response to my suggestion that they've deliberately played down their obvious skills as musicians, "And we learnt from those bands that by going for overkill all the time, it really doesn't contribute that much to the songs. So, with BIo.Torch, we threw all that out of the window, and went back to the basics of writing cool songs. Sure, we can be technical when we need to be, but it's not like we're shouting out to the world, 'Look at us, look how advanced we are as musicians!' We wanted people to remember our album as being about nine good songs, not about this lead or that fill."

And remember it you surely will, long after the final majestic strains have faded away; not just because the band have a knack for a killer tune, as well as a nice line in aggressive intensity, but because their poetic lyrics plumb the depths that human beings can plunge to given the right circumstances.

"We really are fascinated by the dark side of man; what people can be driven to in extreme situations. What makes a serial killer go out and kill others? We really try and get into someone's mind, and discover what could possibly drive them to do these terrible things, but without being all cliched. We try to use a lot of weird metaphors, like insects, and other creeping, crawling things, and we try to keep it as sick as possible, of course!"

Of course! "But there's a positive message in there as well. A lot of our songs are about individualism. Everyone has an intense power within themselves; it's just a case of finding it and tapping into it..."

Album titles don't come much more blatant that Blood Tsunami's 'Thrash Metal' now, do they? Quite a statement of intent indeed, but thankfully there are no empty promises being made here as this Norwegian quartet throw down the gauntlet with a debut album that does exactly what it says on the coffin.

"Since Venom had 'Black Metal' and Dismember had 'Death Metal', we thought it was about time someone used 'Thrash Metal' as well!" laughs drummer Bard 'Faust' Eithun (yes, the very same Faust that played with Emperor and Aborym). "There is no gauntlet involved though... at least not consciously. I appreciate a lot of today's thrash, but this is just our way of paying tribute to the lost heroes of the Eighties; you can hear a lot of those influences in our music, and the title is supposed to completely nail down what we are up to."

So, how does Faust think thrash circa 2007 really measures up to thrash circa 1987? Has Pro Tools leeched much of the raw energy from the form?

"One thing you need to realise – both as a musician and a fan - is that nothing will ever compare with the old heydays... for example, black metal fans will always compare anything I do with 'In The Nightside Eclipse'; that's something I realise but cannot change in the slightest. The same goes for bands as well as individuals: Metallica constantly fight a losing battle because everything they do will be compared to 'Ride The Lightning' and 'Master Of Puppets'... which basically means that everything they ever do will suck, haha! This is the fate of music and musicians, but you need to take things as they are; I appreciate putting on some old shit - preferably something I have had a long relationship with - but at the same time, I like putting on newer stuff like Dew-Scented, Manifest, Hatesphere, Vesen, MX5, or Waklewören. It is important to support the new breed as well; if not, we are just fooling ourselves.

"Still, being a musician myself, and not only a fan, I am dependant on people supporting the band I am in. The bottom line is, the heydays are over, Pro Tools is here to stay, but hey, we're just gonna have to take things for what they are..."

Well, fans of the Eighties will find much to stimulate their aching necks on 'Thrash Metal', with the impressively heavy instrumental, 'Godbeater', even coming across like some dream-come-true amalgamation of the Big Four (that'll be Metallica, Megadeth, Slayer and Anthrax for any whippersnappers still reading!) Elsewhere the old school Kreator influences are in full effect on tracks like the awesome 'Infernal Final Carnage'.

"Yeah, we all love Kreator," admits Faust, "Especially [guitarist/vocalist] Pete, who writes all the music in the band. For me, there is a great distinction between European and American thrash metal; the European one has always been a bit rawer, dirtier and meaner, with a stronger element of black metal (although America had their counterparts with Slayer and Possessed), whereas the American bands always sounded more 'international' and somewhat more professional... if you get my point? I enjoy both types; the professionalism and musicianship of the American ones and the downright dirty and mean attitude of the German ones."

And when the Blood Tsunami crashes over the UK in May as support to Zyklon, readers here will get chance to sample their viciously concise brand of Eurothrash for themselves, hopefully realising in the process that there's a lot more to this band than just a famous drummer.

"It is important to emphasize that Blood Tsunami is my number one priority. My other band, Aborym, is a great studio band and we did one hell of a record with 'Generator', but it will always remain a studio band whereas Blood Tsunami is a band in its own right, rehearsing and doing gigs etc. For better or worse, there will always be some attention given to me being in the band; I realise that it might create a little bit of extra interest, but at the end of the day we need to do our job and make kick-ass music. Fans today are very picky, and very aware of their own desires, and they can't be fooled, so even if you have some famed musician, or some other fucking celebrity, in your band, it doesn't mean shit if the music sucks!"

BLOODLET ~ ISSUE 55 (JUNE 1998)

Bloodlet by Danielle Dombrowski

Clearly always a cut above the average evilcore band, Bloodlet have upped the ante even further with the grave new world that is 'The Seraphim Fall', a record that is already being hailed as the hardcore album of the year so far. Vocalist Scott Angelacos called up Ian Glasper to explain more.

When I finally get to speak to Bloodlet, on the phone from their native Florida, it's not their drummer, Charlie King, on the other end of the phone, as I was expecting. Nope, instead I get vocalist Scott Angelacos, because Chuck is sleeping off the excesses of the previous night, which so happens was his birthday. This is oddly reassuring – that the battery regiment behind this punishing hardcore act can succumb to such a human weakness as a self-induced headache, or even be proven to have been born at all – because a cursory listen to 'The Seraphim Fall' would suggest that some strange, cold alien blood courses through their veins. They could well be the inhuman virus in the rock machine, immune to commercial pressures and restraints that most labels would like to impose upon their artists. Such is the hostility that oozes from 'The Seraphim Fall', like the mucus of a poisonous tree frog.

"Oh yeah," chuckles Scott smugly, "We definitely play a totally selfish style, all for ourselves. We have no concern for how the label might manage to sell it to the people out there!"

They needn't worry too much, tho', 'cos in this Age of Quarrel, there are many of us who thrive on such outpourings of sonic violence. There will always be individuals warped or desperate enough to seek solace in the sounds of madness made music… take Nick Terry, for example, our very own Ed, who shot his - literary, I hasten to add - mess all over this very same disc last issue.

After beaming down the blower at the rave review they received - they're obviously well aware of Nick's high standards when it comes to hardcore - Scott tells me how they don't usually garner such accolades.

"Uh, let's just say that the press have a few problems getting to grips with us! They make up all sorts of things… we get labelled 'evilcore' quite a lot, which is a cop-out, but I suppose it's fairly accurate. It's kinda cool to have our own genre all to ourselves. We've made up our own thing, and people are finally starting to see that, at last. We knew we weren't friendly to any particular genre right from the start, so we went out and made our own fanbase."

And there's only one way to do that – lots and lots of road work, something these guys do not shy away from. In fact, they seem to thrive on it.

"We were out on tour for seven or eight months last year, and rehearsing and writing in between," Scott informs me. "We want to play to everyone, so we'll pretty much tour with any band. We have no real affiliation with one particular style of music – I can't think of one type of band we wouldn't tour with. At least when we're on the road we can support ourselves… when we're at home we get the debt collectors lining up at the door. We have to park the van facing backwards so they can't tow it away!

"Actually, our schedule is really why we're not in touch with any particular scene here at home. We don't get a chance to be. The only bands I meet are the ones we play with on tour, rather than specific scenes or genres. But we attract a lot of different people to our shows, our audience is like a constantly shifting thing. After the Entombed tour we started to attract a lot of metal kids, but after the Neurosis thing, we were getting a lot of punks for a while."

Bloodlet by Danielle Dombrowski

Even if you hadn't heard Bloodlet before, you're probably getting the idea that they're not your average band, right? Right! Hold that thought, and expect to be thrown at every twist and turn, expect to get injured in the scuffle; go in prepared for all this and more, and you might survive 'The Seraphim Fall'. If you're lucky. If you thought their last effort, the bloodcurdling 'Entheogen', was nasty, wait 'til you clap ears on this – it's even more detuned and base and extreme, yet there is also a strange grace to their lurching noises.

"Yeah, we recorded the album in the order we wrote it," he reveals. "We tried to bring the songs together as a constantly flowing thing. It's really a big concept album anyway...," he adds teasingly.

So, do tell. Concept albums are rarer than rocking horse shit in the hardcore genre.

"The Seraphim were a high order of angels, basically the Four Horsemen of the Apocalypse. And when we started this band, we just wanted to be as annoying as possible, to everyone, and the Seraphim made strange sense as some sort of parallel. The album is basically about our fall, some of our life experiences, and some of the people we met out on the road. We're very analytical, we want people to have to think. 'Seraphim' is a sister song to 'Cherubim' off our first record, and we plan to bring back some of the characters from here on our next record. We're trying to be subtle about it, there's a bigger picture, but people won't see it just yet."

Of course, Bloodlet aren't the first band to use such imagery, and nor wiII they be the last. The Little Big Man, GIenn Danzig, has often seemed to hint that he may be a fallen angel himself in some of his lyrics, metaphorically speaking (of course, GIenn!) So, is the Bloodlet concept a similar conceit?

"No, I have no such delusions of grandeur," deadpans Scott, "But I do utilise a lot of religious imagery. It's always been with me all my life. I was brought up a strict Catholic, and it was only natural that I should rebel against that. I was constantly arguing with my mother about it. I learnt the Bible backwards and forwards [most of our Norwegian friends have only managed the former so far - IG] as a result, but I use it all only as metaphor for real life situations."

And what bizarre real life situations they are, ladies and gentleman. When you expose yourself to 'Seraphim...', be prepared to peer into a psyche where the lift doesn't quite go all the way to the penthouse suite. No, I'm only kidding, but just maybe you've been locked up on a tour bus for one too many road-trips? Too much time on your hands for contemplating the uncontemplatable? I mean, what the fuck is 'Dogman With Horns' all about?

"Um, basically that's about me," explains Scott. "It's about an ongoing feeling I've had, an emotion I've tried to communicate. I have a thing with numbers, y'see. Not necessarily numerology, but my own twisted fascination. Numbers appear to me, and take form, and take on greater meaning, it's quite intense. Take the number three, for example. It's a number that fascinates me. It's indivisible by anything but itself. And it's greater than two, of course..."

Okay, I'll take your word for it, Scott (please, no one say anything to alarm him back there). What about 'Seven Hours Of Angel Food' then? "Oh, that was an interesting experience," he enthuses, warming to the topic now. "We were on a bus from LA to Vegas, and we met this very intense guy. He was totally out of it on speed, and spent seven hours babbling to us. He veered from seeming to know everything about us, to being convinced we wanted to kill him. It was very strange."

And, of course, seven is another number of reputed power, and so go the lyrics for a Bloodlet record. As vaguely disturbing as the ominous music they accompany, and oh so wonderfully dark and mysterious. Upon perusal of the booklet art chosen for 'Seraphim...' one could almost be forgiven for saying, uh, Satanic, but nothing it appears could be further from the truth.

"We never set out to be seen in such a negative way," claims Scott. "The whole concept is about healing, the letting of bad blood. It's not meant to be an evil entity, it's meant to be cleansing, a release. We just pour it all out when we're on stage. We try to act out our little story up there, for everyone, as best we can. It's an act of true catharsis. I always learn something about myself every time we play live."

BLUNT WOUND TRAUMA - ISSUE 154

(FEBRUARY 2007)

As previously revealed in our Northeast UK scene report, Newcastle six-piece Blunt Wound Trauma take influences for their violent nasty noises from right across the spectrum of

Blunt Wound Trauma, by Mark Greenbaum

extreme heavy music, although if pushed to tie these guys down more specifically their obvious love for '... Trendkill' period Pantera certainly helps define them.

"Our influences are varied and diverse," agrees singer Idene, one half of the vicious BWT vocal attack, "With each member of the band being into something different to the next; I think it's these varying influences that help to fuse our very own sound. Every single one of us is into something else, whether it be hardcore and metal, old school punk and death, black and extreme metal, stoner, industrial, electronic, metalcore... we all have something influencing us that helps form the skeleton the songs are written to... I could go into naming bands, but it might take up too much space!

"When writing lyrics, we always tend to write about the world around us, or things that are going on that affect us in some way or another. Sometimes we just let it out and keep the lyrics brutally honest and to the point - the track 'Daniel Pollen' is all about the judicial system, for example – but on other songs we'll get all symbolic and full of analogies and images. This way we get listeners to form their own opinions on what they think the song is about. Other influences are obviously life experiences we've had: friends turning their backs on us, girlfriends fucking us over, the council ripping us off... basically, if you fuck with us, we'll write a song about it and we'll be as harsh as we want!"

With the band about to unveil their full-length album, 'The Backlash Of The Damned', that Idene describes as "an unstoppable work of musical aggression", this enthusiastic young troupe look set for bigger and better things.

"It would be a cliché to say we want to be the heaviest band in the world," admits Idene, "There's a million other bands claiming the same thing, but it's the truth. The music is ugly, the lyrics are filled with hate, and in most cases that anger is justified. Our goal is to become what we want to be through music, and to get our message across... hopefully someone out there will be listening! So far, I think we've achieved a great deal in the six years we've been together, and the way it's going now, I hope we can get even further..."

Born From Pain – issue 105 (December 2002)

Born From Pain, courtesy of Rob Franssen

Whatever you do, if you're going along to the Eastpack Resistance tour when Biohazard, Agnostic Front and Hatebreed all hit the UK this weekend, be sure to turn up early. Because the first band on are Born From Pain, one of the heaviest European hardcore bands of all time. They will literally, to use an appropriate cliché, tear your soul apart. And you thought Hatebreed were heavy...

"We've played with them before when they were doing the Sepultura tour," bassist Rob explains how they landed the main support slot on Hatebreed's own headlining tour leading up to Eastpack as well. "We played a couple of their own club dates with them that they did around that tour. So basically, when we knew they were looking for a hardworking European band to support them on this tour, we got in touch with them and they were happy to take us out. We all knew each other a little bit from the shows we had already played together anyway, so it basically all came about very smoothly." The more astute of our readers will have realised that Born From Pain named themselves after an early Earth Crisis song, but it turns out that Earth Crisis aren't actually one of their main influences.

"Our main inspirations are the harder and heavier sounding older hardcore bands like

133

Integrity, Killing Time and bands like that," claims Rob. "Also, some metal bands, Slayer and the like, I would say. The main thing for us has always been the heaviness involved in the sound of the music. We try to take the best elements of both hardcore and metal and blend them into the heaviest kind of metalcore that both sides can relate to."

And that's something these guys have down to a fine art. Their 'Immortality' MCD set a new benchmark in sonic brutality for the Eurocore scene, but even that was eclipsed by the devastating 'Reclaiming The Crown', unleashed by Gangstyle Records last year. Born From Pain take the most furious thrash riffing and boil it intensely until there's nothing left but rage in its purest form. And if you think the band sound good on CD, wait until you see them live; the aggression emanating from the stage is almost palpable. Which all begs the question, where can the band go from here? How can they possibly take their sound to the next level without becoming a parody of themselves? But Rob seems bewildered at the suggestion that they could even consider trying to be anything other than what they are.

"The band's new sound is still brutal and uncompromising. We have incorporated more up-tempo and somewhat faster parts in the songs, but the sound is still as heavy and relentless as fuck! We are not about to evolve in any crazy other directions with the sound. That's just not Born From Pain. However, we do work within a certain framework where anything goes... as long as it's heavy and skull-crushing!"

BORN FROM PAIN – ISSUE 111 (JULY/AUGUST 2003)

Holland's Born From Pain have finally taken time out from their never-ending tour schedule to record the long-awaited follow-up to 2000's 'Reclaiming The Crown'. Ian Glasper receives the beatdown from bassist Rob on the devastating display of evilcore that is 'Sands of Time'.

Dutch hardcore veterans Born From Pain, have gone from strength to strength these last few years; every time I see them live or hear a new recording it far surpasses the previous one - they're gradually clawing their way to world domination under their own terms. The new album for Gangstyle Records, 'Sands Of Time', is their best yet, and they've been keeping busy with plenty of high profile roadwork, not least of all the opening slot on the recent Eastpak Resistance tour.

"Oh, that was just awesome," recalls bassist, Rob, gushing with enthusiasm. "It was great to play with a band like Agnostic Front. They were one of the first hardcore bands I started listening to some fifteen years ago, so it was kind of weird to be on tour with them, but we loved it. I guess for the other guys it was kinda the same with Biohazard. Well, anyway, the tour was great. Everyone got

along really well and it was like one big family. Almost all the shows were great for us, except for a few. Sometimes the sound was kinda fucked up, 'cos we had to open every night and sometimes got used as an extra check for the PA, but mostly that was okay though. Worst show? Hmmm, response- wise, it must have been somewhere in Germany, I think Mannheim, but even there we still sold a lot of merch and CDs, which kinda means they still liked it though. Soundwise, Sheffield was definitely the worst. Damn, I dunno what happened there, but they had the PA off during our set, fucking amateurs, haha! Best show? There were too many to list. Tilburg in Holland was crazy, Dortmund, Paris, London, Italy... there were many really good ones. It was all so much better than expected. The response from the kids, the organisers, the press, the other bands... awesome."

What have the band been up to since?

"Since 'Resistance', we've been finishing writing and recording the new CD. We finished that process at the end of February, when we were done recording. We've been playing out every weekend again and been doing more tours, one with No Turning Back and another one with Terror. Playing out a lot is a priority right now, and we still have a shit load of shows to come this year. We're doing the Madball tour in June and July, and a lot of big summer festivals. Hopefully we'll be back in the UK later this summer or fall for more dates."

Why record in Denmark - was there not anywhere closer to home where they could have achieved the sound they wanted?

"We ended up recording in Denmark after a long quest for a good producer who would fit our budget. We listened to so many CDs from different people, it was unbelievable. Until Theo [Gangstyle head honcho – IG] handed us the NAOP recordings, we were still not sure what to do. But their sound was so good, we ended up listening to more stuff that Tue Madsen had done. We came to the conclusion that he would be the man to finally provide us with the production we'd been looking for these last four years, and went into the studio with him.

"Everything was different than the other times we went to the studio," he continues, "Because we knew he knew what we wanted and how we want to sound on CD. Tue is a metal guy, and we wanted the heaviness and aggression of a metal production plus a big open sound. I think he did an awesome job on it. He just knew what to do with our music. That's the biggest difference I guess – Tue knows what he's doing. The trip was well, well, worth it as far as we're concerned."

It certainly was; 'Sands Of Time' is not only the heaviest and hardest Born From Pain release to date, but also the most accomplished, the band sounding like a particularly well-oiled (killing) machine - finally threatening to slip the persistent Hatebreed and Merauder tags that have haunted them for so long.

"I'm glad you mention this," laughs Rob. "Hatebreed are an awesome band and good friends of ours, and we see them as the perfect example of the road a hardcore band with ambitions should be travelling, so with that in mind it's definitely a compliment. But to be quite honest, we're getting a bit fed up with being compared to them all the time. Yeah, we do sound heavy, aggressive and hard just like them, but we are, just like Hatebreed, a band of our own who tries to do stuff on our own. We don't look at

Hatebreed and compare. Neither should anyone else; I wanna be judged for what we do ourselves, on our own merits, not get compared to everything Hatebreed does all the time. But at the end of the day, I'd rather be compared to Hatebreed than The Mentors, haha."

Well, I've been as guilty as the next journalist of the above pigeonholing; there's just something about BFP's violent rhythms and Che's throaty roar that recalls Jamey Jasta's wrecking crew in full flight. But there has been a marked progression with 'Sands Of Time'.

"l think we have indeed written songs that sound and feel more mature. We had material for the CD that just wasn't like that, which ranged from a longer while back. We dropped that and managed to pack the CD full of stuff that was really powerful and aggressive and, like you already mentioned, 'cohesive'.

"Also, another big advantage is that we have finally found a line-up that 'feels' each other way better musically. Also, we have a way better drummer than Wouter could have ever been now. Not to dis him, but it's true. Another good thing about this CD is that the way the lyrics are put onto the songs is really awesome; the lyrics are a little more direct and less metaphorical, which has led to misunderstandings in the past. The biggest advance though is in the production, of course. We've been looking for that for four years and finally found it. We're well pleased!"

I'm glad the lyrics are mentioned; they are less ambiguous than previous albums, but are BFP really as miserable as a song like 'The Longest Day' suggests?

"Thing is, when I wrote those lyrics I had been going through some rough times where I really felt down on a lot of things. That song just reflects those feelings. The last two years have not been easy on any one of us on a personal level, so a lot of the new lyrics reflect that. I think the whole CD concept does. It oozes the way we feel, and have felt for a long time about a lot of things.

"The general idea behind the CD title is that all the stuff we deal with lyrically is based upon frustration, pain, joy, etc., strengthened or weakened throughout time. Looking at it like that, 'Sands Of Time' just seemed to be a very good title for the CD. I know that everyone says that time heals, but sometimes it also just makes these feelings stronger."

BORN FROM PAIN ~ ISSUE 178 (DECEMBER 2008)

Probably the best hardcore band in the world named after an Earth Crisis song - after All Out War, of course (only kidding, guys!) - Limburg's Born From Pain are taking no prisoners – either musically or lyrically – with their latest offering for Metal Blade, 'Survival'. And it's been all change in the band's boot camp recently, with bassist Rob Franssen stepping up to the microphone following the departure of the mighty-throated Che, prompting the recruitment of a whole new rhythm section in the shape of bassist Andries Beckers and drummer Roy Moonen. That might sound like a virtually

Born From Pain, 2019 – by Claudia Kötters

brand new band to some, but the spirit of Born From Pain remains intact... is renewed, in fact.

"It feels like coming home really, being back on the mic," reckons Rob, of his new role. "I loved playing bass, but it was a little restrictive at times. I'm really hell-bent on getting our message out there, and that is way easier when you are the man at the front and actually able to address people right to their faces. It is what people expect from a front man more than from a bassist anyway, I think.

"But this is nothing compared to all my old bands," he adds, comparing vocal duties with Born From Pain to the previous bands he has fronted, such as Feeding The Fire and Bloodsport. "This is way more serious, a lot tighter... a real-real band, if you know what I mean. So, that only makes it easier for a singer, I think... although grooving to riffs was cooler with a bass guitar, haha!"

And it has to be said, Rob's voice has a distinctly different vibe to those of his predecessor, Che, bringing more of a punkier, hardcore edge to the band's trademark metallic grooves. The twin guitar attack of Karl Fieldhouse and Dominik Stammen is still the equal of anything Hatebreed or Terror are likely to grind out, but the clearer vocals lend proceedings a whole new urgency.

"Of course, that's something that depends on your taste for vocals," offers Rob, modestly, obviously keen not to dis his old friend, Che, who turned in such a sterling performance on the first three BFP albums. "We, as a band, definitely think it has brought something to the mix that was lacking before, and yeah, the vocals have become more understandable, and a little bit more diverse; that was something we were looking to do for a while. I know that people were used to Born From Pain with a more death metal style, those deep, throaty vocals, but that is definitely not me. I try to put a more aggressive edge to the whole thing and, although the vocals are still rough, they're easier to understand. We feel it's something that not too many heavy bands usually do, and being a little different in that aspect is good, I think..."

So, with a clearer vocal delivery, have Born From Pain actually anything constructive to say? Thankfully yes, although, as that album title suggests, they don't feel the world is in a particularly happy place right now, and we'll be lucky if we all survive the coming storm. So batten down the fucking hatches.

"Well, yeah, 'Survival' is basically a call to arms in many ways. It's no secret that more and more people live an everyday struggle for survival, and I'm not just talking about war-time situations; I'm also talking about day-to-day situations in our 'civilised' western world, where more and more families are sinking below poverty level and life becomes a battle in a whole different way.

"And the concept of the record is that we need to get up and voice our dissent and anger," concludes Rob defiantly. "We need to make a fist against those who led this world into the dark ages we are in now; resistance against these people alone is a struggle for survival that everybody will need to get involved with at some point. The ugly face of a new world order is showing more and more, and it is undeniably trying to shut the door on anyone that's a 'have-not'. This is what songs like 'The Wolves Are Loose' and 'Under False Flag' are about; an elite of tremendously powerful people are trying to make us believe they do good, and we have puppets like Bush, Brown, McCain, Obama and whoever else, legislating laws that have not been around since Nazi Germany! They make us think that terrorism is a real threat, they make us think that everybody and his dog is out to get us, they install governments, install laws, they manipulate economy, and they do not care about anything else but themselves. Just look at the situations that gave these people the power and profits they enjoy now; just think what it took to get them there. They create chaos, then restore order... if they can go to war for profit and power and don't care who suffers, do you think they care when a father in Germany, Holland or the UK cannot feed his children every day? I don't think so! The world is in a state of disarray, fear and intimidation right now, and we're at the receiving end. Your hardcore scene needs you... join the struggle - before it's too late!"

FROM THE CUTTING ROOM FLOOR:

Please tell us about the changes in the BFP line-up recently, specifically why you have had to recruit a whole new rhythm section! How has that affected the chemistry/dynamic of the band?

R: Well, yes... first off, we had Che wanting to do other things in his life. He felt he wanted to get away from the touring life and settle down. Fair enough. We had some friends helping out on vocals since we didn't want to sit back for a while without playing, especially to show people we are alive and kicking. That worked out very well,

Born From Pain, 2019, by Claudia Kötters

with a lot of good quality voices helping out. After all that happened no one seemed to be willing to stay because of the lives they lead and how much time Born From Pain takes to do... so a lot of people surrounding the band - and the band itself - urged me to pick up the mic again and try to go on vocal duty. I had been singing for the band in the past and I felt right at home doing it now. After a while of getting back into it and practicing together we hit the road with me on vocals and we got amazing feedback. The feedback on the record is good too, so we are really happy we made the decision since we feel I incorporate the BFP thing the most out of all those singers, and it just seems logical that I have switched to the mic. Since I used to play bass guitar in the band, of course we needed to get a new bassist, which we found in long-time friend Andries who used to play for The Setup. Our old drummer Roel had been suffering from nerve damage in his elbow for a while, and he had been working to get back in the band for the last eight months, until the doctor told him it didn't work the way they expected and they ended up telling him that he at least needed two more years to get back to a point where he could intensely play the kit again. When he called and left, we were very disappointed, but he needs to think about his health as well. Roy, who had been filling in for Roel over that period of time was asked to stay and he did! The feeling in this line-up is just great and it feels like the band is reborn actually. Atmosphere's great, awesome vibe... cool.

BFP seem to be freshly energised politically... was there any one thing in particular that caused this lyrical re-focusing? Or has the band worked up to this gradually? If so, what's next for BFP on the political activism front?

The band has worked up to this gradually, but the situation we have been in with the world over the past two years and the increasing ruthlessness with which we can see the world go down the drain... we just feel it is time to give resentment a voice. There is no shame in trying to help each other and trying to be there for your fellow man. That is why we are getting actively involved in things. We are mainly trying to help out independent, non-government and big company–steered organizations in their fight for justice, and give a helping hand to organizations that are there to help people out. I feel that showing solidarity amongst the people and showing the powers that be that the people can stand together helps a lot. The power of all of us together is the only thing they are afraid about. They can buy anything they want, they can force any decision, but if we stand up against it with billions more than they are, they have no chance.
We are now being active for Amnesty International with some actions; we will do the same thing for Doctors Without Borders, some foster parent organizations and we will be getting active in our local communities helping people out that cannot be self-dependent anymore and are in need of assistance. We are active over the internet with petitions etc., but also get physically involved helping out. We also donate money with the band to just add a little so these people can keep on doing good for our fellow people...

What are your thoughts on the current hardcore and metal scenes? Do you think enough bands are striving to bring about a positive change in their fanbase?

R: I think metal and hardcore are far more the same than a lot of people would like to believe. Hardcore is always looked upon as more political or cooler, and metal is always looked upon as hell-death-fire and couldn't care less, but I beg to differ. Both scenes have an underground that is more and more leaning towards trends and how-cool-one-looks instead of concentrating on things that really make these scenes special and one of a kind. Never forget that both scenes always were pretty knitted together, especially back in the early Eighties, when a lot of the thrash metal bands looked at hardcore and punk for their influences. Both scenes have always been a counter culture against the values, rules and laws that be. I think that trying to bring about a positive change in people and the world in general is eminent, even beyond metal or hardcore. There is a lot in this world that needs to change for us to be able to live in different ways.

You're on another Resistance tour... another great bill too... it's not the first time you've done Resistance though! Is this the best yet?

R: I think it could be the best one! Last year's bill will be hard to top though. Anyway,

Persistence tour has become an institute over the years so I think it is always great to be on it, since people always come out in masses. Last time we were on, we were on a bill with Hatebreed , Napalm Death and Agnostic Front; now we are doing this tour with Terror, Heaven Shall Burn and Sick Of It All, to name but a few. I like the fact that this time round we play with a lot of bands we are friends with and a band we never toured with before (Sick Of It All), which has been always one of the bands that we admire a lot! So, I think this will be quite amazing... Persistence always has so many crazy kids coming out you get to play to, and will be able to get some stuff across to; it's a great time!

Success in a hardcore/metalcore band relies on a heavy touring schedule... how do you deal with being on the road all the time? If hardcore is about family, how do you cope with being away from your own?

R: Well, that's a hard one. It all depends on how your relationship works and how much responsibility one has. Having kids is a whole different ballgame perhaps, but since none of us have kids and all have girlfriends that are amazingly supportive of what we do, we go on the road with a good feeling and not one of having left people out on their own. Up until now, it has been working out really well; it is what we love to do and what we want to do, so it's all good!

BOTH WORLDS - ISSUE 30 (MAY 1996)

Both Worlds

I think it's safe to say that the Cro-Mags were a legend; their 'Age of Quarrel' debut album remains arguably one of the greatest hardcore records ever made. Shame then that they ended under such a black cloud, split in two by the bitter dispute between

Both Worlds, John Joseph, by Danielle Dombrowski

bassist Harley Flanagan and vocalist John Joseph, who is now fronting NYHC 'super group' Both Worlds.

When you learn that John actually started with the idea of Both Worlds back in 1990, upon first leaving the Cro-Mags, you've got to wonder if he regrets not starting it properly back then - instead of trotting out the inferior 'Near Death Experience' Cro-Mags album.

"Well, I only did the 'Near Death Experience' thing to get out of my contract, I didn't even want to do that record," explains John, on the phone from the offices of Another Planet, his current New York label. "In order to be able to do Both Worlds, I had to give them that last record and a tour; that was a contractual obligation. The music was already recorded, tracks that weren't used from [third Cro-Mags album] 'Alpha Omega'. Harley says he didn't play on that record, but that's a bunch of shit 'cos he did play on it.

"I don't regret anything because years ago this wasn't meant to happen. We can make all the plans we want, but sometimes things happen naturally that are out of our control. But now everything's falling into place. And I don't regret anything I did with the Cro-Mags 'cos it was something I really enjoyed, even though I never got paid for putting out those records."

Has the fact that you got burned in the past left you cynical towards the music industry?

"I've always been cynical towards the music industry, 'cos I've seen what happens. Bands get exploited; it's like legal prostitution, they pimp you out on the road. You boost your record sales for 'em and often you don't get shit for it. I don't hold any bitterness, but I learned my lesson to watch what you sign and to keep a close eye on what goes on with the band's business."

This time out, joined by A J Novello on guitar and Porky Mo on drums - both out of Leeway - and with Eddie Coen on bass, an ex-Sick Of It All and Murphy's Law member, John's new band sounds like a NYHC fan's wet dream come true. However, they aren't the stomping metalcore you might expect. Sure, their sound pays homage to their old bands; it's still hard and energetic, but Both Worlds are also a bit mellower, more rhythmic, and more thoughtful. Something revealed on their 'Blind Zero Gravity' CDEP, and also reflected in their ambiguous name.

"When I came up with that name, I'd just left the Cro-Mags and I was going through some hard times in my life. I just realized that even though we are here on this planet, there's knowledge that can elevate you spiritually. And then there's things that can degrade your life. For me, it was using cocaine. I was like, 'Wow, I'm caught in both worlds...' You can either do things in your life that are positive to advance yourself, or you can destroy yourself."

Tell us a bit about the benefit show that a lot of NYHC bands organized on your behalf.

"Well, I don't want to harp on about it, but basically Kevin and Harley from White Devil ratted me out to the military for being AWOL from the Navy, and got me into a lot of hot water. Kevin now has an order of protection against me, where I can't even speak a word to him or I go to jail for 30 days, and Harley hasn't been around since June. He's hiding out 'cos he knows I'm going to fucking beat his ass for turning me in.

"Anyway, all the bands put together a benefit for me to cover my legal fees. That was a godsend, 'cos it helped me get a really good lawyer. It was a great feeling everyone pulling together to help me out; I'll never forget that as long as I live. People can say all they like, but it's their actions that really count. And all those bands dedicating their time and effort and coming through for me says more than any speeches could convey."

Similarly, one listen to the new Both Worlds CD will surely convince you more than 50 of my cheesy metaphors that this is a band who don't have to rely on past glories and who are more than exciting enough to make an impression on their own merits. Roll on the debut album.

BOTH WORLDS - ISSUE 54 (MAY 1998)

Despite the presence of ex-Cro-Mags frontman John Joseph in their ranks, Both World ain't a Krishna band — just another example of NYHC going beyond itself into new musical realms. Ian Glasper hears the singer explain why he needs no guru to be spiritual, and why space travel is bad for you...

Y'know? I do believe that Both Worlds were one of the first bands to feature in our Upfront section, back when it was hardly more than a glint in our eyes. That was for their 'Beyond Zero Gravity' MCD on Another Planet, and even in that embryonic stage you just knew that they could be destined for greater things, and not only 'cos they contained ex-members of such hardcore legends as Cro-Mags and Leeway. No, Both Worlds only hinted at their HC ancestry with their buoyant energy and intensity, preferring instead to cut a new swathe in comparison to their old flames, something decidedly more rock. But then, they vanished! Just like that – until now, and the imminent arrival of their debut full-lengther, this time for Roadrunner, 'Memory Rendered Visible'.

"Basically, we had to get on the right label," explains John Joseph, their highly-charged frontman, on the phone from his label's NYC office, explaining their lengthy hiatus, "And we had to write the best songs we could - we didn't wanna shoot our musical load prematurely, as it were. We wanted to come out with something a little ground-breaking, so we locked ourselves away for six or seven months until we'd written a bunch of good songs.

"Also, everyone in the band was involved in other projects, and to get people to commit to moving on from bands like Leeway was tough, but once we started writing and shopping the demo, and people were interested, the choice that everyone had to make was obvious. We're one band now, tight musically, and as friends."

That's good to hear after the cloud of viciousness that darkened the split in the Cro-Mags' ranks. But I still heard all sortsa rumours that you'd split up, or signed to a major, or whatever!

"Well, we just stopped playing, so we could write this record," John dismisses the rumour, "And as for us signing to a big label, well, people can say what they want, we don't give a shit. I've been playing music for over twenty years. We didn't have anyone telling us what to write, or how to play, on this record. What's on this record is exactly what we wanted to do. We're very thankful that Roadrunner wanted to sign us, they look after their bands... what am I supposed to do? Travel round in a broken-down van all over again? Please, man! Half these bands who talk shit about us haven't been through one thousandth of what I've been through since '81. Breaking down in deserts, getting arrested, getting in fights, c'mon. Bands like the Cro-Mags, or the Bad Brains, or AF, made it easy for all these bands now. It's a piece of cake for these kids, but we paid our dues, and paved the way."

All that experience has come home to roost on 'Memory Rendered Visible', a wonderfully mature record and a veritable smorgasbord of driving, passionate metal and hardcore-tinged alternative rock. There are a lot of influences at work here, from Quicksand and Handsome to Jane's Addiction and, of course, for a band with strong links to Krishna, Shelter. Mr. Joseph is in agreement that he loves all the bands mentioned – except Shelter...

"I don't wanna start any stupid competitions with any other bands," sighs John, "But I don't see eye to eye with those guys on their philosophy. The truth is going to be known in the whole Krishna movement soon – there's been a big cover-up going on for the last twenty years, but that's all being exposed now.

"Shelter's guru, who they're leading all these little hardcore kids to, was nothing but a child molester and abuser. To me, Prabhupada is the only one to be worshipped, but they're worshipping someone no better than you or I, man. People get guru complexes, everyone wants to be a spiritual leader, and I'm involved in exposing the whole scam that went down in the Krishna movement, and showing these people up for what they are - they're criminals."

Now, despite this theological heaviness, don't go fretting that Both Worlds are gonna get in your face over your religious beliefs, or lack of 'em, 'cos age has mellowed John and his merry men considerably, altho' spirituality is obviously the driving force behind his inspiration, and aspiration.

"Oh yeah, that's what we're about. The name Both Worlds refers to the material and the spiritual worlds... you have to live in the material world, but you should be striving to get out of the material and into the spiritual world. We're not this Shelter band who'll come on stage in robes to preach at people 'n' stuff - this band has the same raw energy as the Cro-Mags - but if you can get something out of the lyrics, fine. Come down to the temple and see what s up, but I'm not gonna get up on stage and start preaching at people, and then go away and be a total hypocrite behind closed doors.

"This ain't a Krishna band - everyone's got their own beliefs, but there is a lot of spirituality there. That's just the way I write lyrics, but I ain't no Joe Preacher, and I won't tell people how to live their lives. If you're not down with my words, and just like the music, then that's cool too. And even if you don't like the music or the lyrics, that's okay too. Not everyone's gonna like your shit, right?"

One of the most potent sets of lyrics on the new record is the awesome pairing of 'Spiritual Flu' and 'Space Junkies', two songs that surge with barely tamed power, yet also manage to exude more intelligence than machismo.

"Uh, 'Spiritual Flu' is about society in general, and how fucked up it is. There's no regard for the planet by any of the people in power. They don't care; they're burning fossil fuels, they're dumping toxins, and they do not care. They don't give a fuck about anyone but themselves.

"And 'Space Junkies' is about when they turn around and say, 'We've fucked this planet up, so let's fly to another one and live there instead...' It can't be done, but if it could, how much money would that take? Only the rich will be invited.

"On the news every day I see they're spending hundreds of billions of dollars," John's voice rises incredulously, "On the space programme, yet there's people here starving in the Midwest! Why worry about other planets? Let's make this one a better place to live on! It doesn't make any sense - we're not made to live on another fuckin' planet, we were born here. Our bodies are suited to maintain themselves here, so this is the planet we've gotta take care of."

I take it you subscribe to the chain of thought that the moon landing was a hoax then? It was all shot in a hangar somewhere?

"Yeah, it was a total hoax. There's even astronauts admitting it was a hoax now. All the time, they're just perpetrating scams on the American people, like the Gulf War... if there hadn't been any oil there, we couldn't have cared less. Look at what went down in Haiti, but that Third World country didn't have any oil, but as soon as anyone dared fuck with our oil, you better believe you'll have Desert Storm. It's all about money, they've put a price on human life.

"You've got a president who was a draft dodger, so he doesn't even believe in war, but when his oil's at risk, he gets all gung ho and fired up about it, 'cos it's about money, it's all about the dollar. We need a President who's a vegetarian, who's spiritually enlightened... only then will the world ever change."

Go for it then, John. "No, I don't want the karma of that dude, hell fuckin' no. I'll just tell as many people as I can about Prabhupada. Devotees - well, real devotees – aren't out there killing people and raping the earth. He's the only person that could save the whole planet."

BREACH – ISSUE 24 (OCTOBER 1995)

Breach

Breach are a heavy, heavy hardcore band out of Sweden that I think a lorra lorra Terrorizer readers could get off on. They have a new album, 'Friction', on Burning Heart Records, but when I caught up with vocalist Tomas recently, our talk kicked off about their debut MCD from last year, 'Outlines'...

"Oh, we got a really great response to that," reckons Tomas, "From both press and fans, because it was kind of a new type of hardcore for Sweden. The only scene then was the punk rock thing, and a little bit of a straightedge scene, but we were playing much slower and heavier."

Did you tour at all for 'Outlines'? "We haven't done any major touring yet," bemoans the vocalist, "Only playing in Sweden for week-long tours and stuff. We are playing some big festivals here though, through the summer, which will be good for us."

I know you played the Fagersta Hardcore Festival – how was that? "That was great!" he enthuses. "I think that was one of the best shows we've ever played in our whole career. We played early in the day, and that was our first time playing in broad daylight, but there was a lot of people there, and we got a really great response."

Some bands find it difficult to 'get an atmosphere going' at a large festival as opposed to a small club? "That's true, we were a bit suspicious about it. It was 5:30 in the afternoon, and the sun was shining... would there be anyone there to watch us? But it was great. And there were many other very cool bands - Earth Crisis, Snapcase, and a lot of other Swedish bands, including Fireside, one of my favourite bands... also Refused and Abhinanda. It was a really good festival."

I know that a few of you were in punk bands prior to Breach. What other influences are there in your music besides that? "Mainly early NYHC bands, I would say," he begins cautiously, "Like Judge, Youth of Today, Burn, and early US bands like Minor Threat... that sort of thing... but we ['we' being Erik – guitar, Anders – guitar, Janne – drums and Kristian – bass] all listen to different kinds of music. For example, our bassist likes a lot of pop music, and also the Chicago scene, and our guitarist listens to Swedish punk."

There seems to be a certain death metal element to your sound too... "Some people do say that! Our second guitarist, before he started with us, did play in a death metal band, so he brought some of that to Breach. I also like some death metal, especially the Swedish bands like Entombed and Dismember – I think they're great."

Of course, you recorded the new album at Sunlight Studios, which helped get that guitar sound. What was it like working there? "We really like the sound we got – it's really heavy and really... well, wide! That's why we went to Stockholm to record."

Is Sunlight expensive, considering their reputation? "No, it's not," reveals Tomas. "Actually, it's one of the cheaper studios in Sweden. I was really surprised when I learnt what they charge per hour. They're not expensive at all, but the people who work there really know what they're doing. They really know about music, and they really wanted to know how we wanted to sound. It was just perfect for us."

There are so many bands in Sweden – is there any competition between you all? "No, not at all, there's no rivalry. We all like each other, everybody, and we all watch out for each other, man. We go to each other's gigs, whether a band is straightedge or vegetarian or not."

And that's one of the great things about hardcore – everyone can have a different opinion but still get along.

"People take it in so many different ways... some say it's harder, some say it's easier," says Breach guitarist, Anders Ekstrom, struggling to put into words exactly how their awesome new album for Burning Heart, 'Venom', differs from their previous opus, 'It's Me God'. And anyone familiar with these eclectic Swedes will probably sympathise with his hesitancy, 'cos, just like the mighty Refused (RIP) before them, Breach often defies easy categorisation, taking the generic metallic new school formula and twisting it into all manner of disturbing shapes.

"We've always tried to change style with each release; we've never wanted to repeat ourselves. We went from almost pure hardcore on that first MCD ['Outlines'– IG] more towards metal on 'Friction', which we recorded at Sunlight where all those kinds of bands go, and then we added a much more noisy characteristic to our sound on 'It's Me God', which had a big Jesus Lizard/Shellac influence. And this is another step on from there... we're still looking to combine all that into one, whilst still going forward. At the end of the day, I think this one has better songs that are more mature."

One listen to 'Venom', and you are plunged into a tumultuous sea of discord, where desperate riffs and strident rhythms clash in a tidal wave of undeniably hypnotic power. Its dark brooding atmospherics and eerie harmonies are a million miles removed from the sXe hardcore scene that originally spawned the band back in '93.

"That whole scene has pretty much faded away," claims Anders. "The sXe thing in Umea will never be as big as it was a few years ago. Back then it was huge, a really revolutionary force, but when Refused split a few months ago, they were like the piece that held that whole puzzle together. We were never really a part of all that anyway – we never preached any message at our gigs - and now it seems like we're the ones that've stood the test of time. In a way, it's tempting to say, 'I told you so', but I won't! Even Abhinanda split not so long back, so now we're, like, one of the only survivors from that period. And that's because we never affiliated ourselves with politics too much, and we always welcomed everyone as new fans, whether they were sXe or not."

Making new fans was certainly the order of the day when they opened up the Entombed/Neurosis tour all across Europe in autumn 1997. Surely that was a dream billing for Breach, and a golden opportunity to take their devastating noisecore to a bigger audience?

"Yeah, that was the single best thing to ever happen to the band," recalls Anders fondly. "It was the ultimate tour package for us; the three bands had different styles, but they were still similar enough to make perfect sense. We did about thirty shows across, I think, ten countries, so it was a good way of expanding our fan base.

"We are in the middle somewhere, between pure metal and new school hardcore - so we went down really well with the fans of the other bands, and I would love to do it all over again! We made good friends with Entombed, so maybe we'll go out together again someday, although our differing schedules make it difficult to pair up. And, of course, we'd like to get out to the States if we could... and Neurosis have a brand new album out, so... fingers crossed! But in this business, you never know what breaks you're going to get until you're actually standing onstage to start the tour."

One listen to 'Venom' should be enough to convince you that Breach have truly transcended the confining walls of the hardcore tag. If the spellbinding, wandering guitar hooks weren't enough, nor the huge rolling patterns the drummer batters out, howzabout the inclusion of two instrumentals, 'Diabolo' and 'Black Sabbath'? The instrumental is a medium usually avoided by us cowardly hardcore bands, who tend to prefer utilising the vocalist for added aggression, but this isn't the first time Breach have embraced it, and no doubt it won't be the last either.

"Well, our singer lives a long way away, up in the north," explains the axeman, "While we've all moved to Stockholm, and sometimes we just come up with ideas and riffs that really have no room for vocals. It's a heavy wall of sound we pump out, so why clutter it further with vocals, if they are not needed? I'm very confident in the band, and we know when a song needs, or doesn't need, vocals. We can tell our stories with just music sometimes, without relying on words.

"Besides, it gives our singer chance to walk out into the audience and watch his own band live... and because he has a head start, he's always the first one at the bar to get the beers in!"

So, next time you're at a show, and you're wondering who that sweaty individual stood next to you at the bar is (and just where the hell has the frontman gone off the stage?), be sure to buy him a drink, won't you? Because 'Venom' may not be everybody's cup o' poison, but if you can handle its harsh expansiveness, it's an album of truly epic proportions.

BREAKDOWN - ISSUE 62 (JANUARY 1999)

For how long can a band be cited as seminal, and held up as a shining example of a genre, before they inevitably totter from that prime poll position? Only to be left at the wayside, as the fickle youth forge ever onwards, in search of new extremities to stimulate the increasingly demanding yardstick by which they measure the millions of new bands that crawl, like rats deserting a

sinking ship, from the woodwork of the underground every week? Usually not for too long, so every time a 'classic' band turn out the goods, against the odds, and show all these Johnny-Come-Latelys just how the fuck it should be done, it's an inspirational thing, y'know? Especially for an old timer

like myself! And if any band have finally triumphed in the stony face of adversity, then that band is surely Breakdown, for long regarded as one of the true vanguards of the NYHC scene (by everyone except the record-buying public, that is), but never really achieving the success they so rightly

deserved. All that could well be set to change, at last, with their new album, the awesome 'Plus Minus', having just been picked up for Europe (it's on Eyeball in the

Breakdown, May 2000, by Danielle Dombrowski

States) by Kingfisher, who with the might of Century Media behind them, might finally give the band the push they need to break
them over here.

"This has taken eleven years to happen," sighs their vocalist Jeff, before being brutally honest about their lack of output over the years. "No one wanted to put our stuff out! And it wasn't for lack of trying either – we sent out loads of demos, but I guess it comes to those that wait. You can't play hardcore music for money - well, not many bands can, anyway. We do it for fun, and because our hearts are still in it. As long as it feels right, I'll still be here doing this. I know one thing for sure – if we'd only been doing it for the money, we woulda split years ago.

"I couldn't ever do another band," he adds, when I ask him what drives him onward, him being the only original member 'n' all. Breakdown is it for me. It's the way I feel, and I can't change my outlook, and this band represents it all so well. If we ever split for good, I won't be putting anything else together. I wouldn't know how, for starters. Mike Dijan is the second most senior member, seven years going on eight. He's the evil half of the deadly duo. We have like a good cop, bad cop thing going..."

What, and you're the good guy!? "Yeah," laughs Jeff, "Or so it seems at first!"

Actually, after talking to Jeff for over an hour about anything and everything punk rock, it's easy to forget that his band have a certain, ahem, 'rep' as tough guys. Sometimes it seems that if you don't ramble on about scene unity, all of a sudden you're a thug. Mind you, they did write a song called '(l Wanna See A) Street Fight', but why, oh why, can't people see a wind-up until it bites them on the ass?

"So many people thought that that song was 100% serious," Jeff tells me incredulously.

150

Breakdown guitarist, Mike Dijan, by Danielle Dombrowski

"Maximum Rock 'N' Roll reviewed it, and said it had the worst lyrics ever, and I know that it's, like, anathema to write in and complain about a bad review, but the guy was

Breakdown live, May 2000, by Danielle Dombrowski

such a dick, I just had to. I wrote and told them that it was all tongue-in-cheek, and that he had his finger in his ear, and his thumb up his ass! And, besides, who doesn't stop to watch a street fight, anyway? They're entertaining, in their own way, and I know I can think of worst things to do.

"A lot of the time, people don't even listen to us. They've already made their minds up before they hear us out, but whatever... we can deal with bad press. We've had plenty of practise over the years!"

Well, hopefully the pigeons will come home to roost, when the power and drive of 'Plus Minus' takes the hardcore world by the throat, and Breakdown can take their place in the Hall Of Fame alongside

the likes of Sheer Terror and Sick Of It All as one of the bands who helped define what we perceive as NYHC today.

Jeff is as self-deprecatingly modest as ever, of course. "Oh, l guess we were lucky back then. When we started, the scene was at its peak, and HC was still so fresh. There was plenty of room to move and create your own style. There weren't any other bands around back then for us to copy, so we just ended up sounding like ourselves."

Bring To Ruin - issue 234 (April 2013)

Featuring scene veterans of many years and ex-members of such much-loved bands as In The Shit, This System Kills and Rejected, Bring To Ruin are the South Welsh

Bring To Ruin, by Paul Cussens

response to Good Riddance, playing gnarly but melodic, raging yet intelligent, hardcore punk rock. Their self-titled album, released through collaboration between no less than seven labels (really, count 'em!), including Pumpkin, Righteous Anger and Riot Ska, is super powerful and super catchy – but why record it in France?

"Basically we were over in France playing some gigs with Urban Attack," explains guitarist Payney, "And really liked the sound on their album. Alex was really cool to work with too; he got us an immense sound, and it was cool having several labels to release it. It helps out with costs, and brings people together which is what DIY punk should be all about."

BROKEN BONES – ISSUE 133 (JULY 2005)

Featuring a member of punk legends Discharge, Stoke's Broken Bones have made a little history of their own over the past two decades, influencing some of the most famous thrash bands on the planet. With new album, 'Time For Anger, Not Justice', through US label Dr Strange simmering in the racks, the band are back from the dead in a most convincing fashion. Ian Glasper was despatched to the excavation and he uncovered a band that are anything but fossils.

Broken Bones

Formed in Stoke-on-Trent in 1983 by guitarist Tony 'Bones' Roberts when he left Discharge, Broken Bones were seemingly doomed to live in the shadow of Bones' previous band until they proved their detractors wrong with some of the best punk metal ever committed to vinyl. So potent an outpouring of metallic hardcore, in fact, that they ended up signed to Rough Justice/Music For Nations and have since been cited as an influence by the likes of Metallica, Anthrax and Slayer.

Despite a lengthy hiatus after splitting during the early '90s, the band are still together today and sounding better than ever, as evidenced by the stunning new album for Californian label Dr Strange, 'Time For Anger, Not Justice'.

"Yeah, I think people initially connect us with the Discharge thing," concedes bassist Paul Hoddy. "It's inevitable really, but I think that we have got our own sound and style and I suppose that some people do consider us an influence in our own right. It always surprises me when they say that we have made an impact on them. We just make music that we like and if there are people out there that like it, that's great, but we're just doing this because we love the music."

Influential and with a worldwide following, even a Japanese band blatantly copied the line-up shot Broken Bones did back in the day with one of them hanging from their neck in a churchyard. Do the plagiarists annoy?

"That was a band called Disclose," Paul recalls, "and they're at the forefront of the D-beat cloning scene, you know, where these bands sound and sometimes even look like Discharge. There are quite a few of them around. Disclose have a record with this picture of the singer/guitarist/band mastermind, Kawakami, hanging from a tree. They also have a slogan 'Dis-Bones Attack' printed on all their records! It's actually quite a compliment when bands do that; even though it's mainly Discharge they're into, they've branched out to Broken Bones because of Bones."

There are a million bands out there that have been influenced by Metallica, but not that many that, in turn, can lay claim to having influenced the metal legends.

"We played CBGBs in New York," recalls Paul fondly. "James Hetfield and Scott Ian had come to the show, a matinee, because Metallica were playing in Brooklyn later that evening. After we kicked in the first song, 'Death Is Imminent', a guy tried to get on stage and snapped the wire to my bass, so I had to use Billy Milano's [SOD] bass – a shitty little medium-scale thing! While I was waiting for it, Bones started playing 'Jump In The Fire' by Metallica and James went wild and thought it was amazing that this guitar hero of his was playing one of his songs! The best thing I saw that night was Hetfield, on Scott Ian's shoulders, headbanging to Broken Bones.

"We then got backstage passes to the Metallica show later that day and they dedicated 'Fade To Black' to Broken Bones, one of my favourite songs ever; what a night to remember. I also saw an amazing bass player in Cliff Burton; he didn't influence me as such, but I loved his crazy style onstage. Such a laidback guy, but get him on a stage and he was wild.

"I think Metallica just became too big too quickly," he adds on that band's varying fortunes over the years since. "It must have been hard to handle; they started out doing '80s metal songs, then suddenly, six years later, they are one of the biggest rock bands in the world with millions of dollars in the bank. I actually thought the last album was great, but I've liked most of their stuff. They had to change direction after 'The Black

Album' or it would have become too formulaic, like Iron Maiden. A lot of people hated 'Load' and 'Reload' but I liked them. And I think the last album was a necessary change again, to keep it fresh – really raw with hardly any solos, which Bones doesn't agree with, of course – even though there's actually one song on our new album with no solo in it, shock horror!"

Ah, yes, the new album and what a return to form it is, too. 2001's 'Without Conscience' strongly hinted that the band were about to hit their stride again, but who could have predicted they would do so in such spectacular fashion? 'Time For Anger, Not Justice' is easily the best thing the band have put their name to since their 'Dem Bones' debut over twenty years ago. It features their usual aggressive metal leanings, and, as already mentioned, manic guitar solos igniting all over the place, but it also has a decidedly harder edge to it, possibly a nod towards the intensity of the current metalcore scene.

"In my, admittedly biased, opinion I actually think it's better than the 'classic stuff' we did in the '80s because it's fresher," says Paul. "A lot of people won't agree with that, I know, but there are also a lot of people who've heard it and have said that it blows them away. I think it does have a more hardcore edge but it wasn't a conscious effort to do that. As I said earlier, we write songs for us, and if we like them, then that's it. It was something that just happened; some songs started off a lot slower, but by the time we were used to playing them, they had really speeded up – that's drummers for you.

"But I do think the current hardcore scene is pretty healthy at the moment," he continues. "There are a lot of great bands out there. There are also a lot of commercial ones too, but I don't really include them as part of the scene, as they are more like corporate puppets."

Broken Bones re-recorded two old songs from the dim and distant past to round out the new record. Was that because they could benefit from a more modern production? "It was mainly for the website. We did this poll where visitors voted for their favourite song, what they'd like to hear re-recorded, and 'Decapitated' and 'FOAD' came out tops. The latter is available as a download from the website as well. It was nothing to do with getting a bad production in the '80s, although they do sound a lot better now."

So, when will they tour on the back of this new album? With members involved in other bands, Bones playing in Discharge and Paul playing in Conflict, how are Broken Bones ever going to fit any gigs in?

"It does sometimes feel as if we come third in the line," Paul admits in closing, "So we have to keep in constant touch with the other bands, to make sure that when I book gigs for Broken Bones, they know not to book on those days. The main stumbling block has been Discharge, who've been really busy lately. We've had to cancel gigs a couple of times for them, but saying that, Discharge backed down so our US tour could go ahead. They had some dates in Europe planned for the same period, but our tour was a bit more important as we're promoting a new album. It's not ideal, but we always work something out."

Broken Bones, by Gutterpunk Photography

"No, we haven't split up!" declares Broken Bones bassist, Paul Hoddy, "But [guitarist] Bones has two young kids now, and with [his other band] Discharge doing regular gigs, we're just going to play now and again, maybe just do big metal and punk festivals... but we're definitely keeping going!"

Thank gawd for that, 'cos the band's new album, 'Fuck You And All You Stand For', is the best thing they've done since their 1984 debut, 'Dem Bones', with not a filler track in sight.

"I don't know of another hardcore album released this year that's as good as ours," he says modestly. "That sounds arrogant, I know, but that's how we all feel; it's a truly angry album, and hopefully a lesson for all the lame shit that gets released nowadays under the guise of 'hardcore punk'!"

BROKEN TEETH - ISSUE 271 (JUNE 2016)

Broken Teeth, courtesy of Claire Harris–Nuclear Blast

"Well, Merauder are just one of many influences," laughs Dale Graham, vocalist with UKHC band Broken Teeth, newly signed to Nuclear Blast, when it's pointed out how much they sound like the NYC metalcore stalwarts. "We all worship the 80's/90's NYHC style, but we do like to add ideas from classic thrash metal bands like Sepultura, Venom, Machine Head, and Testament, to name but a few. "When it comes to lyrics, it's all just words of personal frustration at modern society. Hardcore music is a community for people who feel like misfits in the outside world, and for the 30 minutes I get to rage about our problems, it's like therapy. It keeps us sane.

"We've not heard anything negative yet," he adds, of their signing to the German metal label, "But if anyone has a problem, they can crawl back in their hole and cry about it some more!"

BRONX CASKET COMPANY – ISSUE 69 (AUGUST 1999)

Bronx Casket Company

It's not every day that Ian Glasper rings us up practically begging to do a feature, so when he threw his rattle out of his pram over Bronx Casket Company's debut album, we thought it was the least we could do to give him a page to convince us he wasn't getting all hysterical again...

It would come as no surprise to many of you to discover that a band with a dark, foreboding name like the Bronx Casket Company were coming from the gothic side of the tracks, but would it make you sit up and listen if l told you that BCC is the 'side project' of none other than D.D. Verni, bassist with power metal vets, Overkill? Okay, howzabout that their self-titled album for Massacre is one of the most confident debuts I've heard in a long while and is a rich, heady mixture of early Candlemass, Sabbath, (second record) Type O Negative and Life of Agony? Ah, thought that might get your attention...

"l had wanted lo do this for a few years now," relates D.D., sounding justifiably pleased with his creation, "But Overkill is busy all the time, with touring and writing and everything else, and l was always saying, 'Oh, I'm really gonna do this... someday!' And then something else would come up, and I'd be on tour or whatever, so I started doing it piece by piece, a song here, and a song there "

And after hooking up with drummer Tim Mallares, one of his partners in crime in Overkill, guitarist Jack Frost from Seven Witches, keyboard wizard Charlie Calv from

Shotgun Symphony, and last, but not least, Mike Hideous – late of no less than the Misfits – the result is nothing less than stunning, a doom album of great depth and immense dramatic impact, that rises above its 'side project' status on black velvety wings.

"Mike was the final piece of the puzzle," says D.D., before clarifying, "He was only in the Misfits for a short while. He stood in for them on one European tour, his 'main' band is called The Empire Hideous; they're not signed or anything, but they're definitely one of the biggest goth bands in the area. Jack gave me a tape of them, and told me all about this weird guy who did all this sick vampire shit, and I knew we'd found our man!

"So, I did all these recordings with me playing all the instruments, even singing, and sent them out to everyone. Bronx Casket Company have never actually all played together in the same room at the same time yet!"

If their sensual cover of Metallica's 'Jump In The Fire' doesn't spell it out for you ["I've wanted to do that song for a long time... I can't wait to see what James makes of it!"], let me: these guys may utilise dreamy textures and sweeping orchestral keys, but they are most definitely rooted in heavy metal. Songs like 'Mercy Ltd' stomp along with strident power whilst retaining a certain delicate framework to their majestic poise.

"Most definitely," agrees Verni. "A lot of bands who do this sort of music, they get atmospheric, which is great... but they lose the riff. And we treat the riff as the foundation for everything else, and build the keyboards around that – not the other way round. If you listen to a lot of the songs without the keyboards, you'll get that whole Trouble/Candlemass vibe, but the keys, and Mike's vocals, add a new dimension, and throw it more towards that gothic thing."

When someone who is already in such a great band as Overkill (I've said it once, but I'll say it again – they were THE metal band of the Dynamo for me...), it always begs the question as to why they bother putting anything else together. Surely you don't feel frustrated at your creativity being stifled within the overbearing persona of such a popular band with a very well-established sound?

"I don't think there's any frustration in the first place, because I have 100% freedom to write whatever I want in Overkill... but I wouldn't want to do other kinds of genres. Overkill is all about high energy stuff, getting on stage and going crazy and ripping yer face off, and we wouldn't want to play moody, melancholy metal. That's not what we're about, and never will be.

"So, Bronx Casket Company was, literally, just fun to do; it wasn't something building up, it wasn't a reaction to anything. I just had these songs written, and I knew all these guys, and we all get on, and I figured it would be a blast."

And a blast it most certainly is, for the listener as well as the band. Hugely heavy, but also eminently listenable, BCC seem to have stumbled upon a perfect formula to win over metallers and goths alike, including those requisite Anne Rice lyrics!

"I guess I'm a little different to most other lyric writers," ponders D.D. "I always think the song should just mean one thing to whoever reads it. Most bands say, 'It could mean different things to different people, you have to decide for yourself...', whereas if I show someone the colour green, I want them to see the colour green, y'know?"

Bullet Ridden

"We are an aural bulwark against the dark forces of repression and mediocrity; we are at war and these instruments and voices are our weapons," reckons Martin Einon, vocalist with Bristol's latest world-class noisemongers, Bullet Ridden. Strong, confident words indeed, but no idle threats either, because these guys sound for all the world as if Entombed have formed an Antisect tribute band! It's heavy, gnarly shit, but then again, what would you expect from ex-members of Varukers, Black Eye Riot and Bomb Blast Men?

"We are set apart from no one in the scene," reckons Martin modestly, "Except those that need to be shunned from it because of their stupidity, of course! Our special charm is that we are an unknown pleasure to most and as yet remain an elusive force of nature still to be savoured!"

Burning Skies - issue 124 (October 2004)

"The speed with which everything happened was a little surreal, but we've been on the Lifeforce roster for about a year now, and we've settled in pretty well. They heard of us after we'd done our first demo and got in touch with us straight away, and we decided to go with them because they've released such great music in the past. We felt they would do good things for us, that we'd work together well, and so far everything's going to plan."

So says drummer Stu of his band Burning Skies and their meteoric rise through the ranks of underground metalcore. Formed but two years ago in the Southwest of England, and featuring ex-members of such heavyweight acts as Unite and Exit Wound,

Burning Skies, 2002

the band are now signed to the aforementioned German label, and are set to make big waves with their lethally impressive 'Murder By Means Of Existence' debut. A bludgeoning mix of thrash, death and hardcore, complete with surgically precise riffing and the occasional relentless blast-beat, it's sure to be a disc that Terrorizer readers take to heart. It's certainly one of the nastier debuts from a UK band in recent years; Slayer-esque atmospherics going head to head with flourishes of dark melody from the NWOSDM, all executed with an impressively ruthless efficiency.

"We do mostly listen to thrash, grind and hardcore," confirms Stu. "We just combine all the things that we love about heavy music. And the lyrics are mostly about the things that happen day to day in our lives, the grievances we have with this world and all the people who irritate us.

"We don't feel that we're competing against anyone else in the UKHC scene though; there's a lot of great bands from this country who deserve to do well for themselves. We're just doing our thing, and we hope people will enjoy it and want to come and see us. Also, we're not trend-followers; we're not about big, singalong choruses, just straight up brutality, that's what we try to achieve.

"But we don't want to pigeonhole ourselves by saying who and what we sound like," he adds, when asked whether he approves of the 'Hatebreed meets At The Gates' tag they seem to be picking up for themselves. "I'd agree that there are elements of Burning Skies that could be compared to those bands, but it doesn't represent the whole picture. We'd rather leave it up to the listener to decide at the end of the day."

Byzantine, pic by Most Exalted

"We really didn't want a band name with a negative connotation like Casket Full of Babies or Vomit Chunks!" laughs Chris Ojeda, guitarist/vocalist with West Virginian metallers, Byzantine. "The name was too good to pass up really. I was looking through a thesaurus for words that were synonymous with 'intricate' and 'inflexible' and when 'Byzantine' came through, it was perfect. I knew it was the name of the empire that succeeded the Romans and that gave us a real good base to build on... after all, what better to name a band after than an empire?

"Also, I did a check on the internet and no-one else had ever registered the name for their band, so we took it... Byzantine is nice and non-suggestive; it leaves a lot to the imagination."

As does the title given to the band's new album, their second for Prosthetic, 'And They Shall Take Up Serpents'. It actually makes reference to an obscure passage of the Bible (Mark 16) that encourages all true believers to become evangelical warriors, to literally handle venomous snakes as a show of unassailable faith and militantly convert anyone and everyone they meet.

"Our lead guitarist, Tony [Rohrbough], brought up this concept of the religious institutions here in West Virginia that are well known for handling serpents in church and drinking strychnine. He said, 'Let's name the album ... 'And They Shall Take Up

Serpents'! And we all loved it instantly! I ended up reading this book called 'Salvation On Sand Mountain' and got some great lyrical ideas."

And just like the serpents of the title, Byzantine writhe with malevolent intent, an intelligent melding of resilient melodies with classic thrash sensibilities and some truly stunning guitar work. Think the brutality of Pantera, the off-kilter rhythms of Nasty Savage, the dynamic arrangements of Shadows Fall, and the fret-board histrionics of Megadeth in their prime, and you're beginning to grasp the ferociousness of this particularly innovative metallic beast. Hell yes, this is some clever, heavy shit.

"I'm really not at liberty to say what separates us from anyone else," says OJ modestly when pushed as to what he personally thinks might help Byzantine stand out from the current crop of modern thrash bands. "It is totally up to you guys and the fans to say if we are different or not. But yes, I do think the scene is flooded right now with bands - but that just means that metal is coming back in a big way! A lot of bands kinda sound the same, but as long as people are digging it heavy, I'm cool with that.

"We just tried to make a more dynamic album this time, but also we tried to make a heavier album. We made sure we had more solos, more singing, just more ass-kicking and head-banging overall. And I really feel strongly about my lyrics on this album as well. I wanted to make a lyrically abrasive album without cursing on it. Not that I am against cursing or anything, but the English language is so vast, I like to get my point across in my lyrics without expletives. There are some great topics on the new album as well."

Indeed there are, the profundity of lyrics such as 'Ancestry Of The Antichrist' (beginning 'A fabrication woven from a burning Bush...!') and 'The Rat Eaters' matching blow for blow the incredible musicianship on display. And as a special gift to any fans that might care to unlock such secrets, the CD itself is enhanced with all the guitar tablature for the entire album. How cool is that? I can't believe that no one has ever thought to do it before!

"We just thought it would be a way of rewarding the kids out there who play guitar and listen to metal really. As kids we used to shell out big bucks for tab books of Megadeth and Testament, and we thought, 'How cool would it have been if 'Rust In Peace' had come with tabs?' So we worked our asses off and tabbed out the whole album for you guys...

"We don't want to hide what we do; we want kids to see it and be able to work on it themselves and hopefully take it one step further. We just thought it would be a great learning tool for anyone interested in what we do and how we do it. If you can't play solos, then don't, but if you can? Shred away, damn it!"

CHAPTER C:
LOUD, POLITICAL AND
UNCOMPROMISING...

CANCER – ISSUE 134 (AUGUST 2005)

After ten years in remission, UK deathsters Cancer are back, and with 'Spirit In Flames' (Copro) being a convincing comeback, they are poised once more like a malignant tumour hell-bent on consuming the metal scene. Ian Glasper welcomed them home.

"Well, when we split back in '95 [after their major label debut, 'Black Faith' – IG], it was completely amicable," reckons Cancer drummer Carl Stokes, explaining away the band's original untimely demise. "We all just decided that the road at that point had stopped. There was a complete lack of understanding of extreme music from our label of the time, East West; they marketed us totally wrong, promised one thing then did another, and even stopped us playing live. That was the last straw really; it was a horrible time for me and the rest of the band, so we just said, 'Fuck it!' We had to cut off the infected limb to survive..."

Interestingly enough, the creative core of the band, guitarist/vocalist John Walker and Carl himself, both went on to study and teach their respective instruments, which has lent them an even greater understanding of musical dynamics than ever before.

"Yes, I did - and still do - teach," says Carl. "The effect on my playing has been huge; it's made me realise that even if you can play all the drum rudiments at a million miles an hour, it's still what you leave out that makes something killer or not. So, as for our own writing, I'm always trying to find interesting patterns that complement John's riffs, as opposed to covering them all with sixteen beats a second... unless that's what we want... and sometimes we do!"

With lead guitarist David Leitch and bassist Adam Richardson (formerly of Brit-punks Assert, with whom Carl also toured as a stand-in drummer) replacing - respectively – Barry Savage and Ian Buchanan, the Telford thrashers announced their resurrection with a brand new CDEP in 2003, 'Corporations', for Henley-based label, Copro, who have also just issued 'Spirit In Flames', the band's first full-length album in more than eight years. Yet despite the extended hiatus, Cancer have essentially picked up the baton right where they threw it down in disgust after being left high and dry by the fickle industry.

Cancer, 2007

"Yes, well, we can't blame anybody but ourselves," sighs Carl philosophically. "The future was there to be seen in black and white; all we wanted to do was play metal. I just think we put too much trust in someone else sorting things out for us. We've learnt our lesson this time – all we want to do is play metal and study law, haha!

"We wrote this new album the same way we always wrote before," he adds, on the creative process behind 'Spirit...'. "The two of us in a room bangin' riffs and rhythms around, only this time we demoed them all straight away onto PC to catch the vibe. So, when we entered the studio, we had the album there in demo form, and all we had to do was inject life into the thing. It took two weeks of blood, sweat and tears, but we always stayed focused on the finished product."

Still, the end results more than justify the means, 'Spirit In Flames' being an immediate, catchy take on the whole death metal vibe, loaded with primitive heaviness but not pandering to the overly technical approach that has been so dominant these past few years. The addition of some compelling grooves and smokin' hot, melodic leads just add to the impression that whilst this is indeed still Cancer, it's an exotic strain of the disease that might prove a little more difficult to shift this time.

"We have grown from that style and hold it close to our hearts," says Carl of the band's death metal roots. "But we are always looking to do something different to keep ourselves interested, to develop the Cancer sound regardless of the scene we're meant to be a part of. I've never followed anybody, none of us have, and to be honest, I don't think our face ever fitted fully, not even back in the late Eighties/early Nineties... mainly because we had so many influences in the sound. We never just played death metal; we had thrash, hardcore, grind, and lots of other stuff going on as well. When we started Cancer in 1988, I don't think the term 'death metal' was even around, but I'm not frustrated at where we are compared to everyone else. Good luck to anyone doing well, but I can't see this band being on 'Top Of The Pops' any time soon..."

All joking aside though, with so many classic metal bands reforming recently, does he really think that anyone cares that Cancer are back together again?

"I care!" he spits indignantly. "We didn't reform anyway; we were just in remission... and now we've mutated and the disease is spreading. There's still no cure for Cancer, and if there is, blow it out your ass!"

CANDLEMASS – ISSUE 53 (APRIL 1998)

Forget, for a while at least, all those new-fangled (eh?) trendy stoner rock bands, and raise your hands for the return of Candlemass, the best doom band ever to come out of Sweden – nay, the world! Ian Glasper talks to founding member Leif Edling about the band's seventh full-length album, 'Dactylis Glomerata', and discovers how being a doomster doesn't mean you lose your sense of humour...

Okay, enough already, I know some of you may be surprised to see me picking up this feature. You'd be even more surprised if you knew I pursued it with an almost obsessive ruthlessness. I was prepared to go round and round in the car park of the Red Eye with Greg Whalen if necessary, and he's a big lad, but that's how much I wanted – needed – to do this.

Candlemass

Y'see, Candlemass's 'Epicus Doomicus Metallicus' debut was nothing short of miraculous, possibly the greatest doom metal record of all time, and then the cocky bastards went and managed to top it with 'Nightfall', surely a milestone in heavy metal. It was on that tour that I caught them live, and I swear to you, one of my mates, a hardened hardcore punk with 'All Hell Breaks Loose' tattooed across his shoulder, broke down and cried on the spot when they played 'Samarithan'. You may scoff, but it's true, and didn't we all, if we only admit it, have our heart strings tugged more than just a little by 'At The Gallow's End'?

"Oh, I heard a lot of stories like that one," laughs Leif Edling, founder, and only surviving, member of this legendary combo, on the phone from his Stockholm home, "But only years after they happened. It was only really around '95 that we realised we meant that much to people. When we were actually playing in Candlemass back then, well, we thought we were an okay rock band from Sweden, and yeah, we had a fair bit of success, but we were quite naive. At that point we just didn't realise the effect we would have on people."

Of course, being legends has its minus points, too, and I guess it put you under considerable pressure when writing this new disc, not to, you know, sully that great reputation (which admittedly has already been tarnished somewhat by the disappointing 'Chapter VI' record...)?

"Well, yes. People need to know it's a different situation I'm in now, and I've matured quite a lot as a person, and we don't sound that much like the old Candlemass, so doing this new record is quite a risk. To be honest, I'm quite afraid," laughs Leif. "I have no idea how people will take this. They expect such a lot, and actually I'm not sure whether I can live up to those high expectations."

Do you get sick of hearing about Messiah Marcolin (their best-known vocalist), and those glory days of 'Nightfall'?

"Oh yeah, you can say that again. I'm a single person at the moment, so I go out quite a lot, and I literally can't go out in Stockholm without five or six people coming up to me, and asking about Messiah, and will there ever be a reunion, blahblahblah. It's pretty disturbing really, but I mean, I love the fact that people still care. Rather that than be forgotten about, that would be sad. At least they don't spit in my face and call me a cunt!"

Okay, I can take a hint, but before we move on, let's just set the record straight once and for all – was a reunion of that classic line-up ever on the cards? Even a little bit?

"That's a very long story," chuckles Leif. Actually, he laughs a helluva lot for a guy responsible for such monoliths to melancholy as 'Dark Reflections', and seems blessed with a genuine and contagious sense of humour. "I had a band called 'Abstract Algebra', and we did one record, and were about to do another, but we fucking failed completely when we came to record it. It sounded like shit, worse than a demo, so we needed to record it again, only better, but in the meantime, my singer joined Yngwie Malmsteem's band, and my guitarists took off to Memento Mori, or wherever, so I didn't have a band, and the album wasn't finished... so I rang Music For Nations, and said,

'Sorry, things aren't going quite as planned' [that laugh again], and they suggested I record another Candlemass album. I liked the idea, and rang up the old guys, but they all had other obligations, so I asked 'em if I could go ahead anyway, and they said, 'Sure, go ahead...' I made it all a lot heavier and now it's a Candlemass record..."

Which brings us back nicely to where we started, and that new record, entitled 'Dactylis Glomerata'. Now, reading Leif's comments, you could be forgiven for thinking this was a total departure, but nothing could be further from the truth. In fact, songs like

'Karthago' and 'I Still See The Black' sound like they could have just stepped off that majestic debut record, being monstrously heavy, and defiantly solemn and moody. Bjorn Flodqvist's vocals recall Leif's own impassioned warblings (Yes, Mr. Edling himself actually sang for Candlemass before they got in the big guy in the monk outfit), and the atmosphere is recreated so perfectly, it's like they've never been away. But then you get one of the more experimental tracks, and while they're not treacherously at odds with the Candlemass legacy, they'll certainly have you scratching yer heads.

"If only you'd heard the shit I was doing in Abstract Algebra, you would wonder just what the fuck I was playing at," says Leif gleefully. "It was very avant-garde. Maybe one day we ought to release those tapes, and you'll see I was into some very difficult stuff, very violent, and discordant, and this new record is that stuff combined with that old Candlemass feel. We've made it very heavy and dark, and made it so people can actually listen to it. Listen to a song like 'Abstract Sun', but imagine it much more discordant, and that was how we started... and this is where we landed up. AA were totally off-the-wall, but now, well, it's kinda like avant-garde doom!"

It's a very diverse album, pulling in influences from all sorts of unusual places.

"Yeah, I think you should release the stuff you record as soon as you record it, 'cos what you put down on tape is like a documentary of how you feel, of where you're at, at a moment in time. You're letting people know how you feel right now. At the moment I'm on a real retro trip... I love Uriah Heep, I'm listening to them all the time, and you fuckin' hate me for that, but I can't help it!"

But you like Snapcase, too (Leif let this slip earlier before the interview), so you can't be all bad! It's my turn to laugh manically now.

"Yeah, and I love Unsane, and I love Slapshot, and Fu Manchu, basically anything heavy, anything original, anything that isn't mainstream - I fuckin' hate mainstream. I love emotional music, done with feeling, anything that isn't generic. Music should express something, anything - it doesn't matter what, as long as it expresses something. Oh, I dunno," he gives up, and collapses into helpless laughter again. "I'm too hungover to know what I want to say..."

Oh, shit, what's my excuse, then?! Moving swiftly on, your new line-up has some surprising names amongst it, not least of all, certain ex-members of Carcass and Europe... how's that for a spread of influences, then?

"Going back to what I just said, music is all about expression, but it's also about having fun, and friendship. Why play music with people you don't like? I want to have a good time. I don't care if I never make a single buck off this band, but I wanna have fun with some of my mates while I do it. Mike [Amott] is a great guitar player – he's in Arch Enemy, a fuckin' brilliant band, the best death metal band out there, and he's also in Spiritual Beggars, another great band, but most importantly of all, he's my friend. And Ian Hanglund is a brilliant drummer, but people don't realise it 'cos he did that fuckin' Europe shit, but he's a good bloke, too."

And they're his words, not mine - yes, a Swede did say 'bloke'! Obviously his time spent touring over here has rubbed off on him. But seriously, despite his easy-going, likeable nature, there is a darker side to Leif Edling, and thank god, 'cos otherwise I don't think heavy metal would ever have been enriched by Candlemass in the first place. A song like 'I Still See The Black' on the new album seems to suggest that he still finds inspiration in the more depressing aspects of life.

"Oh, I dunno, I just can't seem to write about happy stuff. Life isn't like that, is it? Life is shit, really, and the sooner you realise that, the better. Existence is not a bed of roses, and you have to deal with it the best you can. It's no good just being a miserable cunt. This stinking fuckin' planet is full of people who hate each other, there's no humanism any more, people have forgotten about everything except money.

"What happened to holding the door for the person behind you? Little things like that, just having some respect for others. You can do what you want inside your own apartment, you can want to jump off the next bridge you see – you hate yourself, you hate your life - but when you walk out of

that fuckin' door, you have a responsibility to treat people with some respect...”

CANNIBAL CORPSE – ISSUE 30 (MAY 1996)

Cannibal Corpse – by Albert Licano

With a repertoire cheesier than a French larder, Cannibal Corpse have wormed their way firmly into the sick hearts of the death metal masses. Now, with vocalist Chris Barnes replaced by new kid on the chopping-block George 'Corpsegrinder' Fisher, can the Corpse still cut it? Ian Glasper wrinkles his nose as bassist Alex Webster talks about censorship, films, taboos and why this is one band more than content to stay sick...

Cannibal Corpse, 1996, pic by Stephanie Cabral

If you want clever-ass progressive death metal, then I suggest you turn the page right now! If, however, you can stomach the slime-drenched salivating rabid outbursts of the most frenzied die-hards, come on down to the basement, I've got something to show you...

Cannibal Corpse's (hilarious) name was long synonymous with, well, how can I put it, cheese, each record somehow managing to top the previous in terms of putrid, pile-driving thrash, each lyric plumbing new depths of depravity. The stinkin' mounds of unmentionable innards that most death metal bands didn't dare disturb, the Corpse plunged into with relish, gobbling until full, then disgorging their fly-blown vomit into the upturned faces of their hungry fans.

Ahem, let's not get carried away here. Where was I? Oh yes, the cheese! Before we knew it, our loveable heroes had sold themselves half a million albums, 'The Bleeding' album had gained them unprecedented credibility, and the blackened sky of the underworld was the limit. Then, disaster! The blood-crazed hordes were shocked when the band kicked out longstanding and much respected (in death metal circles, at least) 'vocalist' Chris Barnes, who went off to concentrate on his side project ('til then) Six Feet Under. But despair ye not, gore-fiends, a new growler has been found...

"Well, his name's George," explains talkative bassist Alex Webster, "Or Corpsegrinder as everyone calls him. He came from the band Monstrosity, and he also used to be in a band called Corpsegrinder, hence his nickname, y'know? We'd known him for a while, and we'd always liked Monstrosity, and we'd always thought George was one of the best frontmen we'd ever seen. He had a really strong voice and a good sense of rhythm, and he was a cool guy, so when the time came when we had to make a change, he was the first person we thought of."

There must have been considerable pressure to step into such well-established shoes as Chris!

"He felt pressured to perform well, sure! It's kinda like a new band since he got here. He hasn't thought so much about replacing Chris as just doing good himself. He wasn't worried about doing better than Chris, 'cos for us there was no question he was better, or else we wouldn't have asked him to do it. If we had liked the way Chris had been singing, we wouldn't have asked him to leave!"

No Cannibal Corpse interview would be complete without touching on those lyrics. I wonder if they ever worry about trying to top the gore that's gone before? "It's hard to top it... but I guess you can always get worse," he laughs, before confessing, "Some of the lyrics on this one were a little rushed - rhythmically we did a good job, but some of the concepts are nothing special. I wrote a lot of them, and I think they're cool - they wouldn't be on the album if they weren't good, but it's definitely along the lines of our other albums. The musicality [wait! Time out, surely!] of the lyrics came out a lot better, but the subject matter is not that far off what we've already done. Maybe when we have more time - we actually kicked out Chris during recording, and had to

Cannibal Corpse, by Albert Licano

re-write all those lyrics 'cos we didn't want to use anything by Chris - we can stretch it in different directions.

"One song I'm pretty proud of is 'Disfigured', 'cos that's a lil' bit different. That's about this guy who hates himself; he's some sort of killer or whatever, so one day he decides to carve himself up instead of killing other people. He's looking in the mirror - that's why he hates himself, 'cos he's an ugly bastard - and he cuts himself up and sets himself on fire..."

If only more killers would follow his example! There's definitely a vicarious fascination with serial killers right now. "Yeah, we've met a lot of kids who are really fascinated with the whole thing, and that's why we wanna dig into that whole deal, y'know? I think to study them is one thing...

but to hero worship them? These are people who've made huge mistakes in their lives and have hurt a lot of people, and they aren't good role models, y'know?"

'Orgasm Through Torture' sounds an interesting one, too! "Yeah, that's Paul's! [Mazurkiewicz- drums] We decided that all of the lyrics on the previous albums always had women being the victims or whatever, so we thought there's gotta be some sick woman who can pull off something awful sick, too! I've definitely met a few girls who seemed capable of losing it like that," Alex laughs.

"Now, the vast majority of our audience are male listeners, so what's gonna gross them out more than hearing about a guy getting his dick ripped off, right? We want to get a reaction if we can!"

Some of your lyrics have been seen as misogynistic, so it's good to put the other

174

perspective. "Sure! A lot of that was Chris's lyrics, but I'm not trying to pass blame or anything, 'cos we all consented to use them. We just wanted our stuff to be horrifying if possible... sometimes we succeeded in doing some scary shit, some of it didn't work as well. I think where Chris was coming from was, y'know how in a lotta horror movies, they have a child who's getting scared shitless, like in 'The Shining', and the more helpless the victim, the scarier it is... and generally women aren't as strong as men."

Uh, getting onto thin ice here, Alex! In anticipation of a slew of letters from our female readers, I push on... is there any topic too taboo even for Cannibal Corpse?

"Well," Alex pauses for thought, and just as I think he's going to say 'no', "Child pornography is pretty disgusting, and something we wouldn't want to touch on, although Chris wrote that song 'Necropaedophile' for the third album, but that was such a ridiculous song it didn't seem to be that bad! I mean, it was bad, but that kinda stuff, you won't be seeing in the future. And with all that bad stuff we've written about, and I'm not condemning it, but just like a guy who makes a movie or writes a book, we're not saying 'go out and do this', we're just painting a picture to provoke a reaction. We're just a bunch of musicians, who happen to be doing horror music – death metal!"

Do you enjoy getting up the noses of censorship groups, or is it just a pain in the ass?

"Hey, it's cool when they can't do anything to us," Alex laughs. "It's all funny until you start losing money! Like when we have a tour set up and you miss four shows, but you still have to pay for the bus on those days. And we're not rich, we still have rent to pay, although we're one of the few death metal bands able to get by. There's only about ten of us in the world, as in ten death metal bands out of all those thousands who can actually live off their music alone. And to keep that going we have to really work hard to keep ourselves known, and it's very hard. It fucks up tours when we have problems getting our stuff in stores.

"I can understand our lyrics getting a rating like the cinema," Alex concedes, "An R-rating or summat. I can understand that. But they don't censor books at all, and there's definitely books that could be X-rated for violence that you can buy even if you're three years old. It's so weird what they decide to censor and what they don't."

Are you aware of the bigger political picture of the censorship issue? "It's so hard to tell where everyone's coming from," he sighs. "We know Bob Dole is not our friend – he's made it perfectly clear that he doesn't like our band – and he might wind up being President! I saw him on a show here called 'Beat The Press', and he was on there with our CD cover, saying how terrible is it. He's using it as one of his issues in his campaigning - he wants more moral standards in the entertainment industry. But moral stuff just isn't that entertaining! I don't think he cares really, and he definitely helped us sell more records! It was all done just to get money, 'cos the Christian Coalition fund his campaign, so he's gotta address issues they're concerned about. He must have gotten a list off them or something, 'cos I'm sure he didn't just go looking through record stores. There's definitely higher forces at play in this issue!"

Since their cheese-drenched but face-ripping 1990 debut 'Eaten Back To Life', the band

Cannibal Corpse

have improved upon their production and their playing, but never attempted anything particularly ambitious with their sound. Sure, new album 'Vile' features a new vocalist, but it is essentially your standard Corpse fare. Business (as brutally) as normal... and I wonder if they are deliberately

flying in the face of the current trend that's seen so many once-rabid death metal bands go all rockin' and melodic on us?

"The thing is we love that kind of music, and we've finally got to the point where we're good enough on our instruments and we're good enough at song-writing to really write the music we've always wanted to play, which is fast, heavy death metal. And hey, it's always in the back of our minds that this is what got us here, this is why people like us... they don't want us to add industrial samples or whatever, and neither do we. I don't have a problem with other bands wanting to expand, but it's not our bag!"

The danger is you'll paint yourselves into a corner you can't get out of. "Sure! But it's a corner we want to be in, and we're content to paint ourselves into it! It also creates an artistic challenge, to keep it interesting within those boundaries, to keep it fresh every album when we're doing the same thing every record... if you see what I mean! It sounds impossible, but I think we do okay, when you consider that stylistically we're doing death metal not a whole lot different to the first album - only better! And every album we've got to be a better band, and at least we're reliable," he adds laughing. "One guy who writes a mag in America said he was expecting something different, and I was like, 'It's us, man, it's Cannibal Corpse... what d'you expect?'"

So, it's through sheer doggedness that you've shaken off the novelty tag with which you were seemingly lumbered?

"I think people can feel out phonies, and people know that we genuinely love the music we play. If we wanted to make money, we wouldn't be doing this style, and people can hear that in the music. Maybe there are better bands, this way or that way, but people can tell we're sincere! We play this six nights a week, 'cos we want to! It's also a lot of fun playing death metal, too, and whenever it stops being fun, we'll take a break. But I can't see that happening right now, 'cos I'm really looking forward to playing the new songs live..."

Thinking about the Corpse live, I recently went to see the mighty GWAR in Birmingham, and what an experience! Onstage decapitations, abortions, fire-breathing, and God knows what else! I left covered in fake bile, blood, puke and cum, and raised a few eyebrows in the chippy afterwards - great fun! I wonder if Cannibal Corpse have ever been tempted by the theatrical approach employed by their label-mates?

"We always talk about it, but it would be a lot of money, and we would probably fuck it up!" laughs Alex. 'l can see us being off cue, l just know we'd fuck things up. We're a little disorganised when it comes to that kinda shit. We do have a set list, but it's such a frenzy, and we're so wired by the music, we don't have time to think about much else. We'd probably goof it up, and end up looking stupid..."

Your songs would also translate great into some OTT videos! "God, if we had like a massive budget...," his voice trails off, and I can almost imagine the blood-spattered epics he's picturing

in his mind's eye. "We are doing a video, for 'Devoured By Vermin', but we've got almost no budget, 'cos we're not gonna get any airplay in America 'cos there's no metal show here. We don't have the money to get a million rats, so we'll have to do something more abstract. There's so much stuff that could be done with it! I really wish some horror film maker would use a coupla death metal riffs, maybe something with no vocals on it, some of that real slow stuff, like that English band, Anathema..."

Of course, Cannibal Corpse themselves have already appeared in a major movie. But was it a violent, mayhem-filled blood 'n' guts flick? No, it was fucking 'Ace Ventura – Pet Detective'! Surely there's scarier movies they'd like to get on?

"Sure," laughs the amiable bassist (for someone the Christian Coalition would have you

177

believe boils babies for breakfast, Alex Webster seems an awfully nice bloke). "I like Clive Barker a lot, because it's so weird; there's so much cool shit in his movies, so many cool effects 'n' stuff. The first two 'Hellraiser' movies were a pretty cool take on the whole horror thing."

Do you prefer the splatter movies or the more moody, atmospheric and psychological horror?

"They're both good for different reasons. It's like different kinds of death metal. Like Cannibal Corpse..."

Yeah, you're the 'Texas Chainsaw Massacre' of death metal... "Yeah, we're the splatter side, and then there's some bands that get the horror thing going. Like Morbid Angel, their song 'Hatework' is super heavy and scary, but in the atmospheric way. It's the same with movies, too. I like 'The Shining', but I like 'The Evil Dead' films, too. And those 'Necromantik' films from Germany? Those are pretty disturbing."

What about snuff films and shit like 'Faces Of Death'? "I gotta wonder at some of the stuff on those. They were supposedly done before camcorders got popular, and yet there's a lot of stuff on there where they have two different camera angles! We've always come from the entertainment angle, and it's a lot easier to watch a horror/gore film if you know at the back of your head that it's not real! But if someone has actually suffered, and it winds up as entertainment, then that's not good!"

Despite flirting with mainstream moviedom, on the aptly-titled 'Vile', the Corpse show no compromise; no quarter is given to those who'd like to see a little more melody or a little less speed.

Unless popular tastes change drastically, they've probably peaked as far as popularity goes, destined (but quite happy) to remain underground. Is that where Alex prefers to see his death metal, its intensity undiluted by major label pressures?

"We were only saying the other day that it'd be really nice to make just a teeny bit more money in this scene. A lot of the bands we're friends with are so broke, it really sucks! We do try to take some of those bands out with us when we can. If there were more opportunities for everyone, if death metal had a bit more leverage, it'd make all our lives a little easier. Y'know, if you're a death metal band and people don't know who you are, you're in trouble right now, you're in big trouble. Because there's no way you can get on a tour, clubs don't want to pay you, everything's hard.

"I don't care about being rich, seriously," Alex concludes, "But a little bit more padding would be nice. I wanna carry on making a living doing this. I love playing and I love music, so it's a real joy to be able to do that."

CANVAS - ISSUE 80 (JULY 2000)

Canvas are one of those bands that can only really be termed 'UKHC' by association; they play a lot of UKHC shows, and they're on Household Name, one of the leading UKHC labels. To simply tag them as 'hardcore' is a bit of a misnomer though, because

178

Canvas, courtesy of Kat @ Household Name

they are pretty much out there - way out there, sometimes - on their own, pushing back the boundaries of what's acceptable in extreme music. I tracked them down to their lair deep beneath Leeds, and tried to get to grips with their strange methods.

So, do you actually perceive yourself as a hardcore band then? Either sonically or ideologically?

Gaz: "It's difficult to say really. I suppose sonically we are, but only because that's the closest thing to it. I don't think we're particularly archetypal. Ideologically, I'm not sure if it's fair to say yes or no, because we don't have any band ideology as such. We are all very different people with very different beliefs and attitudes. I think the idea that there is a common hardcore ideology is a myth, anyway. I reckon that fifty percent of the hardcore bands I've met are well dodgy as people."

Dan: "Most of the bands I see are so boring, both musically and as performers. My impression is that the ethos of too many hardcore bands is to just copy others - and I don't think we fit into that at all."

I have to admit that I don't actually 'like' Canvas as such - but I can appreciate what you do! Is this a common reaction? And do you deliberately cause such confused responses?

Gaz: "Yes, I think it is quite a common reaction. For example, last year, we played at a festival which was almost exclusively pop-punk and emo, and we expected to fall flat on our faces, but the audience seemed just as into us as they were into Spy Versus Spy and Month of Birthdays. I can guarantee that the vast majority of those people were not into our garbled rubbish, but they clearly appreciated it and enjoyed the set.

"We get a lot of people who don't just listen to our genre of music coming up and saying

Canvas, courtesy of Kat @ Household Name

they thought we were really good after we've just played, and to me that's much more rewarding than compliments from hardcore fans."

Dan: "Yes, our songs are complicated. Yes, when we have a bad night or a bad mix, we sound like experimental fucking nonsense. But no, we don't write songs to confuse people. I think that when you've heard most of our songs a few times, they're not as weird as you think. Although I do know what you mean, and I hope that not everyone merely 'appreciates' us – because wouldn't that just mean that we're a really shit band?"

Your new album 'Lost In Rock' has more of an expansive feel to it, whereas your debut was much more oppressive/claustrophobic; was this a natural progression, or a calculated one?

Karl: "Firstly, I have to say that I am so proud of 'Lost in Rock', and that in my mind it couldn't have been done any better, unless we'd had a little more time in the recording process maybe. The reason that it's more expansive is that we've all changed as people in some way since we started, in the fact that we've all broadened our minds as to what we listen to and let influence us.

"Some bands keep churning out the same album over and over again, which isn't always a bad thing, but I think we have progressed by always wanting to better each release; sometimes by making it more technical, sometimes more simple... sometimes even giving it all a 'concept feel', which is what we've done with this new one."

What role does the band play in your lives? All-consuming passion or amusing distraction?

Gaz: "Amusing distraction. There are much more important things in life than making a racket. It's great fun, but so are a million other things."

Dan: "Sometimes I think Canvas is the worst thing to ever happen to me! But in the studio, during a show, on the bus on the way to work listening to a new recording – these

are the times l remember why l spend all my money on petrol, cymbals and takeaways."
Do you enjoy fucking with audiences' preconceptions?

Gaz: "Oh god, yes. There is no thrill greater than turning up to play a gig where you're billed as 'Leeds 6 Metalcore', and then watching these big sweaty blokes with furrowed brows and sleeveless Madball T-shirts completely failing to find a suitable beat to stomp their feet to!"

THE CASUALTIES – ISSUE 118 (APRIL 2004)

Casualties 2019, by Morat

The Casualties' last album, 2001's 'Die Hards', was an accurate self-description. Their new album, 'On The Front Line', sees them setting even higher standards for modern American punk, yet not afraid to ring a few changes in the process. Ian Glasper bore witness to the revolution.

New York hardcore has featured strongly in our pages ever since the magazine's inception. But let's never forget that city's fine tradition in punk rock, either, still burning strong within The Casualties, surely one of the best new punk bands of the last ten years. Look no further than their brand new album, 'On The Front Line', for proof. Unfairly dismissed by their right-on detractors who can't see past the retro haircuts, there's no denying that these guys kick ass, and lots of it. Tighter and more raging than ever before, 'On The Front Line' blows the piss out of anything Rancid have done since '96.

Casualties, by Will Binks

"We spent a lot of money on this new record, so I think that it's our best one by far. We're finally getting out of the garage," laughs guitarist Jake. "We've always been a live band before anything else, and the previous studio recordings lacked that energy. But this one is pretty damn close to how we sound onstage. This was our first time with a proper producer, so we sound more together than ever."

Said producer was none other than living hardcore legend, Bill Stevenson of Black Flag/Descendents fame, who recorded the band at his Colorado studio, The Blasting Room. "He's an excellent drummer, so he worked our drummer really hard," Jake recalls, "But he worked all of us hard really, and managed to bring the best out of us as a band. We had a few songs that we were pretty pleased with as they were, but he had a lot of suggestions that changed them for the better. An outside opinion is invaluable when you're in the studio, 'cos in a band you just get too close to your own material to see what sometimes needs to be done."

The new record sees the band not only making tremendous steps musically but lyrically too, and let's face it there's plenty to be outraged about in this day and age. Songs about quaffing homebrew just don't cut it anymore.

"The first few years, we were just taking the piss really, and having a laugh," admits Jake. "We were just a drunken punk band, but the political climate has changed, and that shit is affecting everybody now. And seeing as we're getting popular, we feel a responsibility to the young kids that turn up at our shows to have an opinion, to say something worthwhile with our music.

"I like to party as much as the next guy, but we've lost a lot of friends to addiction over the years, and, although we're not going to start telling people how to live their lives, we have certain things we feel strongly about that we're going to say with The Casualties."

And they say them in style too. Opening with a rousing rally cry, the new album busts straight into the awesome title track that marries that abrasive UK82 sound we all know and love to intricate bass runs and vicious, metallic (in tone, at least) guitars. Coupled with the superb production, it all makes for a storming album that should see the band recruiting for their enthusiastic Casualties Army worldwide.

"It's great that we're still so excited about the band after all these years," enthuses Jake. "We're probably busier now than we've ever been before, and it's a dream come true to be able to live this lifestyle; touring around the world and playing punk rock every day, then getting home and being able to pay all the bills, and still have a little money left over to last you through until you go on tour again. We feel very privileged, especially as we see some of our friends in bands that have to get jobs to make ends meet... so whenever we can, we take some of them out on tour with us as roadies.

"I signed up for punk rock as a lifestyle; it's not a passing phase for us, we're here for the duration. A lot of punks just pass through, they're here for a year or two, and then move onto the next big thing, but for every ten kids like that, you'll get one or two that stick with it and find something positive for themselves in the scene. It's for those kids that we're flying the flag for hardcore punk, and we'll be doing it for many more years yet, I promise you that."

CATARACT – ISSUE 128 (FEBRUARY 2005)

Having brought Swiss heavyweights Cataract into their ranks, Metal Blade are rapidly becoming the first stop for brutal, metal-bolstered Eurocore, and new album 'With Triumph Comes Loss' looks set to become a flagship for the art of uncompromising crossover. Ian Glasper stepped into the ring with guitarist Simon Fullemann.

As if 'Great Days Of Vengeance', their 2003 album for Lifeforce, wasn't heavy enough, Switzerland's Cataract have upped the ante yet again for 'With Triumph Comes Loss'. Not only is it their all-important third album but also their high-profile debut for genre giants, Metal Blade. One could be forgiven for assuming the band had been feeling the pressure to deliver the goods recently...

"No, not at all," smiles their amicable guitarist, Simon Fullemann, sounding justifiably pleased with himself. "We signed the contract with Metal Blade after we'd written all these new songs, so we never knew that they would be so important for us. We just knew that we were writing for our third record, and that's the most important one, whichever label you're on, so the only pressure was pressure that we put on ourselves, but there was none from anywhere outside the band."

Cataract, by Manuel Vargas

And just how did a humble hardcore band from Switzerland end up on Metal Blade? "We started out on an American label [Ferret, for their 'Golem' debut in 2000], but it wasn't working out too well because of distance and time differences, so we switched to Lifeforce in Germany, but even then we were talking to bigger labels, although we didn't take them too seriously then. And sure enough, Lifeforce did really well with 'Great Days...'. That record attracted us a lot of new interest from metal kids, and once Metal Blade got a copy, they called me up and offered to work with us just a few days later. Of course, they're one of the most respected metal labels in the world, so when we had an offer from them there was no way that we could refuse - it's a dream come true!"

Whilst 'With Triumph...' isn't exactly a ground-breaking release, it's certainly weighted with more than enough molten potential to suggest that Cataract may have a seminal album in them yet. Equal parts (early) Hatebreed and Slayer, it's a devastatingly brutal slab of to-the-point metalcore, with eerie, discordant guitar harmonies providing little respite from the bloody-minded bludgeon that is at the core of the Cataract sound. There's no denying the satisfying ferocity of the riffing to be had here, and the whole thing benefits immensely from a phat Antfarm production job courtesy of the ever-reliable Tue Madsen, the man responsible for all those monstrous CDs from Barcode and Born From Pain.

"The first few records were done with an old friend of ours because he understood what we wanted to do, but even as we wrote these new songs it was clear that we had to do something different, try something new. And every record we'd heard that Tue had done made it obvious that he was the one that we wanted to work with this time. Because, although it's really important that we write our songs in our own environment, it's equally important that we work with someone who allows us to recreate that feeling in the studio. And thankfully when he heard the demo of these songs, he was totally into it as well."

Despite its metal credentials, and song titles such as 'Reborn From Fire' and 'Hallow Horns', don't be deceived into thinking that Cataract have sold the scene that spawned them down the river. Nothing could be further from the truth, in fact, with the band still making great efforts to imbue their music with a positive message, and taking the time out to explain that message whenever the opportunity arises.

"Totally, we are nothing else if not a hardcore band. Two things help differentiate a hardcore band from a metal band – where you and your thoughts come from, and what words you choose to write down to represent them. Most hardcore bands try to speak directly to the audience and to say what they think, but we try to be a little different. We still try to say exactly what we think, but we also try to leave our lyrics open enough that metal kids who may never have listened to a hardcore band before can also relate to them as well. And being on Metal Blade has exposed us to a lot of new kids; we're reaching so many kids now who've never heard or read these kinds of lyrics before, and that's a very positive thing for us, to help break down a few barriers."

Cause For Alarm by Naki

Ian Glasper really did give us Cause For Alarm when we asked him to interview said NYHC band to coincide with the release of their new album, 'Beneath the Wheel' for Victory, while on tour with them in Europe, but the doughnut forgot to pack his Dictaphone. So, generous to a fault as we are, all we gave him for Xmas was a deadline, and our New Year's Resolution was to kick his sorry ass if he missed it. As if he would...

"In a way, I am Cause For Alarm; I book most of our shows, I sort out all the merchandise, I got our record deal together... and after doing all that hard work, I have to admit that I have a very short
amount of patience with people who have other priorities, or who would really prefer to be in other bands, or who let their egos get in the way of playing the music. I'm not going to let them stop me, y'know?"
So says Keith Burkhardt, vocalist with (and only remaining original member of) those unsung legends of NYHC, Cause For Alarm, as we discuss the apparent revolving-door policy he has in his band as regards fellow members. They come and go with the regularity of a whore's doorbell, and some could imagine that, just maybe, Keith is a little difficult to work with...?
"l just got to the point where, if a guitar player couldn't tour, or a bass player couldn't make rehearsals, I wasn't prepared to let that slow me down in doing what I wanted to do. In the beginning, I always wanted CFA to be this tight bunch of mates, a band who shared a common goal, the same ideals, who were all the best of friends, but I think

that's a really rare quality in most bands. You do get some bands, like my friends in Texas Is The Reason, who say, 'Well, this is the band, and if anyone leaves, then it's all over...', but I couldn't really ever apply that attitude to my own band. As for me being hard to get along with? Well, I guess some people might perceive me as being somewhat arrogant, but that's because I like to keep myself to myself a lot of the time when I'm on tour. I have a lot of friends on the road, and so I'll go hang out with them, but that doesn't mean that I'm trying to distance myself from the rest of the band or anything." And I can vouch that the man speaks the truth, ladies and gentleman, having just recently spent two fun weeks in his company when Stampin' Ground toured the toilets of Europe with CFA. When I first met Keith, he did seem distracted, preferring to spend his time reading and drinking tea, rather than twatting about with us Limeys, but a common love of Typhoo soon threw us all together, and if there's an easier-to-like bloke on this planet then I've yet to meet him.

Of course, it would have made sense to do this interview whilst on the road together, but you know how it is – the best laid plans of mice and men, and all that - so in the end I had to call him up at his home in New York, New York, on Christmas Eve of all days, and with us both still having some last-minute shopping to do! So, let's cut to the chase, or rather their steaming new album for Victory, 'Beneath The Wheel', and more specifically the interesting liner notes, penned by Keith himself, that seem to reveal a certain disdain for many aspects of the hardcore scene.

"Uh, I guess that it really comes down to me being, at this stage of the game, at this point in my life, more interested in just playing music. I wrote some of those things out of frustration, and they shouldn't be taken totally literally... I mean, if people want to think of us as a hardcore band, as part of that whole scene, that's absolutely fine by me, but in this day and age it's almost impossible to define just what hardcore is.

"On one hand, I would define HC as a particular style of music, that has totally developed and grown, and turned into many different styles, a lot of them totally different to how I would have defined it back in the late Seventies and early Eighties... then you have people who say that hardcore is a specific attitude - that Earth Crisis are a metal band but with hardcore ethics. The thing is, there's lots of other kinds of bands, indie and folk bands for example, who have homogenous ideals, so are they hardcore bands too? I find it really hard to pin it all down anymore! There's so many subdivisions - sXe hardcore, vegan hardcore, sXe vegan hardcore, grindcore, youthcrew hardcore... and at the end of the day all I'm interested in doing is playing music to as many people as possible."

Well, for what it's worth, I think you're definitely a hardcore band, by virtue of your sheer energy and speed, but I don't think you deserve the old school tag you've been shackled with. You might very well be old school 'cos you were around back in 'the day', when NYHC was still in its infancy (possibly still in the womb, in fact), but 'Beneath The Wheel' reveals a band who are actually subtly cutting edge.

"Totally," enthuses Keith. "If you listen to our first 7", and then the split with Warzone, and then 'Cheaters And The Cheated', and so on, we've always progressed. Especially

187

Cause For Alarm by Naki

now, on the new album, which is just a mixture of all sorts of music, basically a crossover rock 'n' roll record. People have been comparing it to all sorts of crazy shit that I had never thought of, even the Chilli Peppers and Motorhead... but those are people who aren't into hardcore, who hear things differently. It's only kids into hardcore who dismiss us as old school. Besides, we were only really old school back when we did that first 7" in '82..."

And back then it was probably called new school, anyway!

"Yeah, right," he laughs, "Exactly. People have also got to remember that a lot of the people who are writing the music in this band hardly listen to hardcore at all. For example, Jay Banks, who wrote the new record - although he played in Sheer Terror, he's way more into rock 'n' roll, and metal, even crazy shit like Savatage..."

Well, whatever the story behind it, and call it what you like, 'Beneath The Wheel' is one of the strongest, and freshest, releases on Victory for a long while, literally bubbling with a quiet intensity, and burning with some razor riffing, all propelled by a lightening-tight rhythm section. And then there's Keith's vocals, not to mention his eccentric stage presence, that really help set the band apart from the rest of the East Coast moshers and their macho posturing.

"I take that as a compliment, because I totally despise all that macho shit. I'm not into that tuff guy thing at all, and the more I see of it, the more it turns my stomach, and the more it makes me want to distance myself from that whole scene. It's so totally bogus most of the time, anyway, just some fake image cultivated for the sake of a few sales.

"I much prefer mixed bills, playing with bands of many different styles, and that's what you'll see at the shows I book over here. I try to mix it up, to attract a varied crowd, and then the show isn't dominated by all these little tough guys running around doing kung fu and enacting their silly dramas."

CEREBRAL SCAR – ISSUE 270 (MAY 2016)

"This is pure metal," declares vocalist Mark Fieldhouse unashamedly, when pushed as to how his new band Cerebral Scar differ from Freebase, the UKHC act he is better known for fronting. "I am deliberately singing in a different tone to Freebase, but still bringing forward the hardcore aggression and vibe... I suppose that runs through my veins naturally! That's probably why I have heard us described as 'thrashcore'...

"It's definitely way more technical than Freebase. For me I didn't want to churn out just 'another' hardcore band. I was looking to wade into more metallic waters, and with [guitarist] Lee [Pidford]'s abilities it was the perfect opportunity. Also, when [drummer] Rhys came along, we knew we could push the boundaries a bit further."

"I'm just a bit older and wiser these days," adds Lee, "But it's a continuation for me from where I left off with Gutworm. I think we touch on various genres; we have heavy bits, fast bits, some of Mark's aggression... I think we have a very good metallic recipe, but we are not limiting our crossover appeal at all. I love the riffs of Testament and early Slayer, and those fast catchy grooves."

Cerebral Scar live Milton Keynes, by Aga Hairesis

Cerebral Scar, by Daniel Bebber

"I grew up in the thrash metal whirlwind of the Eighties," continues Mark, of his primary influences for Cerebral Scar, "And it was a time that changed my life. It helped me venture into crossover music, and quickly onto hardcore as I heard 'Cause For Alarm' and 'The Age Of Quarrel' [by Agnostic Front and Cro-Mags respectively, of course].

"In Cerebral Scar, I'm personally looking towards Exodus and D.R.I... that crisp delivery, aggressive and harsh, and straight to the point. Lyrically? Well, if you take a song like 'Pit Pass', for example, it's a kind of story, documenting what went on over those magical years... a little bit of nostalgia, I suppose.

"'Thrashback' is similar in content [check out the video!], but also about hanging onto your beliefs; there's even a verse which pays homage to some of those classics from the past. But then 'Pessimistic Regret' has more of a hardcore vibe, as it deals with real life attitude... 'Don't hold onto the baggage of your past; never regret life, it goes too fast...'"

With a three-track Russ Russell-produced CDEP, 'No Remorse Required', out now on Mosh Tuneage Records, Cerebral Scar are determined to make their name the old-fashioned way, thrashing their way round the underground circuit, letting their no-nonsense crossover do all the talking for them.

"With Cerebral Scar we will play anywhere with anyone," confirms Mark. "There is no rock star bullshit with this band. We are music lovers, and we intend to play as much as possible... so don't be afraid to ask us, people! It's also another way of going back to the old school; not just the music, but the attitudes and lifestyles etc. Freebase is more picky and select with the gigs, but that's a good thing in its own right. Cerebral Scar is a band starting from scratch, so we have to put the leg work in, and we are not afraid of that.

"An old buddy once said to me, Cerebral Scar is old school thrash bolstered with death metal rhythms and hardcore aggression, and that's us in a nutshell! We want to see the dance floor moving, we want to see people slamming and diving, we want to bring back that old school gig vibe... having fun, yet respecting all. Just like it used to be! Drink and thrash!"

CHAOS UK - ISSUE 11 (AUGUST 1994)

I recently spoke to newest Chaos UK member, bassist Marvin, about what it's like to be the new kid in the punkest band on Planet Earth, mere days before they left for two-and-a-half months of touring over in the States, following the release of their last album, '100% Two Fingers In The Air Punk Rock', some time ago...

What's been happening with the line-up of Chaos UK, and how did you come to join the band? "About two years ago, Vic joined on guitar from Nausea (the New York punk band), and drummer Pat got poached from The Sun Tribe, a Bristol indie band. I joined eighteen months ago; at the audition I had to stick a beer bottle up my ass."

Did you have to play bass at all? "Yeah, a bit at the end, but I'd been accepted before then... for being a fucking idiot, I suppose."

Does having Victor over in New York pose any problems? "Nah, Victor enjoys travelling

Chaos UK, 1994

anyhow, and he'll come to Europe for three months and we'll tour, and then he'll go home for a bit, hop back and forth. We haven't seen Vic, god bless him, since last September in Germany. I hope he's still alive."

Does he know any hardcore legends in N.Y.C.? "Oh yeah, damn straight, Sick Of It All are from the same area as him, and he can remember them in their Iron Maiden T-shirts looking lovely and heavy metal. Yeah, he's known them all. The guitarist out of Samhain, Glenn Danzig's old band, used to nag him to join 'em, but he wouldn't, on the grounds he didn't want to play with Danzig. He's 2' 2", he's too short! Victor even had John and Harley out of the Cro-Mags wanting to kill him for something he said about them in an interview, but he sorted it out in the end."

So, what's been happening with the '100% Two Fingers In The Air Punk Rock' album put out through Century Media a while back? "We toured Germany extensively, drank every bar dry, then America for three months which was fucking murder. We bought an old school bus, but it broke down, and we were stuck in Ohio for five days in a country and western cafeteria, which did our heads in. All the violence stems from there... we all offered each other out. Some sort of male bonding, I suppose. Mexico was good, the kids are crazy, the best punk rockers, totally nuts. "

Do you ever get any groupies, apart from small animals who can't run faster than you? "Oh yeah, but it's usually only in Germany, and they're usually big strappers with moustaches and leather boots, but you'd have to ask Chaos about that. There's generally not many women near our dressing room, what with all the shit flying about. Women and shit don't mix, take it from me, kids."

Regale us with some of your pleasant tour antics then? "In Ireland, our drummer had been drinking for two or three days, and all the way through the tour we'd been doing naked bum farts on each other's necks, and he shat on our driver's back. He actually projected shit two feet onto the dashboard! Gabba's often shitting in his hand and throwing it at us... he interferes with felines everywhere too and enjoys torture and psychological violence, usually on youngsters.

192

Chaos UK

It's really just horrible and cruel jokes non-stop. We even made Chris from M.D.C. up like a black and white minstrel when he was pissed, and took photos of us sticking our cocks in his mouth while he was asleep. We'll publish those one day..."

Do you actually look forward to touring with these animals? "Oh yeah, it's a scream! The thing is, it's like that every Friday and Saturday night in Bristol and Cardiff anyway, so we just take it out on the road. The circus comes to town, y'know?"

So, who's the biggest bunch of assholes you've ever had to play with? "Chaos UK, without a doubt."

Tell us about the next Chaos UK record... "We recorded a demo last year in Ireland – we wrote it in the morning and recorded it in the afternoon, in true Chaos UK tradition – which we were gonna put out as an LP, but we decided to drop half the songs, write some new ones and re-record it. We'll go to Germany later this year to record, and Century Media will bring that out. Hopefully we'll bring out a single off that one was well, called 'Ramraid', which is about some of the band's more dubious activities. I can't really elaborate any further on that!"

I understand you've got some pretty prestigious fans of the band in the metal scene? "We met Sepultura at Tower Records, and they were really friendly. They're into all the old punk rock bands from Bristol, like us, Amebix and Disorder. We got chatting and they're really keen to do some gigs with us. With any luck some shows will come off with them in South America. That'll be a laugh! And a piss up! We got on the guest list for Donnington, but our lift never turned up. On reflection, it was a good thing, 'cos we didn't want to sit round in the rain and watch Aerosmith anyway!"

Captain Oi/Cherry Red/Retch - issue 96

(January/February 2002)

Whether you think they are an indulgent, redundant nostalgia trip or a potent reminder of the sterility of modern music, like it or not, punk reissues are here to stay. And with more and more flooding the market every month, we thought it high time we had Ian Glasper examine a few of them in detail, and maybe even question their validity...

Ask anyone in the know who the king of the reissue is, and they will say Captain Oi! Mark Brennan, ex-bassist of the Business, sometimes releases half a dozen old titles a month, and he always packages them in the original artwork, with exhaustive liner notes, and a slew of extra tracks. They really are definitive works, and a true godsend for anyone who loved their punk rock so much they've worn their old vinyl copies flat. Case in point would be his latest Exploited reissues. 'Punk's Not Dead', 'Troops Of Tomorrow' and 'Let's Start A War' have all been bundled up in ultra-smart digipaks, complete with a poster of the album cover and rare photos of the band, and between the three of 'em there's a whopping 21 (yes, count 'em!) bonus tracks, lifted from various compilation albums and single B-sides. And if you're not already familiar with The Exploited (where the hell have you been?), let me assure you that these albums have more than enough bite to appeal to any lover of aggressive underground music, old or young.

Mark promises me that we have plenty more such goodies to look forward to in the New Year, including the digipak treatment for the first two GBH albums. But he doesn't just exhume and resurrect golden oldies, Captain Oi! has recently turned his attention to coercing some of these ancient punkers back into the studio to prove they can still cut it with new studio albums. Most recently, Slaughter And The Dogs, fresh from conquering the USA, released their first brand new album in an age, entitled 'Beware Of...', and a seriously rocking effort it is too. Watch this space for a new album from the Adicts next...

Anagram (a division of Cherry Red) are no slouches in the reissues stakes either, with their 'Punk Collectors' series being of particular note. The (Metallica-approved) Anti-Nowhere League just got the Collectors treatment, with 'Animal! The Very Best Of The Anti-Nowhere League' being a crackin' compilation of all their most obnoxious biker punk anthems. The track listing is beyond question, and the complete discography and rare pictures help enhance an already great collection.

"The main idea behind it was to put out punk records from the indie labels of the late '70s and early '80s on CD for people who only had the original copies on vinyl or were part of the scene at the time," explains Tim at Cherry Red, about the concept behind their Punk Collectors series. "Also, there is definitely a new generation of fans buying these CDs; they've been listening to newer punk and hardcore bands who are all citing the older bands as their influence."

But there's just so many reissues coming out right now, isn't there a danger of flooding the market?

"Between ourselves and Captain Oi! we are very careful not to step on each other's toes," reckons Tim. "Mark Brennan actually compiles a lot of our punk CDs for us! You'll see a Vice Squad release, for instance, from both Anagram and Captain Oi! but we'll each cover a different period of the band's catalogue. And we've tried to make the reissue much more interesting recently; with all the new technology in the home we've started to put on enhanced video and live footage and releasing them as digipaks that are much more attractive."

Last but not least would be Retch Records, run by none other than Spike, late of the criminally underrated Blitzkrieg and Paradox UK, who has been known to put out the odd reissue through his Retch Files series...

"The inspiration for the Retch Files was to put a fun fresh veneer on an old theme if you like," says Spike of his (particularly bad-mouthed) baby. "I love this music and just wanted to put it in a fun modern package. Plus it's kind of Ronco on speed and trippin' with ownership of nuclear weapons; it's loaded to the teeth and fun in that some of the things I'm reissuing were never issued in the first place! Nostalgia without history – hooray! It's a concept and I like it! So far it's been received okay, especially the Varukers... I mean, everyone loves the old Varukers?"

They certainly do, so it was a luvverly surprise to have their corking 'One Struggle One Fight' coupled with their (not so corkin') 'Live In Leeds' albums for Retch Files One. Thank you, kind sir, but couldn't this preoccupation with the past be seen as a sad indication of our current punk scene?

"No, I wouldn't say so, not really," ponders Spike. "It's more a sad indication of greedy promotors who will not take chances on new bands; they'd rather pack 'em in for Holidays In The Sun and events like that - why don't they do regular events of a smaller nature for new bands?

"Plus, the punters are as equally to blame; they will not take a chance on a band unless they've already heard of 'em, shame on you. Yes, I do reissues, but I also do new bands as well, great new bands such as Airbomb. People have just got to take a chance on some of them and stop being boring conservative bastards!"

CHIMAIRA – ISSUE 93 (OCTOBER 2001)

I normally hate asking bands about the inspiration behind their names, but this time round, I just had to. In Greek mythology, a chimera was a fire-breathing beast comprising the head of a lion, the body of a goat, and the tail of a dragon, and I find it exciting that a band should choose such an unusual and esoteric name.

"I wanted an avant-garde name, something that wasn't obvious, and this creature caught my attention. It was three animals coming together as one, and I figured we were six guys coming together to create a whole new metal beast," laughs vocalist Mark

Chimaira 2001, pic by Todd Bell

Hunter, when I call him for the lowdown on their debut album for Roadrunner, 'Pass Out of Existence'.

And musically you pull together many influences in weird and wonderful ways too.

"Yeah, we don't wanna be a genre. We blend a lot of styles so we can capture the attention of a much less restricted audience. We write like an early metal band, add in the technicality of death metal, some of the simplicity and dynamics of nu-metal, and I try to keep the vocals really hardcore..."

Of course, you guys hail from Cleveland, a real hot bed for brutal hardcore, and your first EP came out on the hardcore indie, East Coast Empire, the label that helped launch Integrity on an unsuspecting world.

"Dwid [Integ's fiery vocalist – IG] actually did some of the artwork on that first release for us," Mark tells me, "And a lot of our old bands played with Integrity. You couldn't be from the Cleveland scene and not look up to them in some way.

"And there's a lot of other great bands coming up too. Ringworm have been around for a long time, but I think they're about to sign to Victory, and you've heard of Run Devil Run and Mushroom Head, right?"

Hell yeah. But don't go thinking that Chimaira are just a Clevo hardcore band. As much as they've built their substantial following from the grass roots up, in that time-honoured hardcore tradition, they owe more to Pantera, what with their syncopated pulverising bass drums and abrasive riffing, than they do to Minor Threat.

"Wow, that's quite a compliment, man, I love Pantera," enthuses Mark. "And I often wonder why there's no one doing that really brutal stuff anymore. We just figured that

if no one was playing the music we love, we may as well just do it ourselves."
And fair play to the man.

CHIMAIRA – ISSUE 110 (JUNE 2003)

Chimaira 2003, pic by Todd Bell

Spawned in the darkest depths of the Cleveland metalcore scene, and poised to spread their wings internationally, Roadrunner's Chimaira have just dropped their second album, 'The Impossibility of Reason' – a work bristling with enough teeth and claws to put their namesake to shame – on an unsuspecting music world. We sent our resident knight in shining armour, Ian Glasper, to see if he could befriend one part of the beast, vocalist Mark Hunter.

Like the fire-breathing creature of myth after which they are named. Cleveland's Chimaira are hotter right now than the toilet seat in Hell's own curry house. Their 2001 Roadrunner debut, 'Pass Out of Existence', hinted at great things to come. but with their recent sophomore outing, 'The Impossibility of Reason', they've blossomed like a poisonous mushroom cloud over the scene, threatening even to cast a shadow over the likes of Killswitch Engage and Shadows Fall with their punishing riff-heavy metalcore. "Um, I think we've always been a metal band," says vocalist Mark Hunter, as we ponder whether they are indeed hardcore metal or metallic hardcore. "But whatever label or subgenre a particular critic wants to tag us with usually seems equally as appropriate, you know? We listen to a lot of hardcore - we grew up around a lot of great bands from this area, like Integrity, One Life Crew and Ringworm. Cleveland has obviously produced some classic hardcore, and we were inevitably influenced by that scene, but there's also elements of straight-up ripping metal and more traditional metal in our sound as well." Classification is in the ears of the beholder. The fact they're housed on Roadrunner and have been on tour with legendary acts such as Slayer, Machine Head and Danzig surely hints at being metal.

"Ha! Well, everybody has different opinions and different ears - we're just glad to be around right now. We don't worry about it too much; we've never sat there writing, thinking, 'Oh, we can't play this chord or that chord, because it's too metal, or not metal enough, or whatever'. We just wanna play, y'know?"

And, in this instance, such pointless pigeon-holing really would do Chimaira a grave injustice, such is the broad diversity of styles they put on display. Although the band specialise in bruising Pantera-like crunch passages, they don't shy away from the occasional acoustic interlude, and the album closes with a thirteen-minute epic that runs the whole gauntlet of their many weird and wonderful influences. If you can imagine the pathos of Alice In Chains delivered via the medium of modern thrash metal, you're halfway there. And, just take a song like 'Pictures In The Cold Room', one minute tearing at your face like a wounded raven black with its own blood, the next tying itself up in knots as it hits the brakes so hard it's almost spun into reverse - it's that slow, twisted and heavy.

"You know what?" Mark gushes with the same enthusiasm for their hybrid creation as Frankenstein has for his monster, "Before that middle section got added, it was just the song that you know... only without the middle part. We knew it was missing something, so we experimented by taking the riff and slowing it down, and as soon as we played it, it felt perfect. It's truly exhilarating when parts like that come out.

"The last record we wrote, we didn't write as a band - it was just me and Rob doing everything," he reveals of their creative process, "But this time around, the entire band was there every single day of the week, writing everything together - we got to feed off each other, which was another huge step for us. A lot of bands, it takes them their entire careers to realise, 'You know what? These other guys have something cool to contribute, too!' We can't wait to write the next one now: we wanna get back in the studio tomorrow," he quips.

What was the reasoning behind recording with a long-time friend, namely Ben Schigel, before setting sail for England to mix with Colin Richardson?

"We figured we didn't need to go to a big studio with a big-name producer to record; we wanted to use the same guy who's done all our demos, who's really experienced with our style and sound. Ben knows our band so well, it's a lot easier to take suggestions and criticisms from him rather than someone who's never heard us before. He's almost a seventh member, to be honest, so we didn't waste any time getting to know him; it was totally comfortable from the very first day. So we decided to keep it on our own terms, and do it right here at home, to keep it as raw and as honest as possible.

"And as for the mix-down with Colin; personally, it was like getting a chance to work with a legend. He has been a part of some of my all-time favourite records by Machine Head and Fear Factory. At first it was quite intimidating, but after a few minutes of being with him, you soon realise that he's one of the nicest guys on the planet."

Both Ben and Colin have certainly helped bring the best out of the band, and, as well as musically, there's tremendous growth on the lyrical front. Although song titles such as 'Pure Hatred' and 'Implements of Destruction' seem to suggest the band's rabid nihilism hasn't been tempered one jot since Mark last spat his hatred for the world into our gawping mouths, the amicable vocalist begs to differ.

"There's a much more positive slant on it all this time. On the last record, it was kinda like we were sat in the corner whining about everything that was wrong around us, but this time we're saying, 'Okay, here's what's wrong, and here's what I'm going to do about it.' I guess the best way we show our positive side is through negative anger – sometimes you just have to scream to get yourself heard or taken seriously."

CHIMAIRA – ISSUE 155 (MARCH 2007)

Chimaira 2007, pic by Todd Bell

Chimaira, the twelve-legged Cleveland killing machine, return this month with their strongest album to date, 'Resurrection', a disc that sees them with a new label, new/old drummer and whole new attitude. Ian Glasper bathed in the good vibes emanating from vocalist Mark Hunter.

It only seems like yesterday when Chimaira were raising the roof with their self-titled third album, but unbelievably it's been two years – and now they're back, rejoined by original drummer Andols Herrick, and laying down the law once again with the Andy Sneap-produced 'Resurrection' for new label Ferret (Nuclear Blast here in Europe). An apt title indeed considering how near they apparently came to splitting last year...

"Yeah, we came pretty fucking close!" reveals vocalist Mark Hunter. "I remember I was drunk one night and saying to [guitarist] Matt [DeVries] and [keyboardist] Chris [Spicuzza], 'Let's fucking quit this band and start something that sounds like Rammstein!' Haha!

"But there were a lot of political things to do with our old label [Roadrunner] going down... mainly in the US – we never had any issues with the staff in the UK and Europe; they were always great to us, and really helped gain a lot of success for our band. But when the last album came out, here in the United States, no one even knew our name at the label... it was really bad! And the CD was so expensive, and you couldn't find it in any stores, and basically the one person at the label in charge of everything to do with our band and our career did nothing for us. And when we confronted him and asked him, 'Why?' His answer was, 'I don't know!' And we were like, 'Dude, this is fucking nuts...'

"We were getting blown away by every band out there... not that we want to be bigger and better than all these other bands, but we'd like to at least be on par with them, and get better tour offers, and more opportunities to play in foreign countries... but with no promotion it's impossible. So I had a heart-to-heart with Monte Connor, the head of A&R there, who's a good friend of mine, and told him how we felt, and to his credit he let us go. And I don't think we would've been able to make this new record in such a positive state of mind if he hadn't done us that huge favour and cut us loose..."

The return of Andols to the fold seems to have rekindled a certain spark in the band's chemistry as well, his re-joining certainly doing much to ease various tensions that were pulling Chimaira in conflicting directions.

"Well, I guess you have to go back to when we had Kevin Talley [formerly of the mighty Misery Index] in the band, and although he is a great drummer, I never really got along with him personally, on the tour bus and things like that... and sometimes he would do things that were disrespectful to either me or the band. And these little things started to add up, and whether he knew it or not, it was as if he was dividing the band, y'know? There were some people that didn't see the negative things that maybe I saw, and I'd get mad at them as well, and things like that, and it just turned into some ugly battles between us.

"And we were on tour in Europe, in the UK with Dark Tranquility, at the end of 2004, and some bad things were happening in that sense, and I'd had enough of him. He's an awesome player, and I enjoy his personality and company – when he's not in my band, haha! It was the last night of the tour, and he was going to San Antonio, and we were flying to Cleveland, so he left three or four hours before us. And I sat down with the rest of the band and said, 'Listen, this guy has got to go!'

"We'd heard that Andols was interested in re-joining, so we got him down to our rehearsal space, and we jammed out the first two songs off the self-titled record, and they sounded perfect and everyone was smiling and happy again. He got off the drums, and I think it was Matt who said, 'Okay, we'll call ya...!' Being a smart ass, y'know? But we knew there and then that he was our drummer again, and it's great to have him back... I'd say he was definitely one of the main factors that helped save this band from breaking up! We were all pretty ecstatic to see him behind the kit again."

Out of adversity comes the greatest art, and sure enough, 'Resurrection' is awash with incredible riffs and some genuinely surprising arrangements and flourishes, making it easily the band's most diverse, satisfying offering to date. A modern thrash album, for sure, but laden with hints of everything from doom to grindcore and back again; there literally isn't a dull moment.

"On the last self-titled album, Rob had a vision, and had a lot of the songs written; everything was in his mind, y'know?" explains Mark. "So me and Matt kinda sat back and let him do his thing, and we were very happy with what he was coming up with. This time round, Matt and myself also had a lot of ideas musically that we wanted to get out ourselves... and the diversity and unpredictability you're talking about just comes from the fact that Matt, Rob and I all wrote an equal share of the new material, and then the other guys threw a few ideas in as well. Our CD collections are very eclectic, and just throwing all those sounds together, and being in this positive headspace again, it was very easy to write. It was like, 'Remember how we used to be when we first started?' We had no record label; we didn't care about anything other than writing music that made us wanna destroy the rehearsal space! And that was our mentality for this album – let's fuck it up and go crazy! We truly had a great time writing it."

So 'Resurrection' is an autobiographical title then?

"Yeah, sure! The song itself is about overcoming shit, and getting through it, and being man enough to stand up for yourself... all those things wrapped into one. It was very disappointing to get to that low point with the band, but if we hadn't gone there, I don't think we would've got to the high point that we're at right now. We would probably have just maintained what we were doing, stayed the same way... not strived for what we've managed to achieve here."

And such a hotly-anticipated release obviously attracted a fair share of bootleggers on the net, a fact that seems to have frustrated the band no end if you read their My Space blogs.

"It isn't the downloading that frustrates us, it's when kids start talking about it," sighs Mark. "I look at it in the same way as a movie... if I'd started reading about 'The Sixth Sense', before I'd seen it, I would be so pissed off – the ending is spoiled, and I already have someone else's vision of what it's meant to be like. And the first time you see it, you're always thinking about that person's vision, not your own. And we don't want that for our fans – we're glad that the people want to listen to our record before it's available, and we hope that they're enjoying it, but we don't want them ruining it for anyone else that maybe doesn't have access to downloading it yet, or whatever.

"I understand it's unavoidable, and I'm just as excited as the next guy at the thought of a new record from my favourite band, but I don't go on message boards and start talking about it! Talk about it all you want – but hold your horses for another month until it's out there..."

CHUCK SCHULDINER TRIBUTE/BENEFIT –

ISSUE 97 (MARCH 2002)

The music of Chuck Schuldiner reached far beyond the confines of death metal. We heard from members of the hardcore community who took influence from the raw energy and attitude of Death, who all incidentally offered their services to the 'Scream Bloody Roar' Chuck benefit show long before his tragic passing. Ian Glasper helped gather their thoughts.

We (being my band, Stampin' Ground) were recently privileged enough to be asked to play a benefit show for Chuck Schuldiner, who at that time was desperately ill, and, most of us being huge Death fans, we instantly agreed. We're actually right in the middle of an enforced hiatus from live work, working on our next album, but we've made the odd exception for special shows, and this was definitely worth emerging from the rehearsal studio to do.

At the time of writing this though, that show is still a week away, but now, with the tragic passing of Chuck, it has taken on a much more sombre tone, having become a memorial show to this (relatively) unsung hero, instead of a benefit, although obviously Chuck's loved ones will be in receipt of any profits generated by the event.

So, instead of joining together in hope for his recovery, 'Scream Bloody Roar' has become a noisy wake, where we can indulge in some of the spirited thrashings Chuck helped propagate, and ponder for a while the words of wisdom, and the notes of chaos, he imparted.

'ALTERING THE FUTURE'

I wonder if, when Chuck Schuldiner wrote that song, he realised the prophetic nature of the title? Already had, in fact. Right from his early demos as Mantas, his uniquely brutal approach to metal music was being digested and regurgitated the world over; and latterly, when he forged out into more technical realms, again, his work was analysed and applied in countless rehearsal pads around the world. Always ahead of his time, the legacy of music he left us will continue to inspire for many years to come. Even those too young to remember first-hand his earliest releases...

"I was only six years old when 'Scream Bloody Gore' came out," recalls Adam Sagir, bassist with London noisemongers Labrat, who are also representing at the Bradford show. "So I got into Death a lot later than most. As a teenager, I was influenced by bands like Obituary, Morbid Angel, Cannibal Corpse and Deicide, and they were all undoubtedly heavily influenced by Death. It was actually those bands that led me to Death; they were all wearing their t-shirts, thanking them on albums or mentioning them in interviews. But I wouldn't say that musically I ever drew too heavily from Chuck. My band before Labrat was a death metal band that just basically plagiarised Carcass, early Sepultura and all the aforementioned bands, which kind of shows through on some of our more brutal bits, but if it wasn't for Death, none of us would have had anyone to copy!"

Of course, not everyone can even remember when they first heard Death – as demonstrated by Mark 'Hic!' Fieldhouse, vocalist with Freebase, one of the UK's leading old school hardcore bands, who were also invited to play the benefit gig.

"The truth is, the first time that I probably heard Chuck's music was when I was pissed up with a load of friends listening to loads of thrash and death metal vinyl and cassettes. At that time the scene was ripe with new bands, and tapes to trade. I initially didn't pay that much attention to what I heard, and even when 'Scream Bloody Gore' came out, if I'm to be totally honest, I was not a real fan.

"That all changed with the release of 'Leprosy'! I picked this vinyl up along with nine other albums the same day, and the only other record that I remember to this day from that lot was Meliah Rage's 'Kill To Survive'. Doesn't that speak volumes? 'Leprosy' struck an instant chord and stood out as such a powerful, aggressive, honest slab of vinyl that I was instantly converted to being a diehard fan of that album. At the time, I remember it being one of my most played records. Thrash was big... but this band topped it all. It was one of the first records I had bought that did not have one single bad track on it!"

Adam agrees, both on the gut-wrenching power of 'Leprosy' and the less-than-instant hardcore appeal of 'Scream...'

"The first time I heard Death was actually on a Terrorizer covermount CD [we didn't pay him to say that, honest – IG], and I'd be lying if I said I was instantly hooked - the track was from the 'Symbolic' album, not one of my favourites. It wasn't until I first heard 'Leprosy' about five years ago that I really got into them. You just can't fuck with that album; it's really stood the test of time and doesn't even sound dated next to newer bands like Nile or Cryptopsy!"

'STORY TO TELL'

Mark mentioned tape trading above, and I'm sure that many of us first heard Death on an unmarked second-hand cassette, sent in the mail with a soaped stamp on the battered envelope! A far cry from the super-slick production and packaging of an accomplished album such as 'Symbolic', but it was the effort made to obtain those recordings that guaranteed them a lasting place in your memory. This wasn't something you could walk into a store and pull from the racks; like the most arcane knowledge, it was something you had to work for, beg for, and earn...

Not to disrespect any of the incredibly talented musicians that Chuck worked with over the years (when you think about the people who helped flesh out Death, it reads like a veritable extreme metal Hall Of Fame: Gene Hoglan, Steve DiGorgio, Rick Rozz, Terry Butler, Bill Andrews, James Murphy, Sean Reinert, Paul Masvidal, Andy La Rocque... need I go on?), but he was the one who was Death. He launched her all those years ago; he steered that vessel through all the turbulent waters when no one gave a fuck about death metal, when all Chuck's peers were labelling him a pariah to work with; he was the one constant in the band's career, and it was his vision that helped shape and reinvent the band so many times over, each time more challenging than the last.

From the sledgehammer blast of 'Infernal Death' that ushered in that bubonic debut album, right up to the triumphant cover of 'Painkiller' that closed the curtain on 'The Sound Of Perseverance', Death were always unmistakably Death. Always ahead of the pack, never content to run with the hounds, Chuck always strove to create something new and exciting every time his band set foot in a studio, and it's testament to his vision that his last album remains, for me, his strongest. His most rounded and mature, where technical precision and hardcore aggression and all the other wonderful ingredients he'd brought to the table with previous line-ups, all came together in one spectacular neck-snapping metal meltdown!

'THE PHILOSOPHER'

What started out as a gratuitous glorification of death and all its gory trappings actually ended up as a celebration of life and the indomitable spirit to overcome all, despite the odds. In the space of fifteen years, Chuck went from 'Sacrificial Cunt' to 'A Moment of Clarity'. It was an exhilarating ride along the way, but if you managed to hang on by your fingertips round some of the hairier corners, one that made perfect sense when the rollercoaster finally slowed to a halt. Over the years, Chuck Schuldiner touched many of us not only with his music, but also with his lyrics, and the way he dealt with his many detractors (not one of them fit to hold his snotty hankies) over the years.

We watched his maturing from the spotty youth mouthing profanities for their sheer shock value ("They torture you by cutting off your cock... Pray if you want/ Pathetic rancid cunt" – 'Torn To Pieces') to a well-rounded human being struggling to find meaning behind his own existence ("Passion burns like fires in the wind/ The end of time/ A time to begin/ It builds you up one way/ And tears you back down" – 'Flesh And The Power It Holds'). Whilst his guitar tattooed its licks into your cerebral cortex, his words cut at your psyche; his doubts were your doubts, his fears were our fears, and a burden shared is a lighter load to bear. And therein lies the beauty that is within even the ugliest of music.

I wonder what Chuck would say if he could read these tributes to his works? Aw, shucks, thanks everybody? Or fercrissakes stop reminiscing about yesterday and get on with living today?

"Oh, definitely the latter; make sure that you enjoy yourself," reckons Mark. "Do as you like, not just as your friends or associates or whoever are saying you oughta do. No one knows your life span; learn, achieve, and enjoy as much as you can. Live each day as if it was your last."

"From my point of view, he seemed to have a dedication to metal that very few can claim to have," says Adam Labrat, on the subject of the huge, yawning void Chuck's passing has left in the metal scene. "He'd been thrashing away for over eighteen years, barely making enough money to live, but still carried on. He died without enough money to pay his medical bills. He was a more than competent guitarist and could have made a fortune doing session work if he so desired, but he stuck to his guns and it's that indestructible metal spirit that I'll miss most."

We'll leave the last words to a true modern-day philosopher in his own right (!), Mark Freebase: "All I'm gonna say is this... if you don't have 'Leprosy', 'Spiritual Healing' and 'Human' in your collection, shame on you!"

Confused

"It's heavier, faster, and has a great old school crossover thrash punk sound!" says Al Del Barrio, vocalist with Confused, of his band's new album, 'Behind Closed Doors'. They have been proudly representing Texan hardcore punk since 1988, and if you dig that whole early Suicidal/DRI vibe, you are going to lose your shit to these guys.

"Yeah, we have a lot of energy on stage, and always try to make it one hell of a great show, guaranteed to make you want to slam, circle pit or stage dive," laughs Al, who also fronts the Worthless Pukes, before adding, of the current Texan punk scene, "The Eighties were great, and a lot of fun, but everything goes in cycles, and it's pretty strong again right now. It is a different crowd, a different vibe... a whole different feel to the scene... but it's pretty much changed for the better."

Congress - issue 35 (October 1996)

"We get a lot of shit from PC morons for encouraging violent dancing, but l don't care. People hold back all evening, but when we come on, we say, 'Go ahead, go crazy!' We do this for everyone who believes in the sheer aggression of a good mean pit. An insane pit and a crazy atmosphere help make a cool show. Aggressive music needs aggressive behaviour on the dancefloor."

The above words are from one Josh Noyelle, guitarist with Belgian psychopaths, Congress. As you may deduce from such a statement, they ain't no hippy peace-punk band either. ln fact, file under the blatantly metal alongside Integrity, Despair and Dark Side. Their debut MCD, 'Euridium', and their first album, 'Blackened Persistence', both for Good Life, are widely regarded as classics of modern metalcore and new MCD, 'The Other Cheek', looks set to continue the trail of destruction.

"It's the best record we've ever done", claims Josh, unsurprisingly. "It's in between our first two releases, death metal mixed with old school hardcore. It's very mean and very aggressive."

What does surprise me is the inclusion of the band's first demo on there as four bonus tracks. Most bands are only too keen to bury their early efforts as deep as possible. Surely it can't be to the benefit of a band to make available such a crude first draft?

"We've left it just as it was, so don't expect any technical shit. It was, after all, the first thing we ever recorded, and with a different line-up. We know we were pretty bad back then, we admit that, but we're not ashamed of our origins at all. We've only put it on there because we've gotten so much mail from all over the world asking for that demo, but it's completely unavailable. It was limited to 150 copies."

As well as the high body-count at their shows, another thing that winds up the right-on punk-police is their apparent preoccupation with the H8000 Crew, a scene within a scene. There's a lot of people who think that the gang mentality will be the downfall of hardcore.

"That's not the way it is at all", he explains with a sigh. "Back in '92 you had the 8000 Crew, so-called 'cos of the postal code you have if you live in west Flanders, but now in '96 we wanted to do something new, so we added the 'H'. Most of the bands play this hateful hardcore music now; back then it was a more emotional style. The new direction has developed out of anger and frustration, but we wanted to keep that link with the old scene."

Perhaps one of the hardest things for a hardcore fan to get their head around concerning Congress might be their bassist, who has been known to wear black metal-style corpse-paint on stage.

"Here, where the kids are familiar with us, they think it's pretty cool, but elsewhere it confuses people, but we don't care. Hardcore is about rebellion and not conforming. He can do whatever he wants, and l know that l can do whatever l want. We are all individuals, all into different things, different styles of music, and ultimately we want to break down all the barriers between hardcore, death metal and straightedge."

Congress – issue 57 (August 1998)

Perhaps the leading un-lights of the now-legendary Belgian metallic hardcore scene, Congress have declared themselves 'Angry With The Sun' on their just-released third album. Ian Glasper caught up with the devilcore veterans' spokesman Josh at the recent Evilfest in order to learn more.

When anyone thinks of the burgeoning Belgian H8000 scene, they can't help but think of Congress, one of the innovators of that brutal edge metal sound. They've brought a

Congress live, by Edward Verhaeghe

fire and spirit to the European scene that had been sadly lacking, and the kids responded accordingly, flocking to their shows like windmilling lemmings hellbent on destruction. And I'm pleased to report that, having just caught up with them at the recent Evilfest, and with my arse well and truly kicked by 'Angry At The Sun', their third full-lengther for Good Life (see the review back in #55), the feeling is still very much in full effect. In fact, the band seem poised on the brink of the kinda success that has until now cruelly eluded them: recently spotted wowing the assembled at the Dynamo, and booked to play most of the continent's other major festivals this summer. But at what price their ever-expanding popularity with their die-hard hardcore following?

"Playing bigger festivals is something we all wanted to do at least once in our 'careers', and we've finally got the chance now, because of the new record and all that, and we are more than stoked to do so," reckons Josh, their guitarist/spokesman. "Of course, playing the Dynamo isn't like playing the Ieper-fest [a well-established underground hardcore meet every August – IG], for example; at most bigger festivals, the crowds don't know, or care, who the smaller bands are, so in a sense it is a challenge to convince that sort of audience. It is very safe to play small, local shows, because you know all the people there, and after a while it becomes predictable and boring.

"As far as receiving criticism is concerned, we're used to that, 'cos the local scene is dying, and they need scapegoats to blame, and our band is one of those. As a band, we see everything we do as a form of expression, an escape, a freedom – every person, whether they are into hardcore or not, has a right to be happy and escape reality – and some people will always have a problem with the way you act, because they envy the happiness you experience just doing your thing."

Congress, by Edward Verhaeghe

You seem a little discontented with the state of the hardcore scene at the moment, especially if you look at the lyrics of a song like 'One More Attempt', which seems a little weird to us Brits, who for a long time have envied the size and strength of Belgian HC.

"You're probably thinking of a couple of years ago, when we had a really cool scene. Right now, tho', everything is kinda divided. There are way too many cliques, who only like to support their own bands, their own little scene. I believe that it is the responsibility of the bands to try and change this. Those lyrics, to 'One More Attempt', say that we are all in this together, and that fighting each other will only destroy our movement. It is hard to please everyone. Even in this supposedly open-minded scene there are people eager to criticise and point their fingers at those who are trying to change their ways."

Well, this is one band who can never be accused of stagnating. They've always strived to push the limits set by their previous releases with every album, constantly searching for new ways to redefine the Congress sound, and the new album is no exception. From the sinister medieval intro, to the odd interludes steeped in sound effects, their experimentation with the unusual could very well earn them the tag of 'the Morbid Angel of hardcore', and like those visionary Floridians, when they clench their musical muscles, someone gets hurt.

Heaviness and diversity can go hand in hand, if handled skilfully enough, and these guys are past masters. Do they think hardcore tends to underestimate its own musical prowess? "Yes, in a way it has become too safe," says Josh carefully. "When we started out in '93, playing metalcore was fresh, new and original, but now everyone does the same thing. Musically, the limits between HC and metal are almost gone, and a band's genre is defined by their image and outlook rather than music. Lyrics and message have always differentiated HC from metal, but sometimes it's difficult to tell the two apart nowadays. "I really don't know which direction hardcore will take next, because everything's already been done. As a band it's really quite impossible to sound original anymore, but you can at least try to be good at what you're doing, and not just try to be cool playing a certain style that is trendy. I can name a dozen bands that were old school two years ago that are playing metal now, but what credibility do they have? Congress have never really deviated from our style, and I guess that's the reason people still respect us?"

Well, that's one theory, and it's as good as any I guess, but whatever the reason, Congress are on the rise, and if Eurocore is your thing, you need to check them out soonest.

CONVERGE – ISSUE 55 (JUNE 1998)

Converge, by Danielle Dombrowski

The dictionary, that ever reliable bastion for anyone struggling for an angle on a feature's intro, defines 'to converge' as the meeting at one point of several things, and Converge, the Boston hardcore band, are indeed a musical crossroads - don't they bury murderers where roads cross or something? - where everything becomes one. No less than Da Ed himself described their 'Petitioning The Empty Skies' MCD - licensed to Equal Vision from Ferret Records, who could no longer keep up with the demand for the disc - as akin to Slayer done by the way of Japanese noise and Voivod, and if that sounds fucking insane, that's because it is.

"The lines are really blurred between genres nowadays," reckons Jake, one fifth of these

Converge – by Danielle Dombrowski

sonic terrorists, on the phone from Equal Vision's American office to promote their latest burnt offering, the malicious 'When Forever Comes Crashing'. "We are very eclectic in our influences. It isn't all just run of the mill hardcore stuff. We all listen to a lot of thrash metal, from Voivod to the Bay Area stuff, right through to the Touch And Go roster, and a lot of the Sub Pop shit. We have very dynamic tastes."

Seeing as you actually recorded a Vio-Lence cover for an ultra-rare 5" a year or two back – needless to say, anyone out there with it for sale, get in touch, I'm in NEED – I take it you subscribe to the train of thought that modern metallic hardcore is, in fact, thrash metal for the Millennium?

"Yes, I guess so, but it's not as well written as it was back in the Eighties. These days, bands seem unable to put together such great songs, and it's really second-rate thrash. They're all too concerned with being as heavy as possible. We're really into trying to write songs, rather than just riff after riff, for the sake of it."

But you have to admit that the lyrics were shit, though!

"Oh yeah, the lyrics were very first level, very basic and stupid," agrees Jake. "Hence we drifted towards hardcore a lot more, especially those DC bands, like Embrace and Scream, that were more emotionally expressive than most HC/metal acts at the time..."

[There then followed a long and anal conversation about the first two Scream records, which I have no intention of boring you all with – IG]. "It was then that we realised we had so much to say, it opened a whole new spectrum up to the band of what we could possibly achieve. Those bands transcended just being bands, just writing songs and selling T-shirts. And we care enough about our band to see it, too, as more than just a collection of songs. We don't have any real goals as such as a band, we're no vehicle for any ethical platform. There is no preachy aspect to what we do, we just try to express what we experience on a personal level."

When pushed for what kind of personal experience could possibly unleash such a vitriolic outpouring as 'When Forever Comes Crashing', Jake will only tell me tantalisingly that it was about "a pretty heavy experience, one moment of desperation, the absolute zero of human behaviour", and having extracted a promise that he'll tell me more next time we speak, I push on. So, what about these Japanese noise and even jazz influences our Nick alluded to? Are we barking up the right tree here?

"In the last few years, I've become more inclined towards that noise stuff. One of our friends from Agoraphobic Nosebleed, who we're going to do a split album with next, has a side project that's

really grown on me, called Japanese Torture Comedy Hour. They're just primarily harsh noise, and he's floated me a lot of tapes of his unreleased stuff. We're even talking about experimenting on a personal level, deconstructing modern music, going for ambience and mood. We've been in a band for eight years now, and we're still growing. You have to push the limits, otherwise it becomes boring.

"As for jazz, well, I listen to a little straight jazz stuff. I'm a jazz novice, but Kurt, one of our guitarists, is into everything – he even plays sax. He's an engineer by trade, he's a fucking robot, and he'll come up with the most difficult stuff possible, just to challenge himself."

And that rational lunatic approach is very evident on the aforementioned new CD, which lurches from one staggering set piece to the next, throwing the listener at every turn, and just when you're reaching for the remote, they lock into such a devastating riff it knocks you back in your seat, and commands your attention all over again. It is not easy listening - it's even less immediate than 'Petitioning...'!

"That's good, that's what we wanted. We want to open people's eyes. We didn't want to write a carbon copy of the last record. A lot of people considered it a defining moment of chaotic hardcore, and it would've been the easy way out to just rewrite it. This is a little more subversive than that one. It gets under your skin, and takes you on an emotional trip."

CONVERGE – ISSUE 94 (NOVEMBER 2001)

Converge by Danielle Dombrowski

For ten years, Boston's Converge have been pushing the metallic hardcore envelope, but with the release of 'Jane Doe' on Equal Vision, they've gone and shoved that envelope right off the damn table, creating one of the most bewildering and compulsively erratic albums of the year. Ian Glasper was dispatched to pick up the pieces, and discovered the emotional wreckage in their midst.

I'm drawn to the new Converge album like a moth to a flame. In a perverse kind of way, I both love it and hate it. I love it when the band hit their stride and the riffs just mow you down like an innocent bystander caught up in a drive-by, but I hate it when they frustrate the listener by doing just what the hell they wanna do, when they wanna do it – how dare they! If you want a nice easy ride, you're on the wrong bus, son. Converge have evolved (devolved?) a great deal since their previous releases, as one listen to the bewildering noises howling from their new 'Jane Doe' disc will confirm, but first we should find out just where the hell they've been these last few years.

"The dramatic three-year wait for an album had much to do with the loss of our drummer, who played on 'The Poacher Diaries' release [the 1999 split album with Agoraphobic Nosebleed on Relapse - IG]," explains elusive vocalist Jacob Bannon when I finally track him down on the other side of the world via the wonders of telecommunication. "The day after the record release show for that record, John decided to leave the band. Though amazingly talented, he simply wasn't cut out for the workload and commitment it truly takes to be in an active independent band. In short, one European tour broke him. And with that, the writing for 'Jane Doe' slowed, and the search was on for a new and integral member of the band...

"We took our time searching out a new drummer; we auditioned a slew of people looking for the right balance of musicianship and personality. After a number of months, we were lucky to find Ben Koller, who was playing in a rock-oriented project with [guitarist] Kurt called Blue/Green Heart at the time. He soon started rehearsing with us, and we then picked up the writing process for the album."

And had you been courted by any larger labels during this hiatus? If so, what is it about Equal Vision that makes you feel so at home?

"We had been approached, as most bands are, at least in a casual way, but we are firm believers in the sense of community that the independent music scene provides. For us, Equal Vision, and the bands that are part of the label (Bane, American Nightmare, The Hope Conspiracy, etc), though stylistically different, are family. They are all close friends, and in many respects, we support and drive each other in a way that few bands can really claim. It's truly a rare thing.

"Equal Vision are an eclectic label who put their all behind their artists. For us, that kind of unconditional support of our work is a necessity. They have allowed us to work with other labels on a regular basis with other releases, projects, and without that kind of understanding and commitment I think that we would suffer greatly. And I would say that there are a number of labels out there who also encourage the same kind of growth and positive environment as EQV, like Hydrahead, Escape Artist and Bridge Nine, but unfortunately there are more out there who limit their artists and are involved for all the wrong reasons!"

This new album is about as twisted and convoluted as I think metalcore can get. And it's got 'opus' stamped all over it! Do you feel it's your definitive work?

"'Jane Doe' was a huge personal work for all of us in the band. For me, it was more of a therapeutic experience in the creative process than any other release we have ever written. For the first time, I feel that we have captured what Converge is wholly about on a record. This is something that has always eluded us in past recordings. And for me, the album is an emotionally complex work... human and altogether grey... and much of that has to do with the rollercoaster of experience I have been part of these past few months.

"I didn't actually let the rest of the band know where I was in my life during the recording process, but it is apparent in the anger and emotional dynamic on the record, that there was an understanding that something wasn't quite right. Recording the album was taking place at the pinnacle of that confusion for me and the work for me reflects that."

The title suggests a concept of anonymity. Is this something you're concerned with in music? Or is it a comment on the facelessness of modern society?

"The title 'Jane Doe' was decided upon while on tour in Europe about three years ago. At that point I had no idea that I was to lose the most important person in my life, and the most powerful relationship I have ever experienced... and in retrospect, it was a self-fulfilling prophecy in many ways. Now, after the recording, I am still left sorting out that emotional wreckage in my life, though the album did save me in some sense. This album is an integral part of that process for me. It's emotionally vulnerable and raw in the truest sense of the word.

"'Jane Doe' as a title represents emotional isolation, loss, and grief - when invested heart fails and you are left to your own strengths. At the point when the album was recorded, and now, I am facing that emotional crisis. And for the first time, it is not a black and white issue with a definitive end. It really has changed me. Friends say for the better, but my gut feeling says for the worst."

Okay, please talk us through the Converge song-writing process - because some of this new material defies easy categorisation, to say the least, and the mind boggles at what inter-band dramas might have played themselves out behind the rehearsal room doors during its inception!

"Much of the musical foundation has always been brought to the table by Kurt, our guitarist," reveals Jake. "At that point we all work towards refining and shaping a song. This album was probably the most collaborative effort that we've ever had in that respect, where all of us were active in the process. I feel that has a lot to do with the unique sound much of the record has. Also, Nate, our bass player added a lot to the album, and I also brought two songs to the record, making it a more well-rounded effort.

"When we began writing the music for 'Jane Doe', we made a conscious decision to disregard the traditional expectations of most people. Many would want us to re-write 'Petitioning The Empty Sky' [their '96 debut - IG], or 'When Forever Comes Crashing' [its '98 follow-up - IG] over and over again. We set out to write a record that would be as emotionally bare and honest as we could create, concentrating on those specifics of song-writing and emotive simplicity."

I'd like to chat too about musical extremes and taboos. Is there anything you guys would rule out doing with your band? I mean, are you very aware of the limits of extremity you can attain without losing your fanbase?

"Art in any form should never have limits, and as a band we have really never been concerned with the kind of limitations put forth on each particular sub-genre of music.

I feel that as an artist you have an obligation to challenge the conservative pre-conceived notions of expression and communication. Visually, musically and conceptually. This is how the bar is raised and doors are essentially opened to new leaps and bounds of progression. Without that kind of experimentation and exploration it would be difficult to discern what was independent, free-thinking music, from the contrived, over-produced emotionless garbage that pollutes commercial music today. Standards are meant to be raised, and creative communication is meant to grow infinitely, without any sort of ceiling.

"As long as there is emotion, there will be creative strides in creative expression. And as long as there is human experience, it will always be interesting and engaging. Thousands of years of art, written word, and music can't be wrong in that respect."

Copro Records – issue 52 (March 1998)

Copro Records – Seizure

In case you were sleeping, we've devoted plenty of coverage to the UK's underground hardcore scene, and more than worthy it is too, of space in these hallowed pages – but what of our underground metal scene? I may spend most of my time in the company of wallet-chained, stage-diving lunatics, but I also know a good metal outfit when I hear one, and Britain, of course, has a reputation second to none in this particular genre, so where are the new bands? The zines? The underground shows? Just like the truth,

Copro Records – Snub

they're out there, somewhere, and now they have one more outlet in the shape of rising label, Copro Records.

"Well, we never saw ourselves as a stepping stone just for upcoming UK bands," claims Jose Griffin, member of death metal veterans, Gomorrah, and one third of the nucleus behind the label. "We always just figured we'd go along and see what happened. Obviously we've been in bands for so many years, we can draw on those experiences. Where we went wrong, we can try and make sure our bands don't make the same mistakes, and we'll try to steer them towards where we went right. The thing that did it for us was the 'Underground Titans' tour – it always comes back to that, just getting out there and doing it. And the bands we want to work with all have the same self-belief, the same self-respect, and are willing to do the work. It's very much a two-way partnership between band and label."

Sounds great! Too good to be true, in fact, but true it appears to be, and a commendable attitude that's pretty close to the ideals of my beloved punk and hardcore music.

"Truth be known," confesses Jose, "We were all involved in the punk thing before we were ever in Gomorrah, and that's where ideas like the 'Titans' tour came from. That's what's got to be done – no one else will help you. If you don't go out and do it y'self, then no one else will do it for you."

"We wouldn't insult the intelligence of the hardcore scene by saying we're a HC band, 'cos we aren't," ponders Geoff Kinch, vocalist of Southampton's Seizure, whose excellent 'Life ln Freefall' debut is the next release on Copro, when we discuss this tentative link between the two scenes further. "We've got a predominantly metal background, but there is crossover there. There is a bit of everything, and hopefully people will pick up on that, rather than just try to lock us into any one scene. We're nice, friendly guys, and we can get on with anyone. We just try to make our own way, and not fuck around with anyone who doesn't fuck around with us..."

Indeed, there is summat for everyone on 'Life ln Freefall', which is a surprisingly thickly produced slab of angsty metal that straddles the spawning pools of Metallica, Sepultura and Entombed.

"Oh yeah," Seizure bassist, Lee, joins the fray for a quick froth at the mouth, "And Biohazard and Machine Head. I've seen both recently, and l was so impressed with how they came across live. Nothing fancy, they just make you want to kick the shit out of someone [laughs]. That's the sorta feeling we're after. We keep it heavy and very simple, really moshing and crushin', without worrying too much about overly technical stuff."

As well as the crunching strains of Seizure, Copro's other unveiling for the spring - apart from the 'Ballistic' compilation CD, that is, which is part roster sampler and part platform for upcoming demo bands - is the '360 Degree Conviction' MCD, by Bournemouth's Snub, which sees them part-trading their patented metallic rapcore for something a little harder and more aggressive.

"Yeah, we've been listening to much heavier stuff recently, a lot of extreme metal, and it's given us a much nastier edge," agrees vocalist Choff, before adding a coupla good reasons for people turning out to see 'em when they get out and about, up and down the country in March, "If you've not heard us before, you'll be in for a shock... and if you have, well, you'll still be in for a shock. We're a lot more accessible — but not commercially accessible - and the new shit should ignite the pit in a big way.

"We completely agree with bands like Congress and Liar," he adds, chuckling evilly, "And like to see a really violent pit. We can't play our local venue at the moment, 'cos our fans just trashed the place last time we were there!"

Sounds like he might nurture a distaste for the emo scene, then? "Yeah, I hate that shit! Getting all emotive and feeling sorry for y'self, I can't really see the point in it at all. Thank God you don't see that sort of behaviour at metal shows!"

CORPORATION 187 – ISSUE 76 (MARCH 2000)

Corporation 187

Here at Terrorizer we give very little column space to covers bands, and for good reason; we expect a little innovation with our extremity. But when those covers bands develop into something fresh and exciting in their own right, then we have to sit up and listen. Especially if it was a Slayer tribute band and they only went and developed into Corporation 187, the latest Swedish speed sensations who have just unveiled their battering ram debut, 'Subliminal Fear', on Earache's underground metal imprint, Wicked World.

Actually, it's a little unfair to harp on about Divine Intervention (as their fling at being Slayer clones was aptly monikered) because they only existed in that guise for three months back in 1995, and did but a handful of shows.

"Divine Intervention helped tighten us up as a band, and obviously it made our playing faster and more aggressive," says their guitarist Magnus, calling me and trying to put it all in perspective. "Slayer is one of our biggest influences, but no more so than, say, Metallica. Back when we were learning to play, we went out and bought books of tablature and learned all their songs too."

Not wishing to sound like a dog with a bone, Slayer still seems to be the predominant influence in your sound?

"We are big fans of their riffing," he admits, "But we do have a slightly different style ourselves. There's a bit more Swedish death metal in our mix; we've always loved Entombed and At The Gates."

Wait just a minute, there's a hint of the Ripper Owens here. From playing metal covers as kids to ending up signed to the very label that all your favourite records were released on. You guys must be on top of the world.

"We were very excited to be contacted by Earache. Like you said, many of our favourite bands came from that label... not just Entombed, but Napalm Death, Terrorizer, Morbid Angel... they obviously have good taste, so it was doubly flattering that they liked us so much.

"We sent it to a lot of other labels too and we did get quite a bit of interest, but Wicked World seemed to be the most interested. They also seemed to be the ones who wanted to sign us purely because they loved the band; they were phoning us every day."

And you're not worried that you'll get lost in either the new wave of Swedish death metal deluge or indeed amongst all the quality metal that Wicked World is pumping out?

"We try not to worry about what we can't really control," says Magnus, in closing. "There's a lot of great bands out there, and a lot of them don't even have record deals, and there's a lot of friendly rivalry between the bands here. So we just make sure that we make the best music we can, so as to stay ahead of the game."

CORRUPT MORAL ALTAR – ISSUE 233 (MARCH 2013)

Corrupt Moral Altar

"Complete chaos," laughs guitarist John Cooke of Corrupt Moral Altar's 'Luciferian Deathcult' EP on Baitin' The Trap Records, and he's not wrong. Relentlessly fast, but also snarky and groovy all at the same time, this new band are certainly Liverpool's most exciting grind export for many a year. "We're living in a pretty messed up world right now," he adds, "And who knows how bad things are going to get? We're just using Corrupt Moral Altar to get our anger out – come and see us live and you'll see what I mean!"

CRO-MAGS 'THE AGE OF QUARREL' CLASSIC ALBUM FEATURE – ISSUE 193 (FEBRUARY 2010)

Cro-Mags May 2000, CBGB, by Danielle Dombrowski

As absolutely seminal albums go, 'The Age Of Quarrel' by Cro-Mags was a watershed moment in not only New York Hardcore, but extreme music in general, influencing everyone from Anthrax to Machine Head and back again. Ian Glasper sought out founding member and original hardcore hooligan Harley Flanagan to find out what coloured it quite so intensely.

219

BEFORE THE QUARREL...

At risk of stating the obvious, New York City's Cro-Mags put the 'hard' into 'hardcore', and in the process dropped one of the most important hardcore punk albums of all time, 'The Age Of Quarrel'. To this day that 1986 debut, originally issued through Rock Hotel, resonates with a ferocious intensity that is hard to define, and even harder to deny: it simply pulses with a violent urgency, oft-copied but never equalled, that was indicative of the crazy scene that spawned it.

"Yeah, there was a lot going on," recalls bassist Harley Flanagan, who played drums for The Stimulators – aged ten! - before founding Cro-Mags with guitarist Parris Mayhew and original vocalist Eric Casanova. "I mean, the scene had been thriving for a while; I'd been around since the Seventies, the punk days, and lived through all of that Max's Kansas City era, of Johnny Thunders and the Ramones and the Dead Boys and all of that. The NYHC scene sort of sprouted from The Stimulators, and the Bad Brains, who moved down from DC, and this other band called The Mad. We had a really young fanbase, not so many of the old school junkie punks from the late Seventies, and there was all kinds of crazy shit going down...

"Even when we were recording the album, we'd be running straight from the studio to [legendary NYC punk club] CBGBs and into these brawls where people were literally getting their fingers bitten off and their heads kicked in... it was totally insane, like 'Spinal Tap' meets 'Clockwork Orange'!"

Hence the relentless aura of chaos that pervades 'The Age Of Quarrel' and makes it so uniquely pernicious: this wasn't an act, this was brutally real; the Cro-Mags weren't just singing about 'Survival Of The Streets' and 'Hard Times', they were living and breathing this grim reality every single day. Yet the band's incendiary attitude was paradoxically tempered with an emerging spirituality, some of the lyrics inspired by [then vocalist] John 'Bloodclot' Joseph and Harley's keen interest in Krishna consciousness and vegetarianism.

SEEKERS OF THE TRUTH...

Another paradox with the Cro-Mags was just how great these guys were as musicians. Considering that some of them were living in squats with no electricity whilst writing 'The Age Of Quarrel', it's a consummate example of early crossover, combining the raw energy of punk rock, the manic speed of USHC and the solid technical skills of thrash metal. Whilst never veering too far into metal territory, even the simplest songs on the album are delivered with such thumping confidence, that only the most cliquey metaller couldn't but help be impressed by the Cro-Mags' grasp of powerful dynamics. Surely the intro to 'We Gotta Know' is one of the most recognisable openings to any hardcore album ever, and the accompanying video, in almost constant rotation on MTV at the time, did much to reinforce the band's well-deserved reputation as the best live band out there – bar none.

"Most hardcore bands were content to just imitate other hardcore bands that had been around before them, or that were around at the time," reckons Harley, "But we were trying to incorporate other elements of music in there as well; for me and Parris, who basically wrote the music together, I gotta say that Bad Brains and Motorhead were the two things that we had majorly in common, but I mean there was other stuff. We used to see a lot of the same old school hardcore bands like Minor Threat and everything else, and all of that influenced us; for me also, Discharge and early Venom, but we had a lot of other influences... we both listened to all sorts of music.

"[Drummer] Mackie was into a few other punk bands like The Damned - but he was also into all kinds of crazy fusion stuff too, like Lenny White, and lots of DC go-go bands. He turned me onto some good shit back in the day. One of my favourite albums he turned me onto was Lenny White's 'Astral Pirates'; I bought it off the side-walk in front of Gem Spa on St. Mark's in like '84 or '85. He pointed it out, and said, 'That album is bad ass!' He was right! We used to bug out on Al Di Meola and Return to Forever, 'Romantic Warrior', all kinds of crazy shit. Even though I was a hardcore skinhead, I was always into music. We were all serious about playing; we weren't just a straight hardcore band that couldn't play... I was listening to all this crazy stuff because I wanted to become a better musician."

DAYS OF CONFUSION...

That's not to say that 'The Age Of Quarrel' is a hotbed of musical diversity – it isn't, it's a no-holds-barred, supremely feral hardcore album, and although the songs are fairly simplistic at first glance, they are delivered so slickly and with such commitment, they never grow old. Harley's throbbing bass chords and John's impassioned cries, Parris and Doug [second guitarist, Holland]'s meaty riffage and Mackie's masterful rhythmic interpretations of those riffs, all add up to an album with frightening focus. Lightning like this can only be bottled once though, and despite a very strong sophomore album – 1989's 'Best Wishes', that saw bassist Harley taking over vocal duties from John, and Pete Hines replacing Mackie behind the kit – the aggressive volatility that defined the Cro-Mags eventually led to their creative demise, a bitter feud developing between John and Harley that still simmers even today, and many different incarnations of the band that could never hope to hold a torch to the line-up that committed 'The Age Of Quarrel' to tape.

"Yeah, when me, John, Mack, Doug and Parris were on it, that shit was something you don't see very often, I'll tell you," concurs Harley, of the band's far-reaching legacy. "I never knew people would remember that album as long as they have, but I knew we were one of the best bands out at that time, and I'm still proud of that shit. I haven't seen many bands that do live what we did back then; I have only seen a few bands that did it for me like I know we did it for others, but hey, that's life... every time I go on stage [Harley now fronts the equally heavy Harley's War] I give it 110%; that's all I can do - that's what I did then and that's what I do now. It's funny really, hardcore and then the Cro-Mags had this huge ripple effect; even though it never made money - we certainly never made any at least! - it had a wide-reaching effect that caused a lot of other things to change and happen, it really did, so hey, people can say what they want about me and the other guys, but people are still talking about that shit we wrote when I was living in a fucking squat with no lights or electricity or running water back in 19-fuckin'-84. So even though a lot of bands that made way more money than us came and went and were forgotten soon after, people still remember us and what we did, and that's something in itself so..."

FROM THE CUTTING ROOM FLOOR:

What was the vibe of the NYHC scene as Cro-Mags were preparing to record 'The Age Of Quarrel'? Tell us about the zeitgeist behind the album...

HF: Check out my new book ['Life Of My Own', published by Feral House]- it will tell you all about not just the scene and the band but the neighbourhood itself, and the type of crazy shit that used to go down. I go into all of this stuff in a lot more detail, and it all influenced us and our music.

What would you say were the band's primary influences as you wrote and recorded the LP?

HF: Well, besides the first songs I recorded I did some solo recording back in like '82 or '83, 'Don't Tread On Me' and a few others that are now out on the Harley's War CD. That kind of started it as far as the direction we were going in, but again, in my book there is a song-by-song breakdown on what influenced each song on that album musically and lyrically. In a way, we kind of capped off that first generation of hardcore 'cos we were doing our thing in like the early- to mid-Eighties, you know...? We weren't like a hardcore band from 1980, we were a little later; our demo and a lot of our gigging was in '84 - that was when we started to kind of takeover. So we had all those bands that had influenced us coming up, everything from Black Flag to Circle Jerks and Minor Threat... all those early hardcore gigs in NY influenced us and who and what we were. I was lucky to have been in it since the pre-hardcore punk days, so I really did see a lot of great shit, and kind of saw the beginning of the whole shit we now call hardcore, and or even crossover and all that stuff that came later. I mean I was there in the punk days chilling with The Clash, Richard Hell, The Ramones, The Dead Boys... all the original punk rock motherfuckers back in the Seventies, so I pretty much seen it all go down from then 'til now.

Tell us about the original cover for the album and why it never got used, and your feelings on the image that did adorn the record?

HF: Well, I picked the cover art, with the explosion; I mean, it was my idea to use the nuclear explosion. We looked at several different pictures, and that was the one we bought the rights to use, and that was what got censored. It was something that we argued with the label about – they didn't want us to use it, 'cos they thought it was too offensive. It was a mushroom cloud with all the 'sinful' activities going on inside it… when I say 'sinful', I mean according to Hindus and Buddhists and so on: acts of violence against animals, children and humanity, drugs, illicit sex, gambling… all the things that are causing world turmoil… the actions of man. One part of it had two gay guys in it, and some people at the label who were gay got all pissed off, but it also had straight people in it too, as well as strippers and pornography and so on, but anyway there was some people at the label who found it offensive. This was Profile, the big hip hop label… yeah, it was too offensive for a hip hop label, which goes to show how long ago this was. Anyway, we insisted that they use it, so they did, but they printed it in a colour that blurred out all the stuff they found 'offensive', so we were like, 'Yo, fuck that! If you're gonna censor our shit, you better print 'Censored' right across it, so people know that you did censor our shit on purpose…' Fuck that shit. And after a short stalemate, that's what they did.

Can you try to define what it is that sets the album apart from every other hardcore album made before or since?

HF: Just good songs. Besides the few classic bands, most other bands just didn't have them. And lyrics that were real; it sounded like we meant it 'cos it was all taken from me and our original singer and lyricist Eric J. Casanova's and John's actual lives. A lot of people don't know this, but John only wrote like four or five sets of lyrics on that album, and I even wrote parts of those as well; the rest of it was all me and our old singer Eric; he and I wrote the majority of the words on 'AOQ', but again, in my book, I'll tell you who wrote what lyric, almost down to each line, and what story inspired each song. A lot of funny and chaotic shit went into all those fucking songs – they all came from real stories, that are all in the book.

How was the record received by the press and fans at the time?

HF: Fairly well, I guess. I mean all that shit was still underground, that whole Rock Hotel thing, and then some of the Metal Blade or Megaforce or whatever other labels started signing bands; I can't even remember all of them, but that was the first era of underground bands on the hardcore circuit and the eventual 'crossover' scene. So it wasn't getting too much mainstream press if that's what you mean, but we got good reactions from the metal magazines… they were always a little confused just 'cos of the whole 'hardcore meets Krishna' image that was being leaned into by everyone who reviewed us, so it was funny in that way, but they liked the record. I don't remember any negative press really, just some dumb stuff here and there 'cos of this weird combination of my skinhead past meets the Hindu/Krishna stuff in this really heavy hardcore, almost pre-crossover, album, all coming from NYC's Lower

East Side. Actually, come to think of it, we did get some mainstream press - Lisa Robinson, who was a big writer, loved us, so we did get some write-ups in The Post and The Times and shit like that. We were also starting to do some big shows around 'AOQ'... I mean we were one of the only - if not the only - hardcore band in NY that could sell out the Ritz back then. I don't know, it was a long time ago now... we did get a lot of press, but it wasn't the way it is now, where it's just ridiculous with all this reality show crap and all the fucking media whores... everyone has MySpace and Facebook and all this crap - anyone can get noticed now.

I know the Cro-Mags have splintered dramatically several times over the decades, but none of that lessens the primal majesty of that debut album - would you agree?

HF: Well, you can't take away from what we did together and I don't know what else to say; I've tried to reach out to those guys several times over the years, 'cos if nothing else I think we did some cool stuff together, and I think it would be awesome to do it again, however unlikely, but I am also onto other things. I just released a Harley's War CD and DVD through MDV Entertainment Group. I just got back from Japan, where I was gigging with Discharge, GBH and The Exploited; while I was there, I got to train a little at a jiu-jitsu dojo in Yokahama; for those of you who don't know, that is one of the things I love. I am a purple belt under Renzo Gracie, and used to compete in grappling and submission fighting events, and have fought some MMA on the underground fight circuit - all of which is in the book as well - but yeah, Japan was great.

Things are good: I have my two sons keeping me busy, and I am in the studio right now, working on some new music. but I tell you, as far as Cro-Mags goes, I do wish everyone could put the past in the past and if nothing else, do one final true reunion gig... maybe film it, put it out on CD and DVD. I think it would be great, and I think we owe it to ourselves as well as the fans, just 'cos so many bands rode our coattails to success, and we seemed to fall short of ever really making it. However, our music seems to have stood the test of time, and that alone is something to be kind of proud of, and I think something that is worth doing a reunion for, but I ain't gonna push the issue any more than I have. I may record more Cro-Mags records in the future, with or without those guys, who knows? In the meantime, I have the new Harley's War release out, and the book coming out. I can't imagine it happening; everyone's got too much beef, and old beefs die hard, especially in the age of quarrel, but I think it's sad in a way. Shit, I told John ages ago, and have told him many times since, if we can't let it go then shit, I'll fight your ass any day of the week - we can film that shit and put it on DVD, and end all the shit talk and all the fake Cro-Mags line-ups can all go to the wind. But honestly, I could really care less about that anymore, it's all old news. Those guys were once my friends and we made some great music together; man, we did some sick gigs and it's too bad most people who have seen some kind of fake Cro-Mags never saw the real shit.

Crossover 2000 - Merauder, by Albert Licano

This month, we're privileged to be on the receiving end of a monster five-header tour that promises to set more than a few venues on fire across the nation. Out of the traps and running straight at us are Merauder, Turmoil, Stuck Mojo and Power Of Expression, the package to be rounded out by one other group. Since we've featured most of these bands already in the pages of Terrorizer, we thought we'd send our man Ian Glasper along to talk to Century Media boss Robert, the man behind the tour concept, and find out a little more......

Shortly, England will be under attack. The invaders will not be repelled, so all we can do is batten down the hatches and hope we survive the onslaught. The perpetrators of this malicious assault? Five of German label Century Media's leading lights! The ambitious banner under which they march across an unsuspecting Europe? 'Crossover 2000 - The New Generation'.

More on these forthcoming mêlées shortly, but first I wanted to know more about the driving force behind it all, Century Media themselves, and who better to reveal all than head honcho [not to mention founder and president!] Robert...

"l formed the label in January 1989, with the first band on Century Media, a German band called Despair," he recalls, casting his mind back to those humble beginnings. "l was actually singing in that band at that time, and we did have a lot of interest from the underground. We got offers from Roadrunner, SPV, Noise, Nuclear Blast and one or two more - more or less all the underground metal labels that were around at that time, but

I had a gut feeling not to get involved with any of those people. I thought they were full of shit, how they treated their bands, and I knew we deserved better, so I started my own label.

"But now, looking back, I have to give those people credit for the job they're doing, because now I know it's not easy to run a record label, and certain things I was seeing back in '89 that pissed me off were just necessary rules of business that you have to follow otherwise you'll sink! Those labels weren't as bad as I thought, but that was the way I saw it at the time, so I followed the punkier,

D.I.Y. route. We borrowed some money here and there and recorded our album, 'Victory Of Hate', and I got some help from SPV and Nuclear Blast, and after a year I'd signed four more bands!"

I know it's a difficult question, but I wonder what his favourite release is, in hindsight... Robert surprises me with an almost immediate reply!

"'Alpha Omega' by The Cro-Mags, which was the best, but also the most painful. It was a very difficult album! First, it was a huge hassle to get the band together, to get them out of old contracts that needed to be resolved and all kinds of other bullshit, then it was very disappointing that the band split up three weeks after the album was recorded! Harley Flanagan just felt he was bigger than God, and wanted to kick out John Joseph and Doug Holland, and the band was more or less finished then! He was more into hanging out with junkie groupies than coming to the video shoots we planned, so all that money was wasted..."

But you did do two more albums with the Cro-Mags... "The live album was more or less to make money back that we'd lost, and we did 'Near Death Experience' which was left over material from the 'Alpha Omega' sessions which just hadn't been properly produced."

Again, with the luxury of hindsight and experience, is there anything you now regret ever releasing?

"Mmmm," he pauses for thought, "No, I don't think so. Looking back, there were some albums that I couldn't see weren't going to do any good. There were certainly a few bands that I had higher hopes for! Overall, though, I don't regret releasing anything by any of the bands I signed."

What inspired you to put together the package tour? "Many times, booking agents and promoters try to rip off the bands by not paying them, or rip off the labels by charging them way too much for tour support and posters 'n' stuff – but the way this tour was planned right from the beginning was that it would benefit everyone, with very low ticket prices, too. It's giving the audience a chance

to see five really good bands, really good live bands that are fresh, with new product out, and not bands that are seen all the fuckin' time in Europe. I think it's a really fair deal. We hope that a lot of people are going to turn out... and like it!"

Merauder are gonna headline the shows, and they play the kind of New York hardcore that's so heavy it's almost death metal. Their brutal 'Master Killer' album shows them as the natural successors to Biohazard's crown. What with Turmoil on the bill, too,

Crossover 2000 – Power of Expression

representing the new-school metallic slow-motion core made so popular by the likes of Earth Crisis and Snapcase, it's a pretty core-orientated bill! Is that a sign of the times? "Yeah, partly," agrees Robert, "But there will always be hard music. Hardcore, after the early Eighties, went really underground, but now it's come up into the public eye again. But there might be a slight change, and industrial might get bigger, or death metal again. Certain trends come and go, and – if there's more to them than a stupid fake image – stay here for a while. But there's always going to be hard music; there's always going to be kids with a lot of anger and hate and frustration and so on, and that's what makes people want to listen to tough, heavy music…"

Well, the above-mentioned kids should have a field day in the pit at these package shows if tough, heavy music is their tonic. As well as the formidable pairing of Merauder and Turmoil, they'll also get an earful of the cast-iron fusing of metal and rap touted by Stuck Mojo, who are also renowned for their incendiary live performances, and the savage crossover of German quintet Power of Expression, featured in these pages only last month, and last seen on these shores kicking off for Voivod.

The Spudmonsters were originally scheduled to join the tour 'n' all, but contractual obligations have prevented that happening, so Slapshot have just been plucked from the label's burgeoning roster to make up the ranks. In the early stages of its inception, Mucky Pup were linked to the package, as were Madball, who are releasing a CD of their early 7"s and studio out-takes on Century Media in April. What happened there?

"There was a similar tour originally planned for February, which had Mucky Pup as headliners," Robert explains, "But for some reason that didn't happen. It was because of Mucky Pup… their album was late, but they're on tour now, with another of our bands, My Own Victim from Kentucky. I'm actually happy that earlier tour didn't happen, 'cos it would have been limited to just Germany, and the organisation would have been handled by other people, and we wouldn't have had so much control as we do now with M.A.D. [the German booking agents], who are really cool.

"As for Madball, they were originally going to headline, but they weren't able to do it, as they just got finished in the studio on their new album, but they can't come out on tour until the end of May, 'cos Matt Henderson, the guitarist, is in college and has some exams he is unable to miss. It's not that they didn't want to come! They'll be over here soon for a short tour with French band Kickback [who have an album due in June on – yes, you guessed it – Century Media], and after the summer they'll be back for an extensive tour." Has it been a major headache to arrange this package? "No, not really. We had a lot of lead-up time. We talked to all the bands... we know what they want, and we know they'll all get along with each other. I don't see any big problems there."

Is it the same running order every night? "It's going to vary from country to country. In Holland and Belgium, Merauder are really big, so they will headline. In Germany it will be Stuck Mojo..."

A lot of tours miss out the UK, because of the extra logistical problems – was it important for you to get the package over here? "Yes, definitely! I'm very disappointed with what we do in England," he reveals, "At least as far as record sales. I hope that people there are at least taping our music and listening to it, otherwise it would be pretty disappointing how low they are. I think that goes for a lot of other labels as well. Techno and dance are bigger in England; metal and hardcore are much smaller markets. Young kids get more enjoyment going to raves and taking Ecstasy; that seems to be the reality of England, or a good part of the truth. I think that's a shame, but there's nothing I can do about it. I'm just glad that Terrorizer is there and that you support the scene as best you can."

Does he think the package tour can change the situation much? "Well, I'm not hoping for too much; I'm just happy that the bands are going to play there, and I hope we don't lose too much money... but we will definitely lose money there as the daily costs are higher than what the shows will make in England – we will just have to see by how much! That shows our dedication, and the bands' commitment, to this music."

Let's prove him wrong, eh, and show 'em that UK audiences are as crazy and enthusiastic as the best of the European crowds, and not just a bunch of stoned losers that would rather go clubbing than see a good live band kicking it onstage! Get along and see the Crossover 2000 – The New Generation festivals, and make sure you get along early to the London and Birmingham shows because they're all-dayers, and as well as the five Century Media bands, you'll be able to see the metallic all-girl Swedish straightedge band The Doughnuts, as well as two of the UK's hardest and heaviest: Above All and Stampin' Ground.

Lastly, I wonder if this is something Robert would like to see done again? "Yes – if it works out! I think the title Crossover 2000 is pretty good, because it shows we're looking to the future. I want to keep that motto and do a tour every year under that name. The next millennium is coming up, and I'm sure that this sort of music will survive, and all of these bands are going to get bigger and bigger in the years to come."

CROWBAR – ISSUE 56 (JULY 1998)

As a certain cinema blockbuster would suggest this summer, size does matter. Often the most effective predators are so feared purely because of their physical bulk and their ferocious roar. We at Terrorizer had learned, through rumours whispered in awe, of the

Crowbar, courtesy of Adam Sagir @ Century Media

return from the brink of near extinction of one such beast, so we sent our intrepid monster hunter, Ian Glasper, into the steaming swamps of New Orleans in search of said creature. This could be the end of civilization as we know it. If this eight-legged, four-headed humongous gets loose again, it'll only be a matter of time before it rampages across the world once more, flattening cities and destroying everything in its path.

"Well, we had a situation with our label in America which forced us to take some time off," sighs Kirk Windstein, vocalist/guitarist with New Orleans' biggest and heaviest export Crowbar, when asked where the hell they've been for the last few years. "After the 'Broken Glass' record, they just kind of fell apart and they didn't do much with it, so we set our sights on securing a new deal and we were involved in a lot of business stuff, behind the scenes shit. Then we wrote for six months and recorded for two, so although to an outsider it might have looked like we weren't doing anything, we were actually pretty busy."

Well, whatever they've been up to, I for one, am more than pleased to see them back. I've been a fan of sludge core, or whatever the hell you want to call it, since I first clapped ears on Crowbar's 'Obedience Through Suffering' debut way back in '92, and they've consistently released quality tomes of brutal weightiness every year, each one reaffirming my affinity to their morosely melodic metal-cum-grind. Over the years I've managed to interview many of their peers, but never the one band who infected me with swamp fever in the first place...

But now my time is come, and with such a devastating new record in the racks as 'Odd Fellows Rest', on Mayhem Records, so too, hopefully, has Crowbar's. It hasn't been an easy ride the last couple of years as Kirk explains; it wasn't just labels they were trying to tie down, it was their own line-up.

"Well, Matt [Thomas, their other guitarist since 93's eponymously-titled second album – IG] left to take over the family business and he moved to Oklahoma. Then we got this guy called Jay in the band, but he had to move to Baltimore so that didn't work out. Then we got Kevin Bond in, but he just wasn't as serious as the rest of us wanted him to be. So in the end we wrote the new record as a three piece, just me, Todd and Jimmy. But now we've got Sammy [Duet, from Acid Bath – IG] in the band since the beginning of the year."

So what is it about Crowbar that these guys can't cope with? Is it musical differences or is it a personal problem?

"No, there's no personal problems at all," Kirk reassures me, and having found him so damn amiable on the phone despite me being a total stranger, I tend to believe him, you know? "Some of them did complain that I took control of everything, but I had no choice 'cos no one else was doing it, writing or anything. But with Sammy it's already working out really good, 'cos he's a good player and a good writer. We've already written some new stuff since we recorded this new record."

The strangely named 'Odd Fellows Rest' (the name of a cemetery in New Orleans, Kirk explains to me) sees the band in fantastic form, mashing out the massive riffs we've come to expect from them, with their usual authority, but also adding a whole new dimension to their now trademark wall of sound.

"Well, the 'Broken Glass' album was like the end of our first chapter as a band," reckons Kirk. "We had wanted to make the perfect Crowbar record with the right production, the right songs, the right packaging, and we were really pleased with 'Broken Glass'.

"After that it was like what do we do from here? We've got to do something different to keep people interested in the band. We'd built this wall around ourselves, and there were certain things that we couldn't do song-wise 'cos we had painted ourselves into a corner. For whatever reason, we felt that we couldn't expand ourselves... so we wrote this album!"

Anyone fearing a drastic departure, can wipe the cold sweat from their brows though 'cos the boys have not lightened their approach by one single gram, but they have had added even more melody to their titanic musical movements, though still more akin to plate tectonics than music. They always could write a great song - it helped elevate them above the other noisy swamp critters - but this time they've penned some incredibly mature sounding numbers, that display a real depth of feeling. The biggest factor in this development is Kirk's voice that has really been given space to shine.

"That was a conscious decision. Jimmy was always saying he liked my voice better when I sang rather than just screamed. I mean, I don't have the greatest voice, but it's not bad, you know? And I'd never use my whole range, never use my real voice, at least not much of it. And I guess I'm just getting sick of the screaming; I can convey more emotion through that painful vocal style. It's also to do with the style of the new material; the last record was flat out aggressive. These songs are still heavy, but also deeper, more sad than angry, so that pained vocal style suited them better."

Leaving the music now, I'd like to talk about Crowbar's lyrics, as I know that they've always been an integral part of the Crowbar experience, for me at least, and I've often sought solace amongst the sombre company of Kirk's words during particularly low moments of my life. They spoke quietly to me, reassuring me that I wasn't the only one enduring that pain, and that given time it would pass. The human psyche is remarkably resilient, but it's comforting to know that there is someone else out there who's been through whatever it is that you're struggling with, and has come out the other end, tattered but basically intact and sane.

"Oh, you know how life is," he says, disparagingly. "It's hard on a lot of people... most people. I just write what I feel, but a lot of people can relate to it, because everyone has been cheated on, everyone has lost loved ones, everyone has lost friends to drugs... I mean, I had a bad relationship experience last year and right after that I got into the song-writing thing for this new record. It's very inspirational.

"It's weird though," he continues, "Because lyrically, the words are all spur of the moment. For the last three albums, I haven't had 90% of the lyrics written before the studio. I might have a melody in my head, and I usually lock myself into a room in the studio with a tape player at the last minute, and just write them on the spot. It seems like there isn't a lot of thought goes into them - they just come out very naturally. They're just there. So it's kinda strange when people come up to me at shows and say, 'Wow, thanks a lot, your lyrics really helped me through some tough times,' 'cos I don't sit there all night working on them or anything."

Perhaps it's because they're so instinctive that they come across as more honest?

"It works for me. I've never felt like I'm a great lyricist anyway. For me, the words always take second place to the music. I'm so involved with playing and writing on guitar. I mean, the words are important, but they just come out so naturally, sometimes in just five or ten minutes. I don't have to worry over them."

A few years ago, it seemed to me that Crowbar were ideally placed to be the next big thing, but then you had all this hassle and you've undoubtedly slipped way down the ranks, and that's got to be frustrating, right?

"Yeah, but unfortunately it's part of this business," says Kirk stoically. "As soon as we started to do good, instead of the label pushing us even more and taking the initiative with more promotion and touring, they were just satisfied with that little bit of success, and they sat back and made a few bucks. Last year, when the label situation dissolved, we all had to sit back and decide what we were going to do. Were we ready to start over again and bust our asses and go hungry and make this happen, or were we old and tired and ready to pack it in? We all said, 'Fuck that, we believe in this band; we love what we're doing, let's get another fucking deal and just do what we gotta do.'

"As soon as we knew that Mayhem was interested, it totally put that fire back in us. We are hungrier to play now than since we first started the band, and that's the truth. It's became like a challenge again; we're practicing more than ever. It feels so fresh again. It's like a brand new band with their first CD coming out; we're very, very excited.

"We've been out of the picture for quite a while," Kirk concludes, "So we've got something to prove. We had to make a record that was a bit special to prove we can still cut it. We've got a lot of lost ground to regain, and we can't wait to get out there again."

Sidebar:
Ever wondered what it's like to have 400 people all yelling, 'You fat bastard!' at you over and over again? Kirk Windstein takes the philosophical view:

"Oh, I think it's hilarious. Believe me, we don't kid ourselves that we're good-looking guys or anything. We know what we're about. We know that we're fat, ugly bastards, but that's why people can associate with us. Half of the people chanting that at us are fatter than we are themselves. We take it all in our stride. I don't give a shit - I'm there to jam and have some fun. We look like we sound, that's all I can say. Although the new guy is really small and skinny at the moment! But we'll beef him up, we'll fill him out with something."

THE CROWN - ISSUE 99 (MAY 2002)

The Crown - courtesy of Adam Sagir @ Century Media

Sweden's masters of death and disaster, The Crown, are back with a new singer, Tomas Lindberg (he of At The Gates fame) returning to his death metal roots, and a new album for Metal Blade, in the shape of 'Crowned In Terror'. Things are looking good for this particular blast troupe, so we sent Ian Glasper to investigate further.

It's been a cracking start to the year for death metal fans. What with the debut from Insision knocking down walls, and The Crown's fifth album, 'Crowned In Terror' more than fulfilling all our high expectations too, it looks like Sweden's on another roll. Not content with fronting Skitsystem (see last issue) and Lock Up, the legendary ex-At The Gates frontman Tomas Lindberg is back again, bellowing yet more anger and hatred, this time at The Crown's helm. So, what exactly happened to old singer Johan Lindstrand? Guitarist Marko Tervonen is more than willing to explain all:

"He just didn't enjoy touring as much as the rest of us," sighs the axeman. "He always loved the music, but in the end, he wanted more of a normal life; there are just so many sacrifices you have to make to be on the road all the time, both financially and socially. We wanted to take the band up to another level, and he realised that he couldn't make that extra commitment. But we totally respect his decision, and it was a very amicable split."

Still, getting none other than Tomas Lindberg to replace him was quite a coup.

"Yes, he was the perfect person to fill Johan's shoes, and actually, when we all talked about what we were going to do next, he was in fact our first choice of who we would ideally like to join the band! We really didn't want a novice with no experience, we wanted someone who knew the real deal about touring in this kind of band. And, of course, we didn't want to lose any momentum either.

"If Tomas had said no, I don't know what we would have done," laughs Marko. "It was weird too, because a few days before, he had actually called up Magnus [Olsfelt, The Crown's bassist – IG], to see if he wanted to join a death metal project he was starting himself. Magnus called him back and said, 'Well, I can't come join you, but maybe you'd like to come join us!' The time was right for both parties to join forces; Tomas had been away from the death metal scene for six years, but now he really has his hunger back."

Apart from the change of singer, it's been quite a ride for the band since the last album [2000's rather ripping 'Deathrace King' – IG], which saw them on the road all over the world with virtually every extreme metal band out there. How did the US audiences respond? They can be pretty intolerant of European bands.

"They were amazing!" enthuses the six-stringer. "We were told by loads of other bands we know that it would be hard, and that we shouldn't get too pissed off at the crowd if they didn't react to us, but we went down just great every single night. It was so good that we're going back soon to headline our own shows for a month! That will be a dream come true for sure, although it's also quite scary; it'll either break us over there or send us bankrupt, haha!"

I'm sure there's nothing to worry about. 'Crowned In Terror' is as accomplished a piece of blinding, (slightly) melodic death metal as I've heard in a long time. From the striking cover imagery (yeah, I know skulls have been done to death, but they sure as hell look cool here) to the Venom-spoof logo on the back of the booklet, from the hell-for-leather pace to the furious riffing that ignites every blast-laden song, this is pure death metal mayhem to rival the unholy leaders of the genre. And with a song on here called 'Death Metal Holocaust', it doesn't appear to be a label The Crown shy away from...

"Well, why deny it? I love death metal; that's what we are! I love the label too, but it doesn't really mean shit nowadays. I mean, both In Flames and Cannibal Corpse are labelled as such, and you wouldn't find two more different sounding bands! All the bands who've been around for a long time [The Crown, albeit as Crown Of Thorns, started way back in 1990 – IG], we all have our own sound now, but we still have our roots in that scene. It helped shape us all, not only as musicians, but as people. We're more than happy with our past."

CROWN OF THORNZ – ISSUE 35 (OCTOBER 1996)

Crown Of Thornz, CBGBs, 1994, pic by Carl Gunhouse

So, what will it be – a coronation or a crucifixion? A coronation, of course, and Ian Glasper is on hand to anoint New York's newest and finest, Crown Of Thornz, with the sainted essence of hardcore...

Yeah, yeah, yeah, they're from Noo Yoik, and it seems that all the bands from there gain instant acclaim, but you know us by now. You know you can trust us to do our homework and exercise some discretion, and any band that gets into these hallowed pages is here 'cos they damn well excite us. And Crown of Thornz are responsible for

many a swollen gland here at Hardcore Towers, not least of all 'cos their debut full-lengther on Another Planet, 'Mentally Vexed', demonstrates the kinda balance between rock melody, hardcore power and metal excess the equal of Leeway's best output... and geographical location can go swing.

"We just got together and jammed, and before we knew it, we had a show", recalls drummer Dimi incredulously. "We'd only practised two or three times together before we played a show with Murphy's Law and Killing Time, so it wasn't just any show either. It was a really big show, it was pretty nerve-racking. We only had four songs, so we turned a fifteen-minute set into a thirty-minute set, you know - lots of talking between songs, lotsa shout-outs to our friends", he laughs fondly at the memory.

Crown Of Thornz, The Wetlands (NYC), 1995, pic by Carl Gunhouse

"From there it took off. When we played out we started to see really great reactions from crowds. Right from the start, it really clicked. We were all in bands before, so we were all clued up on shit like song-writing. The band had only been together about a month and a half before we recorded our first EP, ['Trainyard Blues' for Equal Vision Records – IG], the whole process was incredibly fast. We didn't spend any time cultivating an image or a style like some New York bands do."

I guess it was inevitable that it would come up, eh? It seems there is no denying the influence that that city has had on the hardcore scene worldwide. So much so, in fact, that almost any band lucky enough to originate from there is instantly heaped with accolade... but is it all plain sailing once you've established with the core-hungry public where your band comes from?

"Oh, there's pros and cons to being from New York," reckons Dimi. "The biggest pro, of course, is that you've already had bands go out there and do the legwork, like Sick Of It All, Madball and Biohazard. They've already gone out there and shown everyone the New York style, and paved the way for others to come to places like Europe, and even Japan and Australia, which is pretty amazing, when you consider how far this city's influence has travelled.

"However, people do arrive at preconceptions about you. We don't sound like Biohazard or Madball or whoever, so I hope the kids don't expect us to, especially if we hook up with a band like that."

One band that Crown of Thornz do sound like is the aforementioned Leeway, a fact that Dimi gladly admits to. "Well, Leeway have been a big influence on us, they put out some great records, and A.J. [Novello - Leeway guitarist] did produce the album. He's helped us in a lot of other ways, too, and we give him respect for that."

Including getting the band into the near-legendary - nah, fuck it, the legendary - Normandy Studios under the guidance of Tom Soares, responsible for many a true hardcore classic, including 'Age of Quarrel' by the Cro-Mags, Leeway's 'Desperate Measures', 'Master Killer' by Merauder and Shelter's 'Mantra', to name but a few.

"When we first got there, we were almost in awe of the place", he reveals candidly. "A.J. was telling us all these stories about bands who'd been there, and then Tom was telling us stories, too. It was like 'The Ghosts of Normandy' or something, but it inspired us to make the best record we could. Some of the greatest albums of all time have come out of that studio."

"The audiences are very tough here, tough to please, that is, 'cos they're really spoilt," continues Dimi, on some of the other pitfalls of coming from the scene that some (especially in Europe) would have you believe is the best in the world. "Bands play here every night, not every weekend or every month or every summer, it's every night, so kids see too many bands, and if you're not the ultimate band with the craziest stage-show, you're just another band to them."

When I suggest that the scene may have become over-saturated, with too many purely copycat bands springing up which eventually detracts from the impact of the originals to the untrained outsider, he disagrees though. "I wish there were more bands, to help out, to help spread the vibe of New York Hardcore. You can never have too many hardcore bands... well, I know I can't! Hardcore is slightly different to other musical styles, 'cos it brings together a whole bunch of street sounds, like punk, rap, even death metal, and that's what makes it so rich. You can have that hardcore background, but can take it into a whole new genre, like Quicksand did, or Into Another. You can bring to it what you like, and make of it what you want. That's why it always stays so exciting."

One big criticism often levelled at bands from you-know-where is that all they do is preach about unity or 'the street' (as in life on the streets, not 'Coronation...'), and whilst these topics might mean an awful lot to the bands, and to many who live in cities, if you live in Chipping Sodbury it's all so much hot air, y'know? [Hey, don't diss my hometown! – Irate Country Bumpkin Ed]

"A lot of bands get stuck in one frame of mind when they're writing lyrics, and they often pander to people's preconceptions without realising it", agrees Dimi. "With us, Ezac [their vocalist - IG] takes inspiration from all over, all around him, from comic books to personal experiences, and when you live in Queens, there's plenty of those to draw on. We jump around a lot, and we do that with our music, too. Whatever we think is good will end up on our records, we don't back away from something that's different. Songs come out of us like sweat!"

This proliferation of music might help explain their involvement in a side project, name of Skarhead. Actually, you may well have heard of Skarhead before C.O.T., seeing as they also featured a couple of members of Madball in the incarnation that appeared on their 'Drugs, Money, Sex' MCD, but, as is so often the case with these projects, it appears that the line-up is something that could stay fluid, depending upon circumstance. Dimi elaborates: "Crown of Thornz were set to record a few tracks for the 'New York's Hardest' compilation [a killer comp. CD on Idjit featuring the likes of Full Contact and Vision of Disorder - track it down if you're serious about NYHC -IG] and we were down the studio with Hoya and Freddy from

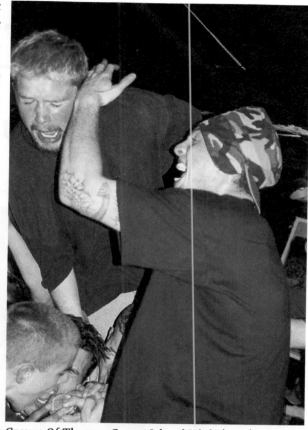

Crown Of Thornz, Coney Island High (NYC) 1995, pic by Carl Gunhouse

Madball. At the time, our bassist was out on tour with 108, so we got together and wrote two songs on the spot in the studio for the CD. We gave those songs to Another Planet, and they said they'd definitely release an EP if we ever recorded one, so we did."

It seems like some bands have all the luck... "It was just a case of the right people being in the right place at the right time. It's a musical outlet for us, we do a lot of one-minute songs, we want to keep that style of hardcore alive, y'know? There will be a full-length Skarhead record, but it'll be done in between C.O.T. touring, and it's a case of choosing who we want to guest on it. We want to use lots of different singers, so we have to track 'em all down and get 'em all in the studio, and that all takes time."

A case of don't hold yer breath, I think, kids, but don't despair, 'cos the cracking debut from Crown of Thornz is plenty to be going on with for now. Just don't confuse them with the Swedish death band of the same name! "We did consider changing our name when we found out about them," sighs Dimi, "But we thought, why should we? They're completely different to us, and on the other side of the world. People had better just learn the difference between Crown of Thornz with a 'Z' and Crown of Thorns with an 'S'!"

CHAPTER D:
LET'S WRECK THE PARTY
(BLOODIED BUT UNBOWED)...

THE DAMNED – ISSUE 92 (SEPTEMBER 2001)

The Damned, 2015, by Morat

Despite what Malcolm McLaren might have you believe, The Damned were the original punk band. Seeing as it's their silver anniversary this year and they've just released a brand new album, 'Grave Disorder' on super-hip punk label, Nitro, we thought we'd better send someone to dig up the dirt. Ian Glasper soiled himself at the prospect.

Wanna know what one of the greatest things about writing for Terrorizer is? You might all think it's the money and the fast cars and the hot women, but it's actually getting to talk to some of your favourite bands after listening to their music for many years (Actually, it's the money and the fast cars and the hot women – Thee Ed). They shaped punk rock as we know it (actually releasing a record and touring the States even before the Sex Pistols did), and as such, I wouldn't be exaggerating if I said they helped shape the whole of my teenage and adult life. Of course, I don't tell Damned vocalist Dave

Vanian this as I'm interviewing him, in case he thinks I'm some kind of stalker fanboy, but when he picks up the phone, with the soundtrack to 'The Day The Earth Stood Still' blaring in the background, I'm a happy man indeed.

"Basically, we're now on a US label, and there was lots of other stuff that we had to do out there at the same time," says Dave, explaining why they ended up recording their new album, 'Grave Disorder' in America – the first time they've recorded anywhere other than good ol' Blighty. "And it made sense with the rate of the dollar to the pound too.

"It wasn't a glamorous thing at all, like how it might sound, but it was an interesting studio we recorded in. It was one huge live room, with baffles set up, and it looked more like a large barn. Dusty who owned the studio had an amazing collection of vintage guitars and keyboards too, so that's why we've got all these weird organs on the album!"

And why did you choose Dave Bianco to produce? He's not exactly renowned for his punk output, is he?

"No, but we really wanted someone who could work with different material. To be honest," he chuckles grimly, "All the producers we wanted to use were either dead or insane! We knew we wanted something that would sound good on the radio now, not dated in any way, and we needed someone who could work with guitars and pianos and drums... real musicians basically, and not just samples and stuff. We liked what we'd heard from Dave, and he'd just finished with Johnny Cash..."

The original punk rocker!

"Yeah, the real man in black! So we knew he was the right guy."

After a hiatus of five years since your last album [the unofficial and definitely-not-Dave-Vanian-approved 'I'm Alright Jack And The Beanstalk' – IG] and what with it being almost fifteen years since you worked last with Captain Sensible [he left after 1984's 'Thanks For The Night' EP – IG], how was it being back in the studio with the Captain on guitar once more?

"Oh, the chemistry was instant again," he enthuses. "We actually did a show together a while back – Captain with his Punk Floyd thing and me in the Phantom Chords – and it was nice to see him again. It had been too long, and it wasn't as if there had been any animosity or bad blood between us or anything... it was more a case of, why didn't we do it sooner?

"We ended up doing a 30-second song for that Fat Wreck compilation ['Short Songs For Short People' – IG], and that seemed to kick-start the whole thing..."

And it certainly does seem like the chemistry is back again, with the new record sounding remarkably contemporary, yet retaining all the rich gothic punk textures we always loved about the Damned first time around – not that you ever split up or anything, but you have been quiet on the recording front these last ten years. Although, with a cracking new album in the racks, more than capable of showing the new school just how it should be done, and hip bands like AFI and the Offspring all citing the Damned as a major influence, it looks like we'll be seeing a lot more of the band again – at last. Even if it's not always in the most obvious venues... I see that you recently played a show in a Butlins holiday camp!

The Damned, by Will Binks

"We couldn't resist it," laughs Dave. "The very thought of it conjured all these images of, like, old seaside postcards and 'Carry On' films, but we had a lot of fun. We all had chalets instead of dressing rooms, and there were red coats doing security; it was all very 'Hi De Hi' and very surreal."

2001 is actually the year the Damned celebrate 25 years of anarchy, chaos and musical destruction, which is a good age by anyone's standards, especially as you've just turned in yet another career-enhancing album. Pray tell, how does it feel to be a punk rock institution?

"Well, there's been so many members come and go, it's been very sectioned," ponders Dave. "Obviously it's still the same thing, but it's also very different now, attitude-wise as well as musically. But the people have always been there for us, and that makes you realise that you're doing something... well, not so much 'important' in the usual sense of the word... but you're a part of all those other people's lives. We've overcome so many obstacles over the years, and we've weathered them all, but without the audience we'd have been long gone years ago."

DANZIG – ISSUE 74 (JANUARY 2000)

Catching up with Glenn Danzig whilst on tour, to talk about his new '6:66 Satan's Child' album, was starting to seem about as likely as finding the Holy Grail in Camden market, but luckily for us we had Mr. Persistent, Ian 'The Mountie' (he always gets his man!) Glasper, on the case - and he scooped us the first full Danzig interview for a UK mag in seven years. Take the rest of the month off, that man!

"Well, I left American - a big scumbag label of rip-off fuck-faces! - and went to Hollywood Records... who were even worse! So I talked to a few other labels, including the big new corporate scumfucks on the block, Virgin, but everywhere I went it was the same old bullshit, and I knew that I'd end up killing someone eventually... "

Mmm, Glenn Danzig, calling me from a hotel mid-way on his latest U.S. tour, sure sounds pissed off. Actually, correction: he sounds like he was pissed off, but now he's sitting pretty with a brand new - and rather killer - album in the racks and his band's name on everybody's lips once again. But be assured, the trials and tribulations of the last few years have helped shape the new album, '6:66 Satan's Child', (licensed to Nuclear Blast from Glenn's own Evilive label) into the brooding monster that is it.

In fact, it's darker than Hell's own out-house, and sees Glenn enjoying an impressive return to form. His tortured howl has never sounded better, and the band behind him - basically the same line-up that did the last album three years ago, with the addition of Todd Youth on guitars - is also shaping up to be a force to be reckoned with, too. But first, let's delve into the difficulties endured by Danzig since that 1996 album 'Blackacidevil', 'cos, let's face it, over here at least, his profile suffered immensely thanks to a criminal lack of push on the part of his label back then, Hollywood Records. Some of us feared that he might even have retired from the music business altogether...

"We actually ended up going on tour with no support off that shitty label! We had no backing whatsoever, so we had to get out of that contract which took a while, and finally we were free to go last summer, which was when we started work on this new record. But for the most part, I've basically been working behind the scenes on all this legal bullshit. The problem in America is, you've got all these idiots who don't even listen to the music we play, yet they're employed to make decisions on behalf of your band? Go and fuck yourselves! I won't gear myself to these assholes anymore, it's got to stop.

"And another thing," he spits, well and truly on a roll now. "What about these bands who moan about the government and the police, and then sign to major labels? They don't seem to care too much where their money comes from then. It cost me a fuck of a lot of money just to free myself to make my music again, let alone having to put up with that shit every fucking day! And I'd like to see some of these other bands go through what I had to put up with, and still come out the other end playing music."

So, what kept you motivated during that frustrating hiatus?

"My anger," he says, without hesitation. "That motivated me more than anything. I sat back and looked at the music scene, and all the hypocrites out there - it's all about fucking money for these people. I know I'm ranting here, but I hate these whining fucks."

Well, whatever negative emotions helped create it, 'Satan's Child' is definitely the album Danzig fans have been waiting for. Where the grating 'Blackacidevil' left many of them nonplussed to an extent, with its quasi-industrial soundscapes and savage noisy edge, here we have the shrieking guitar harmonics and surging riffs of old, and of course Glenn's seductive roar - but all welded to the hypnotic rhythms explored on that bleak last record. Lunging from the speakers with the undulating opener 'Five Finger Crawl' (which will be the first video from the new record), it alternates between simplistic riffs that will nail you to the floor and then kill your family in front of you, all the way through to big bluesy doom passages that will astonish you with their sheer size and depth. It all makes for a wonderfully heavy, moody album, and one totally befitting the Danzig name. With the benefit of hindsight, how do you regard 'Blackacidevil' now?

"It kicked fucking ass," responds Glenn indignantly, "And a lot of people went right ahead and ripped it off, too. All my records are a little ahead of their time, but I'd rather be a leader than a follower, y'know? Some people loved it, and some people hated it, but that's cool with me; I'd much prefer people to be passionate about my music rather than being indifferent and unmoved.

"And contrary to popular opinion, it also did real well, too. 'Sacrifice' had way more radio here than even 'Mother' did, and the album made the top five in rock charts all over the world."

I think some people were a little dismayed that you have this awesome voice, but insisted in drowning it in such harsh vocal effects.

"What can I say?" says Glenn dismissively. "If you wanna hear an album with no vocal effects, go form your own fucking band and record one yourself..."

Uh, okay, point taken... but I think I'm safe in saying that this album will be greeted with similarly mixed reviews. Already I've seen it both revered, and slated, but hey, at the end of the day, opinions are like assholes - everyone has one... and mine is the only one that I really value! And I declare '6:66 Satan's Child' to be a roaring success, dripping with gloomy atmospherics, and way heavier than its predecessor, yet without going all trendy - and Korny - on us. So, good news for diehard fans then, but even better is the fact that there are plans afoot for more Danzig material next year than we've seen in the last five...

"Part of my fight with American and Hollywood was to get the rights to everything back," he reveals, "And now I own it all again. All the live recordings and re-mixes, all the MTV videos from 'Danzig III' onwards [hopefully this means we'll get to see those notorious promo clips for songs such as 'It's Coming Down' in all their rubber-clad, penis-piercing glory! - IG], and every unreleased track from every album session! So all that will now be coming out in different formats and with extra tracks. And I'll be doing another 'Black Aria' [Glenn's soundtrack-style side project – IG] album next Christmas, too."

Yep, you read it right, kids; an album of unreleased Danzig, spanning their entire career,

Danzig, Santa Monica Civic, 1989, pic by Alison Braun Photography

and, at last, a full live album - for all of us who thought 'Demonsweatlive' was way too short for its own good.

"Y'know? Rick [Rubin - the band's old producer - IG] didn't even want to do that live MCD," says Glenn incredulously. "He thought it was too early for us to be doing a live record, and I suppose he had a point, so we ended up doing half and half... and yet that live recording was what launched the success of 'Mother'!

"So now there will be a full live record towards the end of next year. It won't be from a single show: it'll be two hours long, a double-CD, for fans of the band that have been with us from the beginning. They'll be able to hear three or four tracks from each and every era of Danzig... and it might help make redundant some of the bootlegs flying around out there, 'cos we've been bootlegged all to shit."

Of course, one of the talking points for all hardcore Danzig fans is the imminent release of the Samhain box-set. Samhain, in case you didn't know, was the band that Glenn fronted between finishing with the Misfits and starting Danzig itself and sonically, as well as career-wise, they were a stepping stone between the two. All three of their albums, steeped as they are in dark, primal violence, are much sought after by collectors, and now, at last, they will all be available once more at sensible prices. And not only are the discs to resurface again, all repackaged and re-mastered for tender Nineties sensibilities, but the band - well, some of them - are back in action on the live front as well... as a strict one-off [goddamn! - IG], Samhain are actually supporting Danzig on their current US tour!

"Yeah, I'm doing two sets a night; we do a Samhain set, and then I go off for twenty minutes and come back on for Danzig."

What does your throat think about that?

"Oh, my voice is doing okay so far," he laughs. "The other guys in Samhain have other stuff to do, so that is it after this tour. This isn't a full-blown reformation or anything; we won't be coming to Europe with this package, and there won't be any new recordings. This is purely to celebrate the release of the box-set."

And not only do we Brits miss out on seeing Samhain, but we could miss out on catching a glimpse of Danzig themselves - and all because certain magazines over here seem unable to resist making snide personal remarks whenever they write about the band. Oh well, Glenn's distaste towards England is well documented, so not only do I get the honour of doing the first full interview for a UK publication in over seven years, but I can console myself that at least I saw 'em when they came over with Metallica way back when, on the back of their first album (gloat, gloat...).

"We certainly won't be coming there when we tour Europe in the New Year - it'll be way too cold for us, and we'll be pissed off enough already, without being there in the winter, too.

"I have every respect for the English fans, but we haven't played England since '92, when we brought Zombie [that's White Zombie, grapple fans! - IG] out with us, even though we've done Europe a lot since then. We always miss the UK out 'cos there's just such a bunch of shit to deal with to play there. It's too expensive for a start, and some

244

of the promoters try to cross-collateralise your shows... also, I did get really pissed off at the UK press back then, and haven't spoken to them since!"

Of course, we may not have heard much about him over here [apologies to our readers in other lands; I'm writing from a UK perspective here − IG] for quite a while, but Mr. Danzig has been more than busy in the interim. He also runs his own highly successful comic company, Verotik (see sidebar for more details), and although he left his old label, Hollywood, he has been courted fairly persistently by another institution of the same name, too. Yes, although nothing has come to fruition yet, I would wager that it shouldn't be too long before we eventually get to see Glenn up there on the big silver screen. For a start, there were rumours of him starring in 'The Prophecy 2', picking up the role of the fallen angel that Christopher Walken played in the downbeat original; and then there was talk of him starring as Wolverine in 'The X-Men' movie, a part that I, for one, think would have been an inspired piece of casting. Unfortunately, it wasn't to be.

"Uh, I would have loved to have done it, and I was flattered to be considered," he sighs, "But it was up in Canada, and they needed me up there for, like, nine months - I wouldn't have even been able to come home at weekends. It would have completely fucked up my schedule, and I'm a musician above all else. I wouldn't have been able to tour for the new album until the middle of next year! They would have wanted me to sign contracts for another movie, too, and two Wolverine 'solo movies'- it would have just been impossible to do Danzig properly."

But don't despair, there's also the distinctly juicy promise of movie adaptations from some of Glenn's comics, which should be awesome, to say the least, if they retain even a little of the insanely explicit violence and sex that the books rejoice in.

"Well, 'Jaguar God' is with a big studio right now," enthuses GIenn, "And that will get done soon. It's gonna be like 'Conan' meets 'Braveheart' − only with a lot more blood! And we've finally got the budget confirmed for a full-length Satanika animated feature, which I'm really excited about. And I'm working on a screenplay for another of my stories, 'The Albino Spider of Dajette', as well..."

Which sounds, um, freaky!

"Oh it is, it's very creepy and twisted. Dajette is this French fashion designer who was born a freak, with eyeballs for nipples! Obviously she can't have a meaningful relationship with anyone, 'cos as soon as she takes her top off, they see these big eyes looking at them, and they flip out [laughs]. Whenever she falls asleep, her id - this albino spider thing - is out there killing prostitutes! We're trying to get David Bowie to play the albino spider. But if I can't make it the way I want to make it, then we just won't bother, because that Verotik stuff was never meant to be watered down."

Such stubbornness seems fairly typical from an artist who is obviously totally unprepared to compromise his creative vision for anyone or anything. After scaling the giddy heights of sold-out arenas and major labels, it would surely have been tempting to listen to the suits at his label, and go where the pepper grows, but no: Danzig 2000

Danzig

is a much more genuine beast, and all the more dangerous and fascinating because of it. Back on his own label, and once again fully behind the wheel, there is no hint of 'playing it safe' on '6:66 Satan's Child'. From the schlocky title to the unrelenting gloomy vibe that prevails throughout, this is unmistakably an album made by Danzig, for Danzig.

"If I ever had have compromised, who knows? We'd probably be as big as Metallica now," sighs Glenn, acknowledging the grim reality of his situation, "But I'd rather give people the real me. When 'Mother' blew up, it would've been so easy to just keep pumping out 'Mother 2', '3', and '4', but that ain't me. I'm not about that, and never have been. I'll always be spitting in someone's face.

"At the end of the day, I've gotta sit back and be proud of the music that I've done. And in five or ten years' time, I want people to still be buying my records – and they do. It's so cool that the Misfits and Samhain still sell so well, as does the Danzig back catalogue.

"Integrity is of the utmost importance to me. As soon as I stop loving what we do – if I find myself doing it just for the money – then I'll stop, 'cos there's far easier ways to make money than being a musician and dealing with this bullshit every fuckin' day."

Dare I ask how you'd make a living if you weren't in this band?

"I'd be an assassin," he deadpans. And what's just a little bit scary folks, is I believe him.

SIDEBAR ONE:
Five Essential Danzig Moments (according to Ian Glasper):

'Static Age' – The Misfits:
Hard to believe that this was recorded way back in early 1978 – but it was. And that it is still so eminently listenable is testament to the strength of this material, which effortlessly rises above its (no) budget production. Best songs? Well, this session only appeared in its original intended album form very recently, but it spawned the now-legendary 'Beware' 12", jammed full of such punkoid classics as 'Hollywood Babylon' and 'Teenagers From Mars'.

'Earth AD' - The Misfits:
Or, when the Misfits went speed metal! A crazily paced album that was unrelenting in its furious attack. Altho' best known for the songs 'Die, Die My Darling' and 'Green Hell' - that were later covered by 'some rock band' or other! - who can resist titles like 'Mommy, Can I Go Out And Kill Tonight?' or 'Death Comes Ripping'?

'November Coming Fire' - Samhain:
After the Misfits self-destructed, Glenn gave free rein to his dark gothic tendencies, and Samhain was the result. It took them three albums to really hit their stride, but when they did, on 'November Coming Fire', it was a sight to behold. Incredibly atmospheric, as well as tribal and pounding, songs like 'Mother Of Mercy' and 'To Walk The Night' could still only hint at the dark delights to come on...

'Danzig' - Danzig:
The super-cocky debut that stopped everyone in their tracks, and even had Metallica begging the band out as tour support to them on the 'Liberty And Justice For All' trek. This album contains songs so good - I'm talking about 'Mother', of course - it took the rest of the world five years to get with the program and see the understated grandeur of Glenn's diabolic vision. And once you've heard the intro riff to 'Twist Of Cain', you never forget it. Ever.
Best songs: every single fucking one of 'em.

'Danzig lV' - Danzig:
The last album recorded by what many regard as the definitive Danzig line-up, '4' is also the most subtle and insidious of all their albums. From the odd-ball 'backwardness' of 'Can't Speak' to the sensual, moody (black) magic of 'Going Down To Die', this is an album draped in veils of shadowy sorrow, and, after the debut, is my favourite Danzig album of all. And what a line-up shot! Best song: 'I Don't Mind The Pain' – I always listen to it before getting a new tattoo, to psyche myself up!

SIDEBAR TWO:
Paying Tribute To A Tribute

You may recall that several issues back we reviewed a Danzig tribute album by a band called – get this! – Glanzig? As tribute records go, it's the proverbial dog's bollocks, a loving, note-perfect collection of everyone's favourite Danzig tracks, and all wrapped up in stunning packaging that pastiches the upside-down cross fold-out booklet that came with 'Lucifuge'. At the time it appeared, I was eagerly awaiting a brand-new record from the Real McCoy, and it was a nice little stop-gap to kill time and have some fun with... but what did Glenn Danzig himself think of it all?
"It's pretty funny," he chuckles good-naturedly. "If they're that influenced by the

THE WORLD's No.1 EXTREME MUSIC MAGAZINE

TERRORIZER

UK EXCLUSIVE

DANZIG
The Son of Samhain Speaks

CELTIC FROST
Tom Warrior's Morbid Tales

TYPE O NEGATIVE
Will the real Peter Steele
please stand up?

Metallica
Sentenced
In Extremo
Writers' Poll 1999
Stratovarius
As Divine Grace
Static-X
Aeturnus
Primary Slave
Evergrey
UK Metal Class of 2000

ISSUE 74   JAN2000   £2.60
PRINTED IN ENGLAND

9 771350 697042   01

Danzig front cover

band, that's fine, y'know? They sent it to my office with a note saying, 'Please don't be mad, we love your band!', which we all thought was pretty funny too. It's cool how much attention to detail they've applied to it..."

I thought it would be appropriate here to catch up with Tony 'Glanzig' himself (ex B-Thong and now with Transport League – IG) for a few words about this unique tribute. "We'd heard that Glenn can get mad about anything," he reveals, laughing, "We thought he might send a hit squad after us when he heard it, but I'm glad he took it the right way. After all, it is a tribute to Danzig, and Glenn in particular, and it's not like we destroyed the songs or anything. We were just bored of all the tribute bands in our town [Gothenburg, Sweden – IG]," he recalls of the band's origins, "So we decided to put one together that would play all the songs we wanted to hear. And the Danzig songs we were doing were getting by far the best response – people love all these songs – which is when the idea for Glanzig started."

What exactly do you think it is that makes these songs so memorable?

"They're so simple, that's the key: the riffs are simple, the arrangements are simple, and you can instantly hook into the songs."

Or rather, they hook into you. With that in mind, which is your favourite Danzig album?

"Oh, the first one," comes the instant reply, "It has all the best songs. It's really bluesy, and the sound is so genuine; it's all recorded dry, there's hardly any effects. And it has so much attitude too... even that line-up photo is so...um... you know, 'the boys are back in town'!

"We're trying to do this all the right way," he adds, in closing, "The haircuts, the poses onstage, even the tattoos - everything! This is the ultimate Danzig tribute band!"

And until an official 'best of...' compilation appears, 'Danzifuge' on Mascot Records, is surely the next best thing.

SIDEBAR THREE:
Probing The Seedy Underbelly of Verotik Comics

"Basically I started Verotik because U.S. comics suck," scoffs Glenn, of the spandex-and-red-tights brigade. "If you wanna read about anything other than heroes with super powers, you're up shit creek. My comics deliver everything that those comics do not – they're violent and sexy and shocking..."

And this is no idle boast either, readers. Having spent some quality time with a pile of Verotik's tasteful titles, I can admit that there's not many comics that can make me squirm, and get me all hot under the collar at the same time. But such explorations of sado-masochism as detailed in the 'Venus Domina' series are sure to get even the most placid amongst you frothing at the mouth.

The heroine of the title is a brutally-built dominatrix, who has six additional vulvas nestling between her ribs, and as she tortures her victims to orgasm, they greedily suck up the pain in the air and convert it into the life force that Venus thrives on, like some kind of sexual vampire. 'The Dandy', this most certainly ain't.

Elsewhere we have bloodthirsty barbarians wreaking gory vengeance on their enemies, primitive were-creatures that reveal a whole new kind of righteous savagery to nature, and fallen angels fighting unstoppable assassins sent from the very depths of hell to drag them screaming back to purgatory. It says 'Adults Only!' on the cover, and you better believe it, kid. Graphic sex and violence is very much the order of the day, but credit where it's due, the comics are also steeped in a vibrant mythology all their own, and blood is not spilt for the sake of it, at the expense of story and character.

"I write the bulk of the stories," confesses Glenn, "Although we did do a series by Nancy Collins, based on her 'Sunglasses After Dark' novel. And the Verotika ones [collections of short adult horror – IG] were all written by people who don't normally do comics – they usually do horror novels and stuff – which is why it's all so intense and way out there."

New York has long been a healthy breeding ground for fresh hardcore talent, and Dare To Defy are no exception. The band have just released 'The Weight of Disgust', their debut effort, and Ian Glasper reckons it's a beauty. Here he chats to their drummer, Met...

Dare To Defy are a very promising metallic hardcore band out of New York City, who have a kicking debut LP, 'The Weight Of Disgust', out now on Too Damn Hype Records, the label ran by their drummer, Met. He also runs the excellent All That magazine, so he's obviously a busy man... l caught up with him to find out more about his various projects, starting first with his band...

"l guess we got together in '89, or late '88... sheesh, l dunno...," he drawls in his laidback fashion. "Our first 7" was called 'Steamrolling Neo-Nazis ln The Nineties', which was a limited press of 500 on a label called Totally Hot, which is now out of print. A coupla years later we did a self-titled 7" with lnner Rage, which sounded crap. That label's outta France, ran by a guy called Jean Marc, who's real cool. A year or so after that I put out 'Tales From The Drunkside', and that was how the label started, and that had Jerry A. from Poison Idea and Paul Bearer from Sheer Terror doing vocals on a Y.D.L. cover.

"About a year after that, I decided l wanted to put out a Philadelphia compilation, which eventually grew into the 'East Coast Assault' compilation, 'cos I got a lot of interest from bands in Boston and New York. A lot of bands off that comp — Life Of Agony, Only Living Witness, Starkweather - have gone places. Then another year later, we did the 'Philly Dust Krew' album, a four-band comp with us, Starkweather, All Out War and Hard Response, and I guess that's when the label really started to become a label. Right after that, I moved to New York... and here I am!"

How did you hook up with Jerry A. and Paul Bearer? "I just called them up outta the blue," he laughs. "We figured we were a no-name band... we weren't from New York, and everyone paid attention to bands from there, so we figured we needed a little something to help push our record. Jerry and Paul really dug YDL too, and wanted to do the cover, so it turned out cool."

You've got a different vocalist on the new album to when you recorded the tracks for 'Philly Dust Krew'... "Yeah, our old singer, Sean Judge, who was the only straightedge member of the band, is now a full-blown alcoholic! He walks around pissin' his pants and pukin' all over the place! But now we have Les, who was formerly in Patterns, who grew up in Brooklyn, graffitiing... a typical Brooklyn dude! He even has 'Brooklyn, NYC' tattooed on his back - that's what a Brooklyn dude he is! Whatever... anyway, you can hear the vocals a little better on the new shit. The lyrics cover a lot of different things... social, political, personal..."

What's '5 Years Down The Line' about? "That's Les's department really, but I think it's kinda targeted at the NYHC scene", hazards Met, "Or scenes in general, y'know? Where you gotta be part of a certain clique to be popular, act a certain way. Some of it's personal stuff, beefs he has with certain people."

How is the NYHC scene? I heard they tried to reopen CBGB's for matinee shows? "Yeah, they did, but there was a huge brawl there. Someone later died of internal bleeding as a result, so they've stopped doing the really hard shows...since then, Kingsize bookings have done some of the more mellow bands... Dead Guy, Bloodlet, y'know, staying away from the violent bands like Madball and Crown of Thornz – those bands might not be violent themselves, but they bring in a bad element. Some people will say, 'Oh, that's not the way it is!', but that is the way it is! It's proven fact! Go and see Coalesce, Dead Guy and Starkweather, there'll be no fights...but you see Madball and 25 Ta Life, and there's gonna be a million fights, lotsa hostility and tension."

Tell us a bit about some of the upcoming releases on your label, Too Damn Hype... "Any day now, there will be a Negative Male Child album, called 'Little Brother', a Candiria album called 'Surrealistic Madness' – they're a kinda death metal/jazz band, but with a Brooklyn attitude, who have a very interesting live show. Also an Indecision 7", who are a Brooklyn straightedge band, then a Maximum Penalty EP, called 'East Side Story', a Stampin' Ground 7", a Shankbuzz EP... and lots of Dare To Defy split EPs," chuckles the drummer, "With SFA, Dark Side and Negative Male Child. And I'm doing a Smiths covers compilation CD, with Leeway, Slapshot, Lagwagon, Black Train Jack, Down By Law and loads more, which will be out in January. Then there's albums by Sub Zero, Bloodstate and Ninefinger – that band has Mike Dean from COC and Rich Hoak from Brutal Truth in it. God, I hope I've not missed anyone out..."

What prompted you to do a magazine too? "It was a way to push the label and get into shows for free," he admits, laughing, "But it just kept escalating as we came up with new ideas, weird stuff. The next issue has a 'Through The Keyhole'-type expose on Lou from Sick Of It All and Jimmy from Murphy's Law's houses. It's not just features on bands... we even have a sorta pornographic 'Dear Abbey', a guy who'll answer your sick, perverted questions! I've got the print run up to nearly 10,000 and it's still a lot of fun!"

DARKEST HOUR – ISSUE 92 (SEPTEMBER 2001)

You just know by their name that Darkest Hour are going to be a full-on metal assault, and sure enough, their latest full length, 'So Sedated, So Secure' on Victory Records, mauls you around like a bad-tempered grizzly bear, puncturing your eardrums and slicing your face in an attack more akin to some Swedish death metal band than anything else on the Victory roster like Integrity or The Hoods.

"We're a hardcore band live," claims guitarist Mike Schleibaum, "But if you've only heard the record you could be forgiven for thinking that we were five long-haired dudes in bullet belts! Everyone likes to have a definition nowadays, but we prefer to keep them guessing...

"We used to get what we called the 'darkest hour stare', where kids would just stand staring at us at shows, not knowing quite what we were trying to do," he laughs. "Or

Darkest Hour, by Fil Bard

the 'fuck you U', where no one will stand directly in front of the stage because they're so confused by our music!"

Oh well, such is life when people are unfamiliar with your material, but all that should soon change, 'cos the new album, whilst hard as nails, is basically a very accessible metal record, incorporating some abrasive melodies and slick dynamics into the tired old metalcore formula. Even the esoteric artwork, based on constellations of stars, stands apart from Victory's other releases.

"Yeah, we really wanted to capture that feeling of searching for something unattainable, and also that feeling of loss, and of being lost. We didn't want anything too obvious for the artwork, because we're not a typical death metal band; we're not a gore band or anything...

"Most hardcore bands who play metalcore try too hard to be metal," Mike reckons. "But we can sit alongside real metal bands far easier than most. We've toured with Destruction, we've played with a ton of metal bands, so we've got nothing to prove, y'know? We don't need to take sides in any petty musical debates."

When Mike picked the phone up earlier, he related a little story to me that seems an appropriate way to end this piece.

"We just bought a new van today! We have so much touring planned because we had to. We did 250, 000 miles in the old one, and it just died on us... which is a shame, 'cos it had a really cool wizard painted on the side of it..."

A lizard?

"No, a wizard, like the Black Sabbath song. And the words 'Heed the wizard'! It was just a joke that got out of hand, to be honest, but the metal dudes dug it!"

Darkest Hour: metal to the max, balls to the wall, bad to the bone.

Das Oath – by Al Quint

"I just knew these Dutch guys; they had this record label called Coalition that my old band, Charles Bronson, was on," explains Mark McCoy, singer with international noise terrorists, Das Oath, of the band's tumultuous inception. "We met a few times, once in Chicago, another time when I was first living in New York. I hadn't really dealt with them much; they seemed a bit mysterious to me, but I knew they were buddies with the guys in [influential Dutch hardcore band] L'arm and they'd put out some good bands. Anyway, Nate Wilson [original Das Oath bassist, since replaced by Aaron Aspinwall] knew these Coalition guys, Jeroen and Marcel, better than me, and in late '99 he asked me to go with him to Holland to visit them.

"We all hit it off pretty well, and when we were there, we decided to go on this big road trip to Copenhagen. It was a fun drive, but when we arrived, I got attacked by this female drug dealer for taking her picture. She had all these rings on her fingers and just kept

Das Oath, by Al Quint

nailing me in the head trying to get my camera. I couldn't get her to stop, she was really freaking out; I didn't know what to do. I thought perhaps I should just sock her in the face to make her fuck off, but it seemed like I'd really hurt her. Then this huge Danish thug who was like her henchman came and started pushing me around. It seemed pretty serious, like I was going to get fucked up really badly, but I didn't want to give them my camera. My friends were dumbfounded; they just stood there laughing at me, the assholes!

"Finally, Jeroen gets in front of me, and in one sweeping blow takes them all out like bowling pins. He ruled! His eyes popped out of his head, his face flared up, he was like an enraged polar bear. Jeroen, who has never been in a fight in his life, is a savage. It was really amazing; he looks harmless, but he's huge and has this vicious killer instinct that comes out of nowhere. So naturally it seemed in my best interests to stick with a guy like that..."

And from such chaos Das Oath were born, somehow managing to write cohesive music with half the band living in the US, the other half in Holland. Fittingly their self-titled album for Hollywood's Dim Mak Records is quite probably the craziest record you'll hear all year. Tearing along at 1000 mph and drawing influence from many different eras and styles of hardcore punk, 'Das Oath' is a life-affirming exercise in latent musical extremity, a violent and brutal wake-up call for a complacent, self-congratulatory scene. And with song titles like 'Great News From The South Pole' and 'Nobody's Married Me In Years', it's apparent that the band's eccentricities aren't merely confined to the music.

"I don't like to talk too much about the lyrics. I don't want there to be much emphasis on them because it's all implied, isn't it? The going rate of anger isn't worth shit anymore. Hateful music is the love song of the new age. So what? For me, confusion is everything. I don't take many stances; I don't adhere to much other than my own meandering path. I no longer like the idea of looking for guidance in what a band has to say, and I sure as hell don't want to be one assuming that I can dictate anything. I hate bands with their singalongs and sloganeering; it's all bullshit cues for crowd participation and happy, good times. That's the last thing I fucking want; bands really need to shut the fuck up and just play their music. The worst is hearing some asshole condemning meat eaters or ranting about politics between every song; every time it just adds up to another jerk trying to appear smart so people will like him. You can't use music as a vehicle for ulterior motives anymore, because we've seen the failed attempts, we know that these things don't render effective results. I want to be practical. If I did have to give somebody advice, I'd suggest doing something they can achieve: throw out your records and go punch your fists through a wall. After that you can finally go drop all your shitty friends and be alone."

Days Of End ‑ issue 257 (February 2015)

Days of End

Featuring as they do ex-members of Stampin' Ground, Underule and Anger Management (and a current member of Freebase to boot), you just know that Days Of End are going to be a brutal proposition... but you may not realise just how brutal.

"We want to bring the dark side of hardcore music back into today's scene," reckons vocalist Heath, "That same attitude from when I was in Stampin' Ground, back in the early days: heavy, intense, angry... just full of rage. What we were doing with S.G. in the mid-Nineties was pretty ground-breaking, especially for a U.K. band, and we are bringing that same spirit and attitude - but much, much darker!"

DBH - ISSUE 43 (JUNE 1997)

Unless you've had your head up yer arse for the last six months, you'll have seen these young upstarts from Liverpool getting rather a lot of attention in the press recently. They seemed to come from nowhere (well, Merseyside actually, but it's the same thing, innit?), and as most of these potential overnight sensations are over-hyped, I took it all with a pinch of salt. That is, until I heard their last single, 'White Godsent', their second for the Dedicated label, which hinted at something really worth ranting about still to come. And now, their debut album confirms my earlier hopes - that all those praises in all those mags weren't just so much hot air - by being a bloody good slab of molten Brit-angst.

'Unwilling To Explain' is the name of said full-lengther, and its musical maturity - produced by Howard Benson (Motorhead, TSOL, Ice-T), no less – is at odds with the tender years of its creators. They're all still in their teens!

"We'd just left school when we started the band", recalls drummer Paul Sanderson. I'm calling him at his home, but I met him a week earlier at the Earth Crisis show in Dudley, where I was impressed by his quiet modesty. "We'd only really been in shitty bands until then, the usual school-type things, nothing serious. Some of us have known each other since we were four or five, so there was an instant chemistry there from the start."

And on all those accolades from the journalistic world? Paul plays it all down: "I really don't know why they've picked up on us so much, 'cos we're nothing special. There's plenty of other bands out there better than us, so I dunno, I haven't got a clue."

There, I told you that he was modest. Martin Harris, one of their guitarists, who is sharing the other end of the phone with him, chips in: "We don't know why, so we're just thankful!"

So, have they seen any of that scene jealousy that rears its ugly head whenever a band has the misfortune to get just a bit popular?

"We haven't seen any, have we?" asks Martin of his drummer, who agrees, adding, "We don't know that many bands to get jealous in the first place! We're not strictly a hardcore band anyway, y'know - we do listen to a lot of hardcore 'n' that, but we wouldn't class ourselves as such..."

And that seems to be the scene most prone to all that bullshit. "Yeah, but we've not seen any of it. Yet."

I have to agree that dBh aren't specifically a hardcore band. If I had to pick a band from that genre to compare them to, it would probably be Bloodline, a now defunct band who were on Doghouse and, like so many of the bands on that label, combined hardcore, metal, and rock. dBh are similarly heavy

and metallic, whilst also being groovy and rockin' too. Did you consciously try to avoid being pigeonholed by straddling all those genres at once?

"No, not really, we never set out to do anything planned", claims Paul. "It's just the way it turned out. We listen to all sorts of music, y'know?"

One band that does seem to get mentioned with annoying regularity, along with Black Flag, who they share the same intense approach to live performances with, is Korn. Haha, touched a nerve.

"We don't like Korn, and don't like being compared to them", he exclaims. "I don't see why people say that at all. None of us like that band, so, if anything we try not to sound anything like them."

"There seems to be a big Korn bandwagon right now", Martin quite rightly points out, "With a whole bunch of bands ripping them off, and we don't want to get lumped in with that if we can help it."

Oh well such tribulations are all part of being an upcoming band, and let's face it, there's a lot worse bands out there you could get likened to. That name doesn't really help avoid confusion, does it? It sounds a lot like GBH, those loveable UK punkers.

"Yeah, people do confuse us with them at first glance", sighs Paul, "But we don't sound anything like 'em at all, do we? [No – IG] I mean, I haven't really listened to them much, but the few songs I've heard were dead good, but very different to us, too. We just couldn't think of a name, and that sounded good. It doesn't really mean anything, or stand for anything clever. It's not that important really – well, not to us, it isn't... as long as it sticks in people's heads."

"People asking us about the band's name sort of inspired the title of the album", adds Martin. "It's not that we're really unwilling to explain, but there isn't anything to explain in the first place. It was just a good album title."

That's dBh for you, I s'pose. Free of all pretension, and not an attitude in sight. What you see, and hear, is what you get. So, they may not be hardcore in many senses, but keepin' it real, they most definitely are.

"We feel very comfortable with where the band is right now", Paul has the last word. "We're not pretending to be anything that we're not. We're just doing what we do, as best we can."

DEAD TO FALL – ISSUE 129 (MARCH 2005)

"We tend to go both ways; we're a metal band and a hardcore band," reckons Jonathon Hunt, vocalist with Dead To Fall, the Chicago metalcore monster with a sophomore album recently unleashed by Victory Records. "We're a real mixture of the two scenes."

Well, judging by 'Villainy & Virtue', the aforementioned new album, the metal faction in the band had the upper hand in the studio this time, because we're talking wall-to-wall riffs, galloping guitar hooks, sombre lead lines, and some pretty devastating breakdowns. It's all about as metal as you can get without actually up and moving to Gothenburg.

"Yeah, we're pretty much into every single style of metal out there," he admits. "Doom metal, black metal, stoner metal... and yes, of course, Swedish metal."

Indeed. And what could be more OTT metal than making 'Villainy & Virtue' a full-blown concept album? Well, of sorts.

"We never set out to write a concept record but it just ended up that way. The title track itself is about the reality of man and the existence of good and evil, and that whole relationship that exists between the two. But as we continued writing, each new song seemed to touch on the same topic in a different way and they all came together under the one title. Each song takes a little piece of that initial idea and explores it in a different way.

"And once we had the album title, we met with Paul Romano [voted Best Cover Artist of 2004 by Terrorizer readers for Mastodon's 'Leviathan'] a couple of times. We decided that we wanted this mixture of comic books and Japanese rikate, two art forms that have villainy and virtue at their core. We're very, very happy with how it turned out!"

And so they should be, said fold-out booklet being one of the more lustrous lavished upon us by Victory in recent times, the dark, violent images it embraces ably reflected in evocative song titles such as 'Master Exploder', 'Bastard Set Of Dreams' and 'Blood Of The Moon'.

"One of our more cheesy metal songs, I guess," laughs Jonathon self-effacingly of the latter. "That's actually about a trip to Puerto Rico we did as a band. There was a shot that we took in this bar we went to called Moon Blood, which was apparently half vodka, half calf's blood... I have no idea what was really in it, but anyway, it was an insane weekend with a lot of very crazy things going on. Each line of the song is a reference to something that happened. It's kinda vague, but kinda cool as well."

DEADGUY – ISSUE 37 (DECEMBER 1996)

Who just went and threw away the rule book? Deadguy may be on the hip 'n' happening hardcore label Victory, but as Ian Glasper finds out, they wear Satan on their sleeves (almost literally) and worship heavy metal... or is that the other way around?

"I think Iron Maiden suck with Blaze Bayley! I saw 'em once, when I was in seventh grade, and they changed my fuckin' life. It seems like all my heroes go up in smoke... hopefully we'll let some kid down in the future, eh?"

The guy chuckling gleefully on the other end of the phone from New Jersey is actually a Deadguy. No, he's not on death row, a dead man walking or whatever, he's one-fifth

Deadguy – by Vique Simba

of the noise terrorists on Victory who've taken this cheery name as their own. His name's Dave by the way, and he works in a record store, a record store that stocks Terrorizer in fact ("It's a gem! There should be more heavy coverage like that here..."), and he's bemoaning the current state of some of his childhood mentors.

"I just saw Kiss at Madison Square Gardens, for $150 bucks, and it was not worth it. I saw 'em with makeup when I was seven, and I was in exactly the same seats, it was kinda surreal. And the Misfits! I saw them for the first time, after loving them for years, and I was really let down. I almost wish that I hadn't seen them, and had kept the image of them I had in my own mind intact. Now the whole mystique is gone, y'know? I've met them, and hung out with them, and they were cool, and I've collected everything they've released. I have one of everything, including 'Cough/Cool', which I paid $175 for – it goes for about $500 usually! The Misfits market is huge, and I hate them now. But can I bear to part with it all? It took me three years to collect that stuff, and I got lucky with a lot of it. I'd forgive them for everything if Glenn would re-join. They should have died as legends, instead of cashing in. It's just not right, it shouldn't happen this way."

Unfortunately, real life is like that, and not everything we want comes our way, but what the hell? We all die in the end, and you can't take your record collection with you. Which brings us nicely (kind of) to that moniker. It's a bit bleak, isn't it? Are you coming to terms with everyone's subconscious fear of death, or what?
"No, we took it from a John Candy movie, 'Only The Lonely', where people are running about saying, 'Where's the dead guy?'," he laughs.
Oh yeah, that was gonna be my next suggestion, honest, guv'nor. "That's just the way we are. If we like something, we use it. There doesn't really have to be any logic behind it."
This unpredictable, anarchic approach might help explain that picture on their first CD for Victory, 'Fixation On A Co-Worker', of a toy monkey being flattened by a cartoon guy with a roller! Bizarre is the word that sprang to mind.
"We were watching HBO, a special on stalkers, and the title of that first record was taken from a subdivision of that programme. That's who the guy is meant to be on the cover. We want to make people feel a little weird, a little paranoid. On first glance, we're writing about dysfunctional society, the 'hating everyone' type lyrics, but you have to read a little deeper."
Deadguy are as musically unobvious as they are lyrically. They mix 'n' mash hateful guitar violence with spastic rhythms, in ways only previously imagined by the likes of Neurosis or the Unsane. Dave also cites Black Flag as a big influence, and Black Sabbath, too ("Oh, there's definitely a lot of big rock going on in our thing...") This is a whole different kind of intensity to other Victory bands like Snapcase, their closest siblings on the label probably being Bloodlet, but even they tend towards the slow-grind thing, whilst Deadguy flail about, spitting venom, like angry triffids.
"We just did a big Victory showcase gig in New York", sighs Dave, with the masochistic pride of the perpetual underdog, "And it really wasn't our crowd. They

Deadguy – by Vique Simba

Deadguy – by Vique Simba

were all there for Earth Crisis, and those kids just tend to stare at us. I'm sure we have a crowd, somewhere..."

He tails off thoughtfully, before adding, "This new one is even less typical for Victory. It really goes over the edge into the shitty noise genre. We're still part of the HC scene, but we're a more modern, abstract version. 'A big mess' is how I usually describe it! I'm sure we had an idea in mind when we started, and as we went along, we progressed, and defined it a little differently. This is just how we write songs. We've tried other ways, but they always end up sounding forced, so we just go with the flow now."

Well, it's certainly producing some interesting results. New MCD, 'Screamin' With The Deadguy Quintet', a back-handed tribute to the American jazz trumpet player, Miles Davis, is one sick li'l puppy, all twisted outta shape with pent-up aggression.

"It's certainly different to yer average release", comes the under-statement of the year in reply. "Our last one got a good response. Snapcase is recording their new LP where we did 'Fixation', so they obviously liked how it sounded. And the newer one is a truer representation of what we actually sound like, so we'll see who really likes us. "We did a shorter record, 'cos we all have short attention spans," he adds. "I know I can't listen to, like, 80 minutes of Tool. We all prefer shorter records, and we tend to do what we want. We're working on new stuff right now, and that'll be for a series of 7"s, or maybe a split?"

Not only do the Guys, as I affectionately think of 'em, like the short record, they also like the short tour too.

"Oh yeah, we like to do a week or two, rather than five or six. You get a little burnt out, you lose focus. You also get a lot tighter, it almost becomes mechanical, and we thrive on spontaneity when we play live. We maybe did four months touring last year, on and off, but now we're taking it easier. We had an opportunity to come to Europe with the Rykers, but we couldn't get our act together quick enough to make it. When we later learnt how big they are out there, we kinda wished we were more organised, and had done the tour!"

Oh well, I hope they'll get the chance to lacerate eardrums this side of the Atlantic soon, 'cos you just gotta love a band who winds people up this much.

"We have these devil shirts", he sniggers mischievously. "We think it's funny, 'cos we grew up with heavy metal. We played with a few Christian hardcore bands not so long back, and no one was buying shirts, 'cos they've got this pentagram on them. Ah, fuck you. The devil-worshipping lifestyle is helluva lot more entertaining, don't you think? You should do what the fuck you like. I grew up in the heyday of the NYHC scene, too, and a lot of tough guy stuff went on, big guys at the front beating people up, and intimidating people. If we had to fight a crowd, we would, mainly 'cos that's what Black Flag, or the Misfits, woulda done [laughs]. A big, angry skinhead got on stage and wanted to sing along recently, and Pops wouldn't let him, and he dragged him across the stage, and they fell into the crowd together. You've got the fuckin' guitars, you shouldn't be intimidated by the crowd - it should be the other way around."

The undisputed masters of Bay Area thrash are back with their eighth album (their fifth for Nuclear Blast since reforming in 2004), 'The Evil Divide', and as is always the case, it's a blinder, with the band never content to rest on their laurels and just phone in a predictable record.

"We don't pre-plan the direction or anything," says guitarist Rob Cavestany, of their approach to writing a new record. "Sometimes we talk about it when we're feeling creative and when we have ideas and things. Basically, for this record at least, there was an intention to progress and spread our wings further on this album than we did on the last two records, mainly because this is the third album with this exact line-up. We've done a lot of touring and spent a lot of time together, in the studio and on the road, getting to know each other and becoming a solid unit, so the time kinda felt right to loosen the reins and expand the margin of the music that we play, and the style and variety within our music, within one album.

"If anything, it was more of a conscious decision to keep the parameters tighter on the last albums and not be as varied and expansive with our style on purpose, to just kinda give it more of a one-dimensional feel, to really keep you in that headspace and keep that focused vibe for the whole thing, whereas on this album it just felt like I didn't really want to restrain some of the things I felt like playing or writing and interjecting into Death Angel's sound.

"In the past we've had a lot more stylistic variations, like on 'Act III' and 'Frolic Through The Park' especially. We just wanted to narrow in and get a little more focused into one kind of sound over the last two albums. And now on this one we just wanted to let it go more. It felt very natural to let whatever come out and not really try to hold anything back on this new album."

And indeed, this is a spectacularly confident and expansive musical offering, with songs like 'Lost' incredibly moody and melodic, and acting as perfect counterpoints to thrashier offerings like 'Hell To Pay'.

"One thing that's for sure is that we didn't want to make the same album over again. We never do. All our albums sound different; they all have their own character and identity, which marks the moment in time that we wrote and recorded those albums, and the people we were in that moment while it was happening... and we're never the same people years later. I mean, we're the same, but you go through experiences and you grow; you evolve and you learn and hopefully you improve on yourself. And whatever happened to you is expressed in those records; I think each album reflects that state of mind, the emotional state of us all individually as musicians and people when we made the recording.

"So, to be honest, I don't think it's possible for us to make an album that sounds the same as another album. That would actually be difficult for me to do. It might seem a challenge for someone to make albums sound different from each other. With the same band, line-up, producer, studio, you would think that you'd churn out clones of the

Death Angel, 2016, pic by Stephanie Cabral

same thing. But I don't see it happening. There's no way that could happen if years go by in between the recordings. And for me I don't see the sense in doing the same thing twice. It works for other people, because that's their thing and style, and I love bands that sound that way. But our band is the way we are, which involves a progressive evolvement from album to album."

So, does the band actively keep abreast of new musical developments in thrash and metal, and allow them to exert influence as they write, or do they try to write in a vacuum, to keep their vision of the Death Angel sound as pure and true to the source as possible?

"Truth be told, I try to check out new bands when I can but I find that I'm just swamped and my schedule is so fucking busy, dealing with this, that and the other, and working on my own music and everything that has to do with the band... you do sometimes try to distance yourself from music so you don't get sick of it, 'cos it's pounding in your ears day after day, especially metal, and when we're on tour, or in rehearsal, it's just constant. So yeah, I try to get away from it, to be honest with you. I'm not even doing it on purpose; I just need a break to clear my ears and clear my head. These days it won't be new bands that would inspire me; you just listen to music at all times. You usually just let the iPod go on shuffle and you'll have a constant mix of all the things that you love and everything comes in, from Billie Holiday to Carcass. It's just one after the other, and I love what I love.

"But when I'm writing music and creating, I'm not looking to get inspired by other music or other artists. I'm already inspired by the artists that I love and worship; it's running in my blood right now. So the way that I write is that I just focus on things, on events, things happening in my life that are causing intense emotion. When that's happening, one way or the other, then music will start happening that seems to be the soundtrack to these feelings. I draw inspiration from life events rather than listening to other music; I don't really need to listen to a bunch of other thrash when I'm sitting down to write thrash music. I did that a lot more in the early stages. Again, you evolve so the whole process evolves with you. I'm not trying to say that one is better than the other. It's just what it is at this point in time.

"I wish I had the time to sit there and scout around for new bands and stuff," adds Rob. "Usually, it'll just come to me eventually, one way or the other. A lot of the times, the thing that really turns me on about music and artists is their originality. That's kinda hard to find in new bands these days. I mean, I'm sorry, but it just is. I'm not saying that a lot of these new bands aren't good. I see a lot of killer bands, with killer energy; they're hungry, they're coming from the right place. But the thing is it takes time to develop your style and settle into yourself as a creative artist and start to be able to get an original sound and express these inner feelings more so than just flailing around on the instruments, showing what you're capable of doing musically.

"Again, the word that comes hand in hand to me when it comes to music is emotion. That's just where I'm at and it's kinda hard to please me that way. But I love a lot of music and I love the newer releases by bands that aren't so new, so I check that out more than absolutely new bands. But thank God that new bands do exist and music keeps on going. People keep learning music, forming bands and trying to go with it. I'm just this old, jaded fucker that doesn't have time to sort through every fucking demo like I used to...!"

The scary thing is, any old school thrash veteran will remember that when Death Angel came out, they were still ridiculously young, and notorious for having a fourteen-year-old drummer. So do they still feel like kids when they hit the stage every night? Has thrash metal kept them young?

"Yeah, we were just kids when we started – literally still in high school... but as far as us still feeling like kids now? I'm gonna say no, I don't feel the same as when I was a kid. I mean, I gotta be honest about it, physically... that's the reality. I don't know who at this stage can say that they have the agility and energy that they had when they were teenagers. We were filled with energy and vigour as kids, we were just on fire.

"But I'm also gonna say that compared to most people my age, I'm probably kid-like, or acting like a kid, or seen as someone who tries to live his life as a person who's a lot younger than he actually is. I think music absolutely attributes to that. In fact, it is the reason for that. I do believe that music keeps you young. It does for me anyway, and a lot of people I know. There's something about it that has this fountain of youth quality. It's a real kick and a fun, playful kind of thing, even though it's intense at the same time. That said, I don't feel like a kid but I probably feel younger than I should feel at this age, especially with all the mileage and wear-and-tear that this body, mind, and soul has been through. So yeah, thank God for music...!"

DECAPITATED – ISSUE 89 (MAY 2001)

Decapitated, by Justin Bird

Any fan of death metal could not help but be impressed by Decapitated's 'Winds Of Creation' debut last year, and the band are about to assail our shores for the second time since its release, so we assigned Ian Glasper to find out all the latest from Krosno, Poland.

It's been a while since I spoke to Polish deathsters Decapitated, and seeing as how they're over here again in but a few days' time with Immolation, I thought it was high time to see what the band have been up to since the success of their Wicked World debut, 'Winds of Creation', which dropped like an atom bomb and blew the death metal world apart less than a year ago.

"Oh, the reaction has been very good. Actually, we've all been pretty surprised with it; we really did not expect our album to become so successful!" beams a chuffed-to-bits Martin, the band's bassist. "The reception in Europe has been excellent, and we were very well received during our last gigs in the UK, but the US has beaten all the records! We've pretty much gotten really good reviews everywhere. I must say that all this is largely thanks to Wicked World and our management, so thanks to all of those individuals!"

Of course, one of the big talking points when the record came out was how frighteningly young you all were. For the sake of the readers just joining us, how old are all the band members right now, and are you getting fed up with the constant questions regarding your age?

"I guess we're all a year older than when we last talked, but seriously, Vogg and Sauron are both nineteen. I just turned seventeen last June and Vitek [their awesomely talented drummer - IG] is sixteen. Of course, everyone's asking about our age, which is slowly becoming a pain in the ass, particularly when we play live. Our fans, who are mostly older than us, simply do not know how to behave when it comes to this stupid little thing about age!"

Now please tell us a little bit more about Poland. How hard was it 'coming up' as a band in Poland? What obstacles did you have to overcome that maybe western bands don't have to contend with? It might be a clichéd western view, but when my old band toured in Poland (admittedly on the punk circuit), bands had very little equipment, and what they did have was of a very poor quality, and so on...

Decapitated, Switzerland 2002, by Shelly Slater

"Well, that was a long time ago and we're so young, we don't remember it," laughs the bassist. "No, it is true that the situation used to be pretty tough when it came to recording, with no proper equipment or decent studios. But it has all changed now, and I suppose our current conditions are not radically different from what is happening in other countries. We have some decent recording studios - maybe not the same quality as the famous European spaces, but still good. Several really killer albums have been recorded here. As far as the equipment and instruments go - the situation is simple. You have money, you can have anything you want!

"It is also true that Polish bands still encounter a wall of indifference when they contact many labels abroad, but this is slowly changing, too. Just look at Vader, Behemoth or us."

Oh well, that's pissed all over my Cornflakes regarding the next question; I was going to ask you whether these problems actually fire you up to make even more aggressive music?

"No, not at all, that has nothing to do with music. We play aggressive music because we like it. Death metal is in us and we do not need any external sources or inspirations."

So what other rising Polish bands should we be watching out for?

"Believe me, there are so many great acts here," Martin informs me proudly, "But it is all in the hands of the promoters and managers. And of those there are very few in Poland. I think Massive Management is the only one that regularly promotes their own bands. We definitely owe our recording contract to them, and they also manage Vader, Dies Irae and several others. One name to watch out for is Sceptic, the main band of our second guitar player, Jacek Hiro. Personally, I really like Trauma, Lost Soul, Dissenter... I think there are probably about fifteen bands which could and should sign to a label very soon."

Would you say that there is a distinctive Polish death metal sound developing – just as there was a very specific Florida sound, and an unmistakable German sound? And if so, what would you say is the basis of that sound? What shapes it?

"I don't think there exists any particular Polish sound as such," he ponders. "All these bands are so vastly different. One thing I can definitely say is that death metal is very strong in this country and that it really is the most popular metal faction here. Which is probably why all our best bands are death metal bands!"

Lastly, when can we expect to hear another Decapitated album... and, more importantly, what direction can you foresee the band going in from here?

"We hope to record the follow-up album in August, in Red Studio - this is where Vader recorded their 'Reign Forever World' and 'Litany'. I think the label is planning an October release. The tentative title is 'Nihility'; it's pretty cool, isn't it? And even now it's clear to us that the new tracks are even more brutal and technical - so expect the worst!"

DECAPITATED – ISSUE 118 (APRIL 2004)

With their incisive musicianship and determined demeanour, Decapitated are more than capable of living up to their name and removing your head clean from your shoulders. Their new album for Earache, 'The Negation', sees them honing their surgical skills damn near to perfection. Ian Glasper was sent to administer the Band-Aids.

Death metal fans are shuffling from the Bristol Bierkeller shaking their heads in disbelief, shell-shocked at the dazzling display of precision brutality that has just assailed them mercilessly for the last 45 minutes. Decapitated are back in town, to promote their new album, and 'age' (well, turning twenty) certainly hasn't mellowed

Decapitated, Switzerland, 2002, by Shelly Slater

them any. In fact, they are rapidly maturing into one of the finest death metal acts stalking the planet right now. So, it was a pleasure to find that they are still keeping their feet firmly on the ground despite every journalist in the world telling them that they are the great white hopes of extreme music.

"So far the tour is going great, we're getting a good reaction in every city," says quietly spoken bassist Martin, relaxing on the band's tour bus prior to the aforementioned slugfest of a show. "It might be because we've visited all these places before, but we never expected such a good response. When we first started the band, we didn't even think we'd do any demo tapes, so to now be releasing albums and touring the world, it's more than we ever dreamt of. At the beginning everyone was just talking about our young ages. As we've got older, people still want to listen to Decapitated, but now just for our music."

And that's the truth, Decapitated are no novelty one-trick pony, as anyone who's heard their latest opus for Earache, 'The Negation', will testify. Released to almost unanimous critical acclaim, the band's third album is indeed their 'Reign In Blood', their 'Master Of Puppets', their very own 'Covenant' – there being more than a hint of Morbid Angel lurking amidst Decapitated's intoxicating mix of violent influences.

"Yes, generally our biggest inspiration comes from American death metal bands," Martin admits. "In our opinion, Florida is a special place for death metal – Morbid Angel, Deicide, Cannibal Corpse – but I actually think death metal is getting better and better. When we started playing in 1996, there was only black metal around and it was really hard to be a death metal band back then. The popular bands were Emperor and Immortal, but there are more and more good death metal bands from around the world every year."

It's just a shame that the new albums from Morbid Angel and Deicide are a tad workmanlike then. It feels as though Decapitated are picking up the baton from those bands and running with it.

"Well, so many people say the same thing to us," says Martin carefully. "We're still young, and we have a fresh standpoint on the music. We have a long way to go to come anywhere near their achievements. I like the new Morbid Angel, but nowhere near as much as 'Domination'. Also, the new Deicide is great, but my favourite Deicide album is 'Once Upon A Cross'."

So many metal bands peak with their third album. Is Martin worried that it may all be 'downhill' from here?

"I don't know, haha! We don't think that far ahead. Who knows if anyone will still want to listen to Decapitated in two years' time? We're just enjoying the moment whilst we can. But right now, we're thrilled with the response, and almost all of the reviews have been very positive. We're not sure why people have reacted so well to this one... maybe it's the production? This is the best recording we've ever had by far. I mean, it was the same studio where we recorded 'Nihility', but this time the engineers knew us before we even went in there. We had a much better co-operation for this record, we hardly had to talk to them about what we wanted. They just knew."

Once you've got past their unfeasibly youthful visages, the next thing to strike you about Decapitated is the incredibly cerebral quality of their music. Not for these guys some detuned blur of subsonic sound; rather a dizzying tapestry of intricate riffs and rhythms, everything delivered at lightening speed, a crystal-clear mix leaving the individual musicians nowhere to hide. Not that they need any such refuge; if tonight's show is the norm, there wasn't a beat or note out of place, and the only thing flailing around the venue was the band's windmilling hair. Would it be correct to assume 'The Negation' was assembled accordingly during months of pre-production?

"No, we just wrote the songs and then recorded them," smiles Martin. "We even wrote two songs on the spot whilst in the studio that ended up on the new record. The studio conditions are very good for writing; you can hear everything just right, of course, and you are already very focused on the music."

Does he have a mental image of how each album should sound before he begins writing and recording it?

"No, it just comes naturally. Also, almost all the songs we wrote before the studio were used on the album. If we start doing something, we try to do our best, and we like to keep working on it until it's finished... and if we don't like it, we don't waste time on it.

"This one is a little bit more personal than 'Nihility'," he continues. "We're Polish, of course, and our country is very religious; 90% cent of the population is Catholic. Religion has become so commercial in Poland, it's not about God or destiny or whatever, it's all about money. The church is like a big corporation, and the whole album is against that religious commercial shit."

Obviously a band from Poland sounds very different to a band from the UK or a band from the States, so do Decapitated think of themselves as product of their environment?

"It's hard to say because everything that goes on there just seems like normality. But death metal is a universal language. We can tour with bands from Sweden or America or wherever, but we still play the same music, and we have common topics we can talk about. Even if it's only about how much we liked this album or that album."

And how does he keep up with his studies whilst on tour? Does he manage to revise on the road?

"No! I'm studying Polish literature; Vogg, our guitarist, is studying at a music academy in Krakow, and he's studying accordion! But he doesn't bring any of that to Decapitated; it's too different to our music. We listen to classical music and jazz, but we'll never

271

incorporate it into Decapitated; we want to be strictly pure death metal. Just 'cos we listen to other kinds of music doesn't mean we have to try and incorporate them all into the band. [Drummer] Vitek and [vocalist] Sauron are both studying the theory of music too."

They're obviously inherent musicians...

"It does help. We've been playing music since we were seven-year-olds, but it helps that we've been learning all this different music as well as death metal..."

The theory of composition is essentially the same.

"Yes, it's all about music, isn't it? We are so very deeply into music; we have very few other external interests. We are still a very small band; we have a lot to learn, a lot of practising to do! All musicians need to practise, even if they don't realise it. No-one is perfect."

"There is a lot of pressure," Martin replies when asked whether he feels the need to keep pushing the envelope, "But what is more important is that we are satisfied with what we have created. When we're not satisfied with an album, that is when we still stop playing. Without our fans we'd still be nothing, but we please ourselves first and foremost. After all, if we enjoy what we're playing, then there is a good chance that others will enjoy it too. And it's important that we build our fanbase slowly. You can't become a known band after just one album; you have to keep playing, keep touring, keep building a strong foundation for the future. There are no short cuts in death metal."

DELLAMORTE - ISSUE 48 (NOVEMBER 1997)

Dellamorte

Think back to issue 43 – yeah, I know it's hard, you've been to bed since then - and our Greg's rather

rave review of Dellamorte's incendiary debut, 'Everything You Hate', which snuck out on Finn Records. He rightly praised its vicious crossover and concluded that the Swedes were a death metal band playing hardcore, which intrigued me. I would have hazarded that they were in fact a hardcore band playing death metal, but then I would, wouldn't I? No matter which way you approach them, there's no denying that they are as brutal and noisy as all hell, and with their second full-lengther newly exhumed on Osmose subsidiary Kron-H showing they also have a knack for some ('Wolverine') bluesey grooves too, we decided it was high time we ventured inside the heads of a band who, by their own admission, are - to quote the new album title -'Uglier And More Disgusting' than most.

"l usually describe it as Motorhead meets Entombed', laughs bassist, Daniel, at my dilemma. "That's pretty accurate. Johan's been in a lot of death metal bands - he had a chance to be in Dismember, back in '89, but he turned it down - but his most famous band was the legendary Swedish punk band, Asocial. And I'm in Diskonto, a punk band as well, who just got back from a month-long tour of the States where we played with bands like Drop Dead, and Los Crudos. We all love punk and thrash,
but we like the death metal sound, so we tried to mix the two. It's death metal, but with a punk rock attitude, l guess."

It's probably the name that throws the punks off the scent. It has a gothic ring to it, if anything, and doesn't really hint at the crusty mayhem lurking beneath the arty veneer. What the hell does it mean, anyway? Something about death, p'raps? (Call me Poirot, if you will...)

"It comes from an Italian gore movie, called 'Dellamorte Dellamora'. I'm a big fan of Italian horror movies, and I really wanted to have an Italian name. I can't say exactly what it means, 'cos l don't know - it's a difficult language - but yeah, it deals with death of some sorts."

There then follows a brief discussion about various awesome - and mainly banned - flicks. We have some common ground here, 'cos l do like to see some sauce splashed about the screen a bit, and have a soft spot for the spaghetti chunk blower film. It turns out that, like myself, Fulci's 'The Beyond' is one of Daniel's favourites, as is 'The House By The Cemetery', but (also like yours truly) he is unable to reason why he enjoys watching graphic dismemberment so much.

"l really don't know", he ponders. "When l was five years old, I stayed up to watch 'Dracula', and I've loved horror ever since. I love the, uh, odd feeling I get, it makes me feel alive. I even like watching films that deal with topics like necrophilia and suicide, but l don't have any urge to do those things myself [Glad to hear it, mate, l was getting just a tad worried there – IG]. People who do that shit are gonna do it anyway, with or without horror movies."

It turns out that Daniel is actually a film student, so I suggest that a Dellamorte video, horror of course, would be the ideal way to combine his two main loves in life.

"Actually, l have been involved in a few low budget - well, no budget at all, to tell the truth - horror films, but I didn't really like making movies. It was too much like hard work. They are only fun when they are finished. It's like rock 'n' roll. I hate recording, I like to stand on stage and play live... but you just can't make movies live, can you? I did a horror movie, which was never finished, but had some great gore in it, and I've

273

often thought about cutting it together to make a music video, but it would be so extreme, it would never ever get shown anywhere, haha!"

Well, shit, extreme music demands extreme images, to paraphrase some brutal band or other, and Dellamorte are right up there with the nastiest of 'em – like all the most skilled torturers, damn near making brutality an art form. So, if you like Swedish death metal and Swedish grind punk, then this is the band for you, you sick fuck. And on the subject of Swedish death, we'll let Daniel have the last say...

"I only really like Swedish death metal. It's more punk orientated, with shorter songs and more attitude. It's more base and brutal. The American DM is more technical, with clever riffs and longer songs. They don't tune down so far either. It's good, but it's just not so rock 'n' roll."

DEMIRICOUS – ISSUE 144 (MAY 2006)

Demiricous

Let's face it, no one will ever write another 'Reign In Blood' (Slayer included), but Indianapolis metallers Demiricous have come about as close as anyone has in recent years with their debut album for Metal Blade, 'One'. A veritable torrent of molten thrashin' metal soundly built on scabrous riffing, creeping evil harmonies, plus oodles and oodles of old-fashioned speed. Hell, yeah, all the ingredients that got me into metal in the first place.

"Absolutely, we all grew up on Slayer, of course," confirms bassist/vocalist Nate Olp, "And from the very first time I heard those guys it stuck to me like stink on shit. But as for other shit [you'll soon realise that Nate uses the word 'shit' rather a lot!], I mainly like the older shit like Testament, Exodus... all that Bay Area shit, Suffocation, Sabbath, all the obvious shit. And as for newer shit, I've been more impressed with real obscure shit like the local bands around Indy: Angleville, The Dream Is Dead, You Will Die, and, from the surrounding states, bands like Lair Of The Minotaur, Sweet Cobra, Ringworm... there's a shit-load of amazing music here in the Midwest...

"In fact, the scene in Indy fuckin rules, I love it. It's not huge, but it's very, very high quality. Every band here is on their own shit, real original, and the best part is that no matter the style of music, everybody hangs out and has a good time together. We are totally a part of the scene here; it's made up of our best friends 'n' shit... we absolutely love where we are from."

No shit. And there really is no shit to be found on 'One', producer of the moment, Zeuss, having helped this hungry, young band hone their sonic attack to smart bomb precision. Plenty of insane blasting recalls the best of modern death, whilst the harsh staccato riffing and boisterous gang vocals of 'To Serve Is To Destroy' is pure virulent metalcore the way it ought to be.

"Well, I don't hear any metalcore whatsoever in the gang vocals," counters Nate, "Not unless you're talkin' real metal core like the old Ringworm and Integrity shit. I just wanted to make it sound catchy and easy to grab onto, so live shows will just be ragers. There's definitely death metal all over our shit though, but we never sat down and made a conscious decision to sound a certain way.

"The only definite goal was to make an album that didn't sound like most of today's metal as far as production goes. We didn't want it too polished and produced, and I think we accomplished that. And now the future looks filthy with rage and fun and fuckin' metal!"

DESECRATION – ISSUE 56 (JULY 1998)

Welsh nutters Desecration seem the archetypal death metal band, all flying hair and slaveringly brutal music. Hell, their debut album, 'Gore And Perversion' even got banned. And I mean properly banned. Seized and destroyed at the pressing plant, withdrawn from sale and the band up in court, charged with trying to corrupt the minds of the general public. And with titles such as 'Stillborn Climax' and 'Bathroom Autopsy' on their newest offering, 'Murder In Mind' for Copro, it would appear they haven't mellowed much. I'm sure some of you are thinking, 'Oh, gore for gore's sake, death metal cliché...', but vocalist Ollie really is hooked on carnage.

"I'm a mortician by trade," he reveals. "That's where I get most of my lyrical inspiration from. That whole thing just fascinates me; I can't explain it, but I'm just into the whole death thing. I love all those really sick and extreme gore flicks, especially the brutal Japanese films like 'Faces of Death'. The Japanese are fucking nutters; they're mad for anything really extreme, aren't they?"

Desecration, 1998, guitarist Glenn

The band have learned from their experiences with their censored first album and 'Murder In Mind', although obviously dealing with many taboo subjects, plays it a little safer, by keeping the song titles inside the CD booklet. And there isn't a word of lyrics in sight. Who knows? This one might even stay in the racks long enough to be sold.

"We made sure that no lyrics were printed on the new record. We sort of had to strike a deal with the police last time and we said we wouldn't put any of that on our next record. Otherwise they'd come down on us really hard. The whole new album was indirectly inspired by all that censorship bullshit, especially the song 'Obscene Publications', where I really just said what I wanted to do about those guys. But I better not translate the lyrics to you, otherwise I'll be locked up and they'll throw away the key..."

Violence aside, there is also much musically to capture the imagination of deathsters everywhere on their second disc. It is a non-stop riff fest from start to finish that pummels you mercilessly into cowering submission. There is no let up, not unless you wimp out and reach for the remote. And perhaps the most amazing thing about the whole recording is that it is driven by a drummer who had hardly played before in his life... that drummer being Ollie.

"The guy who drummed on the first album hurt himself in a fall," recalls the singer. "He was pissed up or something, and fell over really badly and had to give up playing. We'd been without a drummer for ages. We couldn't do any shows or anything, and after a couple of years I just thought I'd give it a go. And it turned out pretty well. I just thought, 'Fuck it!' and went for it, full on aggression, and it sounds pretty good. But we've got a shit hot drummer now - he used to be in Parricide - so it's going well for us again."

It certainly is too, the band having recently toured the UK with Thus Defiled, as well as landing themselves some high profile supports on the Cannibal Corpse tour.

"I was a bit disappointed with them, to be honest," he sighs. "A lot of it's to do with there being no Chris Barnes, but I don't like the new album at all. That just doesn't sound like the Cannibal Corpse I know and love. But the shows were good to play."

Of course, you did the Fuck Commerce festival out in Eastern Europe with them too, right?

"That was fucking amazing," Ollie enthuses. "There were three or four thousand people there when we played and we went down really well 'n' all, one of the best responses on our day. And Vader were brilliant too. The audience was crazy, stage diving and all sorts of shit. It made me kind of embarrassed at how shit the scene is over here. We've got nothing here even remotely like that."

What's up with our own scene then? And more importantly, what can we do to improve it?

"I don't think it's the bands 'cos there's plenty of good new bands coming through. I think it's black metal really – everyone's into that now and no one turns out for death metal bands. Not unless you're the likes of Cannibal or Deicide anyway. But what goes around comes back around, you know? And death metal will have its day again, I know it will."

DESTRUCTION – ISSUE 230 (DECEMBER 2012)

You can count the number of extreme metal bands that have enjoyed thirty years together on the fingers of one hand, and ones that have somehow retained their youthful intensity are even rarer still. Thankfully Destruction are amongst that elite group, and their new album, 'Spiritual Genocide', crackles with the band's love and mastery of the thrash genre. Main man Schmier was more than happy to contemplate the band's imminent anniversary by taking Ian Glasper on a trip down memory lane...

How does it feel for the band to be 30 years old next year? Did you ever dream it might be so back in 1983?

"It's a bloody miracle indeed! Time flies when you enjoy yourself as we have, but when we started we never ever thought we could go this far. I'm aware of both the luck and the hard work... you need both to stay in the business for this long!"

How does Destruction 2012 differ from Destruction 1983 (apart from being 29 years older, of course...)?

"We were young rookies from the countryside at the beginning... now we are a band that has toured all over the planet, played the biggest festivals in the world, and experienced all these different cultures and crazy ups and downs. All this shapes your

Destruction – 2012, courtesy of Nuclear Blast

character, but we are still as hungry and crazy as we were back in the early days. Thrash metal is pissed-off music, and we are as angry as we were on day one... if you lack teeth, you cannot play this kind of music!"

But how do you keep that hunger going for the music?

"We are still burning for this music and still have something to say. Mike and myself are not married, we don't have families; we have always put our full focus on the band, and no so-called conservative ideal ever attracted us away from it. If you are not hungry and pissed off, you can't play thrash - that's why it's mostly young thrash bands that impress with their energy and freshness. We are aware how lucky we are to still play this underground music at a high professional level, so we sacrifice a lot of normal tasks and hobbies for the music - because this is the biggest gift in life: doing what you love!"

Please tell us about 'The Butcher' - about why you used him in the first place, and why you adopted him as your mascot?

"The first butcher cover was my idea, and we never thought that it would become the best-selling Destruction item in history! He became our mascot because the fans loved him - the followers choose things like this; when you see that stuff has support, you start to work on it. And that's how the butcher became a trademark: the fans have always been a big part of the band's success and history..."

You guys have played all over the world... but where are the best Destruction fans from?

"This is a very tough question, because we've played at many exotic and amazing places, with fans that are more dedicated than us spoiled Europeans can ever imagine! But I think Latin America is the place with the craziest fans in the world - metal is their life; this music gives them the energy they need to fight the hard and difficult circumstances they are often in."

Over the years, you've had many line-up changes... which incarnations of the band hold the fondest memories for you?

"We are all friends again! All the fights and troubles are just history now; we are one big Destruction family now – all the former members and the current band. Of course, the early days with Tommy and the 'Mad Butcher'/'Release From Agony' years have a special place in my memory because everything started then. But all the old members except Marc have contributed something to the new record... backing vocals, solos, or some drumming from ex-drummer Olly..."

You have an incredible legacy of music behind you already... but which would you rate as your best albums, and why?

Destruction, 2012, courtesy of Nuclear Blast

"Well, from the old records: 'Infernal Overkill', because it was our breakthrough and still sounds good after all these years. Most songs off the record are still in our playlist for the live gigs today; not just 'cos the fans like them, but also because it's still fun to play those tracks live... a great achievement if you think of all the years that have passed since we wrote them.

"I still love the 'Live Without Sense' record, 'cos it shows the band at our highest point at the end of the Eighties, and 'The Antichrist' because it made our comeback a success. Some of the songs are the new anthems and are now as important as the old classics. If an Eighties band wants to be on top now, new tracks have to hit hard as well..."

And what about the worst album you think Destruction have released?

"Haha, that's easy! After I got kicked out of the band back in the day, they did some records I didn't like that much at all! But my least favourite album that I did sing on is maybe 'Devolution' or 'Metal Discharge'... but of course you gotta stand behind your work, so I do not 'hate' those records; I just know now that we could have done better at the time."

Tell us a bit about the new album – what inspired the title? And how do you think it stands alongside the younger, modern thrash bands of today?

"The title is inspired by the world's insanity today, and how we all get brainwashed by our governments. When I watch TV, or the news in other countries, I always see how people's beliefs differ from each other; we all think we have found the Holy Grail but in the end all our thoughts are led and directed by our environment, governments and religious leaders...

"But it's great to see the young bands thrashing again, and we are still in the same position: the godfathers that show the youngsters how to thrash 'til death!"

What have been your greatest successes as a band?

"Just to survive all the difficulties and still be here is surely our biggest success? It's fantastic to realize how far this music has travelled, and when we play places like Singapore, Taiwan or Venezuela, I am proud that the heavy metal movement made it to worldwide glory. And there is always more to come... next on the list is Latin America again, then the Phillipines, Vietnam and Malaysia – the world is big enough to keep us busy 'til the end of my days!"

And what about your failures... is there anything you really regret?

"I may have failed on a private basis here and there... disappointed some people that are close because I was never home too much. You lose friends that way; your social life becomes restricted when you are always on the road. The crew and the band and the fans become your family. I learned from that, but I also know that real friends understand my way of life."

What's next for the band? Where do you possibly go from here? Or have you already achieved everything you want to?

"If you are not hungry anymore it's time to stop. We wanna go to all the places we did not play yet on the 30th anniversary tour. And some shows with the German thrash heroes and friends from Sodom, Kreator and Tankard would be another aim for 2013!"

How would you like Destruction to be remembered in a hundred years time? When people are looking back at the metal scene of the Eighties and Nineties etc?

"Unbreakable, fast and furious – and always real!"

DEVIATE – ISSUE 245 (AUGUST 1997)

Deviate, by Bernaded Dexters

Yes, Deviate are from Belgium, and I know we've given plenty of space to covering bands from there already, but these guys have a slightly different flavour to the H8000 stuff I love so dearly, being less death metal and more your Biohazard/Madball kinda thing. I first witnessed them opening for Integrity in France, and they really tore it up, whipping the Rennes audience into a bloodlust with their precise crunching crossover. "The H8000 crew have been around a long time," acknowledges drummer Laurens, "And Edward from Good Life is a great guy, but some of his bands are a little bit separated from the rest of Belgium. A lot of them are militantly straight edge and there's a bit prejudice against people who smoke or drink or whatever, so they segregate themselves from the rest of the scene a bit. In Brussels we have a very united scene, no matter what kind of hardcore you're into. There's skaters and punks and metal kids; it's very openminded and all the kids get together at the shows to basically have fun." Well, Deviate's new album - their fourth – 'Thorn of The Living', should have them all writhing in the pit in furious ecstasy, 'cos it's an accomplished blend of 25 Ta Life's fury and Merauder's brutality. In other words, manna from hardcore heaven. And with hardcore threatening to spill over into the mainstream at any moment, don't be surprised if you hear the name Deviate on the tongues of scenesters everywhere real soon.

"I'll be glad when all the hype about hardcore is gone, and we can just do our thing the way it used to be. I think media hype ruins everything, but I guess that at the end only the true bands will remain standing. And the ones who jumped on the bandwagon will have fallen by the wayside..."

So, you would prefer to see hardcore stay underground?

"Yes, in many ways," claims Laurens. "Of course, with my label head on, I'd say no, 'cos the more sales I make, the better it is [Laurens runs I Scream Records who, as well as his own band, have on their roster, amongst others, Down But Not Out, 8-Ball and Looking Up – IG], but the fashion driven sales will die off soon anyway. And I'd prefer real sales, to a true crowd who loved the music and the bands with integrity, who will be around for years to come."

DIM MAK - ISSUE 71 (OCTOBER 1999)

Death metal legends Ripping Corpse haven't just spawned Eric Rutan's Hate Eternal, they've also bequeathed us Dim Mak and their 'Enter The Dragon' debut. And with a martial arts fixation to their name, we knew the assignment was a job for our man Glasper. After all, he has been known to hang around his local aikido dojo, and not return his 'Out For Justice' videos to the store, so we tracked him down to a monastery in the Himalayas where he was raising hell and playing with a Rubik's Cube, and set him loose...

Dim Mak. Now there's a name to conjure demons with, eh? And this New Jersey quartet, who emerged from the still-smouldering ashes of one-album-deathmongers Ripping Corpse, really do whip up an unholy racket that lives up to their unusual moniker. Drums and guitars lash at the senses mercilessly, breathlessly combining insane speeds

Dim Mak

with awesome technical flourishes. So, is Dim Mak some mythical Sumerian devil? Or maybe the name of some long-lost, unspeakable tome of occult wisdom? No, the truth is just as esoteric, but a whole lot more interesting because it's real.

"Dim Mak is actually an ancient Chinese martial art based on pressure points, that was developed from the acupuncture system," explains Scott Ruth, the band's leathery-lunged vocalist, calling me from his home of Red Bank. "There was a 12th century monk who was an acupuncturist and a martial artist, and he combined the two sciences. Apparently, he lived near a prison he was privy to, and he used to experiment on the prisoners, trying out all the different strikes he was developing!

"Dim Mak is also meant to be the 'death touch'," he adds, elaborating on the name's inevitable darker connotation. "If it's done properly, it can be called 'The Death With One Strike', or even 'The Delayed Death', and by striking a certain point of the body, that area deteriorates and eventually stops the heart – and the person drops dead a week later..."

And one play of their incredibly fierce debut album, 'Enter The Dragon' (on Dies Irae Records out of Singapore) could possibly have a similar effect on the listener, so approach with extreme caution! The ebb and flow of their material is more like the devastation wrought by a tsunami. It features a ripping (Corpse!) thirteen blasts of pugilistic pressure-point-attacking mayhem which will shred your senses as much as – if not more than, by virtue of its unmitigated rawness - the outfit their former-band-mate in Ripping Corpse, Erik Rutan, did a much-mooted stint in, Morbid Angel. And, guess what, the martial arts connection doesn't end with the name of the band... for starters, they named their record after the greatest Chop Suey film of all time. I take it there's a few Bruce Lee fans in your ranks?

"Oh, most definitely," agrees Scott, "And it wasn't just his intensity and his skill that inspires us; he was such an extremely driven individual. And we're a very disciplined band, when it comes to practice and performance; we're always striving to improve on our skill levels. A lot of younger kids who aren't so into martial arts might wonder what all the fuss is about - they probably get more of a rise out of Jackie Chan, or Jet Lee - and not to take anything away from any of the other Hong Kong stars, but there was a lot more to Bruce besides the obvious.

"One of the things I found most interesting about Bruce Lee is that he was an extremely hot-tempered person. His philosophy was strong, but he had a long way to go with that... but that just makes him more of a human being in my eyes. He wasn't always the cool, composed martial arts practitioner; he was an explosive, dangerous thing too, and that's what we aspire for in this band."

"And we all know that the best bands do tend to have that tension within them, that self-destructive tendency that adds to their romantic mystique. Take the Cro-Mags for example, who tore themselves apart because of personality clashes within the band, but perversely wouldn't have been half the band they were if it wasn't for the very trait that ultimately destroyed them.

"As a group of people," ponders the vocalist, "The three of us at the core of the band are very intense. We've been together twelve years, and it's almost like a marriage gone bad... but we're not looking for divorce; we just wanna fight through it.

"And when you added Mr. Erik Rutan [now with Hate Eternal - IG] into the mix, back in the Ripping Corpse days, you certainly had an explosive time bomb of personalities... and the three of us are still like that. But that adds a lot of important chemistry to the band - we've always enjoyed teetering on the brink of destruction!"

Listening to 'Enter The Dragon' is a similarly thrilling experience, kinda like walking a tightrope over a boiling volcano. One moment the guitars are spiralling around your head like hungry vultures above a kill, threatening to vanish up their own arses as the riffs clamber over themselves in their eagerness to assail your ears, and then they pull it all back from the edge with a rock-solid grind section. And the lyrics are equally schizoid, flirting with violence yet carrying an intelligent, vaguely spiritual undertow ["I wanted to let the hammer fly a bit, let myself rage... but I also didn't want to be too obvious..."]. It's a dizzying display of dynamics, and one that I feel could possibly have been even more stupefying if it had been afforded a slightly thicker production, especially in the guitar section.

"I'll admit that the guitar is a little down in the mix," concedes Scott, "And it's less abrasive than we wanted it, too. In actual fact, it's a very good heavy metal guitar sound, and that has a little to do with a minor compromise we made in the studio with the producer. Next time out, I think we want to sound bigger... uglier [laughs]. I love the rawness of the record, but yeah, the guitars could be beefier."

One of the benefits of such a clinical sound is that it's perfectly crisp and clear, which demonstrates the band's confidence in their musicianship, because everything is right there for all to see – there are no walls of screaming distortion to hide behind.

"We wanted that crisp sound, because with all the blast beats, it's easy for things to get messy. We really wanted a crystal-clear edge to it all, and we didn't want to go to a typical engineer and get your typical death metal sound, so we pushed for something a little different. It's a simplified style compared to Ripping Corpse, so we went for a leaner recording process."

And apparently not to everyone's taste either. I've read one review in particular that was especially scathing towards Scott's more shouty hardcore-like vocal style, and it seemed that the writer was yearning for the olden days of Ripping Corpse to be revisited all over again.

"To be honest, I even tried to hold off that growling style back when we were doing Ripping Corpse," he recalls with a sigh, "But they were more in that direction than they are now. They were probably more of a thrash style, if anything, to be honest.

"Listen, I have every confidence in what I do, and so does the band, and I know that I could just hunker down and spew out some of those death metal vocals, but that wouldn't be me – and I can only be true to myself."

Well, I totally dig your sound. As well as the mighty Nasty Savage, it also reminds me of my salad days, when all those technical crossover bands like Beyond Possession, Hirax and Impulse Manslaughter were coming through.

"We are an oddity," agrees Scott. "We hover on the periphery of thrash and death and hardcore. We have trappings of all those genres, and more – but there's a lot of stuff that will throw a casual listener, so it's been a constant battle for acceptance for us.

"We have a pretty aggressive attitude, and we enjoy all those different kinds of music, so it's quite disappointing when people seem to be so polarized. They expect a death metal band before they've even heard us, and they want a death metal band, and then when we don't fit their idea of a death metal band, they're bound to be disappointed."

DISCHARGE – ISSUE 102 (SEPTEMBER 2002)

If you don't know who Discharge are, we can only assume that you've picked up the wrong magazine by mistake. The only bands who've probably influenced as many other artists as them would be Black Sabbath and Judas Priest. Ian Glasper loves the band's early material more than life itself and reckons their latest, self-titled effort for Sanctuary is a genuine return to form... and not before time.

Everyone knows who Discharge are. The band helped change the face of modern music with their ultra-brutal take on three chord punk rock, and no-one who was exposed to their graphic anti-war imagery will have easily forgotten it. But after a series of truly classic releases in the early '80s, the band underwent several line-up and direction changes, and some of their latter-day albums, whilst decent enough metal records in their own right, did little to ingratiate themselves to old school Discharge fans. In fact, for a while back there, each new album was greeted with a nervous groan rather than euphoric

Discharge, 2016, pic by Fabiola Santini

anticipation... until now. Finally, the band have reunited their original line-up – the line-up that brought us such classic EPs as 'Realities Of War' and 'Fight Back' – and their new, defiantly self-titled, studio effort is everything Discharge fans have hoped and dreamed of these last twenty years. A scorching return to the glory days of old, and most importantly, Cal is shouting his head off once again, rather than hitting those high metal notes that turned all the fans' noses up from 'Grave New World' onwards.

I caught up with drummer Tezz, one of the founding members, who left right before the 'Why?' 12" and has seemingly been in every single punk band out there since.

"I left the band in 1982," he recalls, his accent a bizarre mixture of his native Potteries and a distinct American twang, a result of him spending more time on that side of the pond than this these last two decades. "I really wasn't happy with the direction at the time, and wanted us to make more effort with our songwriting. Of course, as soon as I left, it all improved, which was typical, haha! They went on to do 'Never Again' and 'State Violence, State Control', of which I was very envious.

"Anyway, I helped put together the Broken Bones with my brother, Tony, and then I joined UK Subs, before moving to the States. Out there, I was in Billy Club, and Battalion Of Saints, then I joined Ministry, as well as Lard and Pailhead! I just wanted to play with as many cool bands as I could, and I still do. Right now, I play with The Business, and I'm back doing Broken Bones, and I just did my first show with the Dutch band, Discipline, too."

Where the hell do you find the time to do all this stuff? And doesn't it relegate Discharge to the status of 'project band'?

"Basically, this is all I do, and I don't let anything else come between me and music. I just do what I have to do, but all these other bands are great fun, and that's why I enjoy them so much. It's a nice change from Discharge, to be honest, which is all gloom and doom musically and lyrically. Who knows? Maybe I can set a record for being in the most punk bands...!

"But Discharge is definitely a real band again now," he reassures me. "We're all very proud of this album, and there's talk of touring to promote it, hopefully doing at least a year's worth of shows on the back of it, and we're even planning to start rehearsing for the next album soon if we can."

That's great to hear, 'cos this album is too good to just sneak out and then vanish into obscurity, and there must be a lot of people out there like myself, keen to see if Discharge can still cut it live. I'm sure with such a strong set of new songs in the arsenal, the gigs would kick ass.

"Well, Cal had the shit tore out of him during the 'Grave New World' tour," sighs Tezz, "And he's never really gotten over that, so he's a bit reluctant to go out and tour, but the rest of us are dying to get out there and show everyone how it's done."

Here's hoping, eh? 'Cos I know that I would love to see/hear some of this ripping new shit in the live setting. I kid you not when I say that tracks like 'War Is Hell' could sit comfortably alongside the best of the band's back catalogue, and of course recent tragic events around the world just prove that the band's lyrical stance of twenty years ago is unfortunately as relevant today as it's ever been.

"This album was over four years in the making," Tezz reveals. "Me and Tony [better known as Bones to most of us - IG] wrote all the music, on and off whenever I was over here from the States. It came together slowly - we didn't even demo any of the songs until some of them had been written for almost three years, but we had a very clear picture of what we wanted this to sound like.

"I was quite conscious about writing a real Discharge record. I'd written a lot of tunes whilst in America that I knew I could only really do justice to with this band... well, the only other band it might have suited would have been Battalion Of Saints, but I definitely didn't wanna waste the material on those guys, haha! Then I brought those songs here, and Bones did his thing with them, and it was magical. We had a good feeling about it from the start, and it was amazing the chemistry and understanding we still had working with each other.

"We saw Rainy and Cal for the first time in fourteen years at some party, and that was when we started talking about doing this with the original line-up again. The main thing we wanted was for Cal to go back to his original shouty vocal style for this record, 'cos he has a great unique voice that really helped define the classic Discharge sound, and the results were exactly how we wanted them to be.

"We were innovators of a whole style," he ponders, when I ask him what made the band so seminal in their early days. "We wanted to go against the grain; we didn't wanna play the blues scale! So we invented the discord to be an anti-blues scale... try and sing fucking 'la la la' over one of those, haha!

"We were a reaction to all the shit on the TV and the radio at the time, but really nothing's changed on that front. It's all so drab and grey and uninspiring, and that's why there's still a place for a band like us. A lot of the younger kids have heard our name, but not our music, and a lot of them can't put two and two together to see which bands really helped shape the current musical climate. So, none of us have any idea how well it will sell, but we do know that our new album definitely has a place in the modern music scene, and we're very proud of it..."

DISCHARGE – ISSUE 143 (APRIL 2006)

Seminal (in every sense of the word) UK punks Discharge are about to unleash, through Thunk/Cargo, both a brand new EP and their first official DVD, and, with a full UK tour booked to celebrate, we decided it was high time Ian Glasper found out just what's taken them so bleedin' long...

In 2002, Discharge fans around the world were thrilled when their Stoke heroes returned to the fray with a new self-titled album, especially when it turned out to be an old school blast of hardcore punk harking back to the band's salad days that did much to erase the bad taste left by the band's misguided foray into the realms of cock rock during the late Eighties and early Nineties. Unfortunately, original vocalist Calvin declined to participate in any reunion shows, despite singing on the album, so Discharge recruited Varukers frontman Anthony 'Rat' Martin in his place, and toured the world, letting everyone know they meant business once again. Then... nothing! After a frankly disappointing show at 2004's Wasted festival in Morecambe, Discharge vanished off the radar virtually without trace, leaving many to fear the worst: that 2002's 'Discharge' had been a one-off and no further new material would be forthcoming.

"Well, apart from [guitarist] Bones and [drummer] Tezz both having sons and getting married, we have been leaving off the gigging front and working on new material," explains Rat, on their voluntary hiatus. "It's a bit hard to try and sort out both at the same time, but it's paid off at last; for about a year, we had no new numbers, but in the last couple of months we have really knuckled down and now have about seven finished songs, and another five or so to be working on... but we are going to have a break from the rehearsal room again, and go out on the road, just to let people know we are still here. Our - and your - nightmare continues!"

"We sorted out a warm-up gig at Bradford Rios back in January," adds Bones. "And, you know, we were all a bit nervous, but it turned out to be a fucking blinder. We changed the set around a bit, which is normally a recipe for disaster after not playing for a whole year, so after 'Decontrol' [the band's much-loved classic third single – IG] we were going to go back on and do 'You Take Part In Creating The System'... but there was such a fucking

Discharge, by Gutterpunk Photography

buzz, with kids on the stage, all dancing around and shouting, 'Decontrol! Decontrol! We've been shit on far too long!', that we looked at each other and thought, 'Let's leave on that high note, eh?' It was really great, so thanks to all those in attendance, for making it such a memorable night, truly a good 'un to come back with…"

"But yeah, for me, personally, the Morecambe Wasted festival wasn't my best," admits Rat.

Discharge, Newcastle 2008, by Will Binks

"My voice was shot to fuck... it was a big night, a big crowd, lots of nerves... in fact, I puked just before I went on! But you know what? When they had turned off the vocals on us at the end, I turned to the rest of the guys and said, 'Play 'Fight Back', fuck it!' They did, and the crowd shouted their fucking heads off - who needs a PA? It would be an understatement to say it sent shivers up my spine; that helped us leave the stage on a good note."

Of course, all such reunions are greeted with a certain amount of cynicism, but, as anyone who witnessed their first UK show back together, at the Hanley Sugarmill in 2003, the 'new' Discharge is just as capable in terms of intensity and power as the old. And hopefully the new EP, 'Beginning Of The End', will silence the critics who claim that the band now just sound like The Varukers playing Discharge covers! It features three brand new songs, all of them bursting with the ferocious aggression of the Discharge we know and love... so, if you thought the band were irrelevant and surplus to requirements, what with the seething mass of awesome young Discore bands out there today, think again.

"Listen up, this is the way it is," growls Tezz. "Rat is now the vocalist for Discharge – and it's all your fault, Ian, for recommending him to me! Some people are pissed off that it's not Calvin on vocals, but he didn't want to do it... not playing live, anyway. But the rest of us do, and we are three of the four original members, let's not forget that! Doesn't that count for anything? I can tell you that we think it does, and that's why we're still here doing it, for fuck's sake. And of course, Discharge aren't 'surplus to requirements'; this is the style we created! We never realised what an influence we were going to have... still don't either, to be honest.

"Nothing much has changed for us though... well generally the crowds are a little bit older, but there are still youngsters coming through giving it a kick up the arse – and it's great that a band like Discharge can still interest those youngsters. They are the future and keep us on our toes; we can't rest on our laurels, not ever. Is punk still relevant? We would certainly hope so, or else we become irrelevant, and that would never do! So, for those that have never seen Discharge live: what the fuck are you doing? Get your arse down and see a real hardcore punk band, instead of all these pretenders."

"But there is a certain amount of pressure singing for Discharge," confides Rat. "It's such an important band to a lot of people - including The Varukers - and I want to do the best job I can. If I wasn't going to give it my all, I wouldn't bother; I don't just go through the motions. I never had an interest in playing with anyone else apart from The Varukers, but Discharge was my favourite band, so when I got asked to sing for them, of course I said, 'Fuck yeah!'

"And I have said before: even if it wasn't me, but somebody else, singing, and they were doing the stuff that they are doing now, stuff like 'Hear Nothing, See Nothing, Say Nothing' and 'State Violence, State Control', I would be supporting them and him, whoever he might be. I wouldn't be moaning and groaning that it's not Calvin on vocals – it's Discharge doing the shit that I personally have waited to hear them play for a long time. Let me remind you, The Varukers played with Discharge around the time of the 'Grave New World' album, and I'm sorry, but that was not Discharge, even if it was Calvin on vocals and Garry Maloney on drums; that was not the band that so inspired me. And at one time, it was just Garry Maloney carrying on Discharge, and The Varukers were practising at the same place as they were. Garry was even going to have Rocky Shades from Wrathchild singing at one stage... no, no, no! At least this is

Discharge doing Discharge songs, with a guy that actually gives a shit doing the vocals... and of course I have my own style - I nicked a bit of it off Calvin!"

Recorded at Mad House Studios in Crewe, 'Beginning Of The End' is available as either a vinyl 7" or a three-track CDEP, and is out now through Thunk Records, the label ran by members of another renowned Stoke punk band, The Skeptix. The single will be chased into the racks by the band's first official DVD, an entertaining document of the rollercoaster ride around the world the last three years has proven to be for Discharge. "Hmmm, difficult one to answer," ponders bassist Rainy, when asked whether the band had a clear vision of how 'Beginning Of The End' should sound before they even started writing it. "We didn't go into the rehearsal room with any set agenda or anything, it's just what we came up with while we were in there. Some ideas worked, of course, some didn't... I suppose if you took the 'Discharge' 2002 release and the Eighties stuff, and threw it against the fucking wall, whatever survived would sound like the new EP! Does that explain things a little better? No? Thought not! Basically, we just throw ideas at each other and see what happens, but rest assured, we won't be putting anything shit out for the sake of it."

"Discharge was always my favourite band, right from when they advertised their first tape in Sounds," says Rat happily, in closing. "I got straight into it; some people in the punk scene hated it, just thought it was a fucking row. I remember I was living at home with my mother, and the 'Why?' 12" had just come out; I kept blasting it out, and my next door neighbour came round and said, 'I don't mind about the noise, but can he change the fucking record?' Some people have no taste, haha! But people ask me all the time what it's like singing for your favourite band... and it's fucking ace! If I was told by someone twenty years ago I would still be doing The Varukers now, I would've thought they were on drugs – never mind if they'd told me I'd be singing for these fuckers as well!"

Discharge – issue 270 (May 2016)

Ian Glasper digs deep with new Discharge vocalist J.J. to find out what it's like fronting the most legendary punk band in the world, and why their new album is their best since 'Hear Nothing, See Nothing, Say Nothing...'

Anyone who knows anything about punk will tell you that Discharge were the most important and influential band to emerge from the UK in the Eighties, their first four singles, first 12" and debut LP being some of the most ferocious music ever committed to tape. They not only spawned their very own sub-genre, the much-maligned D-beat or 'Discore' school of punk, but ended up shaping thrash metal (with everyone from Metallica to Neurosis paying homage via cover versions), and indeed extreme music in general, such was the intensity of their vision.

Discharge, Newcastle 2008, pic by Will Binks

Of course, when a band makes such an impact with their early material, there's only one way they can go from there, and with Discharge, the downward spiral was a vicious one, and it took them many years to gain back the credibility they lost with their second album, 'Grave New World'. Not a bad album in its own right... but when it was the follow-up to 'Hear Nothing, See Nothing, Say Nothing', an absolute turkey.

Anyway, Discharge are back with a new vocalist and a brand new album, 'End Of Days', on Nuclear Blast, and thankfully it's a blinder.

"I knew the guys for a few years before joining the band," explains said new vocalist, J.J. Janiak. "About six years ago, my old band Wasted Life supported Discharge in Stoke; I was then told [Discharge bassist] Rainy was trying to get in touch with me, so I contacted him and he said he wanted to get together and do some songs. At the time though I didn't realise it was for Discharge, I thought he maybe wanted to do a side project. We couldn't seem to get together for rehearsal though, so the idea just kind of went out the window. Not long after I was asked to sing for Broken Bones, with other members of Discharge, and then the news surfaced about Rat [from The Varukers, Vile and Warwound, and previous singer of Discharge] being out of the band. I had a feeling I was gonna get a phone call, and sure enough I did! They had a gig two weeks later, so I didn't have much time to learn the set, which was around twenty-odd songs. I wasn't quite sure about doing it permanently, so I told them I'd fill in until they got someone, just to prevent cancellations. My first gig with them was in Belgium - in front of about 20,000 people! But it went really well.

"And there's been quite a few more since," he elaborates further, on the rollercoaster ride that joining Discharge has proven to be. "Playing in Greece was nuts. We played in a basketball stadium which was practically full; there were flares shooting off everywhere, the place was engulfed with smoke, and there were beer cans flying in every direction... the place just went crazy. Then after the show a big part of the crowd went down to the Turkish Embassy and started throwing bricks, bottles, etc. at them and the guards... I was told we 'inspired' them!"

And how was it, stepping into the breach, with such big shoes to fill? Discharge fans aren't the most forgiving if you fuck up their favourite songs in the whole world!

"It was a bit confusing at first," J.J. admits. "Like I said, I wasn't sure I wanted to make it a permanent thing, and it was just for that reason – I had VERY big shoes to fill. Especially with a band that's been going as long as Discharge have; people always want to see the original members, and singers are usually hard to replace. But as soon as the live videos came out, the fans accepted me straight away, and I was a bit shocked really... it was really down to the fans; they made the decision for me to stay in the band. It was crazy: I was getting emails from Discharge fans all over the world, begging me to stay with the band, and it's hard to say no to that."

Well, their faith in J.J. has paid off, because 'End Of Days' is a formidable slab of fiery punk rock, and a welcome return to true form. J.J. isn't the only 'new' member of the band though, as they have Tezz Roberts on rhythm guitar now as well. In fact, Tezz is nowhere near being a 'new' member, having been the band's original drummer during the aforementioned seminal early recordings, and is the twin brother of lead guitarist, Bones. But this was the first time they would have written and recorded with two guitarists.

"It was a slow process at first... we did a little bit at a time during rehearsals. Bones and Tezz would normally come up with the riffs. Normally when I hear the music for the chorus, I'll get a line or phrase come into my head, and I'll write all the lyrics around that. As for the arrangements of the songs, we all took part in that.

"There was no conscious decision to make it sound 'old school' or anything; the only thing that was conscious was to keep it short and simple. Less is more. As for the writing, I wanted to touch on some real issues that sometimes get passed off as 'conspiracy theory', which I think is just a term to make you sound crazy... I prefer to call it 'truth theory'!"

There must have been huge pressure on Discharge to deliver the goods, and lots of people expecting you to come up short. Were you conscious of that weight of expectation as you were writing and recording? Did it feel like 'make or break' time – again! - for the band?

"Yes, there was huge pressure on us with this album, especially as it's on Nuclear Blast Records, and they're a label that has worldwide distribution, so it'll definitely be heard... unlike the 2001 [self-titled] album [which briefly reunited the original line-up again] which was a great album but virtually got shelved as soon as it came out. There's still a lot of people that don't even know of that album.

"There was also pressure with it being a new line-up, a new singer and two guitars... it's the first thing we've released with this line-up, of course, so we will ultimately be judged by that. If the first thing we put out is shit then no one will be interested in the next release...

"Anyway, we were ready to record an album, so we went in the studio to record three demo tracks," continues J.J., on how the Nuclear Blast deal came about, seemingly out of nowhere, "But they came out sounding way too good to be demos, one of those songs being 'New World Order'. Darren Green put together a video for us for the song, and we released it on You Tube only, just to get something out there to give people an idea of what we were doing and what this line-up sounds like. Next thing we know is we're getting approached by Nuclear Blast! And the rest is history..."

'End Of Days' is as good a Discharge album as anyone could hope to expect in 2016, and whilst it doesn't mimic the early records, it certainly nods heavily towards them in attitude and approach. One of the most noticeable similarities though is J.J.'s uncanny resemblance to original vocalist Kelvin ('Cal') Morris.

"Yeah, I'm always getting compared to Cal vocally; it's just the sound of my voice and how I've always sung, so I can't change that, but I think that's part of why I was asked to sing in Discharge in the first place. Usually, the singer's voice in a band is what defines that band, and if you do something completely different it doesn't work, because that band has now lost a big part of their defining sound. I think the 'Grave New World' album is a perfect example of that...!

"But I can honestly say I love this new album. As a musician you know when you record something that sounds shit, and you're usually your own worst critic, but this is probably my favourite recording I've done in the last 25 years. We're all really happy with it. I think it easily stands up to the classic Discharge material, but whether or not it will be considered a classic is up to the fans to decide. Only time will tell... I really haven't heard any negative feedback so far, other than from uninformed people saying

Discharge, 2017, pic by Morat

that it's not Discharge because there's no original members - when they don't realise there's actually three out of the four original members in the band still there."

And with tours of Europe and the US, and an appearance at the Maryland Deathfest confirmed for May, it looks like business as usual for the revamped Discharge.

"Yeah, we might have a new singer and an extra guitarist, but nothing's really changed. All the problems still exist that the band sung about back in 1980. We're definitely still angry... older and wiser, without a doubt... and there's definitely more back pains these days too!"

THE DISCHARGERS – ISSUE 141 (FEBRUARY 2006)

The Dischargers

"For too long have we sat back and let the critics and the teachers and the education system and the professors and the academics and society tell us what they think is great art!" spits Malcolm 'Scruff' Lewty, vocalist with one of the angriest bands on our planet at this moment in time, The Dischargers. "There is such a dumbing-down of world art, it disgusts me. Why is a fucking poem by Byron more important than a poem written by a homeless guy on the street? Why is the Mona Lisa more beautiful than a sketch of a fox by a foot-and-mouth artist? How dare someone tell us that something is more important, and therefore more valid, than anything else?"

Oops, I've got Scruff started about the Art War, a tumultuous battle for equality and freedom of expression that rages at the heart of his latest band, The Dischargers, and his obvious passion for the subject translates beautifully into some of the hardest, nastiest, most vital Discore imaginable. With Scruff (whose impressive resume includes Hellbastard, Nero Circus, Sidewinder and The Apostles!) based here in the UK, and the rest of the band (members of The Hellsonics, Reposters and Visions Of War, no less) over in Belgium, many logistical problems have been overcome to bring you their debut album, 'There's No Place Like Hell' for Bath-based Fury 76 Records, but that's not what makes this potent slab of pissed-off hardcore so compellingly savage.

"Hell is other people!" rants Scruff misanthropically. "Awww, fuckin' hell, don't get me wrong; I enjoy meeting new people and interacting with the human race, but there comes a point when I just can't take it anymore. And I have to be alone... would die to be alone. It's just the way it is. I consider myself pretty much a 'people person' as well – I can usually get along with anyone, really easily – but there is always something there that says, 'Enough...' You know?

"But the art-war could be a single lonely man in a rented room painting on cardboard because he can't afford real canvas; the art-war is your friends who continue to write, paint, draw and make music even when they were told repeatedly at school that they were 'useless'. Reading this now you are contributing to the art-war, so well done. Keep it up. Blast those words across humanity!"

FROM THE CUTTING ROOM FLOOR:

"When I knew The Dischargers was becoming a reality, it clashed with my previous/current musical tastes, and I thought it was a bit of a dead horse, but it turned out to be way MORE than a mere 'Dis-band'. Of course, bands like Genocide SS & Wolfpack have rode the Dis-wave and managed to put some refreshing twists & turns into an over-used, over-run style. I think, rather than list WHY The Dischargers is different from my previous musical offerings, it would be more apt to comment on the fact that The Dischargers are similar to what I have done in the past because of the lack of obeying the 'rules' within the lyrical department. Usually when a band releases something that is successful, they regurgitate that same theme again & again, and this, to me becomes stale & very boring. A formulaic pattern emerges and it is repeated and this becomes safe and acceptable – well, fuck that! I actually see no reason why Dischargers cannot have a piano or a complete orchestra on the next album, or even a shedload of monks uttering verbal peaceful offerings to the great Buddha in the sky, and if not, then WHY NOT? Fuck all that 'playing it safe' bullshit. It is all just music, and it brings people together, which, in this day and age of whole communities & nations becoming more & more insular, has GOT to be a good thing. As for things I have done/created in the past, London band The Apostles (of which I was a member for some years), my old hardcore/metal band Hellbastard, and Nero Circus, and my old band Sidewinder were all quite angry. The Dischargers, actually, is the angriest and most brutal thing I have ever been involved with. It really is a bull in a china shop. David, Zen & Steph are all in (and have done) heavy bands in the past, they are certainly not newcomers to this scene, and I think we have made a relevant album for the 20th century. I do know one thing, I have not heard a band like The Dischargers for a long, long time."

"If the Terrorizer readers want to really help, then maybe they could try any of the following? Adopt an orphan from a foster-care home, adopt a cat or dog from an animal centre, commit a random act of kindness for an old age pensioner, or give generously to the West Memphis Three campaign's bust fund. If you are at school, then tell your teacher that his lesson is boring and then demand to have The Dischargers come and play... and I will give free lessons to your class for a week! Support Fair Trade produce, subscribe to Terrorizer, give old clothes to second-hand hand shops, recycle everything you can... or just tell me to shut up!"

"And shit, I have good reason to be misanthropic. My father had an untimely death, and I never knew him as well as I'd have liked... I found my own mother dead after she had committed suicide in 1981... I was eleven years old, fercrissakes. Then I had to put up with all the bullshit of being sent to a children's home and staying there until I was sixteen years old 'cos no one else could look after me...

"I never even got the chance to say, 'Come on dad, I'll take you down the pub for a pint...eh?' He never drank anyway, but that's beside the point. Unfortunately, after this my mother found the WRONG boyfriend, and I'd come home from school and there was blood all over the walls and all over the carpet, the idiot dysfunctional fuck had slashed his wrists, and was high on something, and what with my mum being lonely, and basically lost, what the fuck was I supposed to do? In this day and age, it's commonly known as either paedophilia or child-abuse. Being threatened and seeing my best mate have the shit kicked out of him because a member of 'staff' in the kid's home was more or less angry that day. What the fuck does that shit DO to a young kid's mind? I never did what all the other kids were doing at all. Transfixed with TV and sports, fuck that. I was off to a Riot Squad gig, or Mau Maus at The Station in Gateshead, Newcastle-Upon-Tyne. My brother would put on shows and promote all these cool bands like Antisect, Amebix, Anti-System, The Skeptix, Svart Framtid, Disorder, Chaos UK, Dirt, Subhumans, etc. in between writing regular UK scene reports for the American Maximum Rock 'N' Roll Magazine.

"To top it all, in 1996 (after years of scrimping and scrabbling by on next to nothing) a sister of my father's died in Bristol and left a wealthy estate behind totalling over £200,000. Me and my brother were informed and got a visit from the genealogists; they said it was OUR money (it was) but in the end we never got a penny, it went straight to the state 'cos they couldn't prove that my father was adopted in South Africa in 1924 or some shit, and they didn't even have a kept record of adoptions in the UK until 1926. Some fat fucking politicians have had some decadent meals and probably many bottles of Chateau Rentiere on me and my brother, as well as god-knows-how-many bags of cocaine and prostitutes to boot. So Ian, after three years of sweating my ass off working and studying at the same time, I was awarded my BA HONS in Modern English Studies, then I had to deal with finding out that teaching English wasn't my bag after all, and going from menial job to menial job, is it any wonder I am slightly misanthropic. Sorry, it's just the way it is. I really don't think anyone can do anything, for anyone."

Disfear

Well, it's been a while since we featured a Dis-core band in the mag, but let's face it, it was getting kinda old back there, wasn't it? And any Discharge fan who could string together a few chords was getting a band up, and getting signed. And it all got horribly generic. But as happened with black metal, as happened with NYHC, and as will happen with Belgian straight edge, that bubble burst, the weak went under, and the strong and true remained standing. A natural weeding-out process necessary for any genre's survival.

"Oh yes, absolutely," agrees Bjorn, vocalist for Swedes, Disfear, when I wonder if he's sick of the whole Dis-core thing. "When we had a break in '93, after the German tour, and then started up again. It was like a new band even back then, and we almost changed the name to get away from the 'Dis' tag. In the end though, we decided to keep it 'cos it was what people knew. But the whole scene has gone too far, you know?"

That said, 'Everyday Slaughter', the second album, but their first on Osmose, for all its raging power sounds like business as normal to me, i.e. Dis-core to the max. As only Disfear know how.

"Do you think so? I think it has a bit more variation than 'Soul Scars' [their full-length debut – IG]. It's not exactly typical Disfear, although you know it's us as soon as you hear it, but more a natural progression for the band."

Another genre cliché they seem to fall into again is a seeming preoccupation with war - which suits the apocalyptic nihilism of the music, but how sincere are your sentiments?

"Of course, we have a fear of war, and I think everyone does, as long as there's conflict in the world," claims Bjorn, "But a lot of it when we started out was just to be like Discharge, I guess. That's why we wanted to do something a bit different now. The new lyrics are a bit more personal, about how I feel about all the shit I see around me. We still sing about war, I know, but we try to touch on some other topics too."

Now firmly ensconced on the well-established Osmose label, the future looks bright for Disfear, barring any nuclear disasters, of course, and I'm sure most extreme metal fans will be able to get off on the unrelenting quality of their punk thrash, if they give them the chance they deserve.

"I hope so. We just played a big festival here in Sweden, the Hultsfred fest, and we went down very well. With all sorts of people, not just punks. We want to bring our music to a wider audience, not just the Discharge fans out there."

DISGUST – ISSUE 4 (JANUARY 1994)

Disgust, first album line-up

Latest Earache signees Disgust are about to unleash their debut, 'The Brutality of War'. Outspoken drummer Steve Beatty tells Ian Glasper why they're not simply Discharge clones.

Disgust are the latest addition to the Earache roster, and if you haven't heard them yet, then you soon will do, because they're pretty bloody good – even if they do bear more than a passing resemblance to Discharge. Actually that's probably the understatement of the year... anyway, I recently asked drummer Steve Beatty to put us in the picture about all things Disgusting.

Steve, tell us a bit about how the band came to be, because it's a little unorthodox, to say the least?

"Well, we'd all been playing for years, and we'd all got utterly pissed off playing in the bands we were in... Dave had been in Discharge and Dr & The Crippens, I left Mass a year or so ago, Gary was in Blitz and Blitzkrieg, Lee was in an electro-industrial band, and Dean's currently in Extreme Noise Terror. It just wasn't right, so we decided, seeing as we all knew each other, and were all into Discharge and that style of music, we'd do something like this. The band had never rehearsed, we hadn't written any songs, never played a gig – we just went into the studio for six days, wrote all the songs on the spot, and did the album there and then. Dean only met the band for the first time when he arrived to do the vocals! The first LP will be out on Earache in late January, called 'The Brutality of War'... but we've signed for four albums, and we're recording the next one in February!"

Did you set out with the intention of sounding like Discharge, or was that just how it turned out in the studio?

"I don't actually think we sound like Discharge! For a start, it's a lot faster, and it's more up to date. I suppose the chord structures are what we do have in common – it's definitely the Discharge school of guitar playing, but it's all much faster."

And your lyrics are all anti-war, just like – dare I say it? – Discharge?

"I wrote all the lyrics for the album, and they came out the way they did because of Bosnia. It seems apt that all those bands were singing about war twelve years ago, and now we're still singing about war again, 'cos war's still with us. The lyrics are as relevant today as ever before. I don't think they're cliched... I mean, they're all stuff like, 'Bombs are falling from the sky', but it's fucking true – it's still going on, and it's still shit."

Will you branch into other topics on future LPs?

"I think it depends on how I feel, and what's happening at the time. I think, if anything, the next LP might have more songs about personal violence."

Will the next LP be done totally spontaneously like this one?

"Definitely! We're going to do everything exactly how we did this one, because it was so fresh. It's not like some lame band, who've been on tour for six weeks, or in the studio for over a month, playing their songs time and time again... it gets dull. With Disgust we want to keep it fresh and intense – keep it an enjoyable experience."

You've all been in hardcore bands before – any lessons learnt from mistakes made in the past that you're anxious not to repeat?

"Definitely, yeah! Like we won't pander to a load of scenester wankers. We're going to do and say what we want, and if people don't like us for whatever we do, they simply don't have to buy our records or come and see us. If you want to level shit at us for being on Earache, tough fucking tit, you know? Earache are honest people – friendly, easy to get on with, and they're fair in their business dealings. All the HC punk rock labels I've dealt with, who say they're really cool and nice, are just a bunch of two-faced cunts in the first place."

Disgust, 1993

So, no gigs for expenses only then, as is often the way on the HC circuit?

"It's like, if you're a HC band into the scene and stuff, you're meant to do everything for free, meant to act in a certain way, say and do all the right things, and you're not allowed to be you – it's a joke! Bands have got to eat, and buy equipment and stuff."

Will we see Disgust live soon, perhaps supporting another Earache band?

"There's talk about doing the Entombed tour next year. Apparently their management have heard our tape, and they're really into it. Plus they're into Discharge too... I mean, they're Swedish, haha! We'll almost definitely be doing Japan and the States this year, and maybe a European tour. We'd like to put together a Discharge-style tour, with Disfear and Dischange, if they're into it. The three of us will just go out and take the piss..."

What about asking Discharge to do it? What do you reckon to their new LP?

"I think it's piss... utter fucking garbage. And I'd love to go on tour with them and show them how to do it. Discharge should fuck off and die some place, just pack it in – they're shit. They're not even a good metal band. Discharge were something ten years ago, but these days they're just a fifth or sixth rate pub rock band. Cal's lyrics and vocals are just horrible, nasty, pathetic and childish. When Discharge read this, they'll probably say, 'It would be really easy for us to do another 'Hear Nothing, See Nothing, Say Nothing'...", but it wouldn't, lads, 'cos you're simply past it. You don't know what's going on anymore, and the only reason you did it was to earn money."

Tell us about the near Napalm Death connection – wasn't Barney Greenway originally slated to sing for Disgust?

"In all honesty, Barney came into the studio and started doing the LP but it didn't really work out. We want to go on tour a lot, and Barney's obviously got other commitments, with Napalm and Aston Villa. Basically, it's our band, and we didn't want it being seen as anyone's project or anything. Barney was quite good and stuff, but he's really too busy..."

A few of you work in the music industry... is this an advantage or a hindrance?

"It's a hindrance basically. People are more wary about dealing with us, 'cos we're not wet behind the ears. Plus, if we do a gig and we're ripped off by a promoter, a lot of bands that Plastic Head [Steve's distribution company] handle won't be going back to that venue either! Also, a lot of people will sling shit like, 'You only got this deal because you know so and so...', but that's crap – Earache wouldn't be releasing our album if they didn't want to.

"If you don't like us, or our music, or what we say, then fuck off, you're not invited. Fuck the lot of you! Simply fuck off! Punk rock!"

Or as Discharge so succinctly put it on their first EP – 'Thanks to no fucker', eh?

DISGUST – ISSUE 40 (MARCH 1997)

Way back when, Disgust clawed their way to the top of the Discharge-a-like punk-core pile with their debut album. Years later, they finally got round to making another one. Ian Glasper spoke to Steve Beatty - now the owner of Plastic Head Distribution - and found out what it's like to be making punk rock once more and not just selling it...

Can you remember way back to issue # 4 of your beloved Terrorizer? Shame on you if you can't. I certainly can, 'cos it was my first feature for the mag, and it was this little lot of noise terrorists who I chatted to. It was an entertaining, animated discussion, with drummer Steve, who's also the head hombre behind Plastic Head Distribution, letting fly at anyone and everyone who'd pissed him off, and the arrogant young chap promised a follow-up to their Earache debut within six months. Well, we waited with bated breath (okay, so some of us did), and we waited, and then we waited a bit more, and then newer bands stole our attentions, and Disgust seemed little more than a distant (ahem), discordant (enough of that already!) memory.

Now they're back, with a vengeance, it would seem, with a revitalised sound and line-up, and a new album, 'A World Of No Beauty', nestling like a weeping wound on the new release schedule of Nuclear Blast Records. Just why has it taken you so long to return to the fray, Steve?

"Well, me and Lee [Barrett, also of Extreme Noise Terror] have gotten on fairly well for the last few years", reckons Steve, "Because he runs Candlelight, and I own part of Candlelight, and we were literally sat in the pub one night, remembering how much fun it was, and we both thought that we could make a better record, a more metallic, more powerful one. We talked about it for over a year, and in the end, I went ahead and arranged for us to go into the studio, which made us get our shit together."

'Getting their shit together' implies that they actually rehearsed for this record. Shurely there must be shome mishtake, hic?

"Yes, we did, and I think that it's quite evident that we worked hard on it. We did six or eight weeks where we rehearsed three or four days every week."

It certainly is apparent on hearing the new disc. The intro rips out of the speakers at you, intent on tearing you a new asshole, and then there's no let-up in the pace for a dirty dozen of grindin' metal-punk outbursts, apart from the occasional slow passage that buries you in a landslide of bad-tempered riffs. They do, indeed, sound like a proper band, rather than some studio project, but weren't you worried that intensive preparation might lose the original edge of that first record?

"Nah", comes the confident reply. "Half of those tracks were written just after the last album, anyway. There's been so many bands who've tried to fuse Discharge and Motorhead, and they all failed, but we've finally pulled it off really well. Three of us have been listening to Discharge for years and years, and we've really got a feel for it, and what, with Wurzel coming in..."

Oh yeah, I was saving that little surprise for later, but now that Steve's let the cat outta the bag, he may as well elaborate. Yes, you read it right, that's Wurzel, ex-Motorhead, on lead guitar.

"I've known him for a while, since he came down the PHD offices a few years ago, when he was doing a techno record with Krusher. Even back when Dave was in the band, when we fully intended to do another album straight after that first one, but Gary wasn't into it, Wurzel was who we had in mind, and he was really up for it even then. He definitely wanted to do something more intense; he'd done the rock thing, the big band thing, y'know?"

I guess it was a whole new style for him? "Oh, it was completely new! He had a hard time getting his head around it at first, but once he sussed it out, his stuff was really good. Some of his lead breaks are great. He didn't contribute anything to the song-writing though. Lee writes all the music, and I write all the lyrics. He's really from the old rock school, and he was thinking, 'Oh my God, I thought Motorhead was intense, but this is a complete barrage of fuckin' noise! It was an eye-opener for him. When he came in the studio and I'd finished my drum tracks in two days, he couldn't believe

It. He's used to doing an album in six months, so when we said we were going to do ours in ten days, he didn't think we'd ever manage it, but it can be done if you don't fuck about." Disgust have certainly moved their sound a step up in the game, but there's been very little change in the lyrical department, the words to their songs continuing in the grand Discharge tradition and concerning themselves with the horrors of war.

"It's very easy to write those lyrics", he admits. "You can churn out an album's worth in a coupla hours, but l actually mean very seriously every word l wrote. We still live in a world which is controlled by violence and war, and I think relying on violence as a means to achieving everything is a horrendous thing. The point of those lyrics is repetition. It still goes on, nothing's changed, and if you look out on the world, it's very difficult to maintain righteous values, to maintain some purpose and perspective in your life, when there's all this madness going on all around you. Our lyrics are definitely not for entertainment purposes. They are for information."

DOA – issue 130 (April 2005)

DOA, Gateshead 2015, pic by Will Binks

With both a new studio album, 'Live Free Or Die', and an impressive 'Best Of' compilation, 'War And Peace', in the racks to celebrate over 25 years of unashamed rabble-rousing, Ian Glasper decided it was high time to bring you the lowdown on Canada's greatest living punk band, DOA.

307

Joey Shithead – now there's a name to conjure with. Frontman with Canadian punk legends DOA, he's turned his hand to many vocations over the years, from acting to fatherhood to running his own label, most recently garnering great critical acclaim with his brutally honest book, 'I Shithead, A Life In Punk', published by Arsenal Pulp Press.

"It's like a philosophy I have," begins Joey (née Keithley) carefully, when pressed for the secret to his band's longevity. "You gotta believe in yourself, and think things out, try to change the world and have some fun at the same time. I guess I'm the glue that holds this band together – we've had so many different members along the way – but anyone that's been in the band has been so on a friendship basis, rather than any sort of 'gun for hire' type thing. You've gotta have something in common with the people you play with, and you have to believe in each other. We take the same kind of philosophy as an ice hockey team, right? We're gonna go out and brutalise the opposition and hopefully put a few goals in their net. Something like that anyway... and then have a few beers afterwards."

Fighting talk indeed, but Mr Shithead walks it like he talks it. Over the course of 26 years, more than a dozen albums, not to mention countless singles and compilation appearances, and years of relentless touring (3,000 shows and counting), his band have proven themselves a musical and lyrical force to be reckoned with, treating their fans with an honesty and integrity so often lacking from the work ethic of the modern-day punk rock band. So, how has his approach changed over the years?

"Well, I was 22 when I started, and now I'm 48 or whatever, so it would be strange if it was exactly the same," he reasons. "This attitude's always been there since I was a teenager and started listening to music, whether it be punk or just something with a message that inspired me. The DIY approach hasn't changed, but things are a little different now. I run a record label [Sudden Death] on a full-time basis so that's a big part of what I do these days."

Was the label set up primarily to take control of his own career?

"Well, originally when we did the 'Disco Sucks' EP [1978]," he recounts, "We thought, 'Everybody hates us, no-one will ever help us, we might as well do it ourselves!' Then we did a few more singles in the early '80s, various benefit singles, and basically we went through about eight different labels between 1979 and 1996. We used to say that every label that went with us used to go bankrupt, so we ought to get hired up by Exxon or IBM as their record label division and then we could bankrupt them at the same time, haha! Of course, the one label that has always been good to us is Alternative Tentacles [run by ex-Dead Kennedys vocalist, Jello Biafra], and we still get on good with them.

"Initially it was a way to do it ourselves, but when I started it full-time in '98, I saw it as a way to control what we were doing, and I could put out whatever records I liked; it would be my own financial ruin if they didn't sell! I would have no-one to blame but myself, but even that's far preferable to being at the mercy of some idiot A&R type guy. You can do stuff exactly the way you want."

Now that journey of self-determination has been captured in Joey's aforementioned book. It's a tremendously entertaining read, essential for both fans of DOA and those just interested by underground culture in general. But was it written looking for some closure, to make sense of all those crazy years?

"Well, I'd ranted and raved with all these stories so many times, whilst we were just travelling around with the band, that eventually one of the guys said, 'Instead of telling us these stories over and over again (they'd roll their eyes into the backs of their heads when I started off on one!), why don't you start doing spoken word stuff?' So I started with that, telling some of the stories that ended up in the book, and about three years ago, I had an offer from a publishing company here in Vancouver to do the book, and I said, 'Yeah, let's do it!' I didn't wanna just write another stupid rock 'n' roll book, but more to show that DOA went through some tough times – we weren't down and out or anything, but we had a lot of hassles from cops, and border guards, and violence, and being ripped off by record companies – so it wasn't an easy ride at all. And what I wanted to show with the book is that, you can go through a lot of troubles in your life, but if you always believe in yourself, you can still come out a better person on the other side. I wanted to get across the whole 'Bloodied But Unbowed' kinda thing."

The regularity with which DOA release albums may be decreasing, but every new record is as energetic and diverse as we've come to expect. On the new album the band sound as fired up as they've been in years.

"You've gotta have some enthusiasm when you're making a record, right?" reasons Joey, "But I figure that DOA can't be putting out new studio albums every single year. Everyone seems happy with this one, so we'll probably work it for a couple more years at least. It's good that we don't have to do another record right away. When you're younger, it's okay to do one every year, when you have ideas that are fresh and vital, but to try and grind one out for the sake of it...?

"The thing is with making records, every one has to be a little different. There has to be an echo of what went before, because that's what forms your identity, musically and philosophically as a band, but you don't want to make it predictable."

Can Joey imagine a time when there won't be a DOA?

"Well, people have been saying, 'Here's to another 25 years of DOA!'" he says proudly, "And I'm like, 'Jesus Christ, I'll be 73! Are you kidding?' I can definitely see me doing this for, say, another ten years, but at some point you gotta realise it's time to quit while you're still ahead. It's a bit of a young man's game, I guess, and a lot of the bands out there now are in their early twenties.

"But I look at it this way: one of my idols is Iggy Pop, and he doesn't play all the time, but when he does, he just picks his spot and comes out and plays a great show. And people are all like, 'Wow, I can't believe he just did that!' And he must be, what, 58, right? He gets up there and can still kick ass.

"People keep saying to me, 'Retire!' and I keep thinking that they want me to put new tyres on my van, haha! You can't go on forever, I know that, but as long as there's a call for it, I figure we'll be here. If people wanna hear it, why not play it to them? And even if it's not with DOA, I'll always be writing music; I'll probably be busking somewhere when I'm 70, playing protest folk songs on an old acoustic guitar!"

Sidebar: DEAD CERTS: ESSENTIAL DOA

'SOMETHING BETTER CHANGE' (1980)
The high-octane debut recently re-released by Sudden Death and sounding as vital as the day it was first thrashed out.

'HARDCORE '81' (1981)
The second album, even better than the first, after which original drummer Chuck Biscuits and bassist Randy Rampage went on to drum for Danzig and sing for Annihilator respectively.

'WAR ON '45' EP (1982)
Features the classic tracks, 'America The Beautiful' and 'War In The East' – sadly as relevant today as ever before.

'LET'S WRECK THE PARTY' (1985)
And why not? Best tracks: 'Race Riot' and 'General Strike'.

'LAST SCREAM OF THE MISSING NEIGHBOURS' (1989)
The band's biggest selling album saw them teaming up with Alternative Tentacles mainman Jello Biafra, a truly blistering collaboration that brought the best out of both parties.

'13 FLAVOURS OF DOOM' (1992)
'LOGGERHEADS' (1993)
Two strong mid-period albums, the band neatly balancing their ultra-serious left-wing politics with a wicked sense of humour and an ear for a catchy chorus.

'LIVE FREE OR DIE' (2004)
As good as anything the band have put their name to in years, the latest album demonstrates just why DOA have yet to outstay their welcome – great tunes, great lyrics and unwavering enthusiasm.

THE DOUGHNUTS – ISSUE 33 (AUGUST 1996)

Who said I get all the shit jobs here at Terrorizer? In the past week, I've chatted to two all-girl Swedish bands, which certainly beats arguing the toss with some crusty old punk band, eh?

The Doughnuts

First of all, it was Drain after their support to Fear Factory in Bristol, and now The Doughnuts, but the two are of course cut from completely different cloths. Not to diss Drain [Oh, go on, everybody else does – Ed] too much, but they look much better than they sound, and they pander to the mainstream under the guise of being 'alternative'. The Doughnuts rock with much more menace, huge tidal waves of discord and distortion with a hint of 'South of Heaven'-era Slayer, all topped off with Asa Foseberg's distressed, impassioned vocal pleadings. In fact, when I hook up with guitarist Sara, Sweden's prodigal daughters of darkness have just finished shooting a video for the haunting 'Word Unknown' track in - where else? - a snowy forest, which should win them instant credibility with the black metal hordes, too.

"Yes, it's helped us get some publicity," Sara responds to my rather obvious question about their status as the world's only all-female vegan straightedge band. "It's bound to get us attention. The important thing is that once you've got people's attention, they decide that they actually like you and they want to continue listening to you. And that's down to how good your band is, not whether you're male, female, vegan or whatever." Of course, there is a down-side to their fated gender, too. "We always worry about sexism out there touring - you know, people who don't come to listen to the band, just to leer at them and shout abuse," she sighs, "But it hasn't been too bad. One of the few times we've encountered that was actually at a show in England, but we just ignored them and kept playing. We sort of worried that America would be bad, but it wasn't really a problem, although out there it was a little bit more violent when we toured with Snapcase. A guy got stabbed at one show and was rushed to hospital!"

Wow, you're thinking now - the States with Snapcase, not a bad support slot to land, right? That's one of the benefits of being on Victory Records, who are rapidly earning a reputation as the heavy hardcore label of the moment. In fact, America is slated again for October, this time in tow with Earth Crisis... some girls get all the luck! Victory are obviously pumping some reserves into The Doughnuts, as can be seen on the juggernaut production and lush packaging of their second album, the enigmatically titled 'Feel Me Bleed'. Nothing to do with vampirism or menstruation, though, Cradle fans!

"Asa writes all the lyrics, and in the album title she is conveying the pain of the earth as we destroy it. She is bleeding with the innocent animals we slaughter. It's just about empathising with the suffering of others."

It's not all gloom, though; there is a humorous side to these metalcore mongers that isn't apparent from their music. I mean, what about that name?

"It was for our first show, and we were trying to decide what to call the band," laughs Sara. "Someone suggested The Doughnuts and that we should dress up like monks on stage, because in Swedish, 'monks' and 'doughnuts' are the same word! People started to know us as The Doughnuts, so we kept the name... but not the monk costumes!"

DOWN BY LAW - ISSUE 12 (SEPTEMBER 1994)

Californian punk outfit Down By Law are back with another new album. Ian Glasper reckons it's their best yet and vocalist Dave Smalley isn't about to disagree...

Californian punk band Down By Law are back with a revitalized line-up and their third

Down By Law

and best album to date in the shape of 'Punkrockacademyfightsong' on Epitaph Records. I recently caught up with the guys on a night off during their European tour and began by asking front man Dave Smalley, also the founding member, about their latest recruits.

"Hunter Oswald is the new drummer who also sings one or two songs," says the singer. "He and Sam, the guitar player, are both from Florida. We met Hunter when Down By Law toured there. Sam was in a band called Balance who opened up for us on the same tour. When we needed some new guys, they were both determined to try out and flew out to Los Angeles to audition. They were my favourites by far and they're great guys. John, the bassist came from an LA band, The Leonards, and he's an amazing player. Hunter and Sam are nineteen and twenty, so pretty young, and John's right around my age. He's 30. It's a nice balance."

So how is it having some new blood in the band? The aforementioned bassist Angry John takes the phone. "Oh, it's great to have somebody so young in the band because it brings me back to the original feeling I had when I was sixteen or seventeen and first going to punk shows. Hunter and Sam are definitely a great energy to have in the band. Dave and I are enthusiastic anyway, but they bring a different perspective to our enthusiasm."

This energy seems reflected in the style and title of the new record. "The album title was thought up by Dave," continues John. "We'd written down about 100 titles on the wall of the studio, and that one just felt the best. It really captured the spirit of what we felt while recording the album. We were making a punk rock record. The energy was very upbeat and we were very clear about what we wanted to do."

You recently appeared on the soundtrack of 'The Chase', so why has no soundtrack album been forthcoming? "The company who put that film out, some major movie company, wanted Epitaph to release the soundtrack," says Dave, taking up the baton once more. "Brett said he'd do it, and lo and behold, they sent over the artwork for the cover, and it was this really cheesy airbrushed photo of Charlie Sheen and Kristy Swanson. It looked ridiculous. Brett called them up and said, 'What the fuck is this? This isn't anything to do with what Epitaph's about. I don't like it and their fans won't like it.' They insulted us by using this really bad cover, so Brett refused to do it. They even sent over some posters for it, one of which is up on the Epitaph office wall. Like little kids, we've made graffiti all over it, whited out the eyes and stuff like that."

What are your feelings on Jello Biafra's beating which hit the headlines recently? "I think it's awful. I don't agree with everything he's ever said, but when you think of all that guy's done for punk rock, he deserves everyone's respect. He went to jail for his band over the controversy with that record cover, he's kept all his connections through all these years. In 1981, the Dead Kennedys were one of my favourite bands and really influenced me a lot, as much as The Clash did. I probably wouldn't be here talking to you if it wasn't for that guy. And to have punks beat him up, I can't believe how short sighted that is..."

How does Dave view Maximum Rock 'n' Roll, the US fanzine which is a bible for many, who originally accused Biafra of selling out? "They're very intolerant and closed minded, and I really hate that a lot. I don't think punk rock has anything to do with that. To be intolerant of right-wing politicians is okay - real things that matter - but don't be intolerant of each other. We have a line in one of our songs that says every fascist left or right has a fucked-up set of rules. I really do think it's possible to be a left-wing fascist as well as a right wing one.

Talking of intolerance, what do they think of the hard-line militant straight edge movement in America? "I knew a straight edge band from Pennsylvania called Forthright," Hunter kicks in. "They weren't vegan; they ate meat, but were straight edge. They got a letter from a band called Vegan Reich, cussing them out for eating meat. It went something like, 'If you enjoy meat so much then you won't mind eating the skin off my knuckles...' It was hilarious. I don't really care for it when it gets really militant. We're just a band and we all have different ways of thinking. We're by no means a religion, we're just making punk rock music.

"Straight edge, like punk, should be an inclusive thing," Dave elaborates, "Rather than an exclusive one. If you want to be this way that's great, but if you don't, well, that's great too. It's whatever works for you."

But do you think music can ever change the world? "I really want the world to become a better place," says Dave, "But I don't believe that if we had anarchy, it could actually work. At risk of seeming old, I'll quote a line from The Who to you: 'Meet the new boss, the same as the old boss...' From 'Won't Get Fooled Again'. There's always going to be someone there who will want to try and ruin everybody's lives. The trick, and what we're hopefully doing with punk, is to acknowledge that music can change individuals, and that's where it gets its power."

DREAMS OF DAMNATION - ISSUE 87 (MARCH 2001)

Dreams of Damnation may be a new name to many of you, but lurking within their ranks is a grizzled veteran from the great thrash wars of the '80s. Ian Glasper, our celebrated gore correspondent, donned his combat shorts and went to investigate...

Wait one minute, what's that I hear? It's the sound of a very sturdy plectrum being sharpened for fresh use after years of laying seemingly dormant...the sound of a fast-approaching maelstrom, a blizzard of brutality just over the horizon, that at any second will burst into view and flay the skin from your very bones. Run for cover, whilst you still can - uh, too late. Let the violence begin!

Melodrama is the only way to welcome back none other than big Jim Durkin, the sick fucker responsible for some of the nastiest, most twisted thrash metal to ever defile eardrums around the world. Jim played in - created - the mighty Dark Angel, and so guaranteed himself a place in the echelons of thrash history, but it seems like his appetite for destruction wasn't properly sated, because he's back, after a ten-year hiatus, with a new band, Dreams of Damnation, and a brand new MCD, 'Let The Violence Begin', for Necropolis. It's everything you'd expect - and more.

So, where the hell have you been, Jim?

"I just needed to make some money, and I needed to get my life back together again," sighs the amicable guitarist. "And to be honest, I was slowly losing interest in Dark Angel. I was losing my original members, all the guys I started the band with. They were dropping out one by one, and it started to take its toll on me too. I was starting to wonder who'd be in the band from month to month! And the songs were really moving in a different direction as well..."

They were getting kinda long back there...!

"Oh yeah," he laughs, "That was Gene [Hoglan, their man-mountain drummer, now with Strapping Young Lad – IG]'s influence. He's such a good musician, and he liked to write real long, complex songs; that's just his thing. I'm more to the point, but when we synched, you got the best of both worlds, and we wrote some great songs together. But like I said, I dunno why, I was just losing interest... "

Which of course begs the question: why bother to come back then?

"Well, I did a MCD under the name Dreams of Damnation back in '92, with a few friends, and it was a Metal Church/Judas Priest type band. It was just a studio thing, and we never played out, but it was a lot of fun. After that I just jammed around with some local guys for the next few years until those rumours of a Dark Angel reunion began. Even though that never panned out, it sort of lit a fire under my ass. I started getting mail from all these people asking me what I'd been doing, where I'd been... it was amazing to find out how much people actually cared!

"And right away I knew that I needed to get out there and play again. This is what I do, and I've never been happier since. I mean, I've built a normal life for myself, and I've got a job now, and that's my financial support, but this - music - is what I'm meant to do, y'know?"

So, Jim roped in long-time buddy, Charlie Silva, on bass and vocals, and Al Mendez on drums, and Dreams of Damnation was born, an unholy recreation of the rawest, filthiest, death-thrashin' mayhem - just the way we fuckin' like it! And, c'mon, what did you expect from the man who penned such gems as 'Merciless Death' and 'The Burning of Sodom'? But in his liner notes for the new disc, Jim is keen to point out that this is not Dark Angel part 2.

"You know what? I had a lot of comments like, 'Where are the high screeching vocals like Don Doty or Ron Rinehart?' People were like, 'Those vocals on your new stuff are so harsh', and I suppose some people don't care for them so much. But they gotta realise, this is a new band, and they shouldn't get any preconceived ideas about what it will sound like. There's no point saying, 'Oh it doesn't sound like Ron', because I never said it would!"

But it does sound like you! Right from the first riff of the intro to the first song, you can recognise Jim Durkin's warped playing!

"Thanks, man," he laughs. "Look, I'm not trying to consciously stamp my signature on this or anything, it just turned out that way. But I'm glad that you can recognise my little traits in there. We're obviously not doing this for the money, and we're certainly not worried about appealing to a bigger audience or whatever, so there's no reason at all to change our music. We can go ahead and do exactly what we like!"

So, I guess a grass-roots, in-love-with-metal label like Necropolis is perfect.

"Yeah, it's great. I can call any time, and find out anything I need to know, without having to cut through a load of bullshit label politics. I'm very good friends with some of the guys there, and I met Paul at the label through Jensen from The Haunted..."

Ah, yes, I noticed the huge shout-out you gave Jensen for inspiration on your thanks list.

"It's not so much his playing – although he is obviously an amazing player - as his sheer love of metal, and the incredible energy he has. We listen to all the same old bands, we were instantly on the same page when we first met, but most importantly, he's living the life. He's making music, he's always touring, and his freshness really inspired me to get off my ass and do this."

And will we see you touring this release too?

"Obviously we can't go out for two hundred bucks a week anymore," sighs the guitarist ruefully, in closing. "None of us can afford it. We have houses to pay for, some of us have kids, so we can't just throw it all to the wind and leave on tour... but we'll play wherever we can. I'd love to get to Europe, maybe play some of the festivals...You know what? I left Dark Angel right before they went to

Europe! I never went to Europe, so maybe this is my second chance?

"We know that we've got a job to do, and we wanna do it the best we can. We're not gonna make any money, but what could be more fun, and more satisfying, than doing what you love? Making metal, of course!"

D.R.I. – JUNE 2016

"We are testing the waters to see if we should write a full length," explains D.R.I. vocalist, Kurt Brecht, of why we've had to wait twenty years for the band's new EP on Beer City, 'But Wait... There's More!' "And we have been busy with other stuff, touring extensively all over the world."

With Kurt and guitarist, Spike Cassidy, joined by Walter 'Monsta' Ryan on drums and

Harald 'O' Oimoen on bass, the EP sees a return to the more hardcore style the band pioneered in the Eighties, rather than the more metal direction they pursued after their landmark 'Crossover' LP.

"There was no pressure to write a particular way; we just tried the songs out live, and they went over well enough. We've sort of gone back to our roots with this one!"

But a lot has changed in the thirty-three years since D.R.I. first shook up the U.S. punk scene with their 'Dirty Rotten EP'...

"Yeah, it's easier to promote our band for free!" laughs Kurt. "That being said, records no longer sell as well as they used to. But we still get a great mix of people at our shows: kids, parents and everything in between. We try to play all-ages shows whenever possible.

DRI, by Gutterpunk Photography

317

"We'll be back to Europe next year. It is much easier now with the GPS – we don't spend so much time driving around in circles!"

DROWNING MAN – ISSUE 79 (JUNE 2000)

Drowningman, by Matt Thorsen

Kevin Stewart-Panko gave them a resounding 9/10 in April's review section, so you can rest assured that when I say Drowning Man are one of the most exciting noisecore bands I've heard in a long time, it's not just Glasper getting hysterical over yet another hardcore band who've discovered the wonders of the double bass drum pedal. You see, I joined the Drowning Man story relatively late – missing all their Hydrahead output of the last few years, and only picking up on the band with their recent 'How They Light Cigarettes in Prison' CDEP for Revelation – but so blown away was I when I heard the rabid (yet coldly calculated at the same time) frenzy the band are capable of whipping themselves into, it was only a matter of time before I would have to catch up with them to find out what could drive men to such extremes.

"I just got back off such a crazy tour," sighs vocalist Simon Brody, calling me from his girlfriend's place in Kansas City, attempting to explain why tracking him down has been tantamount to locating the holy grail. "It was the usual insanity, only this time, for once, our van didn't break down so often. We have a really old van, and over the last year we must have got ourselves such a bad name for being an unreliable band to book, because it's broken down on us every other show! But this time we put a load of money into it, and it actually held out...

"Come to think of it, it did break down," he adds laughing. "On the day we left, we were on our way to the first show in Buffalo, and we broke down in a big snow storm. We got it fixed and it ran okay for the rest of the tour, until we were on our way home, and we broke down again – less than five miles from where we broke down a month earlier. It was kinda spooky; I guess there's some evil spirit of the N.Y. freeway that doesn't like us too much."

Such are the trials and tribulations of touring. Do you find you start to lose your own identity halfway through a long stint? You start to become your ugly road-dog alter-ego?

"Oh yeah," says Simon knowingly. "We're all going through that right now. I think I'm the lucky one out of all of us, 'cos I've been flying out here to Kansas to see my girlfriend, so I haven't really 'come home' yet. But the other guys... I was talking to Dave, our bass player, and he's still living out of his duffel bag. And I'm still using my travel wash bag in the bathroom! We're all in denial that the tour has ended, 'cos, of all the shitty places I saw on the road, I think I would prefer any of them to Burlington."

That's Burlington, Vermont, readers, Drowning Man's home town, and if you're thinking that you've never heard of it, don't worry, you haven't missed much by the sound of things. Because it must be a very miserable place, to inspire the kind of violent rage that Drowning Man channel into their hostile blend of noise, metal, emo, and hardcore (never mind those spastic rhythms and demented melodies). One look at the lyrics to a song such as 'Black Tie Knife Fight' hints at a disturbingly anti-social side to the band.

"Actually, I wrote that song about a personal experience," Simon says [sorry, couldn't resist it – IG], chuckling to himself at my crass psychology. "I'm a very laid-back person in reality, but I do have a temper, just like everyone else. I was working the door of a club in Burlington, which is a big college town, and it was at some frat bar. And I was just looking in dismay at all these kids who invade our town, and stumble around, waving bottles in my face, pissing all over the steps of the bar... you know what? If I could've gotten away with it, I would probably have stabbed one of them [worrying laugh]. A lot of our lyrics are violent, but they suit this type of music, and more often than not, they are loaded with sarcasm. They're a joke, because we are not violent people."

Glad to hear it, Simon. But I know that you've got something you need to get off your chest before you go, right?

"Yeah, I fucking hate all the fashion aspects of hardcore, all the stuff that just detracts from the music. Have you got kids out there wearing tennis visors yet? Just you wait... what the hell is all that about? It's ridiculous. Actually, our goal in this band is to get big enough so we can lead the way in some outrageous fashion trend all our own, and see how many kids get suckered into it..."

DRY KILL LOGIC – ISSUE 91 (JULY/AUGUST 2001)

"Oh, it's going fucking great, every night has been amazing. The crowds are cool, all the other bands are cool, so every night it's kicking off. And it's the right bill for us too, 'cos these are the kids we need to be in front of. So we're very grateful for this opportunity; it's a dream come true."

The man who sounds so psyched to be alive right now is Cliff, the singer with latest

Roadrunner signings, Dry Kill Logic, and the reason he is happy is that his band have just released their impressive debut album, 'The Darker Side Of Nonsense', and are mid-way through a huge US jaunt with Fear Factory and Spineshank. Who wouldn't be on cloud nine, eh? But it hasn't all been plain sailing for this exciting modern metal outfit based in Westchester, New York; due to threat of a lawsuit, they just had to change their name from Hinge, under which guise they've been in existence since 1995.

"When we signed our deal, we found that there was a recording studio in Chicago called Hinge, who'd been in business about six months longer than us, and he had a trademark on the name," sighs the fast-talking frontman. "We approached him for consent to use the name, or at least share it and we co-promote each other, but he told us to go fuck ourselves. He was, like, 'Screw you, I don't want your money, I don't need your help, I just want my name!' Which was a little disturbing, y'know? It seems unfortunate when people can't work together."

Oh well, such is life, and personally I prefer the Dry Kill Logic moniker anyway. It certainly helps paint a picture of the band's pounding hypnotic metallic rhythms, that lurk in those dark shadows somewhere between System of A Down and Sepultura. It's nu-metal for want of a better term, and normally I hate nu-metal, but I definitely dig Dry Kill Logic. Must be the hints of Snapcase I hear in some of their grooves, or maybe the almost tangible anger with which they ply their trade.

"My lyrics aren't really directed at any one person or any one particular event, but rather they are about the emotion of anger," Cliff explains, when pushed about the amount of angst they have poured into their album. "Our record can be the soundtrack to anyone's anger, not just mine. The songs that have always meant the most to me are the songs I can relate my own meaning to, instead of having to relate to the meaning of the songwriter. That way you embrace them and make them a part of your life."

DUB WAR - ISSUE 8 (MAY 1994)

Dub War 1994

Newport based 'rock-reggae' band Dub War have just signed to Earache Records, whilst they still have their debut album, 'Dub Warning', nestling in the record racks. Ian Glasper finds out more from bassist Richie Glover.

You may well not have heard of this Newport band just yet, but rest assured you soon will. The ripples they are currently making are rapidly becoming waves. Not only do they have an LP, 'Dub Warning', in the racks, which has the sort of across-the-board appeal required to break out of the punk/metal ghetto, but they've also just signed to Earache – a label not renowned for its rock/reggae bands!

What I want to know first of all is how they got together as a band... "We came together about two years' ago," says the band's bassist Richie Glover. "It was just the three of us playing our instruments [Jeff Rose – guitar and Martin Ford – drums], trying different things out. Me and Jeff can sing a bit, but not very well, so we were doing straight punk, with us screaming over the top. We were feeling pretty limited in what we could do, and decided we needed a singer. We'd heard some tapes of Benj [Clive Webbe], and knew he was a good vocalist, so got in touch with him. From the first jam, where he grabbed the mic and joined in, it just clicked. He added the reggae edge, which we all listened to and were into anyway, but he also introduced the rap and ragga, which pointed us in a new direction."

So what sort of response did they have to their 'Respected' EP and 'Dub Warning' LP (both on Words of Warning Records)? "I've no idea what the sales are, but I know it's doing well – certainly better than we ever thought it would do anyway. We didn't put that first EP out expecting to get in the indie charts or get airplay, so we were surprised when Radio One started playing it and it got the reviews it did. We were amazed when it got Single Of The Week in Kerrang! And the new LP's been received a lot better, if anything. We did our releases real quick, so they don't sound much different to each other, but the songs on 'Dub Warning' are more 'us', because our song-writing's obviously come on."

I take it you were pleased with the efforts of Karl (Words of Warning boss), seeing as he's now your manager? "Well, we had a few people offering to manage the band, and we went for a few meetings with all these sharks in London, but all they could think about was how much money they could make off us. We decided we needed someone we knew, and Karl seemed the perfect man for the job. He's already done a lot of groundwork for us, and the releases have done well for both the band and his label, and we wanted to keep the Words of Warning connection alive."

Hence the song 'Words of Warning' on the new LP? "I suppose it's a tribute in some ways... the label certainly inspired some of the lyrics in the song."

So what tours will you be doing to promote it? "In the book at the moment, we've got some Fundamental and Blaggers support slots, as well as a few headlining gigs of our own. We're off to Ireland in two weeks, and we're touring Russia in May! We had an offer of the Killing Joke tour, but we had to buy onto it, and it was like two grand to play a few shows with them, which is ridiculous. We're not going to pay to play, especially

321

not at this stage of the game, when we haven't got much money to play with anyhow." How was the tour with Gunshot? A lot of the rap scene seems real macho and sexist... "Gunshot are not like that at all! They're pretty sussed; they've got a good message that goes much deeper than that. It was a really good tour for us, we went down pretty well. At first, I think we scared the rap audience a bit, because we're quite heavy, doing the rock thing with the punk edge. But they got into it. They didn't go mad, mind you – except in Scotland, where they were moshing from start to finish! I suppose it's just a case of doing more gigs and getting our stuff better known..."

Dub War 1995, Benji and Jeff

You recently cancelled a few shows because Benji was ill – what was up? "He was having bad pains in his stomach, so we got the doctor out to see him, and he was rushed into hospital, where he had to have his appendix out straight away. But he also had a perforated bowel, which was all brought on by the tour we were doing – sleeping on the van floor, not sleeping properly, eating shit food every day..."

I was a bit surprised to see that you'd signed to Earache – what's the score with that? "One of their people read about us in a zine... 'Throbbing Organ' or something? They thought we sounded good and bought the CDEP and were impressed. They rang us up, set up a meeting and we did some negotiating. There were a few other labels interested, but what the boys at Earache were offering was really good. Most important to us was total artistic control, plus they are a good, respected label. We've signed for a minimum of two LPs, and a maximum of five, if they want to keep us on... I think? I ain't sure about the contracts and all that side of things..."

Are you pessimistic about today's music scene, what with the recession and dwindling gig attendances? "The gig attendance and sales being down really affects the other end of the market, but at the stage we're at, we play to hardly anyone most of the time anyway! Just selling a few thousand singles is great. We're low enough down the food chain to be grateful for everything, and in a way, it's incentive to get off your ass and do it, you know? You've got to try and look at it positively, and take inspiration where you can."

Where does the band stand politically? "Basically, this line-up says a lot racially – a black singer with three white musicians, making music together, speaks for itself really. Politically, our songs are just a reflection of the day and age we live in, all the shit we see going down on the news. They are just our interpretation of things, us trying to make sense of the world."

What would you like to achieve with Dub War? "Just to keep the ball rolling really, carry on creating challenging music, keep trying out fresh avenues, and maybe sell a few more records..."

DUB WAR – ISSUE 16 (JANUARY 1995)

Things are on the up for Dub War, the new Earache signings who recently completed a tour with Manic Street Preachers, have just released their new EP, 'Gorrit', and are gearing themselves up for a full-length debut, due in the new year. Ian Glasper gets the details from the band's bassist Richie Glover.

It was back in issue eight that we last caught up with Newport's Dub War, so it seems high time for an update on happenings in their camp. Finding out all the latest info wasn't easy though – I had to drag bassist Richie Glover away from 'Eastenders'! Really – he was fifteen minutes late ringing me, 'cos he wanted to know what happened to Grant in hospital! Once I've steered him away from talk of Albert Square, I ask him how they're finding Earache... you may recall from last time that they were the first rock/reggae/rap act to sign with the label!

"They're good heads," reckons Rich, in his easy-going tones. "They're easy to work with, there's good communication between us. They've left us to ourselves; they make the odd suggestion, but seem quite happy with what we're doing anyway. It's all business to them at the end of the day, so they've got their 'business heads' on, and leave total artistic control to us. They've not put their foot down with us at all.

"I mean, a lot of people were surprised when we signed to them, but with a band like Scorn doing well, the label's getting more diverse and branching out. And a lot of people told us to watch out for them, 'cos apparently they can be cunts to people, but people say that about any record label, y'know?"

Dub War 1995

Last time we spoke, you were hoping to get to Russia – did you get there in the end? "No, we never got there, because the promoters in Moscow were threatened by the Russian mafia! We had a phone call off the woman organising it, and she was really upset, 'cos it was only three weeks before we were due to go over, and everything was sorted. She was told she had to give them so much money off each gig, some sort of tax and she refused – in the end, she had to cancel the tour!"

You recently did an anti-fascist gig in Maesteg – why there in particular? "That was in September, with the Cowboy Killers. I don't know if you saw it or not – it was in all the papers – but one of the guys from the Ku Klux Klan in America moved back to Maesteg – home to his roots, sort of thing - and there were KKK leaflets getting handed around to all these kids! That was all brewing up there from early this year, but it was a brilliant gig, with no trouble."

So, is racism a problem in South Wales? After a moment's thought, "Up in the Valleys, there's some quite racist places. There are some really isolated communities, like council estates in the middle of the mountains, and they can be a bit backward – a lot of them have never even seen a black guy!"

How much of an inspiration are your surroundings down in Newport? "There's nothing else to do basically. It's a bit bleak, but you've got fuck all else to do except write music... that's why Newport's packed out with so many bands!"

And how did you get Jamiroquai, the Brand New Heavies and Haggis from Senser involved on the 'Mental' EP? "We were thinking of different people who could do some remixes for us..." As usual, Richie plays it down, "And we thought a bit of funky jazz would be a laugh, so we let them have a go. We don't know them personally, we didn't meet them at all - we just picked them as people we'd like to do the mixes. They did their thing without us there basically."

That's one thing I've always wondered about these remixes – how much say do you have in it if you're the original artist? "Well, if you don't like it, you can tell them to go and do it again, so you do have the final say. What they do is take it away and do five or six different mixes of your song, and you choose the one you like the best. If you don't like any of them, you get them to change it – or you don't pay 'em their money, haha!"

On the new 'Gorrit' EP, you've even had a go at your own remix... "Yeah, the 'Black Anadin Toxic Waste' mix, which is amazing, really good. We slowed it right down and made a whole different song out of it by sticking all these different vibes on there."

I've gotta say it – the chorus of 'Gorrit' sounds like Faith No More! "Yeah, a few people have said that to us; I think it's an easy connection to make because of that rock–rap voice. The trouble is, y'see, we're so compatible with everything, so diverse... we could sound like anybody – or everybody!"

Tell us a bit about the tour with Manic Street Preachers? "It was very good. We only had, like, twenty minutes each night, which wasn't long enough – just as you're getting into the vibe of the concert, it's time to get off stage. It was a new audience for us too, so we were breaking new ground – but we did manage to get across to the crowd... we blew the Manics off every night anyway!"

How were they towards you? "They seemed okay. They were cool, friendly enough. Richie was a bit quiet, but James always said, 'Hello'. They kept themselves to themselves most of the time."

Can you think of any bands you wouldn't want to play with? "Mmm, good question," he ponders. "I'd play with anyone; I'm a slag – a whore for music!"

Lastly, what about your new album? Whet our appetites! "It's all finished and will be out in February," he says, before adding modestly, "And it's fucking brilliant basically – what more can I say? It's quite diverse again, it's dub-funk, it's Dub War matured into a real band. There's no remixes, no guests... just us. We have got a song called 'Pain' on there, and we just had to name the album after it, because it's a classic anthem. It's the 'Bohemian Rhapsody' of Dub War - wait 'til you hear it, you'll love it... everybody will love it!"

CHAPTER E:
FORGED IN THE FLAMES
OF CHAOS...

EARTH CRISIS – ISSUE 16 (JANUARY 1995)

Earth Crisis – 27-1-97 – by Danielle Dombrowski

Earth Crisis are hard-hitting straightedgers who have an EP, 'Firestorm', currently nestling in the record racks and a full-length album due sometime in the New Year. Ian Glasper talks here to the band's frontman and vocalist Karl Buechner about the band, their views on music, the straight-edge philosophy and that forthcoming new disc...

Not only are Earth Crisis the first straightedge vegan hardcore band to appear in these pages, they're also one of the heaviest and most intense. Their 'Firestorm' EP on Victory is simply awesome.

I caught up with their vocalist Karl Buechner recently when they flew into the UK for a quick-stop two shows in Bradford. Firstly, I want to know what's been happening with the band recently?

"We've had one line-up change, just last week," begins Karl, in a quiet, measured tone that belies his venomous vocal delivery, "We parted with our old guitarist on good terms. He was having trouble, so it was easier that we get someone new, someone who has more motivation, and Chris has been working out well." (As well as Karl and Chris, Earth Crisis comprise Scott on guitar, Ian on bass and Dennis on drums, and they have an average age of just twenty!)

What about the new album? "We've just finished recording it, and we'll be mixing it when we get back and releasing it in the next coupla months. It contains ten new songs, and we're really happy with the way it's come out. It's gonna be something good."

Aren't some of the guys from Believer helping out with the production? "Yeah, they are. We've come to be good friends with Kurt and Joe, who did the engineering, and did a really good job. Jim from Vigil, formerly of Conviction, has also helped us with engineering. He's our alternate guitarist!"

I know you guys are straightedge (i.e. they don't drink, smoke or do drugs) - what provoked you to take this stance in life?

"As we've grown up, we've seen a lot of people pretty much destroy themselves with drugs and alcohol, relatives dying from cancer because of smoking and so on, and we've seen this suffering first hand, and it's affected us. l myself have never taken drugs, drank or smoked, but I know that doesn't make me any better than anyone else. I definitely think straightedge is survival. When you partake in those kinds of things, it's only a matter of time before you're locked into addiction."

He adds, "Straightedge is a lifetime commitment to abstain from these poisons."

But what about the fashion side of it, and the 'X'-ing of hands etc.?

"It's a totally personal thing," Karl reckons. "We're not out to make everyone straightedge, but we definitely want to expose kids to the benefits of drug- and alcohol-free living. It makes life so much easier, so much more fun - you can accomplish a lot more things in a much shorter amount of time. The 'X'-ing of hands is important to us... the 'X' is the symbol of straightedge, and straightedge is what we love, and we take pride in it. But, if other people are straight and don't 'X' up, that's fine, too."

And what prompted you to go vegan (i.e. they don't eat meat or any dairy/animal products)?

"My grandmother and many members of my family are vegetarian, and I was raised to be respectful of animals. As I got older, I researched things a bit more, and realised the reality of the situation.

Animals are dying, being abused in laboratories, being murdered and turned into meat and leather, and it's an unnecessary and horrific thing. I made a commitment to never go back to that type of diet, because it's destructive and creating even more suffering in the world. Our song 'Eden's Demise' shows how things interconnect - how animals being raised for food destroys the environment as well as the life of that individual creature. Hopefully it might motivate people to make a change."

Don't you think vegetarianism also encourages a more respectful outlook towards other often-discriminated groups? "Yeah, absolutely," agrees Karl. "Freedom goes right across the board.

Earth Crisis – by Naki

Oppression is oppression. Once you go vegetarian, then vegan, you contemplate what you're doing. You're having less of a harmful impact with your life, trying to keep things alive, make the world more peaceful and just. That spills over and keeps growing, and you start considering things like sexism and racism."

Although vegetarianism is on the increase, do you ever get frustrated and disillusioned at how vast the meat industry still is?

"Yeah, there's times of frustration for any vegetarian. They're dealing with people around them who are essentially refusing to face the truth, and they have to put up with mockery from people at school, at work, but you just have to draw off the people close to you who agree."

I know you've songs about militant animal liberation - I take it then that you agree with violent direct action? "I think any action that helps bring an animal to freedom and stop their suffering is a good thing," Karl offers carefully. "We want peaceful change and solutions, but if people are too stubborn or greedy to allow that, then a change has to be forced. We'd only advocate violence as a last and final resort, if all other means have been exhausted or attempted."

EARTH CRISIS – ISSUE 80 (JULY 2000)

Whoever thought that metallic hardcore had evolved as far as it could possibly go needs to think again before they check out the new Earth Crisis album, 'Slither', out now on Victory, because the band have taken their sound into a whole new dimension of catchy heaviness. It certainly took us here at Terrorizer by surprise, so we sent Ian Glasper to talk to Karl Buechner and to investigate the band's blatant reinvention of themselves.

If there's ever been as big a musical jump between two albums by the same band then I've yet to hear one as astonishing as the one between 'Breed The Killers' by Earth Crisis and their latest offering, 'Slither'. And if you go back just an album or two earlier into the band's career (to '96's 'Gomorrah's Season Ends', or '95's 'Destroy The Machines'), the metamorphosis is even more incredible. The vegan eco-warriors from Syracuse have transformed themselves, seemingly overnight, from relentless brutal hardcore angst-mongers into groovin' nu-metallers. Still, their new album rocks - just in different ways to their back catalogue - and they haven't lost any of their lyrical indignation, but all the same, the Terrorizer readers need to know what went down, right?

"We just felt we had gone as far as we could with straight-forward heaviness," sighs quietly-spoken vocalist, Karl Buechner, by way of explanation, "And we decided we needed more dynamics, to make it exciting for us again. We've always done just what we want when we want anyway, and we've never been concerned about fitting into any particular mould or scene.

"We are a very progressive band," he continues. "Each album has been a progression from the previous one; we've never done two that sounded exactly the same... but this time we really went out on a limb. I think this is probably the most creative, innovative record we've ever done, to be honest, and one we're all genuinely proud of."

Of course, the cynical amongst us might perceive this as a move to break into the mainstream.

Someone I was talking to about it suggested that this sounds like the album you should have delivered during your short stay at Roadrunner ('Slither' is on Victory again, the band's original label – IG).

"The main goal of Earth Crisis from day one was to push our message to as many people as possible, and each day we get a little closer; we reach a slightly wider audience. And at least it's still us, doing what we want, and doing it all ourselves.

"Besides, our subject matter, and the musical aggression, will always make it very difficult to achieve 'mainstream' success. We write for ourselves, and no one else, but this album certainly looks set to be better received than anything we've done before, even if it has got people talking!"

And while I'm being devil's advocate here, the return to Victory looks like a bit of a U-turn too.

"The truth is, the day our deal dissolved – and it wasn't just us, either: Roadrunner shed all their hardcore bands in one fell swoop, they just didn't wanna push that style anymore, y'know? - we had four labels interested. Two of them were metal, one was hardcore, and one was punk. Victory just gave us the deal we wanted; we were looking for a big radio push, and a decent budget for a video, and all the other things we'd been lacking until then. Now it all seems to be falling into place a bit more... actually we're doing our first 'real' video - with real actors and actresses, and a proper storyline - next week. It's pretty serious, it's with a guy who has worked with Pantera and Soulfly, so none of us know quite what to expect. This is all new to us!"

The biggest departure, it has to be said, is with the vocals. Karl is now singing. And I don't mean wailing tunelessly, either - this guy can really hit those notes, demonstrating great range as well as natural rhythm. He can still roar with the best of them, but here he's pushed his delivery to the limit, to wring every ounce of diversity out of any given passage. His subtle melodies blend seamlessly with the often-intricate guitars and stomping beats to help create the most challenging, listenable EC material to date. Was this something you've wanted to do for a while?

"Yeah, I've been working towards this for a few years," he admits. "We always wanted to do something like this, but I couldn't pull it off until now; my lungs just weren't up to it. One of the goals with the new vocals was to get the extra dynamics we wanted to bring in, so when the breakdown sections hit, they sound even heavier. You feel them more because there's more depth and texture there. It's not powerful in the same way as the other Earth Crisis records, but it's more energetic. It has a manic energy, not a dark energy like 'Breed The Killers' had."

And I suppose it's pretty pointless having a lot to say if no one can understand a word of it!

Earth Crisis, by Naki

Earth Crisis, 1997, by Danielle Dombrowski

"Yeah, it seemed totally redundant having such a strong message if the lyrics were indecipherable. You have to remember that we've been doing the same style for eight years now - caveman style! – and now it's a lot more fun again, because it's something different. It was a fresh challenge, especially for me. I put a couple of holes in the rehearsal room wall trying to get it all right, but I think it came together pretty good in the end."

I know that a lot of your fans are going to feel disappointed, maybe even cheated, by the new direction. After all you sound like a different band to the Earth Crisis that gave us 'Destroy The Machines'.

"Yes, but that was five years ago," comes the only-slightly-exasperated reply, "And just as many people would complain if we sounded exactly the same, too! Listen, we've given those 'hardcore fans' six albums of brutal basic heaviness that they can listen to over and over again, forever and ever if they want - but this is what we want to do. We're all on the same page, too, as regards this new direction; everyone in the band is pumped up about it."

One thing that hasn't changed for the band is their strong stance against the abuse of animals and the environment. Karl's lyrics are as inspirational and as challenging as ever, but even here, we see somewhat of a development, with his potent words highlighting some new topics, such as the disturbing new atrocities created by modern science.

"Every album has always focussed strongly on animal liberation and the environment," agrees Karl, "But this time, I started to think about how things actually got this bad in the first place. And why no one saw all this coming fifty years ago, and why no one did anything about it back then, whilst there was still time.

"So, with this record, we tried to look into the future, and tried to predict some of the problems that are bound to result from robotics and cloning and genetic engineering. We're trying to sound the alarm, for the animals especially; it's a new millennium, but the future's pretty bleak. Humans have always shaped the animals' environment to suit ourselves... but now we're actually trying to shape the animals themselves. It's pretty scary stuff."

So how does all that fit in with the reptilian cover concept, and title?

"The album is all about how evil is trying to take over, infiltrating everything to the very core; that's why the serpent is crawling around the heart, looking to strangle it."

Y'see, the music might be different, but this is still Earth Crisis, no doubt about it, even if they make you wanna bounce up and down now, instead of doing windmills. Another thing that hasn't changed is the band's willingness to take their music out on the road, with extensive touring imminent to promote the latest offering, and talk turns to one of the more unusual road trips undertaken on the back of the 'Breed...' album. I heard that you guys actually went and played in Columbia, of all places?

"Yeah, we did the Rock in the Park festival down there," remembers Karl, with a wry chuckle. "And that was definitely the craziest thing we have ever done as a band. I was more than a little nerve- racked by the end of it! All the hotel doors were kept locked, and guarded by guys with shotguns... our cab driver wouldn't slow down when we asked him to, for fear of getting ambushed... we had to go through huge blockades to get into our own show...

"All the people we met had really beautiful natures, but there are definitely some shady characters down there. When we went for our shots [he means their inoculations – IG], there was a big disclaimer across the top of all our travel forms saying that Columbia is the most dangerous country in the world to go to if you're an American – in case you get kidnapped there or something. But it was in front of 120,000 people, so it was easily the biggest concert we've ever done... maybe the biggest any hardcore band anywhere has done? It was even bigger than the Ozzfest shows we did, so it was awesome, and certainly an interesting experience..."

To say the least, by the sounds of it. Another noticeable achievement for the band was actually getting the opportunity to address Congress on the topic of straightedge! How the hell did that happen?

"Oh, MTV put a panel together on the subject of teen drug abuse and addiction," says Karl modestly. "It was for a programme called 'Smashed', and we were brought in to represent sXe as a solution. And there were Congressmen there, as well as teachers and parents, and it was an amazing opportunity for us to demonstrate how positive hardcore music can be for the youth. That programme must have aired at least fifteen times since then, so it was well worth appearing."

Lastly, I'll leave Karl to persuade you to check out 'Slither'... it's well worth investigation, despite what you might have heard from the disbelievers!

"I honestly think we've stayed true to the Earth Crisis roots... the lyrical stance is the same, the aggression is still all there... on first listen you might be a bit surprised, but soon you'll realise it's still us, just trying to do something different."

EARTHTONE9 – ISSUE 60 (NOVEMBER 1998)

earthtone9, pic by Tamara

The cover of their debut full-lengther, 'Lo Def(inition) Discord' on Copro Records, may very well be packaged up neatly to look like bubble wrap, but you'll soon see that earthtone9 aren't anywhere near as readily classifiable, their captivating groove built on a solid foundation of powerful riffing, surging rhythms, and super-intense vocal exhortations. So what, you ask? Nothing new, you may think. Until you hear the unique spanner that this Nottingham-based quintet sneak subversively into the machinery of nu metal, intent on corrupting its sterile heart with some real passion, lacing their take on the genre with some truly organic emotion.

earthtone9, live West End Centre, 1998, by Nigel Crane

"Yeah, I like the word 'organic'," agrees Karl, the band's vocalist, explaining down the phone to me just what it is that he thinks sets earthtone9 apart from the rest of the Brit brat pack. "A lot of bands try to be too clever-clever, and it just detracts from their heaviness. I like all that stuff, and I listen to a lot of really savage bands, too, like Kiss It Goodbye and Integrity, but those kind of vocals are hard to take for a full album, so I listen to a lot of singers, too, like Chris Cornell. We try to mix that in, without diluting what we want to do, and I would hope that, on a dynamic level, our lighter shades make our heavier stuff even more of a kick in the face."

Oh, indeed they do. Songs like 'Leadfoot' brutally blend Tool, Helmet and latter-day COC, into a big, nasty rollerball of seductive menace that really gets into your head and dances on all the right synapses. Their sound makes all the right electrical connections up there, but it's still damnably hard to pin down. I've even seen it desperately described as 'Machine Head jamming on Pink Floyd'!

Karl chuckles at this imaginative analogy, "Mmm, I've never really listened to Pink Floyd, but I guess there's some of their sound in there, somewhere, in the way we use processed, delayed guitars, and it all sounds quite soundscapey and interesting. "As long as people liken you to bands they like, then it's a very positive thing, isn't it?" adds the singer. "I mean, Machine Head are quality, they've got class stamped all over them. It's fantastic to be equated to a band like that - they're heavy, and they mean it. I would hope that we sound a little more left-field than they do tho', and not quite so straight-ahead, but, shit, it's still quite a compliment."

And the band can expect more of the same, if all the rave reviews they've been garnering are anything to go by. You, and Copro Records, of course, must be thrilled at the response, right?

"Yeah, we're stoked. I mean, how do you feel when you get to hold your own music in your hands? It's an incredible feeling. And then to have others react so enthusiastically to it, it's just amazing. The ball has started rolling for us, and now it's a case of where we can take it."

Inseparable from the very distinct sound of the '80s thrash scene was its very distinct, apocalyptic imagery. One of the people who helped colour the public perception of thrash was surely Ed Repka, an artist who painted literally dozens of our favourite album covers. Ian Glasper spoke to the man who redefined the wasteland.

"I really didn't listen to any thrash metal until I started painting the covers," admits Ed, when probed as to whether he actually liked the bands whose albums he illustrated. "And then I thought I had better investigate this subject further! After listening to the music and speaking with the various bands, I developed a respect and a taste for it. It was chaotic and powerful, and strongly driven by a message.

"My own introduction to heavy metal came via Kiss, Ozzy and Black Sabbath, and Alice Cooper when I was a little punk in the '70s. These artists appealed to me because their personae were derived from movie monsters and comics. However, I was never really a full-on metalhead. It was later that I became more interested in music. Punk rockers like the Sex Pistols, Ramones, The Cramps and The Misfits were my favourites."

And like any good punk, Ed soon made a name for himself by flying in the face of tradition. As the hottest thrash painter on the block, he tended to specialise in menacing reminders of impending apocalypse, and grim visions of the irradiated aftermath. Years later, his work has truly seared its way onto the retina of the collective underground subconscious, and, of course, the piece of art that everyone remembers him the best for was the 'Peace Sells... But Who's Buying?' album by Megadeth.

"Yeah, that one really put me on the metal map," laughs Ed. "Originally signed to Combat, Megadeth jumped to Capitol to release the album, so the art I created for Combat was suddenly getting major label level exposure. I walked into Tower Records in Manhattan one day and was confronted with a mountain of 'Peace Sells...' covers! That image was everywhere! I also hooked up with Brockum [Megadeth's merchandiser] and created a series of posters and t-shirts, so for a few years there was a lot of product out there with my images on it.

"I look at 'Peace Sells...' today and can still see the energy. Today I could paint it much slicker but not really improve upon the character's body language. I guess that is why Megadeth have used it all these years and have been unable to match it with anyone else. There was - and still is - a bit of magic to that picture."

How much creative input did Ed have with each cover, or was he literally a hired pen?

"All the final imagery on the covers comes from me," claims Ed, "Except where the band had an established mascot design, and even then I would redesign it or enhance it. I was given a lot of latitude to realise a cover concept. Concepts came from me, the band, or a brainstorm session. If I felt the idea was half-baked, I would try to steer them in a better direction. I always worked under the assumption that if I liked it, they would too. I also felt free to change things as I painted to make the painting work better."

As well as 'Peace Sells...', Ed has splashed the red stuff across many other striking covers.

Over the years, everyone from Vio-Lence to Napalm, from The Misfits to Evil Dead called upon his services. Some he recalls with relish, others he deems best forgotten.

"My least favourite cover would have to be 'Piece Of Time' by Atheist," reveals Ed. "It's just a boring hour glass with Stonehenge in it. That's what they wanted. It's like a Spinal Tap cover! I don't even have a printed copy of that one.

"My favourite cover of all is Uncle Slam's 'When God Dies'. Technically it all works, the colour scheme, the large iconic image, the concept, the balance of airbrushing and hand painting. There is no part of the painting that isn't just right. It's just a shame that as I reached a peak of sorts the whole thrash movement was losing steam, and cover assignments suddenly stopped.

"The thrash scene of the '80s was wild," he recalls fondly, in closing. "Indie labels sprouted up overnight and were signing every garage band they could find. The majors were scooping up the best. But as with any subversive element, once it becomes mainstream it loses its edge. Soon bands like Winger were created by the majors to cash in on the success. The true proponents of thrash were like bad-ass prophets of doom who enjoyed shoving their twisted lyrics down the throats of the establishment. But then Pat Boone recorded cover versions of metal classics, including stuff from Metallica and Megadeth. That was the day it all ended."

E-TOWN CONCRETE – ISSUE 79 (JUNE 2000)

E-Town Concrete - by Danielle Dombrowski

New Jersey's hardest, E-Town Concrete, are back, with a brand-new album on Triple Crown, 'The Second Coming', which runs rings around the band's debut from '98. Ian

E–Town Concrete, Brooklyn Bazaar 2019, pics by Carl Gunhouse

Glasper likes a bit of rhyme and rhythm with his metalcore, so he got the job of tracking down frontman Anthony on the mean streets of Elizabeth.

"I know that everybody always says that their new album is heavier than anything else they've ever done, but in this case it's true. And everybody always says how they've matured or whatever, but we really have. A lot of those songs on the first album [1998's 'Time 2 Shine', on Resurrection AD – IG] were written when we were, like, sixteen years old, and now we're all a lot older, and wiser, and better on our instruments... we've all matured in our own way, and it definitely shows."

So says vocalist Anthony, of New Jersey kingpins, E-Town Concrete, on the subject of their latest - and yes, definitely, their best - album, 'The Second Coming', for Triple Crown. It sees the band further developing the metal/hardcore/rap hybrid they helped to spawn five years ago when they first picked up their instruments looking to escape the grim streets of Elizabeth through their music - but more on that later!

"We try not to label ourselves as merely a hardcore band, or just a metal band," growls the frontman in agreement on his band's enthusiastic embracing of musical diversity. "I mean, we're both metal and hardcore, obviously, but we also have a lot of hip hop in there, a lot of different shit going on... we try not to limit ourselves as to what we can and can't do. We'll try anything once! Everyone in the band likes different types of music, from our guitarist at the one end who likes Pink Floyd and Fish, to myself at the other, listening to everything from rap to Tori Amos!"

And it shows, believe me. E-Town are not blinkered in their approach to writing music... from the sledgehammer opener, 'Soldier', to the mellow strains of 'Dirty Jer-Z', they are unafraid of melody and introspection as a counterpoint to their weightier, more aggressive moments. It's an imposing display of musical virtuosity, both colourful and highly listenable, and one that transcends all the bullshit cliques that riddle the hardcore scene.

"People can tell we're real," reckons Anthony. "We come from the heart, especially lyrically; I always tell it just like it is. I tell stories that people can relate to, about things I've seen, things I've done, or had done to me, and so many people can really relate to stuff like that."

And those lyrics are pretty gritty, folks, not to mention more than a bit defiant. You don't have to be a brain surgeon to work that out; their last MCD was entitled 'Fuck The World'! "We do have some songs that are very positive, about where we want to go with this band, how we want to take the world by storm... but I also talk about things that happened to me growing up, in a single parent family... growing up without a father. I even talk about child abuse and stuff like that. I don't just write about the city; I'm writing about life in general. People everywhere can relate to this shit - plus when they see us live, it all makes sense. We put everything we have into our live show, and no one can deny our commitment."

Isn't opening yourself up in such a way a painful thing to do, especially when you have to sing the same words over and over again every night on tour? And doesn't it leave you feeling vulnerable, albeit cleansed?

"Oh, it does," admits the singer, "Especially when people come up and ask you about all this stuff you've written. Sometimes it's people who know you, too, who were there when some of the things you're writing about were actually happening, so they know exactly what you're talking about. It's almost embarrassing, in a way; I write this stuff for myself, but then when it comes out, it leaves you wide open..."

Would you say that you have to be in this band, rather than you merely want to be?

"Well, that's kinda true. I have no idea what I would do if I wasn't in E-Town. It's my main release; it helps me deal with so many things. Basically, it's the only thing I really love in life – every morning when I wake up, the first thing I think about is this band. That's why we wanna make this work, we want to blow up and achieve success... 'cos we really care about this.

"People always talk about selling out, but all we're trying to do is make this our life, make enough money off it so we don't have to do 'real' work, and we can focus on making our music. Once you get to a certain age, and you have a family and bills to pay, you realise that you have to make a certain amount of money just to survive. It's easy for people who didn't grow up in an environment like ours to say that that's selling out, but they're just naive, and don't see what really goes on in the world."

EUROCORE (REVEAL/PUNISHABLE ACT/KICKBACK) – ISSUE 50 (JANUARY 1998)

Eurocore – Kickback's Steffen Bassac and Edward Verhaeghe-Good Life Records, Dour 1999, by Pascale Stolym

Forget ERMs, EMUs and EECs, the real European community already exists, in the continent-wide hardcore scene that's done so much to inspire some of the action over here in Britain. Just ask Ian Glasper, a man who knows what's what on both sides of the

Channel, who here takes you through three of Europe's newest and brightest hardcore prospects, Kickback, Reveal and Punishable Act... no borders here!

Ah, Europe. For long the envy of the UK scene. For so many years, we watched across the grey Channel, all those legendary US bands touring, the sheer size of some of the shows, the wealth of zines and labels and venues, how damn organised it all was, while we skulked in the shadows and apologised for our excesses. But we learnt as we watched, like lab rats, the bars of our cages the tight confines of this cursed island, we learnt and grew stronger. And now we're building a scene that will make the old Roman Empire look like a game of Scrabble.

We've talked all about the UK scene, how it's gone from strength to strength recently, but let's not forget what's happening in Europe, in the scene that, let's face it, inspired us to get our shit together over here. New bands emerge blinking into the glare of the spotlight every week, all deserving of your attentions, and one such band is Reveal, outta Holland, newest signings to the rising star that is Good Life Records.

"No, we're not too happy with the sound quality, the money ran out," explains their bassist, Dave, when I put it to him that the only thing that lets down their 'Dissection of Thought' MCD is the dodgy production. "We just didn't have the time we needed. Our singer was sick when we recorded, and several times we tried to lay down vocals, but he had this virus in his throat, and it didn't work out, but we still got charged for those wasted sessions. And in the studio, it sounded great, but, of course, when we got it home, it didn't sound anywhere near as good."

Ah, that's a common mistake for new bands - you should always take a Walkman in with you, for playback, 'cos those huge studio speakers would make a wet fart sound amazing. Was that your inexperience showing itself?

"Yeah, we'd only been together a year when we recorded, and we didn't know quite how we wanted to sound. Since then, we've done a lot more shows, and now we've started to create our own sound, so when we record again, it'll be a big improvement. That said, for a first CD, we're still very pleased with it."

And so they should be. Minor gripes aside, 'Dissection...' is a lurching Slayer-esque take on the HC thang, almost sounding more Belgian than Dutch. Intensely guttural vocals and razor-edged rifferama are the order of the day, something that Dave is only too happy to talk about.

"Me and the singer were in another band together, a hardcore band, which broke up, and we hooked up with Micha [guitars - IG], and he's from a total metal background. He likes Metallica, and Slayer, and all the classic metal bands; we explained our ideas to him, lent him a lot of CDs we liked, and Reveal is a mixture of the two styles. We never thought we'd get as far as releasing a record, it was just for fun. We wanted to express ourselves and play our music, which is where the name came from."

Berlin's Punishable Act have a very definite metal edge to their sound too, but rather than the detuned evil thing, these five Berliners go for the groovier power trip. Their

Eurocore – Reveal, photo by Jean-Paul Fryns, scanned by Maxime Opsomer

'Where It Came From' MCD on Mad Mob contains four slabs of crunchin' crossover, not dissimilar to early Biohazard meeting the Cro-Mags up a darkened alleyway, and opener 'The Music Has To Manage (To Unite Us Again)' is a real anthemic rallying cry for tolerance in the scene.

"The band has been around long enough to see a lot of changes in the scene." explains vocalist, Mike, down the phone from their promoters MAD's German office, my good friend, David Strempfel translating for him. "There's too many splinter groups - vegan, sXe, people with red shoelaces, whatever. It was different at the beginning – you weren't classified by whether you drank or not. What you ate wasn't important. The roots of the scene should lie in unity and friendship, regardless."

I know that Berlin once had a very tight scene, three or four years back. How is it now? "That's a good question! In '94, the Berlin scene was just coming to life again after a few quiet years, so all the bands were helping each other out, and giving each other a hand. Now the scene's way bigger, and there's a lot more bands, and the bands don't watch out for each other so much. But there's a band called Plain, whose drummer used to be in PA, and we try to help them out whenever we can, and vice versa, so there is still unity between smaller groups of bands."

Like a lot of Berlin bands, do PA often get accused of trying to be tough guys, just 'cos of your tatts 'n' stuff? "Yeah," sighs Mike, "And I don't really know why. It might be 'cos of the tattoos, or something, but from my point of view, the tattoos are not macho at all. Just part of my life, part of my beliefs against society, but I wear them on the outside rather than the inside. Anyway, if anyone actually reads our lyrics, they'll know that we don't have anything in common with those tough guy bands. We don't have lyrics that go like, 'You were my friend, but you Iet me down, you stabbed me in the back, now it's time to pay', and virtually every other sXe band, or youth crew band, has at least one song like that!"

The last band we meet on this brief sojourn through Europe, Kickback, are probably the most successful (so far!) of the threesome, having just released their second full-lengther, 'Forever War', on Century Media, and only the night before our interview played with Machine Head!

"It was really good," says vocalist Stefan, on the previous night's performance. "We went on after Entombed, right before Machine Head. and we got a great response. It was a great show, there were a lot of different people there... hardcore kids to see us, metal kids to see the other bands. We try to do all sorts of shows, to get to as many people as possible. This new album will really open us up to the metal audience, I think."

Last time I saw Kickback, one of our intrepid Terrorizer photographers, Dave Thomas, had his head cut open. The time before, a girl got kicked in the head by a karate dancer. Kickback have the reputation for some of the most violent shows in hardcore – is that something you encourage or what?

"Well, it's violent music, and always has been, so violence is part of the scene," comes the unapologetic response. "When you're onstage, sweating, you wanna see the pit go crazy. As far as people getting hurt, I don't like to see it, but that's the way it goes. It's like sports, you know? If you go ballroom dancing, you won't get hurt, but if you like hockey or wrestling, chances are you will. It goes with the territory - but people don't have to go in the pit."

Talk turns briefly to the new album, and I can confirm that it's ten times the record their previous CD, 'Cornered', was. It's more of the same hard-as-nails crossover, but executed with much more flair and focus.

"The last two years have seen a lot of changes in the band," confirms Stefan. "A lot happened, we have a totally different line-up, new drummer, new guitar player... the album is still the same music, it's still a mix of hardcore and metal, but we really worked on the material this time, whereas the last album was just all the old songs. We didn't pour as much of ourselves into it as we did this time."

And what about that super-aggressive title? "It's just about us, about our attitude to life. You can take it several different ways, but it's about how people will put you down, in many different ways, be it through religion, or any other form of oppression. Your life is a war, from the day you are born, to be yourself. We live in a world that is fucked up, people will fuck with you every day. You've got to be strong, you've got to adapt, if you want to survive."

There you have it then - three exciting new bands to go and check out, as soon as possible, and no real reason not to. In the intro, I talked about nationalities, and I talked about empire building. All bullshit, in hindsight. Europe is only a short ferry trip away, as many of us have discovered, and their scene is our scene, and vice versa. Look how cosmopolitan some of the London shows are becoming! Remember how cool it was to meet a French guy at an English gig? Well, go to Paris, and thrill a French person there that there's a Brit in the crowd! To paraphrase the ever-popular Slayer, hardcore knows no boundaries. So, take advantage of that duty free while you still can...

Excel - issue 278 (January 2017)

When most people think of metallic hardcore from Venice Beach, California, they tend to think of Suicidal Tendencies, or one of their many off-shoot bands like No Mercy, and they're all great bands, make no mistake, but the undisputed kings of Venice Beach crossover were Excel. Mixing street cool with youthful energy, and old school American hardcore with frantic speed metal, into a supremely tight whole, Excel knocked the scene sideways with their 'Split Image' debut, released on Suicidal Records in 1987. And the 1989 follow-up, 'The Joke's On You' (this time on Caroline), was even slicker, a superb fusion of punk and thrash that saw the band's reputation spreading around the world. Those kind folk at Southern Lord reissued 'Split Image' in 2014, and now it's the turn of 'The Joke's On You' to have a welcome reissue, and to wow a whole new generation of crossover fans with its incendiary grooves - but why now, and why Southern Lord?

"We haven't reissued 'Split Image' or 'The Joke's On You' on vinyl since they were originally released in the Eighties, and they've not been available since," explains bassist

Excel – by Albert Licano

Shaun Ross. "Greg Anderson [from Southern Lord] approached us, because he's been into the band since the Eighties. And at the same time, we'd seen how good the Bl'ast reissues he did turned out, so we thought it was a perfect fit.

"We re-mastered it from the original master tapes, and it sounds far superior and modernized compared to the original version. Brad Boatwright at Audiosiege did a great job, and we really do feel that it now sounds much more massive than the original, especially on vinyl. We've also added new gatefold art by our friend Farron Loathing..."

Almost thirty years after it was recorded, 'The Joke's On You' still sounds as fresh as the day it was recorded, positively throbbing with an intensity that's rarely been equaled in the years since. A lot of albums from that period have definitely lost their potency over the years, but not 'The Joke's On You'; it holds its own against today's new breed with seemingly effortless ease. What is the secret of its longevity?

"We've always tried to challenge ourselves and not write your stereotypical verse/chorus/verse songs," reckons Shaun. "We came from the punk scene, where that was the usual formula, and we tried to avoid that. The end result was a unique LP, and 'The Joke's On You' will always have its place in someone's collection.

"Looking back, we feel that the album properly represents that era in Los Angeles, and the diversity of the scene at the time. Los Angeles never really had a big hardcore scene like, say, New York did. There were a handful of bands like Final Conflict, Cryptic Slaughter, or Chain of Strength, which all came from different sub-genres of the scene. Excel was able to bridge the gap between those divisions, and I think you can hear that musically with 'The Joke's On You'..."

Excel, by Albert Licano

There are many stories about the LA scene of the Eighties, and how crazily dangerous it was, and from an outsider's perspective it appeared to be riddled with violence and gang-related crime. However, Shaun remembers it in a much more positive light:

"That was a great time to be in Los Angeles! Individually, we grew up all over town and we always considered ourselves 'All City'. There was a lot of rapid change in the scene from the early to late Eighties. And yes, they were crazy times, taking into consideration everything else that was going on in the city, like the explosion of gang activity, but we were in our late teens and it seemed a pretty rad time.

"By then, we were playing most of the bigger venues here, and supporting the national touring acts of the time. We had our graffiti crew, we were writing this album, and just skating and hanging out as well. 'The Joke's On You' represents our youth, friendships and far more care-free times...

"My favorite songs would be those that are the most fun to play live, like 'Affection Blends With Resentment', 'My Thoughts' and 'Never Denied'. My least favorite would be 'The Stranger'; it was an unfinished song that was pieced together in the studio at the last minute. It could have been way better, but looking back, I don't think that we'd change anything though. It was a special time, and those songs capture the spirit of that era."

The album benefits hugely from a crisp, crunchy and instantly accessible production courtesy of Randy Burns at Hollywood's Music Grinder Studios. Burns was hot property at the time, and the band definitely fell on their feet when they secured him to oversee the production; he allowed them to be themselves, yet focused their many eclectic influences into something cohesive and timeless.

Excel, circa 'Split Image', courtesy of Shaun Ross

Excel, outside Oki-Dog, courtesy of Shaun Ross

Excel, pic by Albert Licano

"It was great working with Randy," enthuses Shaun. "We couldn't believe that the same guy who produced 'Scream Bloody Gore' and 'Seven Churches' was working with us!

"Musically we'd always been influenced by early Exodus, Sabbath, Trouble, Discharge, Crucifix and English Dogs etc. But we were also listening to Robin Trower, King Crimson, early Grand Funk and other Seventies rock stuff around this time too. And lyrically [vocalist] Dan [Clements] was always motivated by what we'd refer to as 'personal politics'…

"Doing 'Message In A Bottle' was a spontaneous idea we had in the studio," he adds, of their surprise choice to cover The Police chestnut – to great effect, it should be added. "I think [guitarist] Adam [Siegel] just started playing the main riff and it sounded cool. We thought that the idea of us covering that type of song was out of context, yet it ended up fitting perfectly on the LP."

Unfortunately following the success of 'The Joke's On You', Excel strayed from the path with their third LP, 'Seeking Refuge', that saw Shaun and Dan recruit a new line-up (after Adam and drummer Greg Saenz left) and pursue a more commercial, 'grunge' direction. Needless to say, it lacked the explosive creativity of their first two LPs, but thankfully three-quarters of this early line-up are back together, playing these classic songs (with new material in the offing too!), and actually sounding better than ever. Catch them live, if you get chance, because they are wince-inducingly tight, and if you slept on it first time around, miss this reissue of a slice of LA punk history at your peril.

Exodus, by Claire Harris, Nuclear Blast

While the so-called 'Big Four' of '80s thrash – Metallica, Megadeth, Anthrax and Slayer – trundled on indifferently into the '90s and beyond, hard times, even harder drugs and the death of their original vocalist, Paul Baloff almost finished Exodus for good. Forever on the fringes of the genre they helped create, the Bay Area legends have finally overcome the problems which held them back for so long and have in the process created 'Tempo Of The Damned', soon to become one of the ultimate metal albums of 2004. Confirmed thrash fanatic and self-confessed 'old timer' Ian Glasper hooked up with guitarist Gary Holt and drummer Tom Hunting as they plotted the return of the riff.

IMPACT IS IMMINENT

This is it, this is the big one. The one we've all been waiting for. For several years now, thrash metal's old-timers have been banging on about a supposed revival that's proving as elusive as Osama Bin Laden, Saddam Hussein and Lord Lucan put together. Sure, storming new albums from bands such as Kreator, Arch Enemy and even Machine Head coupled with sterling live shows from Death Angel and Testament have helped keep the speculation simmering, but come February 2004 it's game over, to coin a phrase. It's been over a decade since their last studio effort, but veteran Bay Area thrashers Exodus (who always could whoop the asses off the 'Big Four' anyway) are about to drop a bona fide bombshell on the unsuspecting world in the shape of the long-overdue 'Tempo Of The Damned'. One listen to this riff-tastic monster will have nu-metallers ditching their pooped in-look baggy jeans and furiously trawling Oxfam stores the land over for leg wear of the skin-tight and none-more-black variety.

It all kicks off, as any truly great thrash record should, with a monstrous, spine-tingling riff that will singe your eyebrows off, before an hour's worth of savage Bay Area battery takes control of your neck, leaving you beaten and bruised but very, very satisfied. Everything that they tell you won't work in modern metal – excessive arrangements, excessive chugging, excessive solos (less has never been more for these guys) – is defiantly present and incorrect, and taking great pleasure in urinating on whining trend-setters from a considerable height.

"We never sat down and planned this," claims livewire guitarist Gary Holt, the man responsible for not only all the music on the new album but also most of the lyrics. "For better or worse, I've never ever written songs with preconceived ideas about what I thought would sell; that would make us no better than fucking Britney Spears or Mariah Carey. Their producers tell them what to write based on what they think will sell to their crowd. I've never written for anyone other than myself. I have to be able to look across to Rick [Hunolt, the band's other guitarist] and think, 'Yes, this is fucking killer!' And then we start high-fiving and getting all excited about it – it has to get us excited."

Summing up the process, he booms, "I just had to find myself really – Gary Holt, bad motherfucker! I just had to realise again that I'm pretty fucking damn good at this. I never have to worry about what other people are doing; I just do it and let them follow."

"I've always looked at us as not really affected by trends," agrees the less-animated but equally enthusiastic drummer Tom Hunting. "We have our influences, for sure, but well, we wouldn't sound good as a grunge band [laughs]! We are who we are, and there's not much else to say about it."

And, as if to prove the point, sitting more than comfortably amongst the brand new material is 'Impaler', a twenty-year-old demo track that has thus far had but one official airing on 1997's live offering, 'Another Lesson In Violence', but which still shreds harder in a few minutes than most MTV-metal bands could hope to in a lifetime.

"We just wanted to get a good studio recording of that song once and for all," Tom explains, "And then maybe everyone will shut up about us playing it, haha! It's undergone an evolution too; you'll notice on the live record that there's some indecipherable lyrics from Paul [Baloff, original vocalist], so we had to go in and figure out what the fuck he was saying! Zetro [Souza, current vocalist] did a good job with it though; I thought he gave Paul props in the way he sang it. You can hear those little Baloff influences coming out here and there...

"The overall album has that 'classic' thrash vibe," he says, wrapping up the thread, "Because there isn't ten thousand guitar tracks, and it isn't all spit and polish, it isn't over-produced. Everything's loud, everything's right, and to have Jack [Gibson, bass, who debuted on the aforementioned live album] play with us in the studio - well, he's fucking amazing. We sound like a full band finally."

FABULOUS DISASTER

So, things are looking peachy for Exodus again, and not before time. Less than two years ago, however, it was a very different story, with the majority of the band more interested in scoring copious amounts of hard drugs than writing music. Which makes the achievement that is 'Tempos...' all the more staggering.

"It's been a long hard road, y'know?" concedes Gary, "We've been through a lot of bullshit. Eighteen months ago, we weren't capable of ever doing this album. Myself, Tom and Rick were still fucked up on drugs, amphetamines, and it controlled our lives. I went through a divorce, through Paul's death... Paul's death should have woken me up! He died of a stroke, but his alcoholism and his fuckin' drug use definitely contributed to it. We weren't snorting; we were fucking smoking, massive amounts. It was hard to concentrate on anything but getting off. It rules your life."

However belatedly, Baloff's premature passing did eventually serve as a severe wake-up call to rest of the band. As the primary songwriter, Gary's rehabilitation was crucial for the band's future.

"This album would've never gotten made if I hadn't cleaned up last September," he sighs, with a palpable air of relief. "I did it for many reasons – my health, I wanted to be a better father to my children, I didn't wanna die like Paul did, or like another very close friend of mine and Rick's who died a year after him. Also, all my girlfriend wanted for Christmas was for me to stop doing dope, and she's so special to me, it was the only thing I was able to give her that really mattered. She's the best thing that ever happened to me. And I've been clean and healthy ever since."

With the Class 'A' kicked and a new found sense of purpose, Gary found his feet at a pace which amazed many, and none more than himself.

"I just started writing!" he beams, still surprised at the simplicity of it all. "I mean, I thought I'd had some kind of writer's block until then, but it wasn't - it was a dope block! The fucking drugs didn't leave me enough energy to put any effort into writing. The funny thing is, I quit doing speed and the songs got faster [laughs]!"

Fans who still mourn Paul Baloff's untimely death must wonder with mixed feelings about the re-energised Exodus and the part he might have played in it had he survived. Gary, however, is grimly clear about one important fact – Paul had to die so that Exodus could live. Harsh? Maybe. True? Almost certainly.

"We'd have never have got it done," he intones sadly. "We'd still be talking about it, like all speed freaks, never really making it happen. Our rehearsals used to be our shows – that was when we rehearsed, when we played a fucking gig. We didn't rehearse before, we didn't even use to soundcheck, we'd roll in with all our gear two hours after the doors opened! We were just treading water; we weren't going anywhere.

"And it's sad to say, 'cos I miss Paul dearly - I'd throw this album in the garbage can to have him back - but the album would've never gotten done if he was still alive, you know?"

"Paul is always going to be the quiet sixth member of the band," says Tom earnestly. His observation offers a unifying and positive vision for their future. "I feel like he's with us every day, he walks the same path we do, and I think he would very much approve of this. I have so many memories of the guy, of so many classic times in my life, that I can never really 'miss him' as such, but yes, his death did eventually snap us into shape."

Sex and drugs and booze have walked hand in hand with rock 'n' roll – and metal –

since the beginning. Although fair-weather friends, they've nonetheless made for a million unforgettable good times. At the bottom of the bottle, however, there must be the music, and with their chemical crutches cast away for good, the Exodus boys have happily rediscovered the reason for doing what they do in the first place.

"The music still does it for me," smiles Gary. "It didn't a year ago. A year ago, I barely played guitar; I just showed up for gigs. I had too many extra-curricular activities, namely scoring and ingesting more speed or fuckin' crank or whatever. But now I've fallen back in love with my guitar, it's my new best friend all over again. I picked it up and these new songs are what happened.

"Time has never really been a factor 'cos I'm still a big kid at heart, I still laugh at farts. I'll know when I'm getting old when I don't find flatulence funny, haha! But I'm not 25 anymore. I have to take care of myself, else I won't be able to do this much longer. Once upon a time, I'd come off stage and I'd be searching for drugs, alcohol and pussy... now I want a sandwich and a glass of chocolate milk! Just an after-show meal, maybe a glass of red wine, and a fucking good mood. But I was like a giant child; I took a lot of things for granted. I've matured a lot these last few years."

BONDED BY BLOOD

And so have Exodus the band. Compared to the meandering complacency of 1992's 'Force Of Habit', their previous studio effort, 'Tempo Of The Damned' sees them firing on all cylinders again, peeling off volley after volley of vicious, lightning-quick riffs. Gary and Rick are still the best guitar duo in the history of thrash, and the whole band are locked so tightly together, it hurts.

"We're all family, y'know?" says Gary. "Right before I cleaned up off the drugs, Zetro actually left, and I fully understood why. He has three children and a wife and a really good job, and he didn't wanna throw all his apples in my cart when I was such a fucking mess. In his position, I wouldn't have either. But I got clean, and we talked, and he saw that this wasn't just a two-week experiment for me, this was my new lifestyle, drug-free, and here we are. We work together better now, because he doesn't have to deal with my cranky bad moods when I can't get any dope and all the other bullshit that goes with it."

One thus-far-unmentioned ingredient went into the revitalised Exodus formula, ensuring success. Rising star of studio wizardry Andy Sneap – a man with a sterling thrash pedigree in his own right – was drafted in to make sure that the patent Exodus crunch was captured just as its creators intended.

"Andy was just the man we needed to pull the performances out of all of us," claims Tom, revealing that the Exodus inner circle extends beyond just the band. "He came out of nowhere when we did the live record. We knew he had played with Sabbat back in the day, we played the Dynamo festival with him, but we didn't know the guy; he just came out of nowhere and said, 'I was born to mix this record'! We were like, 'Oh yeah?' He came onboard and blew us all away."

"Andy is family, I'll never work with anybody else again," asserts Gary, "And that's something we've really got now, with our road crew and management, we've got a real sense of family, people we enjoy being around.

"In the '80s, egos came into play and things like that. It became really big business, and it still is in many ways, but I'm just happy to be here doing this. I just wanna play music and pay my bills, man; I have no delusions of owning a castle on a Bavarian mountaintop.

"You know what?" he exclaims suddenly, recalling a recent event, "We just played a show in Porto, Portugal, and it was the most beautiful town I think I've ever seen. I mean, I've seen beautiful towns but never from the fucking window of the club! This club was looking out over this river port city and I just stood there and soaked it up; I didn't wanna leave, I just wanted to sit there and look at it. In the past, I wouldn't have appreciated that! I would've been like, 'Where's the catering? Where's the booze? How many chicks are outside?' I wouldn't have even bothered to look, but now I know that I'm lucky to be here, and the things I took for granted are truly important to me."

Which brings us back to the music. If the forgettable 'Force Of Habit' was the sound of a band taking themselves and their career for granted, 'Tempo Of The Damned' sees them rediscovering and embracing the spirit which made their early output such a paradigm of channelled aggression and cathartic anger.

"I just got on this writing roll that no one could or would get in the way of," explains Gary. "It was my therapy, I found myself again. In the past I've had the odd identity crisis, I wasn't sure who I was anymore; I was trying to be something I wasn't.

"I've not been this happy in years, yet the lyrics have never been so angry. I'm clean, off the speed, yet the album is so fast. There's a lot of energy. This record was very liberating. I'm very proud of it, not just 'cos of the music, but because of the road we walked to make it. There were pitfalls on either side, and I feel privileged to have come out of that lifestyle alive. I'm proud we made it even happen in the first place."

"It means different things to all of us," adds Tom in closing, on the subject of the album title. "For me personally, we were all living our lives at a very dangerous pace, literally the tempo of the damned. I really thought kicking the drugs would make us slower, but I was wrong. We're a machine right now," he concludes, "And we're ready to crush, believe me."

Sidebar # 1: DESK JOB: ANDY SNEAP ON EXODUS

What was the vibe in the studio during recording?
"It was pretty relaxed really, but that's due to us all knowing each other. It got tiring towards the end as we were sleeping in the studio, on the floor, which I was prepared to do, because there was no money upfront for this album. Gary accused me of being gay when I got a hotel room for a couple of days, but all he did when not tracking was root himself on the sofa 24/7, watching hardcore porn and eating hot-dogs. This album was done on favours by everyone involved, because we all believe in the band. I probably wouldn't be doing this in the first place if it hadn't been for Exodus. Having said all that, I have no problem telling them when something is crap."

Tell us a little bit about the recording process - where the hell did you get that guitar sound?

"We did a few days pre-production in San Francisco, just getting used to the songs, demoing them a bit better, so we could get tempos and any little arrangement ideas sorted. They were pretty well-prepared to be honest. We then went about an hour north of the city to Prairie Sun Studios, where they tracked 'Bonded By Blood', to track the drums for a week. After that, we moved south of the city to Half Moon Bay, to a smaller studio run by some friends of Rick. I then brought it back to the UK and mixed it for a couple of weeks, although I've gone back and tweaked a couple of bits since. With the guitars I've tried to keep that classic thrash feel by doing just one track either side with Gary's modified JCM 800, which is the best sounding Marshall I've ever heard."

Are you at all concerned that you might paint yourself into a corner with the style of metal you're predominantly producing these days?

"I'm always aware of the typecast thing but I've got enough things going on. Some labels see me as a mixer, others realise I'm actually a producer; I've got a good reputation the world over now, so I have quite a wide range of projects getting offered to me. Y'know, I don't want to do emo and I don't want to do out-and-out black metal either, mainly because I don't understand it. You have to believe in what you are working on; it has to be from the heart to be good. Basically, if it's good rock/metal then I'm interested."

Sidebar # 2: RIFF BY RIFF: AN EXODUS DISCOGRAPHY

'BONDED BY BLOOD'
Music For Nations, 1985
Recorded in 1984 and originally to be entitled 'A Lesson In Violence', this is the incredible debut that helped define the classic sound of Bay Area thrash metal as we know it today. What Exodus lacked in finesse compared to the likes of Metallica and Megadeth, they more than compensated for with sheer nastiness. Every song was perfect, and the album was a runaway train of brutal riffs, that stands up to repeated listens twenty years after it was originally unleashed. A truly essential landmark in the annals of metaldom, this should hold pride of place in every metalhead's collection. [10]

'PLEASURES OF THE FLESH'
Music For Nations, 1987
After the success of 'Bonded...', it came as a huge surprise to fans everywhere when maniac frontman Paul Baloff left Exodus to front his own short-lived act, Piranha. The band wasted little time drafting in Steve 'Zetro' Souza, formerly of The Legacy (who, of course, went on to become Testament), a formidable replacement with barbed wire tonsils of his own. Whilst not as jaw-dropping as its predecessor, and despite its embarrassing 'Carry On Up The Jungle' cover, 'Pleasures...' was still a fantastic album, brimming with memorable moshers such as 'Braindead', with the innovative highlight being the menacing 'Chemi-Kill'. [8]

'FABULOUS DISASTER'
Music For Nations, 1988

Another crap cover, but another killer album. 'The Last Act Of Defiance' was possibly the finest opener of any Exodus album, a fast and furious assault on the senses, tighter than any band had a right to be and loaded with shredding solos. The title track followed and was another rifftastic workout, as was 'Toxic Waltz', a crushing mid-tempo chugger (shame about the overbaked backing vocals). But then the album took a turn for the worse, with one too many fillers rearing their lazy heads. Still, it was carried perfectly adequately by its strong tracks, and the CD came with a bonus AC/DC cover, 'Overdose'. [7.5]

'IMPACT IS IMMINENT'
Capitol, 1990

The first thing that hit you about Exodus' fourth album was the guitar sound; it was like a cheese grater dragged across your forehead. It really was so relentlessly in-your-face, it almost detracted from the songs themselves, which was a shame, 'cos there were some good 'uns on here, although nothing to match the best shit from the unholy trilogy that preceded it. Not only was this the band's major label debut, it was also the first studio effort to feature the very able John Tempesta on drums (Tom Hunting having left midway through a US tour only to later turn up again in IR8 with Jason Newsted). [7]

'GOOD FRIENDLY VIOLENT FUN' (LIVE)
Relativity, 1991

A lame live album that had 'cash-in' written all over it. It started promisingly enough, a decent recording with the band hammering into 'Fabulous Disaster' and 'Chemi-Kill' as if their lives depend upon it. Then the set list took a turn for the worse, seemingly doing its utmost to include all the band's throwaway material. And come on, an eight-song live album? Give us break. This sucked, and paled in comparison to the 1997 'Another Lesson In Violence' live opus. Did I mention the crap cover as well? Now there's a surprise. [4]

'LESSONS IN VIOLENCE' ('THE BEST OF')
Relativity, 1991

A rather pointless collection of 'highlights' from the first three albums. They may as well have just reissued 'Bonded By Blood' again. One can only assume that this was another contractual obligation, and no doubt it helped win over a few younger fans to the Exodus style. Hopefully they went out and bought the earlier records as a result and checked out what there really was on offer. Of course, it rocked – it was Exodus after all – but what kind of fucking idiot would include a live version of 'Dirty Deeds Done Dirt Cheap' over 'Deliver Us To Evil', 'Parasite' and 'Last Act Of Defiance'? [4.5]

'FORCE OF HABIT'
Capitol, 1992

This was the record that both introduced fans to new bassist Mike Butler and spelled the end for the first incarnation of the band. By 1992, Exodus had seriously rocked out. The fast songs – once the primary thrust of any album – were now seriously in the minority, and when they did thrash it up, as on 'Feeding Time At The Zoo', it sounded forced. They even tried their hands at ill-advised covers of The Rolling Stones ('Bitch') and Elvis Costello ('Pump It Up') – ouch. The undoubted highlight remains 'Architect Of Pain', an ambitious and atmospheric, eleven-minute epic about the Marquis De Sade. [5]

'ANOTHER LESSON IN VIOLENCE' (LIVE)
Century Media, 1997
This was more like it, a return of the Exodus we know and love. 80% of the original 'Bonded' line-up were back together and firing on all cylinders (only bassist Rob McKillop being replaced by Jack Gibson, who had previously been spotted in Wardance with Gary Holt and Tom Hunting). Recorded in front of a sell-out home crowd of thrashing maniacs, impeccably mixed by Andy Sneap and featuring, not only a set list to die for, but some truly hilarious stage raps from the now sadly-departed Baloff (RIP), this is probably the best live thrash album out there. [8.5]

'TEMPO OF THE DAMNED'
Nuclear Blast, 2004
Taking all the best bits of the first three albums, and conveniently ignoring the crap that padded out the third, this is Exodus's glorious return to form. Reuniting the band with Zetro once again and stomping all over the faddy metal that has polluted our radios for several years, this is an unashamedly retro trip to thrash heaven given a thoroughly modern face lift without anaesthetic. And wait 'til you get a load of some of these fuckin' riffs. Thrash-head revisited, and not before time. Let the shakeup commence. [9]

Exodus – issue 196 (May 2010)

There's only one thing Ian Glasper likes better than hardcore punk, and that's hardcore Bay Area thrash metal! So when the grandaddies of that scene, Exodus, finally decided to drop their new studio album, he got the call to dust off his Hi-Tops and man up for some 'good friendly violent fun'.

Bay Area thrash legends Exodus return to the fray this May with their tenth studio album, 'Exhibit B: The Human Condition', a belated follow-up to 2007's 'The Atrocity Exhibition: Exhibit A' that shows no sign of the band easing off the gas. In fact, it cranks the clock right back to the manic vibe of the band's incendiary third album, 'Fabulous Disaster', but incorporates an occasional subtle vocal melody or guitar harmony, just to remind us that these guys aren't stuck in some well-trodden Eighties rut... which is just as well, seeing as their last studio album was a (rather killer) song-by-song re-recording of their classic 1985 'Bonded By Blood' debut.

Exodus, by Claire Harris, Nuclear Blast

"A lot of people loved it, and a lot of people hated it!" laughs guitarist Gary Holt, acknowledging the risk taken re-recording such a devoutly-worshipped piece of thrash history. "Most of the people that didn't like it had a problem with the whole idea of doing it in the first place more than the actual record. I did one interview with a guy, who's actually a good friend of mine, and I pulled a fast one on him and turned the interview around and started interviewing him... I basically got him to admit that he just loves 'Bonded By Blood' too much, haha! He was like, 'Oh, I thought the vocals were too one-dimensional...' And I was like, 'But if Rob had thrown in two or three extra dimensions, what would you have said?' And he wouldn't have liked that either, because we'd have been, 'Playing with the original too much!' How many dimensions did Paul [Baloff, the band's original vocalist] actually have? One fucking awesome dimension! "We didn't set out to change the world with the damn thing," he sighs. "We released it independently, we didn't even go through Nuclear Blast, y'know? It was something we just did, and I don't regret doing it whatsoever, and 'Bonded By Blood' is still a classic and we haven't taken away from that in any way. We just wanted to expose a few newer people to the original, and as far as old bands re-recording their vintage material goes, we did it far better than any of those other bands. We left it quite raw on purpose; we actually recorded it in less time than 'Bonded By Blood' itself! Someone asked, 'How much time did you spend rehearsing to re-record it?' And I said, 'None! If I can't play 'Piranha' in my sleep, I shouldn't be doing this any more!' If Tom [Hunting, drummer and other founding member] and I had to rehearse before going in to track those old songs, we have some real issues..."

LONG IN THE TOOTH

Thankfully there's no issues with 'Exhibit B' either; it's super aggressive, loaded with crunch and attitude... all the classic Exodus ingredients, in fact. The title obviously implies that it's a companion piece to 'Exhibit A', and when that came out in 2007, we were promised the next installment the following year – and here we are, three years later... so, what happened?

"At first, when we decided to do it, 'Exhibit B' was just going to be an EP," explains Gary. "The whole idea of doing it as two separate things came about because we had an album-and-a-half of really solid, killer material. All the songs were so long on the last album, we couldn't physically fit everything we recorded onto one disc, so we decided to go for the two releases, and then we did a lot of touring, had a lot of commitments... we had originally planned to write two more songs to go with what we had, but we ended up writing nine songs or something, including the various bonus tracks we did – and time just flew by and we were too busy to do it sooner, y'know?"

You worked with Andy Sneap again, and it seems you've finally found the right producer that understands where you guys are coming from...

"Oh, sure, sure... there's a lot of really capable producers out there, but first and foremost, Andy's one of my best friends, so when we're working together, it's kinda like sitting there with a band member, brain-storming and stuff, rather than sitting with some producer that you can't help but think of as being an 'outsider'. And sometimes, in those circumstances, you find yourselves not wanting to absorb ideas because they're not coming from the band. But Andy really knows this band; he's been an Exodus fan for years... we played together when he was in Sabbat... in fact, we still play with Sabbat even now! He knows where we're going with each album; he listens to the songs and we don't have to discuss shit, he understands musically what's happening and everything gets tracked accordingly. He's one of the best engineers I've ever worked with - his mixes are just phenomenal - but more importantly he gets the best out of us and helps us capture the best Exodus record we can make at the time."

DOING THE TOXIC WALTZ

Given the band's formidable reputation, does Gary ever feel under any pressure to deliver on the riff front? Does he lose any sleep trying to churn these licks out, or do they still just fall out of him?

"They still fall out of me, but I do put a lot of pressure on myself," he admits, "Because I'm kinda like a walking contradiction: supremely confident and supremely neurotic at the same time. But that also fuels me and drives me, so when Andy shows up, the riffs are all there, and he'll just come up with arrangement ideas like, 'Why don't we just shorten this section here?' And I'm thinking, 'But that riff's killer...' 'Yeah, but Gary, the song's already eight minutes long!' Haha! But like I said, I'm constantly saying, 'Man, this album's so great, it totally rules...' and the next minute it's, 'Is it even any good? I want to do it all over again!' As soon as this record was done, everyone was so happy with it, but a month later everyone was telling me to shut up, because I was like, 'Dude, I really want to go back in the studio and re-do all the solos!'

"I just strive for excellence, you know? Once you start believing that you've accomplished that, a) you're probably an ego-maniac asshole, and b) what room do you have to improve with the next record? If you already believe that your shit doesn't stink, y'know?"

Most Terrorizer readers would agree that 'The Big Four' of thrash metal should really be 'The Big Six' and include Exodus and Testament for their relentless consistency. Do you ever feel slighted by that term of reference...?

"I'm not one to dwell on and get upset about stuff like that, because I know I was one of the very first... never mind the Big Four of anything, it was like the Big Two back then, y'know? That term's based purely on sales... obviously Slayer are a legendary band, Anthrax are great too... but I'd rather let our albums do the talking – I'd put our shit up against anybody's stuff. Metallica are obviously the biggest rock group in the world, and Megadeth are an amazing band – and Dave [Mustaine] gets double bonus points for being part of Metallica too! But I don't let it bother me because I know exactly where we were when all this shit started, and a lot of other people do too."

FROM THE CUTTING ROOM FLOOR:

I would argue that the Exodus sound is built around your riffs and Tom [Hunting]'s unique, rollercoaster drumming style that interprets your riffs in a very unique way... would you agree?

Yeah, sure, Tom's the backbone, the heart and soul, of this band. I've had the pleasure of working with two other awesome drummers, Johnny Tempesta and Paul Bostaph, but when you listen to those Exodus records, there's something missing...

It doesn't sound Exodus-y enough!

Yeah, exactly! Tom is like a rollercoaster and he gives the songs a huge amount of energy... anyone can bust out killer double bass and amazing fills, but Tom's style seems to make shit seem like it's actually moving! It's like sitting in a parked car and thinking you're rolling down the road, y'know? No matter how fast a song is, when Tom plays it, it has an illusion of being faster...

Your old guitar partnership with Rick was right up there with Hetfield/Hammett and King/Hanneman... how does the one you enjoy with Lee compare? I love the guitar duel you do on the DVD!

That was fun! Lee's just an amazing guitar player, and I've known him for longer than I've known Rick! He's an amazing rhythm player, so it's made our live sound a lot tighter too... he shreds so hard, I sometimes don't wanna play leads anymore; I just want to be a rhythm player, haha!

The new Heathen album's awesome – do the two bands ever clash with commitments?

No, not really... fortunately for Exodus it takes those guys ten years to write a record, haha! But yeah, the album's amazing... if anything, it's hard on Lee because he goes straight out with Heathen for six weeks when we take a break and then goes straight back out with us... he's away from home that much more! But we're more than open to him going out to tour on the back of such an amazing record.

So Exodus are, what, thirty years old now?

Yeah, if you're going right back to the high school band days, it's gotta be thirty years... I don't spend a lot of time thinking about stuff like that; I mean, I had to be informed by someone else that it was the twenty-fifth anniversary of 'Bonded By Blood'! And I was like, 'Oh yeah, you're right!' I kinda look more forwards than backwards...

Where do you draw the inspiration to keep going, and keep writing such violent attacking metal music?

We feel as a band that we deserve a lot more... that's not to say that we're not fortunate though. I make a living doing this, and I'm certainly by no means rich, but I'm lucky that I've been able to continue doing what I love doing. We definitely feel like we've got something to prove, which is why our albums keep getting more intense... plus I'm afraid that if we allow ourselves to take our foot off the accelerator, we might come to a stop, haha!

About your song 'Nanking'... who's the historian in the band?

That'd be me, I'm kind of a history nut... and I've always wanted to write that song for quite a number of years, and when I wrote the music, I just thought, 'This is the one!' It has this slow, ominous, military marching feel to it, like an army storming into a city, y'know? And it was a horrifying event, and one that's always been denied to a large part, so a lot of people don't know about it... this album deals with the atrocities that mankind is capable of... and every day there's something new to write about!

EXTINCTION OF MANKIND – ISSUE 122

(AUGUST 2004)

If the thought of having your head unceremoniously knocked in by some of the most gratuitous and ugly grinding riffs imaginable doesn't exactly float your boat, turn the page and go scurrying for cover, or, more sensibly, subscribe to a weedier magazine! Assuming, however, you live your life to a soundtrack of distorted metallic noise like the rest of us, read on eagerly, because Extinction Of Mankind are the heaviest punk-

Extinction of Mankind, Ste, by Will Binks

metal band you've never heard of. But hopefully their self-released 'The Nightmare Seconds...' CD will at last see them clawing their way to the very top of the crustcore food chain.

"We started our own label just because we wanted to have a proper say in the new album's production," explains guitarist Scoot (who cut his teeth in Doom and also plays with Hellkrusher), as to why they ended up releasing said latest disc themselves.

Extinction of Mankind, Scoot, by Will Binks

"We've always stuck by the punk DIY ethic, not involving big record labels or anything – not that any big labels ever wanted us! But the thing with some of the smaller labels is that they can take forever to put out your records. I'm not naming any names, but they scream at you for a recording and twelve months later nothing is out; or it is out and for sale all around the world, but they haven't bothered telling the band.

"Some labels are great, though," the six-stringer concedes, "Like Profane Existence, who are putting out the vinyl version of 'Seconds...' for us, but we thought this time we'd do it ourselves, and oversee all the mastering, artwork, layout, everything. We got to a point where we didn't care if we sold any or not, as long as we could hold a record in our hands that fucking rocks, and I think we can, we're really proud of it."

And so they should be: such a stirring cocktail of pummelling punk and chugging metal hasn't been heard emanating from these shores in many a year. And included amidst the chaos is a devastating cover of 'Arise', originally by UK crust kings Amebix – a band that Extinction obviously worship a little more than is healthy.

"Yeah, they were a huge influence on us," admits Scoot. "But we listen to everything from Motörhead and Antisect to Slayer and Sepultura. Basically anything heavy with a punk vibe, and we hope the new LP represents a respectful dedication to all the bands we grew up on, and all the bands we like now. Musically, it's quite metal – but we're punk as fuck at heart! When I write riffs, I'm not bothered if they're too metal or punk or whatever, as long as they're just fuckin' heavy.

"The sorry state of the world is a big influence, too," he adds. "Politics, religion and money make the world go round apparently, and I think it's turning us all inside out. That's why the full title of the new record is 'The Nightmare Seconds Of An Endless Time'; it's basically about how, when life is hard and evil, the seconds of pain and hurt seem like an eternal nightmare and the seconds lead to hours, the hours to a lifetime..."

Not that any of this is stopping the EOM guys from getting out there and spreading a little of their own brand of oppressive musical mayhem. As well as trekking around the UK, they've toured the US twice in recent years with Misery, both earning and learning a greater respect for the underground punk scene along the way.

"There are a lot of cool bands out there that deserve some recognition for playing truly brutal heavy punk, because they're the ones that make a difference," states Scoot. "Fuck ya pop-punk shit and cock rock metal, that's just on a par with mainstream music, and it's tragic! Bands like In The Shit, Bait, Bomb Blast Men and Broken Access blow away all the popular so-called 'heavy' bands and really deserve to be checked out. I think we need another classic punk era to kick it all up the arse again!"

EXTREME NOISE TERROR - ISSUE 16 (JANUARY 1995)

Extreme Noise Terror are veterans of the UK metal scene, and they're about to release a 'best of' album in the shape of 'Retro-bution'. But what's been happening to them whilst they've been out of the spotlight? Ian Glasper attempts to find out by speaking to vocalists Phil Vane and Dean Jones.

Extreme Noise Terror are poised to make a welcome return to the scene after a period of relative inactivity; they've signed to Earache and are about to release a re-recorded 'best of' album, 'Retro-bution', on an unsuspecting world. Phil Vane explains what they've been up to during that hiatus since 1992's 'Phonophobia' album:

Extreme Noise Terror, by Gutterpunk Photography

"We were basically getting the line-up sorted out, rehearsing new material, and getting a new outlook on the sort of material we want to put out. There's only so much extreme hardcore thrash you can play before running up against a brick wall. You can't play at 1000 mph for the rest of your life, y'know? It'll bore people shitless after a while, it becomes very dated. We're not going to mellow out or anything, but we'll try to incorporate elements of that hardcore sound with a more modern approach... it's still ENT – you'll always be able to tell us apart from other bands – but it's not totally generic."

So what were the problems that needed ironing out with the line-up? "We had to get rid of our drummer, Stick [of Doom fame, and now also with DIRT], due to his drumming abilities, or his disabilities would be a better way of putting it, and our bassist Mark, who wasn't enjoying the direction we were going in. There were no personal problems – it was just their inability to keep up with what we wanted to do." Phil sighs, "It was a bit of a hard thing to do, because we got really close to them as people, but once you realise they're no good for the band, you just have to do it. So we've got a new bassist, Lee [of Candlelight Records], and a new drummer, Darren [AKA Pig Killer], who was in the original ENT line-up. Also, we've got a second lead guitarist, by the name of Ali. We just wanted to fill out the line-up [completed by Pete Hurley on first guitar], and improve on our musical capabilities, so we could advance, rather than wallow in the pit of hardcore."

I wasn't going to mention KLF, but will the LP they recorded with them ever see the light of day? "No!" Dean's adamant on this one, "It's firmly stuck here in my tape collection, not to be seen or heard by anyone!"

Talk turns to the new album, and I ask Phil if it was fun doing those older songs with so many years of studio experience under their belts? "It's nice to have something I can listen to, and play at people, and say this is what ENT were like, compared to the new material. It's been well recorded, and we're very happy with it. It's a bloody good documentation of what we were about, and it was good fun to do those songs one last time, and in the best studio we've ever been in. Hopefully we'll never have to record them again, haha!"

But it's a bit more than simply a 'best of' collection, isn't it? "We've revamped a lot of the old material on 'Retro-bution'... there's a lot of middle-eights, lead breaks and things added to the songs that they never had, say, five years ago. The new line-up's given us more scope with those old songs – we've beefed them up a bit, made them more relevant sounding. Hopefully it'll be a good introduction to the new ENT... a way of saying, 'We're back!'"

Is the new material really so different? If so, in what way? "It's not really experimental in the sense of true experimenting, but some of the songs are a lot slower and a damn sight heavier. It's a bloody good mix of hardcore and heavy metal. There's a lot of people who would like to see us continue to be the old ENT, but there's no way we can continue playing that for the rest of our lives... no way! We've just advanced, learnt to play a lot better, and you can't restrict yourselves..."

Dean adds, "People who liked us before will still like us, I think. We're a lot tighter and more professional, but it's still good, hard music."

And I'm sure they'll prove it when they release a brand new album in the spring, but until then, there's hopefully a tour with Bolt Thrower in February and, of course, 'Retro-bution', which even though it has 'retro' in its title, possesses a modern ferocity a lot of bands would die for.

Extreme Noise Terror, Leipzig 1993

"Yeah, a lot of bands would love to deliver an album like this," adds Phil confidently, "But there's only one band who can, and that's Extreme Noise Terror."

EXTREME NOISE TERROR – ISSUE 88 (APRIL 2001)

After three years in the wilderness, Extreme Noise Terror are back with a new album, 'Being And Nothing', that's more extreme, noisier and more terrifying than ever. Who better to get the scoop than our very own noise terrorist, Ian Glasper?

It's been a turbulent three years for Extreme Noise Terror. Their last album, 'Damage 381', released by Earache in 1997 (which famously saw ENT virtually swapping vocalists with Napalm Death, albeit for a very short time) wasn't particularly well received, and promptly after, the band seemingly disappeared. Little did we all know that, behind the scenes, a new, improved ENT was beavering away on a new album, and only now comes the rude awakening for the doubters and detractors of the band who were so quick to write them off. 'Being And Nothing', the band's brand new 'come-back' album, recently released by their new label, Candlelight, is as brutal and savage as any of us could have dared hope for, being a veritable maelstrom of hateful metallic grind. Here's hoping that everyone hasn't forgotten about them in the meantime...

"It's such a horrible thing, to see all the music magazines come out every month," sighs drummer, Zac O' Neil, "And know that there will not be anything about your band in any of them. No promotion, no press, nothing going on, and that's a terrible feeling. We knew we had to make a great album that would make everyone sit up and pay attention to us again. I'm not saying that everyone will turn around and like this record just like that, but at least we know that we've made the record that we should have done three years ago..."

Ah, yes, that troubled period for the band that I alluded to in my little intro above. Just what was going on back then? Were you in the throes of some sort of mid-life crisis?

"Yeah, I think you could call it that," says Zac carefully. "The crisis was that whole era around when we released 'Damage 381'. The record didn't do so good, and we're not very happy with it. It's not like we're embarrassed by it or anything, because we've done it now, and it's a part of ENT history whether we like it or not. Besides, I wasn't in the band when they did it, so I had nothing to do with the writing of it [laughs]!

"I was much more involved in the writing of this one though; in fact, me and Dean wrote everything. And we just knew that we wanted to put that album behind us – it was really moving in a direction we didn't want to go, to be honest. Like I said, we're not ashamed of 'Damage', but this album now is really the record we wanted, and needed, to put out."

Well, you've certainly blown the cobwebs away with 'Being And Nothing'. It's as potent a piece of death metal as I've heard in a long time, and it's incredibly intense. I take it that there was a lot of anger and frustration at all the setbacks that got vented in the studio?

"We were just so hell-bent on making this work. We wanted to make Extreme Noise Terror sound like an extreme noise terror again – as opposed to a medium noise terror! If you've got a name like we have, you can't go and play half-heartedly. And it's not like it's something we find hard to do, but we have to want to, and this time we were well up for it. I blasted my ass off in the studio; we all went all-out at it, and yeah, a lot of the band's turmoil did come out in some of the songs."

And talking of blast beats... there's a much more prominent death metal feel to the band nowadays than before. You used to have this heavy UK grindcore thing going on, but now it's more akin to Suffocation or one of those other ultra-brutal US death bands, all detuned squeaking guitars and guttural rhythmic vocals. I gotta say that I approve of the new direction, but why such a drastic change in the space of one album?

"We never had a specific sound in mind," claims the drummer, "But we just wanted to be as extreme and as fast as possible, and the way it came out is the way it came out. On the last album, Ali wrote most of it, and there was a big influence from bands like Napalm Death and Carcass, but this time, it was more me and Dean's influences... and I'm not a grindcore head at all. I'm totally into the death metal thing, Dean too, so this time around we were much more focused and much more extreme.

"There's a very euphoric feeling in the band right now," he adds in closing. "We're all very excited to get out there and play again, and we're all very excited for people to hear the new album too. We're keen to put the last three years behind us now, 'cos we've had a really bad time of it all... all those label and line-up hassles, and European tours being cancelled and stuff... we'll be touring a whole lot more now, I guarantee it. And whether 50 or 500 people turn out to see us, it won't matter, as long as we're out there again, proving to people that we're still a force to be reckoned with."

CHAPTER F: AT WAR WITH THE WORLD...

If you thought you'd seen the last of Marco Aro when he left The Haunted a few years ago, think again, because he's back fronting his old band Face Down. Ian Glasper found out why it took him so long to return to the fray....

"We're trying to put Stockholm back on the metal map, y'know? It's been a bit quiet here recently; it's been all Gothenburg for a long, long time! And there are so many new bands coming up here in Sweden that are just clones of that style, which is why we decided to get some Stockholm sounds out there again. And they do that melodic stuff so much better than we do, so let them keep going at it... and we do what we do better as well – no mess, no fuss, just pure impact."

So says Marco Aro, vocalist with Face Down... although many of you will know him best as ex-vocalist with Swedish metal phenomenon, The Haunted. Now back with his newly reformed original band, he's just finished work on what may actually be the heaviest record he's ever sang on, 'The Will To Power' for Black Lodge Records, and that comes as a surprise to even Marco himself.

"Right before I joined The Haunted, I'd pretty much made a decision that I was through with the music industry," he reveals, "But then I got the call from [Haunted guitarist] Anders [Bjorler], asking me to come down and audition, so I thought, 'What the hell? I'll give it one last try!' And I got the job, and did that for four or five years... but then I reached the same point I was at before – thinking that it just wasn't worth it anymore, with all the old problems I'd had escalating into something even worse. So I decided not to do this shit anymore!"

What kind of problems are we talking about here?

"I was battling with drug abuse at the time," he says candidly, "And all the personal problems that come with addiction – family stuff and shit. I knew I had to do something... something had to go, and unfortunately that was The Haunted. And I'd pretty much decided that I was done with music... until Joakim [Harju], our bassist, called me up, saying he had a record deal for Face Down, and did I want to sing on a new album? This was probably a year after I quit The Haunted, and during that time

I'd started to get the old feeling back – you know, when you watch a band onstage, or listen to a great new CD... and I thought maybe I should reconsider and do it again." You see, music's the biggest drug of all!

"Well, it's been the whole of my adult life; that's pretty much all I know, and it's a big thing to walk away from it. So I decided to give it another go, to see what happens this time... because we can afford to be picky now. Our lives don't depend upon it anymore, and the key word here is 'fun'! To keep doing this while it's fun – if the fun dies, so does the band."

'Fun' is not a word easily associated with 'The Will To Power' though; a veritable sledgehammer of an album lingering with malicious intent somewhere between Slayer, Pantera and Hatebreed, what it lacks in technical flourish it more than compensates for with a frighteningly singular aggression, Marco spitting bile all over the place like a ruptured spleen. So, does he feel as if he's back where he belongs?

"I guess so, because I used to feel out of my depth in The Haunted, 'cos those guys are such tremendous musicians, so productive... such perfectionists. So, even though I felt a part of the band, I always felt a little out of my league... if you know what I mean? It's hard to explain really, and it might sound wrong, but that's the way I felt."

That's interesting, because, against the odds, the new Face Down album is possibly even the equal of the mighty Haunted themselves! Maybe you're underestimating yourself?

"Yes, maybe I am," he admits, laughing, "But I got two important things from The Haunted... the first was experience - a lot of experience, 'cos we toured almost all the time. But the other thing I learnt from them was never hope for anything... and maybe that's why I say all this stuff, because I'm scared of falling flat on my face. So I'm underachieving already, haha!"

FALL FROM GRACE, TUNGSTEN & LEADFOOT

('SOUTHERN METAL') – ISSUE 47 (OCTOBER 1997)

It ain't a scene so much as a loose confederation, if you'll forgive the pun. Call it sludge, boogie, groove or stoner metal, there's no denying that many a band from the American south is taking things slow 'n' easy right now. And what better proof when not one but three such critters crawl forth at the same time? Follow Ian Glasper as he journeys through swamp, savannah and city in search of Fall From Grace, Tungsten and Leadfoot.

Now I've always had a soft spot for something dark 'n' twisted musically, but it was only in more recent years, with the onset of some vague kind of musical maturity, that I began to appreciate a doom-laden groove as a side order as well. And then the forbidden strains of something truly heavy called to me from across the ocean. From a dark, dank swampland, came Crowbar - wielding riffage that combined mood, menace and extreme weight. If we're going to call bands like this Southern 'rock', think a lump of granite, and not some wussy AOR nonsense, okay?

Already done Floodgate, but my craw was in need of further detuned nourishment, so join me on another foray into a dripping, dangerous world, attempting once more to plumb the unfathomable depths that lurk beneath the surface of the American south. And what better place to start than the black, unholy heart of this loose musical confederation, New Orleans?

As soon as he picks the phone up to me, Jay Ceravolo, guitarist with (relative) newcomers, Fall From Grace, takes a shine to me. This is because he's read my review of their self-titled Music For Nations' debut, where I said that his album would be on my playlist for my funeral.

"The funeral thing did it for me, man," he laughs. "No one's said that about us before. That's a compliment and a half, you won me on that!"

If you seem to recognise the name, but can't quite place it, allow me to enlighten you. Jay was once part of the awesome thrash band who plied their wares under the name of Exhorder, as was Kyle Thomas, now fronting the aforementioned Floodgate, but Fall From Grace are far from an extension of that influential act.

"Actually, Kyle went off to audition for COC," the laidback guitarist fills me in with a brief history lesson, "And when he came back, he was really into that type of music. He didn't want to play that heavy Exhorder style anymore, and I was bugged out, big time, but I respected his decision, and said, 'Fine, you go and do what you gotta do'. So, my mission was to find a new singer for Exhorder, and a few people told me about Wil [Buras, vocalist of FFG – IG]. I checked him out, and I knew this dude had a really good voice, but when I put it to him, he said, 'Man, I'm really flattered 'n' all, but I really wanna do my own thing... but we're looking for a guitar player!' They weren't as heavy as I was used to, but they had a lot of potential, and I heard that, and I thought on it for about a month. Exhorder had been falling apart for a coupla years by then, with everyone off doing their own thing, so I thought, 'What the hell'. I loved the guy's voice, and believed we could make some good music, so I jumped in headfirst."

It's this rich vein of melody that Wil manages to weave into every line of lyrics that gives the album such astonishing texture. That, and the titanium production job of Matt Thomas, who was, until recently, busting strings with heavyweights, Crowbar.

"He was so good in the studio, I felt so comfortable that I could almost have left him to take the reins. He has a deep understanding of where we're coming from, he knew exactly where our heads were at, it was like we'd been working together forever. He's apparently retired from music now, but he's said that, when we do our next record, he'll get back in the saddle again to work with us."

And what of the incestuous scene the city's famous for? Are you comfortable to be lumped in with that sludge thang?

"Oh, yeah," Jay drawls. "Even in the Exhorder days, even though we weren't a sludge band as such, we were down [hey, leave the bad puns to me – IG] with all the local bands. I'm so happy to be from this state, it's a great place to be. There's so much talent here brewing over, and it makes me real happy to see some of these bands getting some recognition."

It's obvious talking to Jay that he still recalls fondly those days spent in Exhorder and he doesn't totally rule out the possibility of a reunion when I suggest that it would be well received, but for now, that debut by Fall From Grace is more than enough to sink yer teeth into...

Next stop, Chalmette, a small town seven miles outside New Orleans, and home to the aptly-named Tungsten, who first made an impression on me with their 1993 '183.85' debut on Pavement, which was most notorious for its unmitigated bitterness towards womankind, an attitude that mirrored its hateful line in simplistic metal mayhem.

Four years on, and now ensconced on the Dutch label Lighttown, Tungsten's newie, 'The Tungsten Survival Kit', sees them compromising oh-so-slightly their bleak musical outpourings with some bitter-sweet melody, but that inherent lyrical fury is still very apparent.

"Some people think I'm sexist or something," sighs Al Hodge, the band's sincere, animated frontman, "But I'm not - I love women, but I've always been burnt by them. On that first album, I had just had my heart broken into pieces by this one chick, and at the same time, my drummer had just split with his girlfriend after seven years, but instead of sitting in a bar, crying into our beers, we sat and wrote about how pissed off we felt, and that's what came out on that first record.

"There's a coupla chicks that did some pretty horrible shit to me, and I thank 'em for it now, 'cos you can't get better influence than that. It keeps the fire burning in your belly. A couple of girls say, 'Oh, I know this song is about me', but they're mainly about a girl who was in my life seven years ago. She was the only girl I've ever really put all my faith into, and she walked away, and it was kinda heavy. It really fucked me up, and now I'm at the point where I don't trust girls at all, as far as relationships go. The reputation I have down here is one of a woman-hater, but to hate a girl is the furthest thing from my mind, but to build that trust back takes a very long time."

Well, you've got yer pop punk for when the sun's shining and you're in love, and when it all comes down round your ears, and winter's chill is thick on your heart, you'll come running to Tungsten. I know that when I was reeling from a broken relationship, I found great solace in Al's lyrical catharsis.

Despite the seemingly obsessive preoccupation with his miserable love life, the new album, as I said earlier, manages to be positively uplifting compared to the previous two's gruelling rifferama, mainly due to the incorporation of some killer tunes, and even some occasional moments of levity.

"A lot of the bands around here are just trying to be heavy for the sake of it," reckons Al, "And we wanted to do an album you could listen to over and over again, without always hitting the skip button. We wanted to do a rollercoaster of a record, not just the same shit over and over. When we started out, sure, we just wanted to be heavy, but that was back in '85. We did two-minute songs, no guitar solos, but our bassist is actually a guitar player, and he grew up on the Tygers Of Pan Tang, and stuff like that, with really melodic leads, and it was just another way to stay ahead of the pack around here."

AI has a less complimentary view of 'the pack', i.e. the New Orleans scene, than Jay painted for us earlier, though. "The people down here only want you to play certain chords, in a certain way, to certain rhythms, and if you don't fit in with that, well, you're not cool. We've always been like outcasts anyway. We just got sick of the whole cliquey scene here, so we just stepped back, and let everyone get on with what they were doing. We don't have the right tattoos, the right wallet chains, we don't smoke the right dope, we don't fit in with that whole community, and we don't want to."

Lastly, on this sweaty musical sojourn, I hotfoot it north to Raleigh, Carolina, from whence came COC, of course, and now, Leadfoot, who in fact, feature two ex-COC-ers in their ranks. Karl AgeII and PhiI Swisher were part of the classic line-up who unleashed 'Blind', my personal favourite Corrosion record (excepting, of course, the awesome 'Animosity'), so their involvement in Leadfoot certainly perked my curiosity about the band. And, sure enough, it picks up the baton fumbled after 'Blind', and hits the finishing tape with confidence, walking effortlessly the tight rope between crushing grooves and mellow blues.

"If people said we sounded like the old southern rock thing, well, there might be some truth in that", replies vocalist, KarI Agell, when I ask him if he feels a part of such a scene. "Lynyrd Skynyrd, ZZ Top, Molly Hatchet, those sorta bands as opposed to the New Orleans thing. New Orleans has a whole separate vibe. Their sound is its own entity, which isn't pervasive across the whole southern music scene."

Already I can sense a certain disillusionment with modern music, am I right?

"Uh, yeah, I'd say so," he says cautiously. "Don't get me wrong, I totally respect the new bands, I really do, but I tend to look towards my musical roots for my inspiration. It's hard for me to find a lot of new stuff that I really like! I mean, I love Soundgarden, Kyuss, Monster Magnet, and Fu Manchu and Slowburn are pretty cool, but none of them move me in the same way as, say, AC/DC, Free, or Thin Lizzy."

The influence of the latter is definitely very apparent on Leadfoot's 'Bring It On' debut, especially on songs like 'Ripe', with its cheeky guitar harmonies, but there is also enough power wielded by the quintet to ensure everything is delivered with enough force to satisfy a hardcore metaller like myself. Well, any hardcore metaller with an ounce of adventurous open-mindedness in his blood, that is. So, what exactly is it that Karl feels is lacking in modern music?

"I don't know!" he laughs. "It's not like we do what we do as a response, we're not trying to fill some kind of niche. We didn't get together saying, 'Damn, there's something lacking in modern music, and we're here to save the day', y'know? In my opinion, there's a lack of groove. If people want to hear great riffs locked into a groove, they have to look at the Seventies, and you can't get that from techno or punk. And thrash is thrash, and that end of the metal spectrum is just not going to pursue that need for a bluesy groove."

I then manage to stop Karl dead in his tracks by dragging a dusty old skeleton from the back of his closet... um, weren't you in School Of Violence?

"Oh, Christ," he laughs, amazedly. "You're the first person to mention that! Uh, yeah, I was in School Of Violence for a year, and I did the album that came out on Death Metal Blade. We were big fans of Motorhead and Discharge, and I took vocal inspiration from the styles of Lemmy, Cronos from Venom... uh, Tom G. Warrior [laughs]! It was fun while it lasted, but ultimately it wasn't very satisfying, I was very limited as a vocalist with that material. But everything happens for a reason, and it was part of my musical evolution. That was a time and a place, and I don't regret it, but it's definitely in the past."

And with their current albums sounding so fuckin' good, none of us need dwell on these bands' previous projects, need we? Just turn your right shoulder to the setting sun, crank up the volume and savour the flavour of the swamp.

FETUS CHRIST – ISSUE 199 (AUGUST 2010)

Fetus Christ live

Insanely fast grindcore is pretty thin on the ground in rural Herefordshire, but Fetus Christ are proud to be black sheep with their psychotic blend of early Napalm Death worship and boozy blast beats. The band's 'Grind Violence' demo is not only, ahem, grinding and violent, and sure to please fans of Disrupt, Heresy and Infest, but also pretty damn funny too, with 'Fuck You, Bitch, I'm Growing A Moustache' surely a contender for the most hilarious song title of the year.

"We'd written a song slating the Christian faith, but it didn't have a name," dead-pans vocalist Liam Doverman. "We played a show a couple of weeks later, and the song was still unnamed; I noticed the 'god squad' were in attendance and said, 'This song goes out to the Virgin Mary, it's called, 'Fuck You Bitch, I'm Growing A Moustache!' And it just stuck from there; we're not massive fans of the faith, and moustaches are rad, so why not?"

The Fiend

"I've heard a lot of reformed bands, and most of them are just plodding along the same old path... no new material, no new message... we just wanted to come back and do a proper job of it, with a bigger sound and better songs," says Robby, guitarist with The Fiend, a reformed punk band from the Northeast, and it's no idle boast. Originally formed in 1981, then splitting up in 1987, the current incarnation sound more ferocious and vital than ever on new album, 'Greed-Power-Religion-War', reminiscent of greats like the Varukers and Discharge at their peak.

"We are a one-off, a throwback to the earlier times of the hardcore punk scene, and one of the only bands from that era that hasn't changed their attitude or ideas, and still one of the most aggressive live bands out there by far."

FIGURE FOUR — ISSUE 92 (SEPTEMBER 2001)

"You know, a lot of bands with a 'Christian message' want to be part of some sort of 'Christian scene', but that's not for Figure Four," claims the band's vocalist Andrew, when I wonder just how much their spiritual beliefs actually interact with the band,

Figure Four

beyond the obvious lyrical overtones. "We're just a hardcore band. Yes, we are all Christian, and that's the most important thing in our lives, so of course that's going to affect our lyrics because I sing about life. But as far as playing shows, we would much rather play shows with other regular hardcore bands. So our Christianity doesn't influence us to take certain shows, with certain bands, or anything like that." And it would be a shame if you let the fact that they're Christian dissuade you from checking these guys out too, 'cos Figure Four are simply devastating. I ranted and raved about the merits of their debut CD on Face Down last year ['No Weapon Formed Against Us' – IG], and now their follow-up assault on Kingfisher ('When It's All Said And Done') has had a similar effect on my hapless ears. If you like savage beatdowns and rampant thrash rhythms a la Hatebreed, or maybe even Merauder, slap this on and you'll be in pure metalcore heaven... no pun intended, of course.

I put it to Andrew that religion has been responsible for more wars than anything else in human history and that surely a benevolent god wouldn't allow all this suffering in the world, and, although not converted, I am impressed by his logical response.

"We actually don't believe in religion. I think that religion is a man-made set of rules that people live their life based on. And I agree that it has caused many wars. But what we have to remember is that it's not God who starts these wars. It's the people. People aren't perfect and sometimes they do mess up stuff. There have been lots of people who have started wars in 'God's name'. But is it really in God's name? People misrepresent God all the time.

"No one is perfect. So we all have a choice to do what we want. I don't think that God

Figure Four, courtesy of Jason Dunn

makes the world a cruel place. It's us... the people, and a lot of people are selfish, cruel, and hateful."

And now that you've been licensed to a decent European label, can we expect to see the band tearing it up over here any time soon?

"We're hoping so! We want to come to Europe really badly! I've heard so many good things, and there are so many good bands out there. We're gonna try and do anything we can to get over there sometime this year!"

FIRESIDE – ISSUE 33 (AUGUST 1996)

Fireside

Like a comet blazing its way out of the dark wastelands of northern Sweden come aptly named rising stars Fireside. This infeasibly young fresh-faced quartet truly play music to warm lonely souls during those long winter nights, when dawn seems a lifetime away.

Anyone who's plotted the (upward) course of this band will no doubt have noted the annoying regularity with which they get compared to Quicksand. The more enlightened magazines among us would also scratch a little deeper and cite Tool, Barkmarket and Rapeman. But then we're good like that.

"Yeah, that's where our influences are coming from right now," agrees bassist Franz, down a cracklin' wire from Scandinavia. "All the stuff I listen to comes from the Chicago scene, bands like Jesus Lizard and Shellac. Okay, back when we started, we all listened to Quicksand and liked them very much, especially their first 7" on Revelation Records. Perhaps when we started you could make that comparison, but we've certainly changed.

"People have to put you in a box with other bands to identify you, but that's very boring. I can understand why journalists do it, but it's quite frustrating. Although one writer said we were a mix between Fugazi and Big Black, which was really nice to hear."

From their conception in 1992, out of the post-hardcore scene, things have moved at a frightening rate for the band. With their luscious, compelling debut due in August on the giant American Recordings, the intriguingly named 'Do Not Tailgate', they've also been confirmed for the prestigious Lollapalooza festival tour in the States.

"We've signed for six records," explains a remarkably unfazed Franz, "So this is what we're going to do for the next seven years. So it was a very big step, but obviously it's good for the band. It's much better than working a shitty day job, even though we don't have a lot of money."

When asked the inevitable question for a band who've signed to a major, he adds defiantly, "No, we'll never go more commercial. We'll always write songs just like we've always done. We make songs that we like and want to play live. If anything, we'll go in the opposite direction - more non-commercial."

Now, some of you may declare the inclusion of a band like Fireside in Terrorizer as a faux pas, considering the distinctly rock feel to some of their more accessible material. Well, a) fuck off and b) live they are a much heavier prospect.

"We're a lot noisier with a much harder edge live, but still rockier than your average hardcore or metal band. We're definitely a good live band. There's a lot of energy on stage. I don't think any of your readers will be disappointed by us live."

Five Knuckle — issue 123 (September 2004)

"We were young and it seemed like a good idea at the time," laughs Five Knuckle vocalist Dan Sanfey, about the origins of his band's name. Far from being any sort of flirtation with violent imagery, it actually stems instead from another pastime popular with adolescent males: "When we first formed, back in early 1998, we started out as Five Knuckle Shuffle! Then, a few years ago, it was suggested that we change the name, so we decided to drop the 'Shuffle', figuring that it put a more serious slant on things. And we've been trying to shake it ever since, but it just seems to keep haunting us."

Still, if the new, improved name doesn't convince you that this promising young Bristol

Five Knuckle, courtesy of Katherine Vik @Household Name

Five Knuckle, courtesy of Katherine Vik @Household Name

quintet mean business, one listen to their new record, 'Balance', surely will. As challenging musically as it is lyrically, the album constantly surprises the listener with slippery, rhythmic twists and turns and some wonderfully convoluted riffing, every song walking that tightrope between furious noise and sublime melody. If you have to stick a label on it, it's metallic hardcore punk rock, but imbued with an intelligence and urgency all too often absent from the genre these days.

"When we first started out, we were all sixteen and into the whole American hardcore thing which had a fairly big influence on our general sound," reveals Dan. "As we've gotten older, we've kinda gone our separate ways with our tastes in music. We listen to a wide variety of styles now, everything from easy listening to thrash. But two bands that we've always agreed on as being a big influence on us musically are Minor Threat and Refused – as you can probably tell.

"It's hard to say really," he sighs in closing, when asked whether he feels the current punk scene is too apolitical for its own good. "I think generally as a whole, it is lacking. There may be more bands singing about these things, with the current situation and all, but it's almost as if singing about politics has become cool and fashionable recently. I'm not sure if this is a good or bad thing, but hopefully it'll encourage people to become more aware and dig a little deeper. And then perhaps we may begin to see some more positive ideas coming out of this music."

FLOODGATE – ISSUE 36 (NOVEMBER 1996)

Most bands talk about their difficult second album, but for Floodgate, their 'Penalty' debut proved to be their 'difficult first album'. Ian Glasper learnt all about the trials, tribulations and tributaries of this New Orleans band from singer and guitarist Kyle Thomas.

Me and Old Nick, the Satanic chief-of-staff here at Terrorizer Mansions, had many a high-brow opinion on how and why Floodgate arrived at their unusual name. His Blackness favoured the train of thought that, seeing as they're outta New Orleans, and it's more than a little wet down thataways, that the proximity of so much H2O roundabout influenced their choice of moniker, whilst I, determined not to be out-brained in the theory department (again), preferred to think it somehow signified the release of pent-up frustrated musical inspiration. Nah, nothing so romantic – we were both wrong.

"We just thought 'Flood' was a cool word, but all agreed it needed enhancing," laughs their vocalist Kyle Thomas, obviously enjoying shooting down in flames our pretentious bullshit, before conceding that, out of the two of us, Nick is closest (damn his eyes). "Actually, it does have some significance for us too... the word 'floodgate' appears in our song 'Imitations Salvation', and there is actually a floodgate in the city walls of New Orleans. That's the beauty of the name – it's open to interpretation, it can mean anything to anyone. Penalty was a cool name, and we didn't like parting with it, but Floodgate is less limiting. Penalty sounds very aggressive, but Floodgate is a little mysterious."

"Penalty?", you're probably thinking, "What is he on about now?" Oops, sorry, in my eagerness to let you know all about this exciting new rock band (yes, I said 'rock' - wanna make something of it?), I neglected to tell you just why you should be so excited about them. For starters, they feature one Kyle Thomas, previously of Exhorder, one of the most hostile of the late '80s thrash metal bands, and they've just signed to Roadrunner Records, who have been known to pick a winner now and again, and if that hasn't got you interested, they're a steamin' good band to boot.

As you may have gathered already, Floodgate began life as Penalty, but were forced to abandon that title by the looming shadow of a hefty lawsuit. Yeah, you guessed it, another band already laid claim to the name, right? Wrong again!

"No, it's a clothing line outta Brazil," says Kyle incredulously. "They didn't want us making T-shirts that said Penalty on them, 'cos they were already producing them. At the end of the day, it was all about T-shirts! It was a real blow, an uppercut from Mike Tyson in fact. It took six months of arguing to arrive at something we all liked, and that the label liked. We had contests in magazines and all sorts of cheesy shit."

In actual fact, the changing of names was the last in a long line of trials that could so easily have been the straw that broke the long-suffering musician's back (but didn't). First, their producer's mother-in-law died, then Kyle's girlfriend's father had a heart attack, and to top it all off nicely, an entire week-long mix-down of recording was lost forever to electronic purgatory. Just how the hell is a guy meant to stay motivated through a run of luck like that?

"There were so many hurdles, it was like competing in the goddamn Olympics," chuckles KyIe, hindsight providing him with a happier outlook on matters. "After the first coupla tragedies, each one became just another thing to overcome, and now we're ready to go. It doesn't seem like any of it ever happened, it's so obsolete at this point. It's all part of the trials of life, but unfortunately, it all happened at once. We're all pretty solid, stable people and we just tried to roll with the punches, y'know?"

Well, he might rejoice, because in the face of adversity he's created a great album, name of 'Penalty', as a mark of respect for the defunct trademark. I mentioned 'rock' earlier... don't despair, though. Normally, even the mention of that word has me gagging back sour vomit, but here we aren't talking rock as in Bon Jovi, we are talking ROCK as in COC or Only Living Witness, or let's cut the crap, Black Sabbath. Dark and greasy and subversively groovy, and not a bit like his former outfit, the infamously brutal Exhorder. As an old fan who mourned their demise, I had to ask, just what happened?

"Our biggest mistake was not running our business properly," he reckons. "There would be a power shift, and there'd be one person in charge who wouldn't know what they were doing, or another person would take over and have problems rallying everybody. It was tough times; we had some bad breaks and they just had a domino effect. Towards the end, there was little or no friendship between anyone in the band. Now that we're away from each other, it seems like we're better friends."

One earful of 'Penalty's soulful sneer and it's instantly obvious that Kyle is peddling a very different kinda vibe with his new band. Floodgate seems like quite a departure for him, veering off on a not inconsiderable tangent to Exhorder's vehement trail-blazing.

"My direction's changed, yes, but my tastes? No! People always wanna know why I've made this departure, when in actual fact, Exhorder was my musical departure, 'cos when I was growing up, this was the type of thing I listened to. I actually submitted a lot of material like this to that band, and it got turned down, either 'cos the guys didn't like it, or they didn't think it fit their style.

"I love the Exhorder material," he reflects, "And I'll never deny that for a minute, but to continue would have been an abomination to the integrity we had as a band. I'm having more fun now than ever before, and it's something I can call my own."

The truth of this statement is blatantly obvious from the passion that flows from the album like rancid juices from a garbage truck's press. Maybe I wasn't so far off the mark with my interpretation of the name after all!

"As fantastic and influential as Exhorder were, they were very one-dimensional, in that we could only go over the top, and once you've gone over the top, where do you go from there? It was all angst, which is fine, but with Floodgate, we will tap all the emotions, as well as just anger."

Exorcising your aggression through a more subtle medium, perhaps?

381

"I don't think that you have to sacrifice heaviness if you get a bit more mellow or melodic, and I don't see anything wrong with good, clean vocals either. I've always been a fan of different types of music; I grew up in New Orleans, how could I not listen to blues or jazz, y'know?"

Ah, we are back to their location once again. We've all seen how certain localities seem to grow towards a certain style, creating a very specialised scene. New York hardcore, Seattle grunge, Californian pop punk, and, of course, southern sludge... COC, Eye Hate God, Crowbar, Tungsten, Down, Stressball, Graveyard Rodeo – shall I go on? (I'm glad you said 'No', 'cos I was about all dried up then!) Do you think geography can actually have a bearing on musical style, or is it simply a case of ideas rubbing off on your neighbours?

"A bit of both, I think," ponders Kyle. "New Orleans is a big city, but nowhere near as big as L.A. or New York, and most of the people in metal bands either grew up together or have known each other a very long time. We spend a lot of non-musical time together; we drink the same water, eat the same foods, often play in the same bands. It's a very incestuous musical community down here. It's also a very hot place, and the humidity will drive you insane. A lot of people have a hard time surviving it. I know people who've moved here from, say, Pennsylvania, and they've said that the first summer was horrific. They never adjust to it... we never adjust to it, and we grew up here."

Still, Black Sabbath were from Brum, and that ain't renowned for its tropical heat, so I will leave you to draw your own conclusions. Something about the Sabs obviously spoke to the good folk of New Orleans on some deep level, 'cos more than one of the metal bands down there, Floodgate definitely included, has a hint of the Seventies about them. Are you guilty of being retro, Kyle?

"I guess if it was too retro, we'd all go to the thrift store and buy clothes that were fashionable twenty years ago," he argues. "We can't deny our roots, but we're trying to take a more modern approach. I mean, okay, we recorded it on analogue, 'cos we prefer that warmer sound to the crisp feel of digital, but it's not like we're driving around in 1960's Volkswagens! And I know that they weren't using our effects pedals back then.

"I s'pose you could call it retro, if it makes you feel better, but I'd say that instead of trying to carve a new path, we've decided to stick with the meat 'n' potatoes and write good songs, 'cos it all comes back to songs in the end, anyway."

FREEBASE – ISSUE 76 (MARCH 2000)

Anyone who's frequented even a handful of UKHC shows these last few years is bound to have been assaulted by Northampton's Freebase and their gnarly take on metallic hardcore punk somewhere along the way. Yet despite having been all over the gig circuit

Freebase

like a bad rash, apart from a few compilation appearances, and the split MCD with Medulla Nocte last year, the band's recorded output has been noticeably thin on the ground. All that is about to change however, with the imminent release of their debut full-length, 'Nothing to Regret', on Diehard, or rather, Diehard's hardcore subsidiary, Hardboiled. We figured it was high time to corner the band and get the run-down.

"It's still basically Freebase," claims Mark Fieldhouse, when l ask him to account for the shift in style since that aforementioned split with da Nocte. "It's still that barrage of guitar riffing, and lotsa shouting mayhem; it's not as if Nick has suddenly started doing solos and fancy finger work... not that he can... [laughs]

"l think to say that our album is 'different' to the split would be terming it wrongly, and may even confuse people. As I said, it's still the basic Freebase sound, but not quite as metallic – I think we pushed our sound to its metal limits with that split! I'm not saying that we will never write songs like that again, and I'm sure that it will still appeal to metal fans anyway, 'cos it's certainly still heavy, but we're definitely writing better structured songs now."

One thing that is very noticeable on 'Nothing to Regret' is how much clearer your vocals are – was that intentional?

"Yes, very much so," confirms the heavily tattooed frontman. "l definitely toned down my vocals for the new CD; they are not so 'deathy' now. It's much easier to make out the lyrics."

Ah yes, those lyrics. Freebase have never been ones to suck up to the PC brigade, and I'm sure that if a name like Freebase hasn't already offended many of the self-appointed scene police, then a song like 'Cocaine Nose Job' surely will!

"That's not a pro-drugs song," Mark claims, "But also it isn't an anti-drugs song, either. We're not against SXE at all; I have a lot of SXE friends... but I know a lot of alcoholics too [that wicked laugh again!] It can be interpreted both ways if you read the lyrics; I like to leave topics open-ended. I'm just addressing the issue, read into it what you like... our lyrics touch on a vast range of subjects; we definitely don't concentrate on just one area, that would just be boring. How many times can you sing about the same topic over and over again? All that does is alienate people - not to mention making them doubt your own conversation level! We just sing about whatever we feel like, and the lyrics are just our opinions on the issue. We certainly don't expect people to pick up our CD booklet and say, 'Oh, they reckon we should do this or that'... at the end of the day, it's only a song, and it's done for fun."

Well, whatever, anyone who knows Mark knows not to take everything he says too seriously. If you look up the definition of 'wind-up merchant' in the dictionary, you'll more than likely see his ugly mug gurning back at you! He's even admitted his love of telling porkies in the song 'Payback', so no wonder when I ask about why the album took so bleeding long to appear, the answer is suitably ludicrous. Everybody else would tell you a saga of costly re-recording and re-mixing. but read on anyway.

"It was quite funny actually. We came back from spending June in Denmark doing the recording [this much is true − IG] and on the way home, Nick, our guitarist and myself got so drunk, he actually fell overboard off the ferry - with the fuckin' master tapes, so they were lost forever. It was unlucky, but at the end of the day, it was the label's fault, as they gave us too much money to piss up the wall on the way home, so we naturally pleaded ignorance... we then went into Backstage with Dave Chang, and it's turned out truly heavyweight."

And that last bit is true, too, readers. 'Nothing to Regret' is just the debut album the band needed to put them on the map, fast and furious and loaded with as much humour as it is serious social commentary. With an appearance already confirmed on this Spring's Eurocore festival in Holland, and several UK tours being slated, the future certainly looks bright for Freebase - and for the UK scene in general. In closing, Mark wanted to have his say on what he saw as wrong with hardcore in the Y2K.

"There is still a lot of unity around, but also there are a few twats who are trying to segregate people It's cool people having different opinions on anything, but to cause trouble and spread rumours, and especially to preach without any sort of tolerance, is pretty pathetic, if you ask me. This whole thing - call it hardcore, punk, whatever you like - isn't, and never was, about rules and regulations. It's all about thinking for yourself, and living your life how you feel comfortable..."

Freebase − issue 99 (May 2002)

The UK's own Freebase have been toiling away in toilets the length and breadth of Europe for years now, but finally, with the release of their ripping, less geographically

Freebase

determined second album, 'My Life, My Rules', for Hardboiled, things look set to change for the better. Ian Glasper was dispatched to hear their master plan... only to find out they don't have one!

UKHC stalwarts, Freebase, are back, and with a vengeance. Their new album For Hardboiled, 'My Life, My Rules', is so far superior to their 2000 debut, 'Nothing To Regret', it almost sounds like a different band. There is a quiet, newfound confidence in their ranks as they prepare to promote their sophomore effort. Although that first record was a more than competent slice of punky hardcore, this time out they know they've produced something that is able to compete on an international level.

"The whole thing was much easier this time," laughs vocalist Mark Fieldhouse, when I remind him of the multi-remix nightmare that their first album turned into in the end. "We made sure that we all knew what was going on this time. There was a lot of shit going down behind the scenes before as well, and I suppose that did affect the CD to an extent.

"We have a much stronger band together now than we did then, both musically and visually when we play live. There is actually only Nick, our guitarist, and myself left who were on the last CD, but there are now four fully committed members in this band, and we feel that this really shows. We all contributed to writing the new CD, and were very open with our ideas. It was much more of a band effort. We have 'brewed' the band significantly, and this new CD is what Freebase are really about. All four of us are really proud of it... something that, if I'm totally honest, we could not say about 'Nothing To Regret'."

So what let 'Nothing...' down? The band were pretty pleased with it at the time...

"We were," ponders Mark, "But with the benefit of a little hindsight, it just sounded too weak. My vocals on it were crap, and the songs were executed poorly; too slow, with no feeling. 'My Life' has really captured how we sound live; full-on, in-yer-face hardcore. The tempos are good, the songs are tight, and there is generally a much better feel to it."

The new album has something of a European feel about it, having more in common with, say, Barcode and Backfire than it does other UKHC bands. Even the artwork helps set it apart from all the UK releases of recent years. Was this something they did consciously, to avoid being lumped in with the 'UKHC scene'?

"Well, the new record is just Freebase!" states Mark emphatically. "This is us. I think that we can safely say now, we have carved a familiar sound, the 'Freebase groove'. We certainly made a very conscious effort not to fall into the trap of, 'Oh, we had better do a UK metalcore CD'. Not that we don't like that style, and there are some really good bands out there, but I really feel that they need to start injecting something of their own into that style, just to help make them stand out, and develop their own sound a little.

"And before all the gossip-mongers and shit stirrers start," he adds defiantly, "Stop! Count to ten, read it again and digest what I have just said. We didn't want to turn out a CD that people could say, 'Oh, that's another typical release, just what we expected.' 'My Life...' is in a similar vein, admittedly, but it is also very different. It is a good combination of hardcore and metal and a little punk, I feel. Freebase have always stuck to what we believe, and we just want to help keep some variety in the UK scene."

Judging by the band's response at the recent Chuck Schuldiner Benefit show in

Bradford, they are now more than capable of crossing some boundaries that their first album may have found unattainable. Despite 'My Life...' being as gnarly as any good punk record, it's executed with the sort of professional precision usually reserved for the metal scene.

"Yes, we did very well at that show," recalls the heavily tattooed vocalist, "But why shouldn't we have? As I said, there are certain elements in our music, especially the new stuff, that most people can draw from. It's weird because, when we first started, Freebase were too metal for a lot of the hardcore fans, and now because we are not 'twin guitar', we are not metal enough! Also, because of the way we look, some of the punks will say that we have nothing to do with punk at all! So we just try to avoid the 'category' listings altogether. We're basically a good crossover band. We take elements of all our favourite styles and we blend the 'Freebase Cocktail'."

And an intoxicating little tipple it is too.

Fuck Reading Festival – issue 33 (August 1996)

Fuck Reading – Sick Of It All, by Naki

The UK punk community's been staging its annual Fuck Reading event for some time now, but this year's bash promises to be something else indeed. With US hardcore bands like Madball playing alongside the likes of the Anti-Nowhere League, August 25th promises to be a mighty transatlantic culture clash. Ian Glasper, a man happy on both sides of the pond, found out what hardcore giants Sick Of It All and LA punks Snap-Her thought of playing with their childhood heroes, and what English punk

Fuck Reading – Peter And The Test Tube Babies, Switzerland 2004, by Shelly Slater

legends Peter And The Test Tube Babies and The Business reckoned to sharing a bill with the Yanks...

You know how certain things in music become an institution, and every now and then need a good kick in the ass to puncture their over-inflated self-important world-view? A few years back, the punk community decided the annual Reading Festival was just such a target, with a big bullseye spray-painted on its out-of-shape behind, and they organised a spiky-topped alternative, naming it, in true punk fashion, 'Fuck Reading'. Nothing like a bit of subtlety, is there?

Well, the Fuck Reading event has become as important a fixture in the musical calendar as its fairy godmother, at least to those in the know, and the one coming up in late August looks set to be the strongest bill yet. This year also marks a very pronounced re-unification of hardcore and punk, two sub-genres that were spawned in the same pool, but forked off in slightly different directions as soon as they found their legs. As well as by Madball, the former gets represented by the much-respected Sick Of It All, returning to our fair isle to remind us all they're still out there, prior to the release of their long-awaited new album on East West later this year. They haven't exactly been sat around the big apple kicking their heels for the last two years, though, hell no! They've been wandering the world in support of 'Scratch The Surface', and touching up their tans in Australia, New Zealand and Brazil in the process.

"It's weird," Lou KoIIer, their quietly spoken frontman, tells me, on the band's metamorphosis into a touring machine. "Sometimes we'll be on tour, and we'll all get run down or something, but we'll get a week off, and we're all sat there, saying, 'God,

I wish we were playing!' We love what we're doing, otherwise we wouldn't do it.

"A lot of the kids we met in New Zealand have been in touch," he recalls fondly, "And they said that since we played out there, a lot of old bands have got back together, and some new bands have sprung up, and it's almost like we breathed new life into it out there. That makes me feel really good, very proud of what we've done with the band, y'know?"

Their visit down under inspired more than good feeling, too, ultimately resulting in a song on their new album. "We have a song called 'Us Vs. Them', which Armand wrote after meeting all those people on tour. A promoter we had out in Australia was really very shady, and didn't do any advertising, but the kids helped us out, making flyers and stuff, and made the tour a success.

"We have another song called 'Martin', which is about Pete's old landlord," Lou informs me, warming naturally enough to the topic of their forthcoming new record. "Whenever we went to Pete's house, he'd stand there cursing us, 'What the hell are you all doing here?', but one day, he was really struggling to take the garbage out, and me and Craig helped him out, and ever since we've been best friends, although he still cussed everyone else out. And then when we came home from tour, they'd found him dead in his apartment, just a bitter old man who died alone."

Are you ready for a Terrorizer exclusive? If not, skip on to the next paragraph, 'cos you're about to learn the name of the new record... well, nearly!

"It's a case of deciding which one to use, I guess it'll depend on which one gives us the best artwork, but Armand wants to call it 'Return Of The Dragon', and the rest of the band wanna call it 'Built To Last'. I actually wrote a song called 'Built To Last', and one of our roadies came up with a T-shirt, too, which had a big '57 Chevy on it. It's not really just about the band, it's about the whole way that people should try and keep their spirit alive. And I'm not just talking about the hardcore spirit, but a positive attitude overall."

After assuring me that the next record – whatever the fuck they call it – will be pure Sick Of It All – and then some – Lou ponders the bill they're appearing on in Brixton. As I said earlier, previous festivals haven't seen such heavyweights of punk and hardcore squaring off to each other (metaphorically speaking, of course), so it'll be intriguing to see if the two are as musically compatible as I always paint 'em to be.

"It'll be interesting to see what a guy who hasn't bought a new record since 1982 and has just listened to The Exploited 'til now will make of Sick Of It All! When we first got asked to do it, what immediately came to mind was, 'G.B.H. are doing it, yes!' They were a big influence on us when we started out in the hardcore movement in '82..."

I personally think everything will go swimmingly. After all, this band have penned a few Oi-ish anthems of their own, including covering Sham 69's 'Borstal Breakout', and more recently recording a cover of 'All Hell Breaks Loose' for a Misfits tribute album, due soon on Caroline, which'll see 'em alongside the likes of Pennywise and Rocket From The Crypt. Promises to be a blast, eh? The only mystery I can see is why the band aren't bigger than the sun.

"One reason is we never go to industry functions, 'schmoozing' as they call it," laughs

Fuck Reading – Snap-Her, courtesy of Katherine Vik @ Household Name

Lou. "Just that word makes me cringe! They want us to go and hang out with people who wouldn't give us the time of day if we weren't in a band...? Fuck that! I'd rather go and hang out with my friends! I'm not going to go down on bended knee and beg someone to play our video or interview our band. If they really like Sick Of It All, they'll do it anyway, y'know?"

And that attitude, ladies 'n' gentlemen, is pure punk, as are Snap-Her, a two-thirds female outfit out of LA who kick off an extensive UK tour with a slot at Fuck Reading. Like Lou Koller, vocalist Andrea Beltramo is full of enthusiasm for the bill, even though my phone call has gotten her out of bed...

"I've always loved English punk bands, that whole sound, a lot more than anything else. It's influenced me a lot more than, say, US punk. Ninety percent of my influences are English. I'm stoked, I can't wait to get over there, it's gonna be great."

Most of us know Snap-Her from their 'It Smells, It Burns, It Stings' debut on New Red Archives (and a fine slab of obnoxious snot-rock it is, too), but it's a little-known fact that they were actually Nina Hagen's backing band!

"Oh, that was just a temporary thing," Andi's keen to play the whole thing down. "Nina came to one of our shows about a year and a half ago, and she liked us, and she didn't have a back-up band at the time, so she had us play with her for about four months. We played five shows in LA and two in NYC, but it didn't go any further than that... but the experience was fun!"

The punk scene is renowned for being quick to judge and unforgiving on those that dare to get on. Did you lose any die-hard fans? "A lot of people were talking shit, saying we were sell-outs and rich bitches," she recalls with a derisive snort. "We were completely broke the whole time we played with Nina. When we first started, she required we rehearse seven nights a week to learn all the songs, as well as working our day-jobs. After six weeks of that, she said we could quit our day-jobs and she'd give us a salary, but that never happened. So we were borrowing money from people, we almost lost our homes, y'know? It became apparent we were getting blown out, so we had to go after our old jobs back."

Andi's day-job is working in a bondage store, by the way, restraint freaks, so no doubt she gets her leather and studs at a discount rate! I guess she's had to put employment on the back-burner again though, because their imminent European tour is a biggie, three months that begin at Fuck Reading, then sees them trekking all across the continent, before returning full circle to the UK in November for a handful of shows with The Misfits. England seems to be warming to these colourful punkers, what with London label Damaged Goods doing their next single and even considering a live album...

"Mmm, we'll see. I'm going to be very picky about the recording, the room we record in, the equipment we're using. In other words, I don't wanna release it for the sake of releasing it, but if it sounds good, we'll do it - if it doesn't, we won't, you know what I mean? I don't really know how people will take it, it's very early for us to do a live record."

So, make plenty of noise at the shows, readers, 'cos you may find yourself immortalised on plastic!

Moving our selective spotlight onto some of the English 'talent' who'll be present, and we have Brighton's infamous Peter and The Test Tube Babies, another band who did a live record early in their careers, and it didn't harm them. In fact, said record, 'Pissed And Proud', was their first album, and for me, their finest moment, their studio recordings never quite capturing the naughty chappies' riotous sense of humour. That said, another live record is on the cards, fifteen years on from the first and to be entitled 'Fuck Soundchecks!', which'll be the first album without their original bassist Trapper. "He was a bit of a cunt, really," laughs vocalist Peter matter-of-factly. "We had a big tour coming up to promote our last album ['Supermodels', on We Bite, that did good business here and even better on the continent – IG], 25 gigs in 25 days, a real big tour for us, and Trapper was like, 'Oh, I dunno if I want to do it, I can make more money working for other bands...' He works as a roadie, for bands like Incognito, and crap like that. At the end of the day, I was on my knees at one end of the telephone speaking to Trapper in Japan, begging him to do it, and he just said, 'Nah, I ain't doin' it - there ain't enough money in it'. And Hans, our temporary drummer, couldn't do it either, 'cos he was working with his other band, so me and Del, the guitarist, had this important tour coming up, with no band to do it with!

"Anyway, we got these two blokes in on bass and drums, who were already in a local band together, and we had a week's practise, and it was fuckin' brilliant. It was better than some of the stuff we did with Ogs and Trap. So, we finished practising on a Friday, did a warm-up gig on the Saturday in Chelmsford and went off to tour Europe the following Tuesday. We'd already got a new management deal, new album, new agent, and now we've got a new bassist and drummer as well.

These two guys are really keen. I doubt we'd have done that recent British tour if Trapper had still been in the band. He never wanted to do anything."

Seeing as the band have toured Europe on a regular basis while hardly ever gigging England, it's no surprise they ended up on a German label really. When I ask Peter how they came about the deal, he isn't too sure... "I don't have much to do with the business

Fuck Reading, The Business, by Gutterpunk Photography

side of it, it bores me. I don't mind earning the money then spending it, but actually getting down to percentages, I ain't got a fuckin' clue! That's what managers are for, innit? It was quite funny, 'cos they said, 'This is the gig when the record label are gonna turn up'," says Pete, dredging up another alcohol-tinged tour-story.

"I'd gotten absolutely fuckin' wrecked the night before, slept the whole day on the coach, missed the soundcheck, and about twenty minutes before we were on, I wandered into the dressing room, and there was all these punk rockers, and I'm saying, 'Where's the fuckin' record company? I thought a fuckin' record company was gonna be here?' Everyone was like, 'Yeah, this is them. This is Thomas, from We Bite, this guy with the blue hair is the boss!' I couldn't believe it, I was expecting a ponytail at least, and I got this spiky blue hair!"

Anyone familiar with the Test Tubes will know their penchant for amusing stories like 'Run Like Hell' or 'Intensive Care', but are they fact or fiction? "Ah, should I say or not?" he chuckles, before confessing, "Stuff like 'Transvestite' hasn't happened to me... yet – but it could happen to anyone,

really, couldn't it? 'Cringe' has actually happened to me though, when I was pissed out of my head in a German bar, trying to get off with a fucking bloke with long hair... "

So, metalheads, beware if you're approached at the bar by an inebriated punk clutching a bottle of Merrydown and singing the words to a song like 'Up Yer Bum'!

As well as G.B.H., One Way System and the Anti-Nowhere League, the English contingent is completed by the legendary Business. Despite their (undeserved) reputation, I found vocalist Mickey Fitz to be a thoroughly decent geezer, even if he was still reeling over Germany knocking England out of the European cup. His band have just signed to Boston's Taang Records, and they're working on a new album, which will no doubt be classic Business fare, in other words no-nonsense street-rock.

"We tend to be out on our own. We were never classed as a punk or a skin band, or a hardcore band, we were classed as a bit of each," he reckons. "On the new record, we'll diversify a fraction, but only on a coupla tracks, 'cos if we diversify too much, we'll lose the fans we've worked so hard to get. I think we've changed fractionally, but for the better, each record, but we're not going to go totally different, no fuckin' way. The Business is The Business, and if we changed our tune, excuse the pun, it just wouldn't be right."

I'm talking to Mickey here at home on the phone, and we pause while he watches the Sex Pistols on Top Of The Pops, and naturally enough after that interlude I wanna know what he thinks of all these punk bands reforming... "It depends on who they are, funnily enough," reasons Mickey. "There's been a lot of bands who worked for a long time, like ourselves, who never really split up, but a lot of bands go out there and think they're gonna earn a fortune just by playing a one-off show. A lot of the older bands think it's just gonna come to 'em, but they've gotta realise that punk's been taken over now, and there's a brand new set of bands out there, like Rancid, Offspring and Green Day. And hardcore is getting bigger and bigger now, with all these bands like Biohazard and Sick Of It All. We've worked bloody hard for this, we've stuck it out, and I just want it to carry on."

And like the other bands on the bill, Mickey is psyched for Fuck Reading. "We've spent the last two and a half years playing Europe and America, but now we're going to try and play England again. Let's hope the time is right and there's no trouble at any of our shows. None of us need that kind of idiotic behaviour. l just know that a lot of UK punks are gonna be dead shocked when they watch Madball - they look like really normal people, but when they hear the music, they'll be like, 'Fuck me, this is as hard as any punk music!'"

Well, if that l'il lot hasn't whet your appetite for the gig, then nothing will. You want a happening show? Fuck Reading, be at the Brixton Academy on Sunday 25th August. See you in the pit.

RIP Mickey Fitz

FURY OF FIVE - ISSUE 38 (JANUARY 1997)

Fury of Five

Believe me, never before has a band been more aptly named! Fury of Five are just that, the exorcism, through some of the heaviest hardcore you'll ever clap ears on, of all the angst and tension that can build up in five volatile individuals.

"We take it to its fullest extent", explains their guitarist, Jay Fury, who despite the intimidating connotations of the name is a thoroughly decent geezer. "Look at all the lyrics on our album ['No Reason To Smile', on Germany's Gain Ground Records - IG], it's all about reality today. There's no fantasy, it's not fiction, it's about the hardships of life, everyday things, that either happen to us, or people who are close to us. The assumed names are just extensions of us as people - James lsmean, Jay Fury, Chico Violencia, Mike Terror, Chris Rage... they just sum it up! Come and see us live, see the way we are on stage, and it'll all make sense. We go nuts, it's very intense. We're not joking around, we're in your face, we come out and go for the jugular."

Such an explosive release is always awesome to behold, but it can often lead to trouble on the dance floor. After all, the dividing line between a slam pit and a brawl is a thin one.

"Mmm, we've had our fair share of violence at shows", says Jay thoughtfully, "But I

Fury of Five – by Dave Thomas

think a lot of hard and heavy bands have that also. People come to our shows to vent their anger and stress, and they come there only for that reason. They don't come along to socialise, or to meet their girlfriends. They do what they have to do, and sometimes there's fights, but what do you expect, when so many people release so much aggression all at once?"

Tough words indeed, but this seems to be one New Jersey band who walk it how they talk it, having seen more than their fair share of hard times. Vocalist James Ismean is actually an ex-con, which adds a certain authenticity to many of his lyrics.

"He was present at a robbery", explains Jay, the self-titled purveyor of 'six deadly strings' (hear the album and you'll know why!) "He definitely didn't do anything illegal; he'd left the scene before it went down. The guys who did the crime pointed the finger at him, and he was locked down for two years. He did the time, and when he came out, he rehabilitated himself, stayed outta trouble, and really worked to turn his life around in a positive way.

"That's what I say to anyone who accuses us of being negative. We're not at all, we're very positive. We've all had our hardships in the past. I've been through a lot of drug problems, y'know? We've turned that into this. We come out and let the kids know that we've been there, too."

Jay's rightly chuffed with their debut, 'cos it's a monster, in every sense of the word. Fat riffs boil malignantly over a huge, groovin' rhythm, as James spits out his righteous venom with a vengeance. Any fans of Biohazard or Merauder should make haste and go check these guys out, right now. And everywhere, impossible to ignore, their attitude and self-belief burns in ever bludgeoning chord.

"This is the first thing I've ever been proud of, the first thing I've been a major part of, that's doing something good and going places. Nuthin's gonna stop us, nuthin's gonna get in our way, nuthin' can hold us down. Anger is our driving force, and no matter what happens, no matter what we sound like, that'll always be there, driving us forward."

FURY OF FIVE - ISSUE 52 (MARCH 1998)

Fury of Five - by Dave Thomas

The heaviest thing out of New Jersey since... well, we forget when... Fury Of Five have just declared themselves 'At War With The World' on their second album of blistering, but challenging, hardcore. Though funnily enough, they start in on the Germans first...

"They were kind of weird, man. Usually when we play it's real chaotic, we get a lot of feedback 'cos we put a lot of energy into every show. Out there was dead, y'know what I mean? The crowds were so lame. We tried to do what we do, and all they did was stand there and clap. It kinda pissed me off."

The 'out there' referred to above is Germany, and doing the referring is one James Ismean, vocalist of Fury Of Five, the most aggressive band to ever come out of New Jersey, if not the world. When I last hooked up with these guys, we were opening for them and Integrity in Rennes, France, and they told me then that they weren't particularly impressed with the response they'd got in Germany. I was intrigued to find out why, especially when I witnessed the carnage they inspired in the Rennes audience. As James says above, it pissed him off, and he isn't a guy to trifle with, as one hapless German found out at his own cost.

"Uh yeah, I ended up jumping off the stage and drop-kicking some guy. He was ridiculing us, and that's not what we're out there for. I warned him three times to chill out. I told him to back off, that just 'cos I couldn't understand his language didn't mean I couldn't see he was making fun of us. I was trying to be a nice guy, but he kept pursuing the issue, and I'm not the kind of guy you push, y'know what l mean? And in the end, he paid the price. I gave him the chance to walk away, and he just kept on. And l didn't go all the way to Europe to be ridiculed."

Nosirree, whatever you say, Jim! As any readers out there who've not encountered FoV before will be starting to realise, these guys are driven by some burning inner rage, hence their manic live performances, and hence, l s'pose, the title of their incendiary new album, 'At War With The World', their second full-lengther, but first for new Century Media offshoot, Kingfisher.

"l am at war with the world, I really am," James tells me in his quiet, but deadly serious drawl. "Every day I get up and have to face another issue, another obstacle. Every day's a fight, and I'll probably fight 'til the day I die, I'll never change. The band's my release. I'm an angry dude, and that's where it all goes."

If you've ever met, or seen, James, you don't need to be a genius to figure out that pumping iron is another 'release' he takes pretty seriously.

"Yeah, every morning I hit the gym so I can start the day with a good head. If l don't, I'm likely to vent my rage on someone else. I've been doing that ever since I got out of prison, so I don't end up right back there. I work out every single day, it's good. It's good for anyone with a problem, with low self-esteem. I don't do it to get big, that's just what happens – I do it to keep a clear head, so I don't fall back in to that trap of drink and drugs and acting like a retard. It's something I have to do, to keep myself busy with the positive, to keep me away from all that negative shit."

And the new album itself is certainly pumped up and rearing to go, metal and hardcore fuelled by a rush of pure testosterone and adrenaline. Yet it's also surprisingly progressive and experimental.

"We definitely want to do more than just chunk out E chords," their guitarist Jay tells me. "A lot of bands just do that, but we wanna do something different. We'll always strive for more; we want to take our sound to the next level. The next album will blow this one away, y'know? Just like this one blows away that first one ['No Reason To Smile' on Gain Ground – IG], it's just gonna get better and better."

Well, Century Media obviously share in the band's confidence in themselves, 'cos they've signed them up to Kingfisher for quite a long deal, involving plenty of albums in the future. "A lot of bands would worry about such a long deal," continues Jay, "But for us it's no problem. We have so much fury and attitude, it just flows out of us. We can easily write five or six albums, no sweat, and they'll all be diverse, they won't all sound the same."

If you want to see some of this rage in action, you need only get along early to any of the imminent Pro-Pain UK shows, which Fury Of Five are supporting on - jeez, what a hateful bill that's gonna be... miss it at your peril – and if you need any more convincing, back to James for a taster of what's in store.

Fury of Five, Rennes, by Sam Lennox

"You're gonna see mayhem like you've never seen before, y'know what I'm saying?" he growls. "We're so real, so raw, some people can't even comprehend what they're seeing. We'll bring chaos, we'll come out and go BAM!, and be gone before you know what hit you. If people won't dance, I'll dance myself; if they won't move, I'll go out there and move 'em myself. They'll get involved, one way or another."

CHAPTER G: CAN'T WE ALL JUST GET LONG...?

GAMA BOMB — ISSUE 235 (MAY 2013)

Gama Bomb, 2013, by Ruth Medjber

Those Irish masters of ripping metal, Gama Bomb, are back with album number four and sounding more sprightly than ever, despite the last few years being somewhat of a test of their intestinal fortitude as they've changed labels, changed line-ups and underwent surgery to keep their brand of deliriously high energy thrash metal alive and kicking. But before we get into all the behind-the-scenes shit, let's talk about what an awesome slice of speed metal 'The Terror Tapes' is - and catchier than a bag of fish hooks too.

"When I listen to it now, I hear something to rival 'Among The Living'," says vocalist Philly Byrne proudly, and rightly so, "It's got loads of character, and is quite punky... we really strove to write songs you can get up and shout along to. When I listen to all the bands that I consider absolutely unbelievable... Dio, Priest, Sabbath, Rainbow, Agent Steel... nearly all their choruses are huge, really simple, really great to sing along to, and work really well live. We used to write songs by throwing lyrics all over riffs, and seeing what might work as a chorus, but this time we knew what works as a chorus and we aimed for that unashamedly catchy feel deliberately, which makes the songs more fun to play.

"I don't think we've sacrificed any technicality for it though; there's still riffs on here that would never have happened on other albums, you know? And there's still blazing solos and incredible drum work on it. It's about finding that balance between being really technical, which is what metal people love, and being really catchy... that's, you know, the pop sensibility - maybe this is like the thrash metal 'Thriller' [laughs]?"

And those off-the-wall lyrics that made everyone spit their beer over themselves previously? Thankfully still intact and more irreverent than ever on songs like 'Shitting Yourself To Live' and 'Smoke The Blow With Willem Dafoe'...

"I wouldn't say we've bought anything more serious to the table this time," admits Philly, "But we've kept the same amount of seriousness that we've always had – which is that we approach the lyrics seriously, and we do write the occasional topical song. There is a song on the album about racism and free speech, and we did originally have aspirations to make this a serious concept album, about the world's dependency on nuclear power, which seemed a really worthy direction, but the closer we came to recording it, it was apparent that some stuff was going to fly and some stuff wasn't, and the stuff that was most satisfying and most fun to write choruses for, was the more absurb stuff. Not necessarily the really wacky jocular stuff, but the absurd stuff, the really obtuse topics, so we ended up with songs like 'Beverley Hills Robocop', and we've got the first ever mention on a thrash metal album, to my knowledge at least, of the word 'quiche'!

"The typical tropes in metal really bore me," he continues, "Songs about being depressed, being angry, being a slave to your emotions; those things don't really inspire us, and I don't really believe they inspire the majority of people either. If you're a teenager, or emotionally unstable, you can identify over and over again with songs about being angry, but in general people want to hear songs about cool stuff, something that puts a smile on their face..."

But whilst it's still all fun and games on disc, Gama Bomb have definitely grown up since 2009's 'Tales From The Grave In Space' and have had to take a long hard look at themselves and the aspirations that drive them to make music.

"Yeah, it's been an extremely difficult period for us, especially the last year-and-a-half, because every single obstacle you could put in front of a band was there, and I'm sure that the course of action of most people in our situation would have been to just call it a day. There were so many opportunities to just give up: our guitarist of ten years, Luke, left, then I had a polyp in my throat, a lump on my vocal chord, which I had to have surgery to remove, then Domo, our guitar player, broke a tendon in his finger, and couldn't play guitar for eight months, then we got into these wrangles with our label, then we had to work out who would sign us... all these problems would have been bad enough on their own, but when they all arrived together, it was a shit storm!

"But what came out of all that was a resolve to work harder, and do what we do even better, so we do now take what we do more seriously, and appreciate what we're doing so much more. When you have to have surgery to keep playing, it makes you realise how much you love playing; when you have to fight to keep your band going, it makes you appreciate your fans – we were gone for a long time, at least in metal terms, for a young band, and our fans never stopped asking after us and caring about our music. When you spend months and months and months wading through bullshit to make your album, when you finally make it happen, it hammers home how much it meant to you. So, yeah, hard times, a lot of bother, but in the end we're all the more stronger for it because we had to harden the fuck up..."

So, just what kind of label wrangles forced Gama Bomb to jump ship from such a well-known bastion of extreme metal as Earache and finance this fourth album themselves? "The situation we had with Earache was very fruitful and very positive," says Philly tactfully, "And we got lots of opportunities out of it, but it reached a point where fundamental shit wasn't going right... personal relationships and all that kind of stuff... and eventually we couldn't really continue with the band if we didn't have a say in it, so we had to reach an agreement with them, where we could go off and do our thing and they could continue to do theirs.

"And although there were other labels who were saying, 'Let's talk...', we knew that if we wanted this to happen in 2013 we had to go ahead and make it happen ourselves. It was a bit shit scary really, but everyone really stepped up, to be honest. We hired a studio in Dublin and [producer] Scott [Atkins] came over and we did all the drums in a week, then we hired another studio over here a few weeks later, and did some of the vocals and guitars... I was cycling down after work at 7 pm and tracking vocals until after midnight, and Scott was staying on the floor here. It was really hardcore, and it really reminded me of what it was like when we were unsigned and doing an album – it was very much back to how we did our first album, except we're not nineteen anymore! "Then we went over to England and recorded bass and more vocals at Scott's. And that's why the process took five months; it was self-financed and done ad hoc, as and when we could do it. But it was really good for the songs, because we had a long time to consider them; some of the songs date back to 2010, so we've had ages and ages to argue over them and make them better. And when I listen to it now I'm astonished at how strong and cohesive it is.

"And we've got a really good arrangement with [their new label] AFM now; we've made a great connection with the people, and we were able to approach them on an even footing, we weren't just some schoolboy thrash band being picked up and given their conditions, they actually respect us as artists and we respect them as a label, so we were able to come together in the middle really well... it feels more like a team again. We're very positive once more – but it's a hard-fought positivity, after a year in the toilet!"

Yet despite all the trials and tribulations, Gama Bomb haven't wavered stylistically one iota and have delivered a classic Gama Bomb album to reward all those who awaited their return so loyally.

"We have rules for the band, and we've had rules since day one – you'll never hear keyboards or acoustic intros or ballads or breakdowns with Gama Bomb. We set those rules from the start, and we're still abiding by those rules. We always wanted to be like a thrash metal AC/DC; we have a tone, we have our sound and structure, and we know what a good Gama Bomb song sounds like, and we're just going to stay true to it and refine it. So it's not as if our first album sounds exactly like this one, but it does sound exactly like us, if you know what I mean? We're not surprising anyone; people who know us and love us do so because of the songs that we write, and we're going to continue giving them exactly what they want.

"Don't forget, when we started the band, there was no one talking about thrash, there was no one playing thrash, and we started the band out of our love of straight ahead crossover thrash, and it made sense to stick with that formula. And thank fuck we have, because unbelievably the music became popular again...

"I think this is one of the most significant thrash albums of the last twenty years!" he states in conclusion. "It's different from other albums; it's absurd and irreverent, but the riffs are fucking outstanding and the choruses are all there. I honestly don't see why this album couldn't change the landscape for thrash... I don't care if only 2000 people think it's raging or we make the top of the Billboard charts with it, as long as people get to hear it - and we can start gigging and drinking again!"

GIGANTOR – ISSUE 18 (MARCH 1995)

Gigantor play mighty fast and tuneful hardcore. Well, that's according to Ian Glasper, who talks here to main-men Jens (guitar/vocals) and Jay (bass)...

If you're a fan of fast tuneful hardcore, then may I suggest you go and check out Gigantor, one of the best exponents of the style I've heard for a long time. Although they've only been together since 1991, this German five-piece have a considerable back catalogue on the Lost And Found label, much of which is compiled on latest release, 'It's Gigantic', and it's with that new album that we start...

Jens (guitar/vocals) explains, "The idea behind the new CD is that we put out most of our stuff as 7"s, which are all sold out now, except the last one, so, to make it all available for newer fans, we decided to put it out on CD, along with some stuff we had left, and also three new songs that we recorded just for that.

Gigantor, 1994

Anyone familiar with Gigantor will know that they've covered some pretty unusual songs for a hardcore band, one of my faves being 'Tainted Love' by Soft Cell, of which they've done two versions!

"The secret track on 'Magic Bozo Spin' [their debut album] was our original version, which we just recorded for fun – we never planned it to be a real track on the album, so we made it a 'secret' track on the end. The one on 'It's Gigantic' came about one night when me, Gagu [vocals] and Nico [other guitar - the line up being completed by Jay on bass and Heiko on drums] were sat drinking beer - it was 3am in the morning, and Nico put the tape on half speed, added some keyboards and a weird guitar solo, and Gagu sang to it." Jen adds laughing, "A lot of people don't understand that version! It appeared on a split single with Goober Patrol [the melodic pop-punk band from Norwich]."

What do these bands that you've covered think of your versions? "I met Martin Gore from Depeche Mode, and he totally liked our 'Everything Counts', and in a German mag, Rock Hard, Gene Simmons was reviewing KISS cover versions, and he reviewed our version of 'Beth', and he was, like, 'Who's that? It's really good! Is it The Hard-Ons? Or The Buzzcocks?' No, it's Gigantor!"

Other bands these guys have covered include the Misfits, E.L.O., George Michael, Sting, and too many Jap punk bands to list...! I ask Jens who he'd most like to see cover one of their songs? "It's always an honour if another band does one of your songs, but if any band, it would probably be the Ramones or The Dickies, which are my favourite bands... but it would be great to hear it from any band!"

Gigantor, Japan, 1995

Of course, their name is taken from a Dickies song... isn't it? "Gigantor was originally a comic in Japan – his name was something like Iron Man 28," Jay tells me, before Jen elaborates, "Then they made a cartoon show for the American market and re-named him Gigantor. He's a giant robot, controlled by a young kid, Jimmy Sparks! The song 'Gigantor' by The Dickies was the theme song from the TV show."

And wasn't your song 'Donut Man' nearly a DICKIES song? "The old bass player from The Dickies knows the guy who wrote this song – it's from the '40s or something – he made a demo of it, and gave it to The Dickies, to see if they wanted to play it, but they didn't really like it, and said no. Since he's a friend of mine, I asked him if we could do the song... it's a good song, even if it was rejected by them! We've done a video clip for it too, which we made in the studio. The Dickies were invited to do our Japanese tour with us in March, but they never got back to the label, never answered Vinyl Japan's faxes, so they said, 'Fuck them!'"

Have you got any plans to tour England? "We're trying to," Jens sighs. "Lost And Found have already talked to someone, but I'm not really well informed on all that. We got offered a tour with Black Train Jack, but we couldn't do it, 'cos it was in January and Jay was busy with work..."

And it's Jay who takes up the phone when I ask about the lyrics to 'Gigantor Positive', seeing as he wrote them. "I come from LA, where everyone parties all the time, and there was no such scene as straightedge. So, when we first ran into straightedge, when I first went on the road with Channel 3 in 1983, I was like, 'Wow! I don't get it!' A bunch of kids saying, 'Blahblahblah!' who were too young to buy alcohol anyhow! This movement and that way of thinking is very deep into that music scene. Basically, that's not what we're about... this is supposed to be fun. We know some people base their lives on music, and identify with bands, but it's not our scene at all. If you're into it, fine... if not, that's okay too!"

Lastly, what can we expect from Gigantor in 1995? "We are already collecting songs for the new album," Jens takes up the baton for the final home straight. "We have plenty of ideas, and we'll be rehearsing it before we go to Japan, then we'll hopefully record perhaps twenty new songs when we get home..."

GIGANTOR – ISSUE 28 (MARCH 1996)

Gigantor, 1995

Our man Ian Glasper caught the Tokyo-Hannover shuttle to find out what went on when German pop-punk band Gigantor exported their 'Atomic' album and live show to Japan...

A lot's been happening in the Gigantor camp of late, not least of all the release of their 'Atomic' album on Lost And Found to widespread critical acclaim and their newfound popularity in Japan. I hooked up with two justifiably chuffed Gigantors to hear all about it. "Vinyl Japan contacted our record company Lost And Found first, and Lost And Found told them... uh... to fuck off," laughs Jay, the band's laid-back bassist, "So then they contacted us directly, with

the idea of us going out to tour there, and to make a record to promote the shows, and it worked out great. In all reality, a 'Japanese tour' really only meant three dates in Tokyo, but for us it was an experience that we've talked about endlessly ever since!"

405

"It's like a Disneyland for rock musicians," says Jens, main songwriter and guitarist. "We had to sign autographs everywhere we walked... even at the airport customs when we were leaving. It was unbelievable, all the shows were sold out. Our new record 'Atomic' is coming out on the JVC label, which is the next biggest label in Japan after Sony, and hopefully we'll get back there in May or June."

What were the differences between the Japanese audiences and the European ones you're used to?

"Well, the German audience is something we're still working on," claims Jay. "We get to play in front of a bunch of different audiences, but none of them so far are really Gigantor audiences 'cos we're still an up-and-coming band, and we haven't done like thirty five hundred live gigs. Building up our live audience is something we're still doing here... but there, it was immediately Gigantor mania! The house was full, and everyone knew every word!

"But they don't make one sound between the songs," he continues, laughing, "Not one word! It's not like 'Cheap Trick - Live At Budokan'! During the songs, everyone was bouncing off the walls, but between the songs? Silence! One of my friends who's been over there with heavy metal bands, he said the same thing happens to everyone, and he thinks it's 'cos the people want to concentrate on understanding what you're saying between the songs."

Talk then turns to their latest album, and a fine slab of prime pop-punk it is, too. Now, love or hate that genre, there's no denying that our five dizzy Germans are leaders in the field, and the new record has less cover versions on it than we've previously come to expect...

"We wanted to squash our critics' idea that we are just a copy band," Jay affirms, "And just like the legions of other copy bands out there that no one really needs, bands that can only get by when using other people's songs. That's definitely not the case with us."

The Maxx Payne who does a guest solo... is that Maxx Payne the famous wrestler? "You got it! Maxx Payne the wrestler. Wrestlers also have to pay their dues by working the smaller gigs before they get the big shows, and one of his small gigs was a six-month tournament here in Germany, including six weeks here in Hannover. And we got talking, just two American guys, both music fans, and we kept in contact over the years. When he was over here last, doing twelve shows in Germany with the WWF, he stayed over to do a coupla weeks in Hannover, and we grabbed him one night and said, 'Sit down here and play on our record, fucker!' And he did, and it rocks!"

And lastly, to answer allegations that Gigantor aren't the busiest band in the world when it comes to gigging, Jay takes the line one more time: "We consider all shows, but we haven't any tour offers so far. We could go out and play every shithole... and that's what we do - but only on weekends," he laughs. "Once a week is enough... sports people aren't expected to do it any more often! You have to consider if the most creative thing for you to be doing musically or mentally is to be sitting in a fucking stinkin' bus driving from town to town! We're big believers in using and abusing every fuckin' media source possible these days to spread our evil message. And the live presentation? We're there! We're always ready to go on stage and tear it up... just don't make us go through hell to do it?"

GOD DETHRONED – ISSUE 66 (MAY 1999)

God Dethroned, by Stefan Schipper

After he'd dug his Malleus Maleficarum out from under all those Easter egg wrappers, we sent our very own Witchfinder General, Ian Glasper, off to conduct an Inquisition into Holland's newest death metal phenomenon, God Dethroned, whose third album, 'Bloody Blasphemy', has pretty much ensured that they won't be getting themselves a place behind the pearly gates come the Judgement Day, no matter how good a reference they get off Metal Blade.

Guitars howl around your head like a raging wind, the accompanying crescendo of blur speed percussion flays your senses, as evil rhetoric is spat forth with a genuine venom for Christianity... nope, it's not from Norway, nor Sweden or America either; it's the macabre vision of none other than Holland's God Dethroned, who so perked up last month's cover CD with their 'Boiling Blood' track. Anyone who was kicked into next week by that sensitive little ditty, resplendent with its many Slayerisms, really oughta check out their new (third) album, 'Bloody Blasphemy' on Metal Blade, from whence said song was exhumed. 'Boiling Blood' is but one of nine stunningly malevolent writhing tentacles all looking to drag you in and drain you of life... or something like that, ahem!

"The solo might sound like Slayer, yes," concedes vocalist/guitarist Henri Sattler, "But the song? No! Of course, we knew that when people hear that first guitar riff, they're bound to think of Slayer, but it's a great riff, and a good aggressive song, so why not use it? A lot of people say it's their favourite track, because it's so catchy..."

'Catchy' in the same way that a fish gaff through the neck is 'catchy', you understand, not in some poncey rock song way. Hearing the high level of confidence and musicianship on display on 'Bloody Blasphemy', it's hard to fathom that God Dethroned actually broke up after their first album ['The Christ Hunt', 1992, re-released on Cold Blood Industries in '98 - IG]... what happened there then?

"Well, the reason we split was, the record company we had back then fucked up every single thing that they possibly could," recalls Henri disdainfully. "For example, they didn't even put the band's name on the front cover of the album! So, you can imagine, we didn't exactly sell a lot of CDs, and didn't benefit from any promotion, and after a while, we had certain problems within the band and decided to just call it a day.

"l then joined another band called Ministry of Terror, who played a more old style thrash metal, and when we were on a European tour with Impaled Nazarene, such a lot of people came up to me and told me that they had really liked God Dethroned, I eventually decided to put the band back together."

So, how did you hook up with Metal Blade? Surely any aspiring metal band's dream!

"We recorded 'The Grand Grimoire' album ourselves, before we even had a deal," reveals the (mad) axeman, "And we sent out some tapes to labels; we only sent out five... four to labels we wanted to get on, and one to a label who we knew wanted to sign us anyway. Of course, that label gave us a contract, but it wasn't a very good one, and while we were considering that, Metal Blade made us an offer, which was much better, and a lot more interesting for us as a band."

And the rest as they say is history, 'The Grand Grimoire' garnered almost unanimously positive reviews, and the band landed first the Six Feet Under support across Europe, and then a slot on the notorious No Mercy festival tour, which saw them playing to packed, enthusiastic theatres, and becoming the name on the tips of tongues of extreme metal fans all across the continent. After such a runaway success story, did you feel under any pressure when you entered the studio to record that all-important third full-lengther?

"Not at the start, when we were writing," reckons Henri, "But once we got into the studio to record, we started to worry that the songs weren't as good as the ones on 'The Grand Grimoire', and that was very stressful. But we carried on and finished it, because there was no turning back and we still basically believed in the songs. This album's more extreme, so I dunno, I think we were afraid it wouldn't do as well as the last one, but now we're very pleased with it. There's some shorter songs, there's better playing, more aggression, and the production's better."

And let's face it, what more could you want from a death metal record, eh? 'BIoody Blasphemy' tears along at a frightening pace, but is also imbued with great red clots of visceral melody as well. To put it frankly, 'Boiling Blood' might sound like SIayer, but on the whole, this will definitely please fans of At The Gates even more.

"Yes, we are influenced by all those Scandinavian death metal bands, like Dissection... and At The Gates," he concedes. "Especially 'The Grand Grimoire' had a lot of ATG influence on it, whilst 'The Christ Hunt' was more like early Entombed – we are big fans of those Swedish bands."

Not drawing too much from the Dutch metal legacy then? "There aren't so many good death metal bands here right now – there were, but they've all split up, and there's not many new bands coming up to replace them. There are a lot of fans of death metal music here, just not enough bands...which is obviously quite a good situation for us in a lot of ways!"

One look at the cover painting, of three demons ripping Christ from his cross, and it seems quite ironic that I'm typing this up on Good Friday! And the lyrics to songs such as the title track – which is a charming number about Christ being eaten alive after being stolen off the cross by a cannibal – are just as likely to raise eyebrows with the god-fearing out there as the gaudy artwork. And with the band being credited inside the booklet for not only playing their instruments but also, for example, 'the abduction of the Archangel Gabriel', and even 'the future assassination of Pope Johannes Paulus II', it would seem to be a reputation they revel in.

"But the funny thing about 'Bloody Blasphemy' [the song, not the album – IG] is that it is sort of inspired by the film 'The Life Of Brian'! It's actually very light-hearted, about Jesus thinking someone wants to save him, to help him off the cross, when actually they want to eat him [laughs gleefully]!"

I bet the God Squad don't see the funny side of it, though?

"In Holland. we often play youth centres, that are sponsored by the local government, and their officials come to the centres, to check on their investments and they see posters for all the shows coming up - and they want to know why the centre is letting a band like God Dethroned play there! That's how these religious organisations come to know of us. Holland is very liberal in many ways, but when it comes to music like this, it is not at all tolerant. Now in Belgium... they are liberal. We've even played in a church itself over there!"

And how does it feel to be snarling the words to a song like 'Bloody Blasphemy' in the 'house of God'?

"Well, we didn't have that song in our set back then." he replies, rather pedantically, "But it was still kind of strange. But a church is just a building, just bricks and stones. On our European tour we have coming up with Immortal, our gig in Poland has been forbidden by the authorities, because of the band names. So, in some countries, it can be very strict."

But there's more to 'Bloody Blasphemy' than just taking pot-shots at him upstairs; God Dethroned have also embraced their own country's history as lyrical influence, penning, not only 'Soul Capture 1562' about the Flying Dutchman, but also 'Firebreath', which seems to have - gasp! Shock! Horror! - an almost anti-English feel about it!

"Yeah, that's kinda true," laughs Henri, just a bit awkwardly, "But they're not really intended that way. I wrote that song about Michael de Ruyter. There was the Three Day War between the Dutch and the English in 1667, and he was the only enemy sailor to ever sail the River Thames - not even the Germans in WW2 got that far - so he's something of a national hero here. I just like historical themes; on 'The Grand Grimoire', I wrote a song about a Dutch sailor who sailed to the Indies via the North Pole, instead of the South."

Oh well, at least such academic themes prove that God Dethroned aren't just a bunch of murdering thugs. You're not a misanthropic psychopath, are you, Henri?

"No, I'm not," deadpans the singer. Yeah, right. So, when will we get to hear your fiery brand of melodic death over here? "Um, when the English audiences get over the lyrics to 'Firebreath'!"

God Lives Underwater – issue 27

(February 1996)

God Lives Underwater

You may not have heard of God Lives Underwater before, but Ian Glasper reckons all that will change with the release of their debut album, 'Empty'. Here he talks with band main man David Reilley to hear a little more....

God Lives Underwater are a refreshingly different band from Pennsylvania. Calling their 'Empty' debut album on American Recordings a techno-rock-metal album is copping out somewhat because there's much more going on than first meets the eye. Um, I mean 'ear'. Louise at American's London office linked me up with main collaborator David Reilley (guitar, keyboards, vocals) to discover more...

I know you guys got signed supernaturally quickly, please tell us about it.

"Well, we sent one song out without even having a name for the band to twelve labels and every single label called us the day they got the tape. It also ended up with a DJ friend Destructo, who works at American Records. He played it to the staff there and they didn't like it at all. They thought it sucked," chuckles David. "They thought we sounded like Faith No More, which really pissed me off, 'cos I can't stand FNM and I've never listened to more than one song by them. Anyway, he waited for Rick Rubin to come into the office and slipped him the tape, and Rick was like, 'Fly these guys out here, I want to meet them...' Because Rick, for the last few years, has been trying to combine techno and hard rock and he's been dreaming of a band like us."

Did you find it scary getting signed so quickly?

"Well, I've been working at this pretty much my whole life. Me and Jeff have been working together for ten years and I myself have been playing the piano since I was four, then I learned to play drums; even when I was in high school, I was sending out demo tapes, you know? So I wasn't surprised to get a deal that quickly; I knew we'd get one eventually and I also knew that what we had to offer was something different, and that at the very least it would catch an A&R guy's ear."

One American magazine went as far as describing you as 'the future of music'. What do you think about that?

"It's very flattering, but I don't want to be conceited and say that we are the future of music," he states modestly. "I think that most rock bands out there now don't use computers, only because they've never heard anything other than techno... and techno sounds like computers! I mean, I love techno, I love dancing to techno beats, but it doesn't really have much soul. If they realize that the computer is just like having a different instrument in the band, more of them would be making music like ours. There's some industrial bands that now do it, that also have keyboards and guitars too, but none of them write songs in a traditional rock fashion. We've been doing pretty well; we're living off it, but there's the possibility that people will never get it. It could just be too weird, you know?"

You got picked for the 'Johnny Mnemonic' soundtrack, which is testament to your futuristic sound...

"Yeah, that's why we got the part. I mean, I wasn't crazy about the movie, it stinks. But I was honoured that a William Gibson movie would have a song of ours in it. Originally, they had a U2 song playing for the ending, but they liked our song better, so at the last minute we ended up getting in. They were originally using our music in just an action scene, so we were like, 'Wow! Our biggest accomplishment so far...'"

I know you got into a bit of trouble recently at a show – what happened there?

"We did a tour headlining some radio festivals; it was late and there were about 5000 people there; I told the kids to go crazy – and they did. And the police there had never seen moshing before, and they turned us off. The kids had been waiting for us all day long, so when we got turned off, they rioted. The police maced all the kids, and then arrested me. I spent the night in jail, for fifteen hours, and they taunted me, made fun of me, just acted like exactly every other policeman who's ever stepped on my back, you know?"

Have you been charged?

"Yeah, I actually have a pending court trial and they're charging me with inciting a riot," sighs a bemused-sounding David. "It's ridiculous, I can't believe it. I think I'll get a fine and I'll have to do community service, but I can't see when I'll have time to spend 40 hours cleaning fire hydrants or picking up trash on the highway. I haven't had five minutes to call my parents lately. Things are moving so quickly..."

You guys skate, right? But I don't think your music will hold much appeal for that particular market though?

"We do skate, but I don't think we'll ever cross over to skateboarders 'cos they listen to punk rock and hip hop. They won't have anything to do with us... they'd probably call us fags!"

In their openminded way!

"Yeah," he laughs, "As openminded as they usually are, robbing stores and whatever else they do. But yeah, we do skate; we're just not 'skaters' in that sense of the word."

And you have another odd hobby – collecting snakes, I believe?

"I like snakes, but the other guy Jeff [Turzo – guitar and keyboards, the rest of the band for live appearances being Andrew McGee on guitar and Adam Kary on drums], he's practically a herpetologist. He knows everything about snakes, where they live, what they eat, how long they live. He knows it all. He's turned me onto snakes too, so now I own a couple."

Will we ever see snakes in your stage show?

"Uh, probably not, no. Usually our stage show just consists of us jumping around and going crazy. We like to keep it simple, and let people decide on the music."

GODSIZE – ISSUE 138 (DECEMBER 2005)

Having recently beaten off fierce competition from the likes of Mea Culpa and Breed Apart to win Terrorizer's coveted Unsigned Band of 2005 title (as voted for by you, dear reader), Midlands-based Godsize are justifiably pleased with themselves.

"We were all just really excited to get on the CD," reckons vocalist Kris Chambers. "Then to find out we had actually won proved to us we must've been doing something right; that so many people liked the track makes all our hard work over the last four years feel like it's been worthwhile, and it's very gratifying to know that people out there dig what we're doing."

Hitting the listener hard with a heady cocktail of Eyehategod's twisted intensity and Iron Monkey's filthy grooves, all fermented to maximum potency in a Southern (Brum) swamp, Godsize are not for the faint of heart.

"We're influenced by many styles of music," explains Kris, "Including sludge, doom and hardcore, mixed in with all the old school metal bands like Black Sabbath, KISS, Led Zeppelin and AC/DC. People listen to us and compare us to all sorts of bands, but we never set out to sound like anyone in particular; we just got together and wrote good heavy rock 'n' roll songs that suited us."

With extensive UK touring already under their belts alongside the likes of Out For Blood, Slit, Orius and (Atlanta metallers) Organ, and future shows already being scheduled for Europe and possibly even South America to help promote their 'Rock 'N' Roll Machine' demo, it should only be a matter of time before an astute label pricks up its ears. But until then, Godsize seem more than happy flying the flag for the thriving UK underground.

"The scene is alive and well with a lot of good bands coming through! We've managed to play with so many great bands and become friends with most of them. It's a shame when some people won't check out the really underground bands, 'cos they miss out on a lot of decent and very real heavy metal by only going to see what's popular and trendy.

"Sure, bands change, line-ups change and the music evolves – it's an ever-changing, exciting scene - but the ethics behind underground music never change, which is why it's the most relevant scene in the world.

"And we just try to offer a good live show, with heavy music, plenty of Jagermeister, energy and sweat. We have a good time doing what we do, and we hope our fans feel the same way about us as we do about them. We write heavy, dirty songs which will always be heavy and dirty... and we certainly won't change depending on what's 'in' at the time..."

GOREFEST – ISSUE 30 (MAY 1996)

Are Gorefest just another rat leaving the good ship Death Metal before it sinks? Or is there life after... er, death? Are the Dutch band simply out on a limb or is it the scene that's out of step with the times? Ian Glasper listens to front man Jan-Chris hum a requiem for the deathly days of yore.

When Dutch deathsters Gorefest released their second album, 'False', in 1992, it was widely regarded as a minor classic on the extreme metal underground. 1994's 'Erase' saw them introducing some rockier vibes to the riffs and loosening up some of the arrangements, making for a groovier easier ride, but upsetting some of the thrash purists in the process.

The 'progression', depending on your point of view, of course, started two years ago, and has reached its logical conclusion with their latest album for Nuclear Blast, 'Soul Survivor'. Whether you like it or not, Gorefest, despite what their name suggests, are no longer a death metal band. This new record owes more to Judas Priest than Slayer or Obituary. If it weren't for the 'maddened beast' vocal approach of bassist Jan-Chris de Koeijer, this would be a traditional heavy metal platter.

"Our musical tastes have changed a lot," confirms that self-same front man, on the dog-and-bone from the continent. "We've been listening to a lot of Black Sabbath and Rainbow, or whatever, and we thought we'd incorporate some of that. The first song we wrote after 'Erase' for the 'Fear' EP was called 'Raven'," he recalls. "Boudewijn

413

[Bonebakker – guitar] came up with it, and it had nothing to do with the Gorefest of old. It was a rock-ish doom riff... a rock song in fact. And we said, 'Wow, this is pretty fucking cool...' It was almost like a release for us, and he said he had tons more like it."

So, he's the one to blame, mosh heads! I actually spoke to the six-stringer at the same time, but thanks to the miracle that is modern telecommunications, I couldn't hear a fucking word. Bob bloody Hoskins can blow me! Grinding the phone into my ear like a man deranged, I wonder how many original Gorefest fans have been lost in the transition?

"We lost a lot of the die-hard fans from the 'False' era when we released 'Erase'," sighs Jan, seemingly from ten billion miles away. "But then again, last year we played on some non-metal festivals and we went down really well. We're beginning to reach a wider audience, and seeing as we started off in a very strict tight genre six years ago, we're quite confident about what the future will bring for us."

Is this a direction in which you feel death metal has to go to survive as a marketable force?

"Absolutely. I don't know about the market in England, although from what we hear it's not very good. But we do know the Belgian, Dutch and German markets very well, and death metal has gone back to its underground roots again... and we survived by just playing the music we like, and got crucified for it," he adds incredulously.

"You know, stuff like 'Gorefest call themselves death metal...' even though we haven't since the 'Erase' album, and 'They don't sing about death and hate...' Okay, if you want to be so pure, go ahead, but we don't think that way anymore. We've progressed as persons and as a band. Whether it's a commercial success or not, for me this album is a personal success 'cos I'm very proud of it. It's a healthy, fresh album; we're not repeating ourselves and we're moving in a direction that all four of us are comfortable with."

Musically, 'Soul Survivor' is far more accessible than previous outings, but the vocals remain a guttural bellow.

"Actually, I think they're more intelligible than they used to be in the past, but we didn't compromise the vocals really. It wouldn't be Gorefest anymore. We are four people and we've come a long way together, but people will get used to it... they better get used to it. We already have enough bad vocalists in Holland and Germany, and I don't think the world is ready for another one."

If further proof were needed of the growing stature of the band, it may surprise you to know that they performed on Dutch national TV, playing one of their songs accompanied by a full orchestra. As well as raising - partly justified - parallels with our own Paradise Lost (you might remember the name... they've even been in this mag once or twice!), it's brave moves like this that'll either make or break the band, and at least it shows they're now being taken seriously as musicians.

"Yes, and that was why it was one of our biggest achievements so far. Normally, it's only the vocalists who appear and they rearrange one or two or the songs to fit in with the Metropol Orchestra, but they chose to do 'Goddess in Black', which has a very long and important guitar solo in the middle section. So we said we'd only do it if Boudewijn could play as well, instead of some cheesy session guitarist doing the lead. We basically said, 'Take it or leave it,' and they thought we were important enough to take it.

"It was quite an honour because this TV program only picks like five Dutch bands each year to appear, so it was cool to be accepted by those people, and it was fun. We had a positive reaction from death metal fans as well, so we've re-recorded the 'Goddess' song and made an orchestral arrangement for it, and that'll be a B-side of a single released only in Holland and Belgium. Sepultura are in the charts, and The Gathering have had a hit, so the market's really right for heavy music here."

Before all you English Fest-fans start throwing your dummies out of your prams," Jan adds, "Don't worry, all those B-sides should appear on one CD in the autumn, so it will be available for everyone later in the year."

Would you ever write with an orchestra in mind in the future?

"Oh my God, I don't really know - but if it comes out of us, it'll happen. One thing is certain, we will not limit ourselves. That's the approach we took on 'Soul Survivor'. Five years ago, we would never have dreamed of it. If you couldn't do it on a guitar, it sucked as far as we were concerned, but we've grown up a little."

Also testament to their burgeoning importance as an extreme metal band is the fact that they're on the bill at this year's legendary Dynamo Festival, appearing no less for the third time. Their first appearance at this Metal Mecca, of course, found its way onto one of death metal's few live albums, 'The Eindhoven Insanity'.

"This time it's a two-day festival, and we're playing on the Saturday night, right before the headlining act," Jan informs me proudly, "Which I think is the best slot in the house. Everyone is waiting for the main band, so you have maximum audience attention. We're all talking about it now, saying like, 'Oh can we handle it?' But the moment we get on that stage in front of all those people, we'll shit our pants, no doubt. I know I will, at least," he laughs.

The dizzy heights of success aren't reached without some amount of risk. After all, you can't make an omelette without breaking some eggs.

"I don't care really, because I'm happy with the album, but if it flops, it's all over. That's quite obvious. If it's a success commercially, then the future is unwritten and we can do whatever we want."

Is such a defiant attitude where the album title came from?

"We went back to basics and thought back to why we started playing – it was because we were fans of the music, but over the years we've got too involved with the business, the money, the managers, all that stuff, and forgetting what it all started with - playing music. So, there's the soul. We've found our soul with this album. This is Gorefest. This is who we are."

The Great Deceiver, courtesy of Peaceville

Since the demise of At The Gates, the rent-a-vocalist extraordinaire Tomas Lindberg has done time in some truly killer metal bands, but his pet project, The Great Deceiver, have finally unveiled their debut album, 'A Venom Well Designed' on Peaceville. It may just be his most well-rounded work to date. Ian Glasper went in search of an antidote.

True originality in metal music (or any music, for that matter) is rarer than the proverbial rocking horse shit, which makes the debut album from Gothenburg's latest unruly sons, The Great Deceiver, all the more satisfying. As Chris Chantler so rightly pointed out in his glowing Album Of The Month review last issue, 'A Venom Well Designed' is a grower; it takes time to work its subtle magic on you. One minute you're rattling away on your PC keyboard, with said album blaring in the background, but 45 minutes later, you snap awake from your reverie, realising the album has finished and released you from its spell – and you've hardly typed anything at all. Such is the deceptively intoxicating quality these Swedes have managed to weave into every dark groove of this stunning record. As their vocalist Tomas Lindberg reveals, this was their master plan from the very start of the band back in 1997:

"We decided to search for a sound that would be perfect for us, and that takes time. You can't force it; you have to be totally honest with yourself. Everyone in the band loves Celtic Frost, and they had a totally different sound for each album, but they still always sounded like Celtic Frost... well, apart from 'A Cold Lake', of course!" he laughs.

"We want to be able to develop in a similar way, by keep expanding upon our very own sound. Most bands take four or five albums before they finally stumble upon their real identity, and I had just left a long-term band [At The Gates – IG] that had itself changed a lot over the years. This time I wanted to do things a little differently..."

416

Fast forward two years, as the band unveil the first step of this miraculous journey to the inner ear in the guise of the 'Cave In' EP on Swedish hardcore label, Bridge. The well-respected Trustkill picked it up for the States, their much sought-after seal of approval granting the band instant hardcore street cred in the process, and repackaged it for the American market as the 'Jet Black Art' MCD. It was an impressive debut offering, as noisy and as dissonant as you like, but it certainly never hinted at the fluid grace of the album that would eventually arrive three years later.

"Well, on that MCD we focused on introducing the band, and we had to leave out certain aspects of our sound to do so," explains Tomas. "It had to blow people away, so we were sure to include the more aggressive and in your face side of The Great Deceiver, but on the full album there was much more room for us to develop a proper dynamic. The MCD is actually quite a limited format, and it didn't really give us a big enough canvas on which to portray our whole sound."

And, as I hinted earlier, what a sound they've uncovered; great slabs of hardcore, punk, metal and even alternative rock, all hewn from the Gothenburg underground and blended into a seamless whole. When asked by a fellow scribe to describe the band, I found myself at a momentary loss for words, and then plumped for 'mid-period Voivod meets early Killing Joke'. Perhaps I should have added 'at a Refused show' to that, but even then, it falls way short of actually encapsulating the daringly simple - yet paradoxically complex - sound that emanates from 'A Venom Well Designed' like a long-lost lover's voice calling for you from beyond the grave.

"Yeah, I guess it is hard to pin us down," agrees the front man. "But that makes our mission complete in many ways. A lot of bands are really messy, with just too many styles for their own good, but we've chosen a combination of sounds that are very straightforward in themselves, just that they are being combined in a totally new way. And it sounds really natural for us too; it isn't something we have to force."

The press release quotes guitarist Johan Osterberg as saying, "We are focused on expressing aggression... but not in any typical, clichéd metal type of way." That comment suggests a certain amount of disillusionment with the metal scene...

"Well, when At The Gates split up, I was disillusioned with it all," he admits. "But I've found a new belief in the extreme metal genre. But it's true what Johan says, TGD aren't about metal at all. We take all the elements of what we like as individuals, and put it through our own filter; it's a very creative, inspiring environment within the band. We're free of all boundaries, we set no limits on our sound, and that's how we make it sound just like The Great Deceiver. We've surprised people with this record, and I'm sure we'll surprise them next time too."

A lot of people may well be surprised at how hardcore TGD is in feel, seeing as it comprises members of ATG, Grotesque and Diabolique. They shouldn't be really, seeing as Lindberg recently sang on the new Skitsystem album, and that's pure grinding punk. Sweden has also produced some of the most progressive metallic hardcore bands in the whole world.

"Yeah, there are a lot of great hardcore bands out there," he concedes, "But we really

The Great Deceiver, courtesy of Peaceville

don't see ourselves as being defined by any one sound. I suppose the hardcore scene is the most open-minded though, so if anywhere, we might be accepted easiest there, but none of it can really sum us up adequately.

"We just focus on strong songs. As much as I love bands like Converge, we're not into weird timings or odd riff patterns, although having said that, certain people do apparently find some of our arrangements a bit weird..."

They're probably thrown by the abstract simplicity of it all.

"Well, I learnt whilst in At The Gates, that less is definitely more. You shouldn't have to prove yourself as a musician if you believe in the songs.

"We were friends with a lot of bands like Refused and Breach," he says, going back to the Swedish hardcore connection. "In fact, the drummer with International Noise Conspiracy [the band formed by Dennis from Refused – IG] was once in The Great Deceiver. That last Refused album, 'The Shape Of Punk To Come', was amazing. They had a similar approach to us; they were a band doing exactly what they wanted without fear of the consequences. We don't share the same sound, but we do share the same ideas and approach to writing songs."

And one has to scratch their head in wonder just how any band should arrive at such sweepingly majestic structures, boldly beautiful and compelling in their haunting starkness, and awesomely powerful in their fierce dark depths. And one also has to wonder how such a lofty concept can stay afloat in the face of individual egos and personal visions for the band's future direction.

"You never can say what will happen with a band, but right now, we all feel very positive, and very united in our approach. We actually know each other better than we know ourselves; the friendships are as strong as, if not stronger, than the band. We have a totally diplomatic way of dealing with things; we have long meetings where we check our ideas and reflect on where we're going with all this. We're sure we can face any conflicts with discussion rather than bloodshed," he laughs. "In At The Gates, we would fight for two hours over one riff, like total kids, but we're all much more mature now, and rather than constantly see the problems all the time, we've learnt to see the solutions and possibilities instead."

And was the label you'd end up signed to ever a problem for you? I mean, after all, you were on Peaceville when you were in At The Gates, and you ended up looking for another label back then...?

"The thing is, I never fell out with Hammy [Peaceville's head honcho – IG] when I was in At The Gates," reveals Tomas. "The contract just finished and we kinda ended up falling out of touch when he struck up the deal with Music For Nations. Earache really wanted the band at the time, and that just seemed the natural route to take.

"But when we did the ATG compilation for Peaceville last year, I suddenly realised that Hammy and I were still very much on the same wavelength. If you look at what Peaceville have put out over the years, you can see that they only sign creative bands, as opposed to commercial bands who would be a whole lot easier to sell. Hammy understands where we're coming from, because he runs his label in much the same way as we run our band. He believes in us 100%, and we really wanted to feel safe on a label where we would have total creative control.

"This album just introduced The Great Deceiver, and now we can really start to develop our sound," he adds, in closing. "Knowing that our label is really behind us, and really understands what we're trying to achieve takes away some of the concerns we might have had, knowing what we know about what we have to do with this band in the future."

GRIEF OF WAR - ISSUE 187 (SEPTEMBER 2009)

Grief of War, by Kiyondo Studio

For whatever reason, the thrash revival of recent years has yet to reach Japan; a sad fact that irks ultra-aggressive speed merchants Grief Of War no end, for obvious reasons.

"Yeah, I'm sorry to say, there is no thrash scene in Japan," sighs bassist/vocalist Manabu Hirose. "Power metal bands like Dragonforce or Sonata Arctica, and Scandinavian metal acts like Arch Enemy or Children Of Bodom are very popular, but there is no thrash movement. Apart from the big names, this music is still totally underground here; we usually end up headlining most of our gigs, and they're normally in small clubs in front of seventy or eighty people.

"There are a few great bands, but without the support of a scene, it's hard to help and support each other, so many bands stop their activities, which doesn't really lead to the development of a scene either..."

Sounding like the bastard offspring of (modern) Onslaught and (vintage) Sacrifice, and with a fucking belter of a second album in the can ('Worship', out now on Prosthetic), Grief Of War could just be the band to finally put Japanese thrash metal on the map –

despite having an exceptionally rough time stabilising their line-up since their self-released 2005 debut, 'A Mounting Crisis... As Their Fury Got Released', an opening gambit that had this very writer all hot under the collar when it was reissued last year by Prosthetic as a taster for 'Worship'.

"We ran out of money when we were doing that first album, so we're not very satisfied with it. This time round, we built our own studio, so we could take as much time as we liked. Our influences take in all the good old German and Bay Area thrash metal bands, but, just like the famous Japanese approach to electric appliances, we try to improve on everything we hear.

"We haven't made it to Europe yet, but when we do, your readers can expect genuine thrash metal with the unique atmosphere of Japan – just don't expect us to dress like samurai or ninjas!"

GRIP INC. – ISSUE 63 (FEBRUARY 1999)

Grip Inc. - courtesy of Olly Hahn

If you enjoy getting your head stoved in by pounding bass drums, then we all know that Dave Lombardo is The Fucking Man. His prestigious past has been well-documented, but it's about time he got some accolades for his new baby, Grip Inc. Their new album, 'Solidify', just might see that happen at long last. Ian Glasper wanders in off tour, his head either up his ass or still in Germany somewhere, but obviously now well-practised in the art of beating skin, so who better to get the assignment?

How the hell do you introduce someone like Dave Lombardo? Anyone with any serious grounding in the extreme music genre knows of this man's incredible talent. He is surely one of the most accomplished percussionists in the world of metal, the human octopus, complete with super-human stamina and a built-in sense of timing that would put Seiko to shame. And of course, he played in...

Well, you know who. The 'S' word. Can't say no more about that, because I've taken out a wager that I can get through this interview without mentioning their name. So, it comes as a nice surprise when he turns out to be about as down to earth as a musician can be, modestly downplaying his own ability, preferring to always turn the spotlight of the conversation away from himself, and onto his current band, the underrated (but about to change all that?) Grip Inc., and their new album, 'Solidify', for SPV.

"It seems to have peaked, and be just standing still at the moment," says Dave, on the state of modern metal. "I think it needs to evolve a lot more. It's like everything else; if it doesn't evolve, then it will just stagnate.

"Um, we have a strong rhythmic sound, I guess," he adds, when I ask him what he thinks sets Grip Inc. themselves above the pack. "We have less of that hip hop thing going on, but it's still groovy. It just doesn't have that rappy feel that so many bands rely on. We try to blend good heavy riffs together with cool rhythms. You have to find the right medium for each song."

I especially like 'Challenge' on the new record – that seems to have a very strong interaction between riff and rhythm.

"What number is that?" drawls the drummer, before - to my amusement - going off and finding his own copy of the disc to see what I mean! "I'm still not familiar with the titles... oh yeah, that's a cool song."

'Cool' is one way of putting it, I guess, but it also drastically understates the immensity of said new album, that features eleven slabs of driving melodic power. When compared to their rather disappointing sophomore effort, 'Nemesis', it's like listening to a different band. They've certainly recaptured the intensity of their 1995 debut, 'Power Of Inner Strength', but this time coupled it to the confidence and maturity of experience.

"I think the second one wasn't as focused as it could have been, 'cos we were having a bunch of problems about then," he agrees, recalling, "We were having a tough time with our old bassist [Jason Viebrooks, now replaced by Stuart Caruthers – IG], it was a difficult time for us. This is definitely more focused. We did it in a lot less time; like, less than ten weeks, for the whole thing - writing, rehearsals, recording... well, maybe

Grip Inc., courtesy of Olly Hahn

it was a little longer when you consider that Waldemar [Sorychta, guitar – IG] worked on the material a lot on his own back home."

Ah, yes, I wondered about the logistics of composing albums when you're spread around the globe like you guys are. Do you work with tapes, or is it a case of cramming in as much as you can when you eventually do get together?

"When Waldemar comes over here for two weeks, we do write intensively, but he also works on stuff at home, and sends me tapes of ideas. l listen to them over, we discuss them, decide which are the stronger ones, then he comes back and we work on them all some more, demo what we've done... he goes away, and we do it all over again, and then the third time we get together, I actually go to Germany, and we go in the studio, polish it all up, and record it."

So, it's a process of evolution, rather than capturing an aural snapshot of the band at a specific moment?

"Um, that happens, too," explains Dave. "We have those moments of, like, 'Wow!

423

Listen to that riff, that's so cool, we gotta use it!' There's a lot of that spontaneous stuff on all the records we've done. In fact, I'd say probably half our material was created like that, whilst the other half comes about more gradually."

Well, whatever the process by which it was written, 'Solidify' is a fat, well-rounded album that exudes an air of completeness that was lacking from their previous studio output, no doubt thanks to the diverse influences incorporated into its rich textures. The band have tied together many of metal's various strands into one big gristly knot of sonic pugilism, that is surprisingly dark in its jaded outlook.

"Yeah, I agree, it's pretty dark. I don't think you can really pin down any real influences in our sound, tho'. Waldemar's got his guitar sound, and his guitar style, and that's how he plays. He likes to play the rock style - or the metal style, or whatever you wanna call it, but I prefer to bring it all on down to just plain 'rock'. Me? I like to play different styles, but again, I prefer to play rock, too. When we put it together, that's Grip Inc., how we interact with one another."

The biggest comparison that struck me right between the eyes was a remarkable similarity to Killing Joke, especially on the song 'Foresight' - that's track five to you, Dave!

"Really? Wow! That's totally unintentional, too. Gus [Chambers, vocals – IG] might have had that inside him somewhere, 'cos I'm sure he's listened to them a lot in the past, but that's just the vocals, y'know? But musically? That's weird. The only Killing Joke album I own is one of the later ones, 'Pandemonium', and I'm sure that Waldemar isn't really a fan or anything."

Oh well, different people will hear different things in different pieces of music. I even detect an industrial bent in there somewhere, that really manifests itself at the beginning of 'Amped'.

"Oh, that's always been there for us. It's not like something we strived for, but it's there, mainly in the mix, the way it was recorded, I guess."

And there's definitely less speed passages on this record than in the past... "Yeah, I know, I just got burnt out on that stuff. It's all good, but nowadays I like to put it together with some other beats."

You must have played enough double bass to last you a lifetime! "Exactly," he laughs. "I'm now more into the artistry of the song, the song as a whole picture, rather than worrying about the technicalities of certain components of the playing or the production."

Oh well, enough about the music [just be assured, readers, that this is some mighty fine shit if you like your metal red-blooded and intelligent], let's talk about the new line-up. After your past experiences with Sla... - oops, nearly! - a certain well-known thrash band, I figure that it's of the utmost importance to you to surround yourself with exactly the right people you can tour with happily?

"Yeah, there's certain attitudes that I hate personally. I can't abide all that high school crap, so we wanted someone with a bit of maturity, and Stuart is really cool, very down-to-earth. He was actually recommended by Devin Townsend, from Strapping Young Lad, and he's a great addition to the band. It's the same as any work situation; you wouldn't want to go to work every single day if you had to put up with people who had a shitty attitude towards you, and it's exactly the same being in a band."

You've always seemed to nurture a certain love/hate relationship with the whole touring life style, though, or is that just a misconception I've picked up from inaccurate press over the years?

"Yeah, I guess it is love/hate," ponders the drummer. "Where do I start with this, without seeming ungrateful? Well, for starters, I hate how monotonous it is..."

You only ever see the insides of vans, venues and petrol stations! "Exactly, and you're with the same guys all the time! Your home is a hotel room, and you spend all your time packing and unpacking bags, loading in and loading out... but you get used to that whole lifestyle in the end. Eventually that's all you know. You get home, and a month later, you're ready to go again. It's in your blood, whether you like it or not, and you go from one set piece to the next."

Tell us a little bit about your collaboration with Testament on their next studio record, 'cos I know a whole lot of metalheads who are wetting their grundies waiting for this! What, with big Gene Hoglan having pounded skins for 'em on 'Demonic', those Bay Area guys seem determined to jam with all the best drummers in the genre, don't they? "That was so much fun," he recalls fondly. "Originally they asked me to do a tour of South America with them, and I was too busy, but I said to them, 'If ever you guys wanna work on some new material...', and they were like, 'Wow, let's do it!' And it clicked right from the very beginning, I've known those guys for years. They're only six hours away from me, so I'd go up there for a week every month, working on, and demoing, material, and it all came together great. We just recorded it a few weeks ago, and it's brutal - absolutely traditional, old school thrash metal!"

And that's exactly what we all wanted to hear him say, right folks? But back to the matter in hand, and that being Grip Inc., and that splendid new record, 'Solidify'. It's a strong title for a strong record, and suggests to me a band who are consolidating their position in this oh-so-fickle industry.

"Absolutely. The band has gone through a whole lot of criticism, that we're a one-off project or whatever, and we wanted to show everyone what this band is, what it means now. 'Solidify' was the right name to call it; there were other names, but none of them meant as much to all of us.

"And that's why we put the band on the front cover, to show how strong we are now. We didn't care what we looked like, we just wanted to say, 'We're a band, not a bunch of machines, just four guys who go on stage and reproduce what we played in the studio, not just half of it and a load of samples...' We're a real band, and we've made a very real record."

RIP Gus Chambers

Guttermouth, courtesy of Eelco Klein Overmeen @ Epitaph Europe

Guess what? Guttermouth are yet another high-speed melodic punk band from America's west coast. Can you resist them? Ian Glasper doesn't reckon so as he gets the lowdown talking to drummer Jamie Nunn.

Guttermouth are an aptly-named high-speed melodic punk band from California, who on the surface appear not to give a fuck who they offend with their comical lyrics. After one album on Doctor Strange Records, and countless 7"s, they've just released their second LP, 'Friendly People', on Nitro Records, the label owned by one of The Offspring, and seem poised for much wider success. I caught up with Jamie Nunn, their affable drummer, on the phone from Denver, on the eve of their first European tour. I wondered if he was sick of hearing Offspring's name during interviews? "It was going to happen, 'cos Brian owns the label," he states stoically, "But, although he put it out, it was our band and our music that ultimately had to speak for itself."

Some U.S. mags are even hailing Guttermouth as 'the next Offspring'... "We don't sound anything like The Offspring - we're much faster and harder, and I don't really know where the comparison comes from, except that Brian runs the label! I mean, we've been friends for five or six years, and have played with them many times... but to be compared to them? I don't really see it!"

Despite the name Guttermouth, if Offspring-like success loomed, could you be persuaded to tone down your language for more radio play? "That's a very good question, and one we've been asking ourselves," he reveals. "We did it on this record, as a matter of fact –

we went out of our way to write a coupla songs which were 'clean' and could get played on the radio, but they're still too hard, anyway – so we can't win! I think we're gonna stay true to ourselves, first, and we're not gonna write a song for anyone else but us."

California can probably lay claim to most of the punk bands with comical lyrics... does he think they are products of their easy environment? Because you don't see many hardcore bands from, say, Poland, with humorous lyrics! "I've not been to any of those places," replies the skin-basher, "But I can really imagine it's a lot tougher than where we live, y'know? We live right next to Disneyworld, for Christ's sake! So, we're a little bit more light-hearted about stuff, having fun is the No. 1 thing! We grew up listening to bands that liked to have fun, that joked around, with no serious message about saving the world, just sarcasm and making fun of things, so naturally it blended into our own music."

But there does seem to be an ulterior motive in your lyrics, despite the excessive piss-taking, of wanting to provoke a reaction... "Exactly," agrees Jamie whole-heartedly, "The funniest thing for us to do is to make people angry, because we [meaning the rest of Guttermouth: Mark Adkins - vocals, Derek Davis - guitar, Scott Sheldon - guitar and Cliff — bass], know what we do is just a big joke. When people take it seriously and get offended, that's when we know we've done something right!"

So you're not worried about being misunderstood or branded irresponsible then? "No, because if someone calls us irresponsible, then they just don't understand what we're doing. You can't really listen to the record and take it seriously!"

Isn't the new album a bit short? I mean, thirteen songs in 22 minutes? "That's the only complaint we've had," he laughs. "The only band who have us beat is the Circle Jerks – 'Group Sex' is nineteen minutes long! We didn't write it so short intentionally – it's just that our songs are short, anyway, and we were kind of in a hurry to put a new album out..."

But your first LP was short, too! "We've never been a band for writing long songs. It seems our attention span is so short, when we're playing stuff it just seems too long! We don't play too long live, either... even if we're headlining we only play for 45 minutes – and we can play twenty songs or more in that time! I hate going to see a band when they play too long," he reasons, "It's better to leave people wanting more!"

You borrowed the Voodoo Glow Skulls' horn section for one song on the new album – is that a direction you'd like to explore more? "Definitely," Jamie enthuses, "I really enjoyed using the horns a lot, and everyone who's heard it has said they really enjoyed hearing us mixing it up a little bit. I think you'll certainly hear a bit more of the ska thing on the next album. The Voodoo Glow Skulls are very good friends of ours, too – we've played together countless times, we love 'em! They've signed to Epitaph, by the way... and you can print that 'cos it's a done deal!"

There is at least one thing you're serious about though, isn't there? "We're totally anti-Nazi, racism, fascism, the whole thing, and we won't tolerate it at our shows. Those people know not to come. Our singer has a big mouth, too, and tends to let them know that they're not welcome. If you come to a Guttermouth show," he concludes, "You're gonna be brothers with everyone there, and you're gonna have fun!"

CHAPTER H: SATISFACTION IS THE DEATH OF DESIRE...

H2O - ISSUE 34 (SEPTEMBER 1996)

H2O, CBGB, 1996, by Carl Gunhouse

If you think the New York hardcore scene is a closed shop, then think again, 'cos not a single member of H2O was born or bred in the Big Apple! But, as Ian Glasper finds out from main-man Toby Morse, that hasn't stopped them becoming some of the hottest news in hardcore this autumn.

No doubt some of you will recall the rave review I foisted upon H2O's self-titled debut last issue? Well, this is one band who we just couldn't let slip through our clutches with just a paltry review.

If, like me, you copped an earful of H2O when they opened up for Sick Of It All and Civ, you'll know they've mastered the much-sought-after art of melding heart-felt melody

428

with ballsy punky hardcore, and they deliver it with a big infectious shit-eating grin on their faces. You just gotta love 'em!

And sit yourself down, 'cos here comes another Terrorizer scoop... who should I get on the phone when I link up with H2O, who are holed up in a hotel with Biohazard and Downset somewhere on the East Coast of the States, but none other than new bassist Adam, who until recently was plucking his four strings for Shelter. Adam's a Cockney barrow-boy by birth; I remember interviewing him when he was about to move out of his folks' house in Essex and into a Krishna temple in Brooklyn! Surely a dream come true for any red-blooded hardcore fan... so what went wrong?

"I dunno what happened," he tries to explain. "The band was really cool, y'know, but being in Shelter was so different to being in any other band, with the whole Krishna lifestyle I took on. I tried to be more spiritual, and spend as much time with the band as I could, but deep down I wasn't happy there.

"It was an amicable split, though, there's no animosity there. Shelter toured with H2O twice," he recalls, "And I really liked 'em a lot. They were my favourite band out of almost all the bands we played with, so when I left Shelter and moved back to England, and I was sat around wondering what to do with myself after being in Shelter for two years, and H2O called me up saying they'd lost their bassist, I immediately said, 'Okay!' And it's working out really great. I'm having a lot of fun with these guys."

Adam's not the only one thrilled with the current line-up of this band, as I find out when he hands me over to tattooed-all-to-fuck frontman, Toby Morse. Not only has their bassist changed since we saw 'em on these shores last, but also their drummer and rhythm guitarist.

"It's a perfect line-up," he enthuses. "This is the band I always wanted. Shit is really happening for us now and it's good to have a band who aren't gonna blow me out.

"I was a bit sceptical, real nervous at first," Toby goes on to admit, on the subject of his very own brother joining H2O on guitar. "I guess I was worried that he might step on my toes or something, 'cos I was like the one who got this band started and gave it a name, but he's awesome, a great writer. And Todd Friend, our drummer, is just like a brother to me."

"I know it's a cop-out to talk about the band's formation, but seeing as Toby brought it up, I'm going to anyway, and fuck you! And besides, it's an interesting little story for hardcore fans who like Sick Of It All, 'cos Toby roadied for them for five years, and it seems he often used to hop on stage before their encore and bust out a jam with the guys, which saw him improvising the lyrics to a song which became known as 'My Love Is Real', about his cheating ex-girlfriend. It seems he cut such a fine figure as a frontman forming his own band was the next logical step. Maybe it was that SOIA connection that got them tagged as a NYHC band, 'cos none of them are actually from the NYC.

"Well, I moved to New York in 1995," Toby reasons, "And so many people from that scene have watched out for me since then. I didn't think of us as a NYHC band until we

H2O, The Wetlands NYC 1998, by Carl Gunhouse

H2O, The Wetlands NYC 1998, pic by Carl Gunhouse

did a big benefit show, and I realised I'd been accepted as part of the family, and that was an awesome feeling, and that's what 'Family Tree' is about. Besides, it's not where you're from, it's where you're at. It's very much an attitude, a state of mind."

H2O are from one of the punkier branches of that 'Family Tree', opting to soften their hard edge with some luvved-up singalong choruses. They owe more to Murphy's Law and Civ than to Madball or Agnostic Front, although Toby professes a deep love for all those bands (and more!) It may have been the band's ear for a good honest tune that had Epitaph head-hunting them for a while, but in the end they opted to join the ranks of other NYC legends such as Killing Time and Sheer Terror on the smaller, but nonetheless perfectly-formed, Blackout label.

"I would love to make Blackout into the Epitaph of the East Coast, it's our goal to do that for Bill [Wilson, Blackout's head honcho - IG]; all he has is hardcore, he's given his life to it. He's real excited about us, which is good because it means he'll work hard for us. Our record is like his best-selling release right now. In the big stores on their play posts, it's No. 1 on a lot of radio shows, it's doing so well for a first album."

Originally you were only gonna do a one-off for Blackout, right? I fully expected you do a White Devil on us and sail straight off to major label land! "Bill has put together a very basic deal for us, where we'll be able to tour and pay our rent, 'cos I don't want to be out there worrying that my wife can't pay our rent, y'know? But the fact he loves our band was the deciding factor. To Blackout, we're definitely No. 1 priority. I've got nothing against major labels," he adds, "But we wanted the right label. I wanted someone who liked us for what we are, and what we do, not 'cos everyone's told 'em we're good or something. We didn't want to go with someone who didn't believe in us. 'Spirit of '84' off the album is about a label that wanted to sign the band, but he wanted us to change our lyrics and style. He kept saying that hardcore died in 1984, but he was so wrong – the hardcore scene is stronger now than it's ever been."

One thing that seems synonymous with NYHC these days is tattoos, and you can't help but notice that Toby has more than his fair share. It seems his skin art is extremely important to him, 'cos he even refers to it as his 'salvation' on one song from the debut record.

"It's definitely my salvation," he stresses. "Civ's been giving me them for free for years. I was his guinea pig when he started; he used to fuckin' practise on me, so now I get free tattoos for life!

I've been collecting 'em for years, I've got crazy stuff, from all periods of my life. I've got Sick Of It All tour dates, straightedge stuff, vegan stuff, Madonna, fuckin' E.T., all sorts of crazy shit."

Straightedge and veganism are two other things raising their profile through hardcore music, but for a sXe vegan ("I've been vegetarian since '88, but my wife got me into veganism about a year ago..."), Toby is a pretty tolerant guy. He certainly doesn't feel compelled to impose the discipline he chooses to exert over his own lifestyle on the lives of others. After all, the more you try to force something on people, the more they reject it...

"Straightedge to me is like my personal choice, but it's gotten so big it's kinda scary and kinda funny. It's become something bigger than the music that created it. It's weird to see people who were meant to be really into it fall off 'cos it's no longer flavour of the month. That's what 'Here Today, Gone Tomorrow' is about. I saw one of the guys who used to be in Chain Of Strength [a straightedge band who wrote a song about sXe called 'True 'Til Death' – IG]; he's in Walter, who was in Quicksand's new band, World's Fastest Car, standing at a show, with his hair all slicked back, smoking cigarettes.

"To each his own, I guess," concedes Toby in closing. "Some people are more extreme than others, but those people who are the loudest are the ones who aren't here next year."

Hades – issue 65 (April 1999)

Hades, 2000, by Frank White

On the strength of their name, you could be forgiven for thinking that Hades are a bog standard death or black metal band, but nothing could be further from the truth, as Ian Glasper found out when we packaged him off hell-bound - for leather? - to get the lowdown on the '80s veterans' comeback album, 'Saviour Self'.

If ever there was a name from the past to conjure with, it would have to be Hades (if you are familiar with their album covers, you'll know what I mean!) and lo and behold, against the odds, they're back to thrill us once again with their melodic speed/thrash/technical take on daredevil metal. All this is not a hollow, 'for the sake of it' reunion either, 'cos 'Saviour Self' - the first fruit of their reformation for Metal Blade (who else?) is actually better than their acclaimed 'Resisting Success' and 'If at First You Don't Succeed' albums from the mid-to-late '80s, and they were good enough, you know what I'm saying?

"Believe it or not, there's still a lot of old fans out there," says guitarist Dan Lorenzo, when I wonder whether I'm in the minority as someone who actually remembers them from first time round. "Just over a year ago, I was playing around on a computer with my wife, and it was cool to see all these really nice Hades websites on there. When we were on tour with Non-Fiction [Dan's post-Hades (Mark 1) band, who also have also featured Alan Tecchio, Hades' current and original singer – IG], people were always coming up to me and asking about Hades: would we ever do a live album, whatever? Non-Fiction was better organized and we got around a lot more, but fans were always asking after Hades; that was the band that had captured their imaginations. Non-Fiction fans tended to like a lot of other bands besides us, but for Hades fans, they only had the one favourite band – and that was Hades. We had a real cult following."

So, was it the unabated interest of the fans that provoked this latest reunion?

"Well, one of my buddies insisted that I pick up the acoustic guitar again. I hadn't played guitar for over two years and I got rid of all my equipment; not because I thought that I would never play again, but because I was very aware that I needed a break mentally, and that was one way of proving to myself that I was going to take it. I really needed to do other things, like be with just one woman, travel the world, play sports... but when he gave me that guitar, I wrote the opening riff of 'Saviour Self' almost straight away.

"And as a musician, I get very frustrated when I have good riffs that no one's ever going to hear, so I gave a tape of those riffs to Al and the other guys, and I knew that even without a deal we'd have to one day record these songs, and maybe get a little licensing deal somewhere like Germany, just to pay for the studio. We didn't even think we'd get signed; we just wanted to do a good record and have some fun. That was all we were looking for."

If only all things this good were so easy. 'Saviour Self' really is one of the most convincing and intelligent metal releases I've heard this year, a fine balance of technical wizardry and gutsy power with that unmistakable Hades feel stamped all over it. Love 'em or hate 'em, there's no denying they were innovative... and still are, if songs like the mighty 'Decline and Fall of the American Empire' are anything to go by.

"We had the riff for that song," recalls Dan, "But Al just could not come up with a melody we were all happy with. And I'm a big fan of stuff like Godflesh, where there is talking and noise behind the riffs, so that's what we tried and it worked so well.

"A lot of the time people in America put all the blame on the system, or they say they're down on their luck or whatever," he continues, broaching the lyrical subject of the song, "But so often, that's all bullshit. People who are absolutely fine and healthy often just don't want to work, and they say it's all society's fault. The song draws comparisons with Rome and Egypt, and how their civilizations became almost too advanced and ended up collapsing.

Hades vocalist Alan Tecchio, by Frank White

"People were furious with the lyrics, especially in Germany; they thought we were right wing extremists 'cos we support the death penalty. They said I was a Nazi because of it, and of course I'm not, but if someone kills my mom, then I want that person dead. I don't want them sitting in jail somewhere, wasting taxpayers' money. But the American justice system is so lacking... where else can you just pay a lawyer to get you off the hook?"

Of course, the death penalty always begs the question, what if they've got the wrong person? But that's another debate for another time. Because time is short, and Dan has a message he wants to communicate to Hades fans everywhere.

"In the past, people have been confused as to whether we were sticking together. We did 'Exist to Resist', and that was a one-off reunion record, and a lot of people were disappointed about that, but I can guarantee that there will be another new Hades album next year. We're a real band again for the first time since 1989, and we're already writing those new songs. This is the real deal now."

HALSHUG – ISSUE 258 (MARCH 2015)

"We are hoping to challenge people's restrictive perception of what punk and D-beat is, and please them with some quality hardcore as well," claim Copenhagen noise merchants, Halshug. "Actually, we are trying to reach beyond the punk scene, and make more people feel offended or touched or annoyed or whatever. But most of all this is a selfish project, about ourselves getting off!"

And new album, 'Blodets Band' for Southern Lord, certainly won't leave anyone unmoved with its raging mix of metallic crust and thrashing punk, reminiscent of greats like Anti-Cimex and Skit System.

"We have an uncompromised pace and intensity in our show that will leave your sinuses bleeding for a month!"

HAMMY – ISSUE 121 (JULY 2004)

(Sidebar in a feature on Carcass)

Paul 'Hammy' Halmshaw not only drummed for the popular UKHC band, Instigators, but he later sang for Civilised Society?, and was/is the mastermind behind the hugely respected Peaceville Records. Although now an established international metal label, Peaceville was once a firm fixture of the UK underground; indeed, their first compilation album, 'A Vile Peace', helped launch many a seminal grindcore band, such as Axegrinder, Doom and Deviated Instinct – all bands that shared stages and influences with Carcass during their formative years.

"I don't exactly know what 'grindcore' is, but I remember being around a lot of people

Hammy, and Lisa, pic by Porl Medlock, 1997

who would go on to be considered as such. We just knew it as 'thrash punk' really... the term 'grind' eventually being coined around about the time of the Earache 'Grindcrusher' sampler.

"Carcass were always around the scene. I'd see Bill everywhere when he was in Napalm Death – they really did set the scene alight! – and when Carcass got going, I was really interested in the first album. The cover was beyond anything I'd ever contemplated, and the 'musical' content wasn't much better, haha! Personally, I never liked their stuff as such, but I was always fascinated by the concept... and it was the conceptualist approach that led me to be in Sore Throat too. I guess they were a grind band in many ways too, the first side of the album 'Disgrace To The Corpse of Sid' – the 99-track side! – being a particular milestone in conceptual music... in my eyes, at least.

"Anyway, back to Carcass, I'd heard all kinds of rumours recently about the members, so it's great that they are speaking now, and putting the record straight. They were hardcore's first boy band after all, so it's good that they retained their sanity!

"Peaceville was up and running back then too. We released Jeff's first band, Electro Hippies, but Jeff had left to form Carcass by the time we did them. I guess the closest we came to pure grind was Axegrinder's 'The Rise Of The Serpent Men', which due to new demand we are actually reissuing this autumn. We are also going to be putting out Deviated Instinct's 'Rock 'n' Roll Conformity', to add to the Doom and Electro Hippies re-releases we did. It's definitely a rising tide again, whatever you want to call it!"

Harley Flanagan, pic by Naki

Harley Flanagan is one of the most notorious names on the hardcore punk scene; the tales surrounding him are legion and unfortunately usually involve drink, drugs or violence. But let's not forget the often-over-looked aspects of this intriguing cult of personality - those of a visionary lyricist, talented bassist, devoted father and skilled martial artist. He may have unfortunately entered the mythology of underground subculture as some sort of deranged thug, but his musical contribution is without parallel, not least of all as one of the driving forces behind the Cro-Mags, whose incendiary 'The Age Of Quarrel' debut literally changed the course of hardcore music as we know it. It is no coincidence that such an intense band was born from a fusing of intense individuals, and Harley was probably the most intense of all. To better understand the slow-burning anger that seems to have driven him for the last twenty-odd years, it's necessary to turn back the clock to the formative years of his childhood... to the very beginning, in fact.

Harley was born in the summer of 1967 in San Francisco. "But I'm definitely a New Yorker by blood!" he laughs. "My folks were hippies and they were seriously caught up in the whole drug thing of the '60s. My mom was from NYC, and she was friends with a lot of, like, famous poets, writers, musicians and freaks, the whole Velvet Underground thing and all that Andy Warhol shit. Dad was from Texas, and had left home at, like, fifteen, started riding freight trains and shit... you know, doing that old school hobo thing. He was always in and out of prison; he had some serious alcohol and drug problems... I guess they both did at different times, but he was really bad. It was a rough start; they met in San Francisco, but my mom split on my dad pretty early. They were together for a few years, but then when I was born, she split a coupla years after, and that was that. His name was Harley too, that's where I got my name; I never saw him again until his funeral."

Harley's mum took him to Denmark, where she met and married a guy called Karsten who raised Harley as his own, but when that marriage disintegrated, they returned to the States, where they hitched around and crashed with different friends before ending up back in New York with family.

"I wound up back with my grandparents and my aunts on the Lower East Side which was a total fuckin' ghetto nightmare at the time, in a building with Allen Ginsberg who was a friend of my mom and aunt, and Richard Hell, who was one of the very first punk rockers. It was a freaky building, the only building on the block with white people in it, and we were all freaks and artists, punk rockers, poets and shit, so we all got fucked with a lot. My street was run by a Puerto Rican gang called The Hitmen; they used to have shoot-outs with The Allen Boys all the time. On my block and down near Allen Street, it was all drug wars, fighting over the streets that they would sell on; it was crazy, at least one apartment got robbed in my building every week! I mean I'm really not kidding; the cops were scared of the gangs in my neighbourhood back then, so no one could really do shit. It was just a drag, I had a lot of pent-up anger and frustration over it all, but there really wasn't much I could do; it was rough."

A key moment in Harley's musical development was in 1977, when his mother brought him back from England a copy of 'Never Mind The Bollocks' by the Sex Pistols.

"l was blown away!" he recalls fondly. "It was just so energetic, it was raw and exciting, nothing like

all the crap my friends in school listened to. I mean up until then I was into Hendrix; I used to draw pictures of him when I was, like, seven – I still have some of them. I was really into Bob Marley... I had good taste, haha! I was even into Stevie Wonder, the Jackson 5, and Herbie Hancock; I was into a lot of music, a lot of cool shit for my age. But then this punk rock thing exploded out of my speakers with guys named Sid Vicious and Johnny Rotten, Rat Scabies and Captain Sensible, haha! I was, like, 'WOW!' I was so into it! It was anti everything that everybody around me was into, all the kids at school were into, like, ABBA and shit... it changed everything, it was definitely a revelation for me."

Music was probably the most positive thing in his life at that point, as Harley had already started drinking and taking drugs and running with the neighbourhood gangs, having learnt at an early age that to survive on the Lower East Side, he had to be a "vicious little bastard".

Harley's first short-lived touring band – when he was ten years old – was Little Big Boss. Harley's aunt, Denise, was very influential during this crucial period of his life; she had attended most of the early punk shows in NYC and befriended many of the bands. In 1978, Harley's mom took him to England

where Denise had been jamming with The Damned drummer Rat Scabies in his side project The White Cats. By the time Harley had turned eleven and returned to New York, punk rock had him well and truly in its clutches.

"The first real punk show I saw in NYC was The Dead Boys at CBs. Back then there were seats bolted into the floor all the way to the front of the stage – years later, me and my friends would rip them all out! Yeah, The Dead Boys, it was sick, haha! Stiv Bator came crawling out onto the stage, then threw a jar full of live roaches and water bugs into the crowd of people all seated at the front! And of course, they freaked! It was hysterical, they were mostly 'normal' people who just went to a nightclub to see some live music and had no fuckin' idea what they were getting themselves into! Later in the set, Stiv hoisted himself up to the ceiling with a noose around his ankles, dropping himself repeatedly on his head into a pile of broken glass over and over again! Well, needless to say, they had to eventually take him to the hospital to sew him back up before the second set..."

It wasn't long before Harley joined his Aunt Denise's band The Stimulators. "I joined them replacing Johnny Blitz of The Dead Boys (who had replaced Bob Wire)," he remembers. "He just bailed out the day of a show, wouldn't answer his phone or his door; I think it was just 'cos he was a smackhead and couldn't make it. Anyway, I knew most of their material from having seen them play and having been at their practices so many times, so I jumped in. They had a gig that night at the Cat's Cradle in North

Carolina; I learned all the material in the back of the van, listening to a cassette and drumming on a phone book! We played that night with The Autistics, it was great; I was an instant success, haha! It was hysterical, no one had ever seen a kid my age in a real band and people loved it."

The Stimulators played with everybody from The Cramps and The B-52s to the Bad Brains and Madness, making a name for themselves as a unique and innovative act over the course of several well-received EPs.

"We had two girls in the band, Denise Mercedes - my aunt - on guitar and Anne Gustausen on bass, and this crazy little blond poet dude Patrick Mack on vocals. He lived down the block from CBs; he was really into Iggy and Bowie and was a crazy frontman - he would dive across tables on his face, knocking people's drinks all over the place, do flips onstage, spazz out and get all weird. It was fun, he was a really cool guy. I was never a huge fan of his voice but hey, it was the times; everybody was doing their own thing and he was doing his, so anyway we were a really freaky band. Two girls, a little kid and a crazy 'mo' on vocals; we weren't a typical punk band, we didn't really fit into any of the categories but we were good, that was the great part of it. I mean, looking back my drumming needed work but hey, I was a kid, fuck it, and we were breaking ground, y'know? We were a lot of the reason the NYHC scene even came to be.

"That's when bands like Black Flag and Circle Jerks first started coming east. The Stims played with the Circle Jerks at their first NY show at Irving Plaza; it was sick, all the DC boys came down... Ian McKaye, Henry [Rollins]... all of them... Void... the whole fuckin' crew, all those bands, they rolled pretty deep. That's when NYC got its first taste of real slam dancing; I mean, it was crazy on the dancefloor in NYC but it was more just violent, frenzied pogo-dancing and stage-diving, but the DC boys were doing a whole different thing they had picked up from the West Coast. That's when it all started changing, it was happening all over the place; it was just a new thing that was starting to rise out of the ashes of the old punk. That's when hardcore really started to happen."

The Stimulators went to Ireland in 1980, where they played the Ulster Hall with Aussie punks The Saints, and Harley had his head shaved by one of The Outcasts' roadies. He returned to NYC the first American skinhead, and began shaving the heads of all his friends ("I wanted my own crew that didn't have to take any shit from no one!") Drinking heavily and fighting almost every night ("Like it was a fucking religion..."), it was inevitable that trouble would catch him up, and one night after nearly getting himself killed by a Puerto Rican gang in Tompkins Square Park, he upped and headed back to San Francisco, where he lived for a while in the infamous Vats (a punk squat in an abandoned brewery) and wreaked his own brand of havoc on the local scene. He hitched around Canada, where he got his devil-grabbing-the-world chest tattoo, before returning to NYC where, after co-founding Murphy's Law with Jimmy Gestapo, he eventually hooked up with Parris Mayhew and at last found a solid line-up for the band he'd been working on since leaving The Stimulators. The Cro-Mags were born... and the rest, as they say, is history.

Their debut album, 'The Age Of Quarrel', was unlike anything heard before or since, and, along with Agnostic Front's 'Victim In Pain', helped define the classic NYHC sound. The band were destined for greatness and were soon on tour across the world with both hardcore and metal bands.

"We even gigged twice with Venom, back in the day," laughs Harley. "The first night in Chicago is one of my best memories of any gig. We were getting ready to go on, and it was a packed show, all metalheads, and the local paper had described us as 'Skinheads gone heavy metal mad'! So yeah, anyway, we're getting ready to go on, and the crowd is already hating us! We walk out on stage and the whole place starts chanting, 'Skinheads suck! Skinheads suck!' I'm like, 'Oh shit', haha! I walk out, plug in and my bass isn't working and the chant is starting to turn into, 'What the fuck? What the fuck?' When we finally get Cronos to loan me a bass (he's a great guy, by the way), we go into 'We Gotta Know' with all the energy and aggression we had. They didn't know what the fuck hit them; when we ended the first song, it was almost silent, they were dumbfounded, so we busted straight into 'World Peace' and 'Show You No Mercy' and this crowd started turning into a headbanging frenzy of freaks with their fists in the air!

"A couple of people were giving us the finger in the front row, so I knee-slid across the stage to one guy and punched him dead in the face, and blood started gushing out of his nose, and I kept playing. He did it again, and this time John [Joseph, vocalist] got him, haha! It was funny as shit; now the guy went from giving us the finger to giving us a thumbs up! By the time we stopped long enough between songs for them to react, we had totally won over the most hostile crowd, it was sick; at first they hated us, but after three songs we had turned the place upside down..."

The Cro-Mags were most definitely products of their troubled environment, and the hostility they dealt with every day certainly manifested itself powerfully within their music. There was never any doubt that this band was for real. When they raged about 'Survival Of The Streets', you just knew that they'd lived and breathed it all their lives.

"On Ave. A, there was a club, 'our club', A-7, where we all used to play. It was just two small rooms; there was a couch and a bar in the back, and no stage. It was real small and we would jam a fuckin' ton of people in there; Jimmy Gestapo and Raybeez [the late singer of Warzone] worked the door and Doug Holland [guitarist with Kraut and then Cro-Mags] was the bartender and this crazy black dude, Dave, a total cokehead, ran the joint. He was a nut and this place was a fuckin' trip, there were so many sick gigs there.

"There was the Park Inn where a lot of us would hang and get drunk across the street (even though we were all minors), and Tompkin Square Park was right there too. There would always be a small handful of us out every night... me, my old singer Eric, little Chris... we were on Ave. and 8th or in that park every single night all year round, but on weekends and in the summer time, man, you could get anywhere from 50 to 200 kids just running wild all up and down St. Marks Place.

"In the winter we'd break up park benches and burn them in garbage cans to stay warm, there was always people huffing glue, tripping, drinking, smoking dust or weed, or whatever else anyone could scrounge up, and me and my friends, we were all just little maniacs. There was a lot of fights, definitely, a lot of them, but yeah, it was really busy down there for a while; it was pretty jumpin' and it was still a really bad neigbourhood - you definitely took your chances back then, there were tons of gangs and lots of drugs and crime."

Sadly, all good things come to an end, and what made the Cro-Mags so unique - their unpredictable volatility – ultimately tore them apart. After several further excellent albums, the band split up very acrimoniously. Harley and Parris played together again in Samsara, which became White Devil (and co-starred Bobby Hambel from Biohazard), which eventually became the Cro-Mags once again. Their awesome 2000 comeback album 'Revenge', which also featured Suicidal Tendencies' Rocky George on lead guitar, signalled a genuine return to form, but the reunion was short-lived as, once again, personality clashes within the band destroyed what might have been.

Nowadays, Harley prefers to surround himself with friends from other NYC bands in his Harley's War project, a 'hardcore all-stars' affair whose nebulous line-up has already included members past and present from such NYHC luminaries as Bad Brains, Murphy's Law, Skarhead, Misfits, Crown Of Thornz, Merauder, Dog Eat Dog and Leeway.

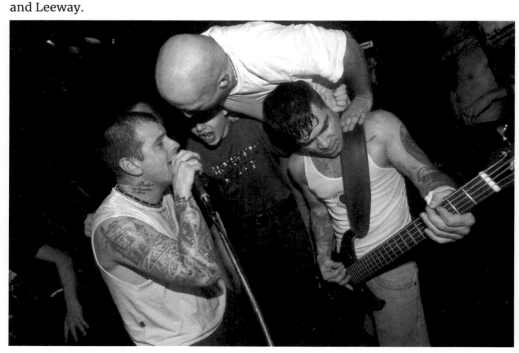

Harley's War, CBGB, NYC, 2002, pic by Carl Gunhouse

"I just like playing with a lot of different players! Someday I hope to be remembered as the Miles Davis of hardcore," he laughs.

As well as a new live Cro-Mags CD in the pipeline, a final farewell release for the diehard fans, Harley is even working on an online Hardcore Hall Of Fame, which will feature contributions from the likes of Henry Rollins. It promises to be something

Harley's War, CBGB's Last Hardcore Matinee, 2006, pic by Carl Gunhouse

a bit special for any fan of the genre, and there's a sneak preview available at the Cro-Mags website.

"I would just like to be successful enough one day to never have to deal with society and the people I don't like ever again, if I don't want to," he muses, in closing. "To be able to live the way I want, maybe live in the mountains or something and just play my music to enjoy myself, and raise my family and watch life go by. That would be nice! But who knows? Maybe I'll move to Brazil and spend my life doing jiu-jitsu, or Europe... Holland? Who the fuck knows where I'll wind up? If I get rich, I'll buy an island and name it Harleywood, haha! But yeah, I'll probably wind up in the mountains with my family, a bunch of dogs and guns, waiting for the Apocalypse..."

SIDEBAR:
Krishnacore?

One of the greatest anomalies of the Cro-Mags was that, whilst they were one of the most aggressive and self-destructive bands on the planet, they were also one of the first hardcore bands in touch with their spiritual side, openly embracing and expounding the virtues of Krishna consciousness long before the likes of Shelter and 108.

"I first started going to the Hare Krishna programs for the food really... I was on the street, shoplifting and stealing food to survive, and they had good vegetarian grub and all you had to do was hang out and listen to their lectures. As time went on, I began to see certain similarities between their beliefs and mine, and they were able to answer a lot of things that had not been answered in my life before – or even asked. In a way, it was the best thing that ever happened to me, 'cos the way I was going prior to that, I would have wound up dead or in jail...

"But that whole Krishna-core thing was a joke, especially 'cos it was kids who used to talk a lotta shit that just had a new bandwagon to jump on. I even heard the term 'Krishna skins'... what a joke! What a contradiction in terms – that one made me laugh. I mean, when I got into it, I really renounced all the so-called titles, like 'punk' and 'skin', and when I was a 'skin', I was a SKIN!

"It's funny, 'cos I had a few skinhead friends that roadied for the band; I guess that's how the term Krishna Skin came about. And we would still get into fights and shit – some people thought we had gone 'soft' 'cos we were vegetarian and stuff, and they'd start with us and we'd have to kick the shit out of them, haha! My boys were all black belts and street fighters, so it was a mistake for the fools who did fuck with us, Hare Krishna or not. But no, I'm not into it so much anymore, 'cos they are corrupt, just like all religions. I still dig Prabhupada a lot, but I'm not a part of their movement; I have my own beliefs."

HATEBREED – ISSUE '50' (INCORRECTLY NUMBERED – IT SHOULD HAVE BEEN 51/FEBRUARY 1998)

Hatebreed '90s - by Danielle Dombrowski

Continuing the east coast assault with a vengeance, here come Hatebreed, armed with their debut full-length, 'Satisfaction Is The Death of Desire', and a growing live reputation. And after a few spins, our resident metallic hardcore fiend Ian Glasper just had to go and find out more about the band's pedigree with singer Jamey Jasta, didn't he?

Whoah, what's up with the east coast of the States? There hasn't been such a slew of killer metallic hardcore releases for an age. Not that I'm complaining or anything, and the new Hatebreed full-length, 'Satisfaction Is The Death of Desire', is, dare I say, the best example of the genre since 'Gomorrah's Season Ends'. Really. You may remember the rave review I gave their 'Under The Knife' MCD recently? Well, I wasn't talking out of my arse either, and, at risk of sounding hysterical, this new album is even better. Within minutes of hearing it, it had usurped the No. 1 slot in my personal Top Ten for the year, so it seemed only a matter of time before Da Ed was on the blower to commission me to do a feature on 'em. And sure enough...

"We're all big Misfits fans, and they've got a song called 'Hatebreeders', and it just seemed to fit," singer Jamey Jasta tells me, when l wonder how negative they really are, with a name like that. A lot of heavy bands seem to tap into some sort of inner negativity... "l think negativity taps into us! The name sounds negative, and I s'pose we are a somewhat negative band, but, like most heavy bands, it's the bullshit of everyday life that drives us, but we certainly don't preach, or breed, hate. We just say what we think sucks. Most of the songs are pretty personal lyrics. 'The Last Breath' is about the finality of death, and trying to accept that, and anyone can relate to it. l know that l like bands that don't alienate you with their lyrics. I've always wanted as many people as possible to respect and understand our words."

Seeing as I've already mentioned 'Gomorrah's Season Ends', and a frequent comparison that crops up for Hatebreed is to the mighty Earth Crisis, talk turns to veganism, and the way in which ideals can be communicated through music.

"I'm vegan, but I'm not drug-free, not completely, although I'm not a drunk either," he begins carefully. "Take, for example, Follow Through from Connecticut, who are awesome band, but they have lyrics like, 'You booze, you lose'. And I know people who are saying that they love the band, but not the lyrics, and they won't sing along at shows. Now, we're into that crowd participation you get at hardcore gigs, we like the audience to have fun. We have a message, but we're not renowned for being vegans or anything, and that's helped us in the long run. We want people to like our band for the music first. That's why Sick Of It All are so big - anyone can relate to their lyrics, anyone can get into them. They're one of the few bands that don't have everything they do analysed, and that's because they've never taken such a strong stand on issues like Earth Crisis have."

Seeing as Victory are the label for this kind of heavy evil shit, it comes as no real surprise when Jamie tells me that signing to them was a dream come true. It seems that, what with EC about to jump ship, and Snapcase sadly now split, and Integrity doing god

Hatebreed '90s, by Danielle Dombrowski

knows what, there could very well be a 'gap in the market' for someone like Hatebreed, and certainly a tidy little niche for them on Victory. But, of course, this is a double-edged sword, because with a bigger, better label inevitably come the cries of 'sell out!' "I'm sure there are kids out there that will say that, but it won't affect them liking the record. People have been saying to me that Hatebreed don't need Victory, that Victory need us, but I know that's not true. The weight of the label's name alone has helped us, to get gigs, to get interviews, to get better guarantees, even before the record came out. Clubs who would never return my calls are ringing me now. All the bands on Victory play different styles now, so we shouldn't get too badly stereotyped either. It won't worry us if we do, 'cos the people doing the stereotyping are still at the shows, and still buying the record. They bitch that Victory only releases metal, but we know that we're a hardcore band through and through. We're not metal kids trying to play hardcore... we're hardcore kids trying to play metal," he adds, laughing.

 The other thing that Jamey discusses quite openly, that is usually a taboo topic for a hardcore band, is the concept of getting 'big', or even admitting that you would like to. "Look, I've been in bands, done a label, and busted my ass for years. I owe people money, I've ruined my credit history, and it would be nice to pay my debts. It'd be nice to be able to go on tour and be able to eat for once, to afford some of life's necessities. No one in this band is a rich kid, who has parents who'd bail them out, so if we did get bigger, and made a bit of money, I wouldn't complain. But if it all ended tomorrow, I'd still be happy with what we achieved. I still want to see the world, and now my music has given me that opportunity."

HATEBREED – ISSUE 116 (JANUARY/FEBRUARY 2004)

Not only has Hatebreed's latest album, 'The Rise Of Brutality', put the New York metalcore bruisers firmly on the map, the band are determined to reach every far corner of it too. Ian Glasper caught up with main-man and 'Headbanger's Ball' presenter Jamey Jasta in the middle of another exhausting tour to chart the band's trajectory to hardcore superstars.

A TOUR DE FORCE

Is there no stopping the inexorable rise of Hatebreed, surely the premier metalcore band in the world today? We may have had to wait for five years after their seminal debut album, 'Satisfaction Is The Death Of Desire', for their sophomore effort (2002's major label debut 'Perseverance') but sensing a distinct advantage and eager to capitalise on it, the band's third and finest album, 'The Rise Of Brutality', is on us already, a mere eighteen months after its predecessor. The band are going from strength to strength, seeming pretty much untouchable right about now, and they got where they are today the old-fashioned way – through relentless touring and self-promotion. And sure enough, where should we find vocalist, Jamey Jasta? On the road, of course; somewhere in Texas, to be more 'precise'.

Hatebreed's current tour started in early September, and it goes until December 14th with barely a night off. Starting with the 'Rise Of Brutality' tour, supported by Madball, Hate Eternal, Cephalic Carnage and Terror, they've proceeded on to the Slayer tour with Arch Enemy and now they're currently touring with Agnostic Front, The Unseen and Ringworm.

And there's more. The 'Rise Of Brutality' world tour will take up the first half of 2004. "We're not sure in what order or to what extent," explains the frontman, still rousing himself from insufficient slumber, "'Cos we're on a new label now worldwide [Roadrunner – IG], so we have to see which territories we're doing best in, where people are responding to the record and stuff."

Hatebreed did 311 shows last year. Doesn't Jamey ever get burnt out on playing live?

"We did at a certain point last year, but it was actually for the best, 'cos it helped us concentrate on finishing up the material we had written. We had time to finally get into the studio and turn the record out just right."

Which came together a whole lot quicker than 'Perseverance' did.

"Well, the material was there, and it was sounding so good, and when we got in the studio we had even more material. We just want to get some good records out – we didn't wanna be a band together for a decade with only two albums to our name! Plus

447

Hatebreed '90s, pic by Danielle Dombrowski

there's enough people who know about us now – we don't have to just try and build on one album too long, 'cos we know our fans are gonna go and get our stuff when it comes out." 'Rise...' is Hatebreed's fastest selling release to date – it's done 100,000 copies in less than three months, whereas 'Perseverance' sold 230,000 copies in eighteen months. In the US. "So, we're thinking, if we stay on the road, we could do 300,000 with this one," says Jamey. He might even have a platinum record on his hands!

"Not sure about that [laughs], but a gold record would be a dream come true. Thing is, we've done this with very little promotion so far, and the big push will only really kick in early 2004. I think Roadrunner will do a good job in the rest of the world, and I'm sure that Universal, now that we've sold this many copies without that much print advertising, will really work it here too. We're pretty psyched."

As are we all. No Hatebreed fan will be disappointed with the new album. It pulses with a terrifying ferocity, yet contains some of the band's most instant material. The anthemic 'Live For This' sounds like classic Leeway meets mid-period Cro-Mags, whilst elsewhere the band hammer home their detuned grooves like a reborn Obituary. And there are none of the generic filler songs that made the last album sound a little rushed.

"I don't think 'Perseverance' was rushed," Jamey counters, "It just took way too long to get out. Then when we sequenced it, I still think we sequenced it wrong. There were some songs that I felt were really strong that didn't make it on that record that are now on 'Rise...'. This time it just felt like we really knew what we wanted, we knew what our fans wanted, and we were really comfortable. There was no pressure, so we just had fun making the record. We had an hour drive home from the studio, and we'd be listening to this stuff every night in the car, and we were just pumped. Our new producer, Zeuss [sic], had always said that he wanted to make the record sound as close as he could to us being live, but with the power and intensity of the drums and guitars being all out in front and not cutting into each other..."

FIGHTING SPIRIT

It seems miraculous that Hatebreed even found time to write a new album at all, considering the huge per centage of their lives spent on the road – thank God for porta studios, drum machines and Dictaphones – but the ever-driven Jasta isn't content with just being at the helm of Hatebreed. He also runs his own Stillborn label – who have new albums from Full Blown Chaos, Sub Zero, Love Is Red and Stigma (Vinnie from Agnostic Front's solo project) slated for 2004 – and has recently been seen hosting 'Headbanger's Ball 2' on MTV.

"I've been doing that for, like, four months now and I've just signed on for another year as well," says Jamey, admitting, "I'm spread a little thin right now. I have to fly in from wherever we are on tour every week or every other week. It's crazy, but I think the show's getting bigger and better, and it's a lot of fun – it's doing a great thing for the music scene too.

"Everyone knows how to do everything, but no one ever takes action," he adds, on his inevitable critics from the hardcore scene. "Some kids are, like, 'The scene sucks! MTV

Hatebreed, Philadelphia YWCA, 1998, pic by Carl Gunhouse

sucks!' This world is full of complainers, but there's a few of us who actually have the balls to try and make a change. When we couldn't get our first record out, we didn't complain, we went and put it out ourselves. And that's always been my outlook. And when they were bringing 'Headbanger's Ball' back, I knew that it could either suck or it could be cool, and I'm trying to help make it cool. I asked if I could have some say, and they said, 'We'll see', and I figured that 'We'll see' was better than 'No!' So, I went in there with an open mind, and it's been great!

"I've played Agnostic Front, Cro-Mags, Leeway, Madball, E-Town Concrete, Shadows Fall, Death, Overkill, Exodus, Testament, Eighteen Visions... and those bands' record sales are all on the up. I mean, Shadows Fall and Killswitch Engage have even just done a 'Headbanger's Ball' tour over here. They're now selling 70,000 records or whatever."

Almost all the lyrics on 'The Rise Of Brutality' are about such personal empowerment – is the band good anger management for Jamey?

"Oh yeah, I'm better off saying 'Fuck you' to whoever I wanna say 'Fuck you' to in a song than I am going up to them and doing it in their face. Right now, I have so much to lose; we've built such a strong fanbase, and a good rapport with our label. Sure, there's some people in this industry that I'd like to punch in the face, but I can't, I'd fuck it all up for us, so I say it in my songs instead."

Does he ever wake up and wonder just how his band got so damn big? As a control freak, doesn't it ever feel like that control is slipping away?

"It feels good right now," enthuses Jamey. "I'm just very grateful to be creating music that people can relate to. And not just people who are into hardcore or metal, but regular people too. We get kids from all walks of life at our shows. We just wanna connect with people. We keep our songs pretty simplistic and heavy, but they're catchy as well. Like, on this record, there were a lot of riffs that we scratched because they weren't memorable enough. A lot of metal bands write songs that are too long, and people just don't have time to sit down and work at getting into them. A lot of people in modern society seem to have ADD or whatever you call it – attention deficit disorder – and we're the ultimate ADD band, haha!"

A quick, easy fix of brutality – just what the doctor ordered!

HATEBREED – ISSUE 149 (OCTOBER 2006)

With a new album, 'Supremacy', for their new label, Roadrunner, still smouldering in the racks, and a new guitarist (Terror's Frank Novinec), what better time could there possibly be to catch up with the mighty Hatebreed than right now? Ian Glasper dutifully volunteered for the smack down...

'Perseverance'... 'The Rise Of Brutality'... Hatebreed don't mince words when naming their albums, and now we have 'Supremacy', aptly-titled because it is indeed the band's most rounded, consistent offering to date. Yes, it's another Hatebreed record (would you want it any other way?), but this time they've nudged the power and intensity needles off the scale, whilst also discovering a new dynamic... the result? Their most listenable release to date.

"I think the best thing to say about this record is that it's our most mature work," offers guitarist Sean Martin. "Not that any of the other records were childish or anything, but on this album, we really came into our own... perfected our formula, y'know what I mean? We have other influences that you can obviously hear, but we opened up just a little bit... we didn't put out the same record again - but we did! We stuck to our musical integrity, stuck to our roots... but at the same time, the album is a lot thrashier, and also a lot more hardcore in parts too. We've just gotten that much closer to really perfecting what we do... we all get along so well, and the vibe was really good on this recording...

"We were technically between labels, going through a lot of red tape and stuff, so in some ways we were in the studio on our own merit, and although everything worked out great in the long run, that situation gave us back a certain hunger. We were just five friends hanging out in the studio making an awesome record again... it was just us at that point. Everything was going fine with the Roadrunner deal, but it was taking some time, and that brought a great camaraderie – and it all transcended into the music. It was really inspirational; we went into the studio with probably seven or eight songs, but when we really hunkered down and started rearranging stuff, this album came out of it. And I really think it's our most mature record to date, musically and lyrically, and you can really feel that, and that sets it apart; we've definitely hit a real peak, where we've really locked together, but this is a new era for Hatebreed. Especially with Frank in the band, because he hasn't really contributed anything to the writing yet, and the next record will be a whole new ball game..."

So he didn't really bring anything to the table for 'Supremacy' then?

"No, not really, 'cos when he joined, we were already in the studio, we'd started recording. Of course, we all know what he's capable of, but it was just one of those things... we decided we wanted a fifth member, a second guitar player, and I thought of Frank right away; he basically came straight into the fold, but by the time he came in, we'd already been in the studio about two weeks, so we were already going, and he just hung out and learnt all the new material while we were recording, y'know?"

And does Frank's presence live free you up onstage a lot?

"Oh yeah, it's great being a five-piece again," enthuses Sean, "Because I held it down for almost five years by myself, and that definitely made me a better guitar player, because I had to take up all the slack and be that much more honed with what I was doing. But now Frank's there, the songs come over much better, because the guitar hangs where it's supposed to while they the other one plays underneath, like on 'Smash Your Enemies', or on 'Empty Promises', where, after the intro, the one guitar's playing, the other is ringing out, y'know? And we were missing that type of thing live, no matter how tight we were... it wasn't 100% how we wanted it to be, and now we're right back to that. Frank is a great player, and we play a lot alike; it sounds really good, and if you loved Hatebreed the last four or five years, you'll love it even more now, 'cos there's even more sonic fury now!"

Hatebreed, Philadelphia YWCA, 1998, by Carl Gunhouse

The thing is, with the band becoming an institution in the metalcore genre, and a horde of rabid fans waiting to hungrily devour whatever you pump out, as long as it says 'Hatebreed' on the cover, isn't there a danger of complacency in the face of such adulation?

"But every record we do has to be better than the last one," counters Sean, with conviction, "For our own peace of mind, so if we ever did a half-hearted record, that would be selling ourselves short, as well as the fans. The band's been together for ten years now, and if we were going to do this half-assed, we'd just stay at home. We take a lot of pride in what we've done, what we've created, and we love our fans, and take our responsibilities to them very seriously. When you've worked as hard as us to achieve the level we've achieved, why not keep trying to go on, to make it better and better? And there's no reason we can't keep doing that."

FROM THE CUTTING ROOM FLOOR:

'Supremacy' feels more dynamic and listenable than 'Rise Of Brutality'....

I know what you mean. It wasn't a conscious effort, it came about naturally; we didn't really plan anything, we just wanted to make it the most crushing record we've done to date. Zeuss did a great job; he's really stepped up his game since we last recorded with him... everyone was just in a great frame of mind, everyone was there one million per cent, and we lived and breathed it to such a point that it really came through. Not that we didn't do that before, on every other record, but the vibe was REALLY right this time.

There's a thousand bands out there who wanna sound like Hatebreed! Are you aware of these pretenders snapping at your heels as you write each new album?

We wanna make every record a step up from the last one, but we don't sit around practising for hours and hours. When it comes to the musicality of the band, we're very loose... we're competent musicians, but we don't sit around practising all day. We tour so much, that's like a rehearsal every single night anyway. If we sat and practised with that mindset, it would probably detract from what we do.
But yeah, we have to make each album better than the last, and hopefully we'll never reach a point where we become stagnant. I think we can definitely top 'Supremacy', but we won't know for sure for a couple of years, haha!

Tell us about the writing process in Hatebreed... is it true that Jamey will hum the tunes into a tape recorder for you to translate into guitar riffs?

Yeah, sometimes he does that! He's even left me voicemail messages of him going, 'Duh-nuh-nuh, duh-nuh-nuh...' You know what I mean? He's definitely the head of the snake when it comes to the band... when it comes to song-writing... I mean, at one time, the kid was our singer, our manager, our tour manager, everything... and he has so many amazing riffs because he is not a guitar player first. He can play guitar... in fact, he's getting better and better all the time, he actually shreds riff-wise... but he can get his ideas out of his head enough for us to figure it out and translate it into a riff. And because he's a song-writer, not a guitar player, the ideas that come to his head aren't muddled up by years of practising and technicalities; he just throws these riffs out, and I'm like, 'Holy shit!' But we all contribute something, we go home and make our own demos and CDs, and then we submit 'em and listen to them, and the best stuff makes it into the songs. No one has an ego in this band – whoever comes to the table with the best stuff, it gets used. We're a really solid unit, and really good friends, and that applies to all aspects of what we do, be it song-writing, touring, whatever; it makes everything that much stronger. There's no inner bickering to take away from what we're trying to do; we're in it to win it, all down for the same cause.

And the writing process for this record was pretty much the same as any other: write a bunch of songs, riff 'em out, and record 'em. It's not hard! I don't want to make us sound cocky or anything, but we're not labouring over this material. We do sweat it in the studio, because we want it to be the heaviest, fastest, most aggressive, most powerful stuff possible, but it's not rocket science.

THE HAUNTED – ISSUE 84 (NOVEMBER 2000)

The Haunted – courtesy of Adam Sagir @ Century Media

The Haunted © Doralba Picerno

Things have most definitely been afoot in The Haunted camp of late, but they're back – and how! – with quite possibly the best metal album you'll hear all year, 'The Haunted Made Me Do It', so we sent Ian Glasper to investigate.

When a band blows up as big as The Haunted are about to, it suddenly becomes that much more awkward to contact them; they're usually jetting off to Brazil to play some huge festival or other. So, my first two attempts to contact them to discuss their phenomenal (the only word I can really come up with to describe it, to be honest) new album, 'The Haunted Made Me Do It' for Earache, fail miserably – but when I finally do catch up with new vocalist Marco Aro, the reasons turn out to be not quite so exotic.

"Uh, we forgot all about that first interview," he laughs, from the bedroom of a plush Berlin hotel room, halfway through a whistle-stop European press trip. "And then we missed our flights to England from Sweden, for that second press day! There was really bad weather that day, and no visibility at all, so we were late getting to the airport, and they'd already closed the gates..."

Hence here I am, sat frantically typing but hours before this issue's deadline. Such is the lot of the lowly journalist! Anyway, many of you will know that Marco Aro was once the singer of Swedish maulers Face Down, but landed himself the gig with The Haunted early last year, and what a gig it's proving to be. First of all, how are you coping with the musical transition from your old group to your new?

"Actually, it wasn't so big a jump for me," he confesses, "Because I was starting to get... uh, not bored as such... I was starting to feel, um, full of Face Down – like when you've had a big meal and totally enjoyed it, but don't want to eat anymore! And I had been thinking of maybe changing style slightly anyway... The call from The Haunted came as a complete surprise, but it was also kind of weird, because I had been thinking about my future in music, and the different bands I would love to try singing for, and The Haunted was one of them. I hadn't really been following their career too closely, so I didn't even know they were looking for a new singer!

"I didn't really know what to do, so I called Peter, the drummer of Entombed, who is a good friend of mine, and he really encouraged me to try out; he told me that I'd regret it for the rest of my life if I didn't at least give it a go, and I knew he was right, so I took him along to the audition with me - because he knows all the other guys – and about a month later I got the call."

And the rest is gonna go down in metal history, as they (sort of) say (sometimes)! So, why exactly did Peter Dolving leave the band anyway?

"It was all down to frustration, I think. He's a very creative, and impatient, person – he has his artwork, all the political stuff he's involved in, and he just got fed up of waiting for stuff to happen after that first album that never ever materialised. The same was true for Adrian [Erlandsson – the drummer who played on The Haunted's self-titled debut album, but who has also since departed – IG]. He just loves playing live, and he had an opportunity to play for Cradle of Filth and tour the world and actually manage to pay his rent, so who could blame him for leaving?"

And how, may I ask, are you fitting into the band now?

"It's really starting to work now," he beams. "In the beginning I was very nervous, trying to fill Peter's shoes; he was such a great vocalist, y'know? The biggest difference was that Face Down were very low-pitched and detuned, so I had to learn to sing in a new key, but it's actually easier, much more comfortable for me now."

Well, one listen to the stunning 'The Haunted Made Me Do It', and you'll all agree with me that Marco fits into the band like the missing piece of a particularly dark, twisted jigsaw. Like the final turn of the box in Hellraiser, he has helped summon from an already great band an album of truly monumental proportions. I'm not exaggerating when I say that '... Made Me Do It' is easily the best metal album I've heard this year. The dramatic and violent intro, 'Dark Intentions', literally explodes into a flurry of unfathomably complex and precise riffing, that even sees Marco tempering his furious roar with a liberal dose of melody that lends songs like 'Hollow Ground' a whole new depth of feeling beyond the purely heavy.

"I think the melody has surprised a lot of people... especially me," laughs the amicable vocalist. "It was an experiment for us too, but it worked well. I'm still not as confident with that style as I'd like to be, but I'm trying it more and more − 'cos I think I know pretty much everything there is to know about just shouting! I actually have a side project up in Stockholm called Mantra, where I can explore that clean vocal style a lot more, and right now I'm still just seeing whether or not I'm any good at it..."

Of course, I forgot that you lived up in Stockholm, and the other guys are down in Gothenburg... how does that pan out for writing and stuff?

"I'm a six-hour drive away from the other guys, so we write everything by mail. When we went in the studio, I hadn't sung one note of the new material actually with the band! I had done all my practising in my car on the way to work − I can't really do it at my place because the neighbours would think I was killing someone or something! It's difficult, but you can always make it work if you want to. Everyone I'm working with is very professional and supports me in every way possible. I would like to rehearse more, but I have a wife and a kid up in Stockholm and it would be too big a wrench for the family to relocate."

So, what about the other components of The Haunted... how do you start writing such a complete and perfect metal record? Do tell (pens at the ready, everybody!).

"Uh, well we all have a lot of different influences that we bring to the table. Per only really listens to jazz; he actually has a John Coltrane tattoo on his thigh! I mean, he was in Artillery and Konkhra, but he basically quit the metal scene a few years ago, cut his hair, learnt the piano, and started playing jazz with old men in smoky bars [laughs]... we had to make quite a few calls to get him out of retirement! It only took us three months to write and record this album; the rest of the time was spent sat around frustrated looking for a new drummer and stuff. As you know, Jensen is very productive [their guitarist extraordinaire, who also plays in Witchery − the thrash metal band who churn out records faster than most bands can mike their drum kit – IG], and we already have half a dozen songs written for the next Haunted album! We're planning to record it next Spring, for a late Summer release..."

Ah, yes, Jensen. And those riffs. The guitarist in my own band took one listen to '... Made Me Do It', picked his jaw up off the floor, and exclaimed that the guitar playing was 'impossible'! And definitely not the work of human hands... surely they weren't forged by machines in the studio?

"Yes, a vibrator!" I hear a laughing Jensen shout in the background of Marco's hotel room.

"It's true, he had a vibrator up his ass in the studio the whole time," confirms Marco. "We're actually a gaycore band," adds Jensen wickedly.

"We were going to call the record 'The Homos Made Us Do It!" comes Marco's defiantly non-PC and heavy metal response...

Seriously though, creating music this aggressive does elicit excessive behaviour (I'm talking about their tasteless humour here rather than the insertion of objects into one's own back passage, of course), and I'll round out the interview with a few of Marco's anecdotes, one of them even from my virtual home town!

"Once I got punched in the face – in Cheltenham of all places. This guy just didn't know what to do he was so excited when we started playing, and he hit me in the face, smashed all my nose open; there was blood everywhere, but I guess it added to the effect of the show! It wasn't a problem really; I suppose it was actually a compliment...

"Like in Italy, where they'll spit at you and flip you off if they like you. 'Fuck you, you're great!' 'Fuck off, we love you!' That's the great thing about being in a band like this, playing this sort of music; you just don't see that sort of behaviour every day!"

Suggested Side-bar: PORTRAIT OF A CEREAL KILLER!

I took one look at the awesome artwork of the new Haunted record, and obviously assumed that they had done helluva lot of research to really get inside the demented minds of serial killers. Assumption, as they say, is the mother of all fuck-ups, and my intended sidebar all about the band's top five mass murderers went out the window when Marco told me:

"No, there was nothing too serious about it all; it's all meant in an ironic way really... a big poke in the ribs of the PMRC. Metal is an easy scapegoat when kids do stupid stuff to themselves... I mean, if you knocked up the sixteen-year-old girl next door, would you blame it on metal?"

Of course I would - why else would I have done it? "Yeah, well... anyway, we have a guy in Stockholm called Andreas who does our artwork, and we asked him for a shirt design, and he came up with 'The Haunted Made Me Do It', and we just thought it would be a cool title."

So, if you're not up for a top five serial killers sidebar, at least tell me how you would choose to kill someone yourself – given the choice. And it has to be very metal. And it mustn't involve a vibrator - see main body of piece if you're late joining us!

"Um... I would wear nothing but a bullet belt and beat them to death with a herring."
Any particular reason for that?
"Just to see how long it would take."
Are there any herrings on your rider for the UK tour?
"You better hope not. Or there could be an incident. Tell the caterers."

Hearse – issue 122 (August 2004)

You wouldn't expect the former vocalist for Arch Enemy, Johan Liiva, to take his eviction from the band lying down. That's why, without further ado, he formed the death/thrash outfit known as Hearse, and after quite a start, the band's sophomore album, 'Armageddon Mon Amour' is about to turn up the heat. Ian Glasper got the handful of dirt.

THE ROAD LESS TRAVELLED
One would expect any band that features an ex-member of such a hugely popular band as Arch Enemy to instantly be granted a certain amount of profile themselves, especially when said ex-member was the Enemy's acclaimed original vocalist Johan Liiva. But Johan's new project, Hearse, has remained decidedly low profile, despite releasing a well-received EP (2002's 'Torch', Hammerheart) and LP (2003's 'Dominian Reptilian', Karmageddon Media). Possibly because, although having just unveiled their thumping second album, 'Armageddon Mon Amour', they have yet to actually play a show together!
"Yes, it's true, we've not played any gigs," admits Johan sheepishly. "But that's all about to change – we're going to the Netherlands and Belgium in September with Dismember. It isn't that we haven't wanted to play out or anything; the right opportunity just hasn't arisen, but we haven't exactly chased gigs either, 'cos we had a lot of work to do, studying and stuff, so we just focused on writing songs and recording..."
It's really hard to promote a band that doesn't tour though; it's any label's nightmare. Maybe that's why the first album passed a lot of people by?
"Yeah, I guess so," Johann admits. "If you want to sell albums, you have to go on the road, but this way I figure we can at least sell two albums at once!
"We got together back in 2000, just a few weeks after I had to leave Arch Enemy," continues the vocalist, on the origins of the band. "They wanted a new vocalist, to take the band to a higher level, and circumstances at the time were a bit chaotic really, especially my own lifestyle. I suppose I was at a crossroads.
"But I haven't looked back since. I even started another band, Non-Exist, at the same time as Hearse. That was very technical death metal, kinda like Meshuggah meets At The Gates; we did one album, on War Music, called 'Deus Deceptor'. Very technical, but not all that groovy, and I personally like groovy music, ha ha! Which is why Hearse is

much more rock 'n' roll, and why I've left Non-Exist now to concentrate and focus on the music I enjoy most."

BEYOND COMPARE

'Dominion Reptilian' was an impressive debut by anyone's standards, but it seemed to go over the heads of its potential audience. How does Johan regard the response it got now, with the benefit of hindsight?

"Well yes, it had a mixed reaction," he agrees. "A lot of people said that it was mediocre and nothing new, whilst others really appreciated it because we were trying out all these new ideas, especially with our guitar solos which we manage to cram into every song, haha! 'Cos that's our trademark, I think; melodic leads, catchy choruses – good songs basically."

And then of course there was the frustration from being constantly compared to Arch Enemy...

"Yes,", sighs Johan, "But we were expecting that anyway. Of course people were going to make those comparisons, and, to be fair to them, a lot of the songs on the first album were in a similar vein to Arch Enemy, really; it's only with the new album that we've started to find our own sound."

Their own sound indeed! 'Armageddon Mon Amour' is about as diverse a collection of death/thrash metal as you're likely to hear anywhere. Alarmingly described on one metal website as 'equal parts funk and crust' (just imagine!), the crux of the Hearse sound actually lies somewhere between the filthy thrash of early Entombed, the majestic plod of prime Candlemass and the off-the-wall eclecticism of 'Into The Pandemonium'-era Celtic Frost. Admittedly it's not quite as awesome as the sum of those parts could be just yet, but they get full marks for setting their sights higher than most. And when they lock together with the bit between their teeth, Hearse are as convincingly heavy as they are ambitious.

"Yeah, that's a good one, I'm pretty pleased with that," laughs Johan at the comparison, especially to Celtic Frost. "Their 'Into The Pandemonium' album is one of my favourite records ever. Just don't talk to me about 'Cold Lake'...!"

What of the Entombed part of the equation though? Once they were the definitive Swedish metal band, before everyone started looking to the States for their inspiration.

"Well, all bands have their own direction, and there's room for all of us, but you're right, a lot of modern bands seem to have forgotten about old school death metal. Some of them avoid it like the plague, and just wanna sound like the latest big thing, but we're pretty old fashioned. We love the dirty guitar sound, all the rough edges to the music. That's why we're so excited to tour with Dismember! They're really old school," he laughs, "And that couldn't suit us better!"

Does he listen to much else apart from metal?

"Oh, we listen to a lot of different stuff, everything from Discharge to David Bowie, really! For example, Max loves Radiohead. He is totally crazy about them; he listens to them on a daily basis. And I'm a big Depeche Mode freak. I like a lot of that '80s UK pop music."

So he's to blame for their ridiculously sludgy cover of Kim Wilde's 'Cambodia' then!

"Well, it's a great song, and she was pretty good-looking too, don't you think? We haven't had too much feedback yet from our fans here about the choice of cover, but I think that as long as it's a heavy, well-performed song, they don't mind too much either way."

It makes a change from yet another Slayer cover...

"Oh, totally. We'd never cover another metal band! At least not on our own album. Maybe on a tribute or something..."

So, does Johan enjoy messing with people's preconceptions of what the band 'should' sound like?

"Yeah, that's what we're all about. We do whatever we want, and we're not afraid of making fools of ourselves, you know? But this time we looked over all the arrangements, and all the mistakes we made, on that first album very carefully. We wanted to make every aspect better, especially the production. The whole sound on that first album was crammed together in a way, and we wanted it all to sound a lot bigger, but not too polished. And I really do think we've found our own style now; it's perfect for us."

UPHILL BATTLES

Not only does the new album sound great, it looks great too, with a gloriously bizarre fold-out sleeve by Marco Jeurissen that suits the melodramatic atmospherics of the album to a tee. It seems to depict the long, harsh road we all face through life as an unforgiving mountainside to be climbed, with little more than summary dismissal awaiting us at the journey's end.

"Well, the record label hired him to do our first album, and we were really pleased with what he did for us. We sent him the lyrics and the music, and then he had free rein to do what he wanted, as long as he kept with the mood of the album. And obviously he picked up on [opening track] 'Mountain Of The Solar Eclipse' as one of the main themes for his illustration."

And what about that provocative title, 'Armageddon Mon Amour'?

"It was a line from a song on the first album. I took it from a book actually, 'Hiroshima Mon Amour', and changed it to 'Armageddon' to bring it more up-to-date, what with all the talk of Armageddon at the moment!"

Does he have more than a passing interest in politics then?

"Well, we're aware of what's going on in the world, and we kind of absorb it. You can't just close your eyes to it, y'know? And in one way or another, it comes out in the music you write, subconsciously if not directly, whether you like it or not."

TO THE POWER OF THREE

"Max [Thornell, drums] and I are really old friends," says Johan, when talk turns to the two rather-less-famous members playing alongside him. "We met back in '84, when we used to play in underground punk bands together. We had a band back in the early

'90s, called Furbowl, and that was a groovy kind of metal too, similar to Hearse in a way, but a lot more primitive.

"As for Mattias [Ljung, guitar], he's been studying and teaching music for a long time, and he's been in a lot of small bands with friends, playing in little venues around Stockholm, but this is his first real band."

It's cool to see a three-piece line-up too. Once that was the classic line-up for a metal band, but nowadays most bands favour two guitarists...

"Haha, three people in the band is more than enough to cope with right now... in Furbowl, we actually only had two people in the band to start with! But of course, when you're playing live, it's a little difficult, with only one guitar, especially if you have a lot of solos, so that's worrying me a bit, that's something we may have to work on. But if we plan to do more touring next year, maybe we'll get another guitarist in just to play live."

Hearse are planning to follow their first shows in September, with a visit to the UK next year, but before then there's the other matter of recording another album this summer.

"Yeah, we have a lot of songs!" Johan laughs. "And we wanna record them all before we get too old. We don't wanna keep our fans waiting for the next record whilst we tour the world, so we're just going to record albums and stay at home, haha!"

HELVIS – ISSUE 102 (SEPTEMBER 2002)

Loudspeaker would have you believe that their gnarliest signings by far, Helvis, hail from a remote island in the north of Scotland from whence they fled once they were caught practising the old religion. It's a nice thought and it really would be fun if the grinding spiteful metalcore that is 'Reverence The Sacrifice', their splendid debut album, had been produced by crusty pagans. A group of pagans in an Entombed tribute band busting out Varukers jams, to be precise...

"Yes, I would be very pleased with that comparison, thank you!" says guitarist Chris Marygold happily. "We've all been Entombed fans for years so I suppose that may have rubbed off on our writing. Obviously [Kevin] Frost plays drums for The Varukers too, so I would expect some bits of the ten pence punk sound to come across, haha! And there really is a Varukers cover on the LP [the raging 'Nothing's Changed' – IG], but I suppose that Discharge were a big influence on both bands so that's going to come over in our faster bits too."

And talking of Discharge, I have to mention the bizarre review you had in one magazine where the journalist in question wondered aloud whether your song 'Black Discharge' was racist?

"It simply came from the fact that we were once described as a cross between Discharge and Black Sabbath," explains Chris. "And I replied 'like a sort of Black Discharge you mean?' So when the next Discharge riff arrived at the practice room it was christened 'B/D'. The lyrics were a quote from a book BK [Bloody Kev, vocals – IG] had by

463

Helvis

Lautremont; 'Melancholy and sadness, are the beginning of doubt. Doubt is the beginning of despair'. And that is what the song is all about!"

So, are you guys metal or punk or couldn't you really give a fuck either way?

"There are certain factions of this band that would say punk, and some metal. We are all metal fans really, just that one of us is a closet metaller... I don't really care how we're described, to be honest. We have influences from all over and have been known to 'recycle' from various sources...!"

"I don't understand your mainland wordings," babbles Steve Watson, the band's 'eastern guitarist' (Chris is their 'western one', you see), the voice of Wicker Man-like reason in the band. "Surely hardcore is building rubble, punk is a person of low morals, and metal is without doubt best played by the band Evil whose classic '80s LP 'Evil's Message' is about as good as it gets."

Uh, okay, mate, best leave the last words to Chris then, eh? Do you ever feel out of place on Loudspeaker's roster at all?

"I don't know why they signed us to be honest," he laughs. "As most of their roster seems to be 'metal-metal', with expansive polished production and sports metal soundtracks, whereas we were just given some pennies and sent to record with our mates at Pristine in Nottingham! Listening to the compilation they put out, it just sounds like we turn up at the end and gate-crash the party!"

Himsa, by Jimbo

I dare say that many of you took one look at my 9/10 review of Himsa's 'Groundbreakingceremony' album for Revelation last issue and thought to yourselves, 'Oh, Glasper's getting all hysterical again...' Oh, the hurt! After all these years and you still don't trust my judgement - have I ever lied to you? No, I think not. Still, even I expected the instant awe I felt for the record to dim a little with time. But hey, I'm listening to it again as I type and it still kicks my ass. In fact, I placed it in my personal top five for 1999, so there. Of course, some of you may be more familiar with Trial, that other Seattle hardcore band whose members it was that spawned the hybrid beast that is Himsa, and who were quite renowned as being rather outspoken about their straight edge ideals?

"Only one of the three of us who were in Trial is still straight edge," explains the band's guitarist Brian, "But none of us label ourselves as such anymore; it's more of a quiet personal thing. There was one point in time, when I was in high school, I couldn't think of anything I would rather be - and to be honest, if I hadn't been straight edge, I just don't know where I'd be right now. But we all got older and things change, in my life and in the scene as well. I'm not old school or anything; when I got into hardcore it was through bands like Undertow and Unbroken. I would go to shows every weekend and it was such an awesome vibe, but then it got really cliquey and a lot of the magic was lost for me. People change, you know?"

And change seems to be one of the primal forces at the very heart of Himsa. Every time you spin their disc, you find something new inside there to move you afresh. It throbs with subtle undercurrents that belie its undeniable brute power. The band have crammed more diversity into 38 electrifying minutes than most will manage in their entire careers. It's quite a step on from their simpler days in Trial (who were an amazing band in their own right, don't get me wrong – 'Are These Our Lives?' on Equal Vision still comes highly recommended).

"Himsa is a whole new level," enthuses the six-stringer, "And I couldn't be happier. I was having to fit myself into Trial musically, and I could never seem to break free of that format. But Himsa is way more me. In fact, I was in a lot of metal bands before Trial... I mean I love Judge, but I love Cannibal Corpse too. We listen to everything from glam metal to old punk rock, and all these styles come into play in Himsa.

"A lot of people get confused when they see such an angry name," he ponders. "It's from a Buddhist word that means wrath and rage and violence, but from all those negative things, a lot of good can result. Protest can be violent, but out of that emerges change. Whatever, the name suits the band. It's very apocalyptic and very intense, so let people make up their own minds when they hear us."

And 'intensely apocalyptic' sums it all up quite nicely too. 'Ground-breakingceremony' is just that: a band rejoicing in the destruction of old sonic cliches, a band ushering in new standards against which all noisy twisted metalcore will be judged in the next century. It really is the purest outpouring of rage I've heard from a Revelation release for many a year.

"Rage is just one of many emotions in there," counters Brian. "It all means something different to all of us. Rage for one means sadness for another. We like to screw with people and go from heavy to mellow to metal, and back again. We have the highs and the lows in both our music and our lyrics, and that's how we try to touch people. And we're getting such a great response too, which is so cool; we never expected it. At shows a lot of people just stand there, which might seem disconcerting to some bands, but the way I look at it is - at least they're paying attention. The Dillinger Escape Plan have told me that they get a similar response, and look at how off the wall they are. I'd rather have people actually listening to what we're doing, and be forced to try and understand it, than just going crazy and throwing their arms around aimlessly.

"Some people have even compared us to bands like 108 or Rage Against the Machine [more like System Of A Down hooking up with Will Haven at a Neurosis show – IG]," he says, still trying to pin down his own band's unique sound. "What the hell is all that about? I mean, we're blown away by comparisons like that; they are such great bands but I don't think you can really pigeonhole us that easily. And we're only going to get more challenging musically, because we like to challenge ourselves!"

Hirax – by Albert Licano

Back in the mid-'80s, Hirax were the darlings of the thrash underground, the first release on an unknown label called Earache, and with an appeal that broke down all barriers. Now they're back together after thirteen years with a new EP, 'El Diablo Negro' and a forthcoming album, 'Barrage Of Noise' featuring The Haunted's Per Moller Jensen on drums. Ian Glasper laid out the red carpet for frontman, Katon W. De Pena

If you ever heard Hirax back in the mid-'80s, you would never forget them. They had a unique style of crossover, a blur of lightning-speed riffing and crazy-ass drumming, whilst their vocalist Katon W. De Pena howled over the top like a banshee loosed from hell. With a logo designed by Tom G. Warrior they managed to appeal to everyone from hardcore punks to true metalheads (even Rykers recently did a cover of 'Bombs of Death'), and their two albums clocked up more than respectable sales worldwide, and then... they disappeared. So, when I saw that there was a brand new Hirax EP available, I was first in line to check it out.

"Well, the last two releases we did were 'Raging Violence' in 1985 and 'Hate, Fear And Power' in 1987 for Metal Blade and Roadrunner," recalls Katon, bringing me up to date with his movements of the last fifteen years. "We also did 'The Anglican Scrape Attic' flexi-disc, which was the first record to ever come out on Earache Records, and later we did the recording sessions for 'Blasted In Bangkok'. Those were the last recordings Hirax did with the original line-up. They'll be released along with the recordings that

Hirax, by Albert Licano

I did with Phantasm, the band that I started with Ron McGoveny [the original Metallica bassist – IG] and Gene Hoglan [drummer for Dark Angel, Death, Testament and Strapping Young Lad – IG]. Both recordings kick ass. They will be out on Deep Six Records... probably by the time this interview hits the streets actually.

"Hirax disbanded right around the beginning of 1988 due to all kinds of personal problems... magnified by alcohol abuse, and then in 1997 this band from San Francisco, Spazz, asked us to do a split 7" with them. The word about the band spread even more after that, and things started to snowball so much. Kids would tell us, 'You wouldn't believe how many people love your band'. So, last year, we finally put up the Hirax website and much to our total amazement it started receiving a lot of hits from all over the world. Thus the band decided to start playing music again. We played our first show back last September, and we recorded a three-song demo the very next day!"

Which of course, became the 'El Diablo Negro' 7" that I gave such a glowing review to last issue. Katon is still with his original bassist, and original drummer too, at least on the EP. Who else is in the band right now?

"Because of the overwhelming support and response from our fans worldwide," enthuses the likable frontman, "We really wanted to put the original line-up back together, but time and age change a lot of things. Scott Owen and I were the youngest and I'm 37 now! But I'm still a helluva lot younger than Lemmy from Motorhead, haha!

"The other guys have children now and houses that they have to pay for, and unfortunately were not able to continue, but there was no chance in hell that the band would not play on! I am 100% into the band, more now than ever before! So we have two new guitarists who are both incredible players. They compliment each other nicely – they are a huge wall of sound – and on the new record we will have Per Moller Jensen, from The Haunted, playing the drums. He has been listening to Hirax and has been a fan since he was eleven years old. He approached us by email offering his services, and we were flattered and replied, 'Yes! We'd love for you to play with us on the new record'. Plus his band totally kick ass; we support what they do 100%. I'm sure he will be working with us a lot in the future on different projects. The bass player who will play on the record is Shaun Ross from Excel. We will probably announce the touring line-up later... depending on scheduling."

Have you been keeping track of the metal scene during your hiatus? If so, have you been pleased or saddened by any trends you've witnessed, and why do you think the time is right for you to return?

"The only thing that really upsets us is alternative music," he spits. "And rap metal. I hate that shit. It's funny, but because I'm black, people think I want to hear that shit. Well, they're dead wrong. I can't stand this new wimpy shit. Seven Dust, Stuck Mojo, Limp Bizkit, Korn, Lit... those bands are all knob jobs. I feel sorry for them really, 'cos for the kind of music they're doing they will burn in hell.

"The reason why the time is right for Hirax is because everything is there for us. We have a very big following in the underground, of die-hard people that are into our music, and we are very proud of that. We will give people the real thing; if they want loud, fast, heavy music, we're the band they are looking for."

And I'll second that. 'El Diablo Negro' is gloriously loud and brash, not to mention unashamedly old school. You seem to have made a concerted effort to stay true to your original sound; was that intentional, or is this the only style you feel comfortable with? I wondered if any of your musical tastes or influences had changed over the years?

"In Hirax we only play what feels comfortable to us. I know for a fact we would never put out anything with the name Hirax on it if it were to shy too far away from what Hirax is all about, which is THRASH. Our influences are still pretty much true to what they always were... Larm, Neos, Neon Christ, Siege, as well as classical music, Spanish flamenco guitar, orchestras, and middle eastern music... but don't let that scare you! These are all just little elements to make our music that much more brutal. The new album will crush everything we've ever done in the past."

One noticeable difference though – for me, anyway – was that your vocals aren't so crazy high like first time around. Again, was this deliberate, or can't you reach those stratospheric notes anymore? Old age and all that!

"No, I can still hit the notes, but on this 7" I wanted to do something different. Plus, the songs are more than a little bit aggressive, so I wanted the vocals to sound really harsh, which was easy to do considering we played a concert the night before. I liked the way it came out, and it's a nice change of pace. But you will hear flashes of the old Katon as well as the new Katon on the next recordings."

Katon has his own label, Black Devil, although the forthcoming album is being released via Deep Six. After all these years, isn't he so jaded with the music that he's tempted to put out the new Hirax album himself? It might seem the next logical step for someone so keen to keep control of every aspect of their art.

"That's a great question. Yeah, Black Devil is run by me and my lovely Norwegian girlfriend, all self-financed on a very small budget. Right now, we are using the label to distribute all of the Hirax stuff that we have, but it's starting to become too hard to keep up with all the orders, and that's the only reason we will probably sign with a bigger independent. I do have a lot of experience with record companies, but once you get to a certain point you don't want to let your fans down and not write back to them, or not send them their merchandise, so to have the backing of a bigger record company helps a lot.

"I am kinda jaded, but I'm also very realistic about the business side of things. And I care about the fans. I had a kid write me a letter - well he's probably not a kid any more – and he wrote to Hirax back in 1986, to order a tee-shirt. He sent his money, and never got it, and then he wrote to us now and ordered more Hirax merchandise! I was so touched, that he was such a diehard fan, I sent him the shirt that he ordered now and threw in a shirt for free that he had ordered back in 1986. We have the best fans in the world, and that's why we're still around."

How's the new album sounding? What can we expect from Hirax in 2001?

"It's been a long time coming, but everything has worked out perfectly," he gushes with fierce pride. "We record in May, for the first time with two guitar players. I will go as far as to say this; it will be in the top three thrash metal records of 2001. Guaranteed. A wall of sound. Extreme, brutal thrash metal music. This record will surprise a lot of people, even people who have never heard of or liked the band. They will all be blown the fuck away.

"Here's a bit of trivia. Almost everything that Hirax has recorded before was recorded in a day or two, and that's including the albums. We are working harder on this new record than anything we've ever done before; we will spend way more time writing, rehearsing and recording. This record will be a masterpiece. We know a lot of people are watching us, and a lot of our fans want this record to come out and kill everything... so we're not going to let them down."

HIRAX – ISSUE 123 (SEPTEMBER 2004)

Cult old school thrashers Hirax are back with a vengeance, a new line-up and the best album of their career in the shape of 'The New Age Of Terror'. Ian Glasper searched out frontman Katon W. De Pena, and discovered why the band are as relevant today as they ever were.

Two snarling wolves glare balefully from the cover of 'The New Age Of Terror', the hotly anticipated new album from cult LA thrashers Hirax. Not only is it the finest artwork to adorn one of their discs since Pushead's crazy 'Murder Of Humpty Dumpty' painting for

Hirax © Maciej Mutwil

1985's 'Raging Violence' (see sidebar), but it sets the tone for the murderous mayhem that ensues when you hit 'Play'. The band lunge and snap viciously, seemingly hungrier and more savage than ever before, and vocalist Katon W. De Pena howls like a man possessed. The spirit of his beloved scene courses so strongly through his veins, it would be a fair wager that he bleeds molten metal when cut. He's steered Hirax through thick and thin since resurrecting them from the dead back in 1997. Consequently, the new LP is both a gauntlet across the chops of many so-called modern thrash bands and a fitting testament to one man's belief in his teenage dreams. It's a real return to the classic form demonstrated on 'Hate, Fear And Power'.

"Yeah, it was kind of a conscious effort to get that vibe back again," beams Katon. "We just wanted to make a record that was in your face. A lot of bands have strayed away from that kinda stuff, but our thing is, we wanna stay true to what we do. We really love this music and we're not ashamed of it, so that's pretty much what the new LP represents: five guys playing metal the way they love to hear it."

Integral to Hirax's recapturing of their classic vibe is the return to a more 'traditional' style of vocals, something that was missing from their recent comeback EPs. Katon is in full agreement:

"Yeah, you're right, but it was really all a matter of time. For the previous records we just didn't have enough time to get everything just how we wanted it. Even on this one we didn't have enough, to be honest; we did it all in four days, but it was still more time than before! We'll probably have longer for the next record, though, 'cos I'm sure that this record will open a lot of doors for us. People are really just getting a taste of what's to come.

"Believe it or not, we really do love what we do," he continues, "and we're not really concerned with the other music going on out there 'cos there's a lot of different trends in metal music today. But we're just playing the kinda stuff that we grew up on, that we love. It's a combination of hardcore and metal, or metal and hardcore, whichever you prefer!"

Yet it's fairly apparent there's little or no influence from more current metal music.

"No, none at all. I guess that music's okay if that's what you're into, but we just don't like that stuff, which is why we continue to write the music we do."

Remarkably, with such a satisfying and cohesive new album in the racks, Hirax 2004 sees a totally different band to the one that recorded 2001's 'Barrage Of Noise' backing up Katon's distinctive shriek. Which obviously begs the question, just what happened to that previous line-up?

"You know what?" sighs Katon, "I was never able to find guys that were crazy enough to wanna go out on tour all the time. But these guys I have right now are probably the most insane guys I've ever worked with as far as hunger and that desire to wanna go out on the road and give it their all. We've all invested our lives in this music, but the old band couldn't go on tour; they all had other obligations. The new guys have other obligations as well, but they make this band pretty much a priority in their lives, just like I do, which is why this line-up is working out so well. When you hear the playing on the new record, you can tell that everybody really wants to do this. I really had to find the right people for it, who all had the same passion as myself, 'cos I've never wanted to stop, I've never given up the dream of Hirax. So right now, with these guys, I'm living out my dream, doing what I wanna do. And hopefully, God willing, we'll stay together and keep putting out great records."

As for those new musicians, youngest member Dave Watson was already something of a veteran musician, a regular on the LA/Orange County circuit. Second guitar player Glen Rogers ("I call the two of them 'The Assassins'," laughs Katon) was a member of both Vengeance Rising, and Deliverance, the latter one of the first bands to start the Christian metal movement. "He's not doing that stuff now," says Katon, "But he should be proud of himself, 'cos to start any kind of a thing is great, especially if it's metal orientated, haha!"

Bassist Angelo Espino was drawn from Reverend, who featured former Metal Church vocalist, David Wayne, while drummer Jorge Lacobellis had played in various metal bands in Argentina.

"I just got guys that knew this kind of music inside out, that's why it sounds so authentic," states Katon. "I don't have time to sit around and bash old musicians, but this is a completely different ball game. The basic idea with this record was to take everything to that new level. We wanted to make something that was better than anything any of us had done before. And I think we've accomplished that, so we're pretty proud of it. We wanted to give the fans something good, so now we just have to go out and give them a good live show too."

2004 is also a big year for Katon, in that it's been twenty eventful years since he first launched Hirax. Yet compare songs from the mid-'80s like 'Bombs Of Death' and 'The Last War' to 'Kill Switch' and 'Suffer' from the new album, and it's a tragic case of 'same shit, different decade' to rage against.

"Absolutely. You read that right, and I hope that everybody who hears the record realises that too. We've been directly impacted upon by what's goin' on around us, especially by the war. We're not putting down our own soldiers, 'cos they're just following orders, but war is never a good thing, no-one wins in the long run. There is an underlying tension; you can feel that in the record, in the music.

"We have something to say, and we're not afraid to say it. We do vote, but no-one listens to us, so bands like us have an obligation to speak out. A lot of metal bands, especially from the United States, won't even touch on that subject, but we're not afraid to speak our minds. That's why a lot of punks like our music too, 'cos they know we're not just your average metal band with nothing to say, writing about killing for the hell of it or whatever. We write about things that actually do matter to us."

Hirax have always worn their influences proudly on their sleeves, a symptom of the band's honesty, and perhaps it's that integrity as well that has always drawn the respect of the punk scene.

"Definitely," Katon agrees, "And we'll always be that way. 'Cos if you stop having something to say, you lose your passion, and that's what this music is all about. We're glad that we've given people a great album, great lyrics, great music and a great album cover. I don't think we're cheating anyone, y'know? Everything we do is completely about the fans; we're doing this for them, and as long as they're there for us, we'll be here for them."

SIDEBAR: Unleash The Dogs Of War: The Hirax Highlights

'Raging Violence' [Roadrunner] 1985
Exploding from one of the most gloriously OTT spoken word intros ever, 'Demons, Evil Forces' set the pace, its insidious opening riff careening wildly out of control into blast beat and fretboard mayhem, while Katon's vocals soared to infinity – and beyond.

'Hate, Fear And Power' [Metal Blade] 1986
With new drummer Eric Brecht from DRI, Hirax managed to scale new heights of manic speed, but also tightened up the riffing for a thrash attack of gargantuan proportions. Its impact wasn't lessened any by the fact the whole record lasted less than twenty minutes. The work of psychopathic genius.

'El Diablo Negro' [Black Devil/Deep Six] 1998
The comeback record that few dared believe would happen. Only three tracks, and not a patch on the Hirax of old, but it still urinated on all the nu-metal wannabes from a great height and paved the way for the lethal urgency of 'The New Age Of Terror'.

The Horror – by Sheep

It was a sad day for UK hardcore punk when both Voorhees and Imbalance chose to call it a day, especially as the last recorded output by either act was their finest to date and hinted at truly great things to come. Thank fuck then for The Horror, who've kinda picked up where Voorhees left off. In fact, The Horror is basically Voorhees, but with vocalist Lecky replaced by Andy from Imbalance.

"About halfway through our last Voorhees US tour, myself, Dave, Arms and Atko all decided that enough was enough," explains guitarist Steve. "We just weren't having fun anymore, and we talked about doing our own shit from scratch. Voorhees was always Lecky's concern anyway; we were just along for the ride and that ride was becoming dull. But we're all still friends with Lecky; there's no gossip here, despite how it might look to outsiders."

"I simply wasn't happy doing it anymore, I'm afraid," Andy from Imbalance cites similar reasons for the demise of his previous band in late 2001. "As far as I was concerned, I felt I'd pretty much come full circle, and I knew that I wouldn't have been able to tour again in that band without completely destroying friendships, so I chose the best option.

"Once back in England, word got round pretty fast that I was leaving. Voorhees was breaking up and they decided amongst themselves that they were gonna ask me to join the new band, and Steve asked me at one of the last Imbalance gigs... it pretty much went from there."

The Horror manage to be even more intense than either of the two bands who spawned it, blasting away at 100mph, each song an uncompromising burst of machine gun speed with clever socio-political lyrics yapped out over the top of the detonation. You could be forgiven for thinking you were dealing with a Misfits-style gothic punk band by the name... but nothing could be further from the truth.

"We look no further than Impact Unit, Negative FX, Gang Green, Out Cold, Black Flag and Poison Idea," reveals Steve of the band's influences. "'80s hardcore is pretty much our sole inspiration. We pride ourselves on our three-chord thrash and childish mosh parts.

"Our lyrics are about the folly of man and how we are all destined to burn. There's very little about this world that's nice, so why pretend otherwise? We live in a world where the bad guys always win. And we ain't no goth schtick costumed Murderdolls goofy Danzig-rip-off party band either!"

The band's first release is the 'First Blood' 10" for NYC label, Chainsaw Safety, a blistering fourteen songs in less than fourteen minutes, all offset by Andy's distinctive and intellectual approach to lyric writing.

"'Let's Get Regional' is about the death of regional accents, the spread of 'Estuary English', which is supported by the media, newsreaders and their entire ilk," Andy explains the ideas behind a few of my favourite songs off the 10". "It's about wanting to hear people who sound like you on TV, being interested by different accents and dialects, and never being made to feel ashamed of your accent and the way you speak.

"'Attack Ships On Fire' has got a bit of everything in it but is loosely about the notion that you get what you work for. Well, for the most part this is true, but occasionally we find people who excel without trying, or they come up with something ingenious based on coincidence; Mary Shelley dreaming up Frankenstein, and particularly Rutger Hauer writing the death scene in 'Bladerunner' ten minutes before it was shot - now that is pure genius!"

As well as The Horror, Steve sings in The Sex Maniacs, who also comprise various members of Voorhees and Drop Nose. Despite the shared musicians, The Sex Maniacs couldn't sound more different from his other turn, coming straight out of the proverbial garage with a much sleazier rock 'n' roll vibe. Their debut CD has just been released by Eccentric Man, entitled 'Mean As Hell'.

"The Horror is fast and dead serious. The 'Maniacs is rock and dead stupid. We're a bunch of fucking idiots. Whilst both bands share many of the same influences it just comes out different in the mix. Both bands are influenced by Black Flag, Circle Jerks and Poison Idea, but we do stuff in The 'Maniacs that we could never pull off in The Horror... especially lyrically.

"The 'Maniacs started out as an AC/DC rip off band, a bit of a laugh between friends and I guess it just got out of hand! I see The Horror as always being a fast political hardcore band that won't be everyone's cup of tea. However the future of The 'Maniacs is clouded... who knows where it will go? I know one thing though - both bands will always blow your tits off."

The Horror - by Sheep

Once described as a cross between Discharge and (seminal Boston hardcore band) DYS, The Horror feature ex-members of Voorhees and Imbalance, and make just as nasty a noise as you'd imagine from such a ferocious pedigree.

"Whilst I hate defining the stuff that we do, that comparison always made me laugh," smiles vocalist Andy. "As for that whole 'Dis-core' sound? God, I didn't realise how much I hate that term, but it has been an influence on the song-writing, particularly on the stuff that Arms has written - he and Steve are the big Discharge fans in the band. There's also a ton of other stuff which gets thrown in in equal measure, so I think people just pick out the stuff that they like and make comparisons from there..."

"The Horror has existed longer for us than Imbalance or Voorhees though, eight years now, and from very early on we always thought of ourselves as a band in our own right, distinctly different from those other bands we were in. The 'ex-members of...' thing doesn't really bother us - no one really escapes their past in that respect – and I'm sure it will exist as long as the band does... and then start all over again - with 'ex-The Horror'!"

One thing that the ripping new album, 'Spoils Of War', does defiantly confirm however is that The Horror are carrying on the strong traditions established by the guys' previous bands, of marrying challenging music to challenging lyrics, and this is indeed a disc that will have you pondering its meaning long after the harsh chords have stopped crashing around your head.

"Age and experience have altered my perspective on the concept of a 'hardcore movement' to the point that I'm resolute in my opinion that it doesn't exist," reckons Andy. "Now, that's not to devalue punk rock or hardcore as musical forms, or the people who identify themselves as punks or hardcore kids and what they do, but to suggest that this loose collection of people, who have a similar taste in music, but have differing views across the political spectrum, and for the most part can't even agree on what 'punk' actually is – never mind anything else – form some kind of collective 'movement' is a little delusional, to say the least..."

FROM THE CUTTING ROOM FLOOR:

The Horror have quite a pedigree as far as UK hardcore goes, was it much of a struggle to establish yourselves in your own right and slip the 'ex-members of Voorhees and Imbalance' tag?

I think in the beginning it was to be expected and it certainly didn't do us any harm. I would go as far as to say that initially things happened for us because of those two bands; but whilst I'm reflecting on it, that tag was not so much of an issue outside of Britain because Imbalance's profile outside of this country wasn't that extensive, whereas Voorhees were very much an 'established' touring band.

Talking of 'UK hardcore', do you still feel a part of a national scene? How has age/experience altered your perspective of that concept of a hardcore 'movement'?

Well, there's a range of ages in the band, and I'm somewhere in the middle. In regards to being part of the scene, The Horror, for 99.9% of the time play DIY gigs with other DIY bands in the back rooms of pubs, clubs and squats, and in the case of the US, basements and houses, so in this respect, yeah, we're part of the scene, and my perspective of it, in terms of what I see, is relatively unchanged from the age I'm at now, 36, to what I saw at 21. However, at 21, I went to a lot more gigs, listened to a lot more new bands, and was a much more social creature than I am today, so I would say that if anything my contact with the scene was much more participatory than it is now.

What progressions do you think have been made between this album and the first?

There have been differences between all the records we've done, but I think to compare 'Spoils of War' to 'First Blood Part I & II', we've certainly slowed down, a lot. 'Spoils of War' has a couple of moments where we do go into the much faster First Blood style parts, but on the whole it's a slower record; there's been no easing up on the intensity, but it does sound different.
With regards to my influence on the sound of this record, my voice sounds very different simply because we spent a lot longer doing the vocals; with 'The Fear, the Terror, the Horror', which was recorded by Bri Doom, he really schooled me in terms

of how to get the best out of my voice as I'd always hated recording. Atko recorded and produced 'Spoils of War', so obviously with our guitarist at the helm, we had an even better idea of what we wanted out of the recording, and the recording process was a whole new experience for us, much more pleasurable – just the five of us, with no 'outside' involvement.

Love the lyrics, mate – talk me through the ideas behind 'Status Hiatus', 'The Zeroes' and 'Spurn', for starters...

'Status Hiatus' is about class structure in Britain and how we tend to measure success – or more significantly deem people as being successful – based upon their job, salary, house, car etc. I also attempted to personalise it a bit because I am lucky enough to have a good job but I'm not particularly interested in cars, or whether my car reflects my salary, or my house for that matter. Being successful in life doesn't need to involve money or acquiring stuff; for some it's playing guitar, for some it's being a good parent, for some it's having time for family and friends, for others it's just aspiring to get the most out of life with the means they have. 'The Zeroes' is about now, this decade, and how we'll view it in decades to come. It's about diet culture, celebrity culture, and a lack of aspiration coupled with a desire for fame. It's not about being a famous singer, dancer, footballer or actor, it's about being famous 'for being famous', it's about people with no discernible talent becoming celebrities and more importantly people's willingness to read about and watch them.
The 'Spurn' in the title is 'Spurn Head' or 'Spurn Point'; it's a strip of land with a lighthouse at the mouth of the river Humber and clearly visible from where I grew up in Grimsby – although separated by a couple of miles of sea water. The song isn't really about Spurn Head though, as I say in the song, Spurn, is a metaphor, it's about the gulf between the government and the people; it's largely about how ordinary people can't enter into dialogue with politicians or participate in politics (other than marking a cross every now and then), and how politicians, particularly career politicians, can't meaningfully engage with the public as their life experiences are so vastly different.

HYPOCRISY – ISSUE 83 (OCTOBER 2000)

Da Ed didn't exactly shoot his load over the new Hypocrisy album, 'Into The Abyss', last issue, did he? But still, such passionate thrashings always merit further interrogation, and Ian Glasper loves it (old school freak that he is!), so he was happy to step up to the plate – as long as he could explore a side of the band that is usually hidden from public view (maybe for good reason?).

Well, Swedish deathsters Hypocrisy have been covered so damn much within these (un)hallowed pages the last few years, there's not much else left to be said, so, to

478

Hypocrisy, courtesy of Claire Harris, Nuclear Blast

mark the release of their eighth album, 'Into The Abyss' (Nuclear Blast), I thought I'd try to confound bassist Mikael Hedlund with some, ahem, probing questions... about life, the universe and bullet belts.

Hi Mike.

"Hello."

So, you ever been abducted by aliens?

"Uh, yeah, several times," laughs Mikael, before adding disappointingly, "No, actually, I haven't. But I would like to be - you never know what's out there; it could be very interesting. You hear and read a lot about it, and it would be nice to experience it yourself..."

What if they started cutting you up to see how you worked inside, maybe to see how you made your new album so brutally old school death metal?

"Well, that wouldn't be so nice," deadpans the amicable Swede.

What's the worse nightmare you ever had?

"Damn, I never remember my nightmares. I mean, I do dream, but as soon as I wake up, they're gone."

Are you scared of dying then?

"No, I don't think about it that much – when it happens, it happens. You can't change fate, and you can't go around worrying about it all the time; you'd go crazy."

Okay, so you're not scared of dying (damn these rock 'n' rollers!), but when you do hang up yer bullet belt once and for all, what song do you want playing at your funeral? Something really morbid, right?

"Uh... these questions are really hard...", laughs the bassist. Then, after a LONG pause, the slightly surprising answer: "I think 'Wish You Were Here' by Pink Floyd, because there's a really good feeling in that song. But I'd be dead anyway, so I guess I wouldn't care..."

I'm not sure if I can accept that answer; it's not metal enough!

"Hey, I listen to every kind of music, from Pink Floyd to the craziest black metal. I couldn't just listen to one style; I'm easily bored. I can even listen to a bit of pop music, as long as it's good..."

Yeah, but can you define 'good'?

"It has to be a mixture of everything; you have to feel the song the first time you listen to it. It has to move you on a deeper level."

Like a bowel movement perhaps? Anyway, imagine your house is on fire, and you have two minutes to get your ass out the front door before it all goes up in smoke. You just have time to grab five things – what are they gonna be, hotshot?

"Well, my bass guitar, of course; then the TV, 'cos that's very important to me. And my stereo, and CD collection, which I value very dearly, and then... um, I think I would grab my photo albums."

Do you not live with your girlfriend then?

"Yeah...", Mikael says hesitantly, knowing intuitively what's coming next. So, would you leave her to burn?

"No, of course not," he laughs good-naturedly. "But you said 'things'…"

Let's just hope she's not reading this, eh?

You mentioned your TV; I take it you're a bit of a couch potato in between tearing up stages worldwide with your rabid take on melodic death – what's yer favourite programme then?

"I love the Discovery channel, you know, all those cool documentaries. I especially like to watch stuff about forensics, and how they catch criminals. I also love comedy, especially a Swedish one called 'Yrrol'; that's always killer."

Hmm hmm, moving swiftly on then. Got any pets, Mike?

"No, not now. I used to have a few cats when I was at home with my parents, but nothing now. It's hard enough to look after myself."

Right then, imagine that your bus has gone halfway over a cliff, and unless you lose one person from your band extremely quickly, it will tip all the way over, and you will all plummet to your death, and there will be no Hypocrisy album number 9. So, who are you going to throw out?

"Myself…"

No, I don't believe that. Really?

"Yes, 'cos I wouldn't want to do something like that to another person. Besides, it's like having to admit you don't like one of them as much as the other."

Okay then, think of it like this: who would be easiest to replace? Surely you'd throw Lars out the door, and get a drum machine for the next album, right?

"No, that would be me again!"

You're just too nice. So, you wouldn't shove Pete out 'cos you were fed up of him being the band member who always gets all the glory?

"Well, he did start up the band," says the bassist diplomatically, "And he had a lot of contacts that helped us get started. Everything was new to the rest of us, so he ended up doing a lot of the press stuff.

"He's a great producer, and he has a strong personality, but we are definitely a band; when we get together there is a really good chemistry. We all have an important function within Hypocrisy, but Pete is like the figurehead of the band."

But he does hog all the press!

"Well, I'm doing this one, aren't I?"

To finish this fiasco on a (slightly more) serious note, do you feel fulfilled in your life?

"No, I don't think so, I don't feel like I've done everything yet. Each new album is a big thing for me, another challenge… and I'd still love to go and play in South America, and Japan… no, there's plenty more that I wanna do just yet."

And I hope you succeed in doing them, mate. Thanks for bearing with me; it's been fun.

SIDEBAR: HEY, MIKAEL, YOUR ROOTS ARE SHOWING…

You may or may not be aware of this, but Hypocrisy have covered both Razor AND Kiss at various points in their recording career, and seeing as 'Into The Abyss' is so unashamedly a back-to-their-roots death metal album, I needed to know what

bands Mikael would like to cover if he was planning a show-us-yer-influences MCD.
"I think I would have to choose all those great songs we used to listen to when we were younger..."

Did you ever stand in front of the mirror practising the riffs on a broom handle?
"No."

Do you now, by any chance? So you can cut a few neat moves on stage perhaps?
"No, not at all, I'm not that kind of person. I just wanna go out on the stage and play our music – all that posing is not my style."

Anyway, about this MCD...
"Okay. There would be a Slayer song, of course – how about 'Hell Awaits'? And Venom's 'Black Metal'. They were a big influence on us when we were starting out. Then Destruction [who the band have just toured with, on the Nuclear Blast festival tour – IG]... say, 'Black Death'... and a Kiss song, too. Oh man, they've written so many good ones... I think 'Detroit Rock City'. And then a Motorhead song – 'Metropolis'. The other guys aren't so into Motorhead as me, but everyone likes Motorhead, right?"

CHAPTER I/J:
USED, ABUSED AND
UNAMUSED...

IOD – ISSUE 77 (APRIL 2000)

"Sabbat was the band that really opened my ears to extreme music! Martin Walker was the lyricist who proved to me that metal songs didn't have to revolve around inane references to the imaginary when there was so much else out there in the real world that was worth talking about. And I continue to be impressed by his word play to this day, especially his work with Skyclad..."

So sayeth Andrew Fox, guitarist with Brummie grinders, IOD, when I ask him to reveal the lyrical inspiration behind their debut album, 'Mundane Existence' for Black Country label Iron Man. And like the eccentric metaller he has just name-checked, his own band also share a healthy distaste for the establishment. Even if you have to wade through a quagmire of glutinous Discore riffing, breakneck blastbeats and demented dual vocals to decipher it.

So how much of your attitude can be attributed to your bleak environment?

"I don't have enough experience of other places to be able to say if there's anywhere else quite like the Black Country," says Andy carefully, "But many of the songs seem to be influenced by the people around us, and it does seem like the intellect of the general public is going downhill fast. Education is substandard, job prospects are minimal and one generation of apathetic, uninspired parents will surely breed another generation of still further apathetic children.

"This lack of hope and self-respect has bred a mentality of greed where everyone is out for themselves at the expense of everyone else. If you read the local papers, it's scary; there has always been someone stabbed, raped or glassed - beaten half to death for no reason at all.

"You can fantasize that murderers are monsters who are either insane or who have some deep-felt motive for what they do, but the fact is most pissed-up dickheads out to prove how hard they are will gladly kill you because they thought you were looking at them 'funny'."

Serious stuff indeed, and the IOD album rages with just such indignation against society's - and their own - shortcomings, one rabid shot of crazy crossover after the other until you're left inebriated by the sheer intensity of it all. But they aren't just about social politics; the band have a considerable and wicked sense of humour, as you can see by the ruthless self-parody of the album sleeve.

"Well, you can talk about serious issues and mean what you say without having to resort to po-faced macho posturing," spits Andy with feeling. "Too many bands take themselves more seriously than they do their music... hardcore punk, my arse. I bet many spend more time in front of the mirror, obtaining the most perfect spiky hair, or the most effective angle of dangle for their toilet chain, than do the trendiest of conformists. Image should come second to musical substance, but unfortunately people would rather use their time on stage to make themselves look good rather than give people something to think about."

ICONS OF FILTH – ISSUE 106

(JANUARY/FEBRUARY 2003)

Back after a five-year hiatus, and just in time to predict the next wave of disaster, veteran anarcho punkers Icons Of Filth are about to unleash the cynic-silencing new album, 'Nostradamnedus', determined to keep all your punk memories - and the future – alive. Ian Glasper donned his combats and discovered why vocalist Stig is now doing it for the kids.

Anyone with a good memory and an eye for detail will be familiar with the tremendous respect I have for Welsh anarcho punkers, Icons Of Filth. I saw them several times 'back in the day', and they always blew me away with the passionate, righteous anger they imbibed every last one of their songs with. They were right up there with the cream of the UK anarcho crop, ie: Crass, Conflict and the Subhumans.

So, it was with great delight – and admittedly a certain amount of trepidation – that I learnt six months ago there was to be a brand new Icons studio album for US punk label, Go Kart; the craftily-titled 'Nostradamnedus'. The trepidation was in case the band sullied the potent memories I cherished of my first encounters with their lyrics and music.

So, why reform right now? In fact, why did they split in the first place?

"We had no real intention of splitting," reveals elusive vocalist, Stig. "The trouble with us lot was that we never bothered to do gigs as much as most bands, preferring to play very much on an ad-hoc basis. We didn't want it to become a chore. We didn't rehearse very much, so long periods of inactivity for us were nothing new. We were all comfortable with that, as none of us were budding rock stars or anything, although five years is a more than reasonable stint.

"It was important for us as individuals to have gotten involved with punk in whatever small way we did. To galvanise that by forming a band gave us the means to sound a collective voice whenever we wanted. A band is just a tool for us really. It's there to pick up and put down at your leisure, so a band like ours forming, splitting up or re-forming is a bit of a non-issue really.

"We've always kept in touch since, as we've all known each other since we were kids," he continues, on the subject of the band's reformation in early 2001, "So I suppose there was always a chance of somebody suggesting we do it again someday. We considered it first around six years ago, so we've really had a good long think about it, but I'd been ill for a couple of years, which stalled things for a bit. Plus we'd all become single fathers! Which doesn't help things when it comes to time away doing gigs, what with the children all being different age groups, so I know that we've all been willing to get involved again, unfortunately just at different stages to each other. It was a question of priorities and our priorities were with our children."

Of course, such is the petty-minded mentality of some insecure punkers, the Icons are bound to enjoy the verbal backlash of wanting an avenue to express themselves again. Already a few snipers are taking pot-shots at the motivations behind the new album, but when a record is as strong as this, it wears its convictions like chainmail and you can't fuck with it.

"I'm not sure how anyone could formulate the opinion of us that we were doing this for the money. We'd have to be really popular and have some sort of track record for ripping people off... and we fall down badly on both points, I'm afraid."

Besides any misgivings about whether the band still have what it takes will soon be steamrollered beneath some ripping new material that wouldn't sound out of place alongside their finest moments such as 'Evilspeak' and 'Brain Death'. The highlight though is the Rudimentary Peni-esque 'Treadmill', an acid bath of acerbic wit crucified by a genuinely tense, menacing refrain. Parenthood certainly hasn't mellowed these guys. Quite the opposite in fact, with youthful nihilism being replaced by a (justified) fear for the well-being of the planet their/our children might inherit at the hands of various present warmongers.

"Lyrically, we're approaching things from a slightly different angle now, but I don't think anything is lost because of that," states Stig in closing. "The subject matter is inevitably still the same, because the same old problems still exist, actually getting more intensified and unstable as time goes by.

"Given that the band only exists as a mouthpiece for us, it would be impossible for us to produce inane songs about falling in and out of love and suchlike. I always think it's such a complete cop-out to have an outlet like a band or whatever, then waste it completely by having nothing constructive or questioning to say. We could only ever operate as a punk band, as we feel so much affinity with the whole ethos of it. I don't subscribe to the notion that punk is dead. I mean, no matter how small its numbers, a population still fucking exists, right? From that perspective, as individual people, we've never been away."

RIP Andrew 'Stig' Sewell

Ignite, Bradford Rios 1996 - by Sam Lennox

'We don't want to be judged by our diets...' say Californian hardcore incendiaries Ignite, a band who are both positive and political, but draw the line at walking the straightedge. Ian Glasper refused to get sanctimonious as he quizzes guitarist Joe Foster.

If you take a moment to look up the definition of 'ignite' in a dictionary (that's the big book of words still in its shrink-wrap balancing up one of the legs of your bed), you'll get summat like, 'to set on fire: to heat to the point at which combustion occurs: to render luminous by heat", and if ever there was a band that lived up to their moniker, this be them. If you saw Ignite opening up for Madball in the summer, you'll need no convincing of this, I'm sure. They possess velocity, melody and smarts by the bucketful, and, contrary to popular belief, they aren't a straightedge band.

"The thanks list on 'Scarred For Life' said in it, 'Be drug free, sober and clean'," sighs guitarist Joe D. Foster, sipping his breakfast juice and slowly waking up to another day in sunny California. Meanwhile I am sat grinding a crackling phone into my ear in grey ol' England, chilly rain lashing my windows. "That was from a combination of band members, when we had Gavin Oglesby still in the band, from No For an Answer. That gave kids the impression that we were a straightedge band, and we're not, and you can print that in big, bold letters! We're not alcoholics or addicted to substances or anything, y'know, but we don't want our band judged by our diets.

"No matter what you do, there's a group of kids out there who will judge you. If you like girls, you must be a sexist pig, or if you wear leather, you must hate all animals... it's insane. There's so many kids strung out on Earth Crisis trying to fit in, and there's no originality anymore."

That said, Ignite are a very positive hardcore band, more than willing to put their money where their mouths are when push comes to shove.

"That's where Zoli [Teglas – vocalist] is today actually," confirms Joe. "He's up at Pacific Wildlife, a sanctuary near here that treat pelicans, and at the moment there's like twenty birds a day coming in with botulism, this disease that affects your nervous system and eventually kills you – you can't even blink, so Zoli's helping these birds, putting drops in their eyes and stuff. We thought more people needed to know about it, which is why we put it in our booklet. It's the same with Sea Shepherd... they're like the police of our oceans, preventing illegal drift-netting and stuff, and they'll mark the furs of seals, so they're worthless and don't get killed. They're a direct action group, but they don't hurt anyone – no one's been killed, although they've sunk a lot of whaling boats.

"So far Ignite have managed to raise about $10,000 for them. We didn't really know about any of this stuff until Zoli joined the band."

These guys aren't just pro-animals though. Another potent lyric on their excellent 'Past Our Means' (their debut for Revelation) is 'Taken Away'. It's about how all the little knocks most of us take in life that seem such a big deal at the time are fuck all in comparison to the hardships some people have to endure. I found it particularly

Ignite, Bradford Rios 1996, by Sam Lennox

poignant 'cos one of my friends was paralysed and the strength he displayed in coming to terms with his disability was inspirational.

"It was written about a true experience Zoli had in Hungary with a kid in a wheelchair," comes the explanation, "But it could be anywhere, any time. All the time we are at band practise, and we'll go out for a Diet Coke, and there will be homeless people asking us for money. Nine times out of ten Zoli will take them across the street and buy them a meal. It's incredible how many times he's done it. He'll never give them money in case they buy alcohol, but he'll go two or three blocks out of his way, pick up food, then go back two or three blocks to hand it out."

Ignite's music has a similarly uplifting quality to their lyrics, buoying you up on a tide of positive energy, rather than swamping you in a surge of negativity.

"We get a lot of mail from incredible places, people in prison, people in Sarajevo, wherever, who say that our lyrics and music help get them through each day. It's awesome to think that your music can have such a positive effect on people's lives.

"The picture on the cover of the 'Family' CD is one I took in Poland," Joe recalls. "We drove through a bad neighbourhood, I guess, and stopped the bus to ask directions or something, and all the neighbourhood kids came running out, and were stood there holding their hands out. It's a real powerful image of Zoli handing out candy to these kids."

It also seems that, like so many other American bands, they've been welcomed over here in Europe with open arms. No wonder that they keep coming back.

"From our very first tour there it was such a positive experience for us, and it just hasn't stopped. We've been back three times now, it's incredible. I'd love to live out there, everyone's so great. I think I have more friends in Europe than I do in America, y'know? I mean, the scene on the east coast of America is great, but here in California it's pretty duff. Hardcore's pretty much overshadowed and swallowed up by punk rock, Epitaph and Fat Wreck stuff. Not only that, but there's not many places to play, unless you get in one of those big college halls and do a rockstar-size show. And we can't just drive across into the next state and be in Boston or Pennsylvania; we've got Arizona, and Texas, and New Mexico to get across. We're pretty isolated over here."

That might explain why Ignite have done a split 7" with Good Riddance, from the Fat Wreck stable, to help marry punk and hardcore, but the ensuing tour the two bands undertook to promote its release seems to have left a pretty sour taste in Joe D.'s mouth...

"We took that tour to try and reach a new audience, cross over and say our stuff to some fresh people, and Good Riddance wanted to play in front of a hardcore audience, so... we started on the east coast, and we headlined, playing club dates with Good Riddance supporting, and we split the door money with them 60/40, and thought that was completely fair. Then the tour reached Canada, and they took the headlining slot, 'cos they've played there before, but we found out it was going to cost us each $280 to enter the country, all our shirts were going to be taxed, gas and food is more expensive there – and out of the $600 they were making every night they were only gonna give us $70! There was no way we could do it, so we had to go home. They're one of those bands who preach against capitalist pigs and all that, but they're as bad as everybody else! Don't believe everything you read."

IGNITE – ISSUE 267 (JANUARY 2016)

Ignite, Coney Island High (NYC), 1999 – pic by Carl Gunhouse

As gaps between albums go, the ten years since Ignite released 'Our Darkest Days' is verging on the ridiculous – after all, they're a hardcore band, not Metallica, right? Well, in the interim, vocalist Zoli has fronted Pennywise, drummer Craig has played with

Ignite, Coney Island High (NYC), 1999, pic by Carl Gunhouse

Strife, bassist Brett with Nations Afire and guitarist Brian with Into Another, and Ignite have kept active on the live front, but it's still safe to say that new album, 'A War Against You' is long overdue for fans of the band.

"It is always a great opportunity to play with different musicians and experience new things," offers Brett, on their lengthy hiatus from recording. "Life experiences, trials and tribulations make you the person you are. I think time away from Ignite, for all of us, let us realize how many people around the world Ignite touches. We received countless e-mails from people begging us to release a new album. This is something very special and something that not too many people get to experience in their lives and we really appreciate this. I also think playing with other people gave us a new perspective on chemistry regarding music. Sometimes there are unexplainable things that happen between a group of people when they get together to write, record and play music. For all of us, Ignite is one of those chemistries that works uniquely well when we step into a room together. But believe me, it is not easy; in the end though, the passion we each have for this music comes through because it is so important to us. We take a lot of pride in this craft."

From the get-go, with the harmonised vocal intro to opener 'Begin Again', it's obvious this is classic Ignite, driven by that energy and unashamed melody that has made them such a unique voice in modern hardcore. With such a long wait for the record though, were they aware of heightened fan expectation for the new songs as they were writing them?

"In the approach to this album we reminded ourselves that there are things that Ignite fans expect from us, and we feel it is important to keep a link to our previous work, but at the same time it is even more important to surprise our listeners with new and exciting elements that they do not expect. When bands try to make a copy of a previous record, they always fall short because it is impossible to capture the magic of a previous work; that was a different time and place. We believe it is important that bands re-create themselves somewhat on each album and keep the energy and creativity fresh. And that is always the biggest challenge, to create something exciting and fresh without losing the sense of the band."

It's safe to say that fans won't be disappointed with 'A War Against You', and one Ignite tradition the band thankfully continues is that of intelligent, thought-provoking lyrics. "The album title is a line from the song 'This Is A War', which deals directly with the media and how their agendas skew the public perception of what is going on in the world. The media is typically either right wing or left wing; rarely do we get a true, centred and accurate view or report of the current events in the world. The media always has titles for current events that have the word "war" in it to scare and intimidate the public; there is always a war on something to help spread fear among the population. In the end, the media is waging a war against truth, and hence it is 'A War Against You'."

IMMOLATION – ISSUE 28 (MARCH 1996)

Immolation

Back with their second album, 'Here In After', death metal veterans Immolation have only just returned from five years in their very own label wilderness. Guitarist Robert

491

Vigna explains the New York band's vision of heaven and hell to our man Ian Glasper.

Immolation! Now there's a word to strike terror into the hearts of any God-fearing music fan! And they're back, with a new album 'Here in After' for Metal Blade that manages to be even more unholy and unrelenting than their first one, 'Dawn of Possession', which they recorded for Roadrunner five long years ago! And it's in the mists of the past that I begin as I wonder why they parted company with their original label...

Their talkative guitarist (and founder member) Robert Vigna is only too happy to explain all:

"They weren't 100% into what we were doing and we were having a lot of disagreements with them. They're a very trend-oriented label, and they're always looking for the next big thing that they can make money off. They were really into putting out our second album but they said, if it wasn't gonna come out at the end of '92/beginning of '93, then it wasn't worth putting out! And we obviously felt a lot different to that!

"Basically, we didn't think they were doing the job they were supposed to with us. I mean, we ended up booking and self-financing our whole U.S. tour, they didn't touch a thing; they were asking for the album, and we were all working our full-time jobs and we were telling 'em, you need to work with us or the album's not gonna be done anytime soon. Either help us out or let us go, put it in writing immediately, and let's be done with it. So we were very happy when it happened. We were both better off, 'cos neither band nor label was doing the other any good."

And what have you been doing during the interim? "We continued in '93, just working our jobs and concentrating on other aspects of the band, taking care of business and trying to make a more solid foundation for the years to come", recalls Robert. "'In 1994, we got back to our mail, got back to everyone, seeing as we were out playing shows and getting more active again. As well as the east coast, we did some shows in Canada and California, and we were even lucky enough to go down to South America and play a show in Peru. We also put together the 'Stepping on Angels before Dawn' compilation CD for Repulse Records.

"When we recorded our new promo, that got the attention of Metal Blade. Brian Slagel had liked our first album, and obviously liked the new demo, and he made the decision to sign us. We were already set to record the new album in July '95, anyway. As far as we were concerned, we were going to record it then, no matter what, whether we had a label or not, even if it meant releasing it ourselves... whatever it took!"

So it was sheer hard work that maintained your fanbase for all those years with no new product out?

"Yeah, but I think the music has a lot to do with it, too. We feel we put enough time into our music so it will last. Our first album has definitely stood the test of time - we put that album out in 1990,

and to this day we still have people picking it up and thinking it only came out last year. They don't realise how old it is, and that's a good sign to us.

"Music should be like that", he claims, with no pause for breath. "You shouldn't just

Immolation

throw something together that is relevant for just a moment. We make music that lasts in people's minds... plus we do keep in touch with everyone that writes to us. We really push it through the underground. We'll never try and change our music to be something we're not. This new album is everything people will expect from Immolation - and more! And to us, taking things further doesn't mean you have to sound rock 'n' roll. We're even heavier and more aggressive, but more emotional at the same time..."

That strong underground fanbase is so important in death metal... "Yeah, of course," agrees Robert, in his New York drawl. "A lot of these bands get all popular, and change their style. They go for the commercial end, and totally deny the underground, and forget about death metal - and those people were who got them where they are in the first place! They don't seem to realise that it usually hurts 'em in the end, anyway..."

How difficult was it touring without a label and tour support? "Well, it was difficult, but it was hard setting up our U.S. tour when we had a label! We booked all the shows ourselves, called up all the clubs, planned everything out and put up the money! It wasn't easy, but we wanted to do it and felt it was important... so we did it. We're a band that's used to doing things on our own, and we don't look to other people to get things done. You have to work hard to get what you want. The fact that we have a new CD out and are about to go to Europe to play is pay-off enough at the moment. We sacrificed everything for this band; this is our life, what we're about... and just to be doing it is enough."

Don't you ever get sick of all the music biz bullshit and wish you could concentrate just on the music? "Oh, of course," he sighs. "Right now, we work full-time jobs and cover all the business end of things as well as the music, so yeah, we'd like to get to the position where we can concentrate more on the music on a regular basis. To be honest, we don't mind dealing with the business side, 'cos we like to be involved in all aspects of what we're doing, to make sure they're being done how we'd want - the right way!"

I think death metal got over-saturated a bit back there? What stood you apart from the crowd?

"At that time, even tho' we shouldn't have been mixed in, we did kinda get caught in the shuffle there. We'd built up a following over a period of years, and when we got to the point of doing an album it was a very natural thing for us, whereas a lot of bands, when death got big, went from being thrash to death and got signed on the back of a demo! Bands were coming out who weren't familiar with what it was all about and that saturated the whole scene, and people got sick of all that generic music.

"Still, it makes it better for the future", Robert reflects, "Because people are being more careful about what they listen to and they're looking for something with a little bit more meaning and feeling."

Let's talk about the lyrics, 'cos I didn't get any on my promo CD... "That's unfortunate that you guys didn't get the lyrics, and we've spoken to Metal Blade about that, 'cos without the lyrics you're missing half the album! Basically, the whole album revolves around religion and its effect on the world, whether it be Christianity or a lot of other religions which our stuff can relate to as well."

Robert is pretty much the ideal interviewee in that once he warms to his subject, he's hard to shut up. "Christianity, for instance, has such a strong hold on the world, and whether you're into it or not, you're always affected by it, directly or indirectly, and so many people are manipulated, controlled and brainwashed by it. People grow up believing these things and just take them as fact all through their lives. It's just people making good off others, who are just victims of the whole thing. To us, we're exposing what seems to be the real evil in the world. People ask us if we believe in what we say, and yeah, we do! What we're saying is more believable than what a lot of these religions preach!"

It's a shame that people will look at the song titles and just dismiss them as the usual death metal shock tactics, and they're not... "No, they're definitely not!" comes the categorical reply. "'Away From God' is about someone who had strong faith in God, but that turned to hatred for God, because God was never there for him when he needed him during difficult times. 'Under the Supreme' is about holy wars, either past or present, and how people go and slaughter others, and justify it in the name of God. 'Christ's Cage' looks at the church, which to us is basically a cage where people are confined within their lives to follow and obey something that isn't real... so each song deals with aspects of religion, but it's not your generic death metal thing."

That cover looks like something from 'Paradise Lost'? "Oh!" Robert is unimpressed. Not the band! I mean the book by Milton! "Yeah, okay, I see," he perks up again. "Well, to us, 'Here in After' refers to our vision of hell. You're looking at a hell where the good and the evil are together, suffering at the same time, and heaven's gates are falling and the darkness is creeping up. Angels and demons, God-fearing or not. l mean, Andreas

Marschall (the cover artist) has a way of really bringing our ideas to life. We tell him what we want, and he adds his creativity, and brings it to life. He also hears the music and reads the lyrics before he puts brush to canvas. He always gets to experience Immolation! We don't go 'Eeny-meeny-miney-mo...' and pick a picture like some other bands; we want the cover to represent what the band is about."

You obviously take a healthy interest in all aspects of an album's production... "For us, if all those elements don't represent Immolation, then it's not correct, y'know? Every song we make should be something that'll last and say something in a profound way. That's what it's all about, not just throwing out whatever's the popular thing at the time!"

Lastly, when will we see Immolation live? "We'll be on the road a lot! In February and March, we're out in the States with Six Feet Under, then we go over to Europe at the end of April with Cannibal Corpse. It's been a while, so we're really looking forward to getting out there and playing our new music, meeting the people and seeing how much they like the new album..."

In Defence — issue 270 (May 2016)

In Defence

"Yeah, we try not to take ourselves too seriously," laughs Jimmy Claypool, guitarist with awesome Minneapolis crossover band, In Defence. "There's enough bands out there with promo photos trying to make them look tough, even though 99% of the time it's a facade. The world doesn't need any more of that; it's boring and uninspired. The way we approach serious issues is with more of a comic bent, while at the same time trying to keep shedding light on them. Our convictions are important to us, but having fun and being socially conscious don't have to be mutually exclusive..."

And if you like the thought of S.O.D. without the brain-dead lyrics, the band's new album, 'Don't Fuck With The Dungeon Master', will hit the spot for you, reminiscent of Municipal Waste at their significant best. Catch them on one of their endless tours; you won't have any more fun being thrashed than with In Defence.

Inhuman, at ABC No Rio, by Jammi York

Like All Out War (featured elsewhere this issue, and who they've just toured the States with), Crisis, Life of Agony and Starkweather, Brooklyn's Inhuman are another band to explode onto the underground after appearing on a Too Damn Hype compilation. Met sure knows a good metallic hardcore band when he hears one. Actually, Inhuman's credentials were already established last year when I gave them a very positive review for their demo, so it's nice to see the boys do good. Witness their new 'Evolver' CD on Eyeball Records, that features eleven of the finest slavering crossover tracks.

Mike Scondotto is on the phone and he's psyched by it all, which is nice to hear 'cos with a band name like that, you could be forgiven for thinking they might all be, um, a bit negative. Or at least, disillusioned with man's inhumanity to man...?

"Well, it mainly came from a lot of personal stuff that was going down in my life," he reveals. "My girlfriend, who I'd been going with for three years, left me, my old band fell apart after four years, I didn't have a job, I wasn't at school, and it was a very depressing time for me. It seemed a very fitting name. A lot of people mistake it as a death metal name, and I love that scene, but I think it could fit any style of music. It's slightly dark, very realistic, but some people are surprised when they hear us - they think we'll sound like Obituary or something, but we're more like, say, the Cro-Mags."

And that's no idle boast either. 'Evolver' has a similar electric intensity crackling through its material. I dare say all lovers of hardcore will love Inhuman. Mike seems to have a slight beef with some sections of the scene, though, judging by the lyrics to 'Good Riddance'.

"That was about some kids I know from Brooklyn," he explains, "Who were in it for a while, who made the most noise about it, but in the end were the ones who left the quickest. They were the first ones to run to the rave scene or the grunge scene; they were never really hardcore, so fuck 'em. I can't believe they could turn their back on this, and I wish them good riddance. 1998 will be ten years I've been into hardcore. My first show was the Bad Brains when I was fourteen, in spring '88, and it really did change my life. Our song, 'My Dedication', is my tribute to this scene. Even though I love metal, hardcore is the one music that has had most effect on me, and stayed with me, and this is all about that commitment."

In The Clear – issue 83 (October 2000)

In The Clear - courtesy of Ian Wiles

Let's face it – England has never been renowned for its old school hardcore. Of course, there's Knuckledust fighting our corner all across Europe, and we had Touchdown and Step Back, two great bands who never realised their full potential, but now we can add Sheffield's raging In The Clear to that oh-so-short list. I caught up with the latter following the release of their criminally cool 'Out of Our Past' MCD for Sure Hand, as the band were finalising a touring stint with Bane from the US.

"Many bands playing 'old school' can be described as generic," counters vocalist Ian, as we discuss the main criticism usually levied at this particular strand of hardcore music. "But a lot of them formed with the sole intention of being generic in order to 'bring it back' or whatever. We've always tried to apply a fairly progressive mindset to our song-writing because we're trying to create something new and carve out a niche

In The Clear – courtesy of Ian Wiles

In The Clear

with our own style... that said, we will always wanna play fast and aggressive hardcore, so we mainly operate within that framework."

You guys are also one of the few wholly straight edge bands in the UK, and without wishing to labour the point, you take a pretty strong stance lyrically on the new disc against smoking at shows. What, would you rather the kids who smoked stay away from your shows altogether?

"Those lyrics, to 'Through The Haze', are basically about people having the respect to keep their filthy habit out of hardcore shows. We want all types of kids to come see us and have a good time – not just sXe kids – but it's our right not to have to breathe that shit in all the time. All we're really saying is 'let us breathe'! If kids want to spend £4 on a pack of cigarettes to slowly kill themselves, then there's sadly nothing we can do about it. The song is about respect for others.

"Shows should be fun!" enthuses the singer. "People can expect to see fire-breathers, topless dancers and midgets doing handsprings off the stage. No, seriously, we put as much energy into our set as possible, at every show, no matter how many people there are, or the reaction we get. It's awesome when you see a positive reaction to a good hardcore band; there's nothing quite like it."

INTEGRITY – ISSUE 66 (MAY 1999)

Integrity – Danielle Dombrowski

When Integrity come out of retirement, add '2000' to the end of their name, and drop a new album that is nothing short of the Apocalypse arriving early, obviously Terrorizer

Integrity, by Chase Corum

go get the scoop for y'all. We needed to put our top, most intellectual, unbiased writer on the case, but he was washing his hair, so we sent Glasper...

Well, it's been a while, but thankfully, one of the most loved/hated (delete as you see applicable) underground bands have deemed to drop another album on us. Integrity are back (but don't go holding your breath for a tour any time soon!) with possibly their hardest record to date, the eponymous 'Integrity 2000' for Victory (who else?) Yep, they done gone changed their name on us, too!

"Well, I've been in this band for ten years," explains vocalist, Dwid, calling me from his home in Ohio. "This is some kind of anniversary for me, and 'cos the line-up has changed, I wanted to add the '2000' out of respect for the old members, as well as to make it a milestone release for the band. I'd always kinda planned to do a band Prohibition 2000 in the year 2000 anyway, but someone else stole my idea when they read it in my Books Of Blood zine... and besides, I didn't much like the name Prohibition, 'cos I drink... but then again, you could ask do I have any integrity too?"

As you may have gathered, Dwid is in a relaxed mood, laughing and joking, despite only having been up less than an hour, and he certainly doesn't sound like the awkward, nasty bastard his detractors would make him out to be.

"I'm the token asshole in the band," laughs Dwid. "I'm very difficult to get along with; I have a problem, I guess. I'm my own worse enemy; I have a very quick temper. And I have a really unusual name, so it's easy for people to pick on me.

"Everything you read is true!" interjects Jason Popson, ex-In Cold Blood and Dwid's vocal collaborator on 'Integrity 2000' [Dwid: "His voice is a lot different to mine, so I

500

figured it would add to the onslaught..."], chuckling on the other phone.

Dwid: "I really oughta go to therapy, but Victory won't give me any time off. Tony's taken my insurance card off me. It's not like Europe over here; you can't just walk into any old hospital."

"He's very Jekyll and Hyde" - Jason again - "nice to you one minute, but the next..."

Dwid: "You see, even in my own interview, people are talking shit about me!"

But Jase has a point - last time I saw you, you were stalking around the stage, in black contact lenses, like a man possessed. Is there a switch in your head that you throw, to slip into that stage persona?

"I might seem a loud talking person," claims the Dwidster, "But I'm somewhat introverted. I'm okay over the phone, or when I have alcohol in me - I can talk then - but one on one, I'm not so good, and the contacts were like a mask in a way, to distance me from the audience. A friend of mine who's a doctor got them for me, but everyone wears 'em now, so I don't do it anymore. I haven't performed live for three years, but yeah, when I go on stage, that is someone else up there. Consciously, I don't know it, but it's like getting into a car. You can drive really fast, but you're not part of the car, are you? I'm up there, driving fast for forty-five minutes... then I run out of gas, and go to a bar [laughs]!

Sometimes it's hard to get out of the car, and get along with the rest of the band - I find it hard to get along with anyone at the best of times - and on that last tour, the car was driving me..."

Ah yes, that notorious Integrity/Fury Of Five/Deviate tour, that virtually laid waste to Europe! Many a tall tale has been told about some of the antics (if you can call mass scraps and mini-riots 'antics'?) that went on. My own band played one of the shows in France – gloat, gloat! – and it was an awesome gig, but really, you should be grateful they never got loose this side of the Channel. So, when will we see Integrity live again? Or are we more likely to see you over here with Psywarfare [Dwid's electronic noise project – IG]?

"You're more likely to see neither," comes the disheartening response. "I have three kids and I live away from everyone. I like being a recluse – it's better for me, and the world, if I seclude myself away. If there's too many people around me, I tend to get troubled and aggressive, and then people get hurt, so why bother subjecting anyone to it all? The last tour was like being in an insane asylum for two months, but it wasn't just me, I can't take all the credit for it. Those other bands were crazy too. It got very, very dark on that bus! I was a devil to the other members of my band... it's no wonder they went off and formed In Cold Blood [laughs]!

"I think they'd printed our lyrics on the backs of the tickets, 'cos everyone was singing along," recalls Dwid, of one Belgian show in particular, when I ask him just what went wrong. "And I just got fed up of trying to drag the mic back off them, so I sat down with a beer and let them get on with it. Plus I was pretty tired, and all busted up from brawling on the bus the night before, so I just said, 'Fuck it!' You see how much I respect

Integrity, Rennes, by Sam Lennox

our audience? I'm actually a very generous person – you're the first journalist to uncover this side of me! – I let the audience participate in our shows so much, I just give them my job as vocalist," he guffaws.

But did you give them your pay-check too? "Um, I don't think we actually got one for that show? So we all lost as much as each other at that gig... well, they only lost the price of admission – I lost my mind!"

Anyways, much as I could listen to the guys gassing about tour adventures all night, let's talk about 'Integrity 2000', the stunning new record, a welcome blast of bleak hostility that goes for the throat and doesn't let up for an hour, a storm of hungry locusts commandeered by those patented soul-in-purgatory howls, that seems intent on stripping you of your flesh. And they manage to throw us with a few spiteful surprises, such as the violin on 'The Burden Of Purity', which acts as the perfect counterpoint to its reptilian riff, or the volatile 'Never Surrender', which not only has an incredibly evil Slayer-ish guitar hook (Dwid: "We've always been guilty of borrowing Slayer's sound, right from the beginning..."), but also a vocal cameo from... wait, I can't tell you, sorry. Contractual obligations 'n' all that crap.

"Let's just say that he's a friend of mine," deadpans the frontman, "Who I grew up with, who we all called The Predator, who looks exactly like Derrick from Sepultura. It's like a magic trick; it's all done with mirrors. No, his label may not like him being on there... actually, this is an old song that we recorded with him years ago, before he became famous... think anyone will believe that?"

But guys, there's a picture of him inside the booklet! "Uh, oh yeah," laughs Jason, "That's just a cut-out..."

"We photoshopped him into that photo," Dwid again, "We cloned him off someone else!" Well, whoever he is, the song kicks ass. You're apparently a band with a healthy disregard for the hardcore scene that spawned you – doesn't it frustrate you that the majority of your audience is from the very scene that you so often deride?

"I don't get frustrated as such," ponders Dwid. "Since the beginning, since our very first seven-inch on Victory - it was only, like, their third release - everyone has always said about us, 'What horrible metal crap! This isn't hardcore!' We were always outcasts; we were never invited to be part of any scene, or any community... but I'm not bitter about any of that. I'm better off isolated from the kind of music I write, I want to write without distraction; I like to keep my stuff – at least the lyrics I write – pure from outside influence. I don't own any hardcore records... I don't even have all the Integrity releases."

"There's a lot of hypocrisy in hardcore," reckons Jason, "But things have come full circle now, and where everyone hated metal back then, most HC kids love it now, so Integrity have gone from being regarded as imposters to innovators. A lot of HC bands like to preach to their listeners, tell them what to do, tell them what to eat, and they find it confusing that we don't seem to care what they do!"

"I'm just saying, the end of the world is coming," spits Dwid, "So get some weapons, and be prepared, 'cos otherwise you'll be left in the cold, and you'll be fucked and you'll die. We created the Holy Terror Church of The Final Judgement out of our own imaginations, and people actually wrote to us wanting to join it. It was meant to be the opposite – there is no church, use your own imagination! We try to emulate artists and authors, rather than revolutionaries; we're not trying to change the world – it can't be changed, especially not by an ugly bunch of hillbillies from Ohio with lots of tattoos. Besides, I wouldn't want to orchestrate any kind of mass movement; I'm rooting for the individual, not people who follow others like sheep."

And lastly, a word about Psywarfare, Dwid's experimental noise project, whose tortured emissions will scare even the most hardened Integrity fan with their unflinching harshness. "I just take the most aggressive elements of metal and hardcore, and remove all the frivolities - and get to the very base of all that aggression - and then just throw it into the audience's face. It's deliberately unfeeling, and hits you on a whole different level. You can't even call it music a lot of the time; it has a disembodied quality that is truly terrifying... imagine watching 'The Texas Chainsaw Massacre', where Leatherface is chasing the girl, the chainsaw is roaring, the girl is screaming, Leatherface is grunting, and you're genuinely afraid. That's kind of what I aspire to create with Integrity too..."

But you cop out by using guitars. "Yeah, that's my little compromise, for the record label's sake. I keep thinking that if I have guitars, Tony might give me my insurance card back!"

JAMES MURPHY – ISSUE 110 (JUNE 2003)

Currently fighting his way back to health after a debilitating brain tumour, journeyman guitarist James Murphy has also begun to rebuild the foundations of his musical life. Ian Glasper reviews the past, present and future of a prolific and influential career.

It's difficult to put a value on the vital contribution James Murphy has made to the death and thrash metal scenes, having made his presence felt on many classic albums and been a part of many seminal bands. It was three young Scots, namely Stewart Whitson, Chris McDermot, and Michael Miller of Putrid Torture webzine, who first made me fully aware of James' plight when they told me about a benefit show they were organising to help him with his medical bills, and I contacted him directly to find out more.

"What I had, and still have, though it's much, much smaller now is called a pituitary macro adenoma," he explains. "That is a kind of tumour which grows on the pituitary gland, just below the brain and just behind the eyes and sinus. They are benign tumours, but they can easily kill you if they grow too large, which mine obviously did.

"It grew to the size of about three golf balls and pressed upward into my brain, leading to extreme memory problems and strange behaviour patterns. It also grew outward into the area of my optic nerves, causing my vision to slowly get fuzzy and just fade away to the point that I was probably legally blind. To top it all off, it wrapped itself around the carotid arteries in my head, placing me in extreme danger of instant death, or at least of being rendered a vegetable.

"It affected me so badly that, before it was diagnosed, I lost everything I had ever had, including my position in Testament, my recording studio and all the gear in it, all my guitars and amps, all my personal belongings and most of the memorabilia from my entire career. I was sleeping fourteen hours a day or more and forgetting everything. If you do this, you will lose everything eventually; girlfriends and jobs will go first, followed shortly by friends, homes, and belongings. This will happen because of the memory thing - you won't remember to pay your bills, and you won't remember to go to, or be awake for, work, so that you can afford to pay those bills. Everything just goes away.

"All of my friends noticed my behaviour and just sort of stepped back from me," James continues with a sigh. "Most of them assumed I had got into heavy drug use, which is not entirely uncommon in the music industry, so that assumption is understandable. Nothing could have been further from the truth though; I'm not into drugs at all. I ended up homeless and eventually my sister sent me a Greyhound bus ticket and got me back to Florida, but my family all ended up thinking I was on drugs too. My father administered a drug test though and discovered I wasn't, so then everyone just thought I had gone crazy!

"My father decided to take me to a free clinic to see a shrink and after the session was driving me back home and decided to stop off at a little eyeglasses store to buy me some off-the-shelf reading glasses, since he knew I was having vision trouble. The optician on duty there saw the difficulty I was having choosing a pair, so he decided to offer me a free eye exam. A couple of minutes into the exam, he told me he thought I had a tumour and he knew exactly what kind. That was how it was discovered. That optician saved my life."

FORGOTTEN PAST

Such are the curious twists of fate and thankfully this happy one means that we haven't heard the last from this talented and innovative player. The metal scene has lost too many key figures in recent years to the big C., one of them unfortunately being Chuck Schuldiner, who James had the privilege to play alongside on 'Spiritual Healing', and whom he remembers fondly.

"Chuck was very open to my ideas during the writing process for 'Spiritual Healing'," he recalls, "I ended up co-writing half of the tracks with him and he never nixed any of my ideas. In fact, he paid great attention when I was just doing finger exercises to warm up on the guitar and even turned some of that stuff into songs, i.e. the opening riff to 'Killing Spree'.

"In the studio he was very cool - he left me alone to do my parts and would only come in the control room afterwards to listen, invariably giving me the 'thumbs up' before heading back out to the lounge. He trusted me in the studio, even though it was my first time. I think he knew from rehearsals that I would do fine. He plays the rhythm guitar on one side of the recording and I play them all on the other, but I've never heard anyone state that it sounded like more than one person playing - we were that tight with each other on the tracks."

But of all the projects you've been involved with, which do you hold dearest to your heart? I would guess Disincarnate, seeing as it was your baby from the start?

"Well, I lean towards saying Disincarnate on one hand, since it was really my thing, and a very personally fulfilling experience. On the other hand, I think that over all I really got to do a lot of great things with Testament, so I have a lot of fond memories there.

"With Disincarnate it was all on my back, there was a lot of pressure, that helped make me proud of my accomplishment but partially leeched away some of the enjoyment. But with Testament all I had to do was show up and enjoy what was going on. There were frustrations involved with not really having any control or even much of a 'vote', but overall it was great to just play my guitar and not worry about the business side too much. There's also the fact that Testament was by far the biggest act I had ever played with to that point, and as such had a lot more going on - world tours, videos, big studios, the whole thing. It was fun."

Is there a particular album you're especially proud of having contributed to?

"Once again I'm torn between Testament and Disincarnate," ponders James. "On the one hand, 'Dreams Of The Carrion Kind' was a very personal effort, and the results still move me. 'Low' on the other hand was very much a collaborative effort that succeeded on many levels - another album that has stood the test of time. There is as great, if not greater, satisfaction in an effective collaboration as there is in a personal work."

What about the flip side - is there anything you look back at with regret?

"Just some of the stuff that I did towards the very end of my time in California, as the tumour was starting to really take its toll on my thought processes. It was all guest appearances - like the stuff I did with Aggressor or Vicious Rumours for instance. It just wasn't what I would have done if there weren't a tumour pressing against my brain; l would have played a lot better."

SPIRITUAL HEALING

So now you're playing again and getting your life back on track, what's next for James Murphy?
"I'm currently planning two new albums; the first is going to be a Death tribute album that I am doing with Deron Miller of the Island Records band CKY - he is a major Death fan, and also a long-time fan of my Disincarnate project. It was his idea and we are working out details now, with the blessings of the Schuldiner family, of course, and there are some very cool guests lined up already. It's shaping up quite nicely.
"Once that is complete, I will begin the final work on the next Disincarnate CD which was
originally planned in 1999, prior to the tumour really kicking in with its worst effects. Nuclear Blast has been very patient and understanding with me so far, considering I blew my advance in '99 on new gear for my studio, most of which was stolen while I was ill. Now I just have to figure out how to make the CD for nothing, haha!"

JIM DURKIN - ISSUE 109 (MAY 2003)

A look at thrash through the eyes of Jim Durkin (Dark Angel/Dreams of Damnation)

"Thrash? Yes please! Well, I guess it was called 'speed metal' at first. Then... aww, hell... thrash is just the word that best explains the music I love to play and listen to. I do believe it's all I've ever played, in fact. Okay, okay, there was this one horrible cover band called Shell Shock I had in High School - we slaughtered the usual staples of metal at the time, but we also played Tank songs and some other obscure (in LA, at least) tunes from NWOBHM bands.
"The funny thing was, because most kids in LA in 1981 had never heard of Tank, they thought the songs were ours! Algy Ward would kick our asses if he saw how badly we destroyed his songs, haha! But as bad as we sucked, we never quit and never looked back, and soon we started writing songs of our own and grew into Dark Angel.
"After seeing Metallica for the first time everything changed! Then Slayer started playing their own brand of Venom meets Iron Maiden, and with two such awesome bands playing locally and often, things started growing. Well, actually, by the time Slayer went heavier, Metallica had moved up to San Francisco, because the fan base up there was super receptive.
"Let's just say that I had a once in a life-time opportunity to watch and get inspired by the greats. Both bands were very kind to me, and I made great friends with the guys in

Jim Durkin – middle – with Dark Angel, 1986, pic by Alison Braun Photography

Slayer. I think I actually sat at a rehearsal while they wrote 'At Dawn They Sleep'; I also watched most of 'Show No Mercy' and 'Haunting The Chapel' get recorded - that's how I met Gene Hoglan and Bill Metoyer. What a fantastic time in my life!

"This new form of metal was exciting and I was always eager for more new bands - to this day I still maintain my demo collection. I remember Slayer would go to San Francisco to play and Kerry would come back with demos and live tapes of bands like Exodus and Possessed. He would play them for me and say, 'Check these guys out!' I would be floored.

"About this time, Robbie Yahn, Don Doty and I had settled on a steady line-up and recorded Dark Angel's 'We Have Arrived' album, but it took so long to come out; it had circulated as a demo, and we soon had Gene in the band, which kicked the song-writing into gear. So, by the time 'We Have Arrived' hit the shelves, we had even heavier songs. Gene and I really wrote well together, and soon 'Darkness Descends' was born and that was truly the turning point for DA, and our biggest contribution to what would eventually be called the thrash scene. Lots of gigs, parties and friends; thrash was and is a way of life. We all knew what moved us musically and, for me, nothing else would do.

"I'm very proud to have seen it start, watch it grow, and then become underground again - only to be reborn through so many new bands with such great talent, like my very good friends, The Haunted, Defleshed, Dew Scented, The Crown... too many to name... but all brought together in the name of thrash. I still carry on my own journey - and hold the 'Flag Of Hate' high, haha! - with my new bands, Dreams Of Damnation and Pagan War Machine... yes, both thrash metal bands. Of course."

ABOUT THE AUTHOR

Ian Glasper has been writing about punk since 1986, when he first started his own fanzine, 'Little Things Please Little Minds'. Although it only ran for five issues, it helped him realise that he could indeed string a few words together, and gave him the confidence – in the early Nineties - to start writing reviews for Record Collector, and a hardcore punk column for Terrorizer, the extreme music magazine that he contributed to for the next twenty years. You hold in your hands one of two volumes collecting every single one of the 350+ interviews he did for Terrorizer during that time.

In 2003, he got fed up of reviewing books about the Sex Pistols and The Clash, and decided to write a book about the particular era of the UK punk scene that was closest to his own heart, the second wave of punk during the early Eighties – or UK82, as it became more affectionately known. The resultant 'Burning Britain' tome, published by Cherry Red in 2003 to much critical acclaim, flew off the shelves and is now widely regarded as the definitive document on that period.

It was followed by 'The Day The Country Died: A History Of Anarcho Punk 1980 – 1984' (2006), 'Trapped In A Scene: UK Hardcore 1985 – 1989' (2009) and 'Armed With Anger: How UK Punk Survived The Nineties' (2012). After then covering the last forty years of UK thrash metal with 'Contract In Blood: A History of UK Thrash' (2018), Glasper joined the Earth Island Books family and gave us 2020's celebrated 'The Scene That Would Not Die: Twenty Years of Post-Millennial Punk In The UK'.

During the whole of this time, Glasper has also been busy writing, recording and touring with his own punk and hardcore bands, keeping his finger firmly on the pulse and staying in touch with the grass roots DIY element of the punk scene that so drew him to it in the first place. Since 1983, he has played bass for Ammonia 77, Decadence Within, Burnside, Stampin' Ground, Human Error, Suicide Watch, Flux of Pink Indians, Freebase, Betrayed By Many, Thirty Six Strategies and Warwound, and he currently plays with Bristol-based anarcho punkers Zero Again and Midlands-based progressive thrash metal band, Sun Of The Endless Night.

A father of two, and a lifelong vegetarian/vegan, he writes for Bass Player, Down For Life and Fistful of Metal magazines, as well as regularly penning liner notes for retrospective punk and metal releases. He is currently hard at work on a full book about everyone's favourite UK punk band, Subhumans.

ACKNOWLEDGEMENTS

Thanks to the following generous, extremely patient people without whom none of this would have happened, blah blah blah: my dad, John Glasper, for all the scanning, Miranda Yardley for the kind permission, Jonathon Selzer, Nick Terry and the other Terrorizer editors, not least of all Louise Brown, Darren Sadler and Rob Clymo (who gave me the job in the first place!), Michael and Andy – Therapy?, Mike Score – All Out War, Welly Artcore for the cover design, Naki, Edward Verhaeghe, Eelco Klein Overmeer @ Epitaph Europe and Peter Ahlkvist @ BHR, Clint @ Organized Crime, Danielle Dombrowski, Morat, Stephanie Cabral, Al Quint, Olly Hahn @ Steamhammer, Claire Harris @ Nuclear Blast, Sam Lennox, Vique Simba, Will Binks, Carl Gunhouse, Stephanie Cabral, Gutterpunk Photography, Jason Dunn @ Facedown, Rachel 'Baz' Ridley – proof-reader extraordinaire (who really shouldn't gloat so much when she finds a mistake...!), Albert Licano, Andrew Giles and Shelley Shells, Igby at Revelation, Michelle Kerr, Alison Braun, Andy 'Tez' Turner, 'Decadent' Dave Thomas, all the bands I interviewed and all the bands that dug out old photos for me, Mark Duncan for file conversions, all the labels that sent me shit over the years, David and Lou Gamage and all the Earth Island family, my 'labelmates' Tim, Alex, Welly, Roy, the guys in Zero Again and Sun Of The Endless Night, Joel McIver @ Bass Guitar, James Sharples @ Fistful of Metal, Miles Hackett @ Down For Life, and everyone who ever took the time to encourage my writings for Terrorizer.

Dedicated as always to my late, great friend Dean Uzzell, who loved his extreme music and would definitely have approved of these collections - RIP